Energy Policy
in Mexico

Published in cooperation with
El Colegio de México

Energy Policy in Mexico

Problems and Prospects for the Future

EDITED BY

Miguel S. Wionczek,
Oscar M. Guzmán,
and Roberto Gutiérrez

Routledge
Taylor & Francis Group
LONDON AND NEW YORK

First published 1988 by Westview Press

Published 2018 by Routledge
52 Vanderbilt Avenue, New York, NY 10017
2 Park Square, Milton Park, Abingdon, Oxon OX14 4RN

Routledge is an imprint of the Taylor & Francis Group, an informa business

Copyright © 1988 by El Colegio de México

All rights reserved. No part of this book may be reprinted or reproduced or utilised in any form or by any electronic, mechanical, or other means, now known or hereafter invented, including photocopying and recording, or in any information storage or retrieval system, without permission in writing from the publishers.

Notice:
Product or corporate names may be trademarks or registered trademarks, and are used only for identification and explanation without intent to infringe.

Library of Congress Cataloging-in-Publication Data
Energy policy in Mexico.
   (Westview special studies on Latin America and the Caribbean)
   Bibliography: p.
   1. Energy policy—Mexico. I. Wionczek, Miguel S.
II. Guzmán, Oscar. III. Gutiérrez, Roberto. IV. Series.
HD9502.M62E57 1988   333.79′0972   88-14381

ISBN 13: 978-0-367-00638-9 (hbk)
ISBN 13: 978-0-367-15625-1 (pbk)

Contents

List of Tables and Figures...................... vii
Preface, Miguel S. Wionczek..................... xi

Part 1
An Overview of the Energy Sector

1 THE MEXICAN ENERGY SECTOR,
  Roberto Gutiérrez........................ 2

2 PLANNING AND DEVELOPMENT IN THE
  HYDROCARBON SUBSECTOR,
  Roberto Gutiérrez........................ 34

3 DEVELOPMENT AND PLANNING IN THE
  MEXICAN ELECTRICITY SUBSECTOR
  Jaime Navarro and Nora Lina Montes....... 65

4 PLANNING AND DEVELOPMENT IN THE COAL
  INDUSTRY IN MEXICO, Nora Lina Montes..... 97

5 NUCLEAR ELECTRICITY PLANNING AND
  DEVELOPMENT, Rogelio Ruiz................ 133

6 MEXICO'S PROGRESS IN PLANNING AND
  DEVELOPMENT OF NEW ENERGY SOURCES,
  Rocio Vargas............................. 166

Part 2
Strategies and Policies for Hydrocarbon
Exploration and Exploitation

7 EXPLORATION AND EXPLOITATION,
  Ana María Sordo.......................... 198

8 THE REFINING INDUSTRY,
  Oscar M. Guzmán and Michele Snoeck....... 247

9	THE BASIC PETROCHEMICAL INDUSTRY, Michele Snoeck	277
10	TRANSPORT AND DISTRIBUTION, Sotero Prieto and Miguel Márquez	302
11	FOREIGN TRADE, Michele Snoeck	334
12	PEMEX'S FINANCES, Oscar M. Guzmán	377
13	DOMESTIC PRICING POLICY, Oscar M. Guzmán	406
14	THE ROLE OF STRATEGIES AND POLICIES IN FORTIFYING DOMESTIC TECHNOLOGICAL CAPACITY, Rogelio Ruiz	421
15	THE IMPACT OF OIL EXPLOITATION ON THE ENVIRONMENT, Miguel Márquez and Roberto López	467

Part 3
Energy Planning between 1970 and 1988

16	ENERGY PLANNING FOR 1970–1976, Manuel Boltvinik	488
17	ENERGY PLANNING FOR 1977–1982, Cecilia Escalante	498
18	ENERGY PLANNING FOR 1982–1988, Manuel Boltvinik	536

Abbreviations and Units of Measurement 553

Bibliography 561

List of Tables and Figures

TABLES

1.1	Structure of primary commercial energy production by source, 1970-1983.......	10
1.2	Structure of electric power production by source, 1970-1983.................	12
1.3	Production and total consumption of energy, 1970-1983.....................	15
1.4	National energy consumption..............	17
1.5	Energy flows, 1983......................	23
1.6	Proven reserves (to 31 December), 1975-1983............................	29
1.7	Regional distribution of proven natural gas reserves...........................	30
2.1	Production and export of crude oil and its derivatives, 1911-1937............	35
2.2	Ratio of exports to production and reserves to production of crude oil in Mexico, 1970-1983.................	50
2.3	Average annual prices for Mexican crude on the international market, 1974-1984............................	53
2.4	Hydrocarbon production, 1983-1984........	55
2.5	Domestic hydrocarbon trade, 1983-1984....	57
2.6	Hydrocarbon exports and imports, 1983-1984............................	59
3.1	Evolution of electricity generation by company of origin.....................	69
3.2	Elasticity in electric energy generation with respect to GNP, 1974-1983........	72
3.3	National electricity subsector installed capacity, 1960-1983...................	74
3.4	Mean electricity prices for 1962 and 1980..............................	79
3.5	Changes in rates in current pesos and pesos of 1962-1980.....................	80
3.6	Electricity consumption by sector........	81
3.7	Expansion plan for the energy sector, 1977....................................	91
4.1	Evolution of Mexico's coal reserves, January 1963 to June 1984.............	101

4.2	Forecast for electric installed capacity, 1983-2000	105
4.3	Coal electricity potential based on resources, 1982	105
4.4	Coal resources	106
4.5	Evaluation of coal electricity programs, 1930-1984	107
4.6	Organization of the coal industry	110
4.7	Cost per unit of electricity generated	120
4.8	Cost-per-unit indexes for electricity generated	120
4.9	Prices for fuel oil and coal at current 1983 prices and 120 pesos per dollar	121
5.1	Market for industrial process-control equipment, 1976-1978	151
5.2	Size and number of local industrial process-control equipment producers, 1978	152
5.3	Industrial process-control equipment imports by country of origin, 1978	154
6.1	Financial resources used in new sources	170
6.2	Distribution of financial resources between new sources	170
6.3	Distribution of financial resources in the photothermal conversion of solar energy	171
6.4	Feasibility of solar technology uses	183
7.1	Regional distribution of proven crude oil and condensate reserves	219
7.2	National hydrocarbon production, 1975-1983	223
7.3	Gas-oil ratio in Tabasco-Chiapas, 1975-1983	235
8.1	Refining programs: Comparison between goals and results, 1970-1983	254
9.1	PEMEX petrochemical program, 1977-1982: Targets and results	284
10.1	Average daily available storage space capacity in Mexico, 1967	310
10.2	Comparative costs of transport and distribution	326
10.3	Installed and utilized capacity for transport and distribution, 1971-1983	327
10.4	Storage capacity	328

11.1	Hydrocarbon and derivative foreign-trade balance, 1976-1983	342
11.2	Natural gas production, trade, and apparent consumption	343
11.3	Petroleum product imports and exports, 1977-1983	356
12.1	PEMEX income, operating, and investment expenditures, 1977-1982	402
14.1	IMP's assistant management for exploration technology: Services lent to PEMEX exploration department, 1973-1982	426
14.2	Number of exploration teams employed by PEMEX, 1970-1982	432
14.3	PEMEX exploration team management, 1972-1981	434
14.4	PEMEX technology inflow according to origin	443
14.5	Technology distribution	445

FIGURES

1.1	Mexico's energy sector	6
2.1	Current organizational hierarchy in PEMEX	47
7.1	Tabasco-Chiapas area	202
7.2	Oil and gas fields of Mexico	203
8.1	PEMEX refining centers, 1983	270
9.1	PEMEX main petrochemical production centers and terminals, 1983	292
10.1	PEMEX oil pipelines, 1983	315
10.2	PEMEX major gas pipelines, 1983	316
10.3	PEMEX poliducts, 1983	317
14.1	U.S. oil-field machinery exports to Mexico, 1970-1982	449
17.1	Economic growth and hydrocarbon production forecast	515

Preface

The objective of the research contained in this work is to provide answers to questions about certain basic issues arising in the energy policy making process in Mexico. The most common patterns in the elaboration of energy policy observed worldwide consist of the sum of sectorial policies that tend to clash because of their particular characteristics and lack of effective coordination. Even in the best of cases, these policies culminate in separate arrangements between the various branches of the energy sector and between the energy sector and a country's energy consumers.

Do Mexico's recent efforts in elaborating and introducing energy policy correspond to these generalized patterns? Which aspects of domestic and international economic policy either condition or restrict the development of energy policy in Mexico? What are the future prospects for Mexican energy policy considering the limitations and uncertainties brought to light during this research?

This work carefully follows the formulation and implementation of Mexican energy policy over the last fifteen years, that is, from 1970 to the present. Although each chapter was the responsibility of a different author, this book should not be viewed as a set of essays written independently. On the contrary, this work is the result of a group effort on the part of full-time researchers in El Colegio de México's Programa de Energéticos and has been undertaken since the early 1980s. Because this volume is a coordinated work, particular attention has been given to avoid repetition, a common feature of anthologies and essay collections. It is clearly up to the reader to decide whether this book offers an integrated view that goes far beyond the numerous works on Mexico's oil policy available in Mexico and abroad. Undoubtedly, the attention paid to the oil industry in the past reflects its relative importance in the present production and consumption patterns of petroleum products in Mexico.

The study consists of three parts. The first part offers a general overview of the energy sector with particular emphasis on the demand for primary energy, according to end-user sector, and on planning in the different branches of the energy sector, which includes hydrocarbons, electricity, coal, nuclear electricity, and new energy sources. The second part analyzes the strategies and policies of the different areas of the hydrocarbon subsector, that is, exploration and exploitation, refining, basic petrochemicals, transport and local distribution of petroleum products, foreign trade in crude oil and natural gas, Petróleos Mexicanos finances, domestic pricing policy, the oil industry's technological capacity, and the impact of oil exploitation on the environment and society. The third part addresses energy planning between 1970 and 1988, from the first energy policy guideline proposal in 1976 to the national energy program for 1984 to 1988.

It will become clear to the reader after finishing this book that although the energy sector is of major importance to the economy of any country, energy planning is an extremely complicated exercise because of its close relationship with the rest of the country's economy and with the world economy in general. An additional complication arises with the need to elaborate energy policy on the basis of at least medium-term forecasts regarding both local and international energy supply and demand.

It seemed relatively easy to build simple planning models during the supposed worldwide shortage of crude oil, the major energy source. However, since the second half of the 1970s, when Mexico began to participate in the international market as a major exporter, building such models has not been quite as easy. Under the conditions prevailing after 1980, world oil market equilibrium became exceedingly fragile, while oil petroleum products continued to play a key role in Mexico's efforts to overcome its deep financial, economic, and social crisis--a crisis brought about precisely by the country's oil-oriented economy. Under these conditions neither models nor forecasts are of much support to countries such as Mexico in energy policy design. Many factors—economic, political, and institutional—must be taken into account but are often very difficult to quantify.

The evidence offered in this study clearly shows that energy planning in Mexico is still at an early stage and that considerable time will go by before real coordination will be achieved between the different branches of the energy sector. In view of the experience of many industrialized and developing countries, be they net importers or exporters of primary energy forms, one can clearly see that progress in energy programming in other parts of the world also leaves much to be desired. It is for this reason, as well as others, that this research effort could be considered a positive contribution to the national debate at all levels on the extent of the problems still to be solved and the energy options open to Mexico between now and the end of the century.

This work would not have been possible without the very generous cooperation of the many experts from the different branches of the energy sector, the interest of the leading figures of the sector in the research work undertaken in the Programa de Energéticos, the support of the authorities of El Colegio de México, and the financial assistance of the Energy Directorate at the Commission of the European Economic Communities in Brussels.

The authors acknowledge the contribution of Pilar Torres and Blanca Aguirre at the program's documentation center as well as the support of the office staff: Leticia Cabrera, Juana Cervantes, Rosa María Valenzuela, and Elizabeth Caso.

Miguel S. Wionczek
Coordinator of the
Programa de Energéticos
El Colegio de México

PART ONE

An Overview of the Energy Sector

1

The Mexican Energy Sector

Roberto Gutiérrez

ENTERPRISES, BRANCHES, AND ACTIVITIES

Artículo 27 (Article 27) of the Mexican Political Constitution grants the state property rights over land and waters within its territory as well as the right to impose on private property the manner of exploitation that the state considers most useful. This chapter explains why the country's two largest energy companies, Petróleos Mexicanos (Mexican Petroleum Company; PEMEX) and the Comisión Federal de Electricidad (Federal Electricity Commission; CFE), whose activities together represent almost all the country's primary and secondary commercial energy production, are state-owned. PEMEX was established with the nationalization of foreign oil companies in 1938 and CFE with the purchase of foreign public utilities in 1960. PEMEX has a monopoly over exploration, exploitation, production, refining, and distribution of crude oil and natural gas and is, also by constitutional decree, the only producer of primary petrochemicals. CFE has a monopoly over generation, transformation, transmission, and distribution of electric power. Only a very small part of the distribution activities in the Distrito Federal and surrounding areas is still in the hands of the Compañía de Luz y Fuerza del Centro (Central Light and Power Company; CLFC); however, CLFC's share of the market gets smaller every day because the company has been in the process of liquidating since the 1970s, with the goal of being absorbed by CFE.

Both PEMEX and CFE have at their disposal institutes dedicated to research. These institutes are the Instituto Mexicano del Petróleo (Mexican Petroleum Institute; IMP) and the Instituto de Investigaciones Eléctricas (Institute for Electric Research; IIE), respectively. The work of both has been decisive in reducing Mexico's dependence in the energy sector on technology from abroad.

The remaining commercial activities in energy are found mainly in the coal industry and in the area of nuclear electricity, both of which are also controlled by the state. The coal industry includes a large number of enterprises dedicated to exploration and commercialization, many of them under concession to private industry and directed toward satisfying the needs of the iron and steel industry, a heavy consumer of coke. The exploitation and commercialization on noncoke coal is undertaken through Mineral Carbonifera de Río Escondido (Río Escondido Mineral Coal; MICARE), whose monopolic client is CFE. The work in electric research and development (R&D) is undertaken fundamentally at CFE by IIE and the Centro de Estudios Carboníferos (Center for Coal Studies; CEC).

Until late 1984 the exploration and exploitation of uranium for generating nuclear electricity was performed by Uranios Mexicanos (Mexican Uranium Company; URAMEX), the related research being done at the Instituto Nacional de Investigaciones Nucleares (National Nuclear Research Institute; ININ). Labor and management problems in this area led the executive to dissolve URAMEX and substitute for it a new organization not yet established. Despite the current institutional reorganization of the nuclear electricity complex, uranium exploration, exploitation, and enrichment for electric energy production will continue to be the prerogative of the state. Also, given the centralized nature of activities related to electricity generation, CFE will continue to be its natural monopsony.

It should be pointed out that the nuclear area's contribution to Mexico's energy balance is still nil. In accordance with the Programa Nacional de Energéticos (National Energy Program; PNE) 1984-1988, its contribution was to start in 1986 when the first unit of the Laguna Verde nuclear electric power plant was expected to come on line. The inauguration of the Laguna Verde plant set finally for early 1987 was again postponed because of the wave of protests of the large groups of ecologists, following the Chernobyl accident in the Soviet Union in the Spring of 1986.

As in most developing countries, a considerable proportion of the population in Mexico does not have access to commercial energy and lives in subsistence agriculture areas with poor communications. Although determining the total number of inhabitants living under these conditions is difficult, the Programa de Energía (Energy Program; PE) 1980-1982 estimated that 28 percent of the country's population --approximately 20 million people-- did not have access to the national electric distribution network.[1] If both electricity and natural gas or other kinds of commercial energy used for cooking are considered jointly, the number of persons with insufficient or no share of commercial energy consumption could be substantially more than 20 million. Instead of these forms of energy, people usually use either candles or kerosene for lighting and use wood and charcoal for heat. The energy required for motion (plowing the land, pumping water, and transporting goods) is generally furnished by humans, with the aid of rudimentary tools, or gravity. The quantity of energy in the form of biomass (particularly charcoal and wood) consumed annually in Mexico to supplement electricity, butane gas, and kerosene is unknown, but there is an awareness that several of the country's wooded zones, such as the northern part of the state of Puebla, have undergone dangerous deforestation as a result of biomass use. Some specialized sources have estimated that in 1980 this energy source supplied 7.7 percent of the total demand (commercial and noncommercial) for primary energy.[2]

Apart from biomass, there are additional forms of energy that have less importance, particularly when compared to hydrocarbons and electricity. Among them are microhydroelectricity and solar and eolic energy, generically known as new or renewable resources. The contribution, if any, of these resources to Mexico's commercial energy supply is marginal. However, given the climatic and physical characteristics of the country, the long-term development of renewable energy sources of all sorts, especially microhydroelectricity and solar, is now considered both viable and indispensable.[3] The progress achieved in several of these areas is still limited to research.

The information contained in this book offers an overview of the constituent parts of the Mexican energy sector. Figure 1.1 presents an integrated view from which several observations can be made. The commercial part of the energy sector is made up of two subsectors: hydrocarbons and electricity, operated by PEMEX and CFE, respectively. The noncommercial part contains a series of expanding areas with great long-term prospects (biomass, microhydroelectricity, solar and eolic energy, and others).

The hydrocarbon subsector has three product lines, oil, gas, and basic petrochemicals. The activities listed in each column, ranging from basic and applied research undertaken mainly by IMP to local and foreign trade, show PEMEX's broad coverage. The electricity subsector is composed of a number of productive areas supplying the necessary primary energy.

These two subsectors are linked (note the dashed lines), on one hand, by the hydrocarbons required by thermoelectric plants to produce electric power and, on the other, by the electricity required by PEMEX to carry out its activities in exploitation, refining, and petrochemicals. These two links, along with others of a purely economic and political nature that are dealt with in Chapter 3 on the electricity industry, have caused discord between PEMEX and CFE, primarily because any move by one partner tends to affect the production costs of the other. Second, if the installed capacity of one is not extended precisely when the other needs it, the other's expansion programs are necessarily held back.

Also shown in Figure 1.1 is the link between microhydroelectricity and the electric research activities undertaken by CFE. This link implies that once a program is set up for utilizing the country's small rivulets and waterfalls for generating electric power, it is difficult for the research activities to remain independent. Most probably, research is tied to the commercial part of the energy sector through CFE. Once this tie is established, microhydroelectricity becomes

FIGURE 1.1
MEXICO'S ENERGY SECTOR

Commercial Energy[a]		Noncommercial Energy[a]
Hydrocarbon Subsector (PEMEX) Areas	Electricity Subsector (CFE) Areas	New Sources Areas

Oil	Gas	Petrochemicals		
Activities	Activities	Activities	Thermal	Biomass
Research	Research	Research	Hydro	Microhydro-electricity
Exploration	Production	Production	Coal	Solar
Exploitation	Distribution		Geothermal	Eolic
Separation	Internal Trading		Nuclear	Other
Sweetening	External Trading		Activities	Current Activities
Refining			Research	Research
Distribution			Generation	Development
Internal Trade			Transformation	
External Trade			Transmission	
			Distribution	

[a] Dashed lines show links between the subsectors.

Source: Based upon information received from PEMEX.

part of generation, transformation, transmission, and distribution of electric power.

The activities related to Mexico's new energy sources are at present very limited in that they consist mostly of R&D. As is seen in Chapter 3, the use of new energy sources by the Mexican industry is very small, a condition that has greatly limited the expansion of these sources. The only area that currently plays a considerable role in consumption is biomass. However, this product is of a noncommercial type and has not received sufficient backing for its use to be extended to industrial activities and energy substitution, as has occurred in Brazil with alcohol produced from sugar cane.

THE ROLE OF THE ENERGY SECTOR IN THE NATIONAL ECONOMY

Mexico's economic development has been closely associated with the energy sector's rate of activity. If we go back to the beginning of the century and the first mention of a national energy sector at the time when carbon production began and electricity production had started on a small scale, it can be observed that the role of energy was to satisfy the development needs prevailing at the time. Mexico was then a primary commodities exporting country and had been so since colonial times because of its tremendous mineral resources. However, during the 1910s a nonmineral product, oil, began to emerge as a main product for export. During the early 1920s Mexico became the world's largest exporter of crude oil, and mining was temporarily displaced as the country's main exporting industry.[4] However, the benefits of this exploitation would be reaped by several international petroleum companies to which the Mexican government had granted limitless exploitation rights.

The energy sector's link with various economic models

The high growth rate of domestic oil consumption, together with the rapid incorporation of important oil producers into the international scene, reduced Mexico's contribution to world crude oil exports after the mid-twenties. This trend was further accentuated after 1938 because of (1) Mexico's temporary isolation as a consequence of the nationalization of the petroleum industry and (2) the explicit decision of the government to utilize its oil mainly to stimulate domestic industrialization. Although the post-1938 energy policy have not become a financial burden for the country, oil contributed only marginally to the fulfillment of Mexico's needs for foreign exchange almost until the abandonment of the import-substitution model, which was in force until the mid-1970.[5] While this model lasted, of the total merchandise exported, the share of raw materials reduced considerably, and the percentage of manufactured exports increased gradually.

Between the late 1970s and early 1980s, oil became a fundamental factor in the new Mexican development model. One might state that the development strategy of this period resulted from the new privileged position of the oil industry, now one of the most dynamic industries in the world. By this time Mexico, as well as other developing countries, realizing the foreign sector's dependence on raw material exports, adopted deliberate export-directed growth policies aimed at promoting the sale of manufactured goods abroad while reducing external dependence on traditional commodities and, thus, their vulnerability vis à vis the import-substitution model. Mexico, however, became less concerned about its vulnerability once it discovered its large oil resources. The country adopted an alternative policy--more for short-term reasons than long-term considerations--that was similar to import substitution in the the allocation of foreign exchange was reduced in almost all sectors and branches of economic activity, including that directed toward export-led growth (as a commodity exporter). Hence, this model can be classified as a neoliberal or external aperture model because a high degree of liberalization was observed in the economy as a result of the oil revenue and the bottlenecks stemming from economic expansion, particularly during 1978-1981. At this time the external sector (exports plus imports) accounted for more than 20 percent of the gross national product (GNP).

Macroeconomic Impact

The GNP growth rate in Mexico from the 1940s on was one of the highest of the developing countries because the energy supply had increased substantially more than the aggregate product. During the first stages of industrialization in any country, the income elasticity of energy demand is considerably higher that one. As a result, it is not surprising that since the early 1950s the installed capacity of the electric power industry has grown at an average annual rate of nearly 10 percent, which means that supply doubled approximately every seven years.[6] Furthermore, between 1970 and 1982 oil production rose at an average annual rate over 16 percent, while the total supply of primary energy increased at a rate of 13.4 percent. This supply increase meant substantial surpluses, which were exported. These exports were one of the main ingredients in the country's rapid economic growth from 1978 onward.

The exportable surpluses of crude oil, petroleum products, and, recently, primary petrochemical products, which together represent the country's main source of foreign exchange (70 percent of the total value exports), have brought about important structural changes in the national economy during the last few years. The energy sector, which had accounted for 3.2 percent of the GNP in 1970, increased its share to 5.7 by 1983.[7] Furthermore, taxes on hydrocarbon exports, which were virtually nonexistent ten years ago, have become one of the most important sources of income for the state.[8] These taxes, together with the duties on domestic sales paid by PEMEX and other energy companies, currently represent more than 40 percent of the federal government's income.

Also, the energy sector has been the one to benefit most from the annual allocation of the federal budget. Naturally, this tendency was greater during the 1970s because of the highest priority given to PEMEX expansion. At that time the share of total public expenditure held by the energy sector was almost 30 percent of the annual average. PEMEX rewarded the state not only with growing levels of tributary resources and a high income capacity but also with the image of great international solvency. Thus, PEMEX became the public enterprise with the greatest external financing capacity, a situation that was used to considerable advantage by the state to expand productive activities.[9] Additionally, the energy sector contributed to the industrialization and accelerated growth of the GNP by granting subsidies to most of the companies selling their output locally.

Finally, the energy sector industry that has contributed most in absolute terms to the creation of jobs during the last few years has been the petroleum industry; the number of its personnel rose from 72,500 thousand in 1970 to 115,800 in 1980.[10]. During the same period the electricity industry's employment grew from 38,000 to 63,000 people.[11] The increased rate of employment sources in this industry helped back up the country's labor policy because the economically active population had been growing for some time at an average annual rate over 3.5 percent.

TABLE 1.1
STRUCTURE OF PRIMARY COMMERCIAL ENERGY PRODUCTION BY SOURCES, 1970-1983* (in percentages)

Year	Oil	Natural Gas	Hydro-electricity	Coal	Geo-thermal Power	Total
1970	55.2	32.6	10.1	2.1	--	100
1975	62.7	27.6	7.0	2.5	0.2	100
1980	75.1	20.5	3.1	1.1	0.2	100
1983[a]	70.5	24.5	2.7	1.2	0.2	100

*If noncommercial energy were included, biomass would represent almost 10 percent of the total primary energy produced in Mexico.
[a]The sum of the parts does not coincide with the total because use of bagasse as energy source has been omitted; its contribution to primary energy is only 0.9 percent.

Source: SEPAFIN and STCE, "México: Balances de energía 1970, 1975-80," in *Energéticos: Boletín Informativo del Sector Energético*, Year 5, No. 11, Mexico City, STCE, November 1981, pp. 9-20; CFE and PEMEX internal statistics, 1983.

STRUCTURAL COMPOSITION: PRIMARY ENERGY PRODUCTION BY SOURCE

An analysis of the structural composition of the energy sector in Mexico shows that the changes in this sector during the last few years have tended toward a concentration in hydrocarbons despite the great variety of resources the country has. The participation of oil and natural gas, both dry and associated, which represented 87.8 percent of the total primary energy produced in 1970, increased to 95 percent in 1983 (see Table 1.1). Oil accounted for 70.5 percent and natural gas for the remaining 24.5 percent. Paradoxically, the natural gas figures show that its relative importance has declined since 1970. This decline can be explained not only by the greater contribution of oil in primary energy production but also by the waste of gas during the first years (the late 1970s) of intensive crude oil exploitation and by a trend observed since the early 1970s of the fall in the natural gas-oil ratio.[12]

The role of the remaining primary energy sources in Mexico's energy balance is measured according to each source's contribution to the generation of electricity. In other words, the sources are taken as subsidiaries of a secondary source. At the beginning of the industrialization period, the main installed plants for electricity generation used available waterfalls; those plants consuming hydrocarbons were substantially fewer. Of the total installed electric power capacity, 43.1 percent was still thermal in origin; by 1983 this percentage had increased to 67.5. This situation can be explained by the great availability of hydrocarbons and the pressure exerted by the demand for electricity (see Table 1.2). This problem is pointed out in PNE 1984-1988, where it is stated that apart from the fact that Mexico is a country with very few waterfalls, it is estimated that there is a usable hydraulic potential of 80 TWh —equivalent to a generation capacity of 22,000 MW—, of which only 29.8 percent is currently used.

Coal production in Mexico has been intimately related to the development of the iron and steel industry, which uses this mineral as fuel and as a reducer. In 1983, however, coal once again became important in electricity plants as a fuel to generate the steam that moves the turbines. This renewed importance can be attributed to the Rio Escondido coal burning electricity plant in the state of Coahuila, which provides 3.2 percent of the total electricity generated. However, the production of coal is still not sufficient to satisfy the country's requirements. The deficit has had to be covered by imports, which represent a significant part of the total coal supply. It is probable that in the long term Mexico will be able to reduce this deficit by turning to its vast potential reserves of both coke and noncoke coal.[13]

TABLE 1.2
STRUCTURE OF ELECTRIC POWER PRODUCTION BY SOURCES,
1970-1983 (in percentages)

Year	Hydro	Thermo	Geo-thermal	Electricity from Coal	Total
1970	56.9	43.1	--	--	100
1975	36.7	62.0	1.3	--	100
1980	27.1	71.4	1.5	--	100
1983	27.5	67.5	1.8	3.2	100

Sources: Poder Ejecutivo Federal, Programa nacional de energéticos, 1984-1988, Mexico City, SEMIP, Subsecretaría de Energía, 1984, p. 146.

The contribution of geothermal power to the national energy supply is still incipient and revolves around electricity subsector, which in 1983 provided 1.8 percent of this supply. The potential of geothermal energy is very broad considering the volcanic nature of Mexico's subsoil. Today, more than 400 zones with geothermal manifestations have been identified. These zones, together with areas in the rest of the country that still have not been adequately explored, give proven, probable, and potential reserves of 2,000 MW, 13,000 MW, and 200,000 MW, respectively.[14]

The history of nuclear electricity goes back to the mid-1960s when it was thought there was a need to promote its development and to build a plant, in this case the Laguna Verde plant in the state of Veracruz. However, because of the lack of technical knowledge about uranium enrichment, the installation of plants, and Mexico's true uranium potential, this project was prolonged for an exceedingly long time. Mexico's hydrocarbon wealth contributed to this delay because it reduced the need to continue energy-substitution efforts. Added to this problem were three others: (1) the long-term maturation of uranium-investment projects; (2) the high economic and financial cost to this type of facility; and (3) the national and foreign political problems involved in its management. Also, because Mexico does not have the uranium-enrichment technology, it has been necessary to send the virgin material to other countries to be enriched, with the consequent problems of dependence and the frictions that it causes.[15] Despite the fact that 1986 was to be the first year of operations at Laguna Verde, development of nuclear-powered electricity appears to become an increasingly controversial issue on political and ecological grounds.[16]

One of the limiting factors in the development of nuclear electricity is the uncertainty concerning the country's uranium potential. Mexico's uranium reserves are said to be extraordinarily large, but there has been no sound data supporting these assertions. Although during the late 1970s several observers did state that total reserves could ascend to nearly 120,000 tons, PNE 1984-1988 numbers them at 14,000 tons, of which only 10,600 are recoverable. According to PNE, with the Laguna Verde plant operating, 60 percent of these reserves will be used. The divergence of opinion obviates the need to intensify exploration efforts in order to achieve precise statistics.

Among the new sources of energy is biomass. Historically, this energy type has been important in Mexico. Most of the rural population, which reaches nearly 35 percent of the total population, uses biomass in one way or another. However, statistics concerning biomass use have not been diffused widely perhaps because they reflect the extent of Mexico's energy underdevelopment, which in turn reflects the country's economic underdevelopment. Therefore, this source is not considered in national energy balances. These balances only take into account energy that undergoes industrial transformation and, consequently, that is commercial and quantifiable. Other types of energy included by PNE 1984-1988 in the list of new sources, such as solar, eolic, and microhydroelectricity energies, are also not included in the national energy balances. Given the financial and technological conditions of the country, the development of these energy sources will be a long-term issue.

ENERGY CONSUMPTION BY SECTOR OF DEMAND

Mexico's economic development has been based on an energy intensive productive structure. In effect, as a result of the discovery of new hydrocarbon reserves during the mid-1970s a rapid increase was observed not only in the rate of energy consumption by the energy sector but also in the growth of the overall product. An increase in per capita consumption also occurred.[17] This high level of consumption was due to a number of factors, among which the following stand out:

- The speed with which oil resources were exploited during recent years, which led to a high degree of waste within the energy sector

- The rapid growth in the GNP since the late 1970s

- The relatively low price of energy compared to both international energy prices and the price of other domestic commodities[18]

The profile of energy consumption in Mexico would have been very different if energy self-sufficiency had not been so high. Table 1.3 shows that although in 1970 exportable energy surpluses in general accounted for barely 4.7 percent of total production, by 1980 these surpluses had risen to 32.8 percent and by 1983 to 44.8 percent.

As a result of the energy sector's rapid development, especially in the oil industry, production increased between 1977 and 1981 at an average of more than 22 percent per year. In 1983 a change was observed in this trend when production levels decreased with respect to the previous year. This change could be the first indication that from now on this variable will tend to grow at a moderate rate, as will consumption.

TABLE 1.3
PRODUCTION AND TOTAL CONSUMPTION OF ENERGY,
1970-1983 (in kilocalories x 10^{12})

Year	National Production (1)	Domestic Consumption (2)	Exportable Surplus (%) (2/1) - 100
1970	475,668	453,115	4.7
1975	678,712	642,114	5.4
1980	1,547,859	1,040,656	32.8
1981	1,837,871	1,146,502	37.6
1982	2,140,093	1,234,531	42.3
1983	2,087,073	1,146,993	44.8

Sources: SEPAFIN and STCE, "México: Balances de energía 1970, 1975-80," in Energéticos: Boletín Informativo del Sector Energético, Year 5, No. 11, Mexico City, STCE, November, 1981, p. 10; and information received from PEMEX.

Despite their source of origin and a production structure heavily concentrated on hydrocarbons, petroleum products and natural gas have the largest share in final consumption of energy, with 89 percent in 1955 and 90.1 percent in 1982. Consequently, the contribution of solid fuels (coal) and electricity has diminished, from 11.1 percent in 1955 to 9.9 percent in 1982. The high consumption of hydrocarbons in the form of petroleum is directly related to its low price as well as to the dependence on hydrocarbons of the industrial and transport sectors for their operation.[19]

Natural gas has begun to gain ground in the final consumption of some productive sectors despite the fact that its participation in overall consumption has declined. This gain is due, on one hand, to its low price and ease of use in relation to other fuels, such as fuel oil, and, on the other, to the recent facilities built by the government to encourage its use in the industrial sector. When the extension and interconnection of the national gas network was completed, resulting in the increased availability of natural gas and lower prices, the national industry's conversion from fuel oil to natural gas began. Its use as a fuel and a raw material in the industrial sector's different areas, for example, in the petrochemical industry has grown by leaps and bounds. Today, natural gas is the industrial sector's most important energy source, making up almost 45 percent of its total energy consumption. Furthermore, a significant part of the oil industry's consumption is satisfied by this product. However, because of a recent reduction in the natural gas-oil ratio of the wells in Mexico, it is possible that, in the future this product might be forced to cede and increasing percentage of the importance it currently enjoys.

According to the energy balances, electricity has maintained a relatively constant share of the final demand: 7.4 percent in 1955 and 7.5 percent in 1982. This energy type is consumed first by the residential, commercial, and public sector and, second, by the industrial sector whose participation has increased slightly.[20]

In accordance with PNE 1984-1988 classifications, the consumer sectors to which energy is destined are energy; transport; industrial; agricultural; and residential, commercial, and public. An analysis of each of these sectors in their order of importance follows.

Energy sector

An analysis of energy demand done by the energy-producing sector itself indicates that it is the country's main consumer. Its participation in domestic consumption increased as a result of intense energy use during 1978-1982, the years of maximum hydrocarbon exploitation in Mexico (see Table 1.4).

TABLE 1.4
NATIONAL ENERGY CONSUMPTION
(in percentages)

Sector	1970	1976	1982
Energy	35.0	33.4	46.4
Transport	25.5	26.8	23.8
Industrial	28.0	27.9	19.4
Agricultural	2.2	2.2	2.0
Residential, Commercial and Public	9.3	9.7	8.4
Total	100.0	100.0	100.0

Source: Poder Ejecutivo Federal, Programa nacional de energéticos, 1984-1988, Mexico City, SEMIP, p. 46.

Although not appearing in the table, transformation losses account for the greatest part of the sector's energy use.[21] It is also in this sector that self-consumption has risen faster than in any other area.[22] The losses occurring in transportation, distribution, and storage are another reason for the high energy consumption in this sector.[23]

Of the two main state-owned companies producing energy, PEMEX and CFE, PEMEX's internal consumption of energy has increased the most. The ratio of barrel consumed to barrel produced was 8.8 percent in 1970 and 12.9 percent in 1980 which meant a reduction in overall energy-use efficiency of 47 percent.[24] This reduction in efficiency did not occur in the electricity subsector, however, because the efficiency of the thermoelectric plants rose from 26.6 percent to 30 percent during the 1970s.[25]

PEMEX's high internal consumption is explained mainly by the magnitude of its operations, its rapid and disorderly growth, and its energy-intensive processes. The national-international price ratio propitiated the situation in which the profit gained from increasing export volume was greater than that derived from making the necessary investment to adequately increase industrial efficiency. The dynamic growth of oil exploration was detrimental to secondary recovery;

it led to the flaring of associated gas and limited the development of other productive activities.

Transport sector

Like the manufacturing industry, the transport sector has increased its participation in the GDP compared to other less energy-intensive sectors such as agriculture. The transport sector has also been one of the most dynamic areas of economic activity; it recently became the second largest energy consumer, although also one of the most inefficient. Several factors explain this phenomenon:

1. The first factor is the rapid growth of private transportation coupled with an accelerated growth of the cities with the greatest concentration of vehicles, giving rise to a kind of "demonstration effect" in respect to the car ownership as a status symbol. In these highly populated areas the underground transport system, one of the most efficient in terms of energy use, is not widespread.

2. Another factor is the low performance of the automobiles, trucks, and buses in circulation. In Mexico annual surveys of motor vehicles fitness are not carried out, a measure that would allow conservation and efficient use of the gasoline and diesel in the sector. Traditionally, automobiles have been large, and only recently have measures been introduced to reduce the number of cylinders in vehicles coming off the production line.

3. Finally, inadequacy of the railroad transport system makes it necessary for passengers and cargo to be transported mainly by automobiles, buses, and trucks, which consume more energy per unit transported.

In 1982 the transport sector reduced its relative share of final energy consumption. This reduction is explained by the relative increase in the energy sector's production, a fall in the transport sector's GDP (-0.5 percent), and the increased price of automobile gasolines and diesel.

An effective way to save fuel might be to establish a minimum performance requirement for fuel use in automobiles, making it the obligation of the manufacturers to adhere to theses stipulations.[26] According to a recent study new federal legislation could result in an average performance of 9.5 to 10.0 km/l for automobiles in circulation.[27] This performance level would mean a savings of more than 422,675,000 gallons of gasoline annually, that is, 1,189,000 gallons daily in 1985 and 1,902,000 in 1990.

Industrial sector

The growth in energy consumption in the industrial sector is slightly lower than that in the transport sector. Nevertheless, in absolute terms its energy consumption has grown substantially during the las ten years as a direct result of industrial expansion and an investment concentration in the sector's energy-intensive areas. The cement, chemical, paper, nonferrous, glass, and sugar industries are experiencing increased energy consumption for similar reasons. Other factors that explain these increases include the following:

. The rapid process of industrialization and the abundant supply of subsidized energy

. The encouragement given to the substitution of capital-intensive technologies for labor-intensive ones

. The substitution of human labor for mechanized processes

. The slow incorporation of efficient technology into the use of energy

. The extremely slow implementation of measures directed toward the conservation and efficient use of energy

In regard to the last point, industry has for many years been the most protected sector in Mexico. The energy sector has supported this protection by charging extremely low prices.[28] This protection has retarded the implementation of energy-saving measures. Despite this protection, however, the industry sector, along with the electricity subsector, has been almost the only area in which any sort of energy diversification has been observed. This diversification has occurred more between various hydrocarbon products than with alternative energy forms. Also, price policy has not been used to favor substitution on the basis of internal availability, production costs, consumer trends and policies promoting certain productive activities.[29] However, the state has encouraged substitution through the reduction in the supply of a given commodity when both price and international demand have been high. But an adequate substitute must be available. In the late 1970s when the United States refused to accept the price of Mexican natural gas, Mexico was forced to use this resource locally and large quantities of fuel oil were freed for export. The strategy of substitution of gas for fuel oil consisted of (1) constraining domestic consumption of fuel oil through increases in its prices because the international demand for it was considerable; and (2) increasing natural gas consumption through subsidized prices and an adequate trunk-line system. Although this method is probably the only way substitution could have been carried out as rapidly as it was, the fact that the industrial sector, as well as PEMEX and CFE, at that time had dual systems of energy consumption was an important contributing factor. Limited results in energy substitution observed in other sectors, particularly in transport, were achieved through official stimuli to promote the use of certain petroleum products over others, for example, diesel instead of gasoline or low-octane gasoline instead of high-octane one.

The possibilities for saving energy in industry are varied. Some of them offer short-term results and do not require investment. Other medium-term measures need, for example, the installation of automatic process-control systems and intensive use of insulators in certain types of equipment. Finally, long-term measures demand high investment because modifications might have to be made to machinery and technology. Applying these measures would lead to a reduction in production costs because expenditure on energy represents a substantial part of theses costs (between 15 and 30 percent).[30] The possible savings for the year 1990 would be around 88.5 thousand barrels per day (TBD) which amounts to 20 percent of the final fuel consumption projected for industrial production and exploitation.[31]

Residential, commercial, and public sector

This sector has stayed relatively constant in its consumption of energy, although it registered an increase in demand in both absolute and relative terms from 1970 to 1982. Hydrocarbons, which are consumed primarily through the use of electricity generated by thermoelectric plants operating on natural gas or fuel oil, continue to account for a substantial part of this consumption (around 70 percent). CFE's subsidized prices have not helped reduce this consumption, which, along with implicit waste, has affected the finances of the company--one of the most indebted of those in the public sector and that with the highest deficit. Nevertheless, as stated earlier, this subsector is much more efficient in terms of its internal primary energy consumption than hydrocarbon sector.

Agricultural sector

Because commercial energy consumption in the agricultural sector is low (only 2 percent of the total), in PNE 1984-1988 the state announced a large project for conditioning rural areas to energy use. The benefits of this project cannot be denied, but its implementation will probably be long term. Therefore, economically this sector will continue for some time to be somewhat insignificant in its use of commercial energy. Charcoal and wood, which, as stated earlier, constitute a very important part of rural energy consumption, can only be substituted by commercial energy once these areas are conditioned for its use.

Energy balance

Reviewing Table 1.5 is perhaps the best way to visualize energy flows and the relationship between energy and the economy. Several extremely important factors are evident. The overwhelming contribution of oil to total supply (extreme left) can be seen along with its use in all branches and areas of end use, including exports. Natural gas, used widely in all areas and activities except transport, follows in importance. The low relative importance of the other primary energy sources is obvious.

The transport sector already surpasses the industrial sector in terms of energy end consumption, and basic petrochemicals have become an important consumer of primary energy, particularly natural gas. Also, a considerable amount of the total energy produced (17 percent) fails to reach any sector or area of end consumption because of its waste during the different energy production stages.

PLANNING PROBLEMS

Planning in general has been a difficult exercise in organization for Mexico (for detailed information, refer to Part 3). In the case of the energy sector, this organization has been especially complicated in part because of the normal exercises in national planning undertaken during the late 1960s, that is, when the country was exporting more hydrocarbons than ever before. The executive's acceptance of an energy program at that time would have meant having to take into account goals for production, internal consumption, exports, the orderly evolution of prices, and so on. This program might have clashed with some of the federal government's macroeconomic objectives, such as rapid GNP growth, financial solvency, a surplus in foreign exchange to service the foreign debt, control of employment, and so on. For these reasons, as well as the unforeseen drop in international oil prices from 1981 to 1982, it is not surprising that PE 1980-1982 was not implemented, even though it had been formally approved by the executive. Considering the current problems the Mexican economy faces, many fear

TABLE 1.5
ENERGY FLOWS, 1983 (TBDCE)*

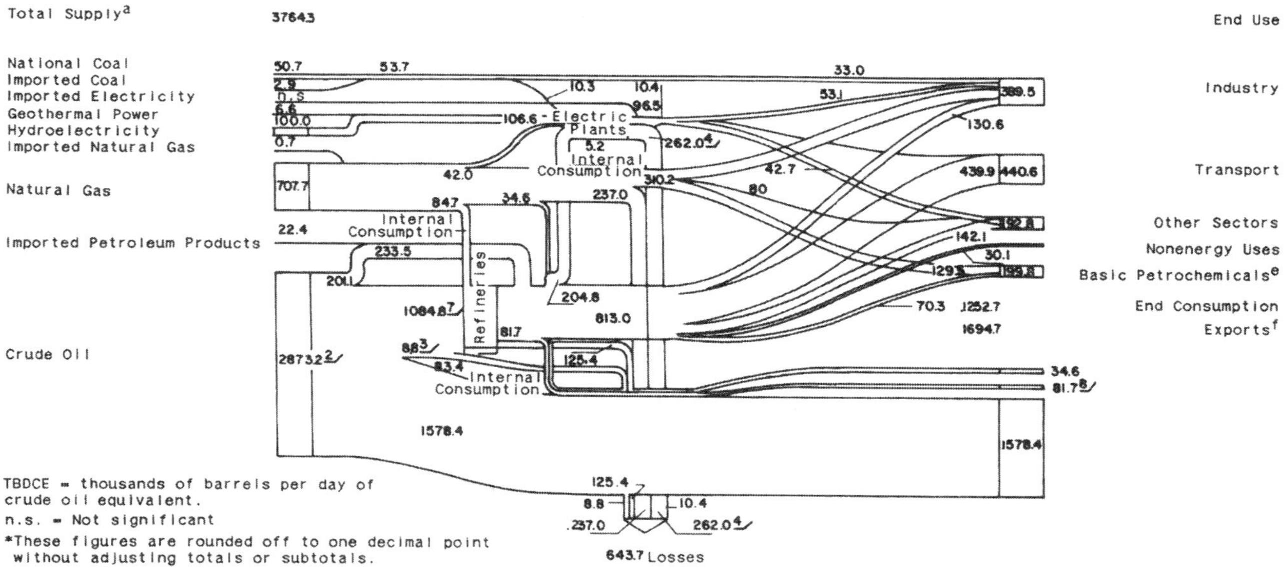

Total Supply[a]	37643		End Use
National Coal	50.7		
Imported Coal	2.9		Industry
Imported Electricity	0.3		
Geothermal Power	4.6		
Hydroelectricity	100.0		Transport
Imported Natural Gas	0.7		
Natural Gas	707.7		Other Sectors
Imported Petroleum Products	22.4		Nonenergy Uses
			Basic Petrochemicals[e]
Crude Oil	28732.2		End Consumption
			Exports[f]

TBDCE = thousands of barrels per day of crude oil equivalent.
n.s. = Not significant
*These figures are rounded off to one decimal point without adjusting totals or subtotals.
[a] includes variation inventory
[b] includes gas liquids
[c] internal consumption plus losses
[d] includes generation transmission and distribution losses
[e] includes raw materials and energy use
[f] includes assemble and net exchange
[g] includes crude oil for separating
[h] Contains virgin load

Source: PEMEX, Balance Energético 1983, Mexico City, PEMEX, 1984.

that something similar might occur with the current national energy program, PNE 1984-1988.

The difficulties involved in energy planning might be clearly understood if the main problems involved in its implementation are isolated. These problems are identified in the following subsections.

Intersectorial problems

Apparently, energy problems have met with serious difficulties in reconciling different interests. These difficulties mean that the programs have been unacceptable from the start or inadequately implemented at some later time. One of the main areas of strife is the industrial sector, which needs sufficient cheap energy to operate. Another is the financial sector, which requires the revenue from energy sales to cover financial commitments to federal government and several other public companies both at home and abroad. Other areas of permanent conflict are urban development; ecology, communication, and transport with respect to human-settlement problems; the deterioration of the environment; and the physical mobilization of resources by the different communication sources.

It is difficult for the four energy-planning agents--executive; the Secretaria de Energia, Minas e Industria Paraestatal (Ministry of Energy, Mines, and State-owned Industry; SEMIP), PEMEX, and the CFE--to think as one entity. This situation is a product of the influence each one wishes to have in the country's energy decisions. The executive's approach is generally global and normally has the support of the energy companies, their general directors appointed by the President of the republic. SEMIP's approach stems from the conviction that the country's development should be based on its industrial sector. It is unlikely that the energy companies, especially PEMEX, which believes that hydrocarbons should be the basis of development, will accept this approach.[32] Thus, each agent vies for increased influence in the country's decision making, which is only complicated by their often differing points of view. Finally, as we see later, it is not certain that these agents are capable of coordinating themselves.

Intrasectorial problems

Within the energy sector planning is made difficult by the participating companies' varying interests. For example, PEMEX has been concerned during the last few years with generating large amounts of foreign exchange, which implies that it is interested in placing better-priced commodities that are in greater demand on the foreign market, leaving the less competitive products for consumption at home. This practice is likely to affect CFE's interests because certain kinds of petroleum products, such as fuel oil, are needed to operate its thermoelectric power plants. If these products become scarce locally because of their demand abroad, CFE will have no other option but to operate with substitute products--if these are available. Another situation of strife exists between CFE and the nuclear electricity community (previously URAMEX). CFE has had to work according to the requirements of domestic demand, depending mainly on fuel oil-operated plants (and to a lesser extent on natural gas-operated plants) where project maturation periods are shorter and less costly. The nuclear electricity community has maintained a long-term approach in which it intends to moderate the importance of hydrocarbons in electricity generation and attempt to reduce nuclear electricity's technological dependence through the accumulation of know-how. This plan implies working well in advance of any increase in electricity demand.

Incompatibility problems between energy policy measures

There are many energy policy measures that if applied could considerably improve the financial situation of the sector's companies. The first measure is an increase in prices and tariffs; another is a reduction of subsidies through energy sales. For several reasons the implementation of such measures has always been controversial in Mexico: (1) the measures are highly unpopular; (2) they contradict anti-inflation policies generally included by the government in its economic policy objectives; (3) these measures tend to reduce activity in key areas of economic growth, for example, in the automobile, iron and steel, oil, glass, and paper industries; (4) they affect the buying power of lower-income groups; and (5) such measures increase the costs of some companies exporting manufactured goods, thus undermining international competitiveness and with it the chance to substitute hydrocarbons as the main source of foreign funds.

Frictions with other countries

In the realm of international policy, it is obviously very difficult for Mexico to maintain good relations with every country of the world and at the same time to obtain the foreign exchange necessary to fulfill its international financial obligations. This difficulty was made manifest during negotiations with the United States for the export of natural gas. It was also apparent when Mexico, under pressure from the international banking system and because of its development needs, made decisions concerning the optimal quantity of exported oil that weakened the oil market and consequently affected the interests and proposals of the Organization of Petroleum-Exporting Countries (OPEC). Recently, such frictions occurred during the creation of the Acuerdo de San José (San Jose Agreement) between Mexico, Venezuela, and the oil-importing countries of Central America and the Caribbean; Mexico was forced to collect payment due on exported crude from some buyer nations, even though their economic situation was possibly worse than Mexico's.

Financial problems

Although a reduction in hydrocarbon production and exports is desirable, the implementation of a plant to achieve this reduction is not easy. This activity is important to the federal treasury because more than 40 percent of the federal government's current income is derived from taxes imposed on the energy sector, particularly from those levied on hydrocarbon exports. Furthermore, the heavy commitments of Mexico's foreign debt could not be covered if it were not for the foreign exchange collected from energy exports. Thus, an awareness exists among economic policy makers that despite the quotas imposed by the energy programs, pressure could be exerted by different sectors to achieve flexibility should Mexico's financial problems worsen or should the policies designed to encourage manufactured exports fail to work.

Difficulties involved in using prices as a regulatory measure

The considerable waste of energy and the rapid growth in Mexico's consumption could be a reflection of the low price of goods and services developed by the energy sector. However, no work has been made public in the country that clearly quantifies the price elasticity of the demand for end-consumption energy. A great number of factor, apart from price, affect consumption. Among them are (1) the energy intensity of the country's industry, which to be reduced requires long-term saving and efficiency programs and structural changes in the industry itself; (2) the high level of internal consumption and waste in the energy sector, which is attributable to the speed at which work is carried out and which to be reduced requires specific long-term programs forslowing the rate of resource extraction, processing, and distribution; and (3) the demonstration effect, particularly notorious in private motorized transport where users are encouraged to use high cylinder automobiles.

Neighboring with the United States has also contributed to energy waste. The relatively low price of Mexican gasoline has acted as a bonus for American car owners who live on one side of the border but fill their tanks on the other. Increasing international prices would help to avoid this situation, but such action has not been taken by the Mexican government because of the inflationary pressures it would provoke. Another option is to close the frontier to

American automobiles, but this plan would affect tourism and create serious international political pressure.

In general, the price policy has been applied rather weakly by the Mexican government. A range of differential prices might help to reduce the consumption of certain sectors and productive areas, leaving others unaffected, but this plan has not been implemented. It is feared that such a policy would increase the federal government's administrative costs and give rise to a black market in sectors such as transport, particularly is subsidies (that is, coupons) were used to reduce the costs of those providing public transportation. This fear is based on experience gained when gasoline prices were increased in 1973.

Limitations to the scope of the subsidy policy

Subsidies in the form of preferential prices for energy consumed are granted to encourage the development of different productive areas. It is hoped this development will increase international competitiveness: Certain petroleum products not in demand abroad can be used internally as substitutes for other sought-after products. Something of this nature occurred with natural gas when negotiations for sales to the United States were thwarted.

This measure has not favored the economy a great deal, nor has it been an adequate medium for energy planning. It has debilitated public finances, and it has accentuated the problems of "industrial infantilism" characteristic of the import-substitution policy, rendering the companies that produce manufactured goods highly dependent on official stimuli. Finally, it has encouraged energy waste and slowed the pace of energy-saving and -efficiency policies.

CONCLUSIONS

Five very important points can be concluded from this chapter. First, not only is there a very close relationship between the energy sector and the country's economic development, but Mexico's main economic and financial variables show an excessive dependence on the production and export of energy.

Second, this sector's productive activity is comprised almost exclusively of two state companies, PEMEX and CFE, that have complete control over their respective productive processes. To a great extent the country's future in energy rests on these two companies.

Third, in just a few years Mexico's oil wealth has led to a substantial increase in the participation of hydrocarbons in the domestic primary energy supply. Given the energy-diversification trends in other countries, this increase could be a serious mistake in the long run.

Fourth, in Mexico energy waste is excessive, prices simply being an inadequate control measure. Undoubtedly, the energy sector has grown under the assumption that supply must satisfy demand and not that demand should be regulated to prevent excessive pressure on supply.

TABLE 1.6
PROVEN RESERVES (TO 31 DECEMBER), 1975-1983 (MB)

Year	Oil	Condensate	Gas Converted to Liquid	Total Liquid Hydro-carbons
1975	3,431.144	522.435	2,384.734	6,338.3
1976	6,435.681	843.232	3,881.974	11,160.8
1977	9,085.729	213.940	5,573.651	16,001.6
1978	25,614.524	2,792.395	11,787.000	40,194.0
1979	30,616.052	2,944.022	12,243.344	45,803.4
1980	44,161.135	3,062.963	12,902.289	60,126.4
1981	48,083.771	8,914.727	15,009.882	72,008.4
1982	48,083.771	8,914.727	15,009.882	72,008.4
1983	49,911.000	7,185.000	15,404.000	72,500.0

MB = millions of barrels.

Source: PEMEX: Memoria de labores, 1975-1983, Mexico City, PEMEX, 1976-1984.

TABLE 1.7
REGIONAL DISTRIBUTION OF PROVEN NATURAL GAS RESERVES (converted to liquid) (MB)

Year	Northern Zone	Angostura Poza Rica (Central Zone)	Southern Zone	Chicontepec	South-eastern Zone	Marine Zone (Gulf of Campeche)
1975	777.78	78.06	970.74	--	--	--
1976	1,584.86	151.63	1,573.29	--	--	--
1977	2,252.04	162.84	2,592.07	--	--	--
1978	2,703.80	195.82	2,980.26	5,355.00	--	--
1979	2,492.29	751.21[a]	3,652.27	5,537.56	--	--
1980	2,029.56	802.61[a]	4,722.77	5,347.33	--	--
1981	2,249.62	756.36[a]	6,659.15	5,344.74	--	--
1982	2,249.62	756.36[a]	6,659.15	5,344.74	--	--
1983	1,715.00	713.00[a]	238.00	5340.00	4,950.00	2,448.00

MB = millions of barrels.
[a] Total for the Central Zone.

Source: PEMEX, Memoria de labores, op. cit., 1975-1983.

Note: The southern zone comprises Agua Dulce, Pemex City, Comalcalco (Tertiary and Cretaceous), El Plan, and Nanchital. The southeastern zone comprises only the Comalcalco district (Tabasco-Chiapas).

Finally, given the very special nature of the Mexican political system and the country's acute economic, financial, institutional, technological, and organizational problems, energy planning is difficult not only to design but also to implement. Consequently, it is probable that energy decisions will continue to be made virtually independent of the objectives and goals contemplated by the energy-planning documents, particularly in the long run (see Table 1.6 and Table 1.7). To revert this trend is the unavoidable commitment of those responsible for future planning.

NOTES

1. SEPAFIN and STCE, "Programa de energía, metas a 1990 y proyecciones al año 2000", in Energéticos: Boletín Informativo del Sector Energético, Year 4, No. 11, Mexico City, STCE, November 1980, p. 26.
2. LAEO, Balances energéticos de América Latina, Quito, Ecuador, November 1981. Percentages are based on several figures.
3. See Poder Ejecutivo Federal, Programa nacional de energéticos, 1984-1988, Mexico City, SEMIP, Subsecretaría de Energía, 1984, various pages.
4. In 1921, 1922, and 1925 crude oil represented 48.3 percent, 50.3 percent, and 43.9 percent, respectively, of Mexico's total exports.
5. Between 1969 and 1974 Mexico's oil balance had a deficit. This period is the only time in the country's postrevolutionary history in which a deficit has occurred.
6. This rate of expansion fell from the late 1970s onward, which can be seen in Chapter 3 on the electricity industry.
7. These figures were based on constant prices of 1970 and include electricity and hydrocarbons.
8. PEMEX, the only net energy-exporting company in Mexico, pays the treasury more than 60 percent of its income from foreign sales. This income has meant from 1981 to 1983, almost $10 billion per year amounting to more than $15 billion. See PEMEX, Memoria de labores, 1981-1983, Mexico City, IMP, 1982, 1984.
9. PEMEX's accumulated foreign debt, which in 1970 represented 10 to 13 percent of the public

sector's accumulated foreign debt, rose to more than 20 percent in the early 1980s.

10. SPP and PEMEX, La industria petrolera en México, Mexico City, SPP, Dirección General de Integración y Análisis de la Información, 1983, pp. 116-122.

11. NAFINSA, La economía mexicana en cifras, 1984, Mexico City, NAFINSA, December 1984.

12. The gas-oil ratio, the first measured in terms of cubic meters and the second in terms of barrels, fell from 20 percent in 1970 to 8.5 percent in 1975, 5.2 percent in 1980, and 4.2 percent in 1982. This reduction occurred despite the fact that in the total for gas we are considering the nonassociated kind produced in the Gulf of Sabinas.

13. Mexico's total coal reserves, including proven, probable, and potential, are calculated to currently be between 2.6 and 5 billion metric tons. These estimates are higher than those of PNE 1984-1988. See Chapter 4 on the coal industry.

14. Guzmán, Oscar, "Nuevas fuentes energéticas," in Wionczek, Miguel S. (editor), Problemas del sector energético de México, Mexico City, El Colegio de México, 1983, p. 176.

15. In the late 1970s, having estimated the national reserves that were supposed large, Mexico asked the United States to provide it with enriched uranium. The American government refused to deliver several tons of this product, arguing that Mexico could make ill use of it, thus jeopardizing the safety of the international community. This refusal noticeably affected relations between the countries.

16. According to PNE 1984-1988 nuclear electricity would represent 2.7 percent of the installed capacity for electric energy in 1986 (the actual figure for this year was of 0.0 percent) and 4.9 percent in 1988. This electricity would come solely from the units at Laguna Verde, which would come on line at different times (at present, late 1987, Laguna Verde plant is still not in operation). Later projects still appear uncertain, their materialization dependent on many random factors.

17. The AAGR for total energy consumption was 7.2 percent for the period from 1970 to 1975 and 7.5 percent from 1975 to 1983. The resulting elasticity for the latter period was 1.7 percent, taking

total consumption into consideration. The AAGR for consumption per capita was 3.8 percent between 1970 and 1975 and 6.7 percent in the following seven years.
    18. Guzmán, Oscar, Antonio Yúnez-Naude, and Miguel S. Wionczek, Uso eficiente y conservación de la energía en México: Diagnóstico y perspectivas, Mexico City, El Colegio de México, Energy Program, 1985, pp. 31-43. See also Willars Andrade, Jaime Mario, "Perspectivas de la demanda interna y posibilidades de ahorro y sustitución de los energéticos en México," in Wionczek, Miguel S. (editor), op. cit., pp. 35-41.
    19. Even when the domestic supply of these products has increased, some of them (gasoline, kerosene, lubricants, and others) have continued to be imported. See PEMEX, Anuario estadístico, 1982, Mexico City, PEMEX, 1983, pp. 123-124.
    20. SEPAFIN and STCE, op. cit., November 1981, p. 11.
    21. Corresponding to this factor, the energy sector's share in total energy consumption was 53.7 percent in 1970 and 47.6 percent in 1982.
    22. Its coefficient went from 31.7 percent in 1970 to 36.4 percent in 1982.
    23. These losses were 14.5 percent in 1970 and 15.7 percent in 1982.
    24. Guzmán, Oscar, et al., op. cit., p. 9.
    25. Idem.
    26. This decree establishes the minimum requirements for automobile fuel efficiency. These regulations were published by the federal government through SEPAFIN in December 1981. See Diario Oficial, Mexico City, 21 December 1981.
    27. Willars Andrade, Jaime Mario, op. cit., pp. 44-46.
    28. In 1977 Mexico tried to sell gas to the United States at $2.60 per thousand cubic feet, although the domestic price was equivalent to $0.32 per thousand cubic feet.
    29. Guzmán, Oscar, et al., op. cit., p. 14.
    30. Willars Andrade, Jaime Mario, op. cit., p. 50.
    31. Idem., pp. 44-46.
    32. This proposal was for the 1976-1982 six-year term, originating serious controversy between the ministry for this area (SEMIP) and PEMEX.

2

Planning and Development in the Hydrocarbon Subsector

Roberto Gutiérrez

The petroleum industry has for many years been one of the most important factors in Mexico's development. The history of this country in the twentieth century would have been completely different if Mexico's subsoil had not been endowed with such large hydrocarbon resources. These resources have affected the country;s history in at least four ways: (1) In political terms hydrocarbons have contributed to the domestic consensus of practically all Mexican post-1910 government and have become a fundamental ingredient in Mexico;s international bilateral and multilateral negotiations; (2) in economic terms hydrocarbons have been the cornerstone of the country's industrial development during all its postrevolutionary history, particularly between 1915 and 1945 and again since 1975, because they have provided foreign exchange without which economic growth would have been much slower; (3) in social terms by stressing the key role of the country;s natural resources they have served as an example for the integration of the different social groups; and (4) in technological terms these resources have helped prove that Mexico has been able not only to manage a modern and complicated industrial sector but also to become known internationally as an exporter of technology.

TABLE 2.1
PRODUCTION AND EXPORT OF CRUDE OIL AND ITS
DERIVATIVES, 1911-1937 (TBD average)

Year	Production (1)	Exports (2)	(1)/(2) (%)
1911	34.34	2.47	7.2
1913	64.92	58.44	90.0
1915	90.17	67.86	75.3
1917	151.49	126.09	83.2
1919	238.56	206.99	86.8
1920	430.33	398.66	92.6
1922	499.39	495.52	99.2
1924	382.68	355.34	92.9
1926	247.73	222.95	90.0
1928	137.40	99.66	72.5
1930	108.30	73.89	68.2
1932	89.88	61.88	68.8
1934	96.36	68.54	71.1
1936	112.40	68.63	61.1
1937	128.51	68.42	53.2

TBD = thousands of barrels per day.

Source: Secretaría de la Economía Nacional, Boletín de petróleo y minas, Mexico City, January 1939, pp. 13 and 15.

OIL NATIONALIZATION AND ITS CONSEQUENCES, 1938-1974

In its beginnings, that is to say during the first few years of this century, the Mexican oil industry was completely controlled by foreign capital. The main companies were American and British, the former holding the largest share of production and investment. The production process followed a rising path from the time before World War I until it reached its height during the early 1920s. It then began to drop primarily because of the overexploitation of existing deposits (see Table 2.1). The main markets for Mexican oil were the United States and Great Britain. During World War I Mexico became the second most important international oil producer, due primarily to oil's essential role as a strategic material for the countries at war and to the suspension of imports from the Soviet Union because of the commercial block imposed by the Western powers after the October Revolution.

During this oil bonanza the first attempts were made to restrict exploitation by foreign companies. With the proclamation of the 1917 constitution and, specifically, its Artículo 27, a long struggle began between the oil companies and Mexican authorities. It was established that the ownership of the subsoil and its riches were the direct and inalienable dominion of the nation (that is, the state), which had the right to grant concessions to individuals or groups to exploit such resources on the condition that the concessionaries operate according to Mexican law. Many attempts were made to prevent this article from coming into force, and the debates to determine its viability went on for a long time. Despite modifications to the constitution, there was virtually no chance for oil legislation at that time.

A new possibility arose with the creation of the Sindicato de Trabajadores Petroleros de la República Mexicana (Mexican Oil Workers' Trade Union; STPRM) in 1935 and the signing of a collective labor contract in 1936. The labor conflict was taken up by President Lázaro Cárdenas in an attempt to force the foreign companies to share both their profits and their administrative functions. In 1937 when Cárdenas intervened to prevent the oil trade union strike, the oil-reform problem became an issue between the companies and the government, the labor conflict being more of a pretext than a real motive.

The nationalization of oil in March 1938 occurred at a favorable moment both domestically and internationally. At home, Cárdenas had considerable support from the popular sector. Abroad, the pressure from the United States was not strong because U.S. attention was centered on the worldwide fascist threat. However, the economic and political pressure exerted by the expropriated companies—and the acute economic crisis caused by a drop in exports—created difficult moments for Mexico in the years following nationalization. Amongst the obstacles to be carefully managed were:

- Organizational problems in the new industry starting with the assets and activities of the former oil company owners

- The substitution of high-level technical and ad-ministrative organizations for existing offices and general administrative personnel, which until completed meant a doubling of staff and offices

- The need to organize technical administration, establishing the basis for the preparation of new personnel, which until nationalization had been supervised from abroad

- Trade union conflicts over work relations, which were made manifest through pressures from the labor representatives to achieve wage-scale equality for the different oil centers and a greater participation in the company's administration

- Financial difficulties during the whole period that worsened at times because of an international boycott and that were exacerbated by the worn-out or obsolete equipment, pipelines, and refineries received by the Mexican oil industry in 1938

Another factor affecting the company's financial situation was the decree of 31 December 1944 that made PEMEX totally responsible for the compensations to be paid by the federal government to the expropriated oil companies. The necessary sums were taken from PEMEX earnings.

During the six-year Cárdenas regime (1934-1940), a series of important reforms occurred, resulting in the consolidation of the new politico-economic model with the state as the central figure. A key element in this new model was nationalism, which acted as a cohesive ideology in decision making in the nation's interests. The element allowed a broadening of the state's functions in strategic activities. Energy, especially oil, became the basis for these objectives and, together with the agrarian reform and the nationalization of railways, implied a break with the enclave-like economy. From the time they were nationalized, hydrocarbons were to opportunely and economically cover the different sectors' oil-related needs. Thus, oil would provide indispensable energy resources for fulfilling development and economic self-sufficiency objectives.

Although nationalism permitted the conscious construction of a centralized political apparatus, oil consolidated the central role of the state in relation to other domestic and external actors. The state demonstrated the autonomy of its decisions before the foreign oil companies in Mexico and before its own workers' union and others which led to a substantial improvement in the oil workers' living standards. However, it was not until 1940, with the change of regime, that Mexico began a period of rapid economic growth, encouraged in part by the outbreak of the World War II.[1] The speed at which this industrialization process occurred largely explains the exportation of agricultural sector surpluses and Mexico's internal energy self-sufficiency.

Rapid industrial expansion occurred from 1940 to 1970. The hydrocarbon subsector clearly manifested the limitations of the low-price and subsidy policy; the delay in key activities, such as exploration; and the priority given to short-term investment as opposed to basic slow-return investments. In 1966 for the first time in its oil history, Mexico stopped exporting crude oil. PEMEX's financial situation had caused the exploration program to advance very slowly. The main hindrance to the company's expansion lay in needing to respond to demand requirements while having to manage with limited financial resources because of very low domestic energy prices. Thus, toward the mid-1970s the reserve-production (R/P) ratio had fallen to the desired minimum--14 years. This fall in the ratio meant that an urgent change was needed in the oil industry's local role and objectives. The company's position had to be reestablished to the point where it was capable of supplying the internal market with oil, gasoline, basic petrochemicals, lubricants, and other products, as was contemplated in the Articulo 27, the "Law of 58." However, PEMEX also had to be able to increase its reserves and suspend imports of these products. This situation was the result of several factors: the particular industrialization stage that Mexico was going through, its position in the international market, and world economic changes with the first signs of recession. By the end of the Echeverria government (1971-1976), the following situation existed: (1) a serious lag in production in certain key economic areas; (2) the political, economic, and social deterioration of the agricultural sector; (3) a progressive weakening of private investment; and (4) a lack of attention to social well-being and the distribution of wealth.

These conditions forced the reformulation of the broad economic policy objectives and paved the way for oil industry development during the subsequent administration. The 1973-1974 energy crisis served to boost exploratory activities in southeast Mexico that had begun early in 1972. Crude oil self-sufficiency was the result; with oil exports starting again in 1974. However, the surpluses for that year and the following two were small because in official circles no one really had a clear idea of the country's true oil potential.

THE OIL INDUSTRY'S VERTICAL EXPANSION

Over a period of thirty years after expropriation decree in March 1938, the oil industry gradually became an essential part of the country's program for internal development, with oil production becoming a major factor in the industrialization process. Mexico was faced with the challenge of having to develop its exploratory, technological, productive, and organizational abilities. As a result, the Mexican oil industry underwent rapid vertical expansion and in a very few years became one of the most integrated in the world.

In the field of oil exploration and exploitation, the country had to realize that the newly formed company's technological knowledge and capabilities were based solely on what was left by the expropriated companies. The challenge lay in operating an industry that had been in the hands of these companies for many years. This task was extremely difficult because support from abroad was no longer available, and there was a lack of sufficient and timely financial resources. A large part of the company's revenue was used to pay the expropriated companies compensation, which directly affected the starting areas of the oil industry's productive chain, that is, exploration and exploitation.

Once most of the debt had been settled, the company began to negotiate direct foreign investment in exploration and exploitation with the major international consortiums. This plan was unsuccessful, and the company resorted to reorienting its policy by offering limited contracts to U.S. exploratory companies. Subsequent contracts would be granted for drilling operations in the continental marine shelf with the stipulation that once expired the contract would not be renewed.[2] Technical and organizational knowledge that was acquired from these groups formed the basis for the later development of the national oil industry. These oil contracts appear to have been a wise decision and can be used as an example for other industries, proving that Mexico has conducted favorable negotiations.

PEMEX barely had sufficient facilities for refining crude oil and natural gas. Its processing capacity amounted to 102 TBD through primary distillation and 12 TBD through viscosity breakers. Although the domestic market was still thin for petroleum products in the late 1960s --diesel sales, for example, accounted for only 11 percent of production--it was considered advisable to continue to expand primary-distillation processing capacity, with the aim of providing a basis for industrial development that would require either fuel oil or natural gas. Because natural gas was not readily available, it was essential to increase fuel oil production.

Primary-distilling capacity grew steadily after nationalization. Its growth index went from 100 in 1938 to 128 in 1940 to 226 in 1951. Over this period no new refineries were set up, but the existing ones were extended by importing technology and the appropriate equipment. A lag existed in disintegration processes involving the catalysis and viscosity-breaking plant because it was not considered advisable to stimulate diesel and gasoline production when Mexico's transport system still did no require it. There were, in fact, exportable surpluses.

From 1947 onward a major boost was given to refining activity with the construction of three new refineries. These refineries meant a substantial increase in total gasoline production capacity, which went from 14 percent of total oil production in 1946 to 25 percent in 1959. Fuel oil production capacity dropped from 54 percent to 42 percent during the same period.

These figures suggest that refining was one of the activities in which the nationalized oil industry had few problems. However, because the expansion of processing capacity was not speedy enough to satisfy domestic demand for gasoline, which had doubled from 1950 to 1959, it became necessary to import oil products; imports increased from 2.2 MB in 1950 (19 percent of production) to 3.1 MB in 1959 (12 percent of production).[3] One reason why demand exceeded supply was a delay in refinery completion because of the company's insufficient revenues. By the second half of the 1970s, the financial problem had been resolved; refining activity was expanded by the construction of three new refineries: Tula, Salina Cruz, and Cadereyta. Despite this expansion, prices continued to be subsidized, as suggested by the fact that a large part of the company's earnings was originated in crude oil exports.

During these years similar percentages of gasoline and fuel oil were produced, 28 percent and 27 percent, respectively. By the end of 1982 the nominal capacity for primary distillation grew 66 percent more than it had from 19?? to 19??, reaching 1.63 million barrels a day (MBD), and the figure for disintegration and viscosity breaking increased by 43 percent, that is, 397 TBD.

In the early 1980s, due to the incentives of previous administrations and a price policy that openly supported PEMEX's efforts to gain financial self-sufficiency, the production of refined products exceeded the domestic demand and started generating considerable surpluses, which are exported. During 1983 and 1984 these surpluses averaged nearly 100 TBD, which meant an income of around $1 billion for each of the two years.

In transport and distribution to be able to continue supplying domestic demand and maintain transport capacity, PEMEX had to take care of the expansion and maintenance of overland and maritime transportation.[4] Although in 1938 the company's maritime fleet consisted of only one tanker and 5 tugboats, by 1941 it had already increased to 17 tankers and 6 tugboats. Furthermore, over the years internal distribution capacity increased substantially with the installation of gas pipelines, polyducts, and oil pipelines, and an augmented fleet of tank trucks, all of which were the responsibility of PEMEX. Gradually, the number of service stations, as well as sales agencies and warehouses, also increased. Thus, the whole national territory eventually was covered.

Another factor in PEMEX's expansion was the inauguration of several representative offices in three of the most important import regions of the world; North America, Europe, and Japan. These offices are located in New York, Paris, and Tokyo, respectively, and although oriented toward coverage of the international market, they have played an important role in the export of Mexican crude oil and petroleum products. The offices have also helped to increase the number of PEMEX clients, which by 1984 was 435, covering 22 countries.[5]

In primary petrochemicals Articulo 27 was the cornerstone of PEMEX's vertical integration because it paved the way for primary petrochemical development. The regulation stated that apart from oil exploration and exploitation, the state petroleum company would hold a monopoly over the following activities in the hydrocarbon subsector: processing, storage, transport, distribution, and sales of petroleum derivatives to be used as basic industrial materials. Thus, PEMEX was given the exclusive right to control basic petrochemical production; private capital was completely excluded from this area. The law established that the private sector could utilize these basic products for the production of intermediate- and final-use petrochemicals provided the respective permits were obtained from PEMEX, the Secretaria del Patrimonio Nacional (Ministry of National Patrimony; SEPANAL) and the Secretaria de Industria y Comercio (Ministry of Industry and Commerce; SIC) (the names of these ministries have changed over time, but their responsibilities have not). The law also assigned the responsibility of applying regulations and the necessary legal baggage for oil industry development to SEPANAL. This baggage has evolved as the hydrocarbon subsector grew, giving PEMEX enough flexibility to allow it a high degree of autonomy.

Although the legal basis for state expansion of primary petrochemical production was established by this law, the expansion was somewhat slow during the 1950s. It was accelerated, however, in the late 1960s when in addition to sulphur, dodecylbenzene, ethylene, and ammonia, which were already being produced, other products of greater complexity were introduced, that is, aromatics, which are fundamental to the development of synthetic fibers and resines, plastics, plasticizers, and detergents. In the 1970s the boom reached its highest point, and in many ways the industry became truly consolidated because of the discovery of hydrocarbons. This discovery made it possible in only six years, from 1977 to 1982, for the total petrochemical production to increase three-fold, reaching 10.6 million tons.[6] Currently, despite international market saturation, PEMEX has a broad exporting capacity in primary petrochemicals, particularly in methanol, ammonia, ethylene, and aromatics.

In R&D the creation of IMP in 1965 allowed PEMEX to develop certain key productive processes for exploration, exploitation, and transformation activities, some of which have been patented internationally. Furthermore, the research in these areas has given the company international recognition, most notably in exploration where it has cooperated with various countries, particularly those in Central and South America. Of course, PEMEX still has a long way to go in R&D; however, with what it has already achieved the oil industry has contributed more than any other to industrial R&D in Mexico. The Mexican government's present crisis with its foreign debt has improved and strengthened the company's technological self-sufficiency. Thus, the imported content of PEMEX's investments, which during the last six-year term (1977-1982) amounted to at least 60 percent, has currently fallen to around 40 percent. Needless to say, this reduction has contributed substantially to the company's internal savings, which at present are the highest in the state-owned industrial sector.

PEMEX's rapid expansion is also evident in its employment figures. In 1938 the number of employees was 17,600; this figure doubled by 1951 and doubled once again by 1971. By 1980, after the oil expansion of the late 1970s, it reached almost 116,000. This figure is considerably higher if casual labor is included.[7] The growth in the number of people employed has meant the creation of many necessary services to cover workers' needs. Thus, PEMEX has become involved in areas completely outside the scope of the oil industry itself, for example, lower-level education, medical services, housing construction, recreational parks, the organization of social activities, and so on.

INTERNAL STRUCTURE AND THE CORRELATION OF FORCES

The Mexican oil industry is administered by PEMEX, which covers all stages of the productive process from exploration to domestic and foreign trade. The company's top executive is the director general, whose decisions are submitted to an administrative council. In practice, however, decision making is fairly centralized, which is logical in a presidential system such as Mexico's. PEMEX's director general and the council members, who hold high posts in other departments either directly or indirectly involved with oil activities, are granted their respective positions by the president of the republic. These members include the following:

- The secretary and undersecretary of state in charge of industrial activities. (The name given to this department has been modified over the years from SEPANAL to the Secretaria del Patrimonio y Fomento Industrial [Ministry for National Patrimony and Industrial Promotion; SEPAFIN] to the present SEMIP. The minister for SEMIP is also the president of the administrative council and is responsible for approving PEMEX's annual budget.)

- The Secretaria de Hacienda y Crédito Público (Ministry of Finance; SHCP) also acts as vice-president of the council

- The Secretaria de Comercio y Fomento Industrial (the name of this department has also been modified over the years and is now the Ministry of Commerce and Industrial Promotion; SECOFI).

- The director general of the main financial development bank, Nacional Financiera, S.A. (National Finance Bank; NAFINSA)

- Five members of STPRM

Seven assistant directors aid PEMEX's director general in his administrative functions (there were nine during the last administration). Below the directors, in order of importance, are general coordinators, managers, assistant managers, superintendents, analysts, and so on (see Figure 2.1).

A variety of individuals either directly or indirectly participate in the oil industry's decision making. Their power is weakened or strengthened according to circumstances. They can be divided into three large groups: the government, private entrepreneurs, and the general public.

As one can imagine from earlier discussions of the PEMEX administrative structure, the first group is in no way homogeneous. The interests and points of view of its members regarding oil's role in development do not always coincide.

The government entities with the biggest opinion gaps between them, at least during the 1976-1982 term, were the oil company as a whole, the representatives of the state-owned industrial sector (SEPAFIN), and the financial sector. PEMEX felt that Mexico's economic development should be based on a hydrocarbon production and exporting capacity strong enough to guarantee adequate operation of the productive apparatus and to obtain the necessary foreign exchange to eliminate bottlenecks.[8] SEPAFIN's policy, however, was oriented toward diversification of the production and exporting capacity so as to minimize the risk of hydrocarbon dependence. Finally, the fundamental concern of the financial sector (SHCP, the Banco de México, and NAFINSA) was to acquire resources both in national and foreign currency so as to reduce the pressure being placed upon public finances. With these policy objectives in mind PEMEX was taxed even further, particularly on foreign crude oil sales, which accounted for a little over 60 percent of the total value of Mexico's merchandise exports. Although Mexico's change in administrations in December 1981 helped to reduce substantially the differences between PEMEX and the industrial ministry (now SEMIP), it still cannot be said that they altogether share the same ideas regarding the oil industry's role in the country's economic development.

The stance of the private entrepreneurs tends to vary according to the ideological nature of the government in office. When the government is in favor of free enterprise, the position of the entrepreneurs is reinforced; however, when the state pushes for greater participation in the economy, their position is weakened. Private enterprise's main concern in the oil industry is production costs, which, as is argued repeatedly, need to be low. This effort, maintain the industrialists, would benefit the society twice over; on one hand, it would allow end-product prices to be kept low, and on the other, it would increase the competitiveness of their merchandise on the international market, implying a greater inflow of foreign exchange for the country. Also, private entrepreneurs have always sought greater participation in oil policy decision making, particularly in regard to export quantities and the country's use of corresponding foreign earnings. They argue that if the income is substantial, part of it should return to them through the financial system for the purpose of servicing their foreign debt and obtaining the imports they need to increase their production and export capacity.

Last, although the general public constitutes the largest group numerically, it carries the least weight. This group consists of intellectuals; journalists; university students; and home consumers, those requiring hydrocarbons for domestic consumption.

FIGURE 2.1
CURRENT ORGANIZATIONAL HIERARCHY IN PEMEX*

President of the Republic
Administrative Council
Director General

| Assistant Director for Primary Production | Assistant Director for Industrial Transformation | Assistant Director for Trade | Assistant Director for Projects & Works | Technical and Administrative Assistant Director | Assistant Director for Planning and Coordination | Assistant Director for Finances |

Coordinators

Managers

Assistant Managers

Head Analysts

Analysts

*This hierarchical diagram should be differentiated from the administrative diagram in which, for normal reasons, the president of the republic dos not appear and the administrative council is placed above the director general.

Source: Diagram of the PEMEX administrative organization, 1984, with modifications by the author.

Its power has been reinforced during certain periods in which the oil policy decision has been the center of economic policy and the subject of national interest, such as during the last few years. Furthermore, their point of view has contributed to controlling and cushioning oil-price increases and has been a crucial factor in considering the adverse ecological effects and the security problems created by excessive exploitation.

THE NEW ROLE OF HYDROCARBONS IN THE GOVERNMENT'S POLITICO-ECONOMIC PROJECT AND OIL PLANNING

The government change in December 1976 occurred in the midst of political and economic pressures. Private enterprise's opposition to the decisions made by the Echeverría government was manifested particularly in the flight of capital and the contraction of private investment. These factors--along with a growing foreign debt, inflation, a marked worsening in the balance-of-payment situation, and the peso devaluation in 1976--made the state change the course of its "conservationist" oil policy in favor of an expansionist one. Food and energy were the main priorities of the José López Portillo administration.

Incorporating the expansionist stance into the company could only be achieved through a revaluation of reserves, which was ordered by the new director general of PEMEX, Jorge Díaz Serrano. This decision was the most important policy change made by the new PEMEX administrators given that conservationist groups argued of the existence of limited reserves and a sustained growth in domestic demand.[9] The expansionists, in turn, claimed that the new oil potential would become the foundation for future economic policy.

The existence of oil was so important for Mexico that despite the monetary devaluation and the agreement for broader support by the International Monetary Fund (IMF), the country was able to conduct itself independently of international financial circles.[10] It is significant that Mexico had a tendency toward oil concentration as an economic, political, and social strategy, while the international energy scene leaned toward energy diversification with a special emphasis on conservation.[11] The state economic policy, denominated "alliance for production," hoped to reestablish alliances with other economic sectors--especially those producing manufactured goods--through incentives for private investment, subsidies, controlled wage increases, and an expansive physical and financial policy. Oil would be the source of foreign exchange that would provide the state with the necessary resources to achieve this goal.

With growing foreign indebtedness and a political unwillingness by the state to transform its tax and subsidy system, to generate additional income the new administration introduced significant changes in the economy's objectives and priorities, which were reinforced by PEMEX in its fortified role as a generator of resources. (As is well known, this proposal did not work, and the nonoil sector of the economy eroded over the years.) This effort had to be convincingly justified in official rhetoric; so, oil became "the lever for the country's development," and incoming foreign exchange was to be reinvested in development activities.

The difference between the Plan Nacional de Desarrollo Industrial (National Plan for Industrial Development; PNDI) 1979-1982 and the Plan Global de Desarrollo (Global Development Plan; PGD) 1980-1982 was that PNDI emphasized the development of industries, such as capital goods, steel, and petrochemicals, and PGD tried to establish the foundations for a more balanced growth between agriculture and industry, thus largely supporting the growth strategy of PNDI.

Of course, a time lapse between the appearance of these two documents was important in regard to the role given to oil. In 1979 when PNDI was released, price raises had just begun because of the revolution of Iran. A few months later, the prices had already doubled, giving PGD an air of optimism. The same situation presented itself again between PGD and PE 1980-1982, which appeared months later.

The optimist forecasts for the international oil market led planners to raise their figures for economic growth and exports, which resulted in generalized but unfounded optimism. The optimism turned into frustration 1+ years later when the Mexican economy went into its worst recession since World War II.

TABLE 2.2
RATIO OF EXPORTS TO PRODUCTION AND RESERVES TO PRODUCTION OF CRUDE OIL IN MEXICO, 1970-1983 (MB)

Year	Production (1)	Exports	Total Reserves[a] (2)	(2)/(1) (%)	(2)-(1) (no. of years)
1970	156.6	--	5,568	--	18
1972	161.4	--	5,388	--	17
1974	209.9	5.8	5,773	2.8	15
1976	293.1	34.5	11,160	11.8	24
1978	442.6	133.2	40,194	30.1	61
1980	708.6	303.0	60,126	42.8	59
1982	1,003.1	544.6	72,008	54.3	52
1983	981.2	561.0	72,500	57.2	54

MB = millions of barrels.
[a]This category includes natural gas.

Source: Based upon information received from PEMEX.

For oil to become the cornerstone of the production alliance, an extensive expansion program was necessary. Thus, Diaz Serrano presented the Programa Sexenal de PEMEX (PEMEX Six-Year Program) 1980-1986, whose main objective was a substantial increase in hydrocarbon production, refined products, and primary petrochemicals. This increase was to be achieved by investing large amounts of money in these production activities. Crude oil production increased from 874.2 TBD in 1976 to 2.25 million barrels per day (MBD) in 1982, almost half of which was for export. Furthermore, the rate of refining activity doubled, and petrochemical production tripled.[12]

Among the company's financial objectives was a reduction in operation expenditures with respect to sales, increased productivity, and careful selection of investment projects and purchasing conditions. Financing from abroad would only be complementary to the resources coming from domestic sales.[13] The most significant changes during the six years were an increase in traded volumes both in the domestic and foreign market and growth in the ratio of total exports to total production and the R/P ratio. These changes are shown in Table 2.2; although exports were virtually nonexistent in 1972, by 1982 they accounted for 54.3 percent of total production. Similarly, the R/P ratio, which had fallen to 15 years in 1974, rose to 52 years in 1982. These changes were possible first because of the discovery of the Chiapas-Tabasco Cretaceous zone in the early 1970s and second because of the Campeche marine platform discovery a number of years later.

However, given the economic productive structure, the utilization of foreign exchange from oil sales had to be defined according to national development priorities. This definition made it necessary to place a ceiling on oil exports in order to avoid and oil-led growth economy. The income from oil exports, it was said, should not surpass "the economy's absorption capacity." In reply to criticism of those who favored an oil-oriented economy, it was said that "Mexico intended to be a country with oil and not an oil country."

This last point of view took shape in PGD and PNDI as well as in PSP 1908-1986. Oil's role should be gradually modified as the overall productive capacity of the economy is stimulated. Thus, although in PGD and PNDI oil was defined as "the lever of development," clear objectives were stipulated later such as determining the quantities of possible resources and the alternatives for their utilization.

In PNDI and PGD optimistic forecasts had economic growth averaging between 8 and 8.8 percent annually; 4 percent more jobs would be created, and the rate of private investment would be around 13 percent. While additional measures were proposed during the first half of the six-year López Portillo administration, an attempt of a profound fiscal reform aimed at strengthenning public finances failed because of lack of governments's determination.

In light of the trade policy established in different social sectors, the trend toward dependence on oil earnings was being questioned as were the high subsidies that the government used to favored private entrepreneurs and that stimulated the wasteful use of hydrocarbons by large public enterprises, CFE and PEMEX being the biggest energy consumers. Also, although operation expenditures were lowered in relation to PEMEX's own income, this reduction was attributable to an increase in sales and not to an improvement in company operations. However, as income began to grow in relation to expenditure and before-tax profits began to increase considerably, the federal government introduced a policy by which surpluses generated by PEMEX would be reassigned to other areas and to projects considered of the utmost priority.[14]

The most important entities in determining the management of petroleum industries and their position in the state organization were the executive, PEMEX, SEPAFIN, SHCP, and the Secretaría de Programación y Presupuesto (Ministry for Programming and Budget; SPP). Although the executive and PEMEX made the final decisions, SEPAFIN was in charge of encouraging private investment through official stimuli and by promoting industrialization to make reactivation, restructuration, and modernization of industrial production possible. Last, SHCP was responsible for the public sector income and SPP for its expenditure and planning and budgeting for the whole economy.

The centralized nature of decision making was highly criticized, particularly in regard to the independent decisions made by PEMEX's, which completely excluded SEPAFIN's director. The situation was reinforced by the changes in the R/P ratio, which endorsed the role of oil as the lever of development. Therefore, in 1978 Díaz Serrano announced that the goals for crude oil production and the export of crude oil for 1982 would be reached by 1980. He then proposed monthly programs for 1979 and 1980 to step up production and exports. Furthermore, this ratio increased, from 24 years in 1976 to 61 years in 1978 and 1979 (see Table 2.2).

THE VICISSITUDES OF INTERNATIONAL HYDROCARBON TRADE

PEMEX's total exports during the 1976-1982 term consisted basically of crude oil, which increased from 95 TBD in 1976 to 1.3 MBD in 1981 and to 1.7 MBD late in 1982. This constituted around 99 percent of the industry's total export volume. The situation that prevailed in the international market until early in 1981 allowed Mexico to benefit from crude oil price increases and to determine its trade strategy in coordination with a domestic oil policy. The period from 1979 to 1981 brought important changes in the evolution of foreign trade not only because of the increasing volume of crude oil exports but also because of greatly improved negotiating power on the part of the producing countries as a result of the Iranian revolution and the outbreak of the Iran-Irak War.

TABLE 2.3
AVERAGE ANNUAL PRICES FOR MEXICAN CRUDE ON THE INTERNATIONAL MARKET, 1974-1984 (U.S. $)

Year	Isthmus (34x API)	Maya (23x API)	Weighted Average
1974	10.66[d]	- -	10.66[d]
1975	11.21[a]	- -	11.21[a]
1976	12.18	- -	12.18
1977	13.39	- -	13.39
1978	13.21	- -	13.21
1979	19.55	21.50	19.60
1980	33.33	28.72	31.28
1981	35.93	31.01	33.20
1982	32.81	25.23	28.69
1983	29.87	23.96	26.42
1984	29.08	25.40	26.90

API = American Petroleum Institute.
[a]This figure was converted to the exchange rate for that year.

Source: Based on PEMEX, Memoria de labores, various years.

Between 1977 and 1979 the sustained growth in the internal demand for oil derivatives contributed to a progressive increase in income from the domestic market. A greater volume of domestic sales was the determining factor in this trend, and the low energy price was reaffirmed because product prices set late in 1973 were not modified.[15]

The international market situation, aided by the production and export of heavy crude oil from the new deposits in the Campeche marine basin, allowed the company's income from foreign sales to rise. The increase in exports and international prices brought the country considerable economic benefits from 1979 to 1981. However, the fall in prices that followed, shown in Table 2.3, marked a change in the role this product might play in Mexico's economic future.

Natural gas exports did not contribute significantly to the oil industry's trade balance until 1980 when an agreement was reached between Mexico and the United States regarding the sale of this product on the American market. These sales did not amount to the 2 billion cubic feet per day (BCFD) that was initially agreed upon; in the final agreement in 1979 it was decided to export only 300 million cubic feet per day (MCFD). This change in the agreement came about because the Mexican government decided to channel greater volumes into its domestic market in order to cover industry's growing needs, particularly in the north of the country. In spite of the fact that gas production rose from 2.1 BCFD in 1976 to 4.1 BCFD in 1981, in October 1984 it was decided to suspend gas exports to the United States, and currently all the gas produced in the country is consumed internally.

In mid-1981 PEMEX's dynamic financial situation began to slow because of fluctuations in international oil prices. A reduction in export value led the company to review some of its investment projects, which mainly affected the petrochemical and refining industries. Toward the end of the López Portillo government's six-year term and despite these changes of fortune, oil had fulfilled an important role in the economy: it had generated approximately $55 billion from exports, having been responsible for three-fourths of the revenue from merchandise sold abroad. In addition, through taxes on domestic and foreign sales, oil contributed to nearly 40 percent of the federal government's income.

Needless to say, the oil industry's extraordinary rate of expansion during the 1970s and into the 1980s meant a heavy drain on the economy. It contributed to an increase in the public sector's total foreign debt, which went from 19.6 billion in 1976 to more than $60 billion in 1982. In 1976 PEMEX's share in the total external debt was 11.3 percent. In 1982,

It was already more than 30 percent.[16] This situation also played a very important role in the accelerated growth rate of public expenditure, which caused the government's fiscal indebtedness to grow and eventually become permanent. In 1982 the deficit had already reached 17.4 percent of the GNP. PEMEX's expenditure, which in 1976 accounted for 15.4 percent of the total budget of state-owned companies, grew to 26.6 percent in 1982.[17] The company was responsible for a large percentage of the previous deficit, a paradoxical situation given its very high income.

TABLE 2.4
HYDROCARBON PRODUCTION, 1983-1984

Product	Year	Year	Annual Variation	Amount Obtained versus Amount Proposed (%)
Crude Oil (TBD)	2,665.5	2,684.5	0.7	99.4
Natural Gas (MCFD)	4,053.6	3,752.7	-7.4	96.2
Petroleum Products (TBD)	1,248.4	1,286.4[a]	3.0	102.1
Liquid Gas (TBD)	154.9	156.1	0.8	91.8
Gasoline (TBD)	355.2	362.7	2.1	98.0
Diesel (TBD)	224.0	232.9	4.0	97.0
Fuel Oil (TBD)	350.2	374.9	7.1	98.7
Other	164.1	159.8	-2.6	159.8

TBD = thousands of barrels per day.
MCFD = millions of cubic feet per day.
[a]This figure excludes virgin stock.

Source: SPP and DGDE, Plan nacional de desarrollo, segundo informe de ejecución 1984, Mexico City, 1985, pp. 127-132.

RECENT RESULTS AND FUTURE PROSPECTS

The plans for production, productivity, foreign trade, the betterment of finances, and energy saving and conservation followed by PEMEX during the López Portillo administration (from December 1981) are part of a new policy designed to confront the present government's economic, financial, and political problems. These problems can be explained partly by misjudgments made during the oil-boom year and partly by the 1981-1982 international economic crisis, which led to a heavy increase in international interest rates, a strengthening of the U.S. dollar, and a new wave of protectionist measures by Mexico's main trade partners, particularly the United States. These problems also help explain the country's heavy foreign debt (the second highest in the world after Brazil) and the reason why Mexico had to resort once again to renegotiation with IMF. The new agreement allowed the country to acquire foreign exchange in the short term to service its debt and to later consolidate refinancing for more than $60 billion that the government still owes to international financial institutions.

So as not to repeat past experiences, during the first year of PNE 1984-1988 it was determined that all the hydrocarbon subsector production targets had to be fulfilled. As can be seen from Table 2.4, with the exception of liquid gas, which attainted 91.8 percent, almost all the results were near 100 percent of proposed production; and petroleum products even exceeded the proposed target. Also, primary refining capacity for crude oil reached 1.35 MBD, an increase of 49 TBD over 1983.

Domestic trading in hydrocarbon products rose to 1.1 MBD on the average, thus fulfilling the proposed target and achieving 5 percent growth over 1983. Sales of fuel oil increased 8.5 percent because this product was beginning to be substituted for natural gas in industrial use, while gasoline sales fell 1.6 percent when consumption shrank because of a price increase in petroleum products and the national economy's slow growth rate. Liquid gas sales showed considerable growth, 16.7 percent, as a result of a significant increase in its use as an automotive fuel, which also affected gasoline sales, and around 1,259 MCFD of natural gas were traded, which practically covered the whole amount proposed for the year (see Table 2.5).

TABLE 2.5
DOMESTIC HYDROCARBON TRADE, 1983-1984

Product	Year	Year	Annual Variation	Amount Obtained versus Amount Proposed (%)
Natural Gas (MCFD)	1,398.7	1,259.0	-10.0	99.9
Petroleum Products	1,031.5	1,083.6	5.1	100.3
Liquid Gas (TBD)	143.1	167.0	16.7	112.8
Gasoline (TBD)	316.8	311.8	- 1.6	95.9
Diesel (TBD)	192.6	199.4	3.5	99.7

TBD = thousands of barrels per day.
MCFD = millions of cubic feet per day.

Source: SPP and DGDE, Plan nacional de desarrollo, segundo informe de ejecución 1984, Mexico City, 1985, pp. 127-132.

Despite an increase in domestic crude oil storage capacity, the flexibility of crude oil continues to be limited; it accounts for only five days of production and nine days of exports. In gas salvaging flaring was cut down to 302 MCFD (annual average), which is equivalent to 8.1 percent of total production. This percentage is less than the 10.7 percent for 1983 and the 15 percent for 1982, an improvement resulting from a greater infrastructure created to aid this reduction. As much as 90 percent of all gas produced onshore was salvaged.

In the area of import substitution, PEMEX's buying power was directed toward industrial promotion, which was aimed at incorporating additional domestic input into oil-equipment manufacture. Thus, the imported component, which was 45 percent in 1982, was reduced to 19 percent in 1984. Efforts continued in the adoption of uniform specifications for the goods needed by the company, which, in turn, contributed to the opening of new suppliers.

In order to improve the saving and efficient use if energy and to modify current energy-use trends, work was undertaken in 1984 on the national energy-saving program. The first results in the energy sector itself showed a saving of 10 percent in internal hydrocarbon consumption, which is equivalent to a daily saving of 110 million cubic feet (MCF) of fuel gas or 16 thousand barrels (TB) of fuel oil.

As for hydrocarbons, in April 1984 there were price increases for nova gasoline (33 percent), extra gasoline (32 percent), and diesel (37 percent). Gradual monthly increases occurred in the price of natural gas (0.60 pesos/m3), fuel oil (0.30 pesos/l), and liquid gas (0.30 pesos/Kg), liquid gas increasing during the first semester only. These increases helped improve the company's financial situation. Its internal savings made it the enterprise with the largest surplus of all the companies in the state-owned sector.

However, hydrocarbon duties and import taxes paid by PEMEX to the federation rose to approximately 1.7 billion pesos, 49 percent more than the previous year. Moreover, PEMEX contributed 657 billion pesos to the public finances in the form of special taxes, which was 89 percent more than the previous year. PEMEX also proceeded to renegotiate $10.5 billion of its foreign debt and to pay off that portion that was not subject to renegotiation.

With the appearance of PE 1980-1982 it became obvious in official circles that there was a need to establish ceilings for Mexican hydrocarbon exports and to avoid going beyond these limits. The ceiling for oil was fixed between 1.5 and 1.7 MBD and natural gas at 300 MCFD. Also considered was the need to diversify exports both in crudes and petroleum products.

PNE 1984-1988 reaffirmed the previous policies, setting a figure of 1.5 MBD for oil exports and as much as 300 MCFD for natural gas. Moreover, PNE was intended to increase the country's refining capacity by 400 TBD and to encourage support to the petrochemical industry, the installed capacity of which had reached 15.3 million tons in 1984.

TABLE 2.6
HYDROCARBON EXPORTS AND IMPORTS, 1983-1984

Product	Year	Year	Annual Variation	Amount Obtained versus Amount Proposed (%)
Exports				
Crude Oil (TBD)	1,537.0	1,524.5	- 0.8	101.6
Natural Gas (MCFD)	217.1	148.0	-31.8	82.2
Petroleum Products (TBD)	84.1	111.9	33.1	159.9
Petroleum Imports (TBD)	17.4	33.1	90.2	--

TBD = thousands of barrels per day.
MCFD = Millions of cubic feet per day.

Source: SPP and DGDE, Plan nacional de desarrollo, segundo informe de ejecución 1984, Mexico City, 1985, pp. 127-132.

In January to October 1984 export average was maintained at over 1.5 MBD . As of 1 November the ceiling was reduced by 100 TBD in a joint effort with other world producers to maintain the stability of the oil market. Thus, for the whole year oil exports averaged 1.524 MBD, a figure similar to that of the previous year. During this same period natural gas exports to the United States totaled 178 MCFD, but because of the suspension of foreign sales on 1 November, the average volume for gas exports was 148 MCFD (32 percent less than in 1983).

The volume of petroleum products exported reached around 112 TBD, which was 33 percent higher than the previous year. Derivative imports totaled 33 TBD (90 percent more than in 1983), 86.3 percent of which were purchases of liquid gas made as a result of an increased demand in its uses as an automotive fuel.

The increased external demand for crude caused a modification in the composition of exports, which went from 56 percent for Maya crude and 44 percent for Isthmus to 59.3 and 40.7 percent, respectively. This change, accompanied by a revaluation of Maya crude, contributed to an increase in the total oil income of $92.8 million over the previous year. In regard to the hydrocarbon trade balance, exports reached a value of $16.338 billion (not including petrochemicals) and imports $355 million, leaving a positive balance of $15.938 billion (see Table 2.6).

The new contraction in international oil prices in January 1985 affected the official redefinition of oil growth in the national economy. Apart from the budgetary cuts that were necessary in light of the $1.7 billion per year loss due to severe price reductions in both Isthmus and Maya crude, the Programa de Fomento Integral a las Exportaciones (Program for the Integrated Promotion of Exports; PROFIEX) was begun with the aim of taking those measures that would achieve rapid progress in the substitution of oil exports for manufactured exports.

During other periods PEMEX's director general tended to announce larger estimates for hydrocarbon reserves in order to justify increased production and exports levels. However, in his speech on 18 March 1985 he announced that these reserves had fallen from 72.5 billion barrels (BB) to 71.7 BB in one year. This fall, he said, made necessary to step up energy-saving programs. Furthermore, he asserted that oil neither could be nor should be the lever for the country's economic development, which reaffirmed PEMEX's new approach to economic development. Moreover, his speech confirmed the ceiling for the crude export at 1.5 MBD, although because of marketing problems such a figure was not reached.

In a review of the most recent years events in the international energy market and of the planning documents, the main objectives for hydrocarbons from 1985 to 1988 are the following:

. To reduce the contribution of crude oil to foreign revenue gained from the export of merchandise from 70 percent to almost 50 percent

- To exercise strict control over supply during periods of pressure on oil prices, just as has happened since 1 November 1984

- To encourage manufactured exports, among which petroleum products and petrochemicals could possibly play an important role (these show great potential and will grow in years to come as a result of the expansion currently taking place at some plants)

- To rationalize the demand for petroleum products through realistic pricing and other measures

- To stimulate energy saving by PEMEX, the country's highest energy consumer

- To increase the company's productivity through a reduction in the use of productive factors without affecting the total quantity of resources produced.[18]

CONCLUSIONS

Since the beginning of the century, hydrocarbons have been a fundamental element in the country's institutional, legal, economic, financial, and political life. Their development has been closely linked to Mexico's economic development. It is here, perhaps more than in any other industry, that the country's technological capability has been demonstrated.

Wealth in hydrocarbons does not justify, however, the waste of energy or its export at all costs. The setbacks of recent years show that the mentality of the Mexican oil man and that of the executive have tended to change in favor of, first, an extension of the useful life of these reserves and, second, a more equilibrated promotion of the whole economy's productive potential. Ex-post, it seems that the "pseudooil economy" into which Mexico has slipped should be reversed and a greater attention should be paid to the links between Mexico's oil exporting capacity and the conditions of international crude oil markets.

Despite the heavy commitments of the foreign debt, which consumes in interest alone about three-fourths of the foreign revenue collected from hydrocarbon exports, it is fairly certain that Mexico will not be tempted to increase its exports of these products. Mexico's energy future will have to be one of increased saving and conservation of energy; greater efforts, though slow, in diversification; and an obvious increase in manufactured exports, particularly nonpetroleum ones.

NOTES

1. Although the Cárdenas period is identified with the rise of the country's most progressive forces, it was marked by economic crisis, diplomatic pressures, internal military frictions, and hostilities of conservative sectors, all of which pressed for the adoption of politico-economic models that were in accordance with existing interests. Mexico's industrialization process reached its most rapid stage of development during the period from 1940 to 1965, when light industry reached full expansion and industrialization was relatively easy. For the later, see Gutiérrez, Roberto, "Cambios de matiz en la estrategia económica de México: Los años setenta y ochenta," in Comercio Exterior, Vol. 31, No. 8, Mexico City, August 1981.

2. Bullard, J. Fredda, Mexico's Natural Gas: The Beginning of a New Industry, the University of Texas, Austin, 1968, p. 9.

3. In many cases prices were even lower than production costs; in 1957, for example, the cost of producing 1 gallon of diesel was 0.87 pesos, and its sale price was 0.68 pesos. See Echaniz, Jorge, Petróleo: Cuestiones nacionales, Mexico City, Fondo de Cultura Económica, 1958.

4. One of the main problems facing PEMEX as a result of nationalization was that the expropriated companies kept much of the relevant technical information, which forced the new state-owned company to operate under conditions of great uncertainty.

5. PEMEX, Informe del director general de Petróleos Mexicanos, Mexico City, PEMEX, 18 March, 1985, p. 13.

6. PEMEX, Memoria de labores, 1983, Mexico City, 1984, p. 116.

7. PEMEX and SPP, La industria petrolera en México, Mexico City, SPP, 1983.

8. This general point of view within the state oil industry is more or less shared by all its members, both unionized and nonunionized, because increased production guarantees greater power and additional job opportunities. However, it is common knowledge that there are coordination difficulties that reflect differences in the interests of the management and the trade union.

9. During the campaign a group of engineers handed the future president of the republic a document that informed him of the risk implied in exporting large quantities of oil given the country's limited reserves. In response to this document a group was formed to evaluate the oil potential. Díaz Serrano and his collaborators were in a position to demonstrate that the reserves of crude oil, natural gas, and condensate amounted to 11.2 BB and not 6.3 as the previous PEMEX team had pointed out.

10. In the agreement subscribed to by Mexico, the third country to sign since its creation in 1974, the stabilization programs was to be in force for three years (1977-1979), during which time it was to have the direct backing and the supervision of the IMF every three months. Mexico opted for this type of agreement because IMF supervision would act as a guarantee and restore the confidence of the international financial community. The package established that devaluation should be accompanied by a pricing and relative-cost policy that would include the liberalization of trade along with a policy of reduced demand and economic activity for the whole public sector. See Villarreal, René, "El petróleo como instrumento de negociación en los ochenta," in Cuadernos sobre Perspectiva Energética, Mexico City, El Colegio de México, Programa de energéticos, 1980.

11. This trend was followed not only by countries with a level of development similar to Mexico's but also by industrialized countries. Thus, with

respect to nonindustrialized countries (in the case of industrialized countries it is obvious), during the period of the two oil crises, Venezuela and Mexico, Latin America's most dynamic countries and main oil exporters, along with Indonesia, were the only countries to continue to consume more energy than other countries with similar economic characteristics. See Guzmán, Oscar, Antonio Yúnez-Naude, and Miguel Wionczek (editors), Uso eficiente y conservación de la energía en México: Diagnóstico y perspectivas, Mexico City, El Colegio de México, Programa de Energéticos, 1984.

12. PSP points out that the intention is to reach a maximum utilization of crude oil components and gas produced; more than 85 percent of PEMEX's exports will be crude oil, and the annual growth rate of total sales abroad will be 53 percent.

13. There was not a radical change in the financial policy of the previous administration. However, Díaz Serrano insisted from the beginning of his administration on the convenience of an adequate selection of investment projects in order to control the indebtedness level and, above all, to generate internal savings.

14. Guzmán, Oscar, Antonio Yúnez-Naude, and Miguel S. Wionczek, op. cit.

15. See Chapter 12 on PEMEX's finances.

16. Banco de México, Informe anual 1982, Mexico, 1983; PEMEX, information about its financial position.

17. BANAMEX, Examen de la situación económica de México, special issue, 1983, p. 14.

18. The achievement of this objective has resulted in much conflict and led to confrontations between the trade union and PEMEX. The conflict originates in the fact that STPRM in its role as employer and worker representative sustains that a reduction in the number of workers should begin with the nonunionized personnel because its numbers have grown considerably during the current administration. At the bottom of it all is the trade union's refusal to rescind some of the progress made in terms of its participation in the technical and administrative decisions of the company.

3

Development and Planning in the Mexican Electricity Subsector

*Jaime Navarro
and Nora Lina Montes*

The aim of this chapter is to analyze the political, economic, technical, administrative, and institutional factors that have determined the development and planning of the Mexican electricity industry, with special reference to the 1970s and the early 1980s. In the section on background events, the most outstanding historical and administrative factors determining the nature of the industry, including its "mexicanization" in 1960, are reviewed. Then, the most relevant aspects of the electricity subsector are analyzed: the electric energy-producing companies, the effects of demand on their growth, the role and constraints of tariff policy, consumption by end-users, and factors related to the expansion of the electric network to outlying regions.

Three essential points of electric industry policy are discussed: sectorial coordination, particularly between PEMEX and CFE; factors that have contributed to CFE's increased productivity and greater efficiency during the last few years; and CFE's financial problems resulting from insufficient capital. This review is followed by a presentation of the industry's planning and prospects, with an explanation of the reasons behind certain policies adopted in the electricity industry and long-term prospects of the industry.

A HISTORICAL OVERVIEW OF THE INDUSTRY:

During the last twenty years of the nineteenth century and the first few years of the current century, many foreign electricity companies were established in Mexico. At this time there were 177 plants servicing the country's most important cities. The first markets for electricity in Mexico were the mining industry (which needed electricity for metal extracting, smelting, and refining) and incipient manufacturing industries (which eventually grew to include factories for the manufacture of cigarettes and beer and articles made of yute, glass, wood, and so on). In 1937 the whole of Mexico's electricity grid was under the control of the Mexican Light and Power Company, Ltd., the Compañía Eléctrica de Chapala, and the American and Foreign Power Company, all foreign-owned. Efficiency was not characteristic of the foreign companies that managed the electric power service, a situation that gave rise to public discontent and provoked a certain degree of awareness about the need to take action against companies failing to respond to users' demands.

Soon, consumer organizations began to protest bad service, high tariffs, and the scarcity of electric energy and to express their disapproval of the companies' behavior. Despite the protests, these companies did not reinvest enough of their dividends in the expansion, maintenance, and improvement of their systems. The services provided were few and the demands of the growing population great. Vast areas of the country were totally neglected. In rural areas, for example, there was not even the remotest hope of ever being connected to the electricity grid.[1] Consumer protests grew louder, sometimes overstepping the mark and making it necessary for the government to intervene. This intervention served a double purpose. On one hand, it established standards and administrative measures forcing the power companies to improve services, and on the other, it led to the establishment of a state-owned agency that was to give electrification "a more modern and just social sense."[2]

Diverse economic and political circumstances overshadowed the government's intention to create this state-owned body, and it was not until 14 August 1937 that President Lázaro Cárdenas' government passed a law establishing CFE.[3] In the interim the foreign companies paralyzed their investments, setting loose a serious crisis in the electricity industry. CFE's limited finances led the government to consider providing the institution with economic resources. Thus, on 31 December 1938 the Ley de Impuestos sobre el Consumo de Electricidad (Electricity Consumption Tax Law) was passed, published in the *Diario Oficial* on 16 January 1939.

The consumer was to be charged 19 percent over the cost of the energy consumed; this amount was to go directly to CFE. The revenue would be used to expand the company's investment capacity; amplify its radius in all areas; and increase the service's use in the domestic and industrial sector, particularly the long-neglected farming sector. The first years were not easy. CFE was forced to sell power in package deals to foreign companies because of their monopoly over distribution. In late 1950s the national company produced more than half the country's electric power and accounted for 41.6 percent of the total generating capacity, 54.5 percent of which was used by the public sector.

In September 1960 the federal executive announced and agreement, whereby it acquired 90 percent of the Mexican Light and Power Co. shares and 100 percent of those belonging to the American and Foreign Power Company and its subsidiaries.[4] The remaining 10 percent of Mexican Light and Power still had to be purchased (of this at least 1 percent still remains in the hands of Canadian and American companies today). The agreement gave rise to a new company that still exists today, that is, Compañía de Luz y Fuerza del Centro (Central Light and Power Co.; CLFC). From the time it became Mexican and later state-owned, the electric subsector began intensive work on integrating networks and organizations as well as eliminating an absurd structure of 168 sets of tariffs for the different regions within the republic. During the 1960s the interconnection of the electric system necessitated the use of units with additional power capacity, with the consequent economies of scale; reduction in investment and operation costs; and in the reserves needed during maintenance or because of inadequate equipment, greater reliability of supply and higher profitability.

Great progress was achieved in just a few years following mexicanization and the integration of the state-owned electricity monopoly. Although in 1960 the electricity generation in the hands of affiliated companies and NAFINSA still represented 6.3 percent of the total, by 1964 it had already fallen to 3.7 percent, and by 1968, only four years later, these affiliated companies had stopped production altogether (see Table 3.1). From this moment on all electric power produced in the country was under state control. Only 10 percent was generated by CLFC, which supplied electricity to the Mexico City metropolitan area and surrounding zones. Although this company still exists formally as an independent unit, its integration into CFE is complete, so much so that CFE considers it its central division and uses it as an important auxiliary in power distribution all over the country. Both CFE and CLFC share the same governing board and general management. Unlike most other state-owned companies, CLFC has an assistant directorship that is relatively independent. Although it works in conjunction with the director general and with certain operative areas of CFE, it is not involved in the construction of new plants. Both companies belong to a group of organizations and enterprises with a government-controlled budget, although the budgetary allowance and expenditure of CFE is about seven times greater than that of CLFC (see Table 3.1).

In regard to the contribution of primary energy sources in the electricity subsector, 59.1 percent of the capacity in 1937 was provided by hydroelectricity and the other 40.9 percent by thermoelectricity produced from hydrocarbons; however, this ratio was inverted over time. Thus, by 1940 the percentages had changed to 49.1 percent and 50.9 percent; ten years later in 1950 they were 44.0 percent and 56.0 percent. Finally, in 1975 40.8 percent of the capacity was provided by hydroelectricity and 59.0 percent by thermo-

TABLE 3.1
EVOLUTION OF ELECTRICITY GENERATION BY COMPANY OF ORIGIN

Year	CFE (1)	Affiliated Companies (2)	CLFC	NAFINSA	Total (3)	(1)/(3) (%)	(3)-(2)/(3) (%)
1960	04,063	544	2,478	1,504	08,589	47.3	6.3
1962	5,183	618	3,153	1,431	10,385	49.9	5.9
1964	8,866	495	2,660	1,439	13,460	65.9	3.7
1966	12,071	648	2,008	1,435	16,180	74.6	4.0
1968	17,923	--	2,096	--	20,019	89.5	--
1970	22,914	--	3,116	--	26,030	88.0	--
1972	28,373	--	3,160	--	31,533	90.0	--
1975	36,718	--	4,162	--	40,880	89.8	--

Source: Based upon information received from CFE.

electricity from hydrocarbons. This trend appeared to be the result of three specific factors: increased hydroelectric plant investment costs; domestic availability of hydrocarbons; and a rapid growth in demand, which made short-term maturation of investment necessary.

During the early 1970s the most important single event in the system's interconnection was the decision to change the central system (Mexico City and surrounding zones) to a frequency of 60 cycles per second. The presidential decree of 23 July 1971 stated that the unification of the electric frequency in all public systems would help everyone concerned. Therefore, with the decree of the 10 May 1972, the Comité de Unificación de Frecuencias (Committee for the Unification of Frequencies; CUF) was created for the benefit of the central-system consumers. In just four years, from 1973 to 1976, Mexico underwent the biggest frequency change ever undertaken in the world. By then, only the Baja California and Península de Yucatán systems still had to be integrated into the national electricity grid.[5]

OVERALL SITUATION;

The electricity industry still faces a wide range of problems in a number of areas. Some of these problems are left to the electric energy companies, such as the design, construction, and operation of new plants as well as transmission and distribution of energy at a minimum cost and with maximum reliability. Other matters, however, are dealt with at the national policy level. Such matters include the following:

. Primary energy use

. Local manufacture of components

. Wage policy

. Tariff policy

. Internal and foreign credits

- Patrimonial contributions

- Rural electrification

The proportions in which primary energy is used, whether it be hydrocarbons, hydroenergy, geothermal energy, coal, or uranium, are normally defined as part of the national energy policy. These proportions are decided as a function of the primary energy reserves available as well as the country's overall objectives. Also taken into account are the current and future alternative uses of the primary fuels involved in electricity generation. The electricity industry's role in relation to the range of primary energy it must have at its disposal is limited by a number of factors. For example, the special characteristics of each generating center, the type of investment to be made, and current expenditures must be taken into account in order to decide the best utilization of fuels.

In Mexico the manufacture of equipment required by the electricity subsector is fundamentally the concern of the capital goods industry. Until now CFE's participation in this respect has been limited to giving technological support through its research center and to programming its installations in order to favor the country's industrial development without substantially increasing costs.

The guidelines of wage and tariff policies are decided by the corresponding authorities. Obviously, these guidelines affect both the electricity plants productivity and their financial situation. The latter is affected also by the company's own financial contributions, which in many cases are quite limited.

Contracting foreign credit depends on the country's foreign-debt management policy. The fact that the electricity industry's indebtedness forms part of the public sector debt implies that the policies for obtaining the credit necessary to expand the system are determined by SHCP.

Last, although the construction and operation of the rural electricity system is an economic burden for the subsector, it will play an important role in promoting the country's integrated development. Consequently, the energy sector's most recent program contemplates the expanding of the national grid in order

TABLE 3.2
ELASTICITY IN ELECTRIC ENERGY GENERATION WITH RESPECT TO THE GNP,
1974-1983

Year	Real GNP (10⁹ pesos of 1970)	Increase or Decline (%) (1)	Gross Energy Generated (GWh)	Increase (%) (2)	Flexibility (2) (1)
1974	578	-	38,413	-	-
1975	610	5.61	41,226	7.32	1.31
1976	636	4.24	44,911	8.94	2.11
1977	658	3.44	49,020	9.15	2.66
1978	712	8.25	53,047	8.22	1.00
1979	777	9.15	58,087	9.50	1.04
1980	842	8.32	62,490	7.58	0.91
1981	909	7.95	68,213	9.16	1.15
1982	904	-0.54	73,225	7.35	-13.56
1983	861	-4.73	74,843	2.21	-0.47

GNP = gross national product.

Sources: Banco de Mexico, S.A., Indicadores econmicos, Mexico City, various years; CFE, op. cit.

to cover the rural population's electricity requirements (see Table 3.2).

THE ELECTRIC POWER COMPANIES;

CFE and CLFC constitute what is referred to as the national electricity subsector and are an entity providing a public service, that is, the country's electricity supply. The Mexican constitution gives CFE exclusive authority to fulfill this task. To do so it must install the plants and equipment necessary to generate, transform, transmit, and distribute electricity as well as provide a competent management to operate the systems and assume responsibility for the different service-related activities.

The duality of the industry's commercial component is accompanied by a duality in the trade union movement, which organizationally has continued unchanged despite the desire for political unification.[6] The trade union's dual nature could contribute the most to the success or failure of the energy policy. Currently, CFE and the Sindicato Unico de Trabajadores Electricistas de la República Mexicana (Mexican Electricity Workers' Trade Union; SUTERM) are partners who do not share the same interests. However, considerable coordination efforts are being made to increase the subsector's productivity, as is shown later in the chapter.

DEMAND

The demand for electricity in Mexico, which is measured in terms of gross energy generation and which includes that used by the generating plants themselves, has tended to increased since the 1950s except for a decline registered from 1975 to 1983. Studies carried out by CFE on electricity demand indicate that electricity prices, which have been relatively low, have had nothing to do with consumer behavior. Although adjustments have been made to correct the average price in real terms, price inelasticity of the demand has still persisted.

TABLE 3.3
NATIONAL ELECTRICITY SUBSECTOR INSTALLED CAPACITY,
1960-1983 (MW)

Year	Total	Hydraulic	Thermal	Geothermal	Coal
1960	3,048	1,358	1,690	--	--
1965	5,237	2,214	3,023	--	--
1970	7,414	3,330	4,080	4	--
1975	11,210	4,116	7,090	75	--
1976	12,978	4,613	8,290	75	--
1977	13,766	4,795	8,896	75	--
1978	16,033	5,297	10,661	75	--
1979	16,381	5,291	10,940	150	--
1980	16,985	6,064	10,771	150	--
1981	19,895	6,621	13,094	180	300
1982	18,390	6,550	11,335	205	300
1983	19,004	6,532	11,667	205	600

Source: CFE, Estadisticas del sector eléctrico, Mexico City, various years.

With respect to the income elasticity of demand, it has been observed that the relationship between the demand and the real GNP is far from satisfactory, at least at first glance. Data for 1982 and 1983, presented in Table 3.2, suggest that the demand has an inertia that does not respond immediately to variations in the overall income level.

A heavy increased in the demand forced CFE to double its installed capacity every eight years between 1960 and 1976. However, a fall in consumption during the late 1970s, together with an international reduction in the margin of oversupply considered acceptable to CFE; allowed installed capacity to be increased at a slower rate during the years that followed. Furthermore, in 1970 geothermal energy started being used as a primary energy source for the electricity subsector (see Table 3.3). By 1983 it represented a significant part of total consumption because of the recent contribution of the Cerro Prieto plant in Baja California. Moreover, by this stage coal, which had become one of the electric subsector's primary energy sources in 1981, already contributed three times more energy than that supplied by geothermal plants because of two coal-fed units at the Rio Escondido complex in Coahuila.

The total demand for energy reflects the amount produced and consumed simultaneously because energy cannot be stored. Therefore, demand adapted itself to production. Now, the output of each new generating plant is absorbed by the demand in the system. This situation indicates, on one hand, that investment in electric energy is necessary and, on the other, that a queuing effect or an unsatisfied demand might exist. The latter would explain the difficulties involved in adequately estimating the price elasticity and income elasticity of demand in the short and longer term.

Electricity generation projects normally have very long maturation periods, and when budgetary adjustments occur, they give rise to cancellations and postponements, which delay plant operations and, therefore, affect demand. Random factors (such as those related to the intensity of the seasonal rains), combined with the risk inherent in the operations themselves, can provoke a reduction in the supply needed to satisfy demand. It has often been said that the subsector's potential reserves, that is, the capacity over and above the maximum demand for a one-year period, are, as a rule, overestimated.

TARIFFS

Electricity rates have played an important role in the electric subsector. Although they have helped stimulate a number of economic activities, they are also one of the structural causes behind CFE's financial imbalance. Electricity tariffs have recently undergone a series of changes and have been reduced from 168 to the thirteen currently in use:

1. Domestic-use rate: As its name implies, this rate covers the residential sector.

1a. Domestic-use rate for hot climates: Introduced in 1973, this rate applies to the residential sector in regions with extreme climates.

2. General rate for demands to 25 KW: This tariff applies to small businesses and offices.

3. General rate for demand over 25KW: This tariff is calculated for small businesses and offices.

4. Special rate for corn meal mills and tortilla factories: This rate is offered for activities classified as a social benefit.

5. Rate for public lighting: This rate applies to lighting in streets, parks, traffic signals, and so on.

6. Rate for drinking water and sewage pumps: The consumption at this rate for certain regions in the country, such as Mexico City, has risen considerably.

7. Temporary rate: This rate applies essentially to services lent to temporary construction projects.

8. General high-voltage rate: This rate basically covers small- and medium-sized industries.

9. Rate for irrigation: This rate was created to stimulate development of the rural sector.

10. Rate for high-voltage electricity for resale: This rate covers electric energy sold to the few remaining private distributing companies, which will eventually disappear.

11. Rate for mining activities: This rate applies to all mining-related activities.

12. Industrial rate: This rate was established to cover long-standing special contracts with large companies.

The low price of electricity has encouraged a number of activities. The first tariff increase was authorized in 1975 when a general increase of 22.9 percent was introduced to cover the cost of electricity. The increases were different for each rate and although some where kept at the earlier levels, other were increased from 10 to 30 percent. In 1976 a new differential increase for each tariff was decreed, and in 1978 a general accumulative increase of 1.5 percent monthly for 24 months was ordered on all tariffs without modifying the differential structure of rates. In 1980 due to a reduction in the electricity consumption tax, a new increase of 10 to 15 percent was introduced.

These increases were motivated by a considerable financial disequilibrium in the electricity industry, which caused a gradual deterioration in the mean price-cost ratio. This deterioration forced the electric utilities to implement an aggressive price policy in order to make prices more representative of costs.

An analysis of the electricity price changes during the period from 1962 to 1980 (see Table 3.4) shows that prices increased by an average of 6.8 percent per year. However, if considered using 1962 prices, the rate actually fell by 3.3 percent per year on the average during the same period as a consequence of inflation. Nonetheless, in the following 10-year period, from 1970 to 1980, because of a rapid increase in inflationary pressures, real electricity prices dropped 4.5 percent annually. The reduction was different for each tariff group, as can be seen in Table 3.5, which shows electricity prices.

The price decreases in real terms during 1962-1980 are an indication of the subsidy granted in each case and the effect that it has on the price-cost ratio. The figures in Table 3.4 show that tax rate number 10 had the least effect on this ratio and, therefore, most correctly reflects the cost of supply. Another rate group is made up of public lighting and government use groups andsmall- and medium-sized industries. The following rate groups are listed in order of their importance in respect to the subsidy size: commercial, domestic, mining, and small businesses. The remaining electricity rate groups, also listed in order of importance, are highly subsidized: irrigation, temporary uses, corn mills and hot climates.

The data in Table 3.5 show that there are two completely different ranges. The first includes those rates that are a closer reflection of actual costs, and the other comprises rates that are a burden to the electric subsector. The domestic rate, which takes into account the rural population, is included in the first group, and in the other group we find those rates applied to industrial activities. This situation exists for two reasons, one social and the other technical. The first reason stems directly from CFE's basic objective, which is to be a social benefit. The second reason is that the amount invested for distribution purposes is noticeably lower for primary users, such as those industrial rates, whose rate is calculated according to relatively few energy-intensive users. The industrial rate contrasts with the domestic rate, which is applicable to a large number of users (nearly 90 percent) whose demand is small and dispersive. Revenue from sales reflects these conditions: Consumption at industrial rates has increased from 35 percent in 1962 to 51 percent in 1983.

SECTORIAL CONSUMPTION

The relative share of electricity consumption by end-consumer groups from 1970 to 1983 does not vary noticeably. The agricultural sector's share stayed almost the same, fluctuating between 6 and 7 percent. The energy sector's share increased slightly, varying from 3.5 to 5 percent. The residential-commercial-transport sector's share fell from almost 48 percent in 1970 to 35 percent in 1983. The industry's share rose from nearly 42 percent in 1970 to 52 percent in 1983. The reduction occurring in the residential-commercial-transport sector was attributable essentially to commerce because the residential part increased its share during the period (see Table 3.6).

SPARE CAPACITY

The spare capacity of the electric energy industry had to be reduced from 27 percent in 1976 to 15 percent in 1982. The budgetary cutbacks dictated by financial restrictions forced the industry to reduce reserves to the recommended minimum (the total liability-capital asset ratio oscillated between 65 and 90 percent year after year). Savings in investment amounted to 28 billion 1984 pesos for every 1 percent reduction in spare capacity.

TABLE 3.4
MEAN ELECTRICITY PRICES, 1962 AND 1980 ($/KWh)

Rate		Average Price (1962 $)	Average Price 1980 (1980 $)	(1962 $)
1	Domestic	41.65	115.36	19.65
1A	Domestic for Hot Regions	36.57	99.38[a]	14.18
2	General, up to 25 KW	49.01	129.83	19.05
3	General, for more than 25 KW	33.61	116.72	17.13
4	Corn Mills and Tortilla Factories	18.52	24.08	3.61
5	Public Lighting	15.33	73.71	9.64
6	Drinking Water and Sewage Pumps	12.28	076.17	09.96
7	Temporary	100.00	195.83	25.60
8	General High Voltage	19.73	79.56	11.94
9	Farming Irrigation Pumps	15.94	35.18	4.31
10	High Voltage for Resale	8.18	53.09	7.79
11	High Voltage for Mining	17.08	51.36	7.71
12	General, 5 MW or more to 66 KW or over	11.24	60.89	9.14
	National Electricity Subsector	25.08	81.67	12.45

[a] These prices are for 1974, which is when this rate came into force.

Source: Based on data received from CFE on the changes undergone in the rates for the electricity subsector, Mexico, 1962-1980.

To achieve this reduction power plant operations had to be cut back, which partly explains the blackouts that occurred all over the country during 1980. The industry's management often cites the cost-benefit analysis of an "overly ambitious" program vis-à-vis a "restricted one." Management also states that under conditions of general austerity, it is advisable to work with an overly ambitious program because it is more economical to postpone or cancel investment than it is to submit the demand to continued restrictions.

TABLE 3.5
CHANGES IN RATES IN CURRENT PESOS AND PESOS OF 1962 TO 1980 (In mean AAGR)

Rate	Comparison at Current Price (%)	Comparison at Constant Price, 1962 (%)
1	5.8	− 4.3
1A	18.1	−17.1
2	5.5	− 5.4
3	7.2	− 3.8
4	1.5	− 9.5
5	9.1	− 2.6
6	10.7	− 1.2
7	3.8	− 7.9
8	8.0	− 2.8
9	4.5	− 7.5
10	10.9	− 0.3
11	6.3	− 4.5
12	9.8	− 1.2
National Electricity Subsector	6.8	− 4.0

AAGR = average annual growth rate.

Source: Calculations are based on Table 3.4.

TABLE 3.6
ELECTRICITY CONSUMPTION BY SECTORS (GWh)

Year	Energy	Residential and Commercial	Transport	Agriculture	Industry	Total
1970	796.5	10,696.5	202.3	1,348.8	9,396.5	22,440.7
1971	891.9	11,645.3	324.4	1,370.9	10,144.2	24,376.7
1972	1,069.8	12,819.8	340.7	1,638.4	11,447.7	27,316.3
1973	1,105.8	14,062.8	355.8	1,740.7	12,679.7	29,944.2
1974	1,336.0	15,427.9	361.6	2,068.6	14,193.0	33,387.2
1975	1,483.7	16,600.0	361.6	2,257.0	15,332.6	36,034.9
1976	1,770.9	17,731.4	350.0	2,437.2	17,369.8	39,659.3
1977	1,889.5	18,311.6	372.1	2,652.3	19,822.1	43,047.7
1978	2,182.6	20,930.2	419.8	2,934.9	20,795.3	47,262.8
1979	2,365.1	22,696.5	411.6	3,333.7	22,760.5	51,567.4
1980	2,711.6	24,380.2	376.7	2,746.5	23,797.7	55,012.8
1981	1,994.2	26,695.3	455.8	3,841.9	26,048.8	59,036.0
1982	3,427.9	29,209.3	455.8	4,801.2	26,998.8	64,893.0
1983	3,326.7	23,087.2	460.5	4,431.4	34,238.4	65,544.2

Sources: Balances de Energa elaborated for 1970-1981 by SEPAFIN, for 1982 by CFE, and for 1983 by SEMIP.

EXPANSION OF THE NATIONAL ENERGY GRID

The expansion of the national energy grid, or the Sistema Eléctrico Nacional (the National Electricity System; SEN), to outlying regions should be analyzed in terms of two concepts: generation and consumption. For technical, economic, and financial reasons, some energy sources can only be utilized where they are available; generating plants are not always situated near where the energy is consumed. Hydroelectricity and coal belong in this category. The most important hydroelectric plants are in the southeast. In the case of coal the plants are in the northeast. Technically, thermoelectric plants can essentially be situated anywhere; however, for economic reasons related mainly to the cost of transporting fuel and equipment and to the availability of water for cooling, plant locations are restricted to certain areas. The hydroelectric plants are distributed all over the country but are more in the north than in the south.

The national electricity system is comprised of three independent subsystems: the Península de Yucatán, Baja California, and national interconnected subsystems. The latter is divided into areas covering the Sistema Interconectado del Norte (Northern Interconnected System; SIN), that is, the northeastern, northern, and northwestern areas of the country; and the Sistema Interconectado del Sur (Southern Interconnected System; SIS), which comprises the central, western, and eastern areas.

Consumption relates directly to areas of high urban and industrial concentration. Thus, demand is greatest in the central region, which includes Mexico City. This area is followed by the western region, where the Bajío and Jalisco industrial zones are situated. Last, is the eastern area in SIS, which basically consists of the state of Veracruz. Greatest demand within SIN comes from the northeast and the Nuevo León industrial zone followed by the northeastern zone, which includes the states of Sonora and Sinaloa. The remaining areas are of little significance.

POLICY CONSIDERATIONS

This section presents an analysis of those areas related to planning and carrying out policy for the electricity industry. The three areas discussed are intrasectorial coordination, productivity and efficiency, and financial problems.

Intrasectorial coordination

This section deals with the relationship in the energy field between the electricity and oil subsectors in an attempt to answer the following questions:

1. How has the electricity policy been adjusted to that of the oil sector?

2. Which aspects of the electricity policy affect the oil subsector's policy?

In order to answer the first question, four factors affecting the electric subsector must be identified: the diversification of primary energy sources, fuel quality, fuel transport, and energy prices. Although diversification plans have been defined within the electric subsector since the mid-1970s, evidence indicates that these plans will not have a visible effect until the time when commercial operations begin at the Laguna Verde nucleoelectric plant. The opening of the Laguna Verde project has been postponed many times both for technical and political reasons.

It was not until 1983 that CFE decided to introduce quality standards for fuel oil and diesel. This decision resulted from a series of findings that stated the operating efficiency of the thermoelectric plants had been affected by the quality of the fuel oil used. Poor-quality fuel oil increased the need for maintenance at these plants in order to avoid their further deterioration.

CFE purchases large quantities of fuel oil from PEMEX; thus, fuel transport is an important consideration. Fuels are moved across the country mainly in the following ways: Diesel is sent by petrol tanker (paid by PEMEX); fuel oil by pipeline and oil tanker (both paid by PEMEX) and by railway in tank car (paid by CFE); and natural gas by gas pipeline (paid by PEMEX).

Energy has become an important issue in the northern part of the country where fuel arrives by oil tanker and railroad. The main problem is that these forms of transport also have alternative uses, the first exportation and the second transporting of foodstuffs. The growth in demand for the northern zone during the last few years has forced CFE to depend on fuels brought from faraway locations for local electricity generation.

Last, the price policy for primary energy sources defined by the federal government with the cooperation of SHCP, SECOFI and SEMIP, as well as PEMEX, has been a reflection of the comparative advantage Mexico has had on the international market. Prices calculated in terms of their energy content have represented a structure that favors fuel oil, then gas and diesel. Although for CFE relative prices have not been affected, the introduction since 1980 of monthly increases (announced every calendar year and subject to change without notice) has encouraged a desire by CFE to participate at least as an observer in the pricing process so that it can acquire a better basis for budgetary negotiation for fuel expenditure. This desire has not been fulfilled, however, because of organizational and political constraints.

The electricity subsector's policy concerning the availability and reliability of its service has motivated the oil industry and others (mainly the iron and steel industry) to reformulate their investment programs and, wherever advisable, to construct their own generating systems. Prior to 1981 when the Mexican peso was overvalued in relation to the U.S. dollar, the cost per unit for investment in self-generation equipment was competitive with the electricity tariff set for industry. It was not until after 1982 that such investment was competitive with electricity purchase costs. Regardless of electricity rates, PEMEX believes the electricity service must be available and reliable. It must be available in order to bring oil projects on line, and electricity generation cannot always be guaranteed. The reliability factor implies CFE's willingness to provide PEMEX plants with special services, which it has never done before. Consequently, for many PEMEX projects electricity self-generation represents a preferred alternative, particularly when it is combined with certain access to CFE's generating facilities.

Productivity and efficiency

In april 1977 CFE designed a program to reduce the annual growth rate of its personnel, which had been increasing at a rate of 8.5 percent. This plan attempted to restrict the number of new workers to 5 percent in 1977, 4 percent in 1978, 3.5 percent in 1979, and 2.5 percent from 1980 on. The two electric workers' unions accepted this program in the belief that it would contribute to the subsector's financial recovery.

In 1976 each operating worker was assigned 140 supply contracts; in 1983 it was 177, an increase of 26 percent in the number of users per worker. The number of energy units sold per worker also went up, from 696,000 KWh per year to 945,000. Although these productivity improvements meant an increase of 36 percent, they were below the target of 50 percent contemplated in the CFE program. Fuel productivity increased mainly because of the new thermoelectric plants, which had better design specifications, and because of improved plant efficiency in energy conversion. This situation led to an increase from 549 KWh per barrel of fuel oil (including natural gas and diesel) in 1977 to 566 KWh in 1982.

The on-schedule completion of projects had an important effect on demand and resulted in particular benefits. Until 1978 project delays were the general rule, but since that time efforts have begun on two fronts: (1) to establish permanent control over contracting schedules and undertake a thorough revision of construction stages so as to improve information systems on projects in progress and to reduce costs and (2) to eliminate technical and administrative red tape, thus reducing paperwork and saving time (those in charge of coordinating construction have been given decision-making authority).

Financial problems

For long periods electricity rates were kept stable while the magnitude of the investment needed to expand installed capacity kept growing. This policy contributed to a deterioration in the subsector's liability-asset ratio. Development programs had to be based on contracted credits, and by 1976 the subsector had fallen deeply into debt. To improve the ratio CFE's debt to the federal government was canceled in equal parts in 1978, 1979, and 1980. The federal government has continued to help the electricity industry since 1975 by covering part of its investment program and granting explicit subsidies for specific tariffs. In 1983 the income from electricity sales represented barely 33 percent of the subsector's total revenue. Given the low rates it became necessary to resort increasingly to subsidies and to internal and foreign loans.

In 1977 the electric subsector defined the following objectives:

- To obtain compensation for the increase in the cost of goods and services acquired both locally and abroad

- To eliminate the difference existing between mean production and distribution costs and mean electricity prices

- To apply specific subsidies for low-income users and those engaged in activities the government wished to encourage

The inflation accompanying the 1977-1981 oil boom, together with a policy designed to disconnect the electricity subsector's revenue from its investment expenditures, caused the rates to lag behind cost once again. This lag was reflected in a mean price-cost ratio of 53 percent. The year 1973 was the last in which this ratio was higher than 100 percent.

PLANNING AND PROSPECTS

A dynamic growth in demand and long project duration are two factors that have encouraged planning the the electric subsector. Planning began in CFE during the 1970s and has been undertaken for ten-year periods. These plans originally were based on information collected by the main distribution centers; now, evaluations were made of the requests to CFE for new services as well as the demand expected as a result of regional or state economic- and urban-development plans.

Since the late 1970s when the idea of integrated planning was introduced in the electricity subsector, other goals have been added to the electricity programs, such as diversification, autonomous technical development, local capital goods manufacture, resource organization, and so on. Thus, in 1978 CFE's first planning program was announced. Its application was not limited to the institution itself. It was the first proposal to consider long-term planning and involved a ten-year program called Programa de Obras e Inversión del Sector Eléctrico (Program of Works and Investment for the Electricity Sector; POISE).

At the same time a long-term expansion plan for the electricity subsector to the year 2000, Plan de Expansión del Sector Eléctrico al Año 2000 (Expansion Plan for the Electricity Sector to the Year 2000; PESE), was made public. It was formulated during the oil boom when it was expected that the country's economic growth rate would rise considerably. Apart from proposing rapid expansion for the electricity industry, this program provided for a high degree of diversification: It was planned that 20,000 MW of capacity in nuclear electricity and nearly 8,000 MW in coal-based generation would be built by the year 2000.

POISE was a planning exercise that attempted to regulate supply and, implicitly, demand and reflected the financial, macroeconomic, and industrial- and regional-development policies to be implemented in the 1980s. The program was subject to annual review so that policy changes and expected growth in demand could be taken into account. For example, the Plan de Desarrollo del Sector Eléctrico (Development Plan for the Electricity Sector; PDSE) 1977-1986 assumed in

November 1977 a mean annual growth in electric energy demand of 9.8 percent; less than one year later in July 1978, this figure was revised upward to 10.1 percent. In 1983, the expected growth rate for the period from 1984 to 1986 was 7 percent per year. The industry's investment decisions were adjusted on the basis of these forecasts. Evidently, the important ingredient here was the projected maximum load on the national electric system, which was used to determine the amount of energy that must be generated to satisfy demand. This amount, together with the appropriate generation capacity margin, in turn defined total capacity requirements.

The growth in supply was planned on the basis of forecasts for medium- and long-term demand. For the medium term (3-5 years) concerns about access to power supply that were expressed by the industrialists directly to CFE were taken into account. The management of each CFE division annually collected applications (both new and revised) from the various economic sectors that defined their energy requirements for future projects; this information provided the basis for a first estimate of demand. For long-term demand econometric models were used for determining the impact that aggregate variables, such as the GNP, mean price, population, and so on, would have on electricity demand. This approach complemented medium-term analysis. However, although it helped electricity market analysis, it still has not been designed at sectorial and regional levels to assist in the decision making related to production. One of the limiting factors of particular importance in the analysis of supply and demand was the quality of the information itself. The definition, measurement, structuring, and viability of pertinent variables were not necessarily provided, and often proxies had to be used to analyze the relevant aspects of the electricity market.

As an example of the planning exercises undertaken from 1977 to 1982, it might be useful to look at the program proposed at the beginning of this period, the Programa del Sector Eléctrico (Electricity Sector Program) 1977-1982. It estimated that generation needs in 1982 would be slightly more than double that generated in 1976, that is, nearly 92,000 GWh; therefore, the program called for installed capacity to be raised to 19,800 GWh, with an approximate reserve margin of 20 percent. This plan implied an increase of 9,200 MW over six years distributed in the following way: hydroelectricity, 2,374 MW (25.85 percent of the total); thermoelectricity, 4,043 MW (43.97 percent); coal-based electricity, 1,200 MW (13.05 percent); nuclear electricity, 1,308 MW (14.22 percent); and geothermal electricity, 270 MW (2.94 percent).[8]

If one compares the goals of this program with the results achieved during this period (see Table 3.3), the following is evident:

- The total generation capacity increase was not 9,200 MW but 5,412 MW

- No contribution whatsoever was obtained from nuclear electricity

- The coal-burning power plants' increase in installed capacity missed its target of 1,200 MW, achieving only 300 MW

- The best performance with respect to the program was the geothermal plants

These results show the high degree of uncertainty associated with medium- and long-term planning, although such is not true in all cases; for example, in geothermal electric plant construction investment was linked with energy-export contracts to the United States.

From the time the idea of integrated development was conceived, planning of the whole energy sector, particularly the electricity subsector, was governed by demand assumptions, plans for other sectors of the economy, or the global economic plan. Thus, the electricity industry had its own plans but was influenced by many others as well. Programs that have indirectly affected the electricity subsector's programming are PNDI 1979-1982 dated 1979, PGD 1980-1982 dated 1980, and the Plan Nacional de Desarrollo (National Development Plan; PND) 1983-1988 dated 1983.

Programs that have had a direct influence on the electricity subsector are the energy programs for 1980-1984 and POISE and PESE 2000. POISE is the product of an electricity market analysis of requests for CFE services and of demand expectations based on economic and social development. With this information and an account of the most representative historical period, an exponential curve was calculated with which a preliminary energy forecast was to be made. The study covered a period of ten years. Every year it was revised, incorporating changes in basic assumptions. The resulting document on the development trends of the electricity market contained estimates of maximum growth, minimum annual demand, electricity generation, and expected sales. PESE 2000, however, considered long-term forecasts for growth in electricity demand that were made on the basis of econometric models integrating global variables, such as the GNP and population.

Late in 1977 CFE elaborated the first of a series of Planes de Expansión para el Sector Eléctrico (Expansion Plans for the Electricity Sector). This document assumed an average demand growth rate of 9.5 percent per year and a high degree of diversification in supply and proposed the doubling of facilities every seven years. Calculations were based on a theoretical hydroelectric potential totaling 80 TWh per year, the availability of 500 million tons of proven noncoke coal reserves (of which 6 million tons, equivalent to 15 TWh per year, were to be found in Coahuila), and a theoretical total geothermal potential between 8.4 and 40.0 TWh per year.

The generating capacity to be added to the electricity subsector during the ten years would be distributed by source in the following way:

Type of Plant	MW
Hydroelectric	3,730
Thermal (HC)	4,200
Coal-Burning	2,400
Nuclear	1,300
Geothermal	215
Total	11,845

In 1976 installed capacity was 10,523 Mw, less than the new capacity to be created between 1978 and 1988. This plan not only contemplated the objectives to be reached within the next ten years but also started long-term planning, taking into consideration CFE's future need for numerous additional electricity projects. These forecasts were made on the basis of econometric models that in essence correlated electric power consumption per capita with GNP per capita. The goals for the different stages and energy distribution by sources are shown in Table 3.7. Early in 1978 when POISE was officially introduced, the only change from the previous document was in the average annual growth rate (AAGR), which was now calculated at 10.1 percent for 1979 to 1987.

TABLE 3.7
EXPANSION PLAN FOR THE ENERGY SECTOR, 1977

Energy	1982		1986		1999-2000	
Type	MW	%	MW	%	MW	%
Hydro-						
electric	6,587	39.9	8,555	35.4	21,900	27.0
Thermal						
(HC)	9,795	54.9	11,575	47.9	23,000	28.3
Coal	630	1.0	2,430	10.1	9,500	11.7
Geothermal	180	3.5	290	1.2	5,400	6.6
Nuclear	654	3.7	1,308	5.4	21,400	26.4
Total	17,846	103.0	24,158	100.0	81,200	100.0

Source: Based upon information received from CFE.

In 1980 SEPAFIN published a profile of the energy sector in which it referred to the electricity program presented in 1977 as the beginning of the new administration. In that program it was proposed that by 1982 the electricity generated would reach 92 TWh, and there would be an installed capacity of 19,800 MW with spare capacity of 20 percent. The new works to be undertaken in the subsector were to provide within the span of five years (1978-1982) an additional 9,200 MW, distributed by source in the following way:

Type of Plant	MW	%
Hydroelectric	2,374	26
Thermal	4,043	44
Coal-Burning	1,200	13
Nuclear	1,308	14
Geothermal	270	3

    The 1980 program intended to build only 77 percent of the projects proposed in the 1977 program in six years as well, but to increase the installed capacity in 1982 to 11 percent more than was previously planned. The additional installed capacity needed to generate this much energy was to come from new plants that were to come on line sooner than expected. By this time the potential of primary sources had also increased. Proven coal reserves were already estimated by some at 480 million tons and uranium at 8,400 tons; hydroelectric reserves were calculated at 500 TWh per year, with generating capacity at 172 TWh. In the long term (year 2000) the contribution of nuclear electricity was to reach an extremely high level, whereas coal's contribution was set at 8,400 MW.

    In 1980 PE 1980-1982 was announced. For the electric subsector it proposed diversification, energy saving, productivity, and regional-development policies, among other plans. The basic assumptions for this subsector consisted of growth rates in electricity consumption between 12 and 13 percent in the 1980s, which meant that by 1990 electricity had to be generated at a rate of 208 TWh per year.

    As part of the diversification policy, it was hoped that by 1990 two 2,500 MW nuclear electric plants would be operating. Together with the plants under construction, these plants would provide a total installed capacity of 20,000 MW for the year 2000. The figure proposed for coal was 4,000 MW; proven reserves of 600 million tons provided sufficient justification for new projects. In 1990 geothermal power would contribute 620 MW. It must be kept in mind that this program, as was PESE 2000, was conceived at the time of the oil boom, when rapid economic growth was expected in the country. The economic crisis that began in the years that followed changed these assumptions radically, forcing the government to adapt their programs to these changes.

The program that currently covers the energy sector is PNE 1984-1988, which was announced in August 1984. Included are the following general objectives for the electricity subsector:

- Diversification

- Efficient use of energy

- Regional development (rural)

- Environmental conservation

- Integrated, flexible, and competitive industries

- Cost-reflecting prices

- Increased productivity

- Financial equilibrium

Specific goals based essentially on the completion of current construction projects include reaching an installed capacity of nearly 27,000 MW in 1988, distributed by sources in the following way:

Source	MW	%
Hydroelectric	7,814	29.1
Thermal (HC)	15,925	59.2
Coal	1,200	4.5
Nuclear	1,308	4.8
Geothermal	645	2.4
Total	26,892	100.0

With diversification this capacity is equivalent to bringing the two units at Laguna Verde on line, completing the first coal-burning electricity plant with its four 300 MW units, and concluding Cerro Prieto projects II and III. Furthermore, although not altogether explicit in the energy program, among CFE's goals for 1988 (which were confirmed in 1985) are:

- To increase the number of electric installations from 25,000 to 30,000 and the number of users by 10 million

- To build between 12,000 and 13,000 kilometers of transmission line

- To reach an installed capacity of 27.3 million KW (446,000 more than that proposed in PNE), implying an annual growth rate in capacity between 7.5 and 8.5 percent (by the end of 1985 alone, a figure of 21.5 million KW was to be reached

- To bring on line twelve new thermoelectric plants, five hydroelectric projects in Guerrero (El Caracol) and Chiapas (Peñitas), the Laguna Verde Plant, and several geothermal and coal-burning electricity plants.[9]

Last, the dual plants (coal- and fuel oil-burning) did not begin operation in 1986, which raises doubts about the utilization of the coal Mexico agreed in principle to buy from Colombia some years ago.

CONCLUSIONS

The purpose of this chapter was to show, among other things, that the electric industry's expansion has been affected by a variety of factors: (1) the energy policy in general; (2) the quality of fuel; (3) fuel transport; (4) overall energy-price levels; (5) labor and fuel productivity; (6) efficiency in project implementation; (7) electricity rates; and (8) the planning difficulties brought about by technical and financial problems as well as problems of a political and institutional nature.

An important conclusion to derive from this chapter is that the lack of intrasectorial coordination, particularly between PEMEX and CFE, imposes serious constraints on the adequate implementation of electricity industry policy. Furthermore, the difference between political and institutional commitments and the viability of investment often make optimum choices for the country's electricity development difficult.

Also, the subsector's financial position is extremely vulnerable because of the absence of rate adjustments, which in the context of continued inflation tends to persist when a subsector's internal policy treats separately its revenue and its investment program. The outdated rates are a product of political pressures: individuals utilize electricity price variables to achieve political objectives, particularly in the north where electric power expenditures reach levels considerably higher than in other parts of the republic. Last, evidence shows that increased working force and fuel-use productivity are the economic factors that would most favor the implementation of a healthy and adequate expansion policy for this industry.

NOTES

1. CFE, "La evolución del sector eléctrico de México," Mexico City, CFE, 1977.

2. Idem.

3. The original objective of this organization, which considered electric energy a social benefit, was to generate, transform. transmit, and distribute electric energy without profit.

4. The political importance of the electricity industry's mexicanization and its background and impact on national life are analyzed in great detail in Wionczek, Miguel S., "Electric Power, The Uneasy Partnership," in Vernon, Raymond (editor), Public Policy and Private Enterprise in Mexico, Cambridge, Harvard University Press, 1964.

5. SEPAFIN and STCE, "Perfil energético de México," in Energéticos: Boletin Informativo del Sector Energético, Year 3, No. 8, Mexico City, STCE, August 1979.

6. Traditionally, the electricity workers have had one of the strongest unions in Mexico, and with the oil and telephone workers form the most important coalition of trade unions in the country.

7. For further information on this relationship, see Chapter 1 of this study.

8. Ibid.
9. *El Nacional*, Mexico City, 28 February 1985.

4

Planning and Development in the Coal Industry in Mexico

Nora Lina Montes

Manifestations of all types of coal--fossil coal, subbituminous, bituminous, semianthracite, anthracite, and graphite--have been found in Mexico. The resources quantified to date are distributed in a few geographic areas mainly in the states of Coahuila, Tamaulipas, Oaxaca, Sonora, and Chihuahua. Proven coal reserves are rather small mainly because of limited exploratory activity. In spite of the fact that Mexico imports coal, it is not widely used in this country, which is rich in oil resources. Because petroleum products are sold by the stated under subsidy, only lately have there been efforts to stimulate alternative energy-source development.

If proven, probable, and potential reserves are taken into account, within a few years coal could become a fairly important form of energy in Mexico. Furthermore, if the right measures are taken, coal could even triple its share in national primary energy production, which currently amounts to only 1 percent. Coal's participation in generating electricity in 1983 was barely 3 percent of the national total but is liable to grow to around 9 percent before the end of the decade.

In order to fulfill these objectives the following matters must be attended to: Exploration efforts must be intensified and the technological, financial, human, and institutional conditions created so that this work can be done at cost equal to or lower than international ones; cooperation between the coal and capital goods industries must be strengthened so that the tools, machinery, and equipment needed can be produced at as low a price as possible; the support of the financial sector must be obtained so that work on exploration and exploitation is not interrupted; skilled labor must be made available; modern exploration methods, such as gasification in situ must be introduced; and last, the continuity of coal-based electricity programs must be assured through the coordination of the coal-related entities and foreign enterprises participating either directly or indirectly in the projects.

In Mexico the coal industry presents major planning and management challenges, although the state's efforts in this areas should not be underestimated. This chapter tells of these efforts, which started mostly in the mid-1970s. The introductory section deals with coal industry development in Mexico, covering both coke and noncoke coal recovery and uses. In the second part the agencies and enterprises involved in coal production and coal uses are described. Part 3 is dedicated to a detailed analysis of the main points of controversy that have hindered the country's development of coal. Last, a section on future prospects offers a possible scenario of the industry from now until the year 2000.

COAL DEVELOPMENT TO THE MID-1970s

The use of coke in Mexico has always been closely linked with the development of the iron and steel and mining-metallurgical industries, which started at the beginning of this century. Until 1930 coal mines were in the hands of private companies. When this resource became nationalized, it was decided that unlike oil it could be mined under concession to private enterprises. At the same time the state established agencies responsible for overseeing coal production and management. On the whole, however, these agencies developed according to the interests of private enterprise.

During World War II the country faced serious steel-import distribution problems with its traditional suppliers in western Europe and North America. The need arose to develop a domestic iron and steel industry and with it a coal industry.[1] Based on the geologic knowledge available at the time, exploratory work was undertaken that resulted in measuring the Coahuila coal reserves. As a result, coke production began to develop relatively rapidly within the limits set by the needs of the iron and steel industries, and mining was undertaken mainly by private companies under concession arrangements, as it still is today.

Once the problem of external dependence was solved, domestic coal grew in its importance to the iron and steel industry, but the supply was no where near sufficient to support the industry entirely: Although this resource is an input for a strategic industry and is important in the production of steel, its role in Mexico after the war has been secondary because it can be acquired from abroad under favorable economic conditions.[2] Furthermore, coal is less important than the other mineral input, that is, iron. In the mid-1970s the person in charge of a state iron and steel company referred to coal exploitation in Coahuila in these terms:

> It is probable that although results are stimulating, exploration will be cut back for some time as it is not economically advisable nor necessary to have enormous proven reserves, as exploration involves large expenditure which must be met. In other words, work is being done to increase known reserves and to assure supply to the plants as required over periods in which it is possible to amortize initial investment.[3]

This somewhat generalized point of view implied that the country did not dedicate serious attention to a specific coal-development and -promotion policy of any importance. From the legislative point of view this resource was regulated under the mining law, but its development was subject to the interests of the iron and steel industry.

The use on noncoke coal as fuel dates from the end of the last century when it was used in railroad transport. Later, in 1930, it was used in the country's first coal-based electricity plant.[4] This plant operated more or less continuously, and during the late 1950s two turbogenerators of 15 and 33 MW were added to its installed capacity. At that time the electricity industry was still in the hands of private enterprise, its nationalization not occurring until the following decade.

In the 1960s the country's energy-related activities were already based on oil. Hence, electricity industry expansion was planned on the basis of thermoelectric facilities, which began to replace hydroelectric plants. The massive utilization of oil was then the predominant criteria within CFE and the energy sector in general. In spite of this the first ideas on diversification had already emerged. A number of projects were begun in CFE with the intention of expanding coal use for electricity purposes. Consequently, in the early 1960s the first coal-exploration company started operating in the country's most promising region, Coahuila. The favorable results justified the construction of a pilot plant that generated coal-based electricity. This plant operated until the end of 1978, using only 104,000 tons of coal per year.

In 1972 CFE's second exploration campaign started. It lasted a number of years and added 133 million tons to the reserves. In 1976 when diversification gained popularity in the country as a result of the 1973 energy crisis and before Mexico's present hydrocarbon potential was made known, a coal policy was formulated for the first time. This policy led to the Programa Nacional de Exploración de Carbón (National Coal Exploration Program; PNEC), in which CFE, PEMEX and the Consejo de Recursos Minerales (Council for Mineral Resources; CRM) participated. Although the detailed results of this program were kept within the institutions involved, toward the end of 1976 CFE reported 172 million tons of proven coal reserves. These reserves justified a large coal-based electricity program, starting with the decision to build a plant at Río Escondido, Coahuila, with an installed capacity of 1,200 MW.

TABLE 4.1
EVOLUTION OF MEXICO'S COAL RESERVES,
JANUARY 1963 TO JUNE 1984

Year(s)	Millions of Tons	Type of Reserve	Company	Type	State
1963	12	Proven	CFE	Noncoke	Coahuila
1967-1968	39	Proven	CFE	Noncoke	Coahuila
1972-1976	172	Proven	CFE	Noncoke	Coahuila
Nov. 1976	8,000	Total Resources	SEPANAL	--	Country
Mar. 1978	2,000	Proven	CFE	Total	Country
Mar. 1978	1,500	Proven	CFE	Coke	Sabinas, Coahuila
Mar. 1978	300	Proven	CFE	Noncoke	R. Escondido, Coahuila
Mar. 1978	200	Proven	CFE	Noncoke	Oaxaca, Sonora
Aug. 1979	3,274	Total Resources	SEPAFIN	Noncoke	Country
Aug. 1979	2,736	Total Resources	SEPAFIN	Noncoke	Country
Aug. 1979	1,494	Proven	SEPAFIN	Coke	Coahuila
Aug. 1979	1,241	Probable	SEPAFIN	Coke	Coahuila
Aug. 1979	480	Proven	SEPAFIN	Noncoke	Coahuila
Aug. 1979	58	Other Resources	SEPAFIN	Noncoke	Oaxaca, Sonora
Nov. 1980	600	Proven	SEPAFIN	Noncoke	Coahuila
Aug. 1982	643	Proven	MICARE	Noncoke	Coahuila, Oaxaca, Sonora
Jun. 1984	643	Proven	SEMIP	Noncoke	Tamaulipas, Chihuahua

CFE = Comisión Federal de Electricidad.
MICARE = Minera Carbonífera de Río Escondido.
SEMIP = Secretaría de Energía, Minas e Industria Paraestatal.
SEPAFIN = Secretaría de Patrimonio y Fomento Industrial.
SEPANAL = Secretaría del Patrimonio Nacional.

Sources: SEPAFIN, Lineamientos de política energética, Mexico City, SEPAFIN, September 1970; Castañeda,

Miguel, and Roberto Iza, Plan carboeléctrico nacional (mimeograph), Mexico City, September 1982; SEPAFIN, Programa de energía, metas a 1990 y proyecciones al año 2000 (resumen y conclusiones), Mexico City, SEPAFIN, 1980.

Thus, during the mid-1970s coal was considered of sufficient importance to be included in energy-diversification projects. Therefore, it was agreed that the coal industry would become part of the electricity subsector and that the state, through CFE and its mining subsidiaries, would promote its development. With its participation in both the iron and steel and energy industries, coal became important at a national level. Its administration and regulation were assigned to government organizations. Similar policies were also established for the coal consumer companies (steel and electricity) and also partially for state mining entities (exploration and mining). The policy guidelines provided for concessions to the iron and steel industry for utilizing coke resources in the Sabinas, Coahuila, area. The rest of the country's noncoke potential was placed with CFE so that it could be mined for the electricity industry. Additionally, although the quantification of reserves was left to these same institutions, the head of the sector, that is, the ministry in charge of industrial and energy issues, was to report the pertinent data officially.[5]

Until the mid-1970s the amount of proven reserves was of little importance, and the only official data was that reported by CFE (see Table 4.1). The access to figures used by other state and private mining institutions was restricted as a result of the conditions prevailing between 1950 and the mid-1970s when coal had little importance in a national context. The scant amount of information available was dispersive and vague, and the figures published for the reserves differed in concept and in value.

PLANNING FROM 1973 ONWARD

The period from 1976 to 1983 was characterized by a policy of rapid economic growth, although in the last few years this growth slowed in part because of a fall in international crude oil prices and the subsequent contraction of the overactive economy. The energy sector was given the mission of promoting vigorous development in the oil industry, taking diversification into account. This plan was to begin in the electricity subsector, where coal was to contribute significantly. In the first plants for electricity expansion during this period, a coal-based electricity program involving approximately 5,400 MW of capacity was to be built between 1981 and 1984.[6] This program began with the Rio Escondido plant, which was decided upon in 1976. With the corresponding engineering studies completed, construction was to begin in January 1978.

To assure the project's coal supply, in 1977 MICARE, a state-owned company was created and made responsible for the mining and sale of noncoke coal to its only buyer, CFE.[7] In 1979 the electricity expansion program was officially made public with the introduction of POISE and PESE 2000. Coal was to contribute 2,430 MW to the electric energy capacity, increasing to 9,600 MW by the end of the century. The later figure was subsequently revised to 6,800 MW.

PNDI, made public in 1979, proposed even greater growth in the electric subsector than that planned in POISE and PESE 2000 in view of the considerable industrial growth forecasted. Thus, the national total for electricity generated in 1982 was supposed to be 92 TWh, corresponding to an installed capacity of 19,800 MW. Coal would contribute 6 percent of this capacity (1,200 MW) and would generate 7 percent (7 TWh). This plan meant that the whole Rio Escondido plant, that is, the four 300 MW units, had to be on line by the end of 1982, even though construction on the first unit was only started in 1978.[8]

The energy sector's other planning document, PESE 2000, was revealed in November 1980. The project was derived from PNDI, the industrial-development plan, and was mainly concerned with hydrocarbon policy. By 1990 in both iron and steel and electricity applications, coal would cover 8.5 percent of the demand for primary energy, or 4.4 million barrels of crude oil equivalent (MBCE). The program planned for the building of two 1,400 MW coal-based electricity plants in addition to the 1,200 MW that would be produced by plants under construction in order to reach a total coal-based electricity capacity of 4,000 MW by 1990. By this date these plants would be generating over 11 percent of the country's total electricity production.

PESE 2000 was more concerned with discussing the advantages (or disadvantages) of using coal as opposed to natural gas, in the oil and steel industry than it was with proposing a coal-development policy. Its conclusion on the subject was limited to the suggestion that the possibility of mining domestic coal should be closely analyzed and that the development of the international market for natural gas should also be considered carefully. However, the document considered the importance of coal in the national energy-diversification process as a function of its participation in the electricity subsector. The corresponding mining policy would be determined by the coal electricity program's rate of development.

The only government planning measures taken during this period were these two documents. However, the coal industry's dynamic growth soon reached a point where careful and detailed planning in this area became as important as nuclear energy planning. A change in policy toward the institutionalization and decentralization of the coal industry and its recognition as a project in its own right was badly needed so as to distinguish coal-related efforts from other CFE projects that might or might not have come to fruition. The Plan Nacional de Desarrollo Carbonífero (National Plan for Coal Development; PNDC) was thus elaborated in August 1982. Its design was left to a group of local and foreign experts and consultants who also lent their services to CFE and MICARE but not to any government agency in the coal industry. The plan proposed the coal industry's development on the basis of POISE and PESE 2000's revised goals and called for the construction of five plants with a total installed capacity equivalent to 6,800 MW. The schedule for starting operations at the plants and the expected accumulated capacity are shown in Table 4.2.

Recognizing available coal reserves, the designers of PNDC suggested the possibility of a coal-based electricity potential of slightly more than 21,000 MW, which is similar to the installed electric energy capacity for 1983. Distribution according to type of reserve is shown in Table 4.3 and the quantity in tons in Table 4.4. The plan covered all the aspects involved in a project of this type and proposed specific measures for each area.[9]

TABLE 4.2
FORECAST FOR ELECTRIC INSTALLED
CAPACITY, 1983-2000

Plant	Year Operation Commenced	Capacity (MW) Total	Accumulated
J.L.P.	1978	1,200	1,200
C-II	1987	1,400	2,600
C-III	1989	1,400	4,000
C-IV	1994	1,400	5,400
C-V	1998	1,400	6,800

Source: Several authors, Plan nacional de desarrollo carbonífero, Mexico City, August 1982.

TABLE 4.3
COAL ELECTRICITY POTENTIAL BASED ON RESOURCES, 1982
(MW)

State	Type of Reserve Proven	Probable	Possible	Additional Resources	Total
Coahuila	3,780	900	1,190	2,250	8,120
Tamaulipas	315	393	715	2,145	3,568
Sonora	43	65	1,150	3,287	4,545
Chihuahua	- -	- -	250	2,570	2,820
Oaxaca	121	213	213	1,420	1,967
Total	4,259	1,571	3,518	11,6672	21,020

Source: Several authors, Plan nacional de desarrollo carbonífero, Mexico City, August 1982.

It was thought that the reserves in the northeast (Coahuila and Tampico) justified installing only 4,000 MW. Therefore, to reach PNDC's objective and additional 2,800 MW had to be installed, requiring around 420 million tons of coal. This goal could be achieved only if the proven and potential reserves in other regions could be reclassified as proven reserves. However, time has shown how difficult it was to achieve this goal under the conditions prevailing in the energy sector, not to mention organizational, financial, and technological constraints.

TABLE 4.4
COAL RESOURCES (MT)

State	Proven	Probable	Possible	Additional Resources	Total
Coahuila	576	140	185	350	1,251
Tamaulipas	44	65	100	300	509
Sonora	6	9	160	800	975
Chihuahua	--	--	40	400	440
Oaxaca	17	30	30	200	277
Total	643	244	515	2,050	3,452

MT = Millions of tons.

Source: Several authors, Plan nacional de desarrollo carbonífero, Mexico City, August 1982.

From the mid-1970s coal's application to the iron and steel industry followed the same trend as its application in energy production. Rapid development for the coal industry was forecast in light of PNDI objectives, which planned accelerated growth for iron and steel. However, these objectives were later revised in response to the budgetary cuts that arose as a result of the country's economic recession.

In 1980 within the iron and steel industry, a technological discussion arose about whether this industry should be developed using coal-based blast furnaces or direct reduction with natural gas. The easy accessibility of natural gas through the Cactus-Reynosa pipeline clashed in the short run with the work being done in coal exploration and mining. The debate remained officially unresolved, and a large national oil and steel project, Siderúrgica Lázaro Cárdenas-Las Truchas (Lazaro Cardenas-Las Truchas Iron and Steel Company; SICARTSA), was undertaken despite the fact that it would probably consume imported coal. Thus, from 1976 to 1983 the policy for coke was essentially no different from that of the previous period: The responsibility for exploration and mining was still left to the consumer company. Nationwide policy in this respect never materialized.

TABLE 4.5
EVALUATION OF COAL ELECTRICITY PROGRAMS, 1930-1984

Date	Installed Capacity (MW)	Total Primary Energy (%)	Organization and Policy
1930	12	--	Private electricity company to satisfy local needs
1950s	50	--	Private electricity company to satisfy local needs
1964	36	--	CFE pilot plant: Initial stage in coal electricity development
1976	9,000	15.0	SEPANAL, Comisión de Energéticos; proposed participation in coal electricity to the year 2000
1976	1,200	--	CFE Río Escondido; country's first industrial coal electricity program still to be defined
1978	5,400	--	CFE Programa de Expansión Eléctrica: Target between 1981 and 1984
1979	2,430	10.1	CFE POISE: Target 1986; 630 MW in 1982
1979	9,600	--	CFE PESE 2000: Target year 2000, short-term revision; 1,299 MW in 1982
1980	4,000	8.0	SEPAFIN Plan Nacional de Energía: 1990 objective
1982	6,800	--	CFE revision of PESE 2000: Year 2000 objective

(Continued)

TABLE 4.5 (Cont.)
EVALUATION OF COAL ELECTRICITY PROGRAMS, 1930-1984

Date	Installed Capacity (MW)	Total Primary Energy (%)	Organization and Policy
1982	6,800	--	PNDC: 5 plants (four 1,400 MW plants and one 1,200 MW plant)
1984	1,200	8.0	SEMIP Programa Nacional de Energéticos: 1988 objective
(2000	9,100	10.1	Year 2000 objective: 10.1% coal electricity participation only; approximately 17.3% when dual plants are included)

CFE = Comisión Federal de Electricidad.
PESE 2000 = Plan de Expansión del Sector Eléctrico al Año 2000.
PNDC = Plan Nacional de Desarrollo Carbonífero.
POISE = Programa de Obras e Inversión del Sector Eléctrico.
SEMIP = Secretaría de Energía, Minas e Industria Paraestatal.
SEPAFIN = Secretaría de Patrimonio y Fomento Industrial.
SEPANAL = Secretaría del Patrimonio Nacional.

Sources: SEPAFIN, "Plan carboeléctrico nacional," in Energéticos: Boletín informativo del sector energético, Year 1, No. 1, Mexico City, SEPAFIN, August 1977; SEPAFIN, Year 2, October 1977; SEPAFIN, Year 3, No. 8, August 1979; and CFE, Programa de obras e inversión del sector eléctrico, Mexico City, CFE, 1978.

In general terms planning for coal's thermal application would be subject to the requirements of the coal-based electricity program. Exploration and the coal used for generating electricity would be CFE's concern, and its subsidiary, MICARE, would be responsible for mining. The organizations for mining--CRM and the Comisión de Fomento Minero (Commission for the

Promotion of Mining; CFM)--and energy planning--SEMIP --would be involved only in formalizing this policy.

With the exception of PNE 1984-1988 real changes in coal policy to date have been minimal. The iron and steel industry continues to work along the same lines, its development defined as part of industry and mining (not energy). With regard to coal's thermal applications, a reduction in the growth rate of "pure" coal electricity programs was proposed in the short term, but the plans for the year 2000 remain unchanged. The exploration and mining policy was to be defined in accordance with these programs, which tend to move in the same direction as before. (For a complete list of coal programs, see Table 4.5.)

However, an old idea is currently being resurrected that concerns building dual plant on the east coast, that is, plants consuming either coal or fuel oil. Coal's participation in the electricity subsector would increase, although exploration and mining programs would need to be reinforced. If such a project were to be approved, the lack of domestic coal resources apparently would not be argument enough to modify the decision to introduce this type of plant because the coal supply would probably be assured by imports.

ORGANIZATION OF THE INDUSTRY

The coal industry consists of a large number of agencies and institutions from both the private and public sectors (see Tables 4.5 and 4.6). Coal is Mexico's only energy resource not administered by a single specialized enterprise, which is the case with oil (PEMEX), uranium (URAMEX), and electricity (CFE). This situation apparently originates from coal's various applications, which have determined its development from the beginning of the century. Coal is legally governed by the (Mexican Mining Law); its most recent regulations were introduced by SEPANAL in 1975. According to the mining law coal is considered part of "national mining reserves"; general clauses are concerned with concessions, mining promotion, and other areas related to national reserves.

TABLE 4.6
ORGANIZATION OF THE COAL INDUSTRY

Industry Stage	Product Uses	
	Iron and Steel	Energy
Mining	Exploration and Exploitation	Exploration
	. Large-Scale Mining	. CFE
	– Iron and Steel Companies:	. CRM
	Private: Several	Exploitation
	Government: SIDERMEX; FMMNM	. MICARE
	– Mining Companies: Industrial Minera Mexicana	. CFM
	– State: CRM; CFM	
	Exploitation only	
	. Medium- and Small-Scale Mining	
	– Mining Companies: Several	
	– Productive: Individual Miners and Others	
Benefit	Washing	Washing
	. Iron and Steel Companies	. MICARE
	– Private: Several	
	– Government: SIDERMEX; FMMNM	

(Continued)

TABLE 4.6 (Cont.)

Industry Stage	Product Uses	
	Iron and Steel	Energy
Transformation	Coking, Blast Furnacing, and Tempering . Iron and Steel Companies: Private and Government	Electricity Generation CFE

Planning and Regulation	. Private
	  – Mining Chamber
	  – Cámara Nacional de la Industria Siderúrgica
	. Government
	  – SEMIP: CRM, CFM, Department of Mines, and so on
	  – SECOFI
		. SEMIP: CRM, CFM, Energy Policy, Operations Department, and so on
		. CFE
		. SPP; SHCP; SECOFI

Research	Instituto Nacional de Investigaciones Siderúrgicas	. Estudios Carboníferos de Coahuila . IIE

CFE = Comisión Federal de Electricidad.
CFM = Comisión de Fomento Minero.
CRM = Consejo de Recursos Minerales.
FMMNM = Fideicomiso Mexicano de Minerales no Metálicos, a branch of NAFINSA.
IIE = Instituto de Investigaciones Eléctricas.
MICARE = Minera Carbonífera de Río Escondido.
SECOFI = Secretaría de Comercio y Fomento Industrial.
SEMIP = Secretaría de Energía, Minas e Industria Paraestatal.
SHCP = Secretaría de Hacienda y Crédito Público.
SIDERMEX = Siderúrgica Mexicana.
SPP = Secretaría de Programación y Presupuesto.

Source: Castañeda, Miguel, and Roberto Iza, Plan carboeléctrico nacional (mimeograph), Mexico City, September 1982.

Coal's industrial uses (iron and steel) are currently covered by a state enterprise called

Siderúrgica Mexicana (Mexican Iron and Steel Company; SIDERMEX), which includes three companies: Altos Hornos de México, S.A. (Blast Furnaces of Mexico; AHMSA), Fundidora Monterrey, and SICARTSA. All these companies are vertically integrated; that is, they engage either directly or through subsidiaries in all activities involved in steel manufacturing.

Coal mining, which is currently in private hands, can be divided into large-, medium-, and small-scale enterprises. The only large one is Industrial Minera de México, S.A., which carries out coal-exploration activities under concession; its branches mine, wash, and produce, coke. In medium- and small-scale mining there are a large number of enterprises, although in small-scale mining, the so-called poceros,[10] or individual miners, predominate. All these companies sell coal to public and private consumers.

The public side of mining administration is concentrated in SEMIP, which assigns this task to several of its subordinate bodies. The Dirección General de Minas (General Director of Mines) is responsible for policy guidelines, the Consejo de Recursos Minerales (Council for Mineral Resources) for mining resource evaluation, and the Comisión de Fomento Minero (Commission for Mining Promotion). NAFINSA manages the Fideicomiso Mexicano de Minerales no Metálicos (Mexican Fideicommissum of Nonmetallic Minerals).

Apart from these state agencies, other entities are also involved in coal-related energy applications: the Gerencia de Exploración y Estudios Carboníferos del Noroeste (Northwest Coal Exploration and Evaluation Department) (a branch of CFE for exploring and evaluating reserves); MICARE for coal mining and trade; CFE's Subdirección de Operaciones (Operations Vice-Director) for the operation and administration of coal-based electricity plants, which is the superintendent's office at the Río Escondido plant; and IIE, which undertakes coal R&D for electricity purposes.

MAIN AREAS OF CONTROVERSY

Numerous controversies surround the coal industry. The major problems to be covered in the following subsections are reserve volumes, importing needs, financial dependence, environmental effects, and coal washing.

Reserve volumes

Undoubtedly, one of the most debated points in the coal industry relates to reserve volumes. This problem arose during the period from 1970 to 1976 when coal began to be considered within the energy sector as a diversifying agent in the electricity subsector's energy-source supply. This proposal was brought up officially for the first time midway through the Echeverría administration (1970-1976) but did not become controversial until late in the term. The opposing opinions arose, on one hand, in the Comisión Nacional de Energéticos (National Energy Commission; CNE) and, on the other, in CFM and the iron and steel industry.

From the beginning the reasons behind the disagreement were not very clear, but different explanations can be suggested. Confusion might have arisen about the type of coal to be utilized in generating electricity or about some sort on governmental intervention in the areas under concession to the iron and steel industry. This explanation does not seem valid, however, because the classification of proven coal reserves clearly shows that Sabinas coal is actually coke and, therefore, good for iron and steel purposes and that the rest of the country's coal resources are noncoke and can be used for energy purposes only.

Another possible reason could be the interest that arose in coal at this time and the proposal that the first stage of coal development should be the quantification of total domestic reserves. PNEC was created for this purpose in 1976 with the participation of PEMEX, CFE, and CRM. This program began its activities in the Rio Escondido region and planned to explore the area around Sabinas and Rio Escondido; in its second stage it was to look also into probable coal resources in Durango and Chihuahua. For some reason these geographical areas did not agree with the interests of the iron and steel industry, which feared perhaps that the results of this exploration would affect their political position with respect to coal-reserve availability. Another reason could lie in the fact that those in charge of coal exploration and mining during this period felt that their budgetary and management programs could be affected. Once again, there is nothing to indicate that this situation would arise because the idea of creating a single organization such as PEMEX, that is, Carbón de México (Mexican Coal Company; CARBOMEX) for the management of all coal-related areas did not prosper. One could also assume an eagerness on the part of a certain agency or agencies (which refused to accept evidence of coal deposits in several regions of the country) to obtain financial resources for exploration. However, their stance was decisive: Certain regions were written off as of little interest, thus eliminating the need for exploration where previous geological studies had shown the possible existence of coal deposits.

If the legal aspects of exploration are analyzed, Artículo 96, Chapter XII, of the mining law promotes the discovery of resources that "can be incorporated into the national mining reserves" through a recompense or preferential concessions. The rewards would be determined by the importance of the discovery and could amount to 50,000 pesos. However, the concessions for the iron and steel industry had been granted before this law came into force. Also, in Artículo 82, Chapter IX, of the same law, which deals with the tax or royalties that coal miners must pay CFM, the amounts charged are a function of production level and not the reserves themselves. Thus, when you consider a company's policy about amortization of exploration costs, the mining law is less an incentive to discover new reserves than Artículo 96 seems to suggest.

Another reason for disagreement was the basic criterion used in defining the different types of reserves. As some experts point out, this problems is worldwide. The reserve definition only implies a certain depth and width for each coal category; the criteria by which these reserves are determined differ from one country to another. Every definition does, however, include the concept of resources "economically recoverable with the current techniques." This situation depends, though, on the access of a given country to such current technology. The magnitude of proven reserves would be a function of the economic profitability of mining at a given moment.

It appears that the lack of general agreement on a technical concept was not the whole cause of the problem in Mexico especially because the geologic evidence at hand (although inadequate because of insufficient exploratory activity) tended to indicate the existence of large coal resources in Mexico. Therefore, it might be useful to discuss the viability of mining, both the cost and technical constraints and the legal disputes that could arise from the expropriation of land. However, even after figures on reserves were certified by the state agencies involved in PNDC and approved by international advise, including Sofrimènes of France and the National Coal Board of Great Britain, the internal controversy continued about the exact amount of reserves. Officially, the accepted figures are those announced by SEMIP, the ministry at the head of the sector.

Resorting to Imports

The importation of mineral coal is a long-standing practice in Mexico and has been the most common form of supplying the iron and steel industry. Even when large coke reserves were discovered, this industry continued to import coal, arguing that the quality of the local mineral was inferior because of its high-ash content, which meant higher costs in the washing process and in the production of clean coal. Apparently, this explanation satisfied those in charge of granting import permits because no restriction was ever placed. Thus, SICARTSA planned its development on the basis of imported coal.

An alternative to importing noncoke coal was announced for the first time with the introduction of PESE 2000, wherein the installation of seven coal-burning plants with a capacity of 9,600 MW was planned. Current proven reserves, however, could only guarantee supply to the first three plants (4,000 MW). Here, there were two options: (1) to develop a dynamic exploration program converting probable and possible reserves into proven reserves or (2) to import coal. In essence, the second option appears the most advisable. The exploration program's success was not assured, although the geologic information available offered good prospects. With the possibility of buying mineral abroad, MICARE presented CFE with a preliminary study for importing coal along with several alternatives, among which were spot-market purchases, joint investment, and long-term contracts. No decision was made, but the spot-market alternative was taken up by PNDC. Among other things, PNDC suggested the creation of a trading company that specialized in this type of international transaction, such as those in Spain.

In regard to joint investment a trinational consortium, with the participation of Mexico, Brazil, and Colombia, was created in 1983 first to carry out preliminary feasibility studies and later to mine the El Cerrejón deposits in Colombia. Apparently, each country contributed $5 million to the study, but the progress of this research venture is unknown.

Early in 1984 after the president's visit to Colombia, official Mexican circles announced that Mexico would buy 1 million tons of coal from that country for energy purposes. At present, it is not known whether the idea of importing the coal still holds or whether it will be substituted by joint investment. The recent PNE did not clarify the official position regarding the imports; it only mentioned "selectively establishing joint participation projects with other countries favorable to the development of the national coal-based electricity program." This document leaves acceptance of joint participation to personal criteria because some believe that the transaction involves direct purchases from the company currently mining and trading the Colombian coal deposits (Exxon). Some assume the intention is still to invest in Colombia, and others suppose bartering will be resorted to, but nothing is clear as yet. Nevertheless, it is a fact that Mexico will receive coal from abroad because MICARE is carrying out the necessary activities for opening a port at Lázaro Cárdenas, Michoacán, where the first dual plant with an installed capacity of 1,400 MW is located. Later, it is thought that a similar plant will be set up in Altamira, Tamaulipas. There are serious questions regarding the decision to set up dual plants in areas far from domestic coal-production centers, unless, of course, this decision was made in anticipation of importing the mineral.

Although SICARTSA was planned on the basis of coal imports, it is implementing a coal import-substitution policy by acquiring coal from Coahuila using railroad transport that operates on a government subsidy. The utilization of this infrastructure for transporting noncoke coal could be contemplated, but apparently cost criteria eliminate this option. Added to this situation, say the experts, is the cost of the special infrastructure necessary for loading and unloading the coal from the railroad. However, heavy investment is being made in the Michoacán plant, which, according to some observers, has design defects involving excessive infrastructure and, therefore, increased costs.

Thus, the study of the different economic parameters influencing coal imports is recommended, preferably based on cost-benefit criteria. It has been suggested, on one hand, that domestic investment be made in productive development (exploration and mining) and infrastructure (transport systems), and on the other, that purchases from abroad be made. All these suggestions require foreign exchange that it was assumed would most probably come from foreign loans. Under present conditions and given the magnitude of the country's debt, such an assumption is no longer valid.

Financial dependence

The financial resources for the coal mining and electricity project have come from different sources. At the beginning of its activities MICARE successfully negotiated a loan from the Inter-American Development Bank (IDB) for $188 million (U.S. $) basically for the purchase of equipment. CFE obtained funds from several different sources for developing its program, such as its own income from sales (the lesser part), contributions from the federal government, and foreign loans (the greater part).

A number of points contained in the IDB loan agreement are worth going over:

- MICARE is committed to operate at a profit for a period of at least 15 years.

- It must increase its equity to 1.2 billion pesos.

- It must give a commission of 1.25 percent to IDB, which is charged annually on the unpaid part of the financing and which is due 60 days after the signing of the contract.

- It must pay interest of 7.5 percent per year on the loan obtained plus transfer and management costs.

- It must pay 1 percent of the total loan for financing inspection and monitoring costs.

- It has an amortization period of fifteen years and a six-month grace period.

- It accepts the commitment of a national contribution calculated at $151 million, of which $52 million would be covered by MICARE's partners.

- It accepts a restrictive clause to the effect that MICARE will not distribute dividends during the period of the project's execution and another clause regarding the way these dividends should be handled once the term is over.

- It accepts a 60/40 ratio of total debt to total equity and a present liquidity index of no less than 1.3.

- It promises that equipment purchased for sums greater than $100,000 will be subject to tenders adjusted to the procedures and policy established by IDB.

- It excludes the possibility of accepting tenders from nonmember countries of the IDB.

Furthermore, as part of the negotiations, IDB requested the withdrawal of the local pit-prop manufacturers. However, it seems that the Mexican manufacturers were able to show that the quality of the local equipment was better than that of the foreign manufacturers, and they assured its continuous supply, a worthwhile achievement for Mexico in the negotiations.

One point that apparently could not be worked out was the participation of nonmember countries of IDB in providing capital goods for the project. At the time CFE had signed protocols with KOPEX (a Polish company) in which it promised to invite the latter to take part in biddings to $10 million; the penalty for nonfulfillment was the loss of a $1.5 million guarantee deposit. It was suggested that equipment be purchased from this company at competitive prices but without tenders, but the negotiations were not satisfactory because of their length. In fact, no one knows the real reason for their failure, and the consequent loss for Mexico was probably more than $1.5 million.

The commitment to operate profitability is a responsibility that MICARE has transferred to CFE through coal prices and that is established in the two companies' sales contract. The contract stipulated that prices would be set in such a way that MICARE would be compensated for "all costs incurred in reaching its objectives." This statement could be interpreted to mean whatever price MICARE set to reach its objectives would have to be paid by CFE whether it is reflected in the price per kilowatt-hour of electric energy or in greater state subsidies.

It is not easy for two companies to discuss prices when one is the sales monopoly and the other is the monopsony. Therefore, the transfer-price concept is used most often, which means prices are subject to periodic revision every six months, as established in the contract. Although at first glance it seems logical to share the cost per ton supplied, a formula was established in the contract to calculate the reviewed price.[11]

The basic coal price established when the contract was signed in August 1978 was 400 pesos per ton; there were no exact parameters for its evaluation. At the time deliveries commenced the first reviews had already been requested; thus, for the first semester of 1981 the price was increased to 700 pesos per ton. In early 1983 a price of 2,500 pesos per ton was proposed and the last official figure obtained in June 1984 was 4,128 pesos per ton.

TABLE 4.7
COST PER UNIT OF ELECTRICITY GENERATED
(in percentages)

	October 1982[a]			July 1984[b]	
Type of Cost	Fuel Oil	Coal Imported	Coal Local	Fuel Oil	Imported Coal
Investment	25	45	54	24	49
Fuel	69	42	30	74	46
Operation and Maintenance	6	13	16	2	5
Total	100	100	100	100	100
Cost in Relation to Fuel Oil	1.00	0.74	0.61	1.00	0.74

[a]Exchange rate is 50 pesos/U.S. $.
[b]Exchange rate is 120 pesos/U.S. $.

Source: Castañeda, Miguel, and Roberto Iza, Plan carboeléctrico nacional (mimeograph), Mexico City, September 1982.

TABLE 4.8
COST-PER-UNIT INDEXES FOR ELECTRICITY GENERATED

	October 1982	July 1984
Investment Amortization	1.35	1.54
Fuel	0.45	0.46
Operation and Maintenance	1.67	1.67
Fuel Oil Ratio	0.74	0.74

Source: Castañeda, Miguel, and Roberto Iza, Plan carboeléctrico nacional (mimeograph), Mexico City, September 1982.

The exact current figures on coal prices are only known within MICARE and CFE. Furthermore, previous figures could reflect the interests of either one of the parties. Consequently, some observes have tried to calculate a coal transfer price, which they put currently at around 7,300 pesos per ton. In 1984 this figure was fairly close to the international coal price, which was 7,730 pesos per ton at the peso-dollar exchange rate average for that year.

TABLE 4.9
PRICES FOR FUEL OIL AND COAL
AT 1983 PRICES AND 120 PESOS/U.S. $

Fuel	Pesos/Unit Inter- national	Pesos/Unit National	Pesos/10³Kcal Inter- national	Pesos/10³Kcal National	Pesos/KWh Inter- national	Pesos/KWh National
Fuel Oil (m³)	16,0548	2,130	1.6028	1.2126	4.111	0.545
Coal (ton)	4,631	4,128	0.6668	0.9549	1.830	2.620
Fuel Oil Ratio	--	--	41.6	449	44.5	480

Source: Castañeda, Miguel, and Roberto Iza, Plan carboeléctrico nacional (mimeograph), Mexico City, September 1982.

The coal-price debate also concerns the veracity of the figures because MICARE is nowhere near completing the production program established initially. Not all the problems stem from this company. In the sales contract CFE had an obligation to supply MICARE's coal requirements on the basis of a five-year generating plan and a monthly calendar of its annual needs. Because the Rio Escondido plant should have been completed by August 1984, and only two units are operating at the present time, CFE has not fulfilled its part of the deal; MICARE has thus been forced to reduce its rate of production. However, MICARE has not fulfilled its commitments either because of technical problems that have plagued it from the beginning (floods and insufficient backup studies prior to the installation of equipment resulted in the extraction of an inadequate amount of lower-quality coal). At first, MICARE was able to fulfill its commitment with

CFE: The high productivity of the cuts compensated for the slow progress in mining. Later, various problems arose. A lack of spare parts was solved by using parts from equipment lying idle, but the lack of specialized personnel and the continuous rotation of staff has affected productivity and equipment maintenance.

To summarize, the CFE-MICARE project needs to be revised. There is no suggestion of reducing or canceling it, especially not the mining part that backs up the coal-importing policy, but changes in the way the project is executed could be the answer. In support of this proposal certain figures CFE uses to formulate its investment projects must be mentioned. As shown in Table 4.7 and Table 4.8, despite the heavy increase in domestic coal prices, in over two years the total cost ratio between fuel oil and coal has not changed, with coal maintaining the position of advantage. Furthermore, these evaluations were made using international fuel oil prices. For domestic prices the ratio would certainly be inverted more than proportionately because the domestic coal price is between 4.5 and 4.8 times greater than that for fuel oil (see Table 4.9). However, if the decision to introduce a coal-based electricity program has already been made, modest though the project might be, it would be worth studying coal resources in depth because an analysis of the figures in tables 4.7 and 4.8 shows no substantial advantage in using international coal over local coal.

Effects on the environment

Three elements of a coal electricity project can affect the environment:

1. The water needed in mining and in cooling at the electricity plant

2. The emission of gas from coke combustion

3. The residual ash from burning the mineral

In regard to the first point, because the plant is located in a desertic zone, in-depth geohydraulic studies had to be done to ensure water supply. The alternatives were as follows:

- To utilize the underground aquiferous reservoirs for both the project and the benefit of the community, particularly for the productive sectors (farmers)

- To build an aqueduct measuring 20 to 30 kilometers to bring water from the Rio Bravo

Both options were decided upon. Negotiations were held with the United States for the use of water from the frontier. It was decided to build an artificial lake with a volume of 18 million cubic meters. The lake was filled with water from the region's underground aquiferous mantles, which, together with those found in the mines themselves, caused a heavy fall in the region's water level,[12] and the region's climatic conditions reduced refilling to a minimum. Although the coal-based electricity project was responsible for the scarcity of water in the region, it has not been possible to convince the farmers to use water from the lake. Apparently, because the conditions of the region are not favorable for farming development, the farmers receive a subsidy from the authorities to promote this activity. If water was to become so readily available that the soil's characteristics changed, it is likely that the promotional measures for farming would be modified, an unwelcome change for those farmers whose economic condition forces them to rely on this subsidy.

The problem of gas emission was solved by means of an apparatus placed on chimneys (filters and electrostatic condensers), which prevented safety levels for both combustion gases and ash in the air from being exceeded. The region's cloudiness, therefore, is not due to the smoke from the electricity plant but from the coal ash dumped on the land adjacent to the plant. This ash, amounting to nearly 1,000 tons per day per unit, has been one of the most serious political problems the project has had to face. When the project was conceived, the multiple industrial uses for the ash were listed, and it was stated that "in any of these applications, the corresponding commercialization would be completely assured."[13] At the time, negotiations were conducted with cement industries for the purchase of the ash. However, nothing could be agreed upon, and the official version was that no satisfactory arrangement had been reached about price or the investment needed for transporting ash to the industrial centers.

However, another version of this story exists. In 1984 CFE and MICARE had still not decided which of them was to be responsible for the ash disposal. CFE said that because ash was an inert product of coal, it did not form part of combustion and should be MICARE's responsibility. MICARE argued that once the mineral was acquired, everything associated with it pertained to the buyer. Discussions were even held about whether the ash should be considered national property. In March 1984 a young company, Cenizas de México, S.A. de C.V. (Mexican Ash Company; CEMEX), presented CFE with a proposal for purchasing the ash. A price between 500 and 600 pesos per ton was mentioned along with a five-year program to acquire the ash, starting with 12,000 tons in the first year and increasing purchases yearly to reach 25,000 tons in the fifth year.

Although this proposal would not solve the problem altogether, it would have been a first step toward a solution. However, CFE never responded to the CEMEX proposal, and after much insistence the company was told that MICARE already had someone in charge of the problem who was making the necessary arrangements to solve it. It was mentioned that contact had been established with a U.S. company and with Cementos Monterrey (no details were given about the progress of the negotiations). Also, the construction of a railroad line, financed by CFE, was being advanced to remove the ash from its land, and a study on the classification of the ash had been requested from the Universidad Nacional Autónoma de México (National Autonomous University of Mexico; UNAM), a necessary step for determining its possible uses. The fact is that the ash continues to pile up outside the plant, and the problem remains with very little hope for a solution.

Washing

Coal washing has been another area of disagreement in coal-based electricity programs. In coal's thermal applications, such as in the iron and steel industry, coke washing is an unavoidable process. The reasons behind introducing washed coal into the electricity industry were essentially based on the technical and economic factors related to working with coal and as well as on operational problems. As a result of the washing process, time spent in the homogenization of the mineral and the maintenance and operation of the boilers is reduced, with a consequent reduction in costs. Apart from these advantages are others dealing with ash; use of washed and unwashed coal; and the use of by-products, such as alumina and earth silicon.

At the start of the coal electricity project, CFE requested a technical and economic study of coal washing. The results apparently were not in favor of establishing a plant of this kind. The plant continued to operate without the coal-washing process, but management and operational problems gradually grew worse. CFE has now gone back to the washing alternative, and it has been decided to install a washing facility for treating thermal coal at the Rio Escondido plant, Carbón I.

FUTURE PROSPECTS

PNE 1984-1988 provides the best indicator of the course the coal industry might take in the future.[14] From this program the following possible approaches can be deduced.

Among strategies are the following:

- Coal is considered a means of achieving energy diversification.

- The main activities in this process should be undertaken in the electricity subsector with coal-based electricity.

- Exploration will be one of the strategic backup phases in diversification, so activities should be concentrated in this area.

- The option to import this resource should be considered, however, in order to assure adequate use of domestic coal resources.

Schedules for expanded use of coal are as follows:

- To begin new coal-based electricity projects in 1983-1984

- To proceed with the Rio Escondido complex, continue designing the Carbón II plant, start work on a new plant by 1987-1988, and undertake studies for new long-term projects

- To improve coal industry management, utilize residues, and tighten control over environmental contamination

- To selectively establish joint-participation projects with other countries

Targets for 1988 are as follows:

- To annually increase solid-fuel (coal and uranium) production between 10 and 11 percent

- To raise coal's contribution to the total energy supply to slightly more than 3 percent

- To raise coal's contribution to the additional electricity capacity to 8 percent

Targets for the year 2000 are as follows:

- To raise coal-based electricity's contribution to total installed capacity between 8.6 and 10.1 percent, 17.3 percent of which to be generated by dual plants

Although these targets are clearly very ambitious, there is obvious interest in developing the coal industry. If exploratory work is not encouraged, development will be forced to depend largely on coal imports; but, given the foreign-currency restrictions foreseen for Mexico during the next few years, it is most likely that the country's coal fields will have to be developed to satisfy a considerable part of the program's goals. However, the possibility has already been considered that coal utilization could change radically: instead of its direct use as a mineral, synthetic fuels derived from coal could be employed. Internationally, the growing demand by miners for better working conditions has not only made mining expensive, it has also reduced the availability of this type of worker. The reasons behind this situation are more of a social than of a technical nature and are helping to speed up research on coal gasification, preferably in situ.

In Mexico progress in coal-related technological R&D has been good; there are companies already capable of developing this type of technology with perhaps a minimum of external assistance.[15] The use of gasification in situ would affect both the energy and industrial sector because the mining problem has nothing to do with the distinction of one type of coal from another. The iron and steel industry might opt for a direct-reduction technology based on natural gas obtained from coal gasification. Whereas, in the energy sector the problem of competitiveness might arise, that is, deciding whether to use synthetic gas as a fuel or as a raw material for the petrochemical or other chemical industries.

In analyzing the forecasts for coal's contribution to the electricity subsector, one realizes that the future coal based plants represent multiples of 350 MW, which seems to indicate CFE's intention to use this particular technology. The first coal-based electricity programs founded on technology brought from Japan and detailed engineering developed in Mexico, were designed on the basis of 300 MW units. The new CFE administration changed its programs in late 1976 to 350 MW units, arguing that this change would mean lesser cost, greater efficiency, and component standardization. The technology for the new units had to be negotiated, and CFE had to muddle through the red tape involved in choosing among the open bids required by the public sector for the purchases of the new units. The earlier technology would be used exclusively at the existing plants, and at some future point the existing engineering designs would no longer be used.

Last, the target to increase solid-fuel production between 10 and 11 percent per year does not specify the type of coal to be used. However, it probably would be mainly coke. This assumption was based on the schedule for operations at the Rio Escondido complex, whose last unit was to come on line in 1986 but which at present is still not in operation. If one takes into account the latest data on noncoke coal production, which showed 1.7 million tons in 1983, and compares the figure with the requirements for 1988 when the four Rio Escondido units would be operating, total annual coal production rises to around 4.5 million tons. To reach this level mining would have to increase 21.5 percent per year. If the coal requirements for the dual plants were added, the increase in this activity would be even greater. These figures raise the question about whether the growth rate proposed for PNE 1984-1988 would limit domestic coal activities to a certain extent, thus justifying or reinforcing the option to import, which would be extremely onerous for the country under current financial conditions. However, if the 10-11 percent growth refers to both coal and uranium, the figure could be interpreted as an average value for the exploitation rate of both. If coal failed to progress, then uranium could take the place of both. This option seems very remote. In February 1985 SEMIP announced that because of Mexico's financial restrictions resulting from the drop in oil prices, the nuclear electricity program would be suspended temporarily, the only exception being the first unit at Laguna Verde, which would begin operations in 1986 as planned,[16] but which, as mentioned in Chapter 3, has also been suspended. Thus, not only are the PNE 1984-1988 proposals for the future development of the national coal industry ambiguous, but the short-term plan seems to permanently modify the original proposals.

CONCLUSIONS

The points discussed in this chapter suggest, on one hand, that Mexico's coal potential is considerable or at least larger than what many experts had traditionally supposed and, on the other, that large-scale coordination efforts will be needed to place coal in the position it deserves.

Coal already plays an important role in many countries, for example in those with centrally planned economies where the contribution to the domestic primary energy supply is already greater than 48 percent. In western Europe coal's energy contribution is more than 21 percent. These figures represent an increment of several percentage points in less than a decade.[17]

In Mexico much time has been spent discussing the advantages and disadvantages of developing the coal industry. The political discussion has not favored the extended use of coal nor have some groups that advocate taking full advantage of domestic hydrocarbon resources. Within CFE thermoelectric plants have been given the most attention, whereas PEMEX has provided many opportunities for utilizing hydrocarbons in the iron and steel industry. Although some experts and observers have spoken in favor of encouraging exploration and mining work, others have opposed it, arguing that it is preferable to resort to imports because production costs per unit are lower abroad than in Mexico. This situation seems logical because Mexico was never fully committed to encouraging this mining activity, believing it prevented it from cutting costs and achieving economies of scale.

The Mexican coal industry is fragmented: Although coke production depends upon the growth of the iron and steel industry, noncoke coal responds to the requirements of CFE, Mexico's monopoly in charge of generating and distributing electric energy. This monopoly, in turn, represents the interests of the state, whereas some of the iron and steel companies providing the outlet for coke production are either totally or partially in private hands.

However, state policy on coal-based electricity is not completely clear: Although the coal industry has been nationalized, the measures to date have not showed any clear orientation toward promoting its development. Far from encouraging domestic coal production, several coal-consuming state companies, SICARTSA for example, have decided to import it.

Last, an optimum plan by which the state can coordinate coal industry development is not easy to produce. Nevertheless, a reduction in hydrocarbon-price subsidies, direct state participation in exploration and coke and noncoke coal mining, the coordination of financing activities, the expansion of capital goods production, and the smoothing of tension within the energy sector in general could all contribute substantially to the expansion of demand for domestic coal in Mexico.

NOTES

1. The first state-owned iron and steel company, AHMSA, was established in 1942.
2. For every ton of steel produced, the Mexican iron and steel industry required 1.4 tons of clean coal.
3. Unpublished paper by Padilla Segura, José (mimeograph), general director of AHMSA, Mexico City, 1976.
4. At this time a plant with an installed capacity of 12 (2 x 6) MW was operating in Gómez Palacio in the state of Durango.
5. The iron and steel companies were to report on the resources and the public sector would report on thermal coal through its mining entities and CFE.
6. This figure would be equivalent to a plant with an installed capacity of 1,200 MW plus three plants of 1,400 MW.
7. The major partners in this company were CFM with a share of 43 percent, CFE with 32 percent, and NAFINSA with 25 percent. Two minor partners were also invited to participate because of their broad experience and excellent organization in coal mining: AHMSA and Industrial Minera de México.
8. The lead time of a coal-based electricity project is between 6 and 8 years under optimum conditions, which is usually not the case with domestic electricity projects where lead times tend to

increase, particularly in new projects such as the nuclear program.

9. The different aspects generally dealt with in a coal electricity project were mining; exploration and mining programs (strategy for opening mines); benefits; coal-washing analysis; coal use in plants; programs for plant construction; human, technical, financial, and physical resources (geohydrology, equipment, and so on); ecology, particularly in relation to ash and other associated minerals (aluminum and silicon); capital goods; commercialization of energy and coal; inputs; and organization.

10. <u>Pocero</u> is a person who mines with rudimentary techniques and minimum investment, therefore producing very small volumes.

11. $Pr = Pa (19.6I \times 19.9I_2 \times 9.0I_3 \times 24.1 \times I_4 \times I_5 \times 27.4I_5)/100$, where Pr = reviewed price; Pa = previous price; I = index determined by the wage increase of MICARE's unionized personnel; I_2 = national wholesale price index; I_3 = national cost index for social-benefit housing construction; I_4 = wholesale price index in the United States; and I_5 = controlled exchange-rate variation index for the Mexican peso with respect to the American dollar.

12. The underground water reservoirs that were discovered caused serious operating problems because of flooding. The water had to be pumped into the Rio Bravo without being put to any productive use.

13. It was proposed that in this region ash could be used industrially as a partial substitute for Portland cement for manufacturing concrete, a light additive for construction materials, and a fine additive or filler for asphalt mixtures.

14. The analysis of future prospects was based on PNE 1984-1988 because it is the most recent document for this purpose and because PNDC, published in 1978, is virtually outdated.

15. The introduction of PNDC favored the creation of some of these enterprises, such as that set up in Querétaro whose main line is soft-metal mining. Moreover, coal-development expectations in the early 1980s were very high. PNE 1984-1988's plans for coal would contribute to the recovery of those enterprises whose present installed capacity, that is, coal-mining machinery, is lying completely idle.

16. "Insta Mendoza Berrueto a reducir al 75% la dependencia petrolera," in *El Nacional*, Mexico City, 2 February 1985.

17. This information is based on British Petroleum Company figures.

5

Nuclear Electricity Planning and Development

Rogelio Ruíz

In Mexico one cannot really talk of a nuclear industry because there isn't one. Although the foundation has already been laid, the industry probably will not start contributing to the domestic product until Mexico's first nuclear plant come on line at Laguna Verde, and at this early stage the contribution will be marginal. Thus, at least for the moment it seems appropriate to talk of nuclear energy as a branch of the electricity subsector. The fact that this energy is subsidized implies considerable dependence on the decisions made in the area. Rather than being strictly nuclear related, these decisions until now have been related to nuclear electricity and will continue to be so for some time. Thus, the purpose of this chapter is to present the most important historical and analytic events in the history of nuclear electricity and to show the way in which the industry's planning has evolved.

As was the case in many countries, Mexico's interest in developing nuclear electricity arose around the time of the Atoms for Peace Program (1953) and the International Conference on the Pacific Uses of Atomic Energy (1955) when great expectations were held about the pacific uses of atomic energy. On 19 December 1955 the Mexican government passed a law creating the Comisión Nacional de Energía Nuclear (National Nuclear

Energy Commission; CNEN). This commission was founded on those principles and ideas presented at the Geneva Conference, which was aimed at the establishment of government agencies responsible for nuclear development.

In 1966 CFE decided to move into the field of nuclear electricity. It undertook superficial economic analyses that indicated the competitiveness of nuclear electricity compared to other sources of electricity. The government, in turn, agreed to consider the feasibility studies for 500 MW nuclear plants. CFE established a nuclear department comprising three experts educated abroad. With the backing of internationally renowned Mexican scientists, CFE signed an agreement with then Stanford Research Institute (now SRI, Inc.) to design a model for analyzing ways of expanding the electricity grid, which included nuclear electric plants as one of the possible means of generating energy. The results of the evaluation indicated that the cost of installing a nuclear electric plant was the main problem to overcome.[1]

THE LAGUNA VERDE DECISION

During the mid-1970s with the consent of the president of the republic, a working group was formed to consider the advisability of continuing studies for the installation of the first nuclear electric plant. At this point the country's hydrocarbon production was insufficient, and it was necessary to import crude oil. Furthermore, people were already talking about the advantages of energy diversification. Thus, in July 1970, a few months before the change of the government, the group reached its decision to install a nuclear electric plant in Mexico. The following considerations prevailed in this respect:

- The pressures exerted by electricity consumption were great. An 800,000 KW demand per year had to be assured from late 1975 onward by the interconnected systems in the south of Mexico alone.

- There was a need to partially substitute demand for hydrocarbons with nuclear materials. The lack of new large-capacity hydroelectric generating plants that would be put to use in the short term implied a greater contribution from the thermal plants, which consumed natural gas and fuel oil. The proposed nuclear plant would allow approximately 8 MB of fuel oil per year to be substituted.

- Although the estimated investment in the nuclear electricity project was approximately 60 percent larger than that needed for an equivalent conventional thermoelectric plant, the lower fuel costs for the nuclear plant meant than the total electricity generating cost would be almost the same for the two kinds of plants, assuming a thirty-year operation period.

- Financing for a nuclear plant was available to CFE at better terms than that for conventional plants.

- The working group considered that the additional investment needed for the nuclear electric plant (compared to the investment in conventional thermoelectric plants) meant an average increase of less than 3 percent in CFE's investment program from 1971 to 1975, that is, while the nuclear plant was being built.

- Although the imports necessary to install a nuclear electric plant were greater than for the equivalent conventional thermal plant, if fuel costs were taken into account, the installation of a nuclear electric plant would have an impact on the balance of payments similar to that caused by the installation of a thermoelectric plant. Fuel oil not needed for the nuclear electric plant could be sold abroad at an attractive foreign-exchange price, improving the country's balance-of-payment position.

- Electricity generation by nuclear plants would allow the utilization of still unexploited

- energy resources and promote the development of uranium mining and the industrial production of components and spare parts.

- There was the possibility of assuring the enrichment of Mexico's uranium through an agreement with the International Atomic Energy Organization (IAEO), thus eliminating the need to come to bilateral agreements with those countries possessing uranium-enrichment technology.

- The nuclear electric plant would be a demonstration of Mexico's interest in the pacific utilization of nuclear energy, congruent with the country's posture as a promoter of the Tratado de Tlatelolco (Tlatelolco Treaty).[2]

By 1971 when the new administration took office, the financing for the plant was almost totally contracted. The World Bank manifested its goodwill by providing credit for a significant part of the investment. It offered long-term credit for $41.3 million for acquiring complementary equipment and for part of the construction, with the possibility of additional financing amounting to $11.6 million for the acquisition of the first load of fuel. The U.S. Eximbank offered $34.24 million and the Japanese Export Bank $9.84 million for the same project. It was hoped that financing could be obtained for the transportation of foreign equipment and materials; if this financing could be achieved, it would only be necessary to spend $29.6 million of the CFE budget during the five years the nuclear electric plant was under construction.[3] By the time the financing was completed, IAEO had approved the site chosen for installation of the nuclear electric plant (Laguna Verde, Veracruz).

SELECTION OF NUCLEAR ENERGY TECHNOLOGY

Despite the government's interest in the Laguna Verde project, it was necessary to reconsider a number of the issues regarding the political advantages and disadvantages of a light-water reactor (LWR), even though it had been looked upon favorably in the first equipment analysis, which opposed emphatically contracting technology for uranium enrichment. The use of enriched uranium, it was argued, would force the country to depend forever on foreign suppliers for its nuclear fuel. Within the working group there was still some disagreement on technological issues because some members considered that the LWR technology would become obsolete by the time the plant came into operation. Another concern among these experts, mainly the representatives of the Instituto Nacional de Energía Nuclear (National Nuclear Energy Institute; INEN), was the lack of attention paid during the supply analysis to local participation in the construction of the nuclear electric plant. Also questioned was CFE's capacity to carry out the nuclear electricity project with a minimum of setbacks as well as the positive impact the larger degree of local expert involvement would have on the country's scientific development.

In May 1972 it was decided that General Electric would be the supplier for a boiling-water reactor (BWR), and Mitsubishi would produce the turbine generator. All the suppliers making offers tried to fulfill one of the most important requirements of the contract —the effective transfer of the nuclear fuel-cycle technology. Once this requirement was assured, letters of intent were signed in September 1972 with the equipment suppliers for the first unit, leaving the option for the second unit to be contracted later.[4]

In 1973 CFE had already completed a new study of the advantages of acquiring the second unit for Laguna Verde. This study was contested by the Gerencia de Planeación y Programas (Direction of Planning and Programs) of CFE, which pointed out that for several reasons it would not be worthwhile to undertake the project and that it should be canceled. Despite the recommendation, in August 1973 an agreement was signed with the supplier for the second unit.

Problems at Laguna Verde

The Laguna Verde project has had problems both at home and abroad. At home problems have been political, economical, financial, industrial, scientific, and technological. The structure and modus operandi of the Mexican political system itself has had a direct impact on the progress of Laguna Verde. The changes in CFE's top positions, the closeness of these people to the president of the republic, the disagreements within CFE, and the problems CFE has had with prominent members of the nuclear community and other government interest groups have hindered the project's progress.

In economic terms nuclear electricity has suffered the impact of inflation, the decline in levels of economic activity, and successive devaluations of the peso. Moreover, the cost of installing Laguna Verde has escalated excessively because of the changes in the project's top management, the capital cost, the difficulties involved in getting parts from suppliers that were no longer interested in producing them, the additional cost of modifying equipment, and so on. In February 1971 the cost of the nuclear electric plant, including the first load of fuel, was estimated at $128 million (U.S. $), and in 1979 the total estimated cost reached $405 million. No one can be certain exactly how much the first nuclear electric plant will cost when it is eventually finished, and no one has calculated how much the user will have to pay for each kilowatt-hour of nuclear electricity.

The Laguna Verde project has required very large amounts of additional capital. The effect on CFE's finances has been severe and has consequently resulted in an even greater dependence on foreign capital. In this sense the federal government has been very cautious, and no significant foreign loans have been involved. However, even if the government had been willing to obtain additional foreign capital, in the late 1970s the federal debt was so enormous that it would not have been allowed.

Certain technical circles admit that the learning process in building a nuclear electric plant has a cost that must be accepted. These experts argue, however (and not without reason), that the experience thus acquired at Laguna Verde has involved an excessively high cost for the country because the equipment built in Mexico was more expensive than if a ready-to-operate plant had been bought abroad. Laguna Verde has made it possible, though, to achieve greater technological integration and independence and to produce equipment with an even greater degree of complexity for future nuclear electricity programs.

What has been the outcome of all this effort? National production has been unable to satisfy--even minimally--Laguna Verde's technological requirements because of formidable problems. One such difficulty is linked to the general problem of the Mexican capital goods industry, where backlogs can be observed from beginning to end in equipment production cycles, that is, in material and test laboratories. Consequently, many local manufacturing problems concern the assembly of imported components that have to be sent back to the country of origin to be finished and tested.[5] Although industry is developing a certain degree of capability in the handling of materials and equipment, it still does not have the capacity to produce technology good enough to compete in international markets and generate foreign exchange.

The import figures for incorporated and nonincorporated technology for the Mexican energy sector (PEMEX and CFE) and the local capital goods sector show that local industry does not have the capacity to cover the demand in these sectors. However, the quality of local production, save worthy exceptions, is so dubious that it becomes an impediment to international sales. This situation results from a lack of economic resources for basic research, technological development, and quality control in private industry. Moreover, industry does not have the support of local laboratories (IIE and IMP), which could help considerably to improve the quality of machinery, tools, equipment, systems, and the services available for locally satisfying the technological needs of the energy sector.

When building something such as a nuclear plant, from another point of view, perhaps the most serious obstacle is the underdeveloped scientific and technological system. This statement does not imply that there are no individuals capable of understanding and working with certain aspects of nuclear energy. Although in 1955 groups of technicians had already begun to form, they have been incapable of sustaining adequate progress in the areas of basic research and technological development, the organizational structure having determined the limits of their activities.

Research capacity continues to be very poor, and the research itself lacks tangible results.

It seems that the technical and scientific aspects involved in the development of a nuclear industry have still not been mastered in Mexico. Mean-while, other countries have already started operating experimental second-generation reactors, and innovations have been made in installed reactors that tend to achieve better security margins, although they increase costs.

The problems that this project has had to face abroad have been of a political nature. The changes in the technology suppliers' export policies have had a significant impact both on the conceptualization of the project and its implementation. If one adds the technical problems that have arisen during plant construction, it is probable that in the future Laguna Verde will face licensing problems because of certain design changes and the loss of quality control in its construction. These concerns stem from the contracting of the Laguna Verde units, when it was agreed that licensing would be granted in the supplier's country of origin. Because the design belongs to General Electric in the United States, the decision to authorize the start-up of the plant is made by the U.S. Nuclear Regulatory Commission (NRC). Several of those responsible for the project believe that the most serious problems facing the plant will be its licensing by U.S. authorities.[6]

Hopes of achieving independence in the field through an agreement with IAEO that would guarantee fuel enrichment and supply to Laguna Verde have been dampened. A number of obstacles have arisen that can be attributed basically to the restrictions introduced by the U.S. nuclear nonproliferation policy.[7]

PROGRAMA NUCLEOELECTRICO NACIONAL DE 1980

In 1980 in an attempt to integrate economic and social policy, the López Portillo administration formulated PGD, which was conceived as a frame of reference for the federal government's sectorial plans, programs, and projects. One of these programs, PNDI, contemplated the energy component as a "lever for progress" and not as an end in itself. To achieve this objective and in an attempt to clarify the energy policy's outlines, SEPAFIN presented PE 1980-1982. Here, the concrete goals for 1990 are stated, and forecasts are made to the year 2000.[8]

The prime objective of PE was to utilize the abundant endowment of energy available to "strengthen, modernize, and diversify Mexico's economic structure <u>oil being the axis and privileged instrument of the economy's structural transformation process</u>" (underscore added).[9]

The specific objectives of the program were as follows:

- To satisfy the country's need in primary and secondary energy

- To diversify primary energy sources with particular attention to renewable resources

- To integrate the energy sector into the development of the rest of the economy.

- To strengthen the scientific and technical infrastructure capable of developing Mexico's potential in this field and of utilizing new technologies

- To rationalize the production and use of energy

- To determine precisely the extent of the country's energy resources

Moreover, the program proposed to "expand the production of energy as a function of the country's general development needs and not of the volume of reserves per se, nor of the requirements of other economies or interests foreign to our own."[10]

The Programa Nucleoeléctrico Nacional (National Nuclear Electricity Program; PNN), established at the same time as PE was based on PE's first four objectives. PNN also contemplated the possible cost advantages associated with nuclear electric energy as well as the assured availability of nuclear fuel, setting as its objective the gradual increase of the country's nuclear capacity to 20,000 MW by the year 2000.[11]

The planners for the electricity subsector did not foresee immediate energy alternative than nuclear energy, given the electricity subsector's need to expand at an annual rate between 9.5 and 11.5 percent for the next twenty years and assuming continued economic and demographic growth, the distribution of income patterns, and increased efficiency in energy consumption.[12] Despite CFE's vision, PE itself stressed that hydroelectric, coal, and geothermal potential could be increased over and above any known estimates and recommended that grater emphasis be put on these fields. In regard to hydroelectric resources, the document reported that "there is a ratio of 5:2:1 between identified reserves, those that could be developed by 2000, and those that can be exploited by 1990, respectively." The theoretical potential is considerably greater than these figures suggest. There is still large hydroelectric potential, although the most important waterfalls have already been exploited, and many new projects are under way. Efforts are required to initiate an even greater number of hydroelectric projects, particularly on a medium or small scale.[13] Therefore, "it is important to point out that although hydroelectricity is not abundant, there exists sufficient potential to produce more than three times the electric energy generated currently by all the different plants in the country."[14]

PE indicated that 600 million tons of proven coal reserves have paved the way for the construction of the first coal electricity plant with a capacity of 1,200 MW, and the construction of two additional plants of 1,400 MW each is foreseen. The impact of this source on the future energy balance could be considerable because it would account for almost 11 percent of gross electricity generation by the year 2000, a figure equivalent to that obtained jointly from geothermal and nuclear energy. Additionally, research would continue to determine the real potential of this source.[15]

PE also stated that the prospects for geothermal energy utilization could increase considerably if the necessary resources for its exploration and exploitation could be obtained. In addition, the potential benefits could be considerable and achieved at very low cost. PE established a minimum goal for geothermal energy of 620 MW by 1990. This minimum was set because the industry is working with a resource that as yet is practically untouched.[16]

These recent proposals make it urgent for the extent of potential nonnuclear energy sources to be quantified. As information on these energy sources is obtained, the nuclear goals that seem to be far from realistic can be modified. As PE stresses, "above and beyond everything else, Mexico needs to strengthen its scientific and technical infrastructure for quantifying and developing its energy potential, utilize new technology and be permanently up to date in this respect" (underscore added).[17]

The feasibility study done for PNN preliminary looked into some cost factors but failed to consider others so important they could become determining factors in the decisions related to the future of the nuclear electricity industry. The considerations put forward in favor of nuclear plants were not exhaustive, nor did they consider the actual future costs of nuclear energy. All this reflected negatively on what could have been an objective evaluation of the various energy sources. According to the defenders of the nuclear industry, the cost per nuclear kilowatt was more favorable than the cost of other alternatives.

Nevertheless, there were vast information gaps in the PNN feasibility studies. One area left untouched was the impact of a whole range of factors on the installation and operation costs for nuclear plants. The nuclear plant costs that the analysts did take into account were calculated according to existing conditions in Sweden, not the possible conditions in Mexico. These costs were compared to those of several local thermoelectric plants, taking into account Mexico's experience and capabilities in this field. Because the experts wrongly assumed that for the rest of the century international crude prices would increase in real terms by 3 percent each year, it was easy to arrive at the conclusion that nuclear energy generation costs would be low. The comparative analyses omitted the evident fact that in some of the industrialized countries, mainly the United States, the installation costs for nuclear plants had risen year after year to the extent that the economic viability of nuclear energy was seriously questioned.

The estimates of installation costs were perhaps the weakest part of PNN. In the available documentation it was impossible to find data necessary for objectively evaluating all the capital costs that could be incurred by the country if it decided in favor of nuclear energy. Thus, the PNN proposal was clearly inadequate as a basis for the country's nuclear strategy: important cost factors and critical considerations for any national nuclear electricity program were either omitted or not dealt with adequately.

Uranium availability

Another major reason given in PNN for fostering nuclear energy was the existence of uranium resources. The PNN feasibility study pointed out that by 1990 there would be an accumulated demand for uranium (U_3O_8) of 1,800 tons; by 2000 the accumulated demand for uranium concentrates would reach 34,000 tons. It was also estimated that during the 1990s the industry would require an average of 3,200 tons per year, depending on the fuel cycle decided upon.[18] It was on this last point that the nuclear program's feasibility was based, although the fuel requirements for each reactor technology under consideration were not indicated in any of PNN's basic documents.

Although there are many speculations about Mexico's uranium potential, sufficient proven reserves for the useful life of the Laguna Verde reactors and perhaps for one other plant of 1,000 MW have been identified. Thus, the country's uranium reserves might not be sufficient to meet the requirements of a 20,000 MW nuclear program to the year 2000, even if such reserves were two times as high as it was hoped and $14 billion (U.S. $; around 925 billion pesos at 1981 prices) made available for this purpose.[19] Total potential reserves might well have been high, but the figures do not justify the excessive optimism of those who stated that "from the point of view of primary products for nuclear fuel, such as uranium, Mexico can sustain nuclear power production of 20,000 to 30,000 MW, long enough for the transition to second generation reactors to occur."[20] To contemplate a program of 20,000 MW without the guarantee of proven reserves is hazardous for the country's energy future. Mexico still has not produced one single kilogram of uranium concentrate that fulfills the internationally established quality specifications.

Despite the limited uranium proven reserves and even probable reserves, the CFE nuclear specialists do not consider the country's uranium-resource situation to be a real hindrance to establishing a 20,000 MW nuclear electricity program. They argue that "the worldwide availability of uranium guarantees that there will be no restrictions in the supply from abroad if, for economic reasons, Mexico were to decide to import it and conserve its reserves or exploit them only partially."[21]

This simple reasoning grants no importance to the national objective of energy self-sufficiency. It proposes very ambitious goals for generating nuclear electricity without the guarantee of independent local fuel supply. It does not appear to consider the complex problems associated with the demand and worldwide availability of uranium and the services for its enrichment. The estimates of uranium supply and demand run into a problem somewhat similar to oil's: Any conclusion concerning the extent of economically recoverable deposits runs the risk of seeming foolhardy in light of the major and rapid changes occurring in the technological, financial, and sociopolitical fields of the world today.

In Mexico it is important for one to ask the following questions regarding the country's uranium reserves: Are there sufficient reserves to cover the demands of a nuclear program of this magnitude? Just how adequate and stable are the plant licensing and regulatory requirements for estimating capital and operational costs and, thus, for determining the price policy for nuclear fuel and for the electricity generated? Could the government establish a nuclear fuel -enrichment industry? If so, with all the imponderables involved, would it be a profitable industry? These questions and many others are valid when evaluating nuclear program costs and cannot be dealt with indifferently. These issues should be confronted, or the nuclear program will be no more than a well-intentioned exercise devoid of realism.

Even if these uncertainties were to be dealt with favorably, another hindrance to the development of nuclear energy is the length of time needed to rationally coordinate the different phases of the fuel cycle: Ten years for the extraction and refinement of the uranium (from exploration to the production of the yellow retort), four years for the conversion, eight years for the mineral enriching, five years for the actual fuel manufacturing, and ten years for the reprocessing. Obviously, these schedules are interactive, not sequential. The investment for certain phases could be delayed if there was not a reasonably certainty of other phases being completed on time. Installation and operation schedules for the different technologies involved in coordinating the nuclear fuel cycle depend on important factors such as coordination, capability, and institutional responsibilities.[22]

A definite policy needs to be defined for reprocessing fuel residues. In PNN's feasibility analyses and diagnoses this point was not mentioned, even though it might have been important to the country's energy self-sufficiency, helping to improve the management of the country's uranium reserves. In these nuclear studies feasibility reprocessing was noted as an essential step in establishing the fast-breeder reactor cycle but not in light-water and Candu reactor cycles. This perspective lacks foresight because it turns a blind eye to the implications of not guaranteeing nuclear plant fuel supplies. The decision to reprocess used fuel depends on whether it is economically and politically worthwhile. However, if basic uranium were not available in sufficient quantities for a nuclear program of major importance, it would be necessary to reprocess the fuel utilized and keep part of the uranium base as a strategic reserve.

The importance of recycling uranium and plutonium lies in the reduced demand for both natural uranium and enrichment services. Possible savings have been calculated at 35 percent with enrichment capacity. The fact that these residual materials represent an exploitable resource should render them a powerful incentive to invest in recovery technology. The savings in the fuel cycles associated with complete recycling (that is, uranium and plutonium) are calculated between 5 and 20 percent, depending on the impact the recycling has on the cost of the uranium mining.[23]

The disadvantages of uranium and plutonium recycling coincide with the arguments on nuclear arms proliferation, public health, physical safety, and the conservation of ecological equilibrium. The question of nuclear arms proliferation raises serious doubts about the disposition of those countries with recycling equipment to transfer the technology. Reprocessing and recycling might be optional, but it is the industry's obligation to assure the adequate economic supply of fuel to cover the demand. A substantial increase in supply can be obtained through recycling technology. France, Great Britain, West Germany, and Japan consider fuel recycling an absolute necessity, but in developing countries with dependent nuclear programs this urgency does not exist. The technological progress in recycling is not easy to transfer to developing countries; they are given nuclear technology that must be kept under the control of the supplier. Thus, it is imperative that a serious analysis be made of nuclear fuel reserves and reprocessing feasibility so as to guarantee the country's energy future.

OBSTACLES AND LIMITATIONS IN NUCLEAR ELECTRICITY DEVELOPMENT

Nuclear energy has been introduced in Mexico mainly in response to priority energy objectives, with no consideration of other civil uses to solve certain social problems. Nuclear energy should not simply imply a nuclear electricity program; its use should be a scientific venture with a broad impact on agriculture, health, education, pure and applied research, the relations between Mexico and the rest of the world, and the political relations between members of the "nuclear community." The question is how to coordinate a national atomic program so that it has an impact on various spheres of Mexican society.

The Mexican state responded to this issue by introducing a law aimed at making meaningful and rational use of the financial, technical, and human resources that nuclear energy programs require. Although this law has its inconsistencies and imperfections, it is a serious attempt to organize this social field and to guarantee certain access to nuclear fuel—the axis of any nuclear program—and the technology associated with it.

On 26 January 1979 the Ley Reglamentaria del Articulo 27 Constitucional en Materia Nuclear (Constitutional Article 27's Regulations on Nuclear Issues) came into force and gave the state the principal task of nuclear development, thus eliminating the participation of local and foreign sectors in exploiting and commercializing nuclear fuel.[24] The nuclear law also reorganized the functions of INEN, subdividing it into two different decentralized public agencies: URAMEX and the Instituto Nacional de Investigaciones Nucleares (National Institute for Nuclear Research; ININ). Both are coordinated by the Comisión Nacional de Energía Atómica (National Atomic Energy Commission; CNEA) and integrated by the minister of SEPAFIN as president, and an executive speaker and a secretary who are appointed by the president of the republic (Chapter III, Article 2). Under this law the Comisión Nacional de Seguridad Nuclear y Salvaguardas (National Commission for Nuclear Safety and Protection; CNSNS) was created as a decentralized organization under the jurisdiction of SEPAFIN (Chapter VII, Article 37).[25]

The state then established institutions with well-defined functions to take care of those tasks specific to their corresponding fields. With these institutions came a vast amount of bureaucracy that given the extent of Mexico's present sociopolitical development has had a negative effect on the implementation of nuclear activities. Work within the nuclear institutions themselves reveals disorganized objectives, goals, and action strategies. There is no rational action directed toward stimulating the country's interest in this field. Activities in the field of nuclear electricity have been carried out according to the interests of established institutional groups, indicating that the legitimate authority contained in the nuclear law has been completely ignored. In practice, CFE has acted independently of URAMEX (now nonexistent), ININ, CNSNS, and other top organizations, which is evident in the diverse plans and ideas for Mexico's nuclear development that have been promoted.

The differences between the groups, which are bound by law to assist the rational use of atomic energy, go far beyond technological factors. With the debate surrounding the rate and magnitude of the country's nuclear development, these differences become acute. Several members of CFE have promoted installing 20,000 MW in eighteen years. Members of ININ, URAMEX, and SEMIP (formerly SEPAFIN) believe the goal should be significantly lower (5,000 to 10,000 MW) in view of the immense range of problems that must be solved to adequately face the nuclear challenge.

The conflicting interests in the nuclear community imply both a political and a social cost. These conflicts perhaps explain why the Mexican government has been somewhat reluctant to channel financial resources into the institutions to fulfill the assigned task. Nuclear energy by nature requires great concentrations of financial, technical, and human resources, all of which give rise to groups whose obligations is to coordinate activities so as to minimize the social cost of nuclear energy in Mexico. It seems too that nuclear energy requires considerable modifications to political and institutional conduct. Neither negligence nor improvisation in planning are acceptable in ventures of this kind. Pending in the nuclear community is a strategy reconciling the social and political commitments of specialists with the high-level scientific and technical abilities that nuclear development in this country truly needs. The future of nuclear energy in Mexico increasingly depends on the capacity to overcome the political, technical, economic, financial, and institutional difficulties hindering sure access to fuel and nuclear technology. This goal must be adapted to the rate appropriate for assimilating this technology, which is not easy to control in advanced countries, let alone in those where there is no quality control. Also, the human resources do not yet exist for setting up and operating the facilities and supervising and regulating these complex and hazardous processes, which could affect national security in its broadest sense.

The results of the PNN feasibility studies indicate that Mexico should commit itself fully to the manufacture of equipment and components for the nuclear plants as well as to the handling of the whole fuel cycle, excluding reprocessing, before the year 2000. Just how feasible are these recommendations in Mexico today, and what benefits would there be for the country?

These questions require consideration of the external and internal factors restricting local industry's participation in the integration of nuclear technology. The first of these considerations, which was discussed earlier, is the obstacles arising from the issue of nuclear arms proliferation, which must be overcome to achieve an adequate inflow of nuclear technology. The content, purpose, and value of the documents of international law for reducing the proliferation of nuclear arms need improving. Mexico cannot have unlimited access to nuclear technology for civil use because of the control held by the nuclear powers, and in the near future no real change is foreseen in the basic provisions of the nuclear nonproliferation policy.

The second consideration concerns the financing required for an enterprise of this magnitude. It is an obstacle that appears insurmountable in the short term. If the necessary funds became available as a result of a price rise in the world oil market (oil has been the financial axis of the nuclear electricity program), which is unlikely, it would still be necessary to reorganize numerous activities, and who knows how this could be done.

Among the PNN requirements are the formation of a good number of highly specialized personnel (which takes time), the mobilization of financial resources, and the coordination of the institutions responsible for achieving these objectives. The truth is that the country lacks the necessary funds and interinstitutional coordination. The latter is perhaps the greatest obstacle to the implementation of any nuclear program. "Perfect harmony" between institutions is not necessarily required but certainly a minimum degree of interaction must exist in order to achieve these national objectives.

TABLE 5.1
MARKET FOR INDUSTRIAL PROCESS-CONTROL EQUIPMENT,
1976-1978 (in millions of U.S. $)

Equipment	1976	Year 1977	1978
Electric and Electronic Instruments			
Production	0.5	1.1	2.1
Imports	23.1	27.8	29.1
Exports	--	--	--
Market Size[1]	23.6	28.9	31.2
Nonelectric and Nonelectronic Instruments			
Production	7.9	8.8	10.0
Imports	6.4	6.3	6.4
Exports	0.3	0.6	0.5
Market Size	14.0	14.5	15.9
Control Valves			
Production	9.9	10.8	12.5
Imports	15.6	16.5	18.4
Exports	--	--	--
Market Size	25.5	27.3	30.9
Computers and Process-Control Accesories			
Production	--	--	--
Imports	2.4	2.3	5.4
Exports	--	--	--
Market Size	2.4	2.3	5.4
Totals			
Production	18.3	20.7	24.6
Imports	47.5	52.9	59.3
Exports	0.3	0.6	0.5
Market Size	65.5	73.0	83.4

[1] The size of the market is equal to production plus imports minus exports; excludes parts and spare parts.

Source: U.S. Department of Commerce, International Trade Administration, Office of Export Planning and Evaluation, country market survey 80-210, Industrial Process Controls: Mexico, Washington, D.C., September 1980, p. 3.

Another very important factor is available industrial capacity. Although the state has contributed to organizing industrial infrastructure, the industrial sector has been unable to develop technology with a sufficiently high degree of precision and quality to compete even minimally within the country itself, let alone in international markets. This situation results from many factors, although perhaps one of the most important is the lack of significant investment in R&D in the different industrial areas.

TABLE 5.2
SIZE AND NUMBER OF LOCAL INDUSTRIAL PROCESS-CONTROL EQUIPMENT PRODUCERS, 1978[1]

Type of Establishment	Number of Establishments Large	Medium	Small	Total Number of Employees
Mexican Owned (51%)	1	--	--	70
American Subsidiaries	6	1	3	932
German Subsidiaries	--	--	1	5
Total	7	1	4	1,007

[1]The size of the establishment is based on the number of employees as follows: large—more than 50 employees; medium—between 10 and 50 employees; and small—less than 10 employes.

Source: U.S. Department of Commerce, International Trade Administration, Office of Export Planning and Evaluation, country market survey 80-210, Industrial Process Controls: Mexico, Washington, D.C., September 1980, p. 6.

The argument in favor of integrating nuclear technology implies that the quality of local industry would improve because of the technology's extension into other industrial processes. In the light of the experience gained from nuclear technology transfer, however, there is no real indication that such would be the case. In Laguna Verde's final reckoning the truth will emerge, whether it be the isolation of the country's industrial sector or its participation in the nuclear technology integration process. With its current energy system Mexico faces a dangerous dependence on foreign countries in a number of technological areas but especially with automatic process-control equipment. In 1978 the sources for these capital goods, which are mostly destined for the energy sector, were primarily foreign: 93 percent of electric and electronic instruments, 40 percent of the nonelectric and nonelectronic equipment, 60 percent of the control valves, and 140 percent of the computers and process-control accessories came from foreign suppliers (see Table 5.1).[26] Local manufacturers, mainly branches of large American companies, undertook the assembly of simple equipment; however, they used components imported from the United States because they lacked the capacity to produce the quantity and quality of the process equipment required by CFE, PEMEX, and other clients (see Table 5.2 and Table 5.3).

If such problems as these are left unsolved, there will be considerable difficulty in maintaining the project's viability. If 20,000 MW is installed at the rate proposed by CFE, a disruptive effect on the country's economy can be expected, with the consequent political, social, economic, and financial costs.

American suppliers occupy an advantageous position in the Mexican market for process-control equipment because of their experience in working with the Mexican energy sector; Mexico's low scientific, technological, and industrial productivity; and the lack of financing for acquiring capital goods and high technology. In 1978 American producers covered 64 percent of Mexico's demand for process-control equipment, and it was calculated that this share would increase to 74 percent by 1983.[27]

Current situation and future prospects

In many countries nuclear energy, if well planned and well administered can be an important and positive contribution to the future well-being of society. If nuclear energy is to contribute to Mexican society, those who formulate and implement energy policy must realistically consider the feasibility, compatibility, and need for this energy alternative as opposed to others. Mexico's official position regarding energy should be understood within the context of its policies for defending state autonomy. This perhaps explains the official reluctance to develop nuclear energy, which, in turn, gives the government time enough to adequately ponder the pros and cons of an issue of this magnitude.

TABLE 5.3
INDUSTRIAL PROCESS-CONTROL EQUIPMENT IMPORTS BY COUNTRY OF ORIGIN, 1978 (in millions of U.S. $)

Equipment	Cost
Electric and Electronic Instruments	
United States	25.45
United Kingdom	0.33
West Germany	0.31
Other	3.02
Total	29.11
Nonelectric and Nonelectronic Instruments	
United States	3.27
United Kingdom	0.54
West Germany	0.33
Other	2.26
Total	6.40
Control Valves	
United States	5.08
United Kingdom	1.02
West Germany	2.54
Other	9.77
Total	18.41
Computers and Process-Control Accesories	
United States	4.14
United Kingdom	1.26
West Germany	--
Other	--
Total	5.40
Total	59.32

Source: U.S. Department of Commerce, International Trade Administration, Office of Export Planning and Evaluation, country market survey 80-210, Industrial Process Controls: Mexico, Washington, D.C., September 1980, p. 4.

The Mexican government does not advocate large-scale accelerated and dependent nuclear development, but it does recognize the importance that atomic energy could have in Mexico's future energy supply. The government believes that this development should be on a par with the country's rate of growth and capacity so that nuclear energy can be adopted in an independent and orderly manner. This position is an attempt to coincide with the maturity of Mexican society and, at the same time, to consider external factors, such as the crisis currently facing the producers of nuclear technology, the social concept of nuclear energy, and its effects on the international system. As stated in Ley Reglamentaria del Articulo 27 Constitucional en Materia Nuclear, all this "converts nuclear energy into a valid option only if it is understood in terms of the nation's social well-being and political stability." If this condition is not fulfilled, nuclear energy in Mexico will become a high-risk political instrument.

Until now, the Mexican government has always followed a nuclear détente policy despite incredible pressures at home and abroad for it to become involved in promoting growth in nuclear energy "to cover the energy demands of the Mexican economy." The objective of a nuclear electricity program for Mexico has become increasingly distant and certainly less clear--it is only one of many national priorities.

Despite these official guidelines, early in 1982 CFE tried to speed up the purchase of the units for the second nuclear electric plant, Laguna Verde II. Thus, a weakness in the energy sector's planning capacity was revealed, forcing CFE, under the instructions of the economic cabinet, to officially announce on 10 June 1982 that bidding for the second plant had been canceled.

The administration of Miguel de la Madrid, who took office in December 1982, concluded that Laguna Verde had become a very demanding project. The need for additional capital had had an adverse effect on public finances and, consequently, it became necessary to depend heavily on foreign capital in order to complete the project.

In its diagnosis of the Mexican energy scene, the administration pointed out the following through PNE 1984-1988:

> Up to date the existence of around 14,500 tons of uranium has been confirmed, of which it is estimated that only 10,600 tons can be extracted. With the installation of 1,308 MW at the Laguna Verde nuclear electric plant, nearly 60 percent of proven reserves will have been committed, leaving potential resources for an additional 1,000 MW to be installed. To date the true magnitude of Mexico's total uranium potential is still uncertain.[28]

PNE 1984-1988's energy-diversification strategy for nuclear electricity was:

> Work will continue on Laguna Verde, with the start of commercial operations for the first unit being planned for 1986. At the same time, studies are to be undertaken allowing the foundations for future nuclear electricity development to be established within the framework of the present program. As part of these studies, the sector will undertake preparatory work for the construction of a second plant.[29]

By 31 January 1985 these preparations had already been suspended because of a drop in the Isthmus crude price, implying a budgetary readjustment equivalent to a year's saving of 1.2 billion (U.S. $).

The position of the present regime is clear; in PNE 1984-1988 it indicates that

> energy diversification in the direction of nuclear electricity generation <u>at a rate congruent with the country's financial possibilities</u> is inevitable as we are dealing with an alternative source providing massive amounts of energy, the importance of which will increase in the long term (underscore added).[30]

The action contemplated in PNE 1984-1988 for nuclear electricity is as follows:

- "An improvement of the efficiency and productivity of the activities aimed at determining the country's uranium reserves and continued work on the construction of the two Laguna Verde facilities

- "feasibility studies for building the new facilities and consequently strengthening Mexico's technological and industrial participation

- "a stepping up of the preparation of specialized personnel and research and development activities in reactor science and technology and in the different stages of the fuel cycle

- "a strengthening of the national nuclear safety system, the completion of programs for the prevention of environmental deterioration and hazards, and the development of the infrastructure required to dispose of radioactive waste"[31]

It is expected that like its predecessor, the new regime will give moderate support to national nuclear electricity development after an effective political lapse of three years; in other words, it will not be open about its support. This expectation is based on estimated uranium reserves, the great recession in the world's nuclear industry, the country's financial possibilities, the priority given by the government to energy sources capable of broadening coverage to rural areas, and the enormous obstacles that must be faced with nuclear electricity activities.

On 8 November 1984 during his appearance at the House of Representatives, the minister of SEMIP, Francisco Labastida Ochoa, announced that URAMEX, the organization responsible for determining the country's uranium reserves, had been abolished.[32] The reason for this decision was that

> we have not had the success we should have had. The country's scant reserves, most of which cannot be exploited economically, imply that this activity has not been as successful as it

should have been if the amount of economic resources assigned to URAMEX for this purpose are considered.

Labastida Ochoa added that "the nation's sovereignty in nuclear energy cannot be relinquished, nor can private companies be permitted to exploit or benefit from uranium. We will continue to act according to this criteria."[33]
Furthermore, he announced

the possibility of establishing an organization under the exclusive responsibility of the state for prospecting, exploring, and searching for uranium. Whether it is called URAMEX or whatever, the important thing is not the name of the organization but with whom the responsibility for these functions lies (underscore added).[34]

In November 1984 the executive sent a project for new regulations dealing with nuclear energy, to be substituted for Ley Reglamentaria del Articulo 27 of the constitution, to the House of Representatives for consideration.[35] The proposals of the project of law were to guarantee state control over fissionables and it intended to reinforce the capacity of CNSNS; exploration and exploitation were to be assigned to public federal organizations, thus avoiding the duplication and unprofitability that had existed in the past. The other stages of the fuel cycle were to be left under the direction of SEMIP as well as the responsibility for the disposal of fissionable and radioactive waste, thus filling the gaps in the 1979 law. ININ research efforts were to be reinforced, as well as the coordination between this and other research areas. Last, CNEA was to be eliminated because of its ineffectiveness.[36]

In synthesis, the project intended the new nuclear law to became an instrument allowing the state to fulfill "its obligation to look after the people's interests—for it is their taxes that pay for the operation of the state-owned entities. Only when a public company fulfills a social role is government financial support justified."[37] In the energy sector sustained efforts should be made to defend the fundamental resources needed for the nation's development and the supply for future generations as well as to promote increased productivity.[38] The strategic nature of radioactive minerals and nuclear energy generation already established in the constitution was also emphasized: "The nation is guaranteed exclusive federal government participation in the different activities in these areas, keeping in mind the interests of the majority, the safety of the population, and the nation's sovereignty."[39]

The new law was intended to rescue nuclear energy from duplicated expenditure and efforts, which in the past always resulted in wasted resources, unprofitability and inefficiency, obviously to the detriment of the country's needs and priorities.[40] The project also envisioned nuclear energy as a means and not an end in itself.

Many members of de la Madrid's cabinet saw nuclear energy as a reasonable alternative, but they also acknowledged that as a technological option, it is not altogether neutral and could actually be a highly political experiment. Moreover, all are aware that nuclear energy should be complementary to a general strategic function that assures the country's independent development, making opportune planning possible in the medium and long term. All these measures proposed by the federal government should be introduced to avoid duplicity, excessive cost, and inefficiency, which place an unnecessary load on the population's economic situation. The support given to nuclear energy would be adjusted to the financial possibilities of the federal public sector, based on its real needs and the rate at which the nuclear program would develop under the auspices of the national energy program. In summary, the project of law stated that the legal modifications were proposed "for reasons of unwaivering national security, obliging the federal government to become directly involved in activities of extreme strategic interest, in accordance with the principles of selfdetermination and independence".[41]

This project of law set fire to considerable nationalistic passion, and the members of the Sindicato Unico de Trabajadores de la Industria Nuclear (Nuclear Industry Workers Trade Union; SUTIN) attacked the federal executive's proposal as "entreguista."[42] SUTIN's leaders argued that the measure was designed to eliminate the union because it had become the conscience and voice of the people. The leaders approached the general secretary of the Confederación de Trabajadores de Mexico (Mexico's Workers Confederation; CTM), Fidel Velázquez, but despite his willingness he could do little to avoid the collapse of what he called "the independent trade union," which identified with ideologies different from those of the Mexican revolution. On 27 December 1984 the new nuclear-energy regulations for Artículo 27 of the constitution were passed by the House of Senators (they had already been approved by the House of Representatives) and published in Diario Oficial on 4 February 1985; they came into force on 5 February 1985.[43]

According to PNE 1984-1988 the first unit of the Laguna Verde nuclear plant was to start operations in 1986, with a nominal installed capacity of 654 MW, and it was hoped that two years later when the second unit came on line, 1,308 MW would be reached, which would represent 5 percent of the nation's installed capacity for electric energy at the time.[44] PNE 1984-1988 also indicated that during the period from 1986 to 1988, construction would begin on a new nuclear plant.[45] However, in light of the 1985 budgetary adjustments, a high SEMIP official pointed out that "nuclear energy implies an expenditure of many millions of dollars, which we do not have. This prevents us from thinking of a second nuclear electric plant for the moment."[46] As we saw previously, the rate at which hydrocarbons are substituted with nuclear power tends to be much more modest than the targets proposed in PE 1980.

After 1988 the future of Mexican nuclear development might not depend so much on local conditions as on the course that international hydrocarbon prices will take and the nuclear industry's competitiveness internationally. On the international scene the tendency is for hydrocarbon prices to drop, whereas in the nuclear industry installation, operation, and maintenance costs increase daily. In the United States this negative correlation poses a serious problem for nuclear electricity's future expansion. There are no financial incentives, and practically all credits for new nuclear electricity projects have been canceled.

Until 1983 the nuclear industry seemed to be working, even though it was not growing rapidly. A slow growth such as this lasting three to five years would not be disastrous for the American nuclear industry. However, to try and foretell what might happen after ten years is difficult, although one assumes the nuclear power industry will not disappear altogether, at least not while nuclear programs are still in force in other countries.[47]

The problems affecting the American nuclear electricity industry have been a determining factor in the development of nuclear technology in other countries. However, where different institutional structures for electricity production exist and there is interest in avoiding dependence on hydrocarbon imports, as in France, Japan, and West Germany, the nuclear industry might prove more successful than in America. It is evident that the 1980s will not be easy for the world nuclear industry. Mexico will continue to observe nuclear energy's progress abroad, but has already commenced nuclear development that is compatible with the nation's society, its politics, and its geography.

CONCLUSIONS

For Mexico, having nuclear energy means analyzing and understanding the role electricity will play in the country's future energy system. In many industrialized countries the task has not been easy, and in Mexico it has been even less so because of an inadequate knowledge of electricity demand and distribution as a result of a society that is constantly and sometimes unpredictably changing.

When Mexico's energy policies were introduced, the energy-saving issue had very little effect on the amount of energy distributed. A pattern of consumption was established similar to that seen in the industrialized countries when oil was cheap and easy to secure. In Mexico correcting this pattern implies curbing the growth in the demand for electricity without causing a negative effect on economic growth. Generally speaking, energy policy planners recognize the urgent need to modify patterns of consumption and increase energy-use efficiency through major planning, but the concrete measures that must be established to achieve this objective have barely been formulated.

Electricity generation by nuclear reactors is complicated and initially very expensive, and no country can justify its use unless it has a very clear idea of its future energy needs and how they can be satisfied. If we assume, optimistically, that these needs are already known, what remains is to demonstrate that Mexico has (or can obtain) a reasonable guarantee of capital and credit that is acceptable economically and politically; can avail itself of personnel trained in theory and in practice; is able to install plants under conditions that assure the population's safety; and has at its disposition the nuclear fuel, technology, and equipment the program requires. The real impact that young technicians and scientists have on nuclear decision making in Mexico is on the increase. Their effect on the future can be considerable as they begin to occupy important positions as energy policy consultants and as the country emerges from its current economic financial crisis.

Nevertheless, it seems that in Mexico the relationship between scientists and technicians, on one side, and political leaders, on the other side, at the decision-making level does not particularly favor the technical advisers. Certain groups and individuals can influence nuclear policy if and when they move in the direction favored by the political leaders, but their influence can dwindle and their persuasive powers diminish if they put too much pressure on these leaders. The decision to establish a major nuclear program in a country such as Mexico implies something more than the simple administration of a new energy source. Nuclear technology is a very important political issue, whether one looks at it financially or socially. Undoubtedly, the results of opting for nuclear technology will radically transform Mexico's sociopolitical structure, although in what way is still unclear, even for pronuclear interest groups.

The most important aspect to consider in Mexico is that the use of nuclear energy will have to be compatible with the country's social, economic, and technological character. Its use will have to be adapted to its existing energy programs and international policy, the prevailing level of education and technical and scientific development, and the model of development desired for the future well-being of its ever-increasing population.

NOTES

1. Eibenschutz, Juan, "Mexico," in Katz, Everett J., U. Marwah, and S. Onkar, <u>Nuclear Power in Developing Countries</u>, Lexington, Mass., Lexington Books, 1982, Chapter 13, pp. 247, 250.
2. Secretarías de la Presidencia, Hacienda, SEPANAL, SECOFI, Relaciones Exteriores, CFE, PEMEX, and CNEN, <u>Dictamen sobre la conveniencia de instalar la primera planta nucleoeléctrica</u> (mimeograph), Mexico City, 16 July 1970.
3. Secretarías de la Presidencia, Hacienda, Industria, PEMEX, and CFE, <u>Dictamen sobre proyectos nucleoeléctricos de la Comisión Federal de Electricidad</u> (mimeograph), Mexico City, 11 February 1971.
4. Eibenschutz, Juan, <u>op. cit.</u>, p. 253.
5. Aburto Avila, José Luis, "Costos y beneficios de la fabricación nacional de maquinaria y equipo para el sector eléctrico," paper presented at the round table discussion "Reunión popular sobre los energéticos en la industrialización y sus impactos regionales," in <u>Consulta popular para la planeacióan de energéticos y desarrollo nacional</u>, organized by the Instituto de Estudios Económicos, Políticos y Sociales del PRI, Mexico City, 25 May 1982.
6. Eibenschutz, Juan, <u>op. cit.</u>, p. 254.
7. In another essay is a review of how the American nuclear nonproliferation policy could affect the operations at Laguna Verde. See Rogelio Ruíz, "La problemática de la planta nuclear de Laguna Verde," in Wionczek, M. S. (editor), <u>Problemas del sector energético en México</u>, Mexico City, El Colegio de México, Programa de Energéticos, 1983, pp. 145-150.
8. SEPAFIN and STCE, "Programa de energía, metas a 1990 y proyecciones al año 2000" (summary), in <u>Energéticos: Boletín Informativo del Sector Energético</u>, Year 4, No. 11, Mexico City, STCE, November 1980.
9. <u>Ibid.</u>, p. 13.
10. <u>Ibid.</u>, p. 2.

11. Escofet, Alberto, "El programa nucleoeléctrico mexicano," in Energéticos, Year 5, No. 12, Mexico City, STCE, December 1981, pp. 1-5.

12. Grupo Nuclear de la CFE, Programa nucleoeléctrico, Mexico City, August 1981.

13. SEPAFIN and STCE, op. cit., p. 33.

14. Wionczek, Miguel S., "Fuentes alternativas de energía," paper presented at the Foro sobre alternativas energéticas, Jalapa, Veracruz, 20 August 1980.

15. SEPAFIN and STCE, op. cit., p. 54.

16. Ibid., pp. 53, 54.

17. Ibid., p. 9.

18. SEPAFIN, ININ, and CFE, Informe sobre los estudios de factibilidad del programa nucleoeléctrico nacional, Mexico City, September-October 1980, study undertaken with the participation of three consultants: ASEA-ATON of Sweden, AECL of Canada, and SOFRATOME of France.

19. Unomásuno, Mexico City, 15 February 1982.

20. El Día, Mexico City, 22 November 1980.

21. CFE, Implantación del programa nucleoeléctrico, Mexico City, CFE, July 1981.

22. Atlantic Council's Nuclear Fuels Policy Working Group, Nuclear Fuels Policy, Lexington, Mass., Lexington Books, 1976, p. 43.

23. Ibid., p. 28.

24. "Ley reglamentaria del artículo 27 constitucional en materia nuclear," in Diario Oficial, Mexico City, 26 January 1979.

25. Ibid., pp. 6-13.

26. U.S. Department of Commerce, International Trade Administration, Office of Export Planning and Evaluation, Industrial Process Controls: Mexico, country market survey 80-210, Washington, D.C., September 1980.

27. Ibid., p. 3.

28. Poder Ejecutivo Federal, Programa nacional de energéticos 1984-1988, Mexico City, SEMIP, Subsecretaría de Energía, August 1984, p. 44.

29. Ibid., p. 64.

30. Ibid., p. 264.

31. Ibid., p. 83.

32. Labastida Ochoa is the current head of the sector.

33. "En empresas públicas no hay margen para corrupción," in Excélsior, México City, 9 December 1984.
34. Idem.
35. Poder Ejecutivo Federal, Iniciativa de ley reglamentaria del artículo 27 constitucional en materia nuclear, Mexico City, November 1984.
36. Ibid., p. X.
37. Ibid., p. III.
38. Ibid., p. III.
39. Ibid., p. V.
40. Ibid., p. VI.
41. Ibid., p. XII.
42. SUTIN, "Frente a la iniciativa de ley nuclear, la defensa de la soberanía nacional: SUTIN," in Excélsior, Mexico City, 18 December 1984. To my knowledge there is no direct translation for this term, which refers to a person or persons conceding the exploitation of mineral wealth and the operation of essential services to foreign companies.
43. "Ley reglamentaria del artículo 27 constitucional en materia nuclear," in Diario Oficial, Mexico City, 4 February 1985.
44. Poder Ejecutivo Federal, op. cit., p. 156.
45. Ibid., p. 112.
46. Declarations of the Vice-Minister of SEMIP, in El Nacional, Mexico City, 9 February 1985.
47. U.S. Congress, Office of Technology Assessment, Nuclear Power in an Age of Uncertainty, OTA-E-216, Washington, D.C., 1984.

6

Mexico's Progress in Planning and Development of New Energy Sources

Rocío Vargas

The United Nations classification of new energy sources includes solar, geothermal, eolic, tidal, biomass (firewood, vegetable coal, and peat), oil shale, tar sands, and hydraulic from small waterfalls.[1] In this chapter we address those new sources that because of their current state of technological development in Mexico are not yet able to contribute significantly to the country's energy supply, even though they could occasionally be utilized in productive activities and for localized demand. Therefore, we deal here with solar energy, biomass, (which includes firewood and vegetable coal), eolic energy, and microhydraulic potential. Although geothermal power has a certain advantage over other sources in the country, it is normally excluded in national energy programs for new sources because it already contributes considerably to electric power generation.[2] However, its contribution and development are marginal compared to hydrocarbons and warrant its inclusion in this group.

The development of new energy sources is a relatively recent interest, dating back only to the late 1970s. However, progress has been very slow because energy-diversification policies aimed at promoting these sources have not been given priority in national planning. The attention afforded them has been limited compared to other sources, such as hydraulic energy, nuclear energy, and coal.

This chapter provides a general overview of the extent to which the nonconventional energy forms have been developed, the obstacles and constraints encountered in their diffusion, and their prospects for the future in a country with an ample endowment of hydrocarbons. The overwhelming participation of hydrocarbons in energy production and domestic consumption and the low price at which hydrocarbons, once processed, have traditionally been sold to the final consumer have restricted and, in many cases, even excluded the development of other energy sources. Their future expansion will depend first on the state's organizational and planning capacity in this particular aspect; second on the importance given to these sources within the energy-diversification strategy; and third on the quantity of resources available in certain zones in relation to their potential demand. At present, precise estimates of such potential are required. Later, the organization and planning stages will have to be reinforced. Finally, it is essential that well-defined development and diversification programs be established.

BACKGROUND AND THE CURRENT SITUATION

The international development of some of the main nonconventional energy sources dates from the mid-1970s. A major thrust in the technological advancement occurred in response to the oil shock of 1973-1974 and 1979-1980, when there were fears of an oil shortage and a feeling of vulnerability by some countries heavily dependent on foreign oil resources. The rapid growth rate in the demand over time and particularly the rise in fossil fuel prices, together with the prospect of further price increases, created the need to define policies that guaranteed energy supply, a major concern of the industrialized countries. In light of these considerations some countries began promoting the development of nonconventional energy forms. In many cases the progress made was substantial, although it was restricted to certain regions because of the competitiveness of conventional energy sources.[3]

By the mid-1970s Mexico's energy situation was favorable because of the new hydrocarbon discoveries. Although the abundance of hydrocarbons clouded the foresight of the experts about the importance of alternative energy sources, the first serious energy-programming attempt in 1980 established among its objectives primary energy-sources diversification, which included the exploitation and use of alternative energy forms.[4] Although the potential importance of solar energy was noted, the program stressed that the only nonconventional source that could offer any significant contribution was geothermal power, which it was hoped would be 0.4 percent of the energy produced in the country in 1990. The 1984 energy program confirmed that in the long term solar energy would offer the most opportunities because recovery investment in R&D was almost assured as a result of the resource's potential and technological flexibility.

According to a number of experts, an abundance of fossil fuel deposits does not eliminate the need for energy diversification.[5] However, diversification projects in other energy sources would not have to be undertaken as hastily as in other industrialized economies because the benefits derived from oil gave flexibility to the rate of investment in developing these alternative sources. The translation of these ideas into a concrete energy program, though, was somewhat less than satisfactory. First, high priority was not ascribed to alternative energy sources, and how to carry out a diversification strategy was not defined. Second, the link between these and other energy policy objectives was not made explicit, nor was their relationship to macroeconomic policy clarified.

The energy program included the use of alternative sources in power projects designed to satisfy the energy requirement of isolated and dispersed rural communities where the expansion and integration of the national electricity grid would have been very costly and practically impossible. These sources were considered then as a means of satisfying localized demands and not as part of a program for conventional sources designed to satisfy massive demand. This order of priorities was reflected in the limited economic resources made available for the development of the alternative sources as opposed to the volumes of investment in other relatively recent energy developments such as nuclear power.

New sources are at an economic disadvantage compared to hydrocarbons because of the abundance of the latter and their subsidized domestic prices. The current cost of technology, the investment required to install plants and equipment, and the minimum acceptable production scales and investment-maturation periods create an unfavorable short-term outlook. The noncompetitiveness of new energy sources in terms of cost is one of the fundamental problems in promoting its development.

Most of the technology on alternative sources in Mexico is at the research or pilot-plant stage. Any advancement is confined basically to teaching and research institutions, certain public organizations, and to a lesser extent, professional associations. The scope of the institutions working on the development of these sources is limited by economic factors; thus, despite the progress made in pure and even applied research, the diffusion of conversion equipment has been marginal. This limit has meant that knowledge of the possibilities, range, and function of this equipment has been restricted to very specialized circles.[6] It is obvious there is a lack of communication between scientific and technological research organizations and the industrial sector. Industry firms utilizing these energy sources are practically nonexistent.

The degree of technological progress achieved has been a function of the resources (financial, economic, and human) allocated to developing each different field. Most of these resources have been concentrated in harnessing solar and geothermal energy. Resources for developing biomass and eolic energy have been very limited (see Table 6.1, Table 6.2, and Table 6.3). Despite this inequality, sufficient scientific and technological capacity has generally been acquired so that at a given moment practically all the nonconventional energy sources considered important for the country could be used. Therefore, technology in itself does not constitute an obstacle to its diffusion.

TABLE 6.1
FINANCIAL RESOURCES USED IN NEW SOURCES
(in thousands of U.S. $)

	Energy							
	Solar					Biomass and		
Year	Photovoltaic Conversion	Photothermal Conversion	Total	Geothermal	Other	Eolic	Tidal	Total
1980	969.0	3,562.6	4,531.6	1,954.6	182.1	168.9	25.4	6,862.3
1981	1,575.7	5,406.2	6,981.9	2,275.5	381.9	174.4	10.8	9,824.5
1982	1,568.0	16,883.0	18,451.0	2,878.2	341.8	170.9	25.4	21,867.3

TABLE 6.2
DISTRIBUTION OF FINANCIAL RESOURCES BETWEEN NEW SOURCES
(in percentages)

	Energy							
	Solar					Biomass and		
Year	Photovoltaic Conversion	Photothermal Conversion	Total	Geothermal	Other	Eolic	Tidal	Total
1980	14.1	51.9	66.0	28.5	2.7	2.5	0.3	100
1981	16.0	55.0	71.0	23.2	3.9	1.8	0.1	100
1982	7.2	77.2	84.4	13.2	1.5	0.8	0.1	100

TABLE 6.3

DISTRIBUTION OF FINANCIAL RESOURCES IN THE PHOTOTHERMAL CONVERSION OF SOLAR ENERGY
(in thousands of U.S. %)

Year	Flat Collectors and Selective Surfaces	Solar Refrigeration	Helioarchitecture	Integrated Projects	Solar Electric Generator	Other	Total
1980	616.9	294.7	1,026.0	530.6	1,070	24.4	3,562.6
1981	743.5	404.4	242.7	2,582.1	1,367	66.5	5,406.2
1982	504.0	390.0	2,716.0	12,256.0	954	63.0	16,883.0

Source: Guzman, Oscar, "Las nuevas fuentes de energía en México: Situación actual y perspectivas de desarrollo," in Cuadernos sobre Prospectiva Energética, No. 30, Mexico City, El Colegio de México, Programa de Energéticos, 1982, p. 48.

However, this situation in no way implies that the resources invested in these activities are sufficient for alternative energy sources to occupy an important place in the energy balance in the short and medium term.

ANALYSIS BY TYPE OF SOURCE

The following subsections are analyses of the various new energy sources available to Mexico. These sources are geothermal power, microhydroenergy, biomass, solar energy, and eolic energy.

Geothermal Power

Geothermal power is one of the nonconventional energy sources whose development has reached a relatively advanced level. Mexico occupies a privileged position in the world because it has two large geothermal regions within its territory. The most important region is located in the Mexicali Valley in the northeast. In the central region there is the neovolcanic belt that crosses the American continent and creates numerous sites with hydrothermal activity. To date, 400 sites with thermal wells have been identified, and 150 of them have been drilled. Of these, 110 correspond to the Cerro Prieto complex in Baja California Norte and 34 to Los Azufres in Michoacán. There are important sites in several other states, including Jalisco, Puebla, Querétaro, Hidalgo, and Morelos.

It has been estimated that there are high-enthalpy reserves that could provide between 11,000 and 13,000 MW, with an even greater potential in possible reserves calculated between 11,000 and 13,000 MW.[7] There are also vast undersea reserves, although with the inexact estimates of their potential and the lack of appropriate technology these reserves will probably not be exploited in the near future.[8]

Although proven geothermal reserves constitute barely 6 percent of total primary energy reserves, their long-term incidence is attractive when both probable and potential reserves are considered. Probable geothermal reserves are greater than probable uranium resources, and potential geothermal reserves make this energy source the second largest after combined liquid and gas hydrocarbons. Therefore, it is calculated that its participation in total energy reserves could amount to 15 percent.[9]

Mexico is one of the pioneers in geothermal resources exploration. CFE began activities in this field in 1955 and by 1959 had already installed the first geothermal facility in the state of Hidalgo, with a capacity of 3.5 MW. With the aim of increasing installed capacity to at least 4,000 MW in 1977, IIE elaborated a geothermal program aimed at promoting exploration, exploitation, and electricity generation by this means. Efforts have since been made in exploitation and electricity generation in particular, with activities ranging from applied research to basic engineering. Despite these efforts, the energy generated from geothermal resources currently provides less than 0.5 percent of the primary energy utilized in the country and only 2 percent of what CFE requires to generate electricity.[10]

The technology needed for utilizing high-enthalpy reserves to generate electricity is not a major obstacle because to a great extent the technology is already available. What has prevented an extensive utilization is the lack of financial resources for these projects, which require heavy investment and involve long lead times before operations can begin. Once on line, operation and maintenance costs become competitive.[11]

Geothermal energy for nonelectric purposes is a promising field in this country because of Mexico's abundant low-enthalpy reservoirs. It can de used for heating and for heat generation for certain processes in the chemistry, mining, and food industries as well as for hothouse crops and grain drying in agriculture.[12] Until now geothermal energy has been used very little in these activities because of the cost of technology and the reduced demand in the areas where the reservoirs are located.

On the basis of Mexico's abundant potential, the national energy program has placed special emphasis on geothermal energy in the medium and long term. With the continued work on the Cerro Prieto project and additional units coming on line there and at Los

Azufres, long-term electricity generation requirements to 3,900 MW can be satisfied. In short, "the exploitation of geothermal resources belong to the field of new sources where currently development programs are more clearly defined, and there is a higher probability that they will be completed."[13]

Microhydroenergy

Although not comparable with South American countries, usable hydraulic potential in Mexico is considerable.[14] According to a number of studies that take into account all the rivers and streams with "considerable pressure and volume," this potential amounts to 80 TWh, equivalent to a 22,000 MW generating capacity, a figure similar to the country's current total installed power capacity, which includes thermal, geothermal, coal burning, and hydroelectricity. Paradoxically, only 29.8 percent of this potential is utilized.[15]

IIE has estimated that there are around two hundred communities without electricity that have some kind of permanent or temporary hydraulic source for satisfying their energy requirements.[16] Of the remaining deposits a capacity of 25,000 MW could be reached using small- or medium-sized facilities. The figures for this potential are only tentative, which appears to support the fact that priority is given to the development of large hydraulic sources for satisfying energy needs rather than small rivers and waterfalls. This order of priorities corresponds to the limited financial resources available, and as a result, hydraulic resources from microsystems and plants with little potential have not been given much importance in the electricity distribution strategy because their generating coasts are high compared to the large thermoelectric and hydroelectric plants.

Generally speaking, microhydraulic development and the gradual substitution of hydroenergy for thermoelectricity have been given little attention during the last fifteen years for the following reasons:

. The speed with which new electricity generating plants had to be installed as a result of the

- country's high rate of population growth and its rapid industrialization

- The interest of CFE planners in creating economies of scale, which has led to the postponement or the abandonment of projects for small- and medium-sized waterfalls because their cost per kilowatt-hour is higher than that of larger waterfalls and thermoelectric plants

- Mexico's vast fossil fuel resources

Currently, microsystems are being used by private enterprises for generating mechanical and electric energy for a number of uses in approximately two hundred coffee plantations in Chiapas, Veracruz, and six other Mexican states. Only recently has the electricity subsector begun to consider Mexico's hydroelectric potential[17] and elaborate plans for a small hydroelectric plant.[18] CFE, the Secretaria de Agricultura y Recursos Hidráulicos (Ministry of Agriculture and Water Resources; SARH), and SEMIP have recently begun a project to build a demonstration plant at Tomatlán in Jalisco, which will have an installed capacity of 50 KW. When it is completed, a full-scale 1.6 MW plant will be built; when this plant is finished, the region's potential, evaluated at 5 MW, can be exploited.[19] CFE also operates small 121 MW plants with an average capacity of less than 5 MW, representing 0.64 percent of the total installed electricity capacity. These plants generate close to 500 GWh per year, which is equivalent to 0.73 percent of the country's total electricity production.[20]

Some research efforts are under way to develop small hydraulic plants. IIE has worked in hydraulic microgeneration, particularly in basic engineering, with the aim of developing the technology necessary to optimize design, construction, and operation of this type of plants.[21,22] The technology needed for tapping hydraulic potential through microsystems does not involve in-depth studies in totally unknown fields. Hydraulic technology used in the large electric plants can be modified and adapted to the conditions and specific requirements of the area. In effect, rather than specific investment in technology, new lines of production need to be developed for small hydraulic plants, taking advantage of existing local technology or technology from abroad that can be adapted to the country's specific needs.[23] There are, however, numerous problems involved in producing these capital goods. To install small hydroelectric plants Mexico would have to start manufacturing electromechanical components.

The heavy investment needed for projects of this nature has been a deterrent to the rural communities for which these schemes have been planned, and their viability cannot even be considered without resorting to external financial backing. However, the disadvantages are counteracted by several factors that reduce the amount required for investment: (1) the possibility of utilizing local materials and labor; (2) the capacity to produce the equipment needed even for power ranges greater than 1,000 KW;[24] (3) the experience in civil technology and in the construction of small- and large-scale works; and (4) the low operation, maintenance, and repair costs once the plant is installed. All these factors considered, the cost of generating hydraulic electricity would, in fact, be competitive with the cost involved if the community were to be integrated into the national electricity grid.

Biomass

A wide variety of natural resources can be classified as biomass for producing energy.[25] Among the most important of these are organic matter from trees, bushes, farming and forestry production residues, and urban and industrial waste. On the basis of this definition the country's biomass potential is enormous. Livestock produces around 20 million tons per year of dry manure, and another 25 million comes from bagasse or stubble. According to the Alonso and Rodriguez estimates for 1982, if all animal waste were to be utilized for energy purposes, 4 million cubic meters per day of biogas could be produced. The maximum amount of energy obtainable from this potential source is equivalent to approximately 30×10^3 TJ per year. The usable energy from total farming residues could reach

52,500 TJ per year, which is equivalent to 1.14 percent of the national primary energy consumption in 1980.[26] Of this residue total the dry residue from maize constitutes and excellent energy resource because there is an available potential of 1.52 million tons, which in 1980 constituted 47.6 percent of total farming residue.

Another rich biomass source is wood and forestry residues. Mexico's forests contain 54 million cubic meters of wood, which is comparable to 16 million tons of coal with an energy content equivalent to 12 percent of the national commercial energy consumption in 1982.[27] Another potential source of biomass is the mountains of urban waste produced as a result of accelerated population growth and industrial expansion. The most important of these sources is domestic waste and liquid effluent from organic industries, food-stuff manufacturers, and organic acid and carbonization facilities, among others.

Although the potential resources are many, because of the alternative uses of the sources, there are constraints to transform them into fuel. Residues from farming production, especially chaff, have traditionally been used as feed for cattle and as a fertilizer. Because most animal waste is from bovine cattle (around 70 percent of the total) and the cattle are put out to pasture, only a small fraction of this waste is recoverable (15 percent). The use of wood and crops such as sugarcane to obtain ethanol is restricted because of deforestation and soil exhaustion and their priority use in foodstuff production. It is almost impossible to expect land to be used for energy-producing crops because this use would clash with food production and the growing of traditional forest products, which is one of the nation's priorities.[28] Unless great thrust is given to reforestation or the elaboration of a program for crops with efficient photosynthesis, the order of priority in soil use will continue to limit the utilization of biomass for energy production. For the moment the feasible resources for this use are certain residual forest products; animal waste (manure); and, to a lesser extent, sewage from urban waste.

The only biomass technology studied systematically has been anaerobic biodigestion. Research efforts have produced positive results in the field of biodigesters—particularly the mesophilic type that range from smaller, family-sized equipment to industrial-size digesters designed to cope with large volumes—and plants for treating organic waste in rural communities.[29] In Mexico there are currently around one hundred digesters with capacities ranging from 10 to 100 cubic meters with a yield of 1 cubic meter of biogas per 1 cubic meter of reactor.[30] Technology in this field is adequately advanced so it is not a barrier to diffusion, but economic resources channeled into the area have been insufficient; however, the relatively low cost makes this equipment accessible to the rural community.[31]

Biodigesters can be used for treating sewage and other kinds of organic waste. Biogas, which can be utilized as fuel for food preparation, lighting, heat generation, and motion, is obtained from this matter. Furthermore, biogas leaves a residue that can be utilized as a fertilizer. This energy source has no fuel storage problems and provides continuous energy, an advantage not shared with solar energy.

A number of designs for biodigesters have already been introduced in rural communities, although for the moment they are mainly used in milking sheds and stables because it is here that the primary products needed to feed the units are found. Other experiments related to sewage treatment have been done in Mexico City's metropolitan zone and in the Peninsula de Yucatán.[32]

The implementation of biodigesters has created a number of problems not uncommon in this type of project. These problems range from friction between local authorities and the community itself to the difficulties involved in organizing a proper infrastructure to collect waste and process water and residues in urban zones and in determining who is responsible for operating the digester. Strategies for integrating this technology into the whole electricity generation process have never been defined in rural electricity programs. Also, responsibility for the diffusion or development of technology has never been assigned to anyone; that is, it has not been decided whether CFE will take charge or the rural community itself will organize operations. For the moment, the absence of a policy promoting its diffusion and the lack of support for the massive manufacture of equipment reduce the possibility of biomass becoming a viable short-term energy alternative in the country's electricity strategy. It is likely that the propagation of biodigesters in the rural sector will continue for the time being to form part of the R&D projects in those centers dedicated to this work.

According to the Plan Nacional de Electrificación Rural (National Plan for Rural Electrification) 1979-1982, in Mexico there are 78,668 rural communities with no electricity.[33] This figure implies that there is a very large potential demand (certainly more than 20 million people) that has to be satisfied with other resources. This sector's consumption is never considered in national energy balances, which cover only commercial energy. According to the current energy balances, the potential demand for heat and power in this sector is between 5.2 and 17 percent of the country's energy consumption.[34]

Under certain conditions overall consumption of biomass in the form of vegetable coal and firewood could be between 5.4 and 15 percent of national energy consumption, indicating the importance of these reserves in satisfying the demand, especially if one considers that they provide around 90 percent of the energy consumed in the sector. Of these fuels firewood is the most important because vegetable coal, which is produced in inaccessible areas, with the consequent supply and distribution problems, is costly in certain communities.

In terms of useful energy, changes in the consumption pattern have been introduced that have caused a reduction in the amount of firewood used and an increase in the use of commercial fuels, mainly liquefied gas. The alteration in the traditional pattern became evident at the beginning of the 1970s when the number of firewood users became stable; by the late 1970s firewood's share in the total domestic-rural energy consumption had dropped from 64.8 to 43 percent.

Diverse factors have initiated this change: (1) the reduced availability of forestry resources (in many communities supply can no longer be guaranteed because of excessive consumption and overexploitation of certain species, which, in turn, has aggravated ecological degradation); (2) the inefficient utilization of these resources; (3) the higher opportunity cost of commercialized firewood in relation to conventional fuels; and (4) the easier commercialization of conventional fuels, particularly liquefied gas.[35]

Solar Energy

The geographic location and climatological characteristics of most of Mexico's territory favor the use of solar energy.[36] Mexico is located within the insolation belt, with maximum rates around 700 cal/cm^2 per day in the summer and minimum rates of 250 cal/cm^2 per day in the winter.[37] Compared to other sources, solar energy has received most of the financial resources assigned for research. The two energy programs introduced to date (1980 and 1984) emphasized solar energy's importance, although no quantitative evaluations have been done to estimate its potential contribution to Mexico's energy supply.

Considerable technological progress has been made in this field, and some of the equipment and mechanisms used have become competitive internationally. The following equipment is technologically feasible: (1) flat collectors for heating water; (2) passive thermal systems generally related to helioarchitecture; (3) flat collectors (for air) associated with systems for drying different types of organic matter; (4) photovoltaic cells for application in places that are far from electricity distribution networks and that require very little installed power capacity (however, these cells are only applicable in very specific situations); and (5) other systems, such as solar lakes or concentration systems, for producing industrial heat.[38] In only very few cases has economic feasibility been evaluated.

Solar technologies can be classified according to the type of process being utilized: (1) photothermal processes; (2) photovoltaic processes; (3) photochemical processes; and (4) thermionic processes. Research institutions have worked mainly on the first two processes, particularly photothermal conversion, so it is here that the most progress has been made. Considerable progress has been made in the design, construction, and standardization of flat solar collectors. This particular technology is the only to date that has developed a commercial market, although it is small.[39]

In the field of photothermal systems there is adequate technological capacity in systems for tapping solar energy and for helioarchitectural housing, and helioelectric plants. Small-scale photothermal systems for generating electricity in remote areas are technologically viable but are still not able to compete economically with electricity produced by conventional generators.[40] Some of the components for photothermal systems were imported until the drastic changes in the parity of the Mexican peso with the U.S. dollar obliged almost complete suspension of foreign purchases. These imports were part of different scientific collaboration agreements that had been entered into between the Mexican government and France,[41] West Germany, Italy, the United States, and Japan[42] since 1973. However, local techniques and resources have prevailed, and in certain cases product results have come from the adaptation of foreign technology to local needs, a feat achieved more by maintaining and dismantling equipment than by any real transference of know-how. The manufacture of helioarchitectural design prototypes shows how the technological experience already obtained is being incorporated into a number of housing projects. These constructions are designed to utilize solar energy for water heating, air conditioning, and electricity generation.[43]

Technological progress in photovoltaic systems has lagged behind photothermal technology because of differences of opinion regarding production chains. The many technological innovations made abroad in this field have been a consideration in deciding whether to carry out technological projects of this magnitude. The priority given to photothermal conversion systems is reflected in the economic resources assigned to them, amounting to 77.2 percent of the 1982 solar energy R&D budget. In 1982 photovoltaic systems absorbed only 7.2 percent of the total resources assigned to R&D. The existing technological capacity for these systems is sufficient to generate decentralized electric energy of less than 1 KW. Despite the potential for these systems in small rural communities, cost is undoubtedly a limiting factor.[44]

To date, the competitiveness of photovoltaic and photothermal systems has been evaluated only in relation to conventional fuels. The estimated cost of these devices is rough because performance tests have only been done under experimental conditions. Hence, other factors specific to operation under real conditions could modify the evaluation. Furthermore, other considerations concerning environment and social well-being have to be pondered in projects promoting these energy systems.

Meanwhile, the criterion carrying most weight appears to be relative cost. The progress in photothermal technology makes it somewhat easier to forecast the medium- and long-term contributions of this system to the country's energy balance. The future of both these technologies will depend, moreover, on whether certain technological problems, such as dispersion and intermittence, can be solved, which could have a favorable effect on costs and make solar energy attractive.[45]

Many small-scale solar-technology applications are useful for farming activities, as shown in the following list:

* Photothermal systems

    - - Applications requiring energy for heat generation

        1. Central heating
        2. Water heating
        3. Refrigeration by absorption
        4. Cooking
        5. Drying of farming products
        6. Water purification
        7. Heat for agro-industry

    - - Applications requiring mechanical energy

        1. Water pumping
        2. Milling of agricultural products
        3. Utilization of mechanical equipment for handicraft and agro-industrial activities

TABLE 6.4
FEASIBILITY OF SOLAR TECHNOLOGY USES

Use	Solar Energy Type						
	Stationary	Passive	Collectors	Ponds	Mobile	Distributed	Central Tower
Air Conditioning	4	4	4	4	4	4	4
Heating	4	1	1	4	4	4	4
Refrigeration	4	1	2	4	4	4	4
Domestic Water Heating	4	4	1	1	4	4	4
Industrial Water Heating	4	4	1	1	4	2	4
Centralized Electricity	4	4	4	2	4	3	2
Decentralized Electricity	4	4	4	2	4	2	4
Water Pumping	4	4	4	2	4	1	4
Water Purification	4	1	2	2	4	2	4
Cooking	4	4	2	4	4	2	4
Drying Agricultural Products	4	1	1	1	4	4	4
Industrial Heating	4	4	1	1	4	1	3
Irrigation	4	4	4	2	4	2	4
Greenhouses	4	4	4	2	4	4	4

Preservation of Agricultural
Products   4   4   1   2   4   4
Refrigeration   4   4   2   2   4   2

1. This category indicates uses that are technically and economically feasible.
2. This category indicates uses that are technically viable.
3. This category indicates uses that require research and development.
4. This category indicates uses that are not applicable.

Source: SEMIP, Diagnóstico sobre fuentes alternas de energía, Mexico City, SEMIP, Dirección General de Investigación y Desarrollo, June 1983, p. 42.

-- Applications requiring electric energy

1. Water pumping
2. Refrigeration
3. Lighting
4. Communications
5. Electric equipment

* Photovoltaic Systems

-- Applications requiring heat-generated, mechanical, and electric energy

1. Lighting
2. Communications
3. Television relay
4. Portable equipment
5. Refrigeration
6. Water pumping
7. Electric equipment

In several of these activities energy can also be supplied from other nonconventional sources. Solar technology is applicable to other areas as well, such as the industrial sector where primary energy is used mainly to generate heat. Its introduction could be immediate because a high degree of technological expertise has been attained in systems requiring temperatures no greater than 150x C. The textile, food, and chemical industries could utilize these thermal solar systems successfully in several of their production phases. The choice between photothermal and photovoltaic systems for generating electricity will depend on technical and economic feasibility (see Table 6.4).

Eolic Energy

The financial resources for R&D in energy generated from wind have been scant compared to other energy sources, such as solar and geothermal power and even biomass (see Table 6.1 and Table 6.2). Among other things this financial limit has meant that only elementary equipment for evaluating eolic potential is available and that no in-depth studies have been done in the area. The most favorable windy areas known to date for exploiting this potential are the following:

- Areas with strong winds (annual average of 7 m/s): La Ventosa, Oaxaca; and La Bufa, Zacatecas

- Coastal zones (annual average of 4.5 m/s): Guerrero and Baja California

- Central plateau (annual average of 3.0 m/s)

Technological development is limited to experimental units located fundamentally at research centers. Only three institutes and one civil association undertake activities in this field; they are involved mainly in the design and construction of small eolic energy conversion systems, which are usually adaptations or redesigns of commercially available converter systems.[46] Prototypes have been designed and built for low-power units (for example, 10 HP pumps and 2.5 to 10 KW aerogenerators) adapted to the country's wind conditions.[47] The purpose of these experiments is to develop windmill aerogenerator and water pump prototypes that can be used in agro-industry and the domestic-rural sector

The country's wind conditions and the difficulties involved in storing this kind of energy because of its irregularity have for the moment limited its use to traditional activities such as water pumping and grain milling, activities where the accumulated effect over a given period and the initial cost of small-scale equipment are important. These difficulties explain why its use is practically limited to mechanical wind pumps in certain rural communities in the north of the country and in the Península de Yucatán.[48] Industrially produced equipment of this kind is scarce, and there are only two branches of a North American corporation that export some of their units.[49]

Because equipment cost must be calculated for each specific case according to requirements, the comparison of eolic power with other energy sources is difficult. Estimates have been made for small- and medium-scale units where costs could be between $1,000 and $2,000 (U.S. $) per kilowatt installed or between 0.4 and 0.5 KW per square meter of harnessing surface.[50] However, generation costs amount to approximately $67 (U.S. $) per KW, which is much higher than the cost of generating electricity by conventional means; such costs place this equipment at a disadvantage.

CONCLUSIONS AND FUTURE PROSPECTS

Currently, Mexico has scientific and technological knowledge enough to stimulate development of a number of nonconventional energy sources. However, because equipment is not standardized, the contribution of these sources to domestic energy supply cannot be considered important in the short and medium term. Thermopower is the exception, however, because it already contributes 2 percent of the country's electricity, and its future growth in the electricity subsector shows considerable promise.

According to a number of energy sector representatives, the foundations have been laid for structural change; long-term efforts include measures for saving and conserving energy and diversifying energy sources. However, production goals and the share of alternative energy sources in the country's energy supply have not been made explicit in quantitative terms. The diversification strategy has given priority to other forms of energy; therefore, a marginal contribution is expected form alternative sources in the medium term. Their contribution to energy supply will be conditioned by the measures taken now that consider technological maturation requirements and market penetration.

Within the energy sector's programming, the development of alternative sources is considered an option that would give small or dispersed rural communities access to electricity. In such cases the cost of the technology involved often makes projects of this kind inaccessible to the community. Sometimes cost-benefit analyses are reduced merely to the question of finances, with no detailed resource evaluation of the area having been done. Often, local manpower is cheap and readily available and could help cut project costs considerably. Undoubtedly, the social benefit derived from this sort of projects should carry more weight in these analyses than economic criteria. The introduction of these systems into the rural sector would help increase productivity in seasonal farming zones where human and animal energy currently predominate and would also improve domestic-rural sector conditions.

The development possibilities of alternative energy sources should be evaluated within a different international energy context than that prevailing during the 1970s.[51] The changes occurring in the oil market, for example, created uncertainty in regard to technological progress because of the increased cost of technology. Despite the lower cost of conventional fuels, it is worthwhile to develop technology in alternative energy sources in order to accomplish the following:

- To fulfill the energy-diversification policy

- To create alternative energy sources for rural communities

- To fully utilize the country's energy potential

Thus, the price of oil should not be the only consideration in the development of alternative energy sources. In addition, other factors related to the country's financial problems have restrained the progress of development, which, in turn, have made it necessary to reduce the budget for new projects. However, proper channeling of economic resources and fiscal incentives and a policy designed to promote these technologies would help to achieve a certain degree if industrialization and commercialization.

Policies designed to promote alternative energy sources require that certain guidelines be defined and established. These are as follows:

- The role these sources are to play in the energy sector as a whole, both in regard to energy diversification and to rural energy development, must be defined. This effort involves the undertaking of a strict analysis of the potential of these resources and their end use as well as the

- appropriate technology under special conditions, such as seasonality; investment requirements; production scales; and economic, social, and political implications. It is essential to gather these data so that sufficient information on relative costs and their trends can be made available to determine the range of energy options.

- The sector's research institutes, the federal government, and industry in general must be oriented and coordinated in order to establish priorities and assign financial resources to R&D.

- There must be greater interaction between research centers and the industrial sector, the capital goods industry in particular, with the object of standardizing equipment and reducing production costs.

Thus, to assure future progress in this field, the state must create favorable conditions for the production and commercialization of this equipment.

These systems can be established in the rural sector if greater coordination is achieved between the energy institutions and if their supply monopoly of a number of their activities is relaxed. The legal framework needs redefining to grant the local communities the right to take over from CFE the operation and maintenance of the equipment, as was the case with electricity generated by small-scale plants. In many cases the energy sector's entities could not take charge of development and operation, but it is hoped they would undertake the task of training the community to operate the equipment. The correct functioning of these strategies can only be guaranteed if the rural energy projects are closely coordinated with national development plans.

Last, when bringing the benefits of energy to rural areas, it is advisable to adopt strategies for utilizing renewable resources in situ by installing microhydroelectric and geothermal plants as well as small aerogenerators, solar ponds, digesters, agro-industrial biomass gasifiers, and so on. However, this development requires considerable federal and municipal support of a financial and technological nature. Implicit here is the need for a serious coordination effort, which under present conditions would be somewhat difficult to achieve.

NOTAS

1. UN, Preparatory Committee for the United Nations Conference on New and Renewable Energy Sources, 30 March to 17 April 1981 (Synthesis of technical group reports), New Delhi, UN, 1981.
2. Poder Ejecutivo Federal, Programa nacional de energéticos, 1984-1988, Mexico City, SEMIP, Subsecretaría de Energía, August 1984.
3. These countries are mainly members of OECD. Here, oil's share of total energy resources fell from almost 50 percent in 1973 to slightly more than 40 percent in 1983, and it is expected to fall to 33.3 percent in the year 2000. See OECD, Energy Policies and Programs of the IEA Countries, Paris, PCED, 1984.
4. SEPAFIN and STCE, "Programa de energía, metas a 1990 y proyecciones al año 2000" (summary), in Energéticos: Boletín Informativo del sector energético, Year 4, No. 11, Mexico City, STCE, November 1980.
5. Corredor, Jaime, "El significado económico del petróleo en México," in Comercio Exterior, Vol. 31, No. 11, Mexico City, November 1981, p. 1314.
6. Guzmán, Oscar, "Las nuevas fuentes de energía en México: Situación actual y perspectivas," in Cuadernos sobre prospectiva energética, No. 30, Mexico City, El Colegio de México, Progama de Energéticos, 1982, p. 2.
7. IIE, Diagnóstico y pronóstico sobre fuentes de energía en México, Vol. 1, Mexico City, October 1982, p. 3.
8. It is calculated that this potential amounts to 97,000 MW, the Gulf of Baja California being the region with the greatest concentration of these energy resources.
9. Guzmán, Oscar, op. cit.
10. Mulás, Pablo, and Sergio Mercado, "Investigación y desarrollo en apoyo de la geotermia," in Wionczek, Miguel S. (editor), Problemas del sector

energético de México, Mexico City, El Colegio de México, 1983, p. 233.

11. At July 1982 prices and on the basis of a 10 percent discount rate, the following list presents the generating cost per kilowatt-hour using different types of primary energy. The generating cost of a geothermal complex equipped with two 110 MW machines are even lower than those of a thermoelectric plant fed with fuel oil with the same number of machines but with greater power (30 MW).

Energy	Dollar/KWh	Plant Power
Fuel Oil	2.24	2 x 350 MW
Coal	2.04	2 x 350 MW
Uranium	2.37	2 x 1,000 MW
Geothermal A	1.98	2 x 110 MW
Geothermal B	2.43	1 x 55 MW
Hydroelectric A	3.36	3 x 190 MW
Hydroelectric B	1.81	5 x 300 MW

Source: Hiriart, Gerardo, "El papel de la geotermia en la expansión del sector eléctrico,", in UNAM, Programa Universitario de Energía, Tecnologías energéticas del futuro, Mexico City, UNAM, 2 March, 1983, p. 147.

12. See Mercado, Sergio, "Posibilidades de participación de la UNAM en el desarrollo de la energía geotérmica," in UNAM, Programa Universitario de Energía, op. cit., pp. 162-169.

13. IIE, op. cit., p. 6

14. The geographical distribution of hydroelectric potential in Mexico is such that 74 percent of it is concentrated in 15 percent of the country's area. Forty percent of the potential is generated at the Grijalva-Usumacinta complex and 34 percent in the Balsas and Papaloapan rivers' basins.

15. Poder Ejecutivo Federal, op. cit., p. 44.

16. SEMIP, Diagnóstico sobre fuentes alternas de energía (mimeograph), Mexico City, SEMIP, Dirección General de Investigaciones y Desarrollo, June 1983, p. 152.

17. At some point SARH began to calculate the usable potential in the irrigation systems, including the use of microplants. However, the investment bud-

geted still does not take into account the possibility of installing medium- and small-scale plants for at least another ten years. SARH, Plan nacional hidráulico, Mexico City, SARH, March 1981, pp. 96, 138.

18. According to the LAEO classification, microplants reach a power limit of 50 KW, miniplants have a range going from 50 to 500 KW, and small hydroelectric plants from 500 to 5,000 KW. See LAEO, "El desarrollo de pequeñas centrales hidroeléectricas en Latinoamérica y el Caribe," in Boletín Energético, No. 16, LAEO, October-December 1980, p. 9.

19. "Energía hidráulica," op. cit., p. 19.

20. Ibid., p. 6.

21. Ferrán Riquelme, Flavio, "Energía hidráulica para generaciones de electricidad a pequeña escala," paper presented at the Foro Interdisciplinario sobre Fuentes Alternas de Energía, Mexico City, IPN-ESIA and IIE, 2 April 1984, p. 6.

22. This project was undertaken in the old hacienda at Dolores, Michoacán. See Ferrán Riquelme, Flavio, "Formulación de un programa de investigación sobre pequeñas centrales hidroeléctricas," Mexico City, IIE, November 1980, p. 10.

23. Ibid., p. 6.

24. Ibid., p. 2

25. Biomass is the chemical conversion of human, animal, and vegetable waste into gas and liquid fuel through the action of microorganisms and solar radiation.

26. Alonso, Antonio, and Luis Rodríguez, Diagnóstico y pronóstico sobre energía solar, biomasa y eólica, Vol. 3, Part 2, Mexico City, UNAM, Instituto de Ingeniería, November 1981, p. 646.

27. Martínez, Ana María, "Biomasa,", in UNAM, Programa Universitario de Energía, op. cit., p. 94.

28. For example, currently 60,000 to 150,000 acres of sugarcane-producing land would be required to produce sufficient bioalcohol as a fuel substitute for motorized vehicles, electricity generation and other uses. Troeller, Ruth, "El futuro de la obtención de energía, con especial referencia a las áreas rurales de los países del Tercer Mundo,", in El Día, supplement, 16 March 1984,.

29. Guzmán, Oscar, op. cit., p. 18.

30. A larger digester (450 cubic meters) forms part of the Xochicalli project called Casa Ecológica Autosuficiente; it was installed for R&D purposes.

31. Initially, it was calculated that the cost of a 40 cubic meter digester was around 150,000 pesos; a 10 cubic meter digester would cost 40,000 pesos. See Castellanos, Alfonso, and Margarita Escobedo, La energía solar en México, situación actual y perspectivas, Mexico City, Centro de Ecodesarrollo, 1980, p. 69.

32. The project is called SIRDO and is being undertaken in the Colonia México Nuevo situated on the outskirts of the city. In this case the biodigester requires the cooperation of the community, which takes care of its maintenance.

33. CFE, Plan nacional de electrificación rural, 1979-1982, CFE, Gerencia General de Electrificación Rural, Mexico City, 1979, pp. 50-59.

34. SEMIP, "Demanda de energéticos alternos, diagnóstico preliminar de fuentes alternas de energía," in Energéticos: Boletín Informativo del Sector Energético, No. 1, 2d Series, Mexico City, Dirección General de Investigación y Desarrollo, 1983, p. 30.

35. Some factors influencing this commercialization were: (1) the ready availability of gas for use as a domestic fuel at a relatively lower price than wood; (2) the increasing number of the population employed with a set wage, which means that wood has a greater opportunity cost for men and young people working in other kinds of activities; and (3) the normal changes in the rural sector's life-style. See White, Margaret Evans, "Aspectos socioeconómicos de la carencia de combustibles domésticos: Un estudio empírico del México rural," in Cuadernos sobre prospectiva energética, No. 55, Mexico City, El Colegio de México, Programa de Energéticos, 1984.

36. Solar energy is used in its restricted sense, that is, energy whose direct source is the sun; there are those who include solar energy in its indirect forms, such as hydraulic and eolic energy, biomass, and so on.

37. Hernández, E., La distribución de la radiación global en México evaluada mediante la fotointerpretación de la nubosidad observada por satelites me-

teorológicos, MSc thesis, Mexico City, UNAM, Facultad de Ciencias, 1976.

38. Alonso, Antonio, and Luis Rodríguez, op. cit., Vol. 1, p. 75.

39. There are twenty five companies producing solar collectors for swimming-pool heating and domestic use. The production method could still be considered semicrafted.

40. Almanza, Rafael, and Gerardo Hiriart, "Conversión fototérmica de la energía solar a electricidad y a energía mecánica," in Boletín IIE, Vol. 2, No. 6, Mexico City, IIE, 1978.

41. In 1973 the Mexican government came to an agreement with France to undertake the Tonatiuh project, which involved installing solar pumps.

42. "Energía solar, promesa para la humanidad," in Tiempo, Mexico City, 23 March 1981, p. 27.

43. In Mexico City construction of this type of housing by the Instituto del Fondo Nacional de la Vivienda para los Trabajadores (National Institute for the Workers' Housing Promotion; INFONAVIT) is in progress. The cost of each unit has been calculated at 10 percent more than the cost of traditional housing; the construction of more units will depend on success of this project.

44. In 1978 IPN estimated costs between $15 and $20 (U.S. $). To be competitive with traditional energy prices, these costs would have to be reduced to 0.5 dollars per peak watt. (A peak watt is the efficiency of a photocell under a 1,000 watts/m^2 luminous breeder.)

45. It has been proposed that the problem of storing solar energy could be solved with the joint use of another energy source, such as coal or fuel from biomass, that can be stored. See Galindo, Ignacio, "Situación actual y perspectivas de la energía solar en México," in Problemas de desarrollo, Mexico City, UNAM, February-April 1979.

46. Alonso, Antonio, and Luis Rodríguez, op. cit., Vol. 2, p. 355.

47. Guzmán, Oscar, op. cit., p. 17.

48. Castellanos, Alfonso, and Margarita Escobedo, op. cit., p. 75.

49. These are MOVISA, S.A., representative of Demster, and a group called Fuerza, S.A., a branch of

the North American company Hummingbird. In 1983 MOVISA produced aeropumps with diameters ranging from 6 to 8 feet, and Fuerza manufactured an aerogenerator known as "Colibrí."

50. Programa de Energéticos, "Energía eólica" (mimeograph), Mexico City, El Colegio de México, March 1985, pp. 35-57.

51. See the work of Styrikovich, M. A., and Ju Sinyak, "Posibilidades y limitaciones de la utilización de fuentes de energía renovables," in Cuadernos de prospectiva energética, No. 42, Mexico City, El Colegio de México, Programa de Energéticos.

PART TWO

Strategies and Policies for Hydrocarbon Exploration and Exploitation

7

Exploration and Exploitation

Ana María Sordo

Planners in hydrocarbon exploration and exploitation have always used the fundamental objectives of the national economic development programs as a frame of reference. Since PEMEX was established in 1938, the state has assigned the oil industry the role of supporting the country's industrial growth, thus subjecting the company to the changing patterns and needs of the state. Every six years at the beginning of a new presidential term and, thus, a new PEMEX administration, targets are set and guidelines established for crude exploration and production. The objectives of the six-year programs have not been solely to develop and integrate the various areas involved in oil and gas extraction. The formulation and implementation of the objectives and targets for hydrocarbon exploration and exploitation were also conditioned by the political considerations and the economic priorities set by the government entering office. Consequently, guidelines and criteria indispensable to coherent and continuous development of resources were sometimes forgotten. In other words, at certain times macroeconomic objectives prevailed over those inherent in the expansion needs of the oil industry, constituting, in turn, serious constraints for economic planning itself.

A clear example of this conflict has been the limited financial resources available to PEMEX as a result of the long periods when the price of its products was frozen. Such a pricing policy, which has been contemplated for the different macroeconomic programs since 1954, has led to a shrinking of oil industry investment funds and to the subsequent reduction in capital expenditure for exploration activities. Thus, proven crude reserves dropped progressively in response to the continuous and growing extraction of crude oil and gas. Furthermore, during the mid-1970s priority attention to macroeconomic objectives meant that hydrocarbon-exploration and -exploitation programs lacked adequate means of technical evaluation, which would have allowed improvement in the efficiency and productivity of these activities.

In this chapter the policies for exploration and exploitation, whether explicit or implicit, are analyzed with reference to the conditions under which they were implemented and the subsequent results. The search for oil, and crude oil and gas production (with special emphasis on those factors influencing policy formulation and execution), achievements, and difficulties are all examined. An analysis of the changes introduced in the field during the mid-1970s is preceded by a review of prior events.

OIL PRODUCTION BEFORE 1977

Early in the 1970s it became evident that exploration activities had not led to the discovery of new locations, thus preventing the drilling of development wells at an adequate, steady rate. Consequently, hydrocarbon production fell behind, unable to keep pace with the rapid growth of domestic fuel demand.[1] Because of the slow expansion of new oil reserves, which was accompanied by continued crude production, the safety margin of proven reserves diminished considerably. Thus, the ratio of reserves to production went down from 28 years at the time of expropriation in 1938 to 18 years in 1970, and an even greater decline was foreseen for the following decade. This trend forced limits on increases in hydrocarbon production; hence, the need to import crude oil became inevitable. If the demand was to be satisfied with domestic crude output, new mantles had to be found quickly to replace the volumes extracted. Otherwise, there was a growing risk that the accelerated exploitation of proven reserves would have a negative effect on the technically sound utilization of the known deposits.

When he assumed his post as director general of PEMEX in 1970, Antonio Dovali Jaime was aware of the exploration lag and the company's productive difficulties. Consequently, exploratory activities, including prospecting studies and evaluative drilling, were dedicated to adding at least 6,000 MB to the proven hydrocarbon reserves within six years. Otherwise, by the mid-1970s Mexico would be faced with a serious energy crisis.[2]

PEMEX management decided that a reserve security margin of at least twenty years had to be reached by 1976 in order to guarantee a certain flexibility in the production required to satisfy domestic demand, 90 percent of which depended on hydrocarbons.[3] This decision was an attempt to establish the conditions for long-term planning because these R/P ratios were considered one of the main parameters behind the proper allocation of investment in the oil industry.

With the fulfillment of these objectives in mind, the company reevaluated prior exploratory activities in order to correct the policies and procedures in practice.[4] At the same time it provided a digital processing center with exploratory information that would facilitate the classification and analysis of geologic and geophysical data. A review of the activities undertaken during the previous administration (1964-1970) and the knowledge that the shallow deposits were exhausted prompted the decision to drill in Tabasco and Chiapas at a depth of more than 3,500 meters in search of oil accumulations in Cretaceous layers.[5] The presence of oil in this part of the country was suspected as early as the 1920s.

From this point on exploration activities were given priority according to their probable contribution to the increase in reserves; thus, resources were allocated to the most promising zones. The intensification of exploratory work produced satisfactory results. The most promising discoveries in the post-1938 history of the Mexican oil industry were made in 1972 at Sitio Grande and Cactus in the Cretaceous oil province of Reforma, which is situated in the Tabasco and Chiapas states (see Figure 7.1). The first test wells drilled in this area indicated an average productivity twenty times larger than the national average, which raised hopes for deposits with great potential.[6] Drilling to greater depths in the adjacent areas during 1973 added to the already discovered reserves, allowing the rapid incorporation of new fields into production.[7]

After these discoveries the initial targets and objectives changed because the goal of 5,000 to 6,000 MB of new reserves by 1976 had been reached ahead of time. The zone for future additions had been located, and it was no longer considered necessary to extend exploratory activities to other regions (which was contrary to Mexican oil policy in the subsequent PEMEX administration under Jorge Díaz Serrano). Hence, exploration had given results that allowed the adverse conditions of primary production to be reversed, eliminating the bottlenecks caused by the reduced availability of hydrocarbon resources.

However, exploration had to be continued to verify the magnitude of the new discoveries and to certify the oil reserves in Tabasco and Chiapas as proven. The increased cost of oil imports following the international crude price rise in 1973 was an added burden for PEMEX's already difficult financial situation, and this factor, among others, was an obstacle to exploratory drilling. Fortunately, a policy change was introduced toward the end of 1973 when PEMEX's financial position had improved because of an internal price increase for its products. By this time development of the Reforma fields indicated that self-sufficiency in crude oil would surely be achieved within a relatively brief period.[8]

Thus, a program was elaborated to extend exploration and had an investment of 3.5 billion pesos in studies and surveys and 10.8 billion pesos in test drilling ($278 and $861 million [U.S. $]), at current prices and exchange rates.[9] Intensive drilling was undertaken in the new oil province (Reforma - Villahermosa) in an attempt to find the extent of the deposits toward the north and the south, to determine their characteristics, and to start production at an early date.[10]

Since this time because of the exploratory evaluation of the whole Tabasco-Chiapas area, development activities have involved sufficient additional loca-

FIGURE 7.1
TABASCO-CHIAPAS AREA

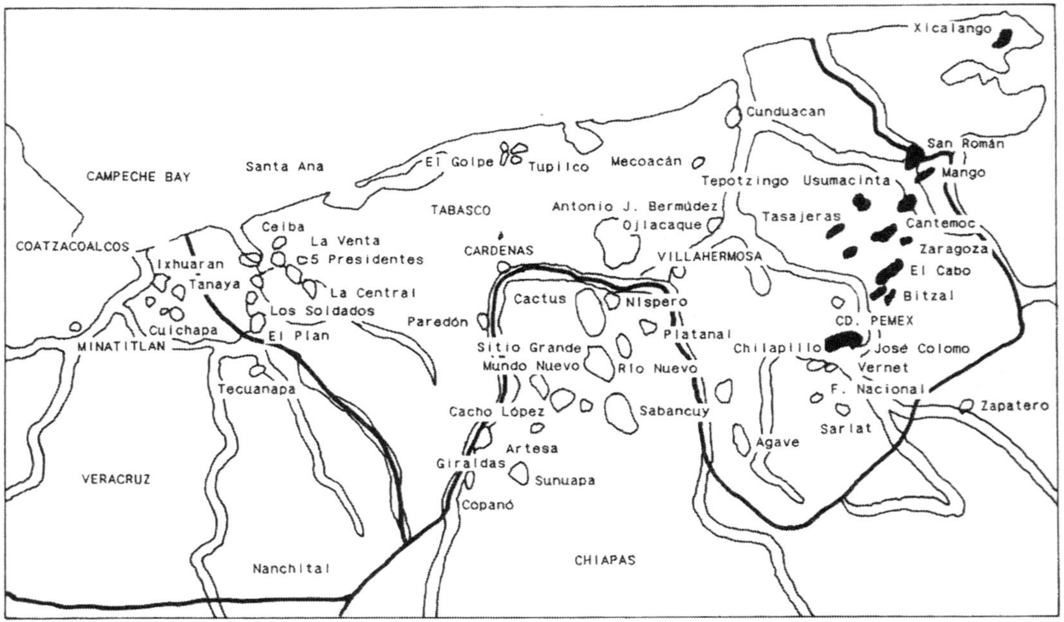

Sources: "The Latin America Oil Report," in *Petroleum Economist*, 1978 (special edition); *International Petroleum Encyclopedia*, Vol. 17, Tulsa Ok., PennWell Publishing Co., 1984, p. 96.

Total Land Area: 1,972,363 km
Continental Area: (0-200 m) 378,900 km
Offshore Area: (200-3,000 m) 734,000 km
Main Sedimentary Area (onshore): 782,100 km

FIGURE 7.2
OIL & GAS FIELDS OF MEXICO

Legend:
- Oil field
- Gas field
- Oil Pipeline
- International Border
- State Border

Total Land Area: 1,972,363 Km.
Continental Area (0-200 m): 378,900 Km.
Offshore Area (200-3,000 m): 734,000 Km.
Main Sedimentary Area (Onshore): 782,100 Km.

PEMEX Division by Zones
Northern Zone: Comprises Northeastern, northern and Southern borders, including the states of Tamaulipas, Nuevo Leon and Baja California
Central Zone: Poza Rica and Papaloapan City districts in the State of Veracruz
Southern Zone: Agua Azul, El Plan, Nanchital and PEMEX City districts in the State of Tabasco
Southeastern Zone: Camalcalco and Villahermosa in the States of Tabasco and Chiapas
Marine Zone: Gulf of Campeche

Source: "The Latin American Oil Report", *Petroleum Economist*, 1978 (special edition); *International Petroleum Encyclopedia*, Vol. 17, Tulsa, OK, Penn Well Publishing Co., 1984, P. 96

tions to allow pulley shafts to be drilled. There were finds at Cunduacán and to the east and west of Sitio Grande and Cactus (see Figure 7.1). Ten areas were discovered and broadened considerably the possibilities of the accelerated growth of crude production. The discoveries also revealed that the magnitude of the region's deposits was much greater than that originally calculated.[11] Consequently, by about the middle of 1974 self sufficiency in oil was restored with a marginal surplus available for export.[12]

Between 1974 and 1976 slightly higher priority was given to exploratory fieldwork than during the first stage of the Dovall Jaime administration, with similar attention given to work in surface geology and in seismology. Thus, the activities of geophysical and geologic teams allowed thirty new productive structures to be identified in Tabasco-Chiapas. In the same period exploratory drilling showed a decrease of 21 percent over 1971-1973 because it was concentrated only in the Tabasco-Chiapas region. Since drilling here had to be done to a greater depth than in the other Mexican oil provinces, it lengthened the process and reduced the total number of test drillings.

Parallel to onshore exploration in the southeast, in 1971 PEMEX began the first prospecting work in the region; by 1980 this area was to become the center for the country's hydrocarbon production, that is, Campeche Bay (see Figure 7.2). Marine geophysical studies (magnetometric, gravimetric, and seismological) resulted in the identification of thirty structures, leading to the drilling in 1974 of the first test well (Chac I) 80 kilometers off the coast of Isla del Carmen. The search was based on the hypothesis that the geologic structures of the Reforma-Samaria mantles extended to the continental shelf.

Because of the technical difficulties of offshore drilling and the country's lack of experience in this activity, the drilling of the Chac I well lasted until 1976 when it began to produce 952 barrels a day (BD) with the reaching of the Jurassic structures at a depth of 5,000 meters.[13] By the end of 1976 there was still insufficient information for the proven offshore reserves to be estimated. However, on the basis of previous detailed studies, it could be assumed that the richest oil formation in the whole country was to be found here.

An analysis of the reserves quantified between 1974 and 1976 indicates that the volume of new proven reserves grew considerably--by 5,477 MB; between 1971 and 1973 this figure was only 24 MB. Nevertheless, this increase was due not only to the intensification of exploratory activities but also to a change introduced in 1976 in the reserve calculation. With the new method those reserves that had previously been considered "probable" were now classified as "proven." This change in the evaluation method led to an announcement by PEMEX's new director general, Jorge Díaz Serrano, in December 1976 immediately after the government changeover. Díaz Serrano calculated that Mexico had total proven hydrocarbon reserves of 11,160 MB, distributed as follows:

Hydrocarbon Reserves	Millions of Barrels
Proven Reserves	6,572
Proven Reserves under Development[a]	2,034
Proven Secondary Reserves	2,554
Total	11,160

[a]These reserves are still to be confirmed by the drilling of new wells and the installation of development plants; they do not take into account the reserves from the Campeche continental shelf.

With this amount of reserves the R/P ratio rose to 22 years, thus recuperating the margin of safety lost in the mid-1960s. The considerable increase in hydrocarbon reserves that was announced in 1976 was closely related to the current government's global economic and international policy and contrasted with the energy-resource policy in force during the Dovalí Jaime administration. The position that hydrocarbons should primarily cover the energy requirements of the domestic market, with their exploitation and end uses regulated so that they are available for future generations, constituted the basic principle behind PEMEX activities between 1971 and 1976. Associated with this nationalist-conservationist attitude toward hydrocarbon exploitation was an extremely cautious evaluation methodology and information policy for proven and probable reserves. PEMEX management and the federal executive followed this approach after the discoveries in Tabasco-Chiapas in order to allow themselves greater flexibility in defining a future course for the oil industry and, in particular, the crude volume to be extracted, thus keeping open the possibility of surplus exports. After the oil discoveries in the southeast, attempts were made to avoid political and economic pressure from the United States, which, as a growing importer of crude oil at that time, had been affected by the radical changes in the international oil market between 1971 and 1973. For the United States the exploitation of Mexico's oil reserves and the export of the Mexican surplus to its "closest natural market" seemed to be the fundamental means of assuring crude supply and at the same time counteracting OPEC's control over oil prices. Under the circumstances there was much speculation in the United States after 1974 about the volume of Mexico's probable hydrocarbon reserves. Many official and private sources stated that the amount of these reserves was 20,000 MB, with a potential crude export capacity of 2 MBD by 1980.[14]

Because such prospects would undoubtedly have repercussions on relations between the countries at all levels, both the Mexican government and PEMEX refused to confirm this alleged reserve figure. In November 1974 it was officially announced in Mexico City that the proven reserves in Tabasco-Chiapas could reach 1,000 MB, and no figure of probable reserves was mentioned.[15] The complex political and economic implications, both domestic and international, of Mexico emerging as an important producer and exporter of crude determined the cautious attitude adopted by the Mexican government.[16]

The argument that detailed technical evaluations were required to verify the estimates left the issue of the size of the Mexican crude reserves undefined for a few years. The technical criteria prevailing in the mid-1970s in Mexico for estimating reserves reinforced this attitude. PEMEX sustained that although the characteristics of the geologic formations were known, it was not certain whether all of them would be productive. Therefore, the formations had to be verified through large-scale test drilling.[17] The position of the industry's management was reinforced internally by the opinions of a group of key technical experts. In a document made public in early 1976, these experts pointed out the danger of Mexico losing its oil self-sufficiency in the short term if new deposits were not incorporated into production.[18] They also recommended keeping crude exports to a minimum.

The attitude about reserve information began to change during the final months of the outgoing administration when the presidential candidate José López Portillo intimated that hydrocarbons might be a key element in the country's economic development. Although PEMEX did not change its stance, the ministry in charge of energy issues announced in May 1976 that the probable hydrocarbon reserves were between 30,000 and 60,000 MB.

In short, although during the first half of the Echeverría administration public information about the size of the oil reserves was subject to technical and political constraints, both surveys and test drilling from 1973 to 1976 produced extremely favorable results and excellent prospects for the industry's future planning. The policy of concentrating financial resources and exploration activities in the Tabasco-Chiapas oil province and, to a lesser degree, in Campeche Bay turned out to be highly successful in the immediate and long term because of the vastness of the discovered deposits. Although some geologists argued that it was a planning mistake to postpone detailed surveys and studies in other parts of the country with possible crude deposits, the exploration provided essential elements on which the country's oil boom was to be based from 1977 on.

In 1971 early in the Echeverría administration, PEMEX was faced with serious difficulties in making oil production expand at a rate equal to current domestic demand and the demand forecast for the next few years (nearly 7 percent per year). The biggest obstacle was the insufficient incorporation of new reserves that would compensate for those being extracted from the subsoil and provide an adequate margin of potential exploitation capacity. The disequilibrium between exploration and production was a legacy from the financial resource-allocation policies of the previous administrations, which affected the rate and the manner of crude-deposit exploitation. In effect, during the late 1960s and early 1970s crude production consisted of draining previously discovered reserves. Hence, the productive capacity of the fields that had traditionally sustained national crude production was declining, or where potential capacity was still relatively large it was difficult to increase crude production.

PEMEX management was fully aware that during the forthcoming six-year period it might be necessary to resort to importing increasing volumes of petroleum products or to undertake crude oil purchases abroad in order to supply the domestic demand.[19] The second option had been rejected by PEMEX during the late 1960s although it was perhaps less burdensome financially that the first, but either choice would put in doubt the state's efficiency as manager of the oil industry. A point had been reached where the financial constraints resulting from the lack of internal resources impeded the industry's adequate planning and reasonably balanced development, thus endangering its vertical integration and the political mandate conferred on the company at the time of nationalization in 1938.

The recovery of domestic-supply self-sufficiency and the conservation of the oil wealth for the future were the two main objectives of PEMEX's development policy for 1971-1976.[20] Both objectives related directly to the industry;s primary production, the intention being to recover the productive capacity in this area. In order to increase oil production, it was decided to give a greater thrust to exploratory activities, to widely use secondary recovery methods on the basis of injection, and to recondition those wells that had stopped producing.[21]

The need for resource conservation placed a constraint on the attainment of self-sufficiency because attempts to achieve the latter risked accelerating the extraction rate to well above the technically advised limit that would assure maximum utilization of the subsoil's content. However, the measures proposed and implied were not sufficient enough to avoid importing crude oil between 1971 and 1974. The fall of crude production in Poza Rica (the main producing center) from 1971 to 1973 greatly contributed to the crude-supply deficit.

The new deposits discovered during 1972 and 1973 in the Tabasco-Chiapas region were immediately set to work because of the closeness of the crude-transportation facilities in Coatzacoalcos, Veracruz (see Figure 7.2). If these fields had not come on line, PEMEX would have been forced to exploit the older declining production areas or, as another option, to increase the dependence on imported crude. consequently, the PEMEX investment program for 1974-1976 called for an increasing amount of financial resources to be channeled into the new Tabasco-Chiapas area in order to substantially increase its crude oil production and eliminate imports.[22] This decision implied an important switch in regional resource allocation because until this time investment in well development had been undertaken basically in the deposits known about since the expropriation of 1938, that is, Poza Rica, the southern zone and Ciudad Pemex (see Figure 7.2). Later, under favorable world-market conditions, the company decided to start producing some crude oil for export. This decision was possible in 1974 because the production from the Tabasco-Chiapas fields provided sufficient crude to cover the domestic demand. Thus, PEMEX set out to obtain the necessary foreign exchange that would allow it to import the necessary equipment, technology, processes, and other services to operate and construct new refining plants.

The possibility of increasing crude exports further caused a considerable controversy in Mexico among the higher-level oil decision makers.[23] This policy conflicted with PEMEX's nationalist-conservationist position in favor of safeguarding the reserves from the new fields through technically rational exploitation, that is, in accordance with the wells' pressure and the life span of the deposits.

The limits and scope of this nationalist-conservationist policy were determined by the president of Mexico when he set the level of exports as a function of the technically reasonable production level that could be expected from the new deposits.[24] The volume of exports gradually became a decisive factor in this production level. Between 1974 and 1976 primary production and distribution for domestic consumption and export reflected this trend. Although in 1974 exports represented 3 percent of crude and condensate production, in 1976 this proportion reached 12 percent, with an increase in production of 40 percent during this period. This increase was basically due to the exploitation of the Tabasco-Chiapas fields where nearly 60 percent of total crude production was obtained during this three-year period. However, in 1976 in deference to prevailing opinion, PEMEX management decided to limit the rate of extraction in the new fields so as to avoid surpassing the optimum safe limit.[25] Otherwise, there was a risk of reducing ultimate oil and gas recovery in situ and endangering future production capacity.

From 1970 to 1976 PEMEX went from a production deficit to national self-sufficiency in crude production and managed to overcome the imbalance between exploration and exploitation, reinforcing the vertical integration of the industry. It also began to participate in the international crude oil market where both price and demand were favorable. Technically, the exploitation policy was characterized by a deep concern for maintaining production rates that would most favor the utilization of available reserves as well as the application of secondary recovery techniques in the extensively exploited areas. Oil came from the subsoil with a high proportion of associated gas originally flared. The recovery of this gas for consumption became essential to the energy self-sufficiency goal and the efficient use and conservation of hydrocarbons as a whole.

NATURAL GAS PRODUCTION BEFORE 1977

During the 1960s there existed no policy concerning the utilization of natural gas. Because of the haste with which oil production was undertaken, no financial resources were assigned to carrying out the necessary work to harness and utilize the gas associated with the crude. The inadequate field facilities (systems for collection, compressors, regulators, and machines for desulfurization) and the absence of transport were a great obstacle to the development of a consumer gas market. Because of this negligence or oversight, 22 percent of total hydrocarbon production was wasted in 1965; in 1970 this waste rose to 26 percent.[26] The fact that production capacity exceeded that of the required facilities shows not only the magnitude of the financial restraints imposed on PEMEX's expansion programs (if they were to lead to the proper use of natural resources) but also a lack of interest in the utilization of natural gas.

Putting in motion a production-consumption chain for natural gas requires the well-planned and -coordinated execution of a series of projects. Apart from the facilities needed to collect the gas and improve its quality, a transport and distribution system is required, assuring a continuous flow from the wells to processing facilities and then to final users; otherwise, costly storage facilities are needed. The absence of these technical requirements during the early stages of natural gas development in Mexico placed serious limitations on the possibility of gas use, particularly when the oil industry was faced with financial problems.

Because natural gas is, in principle, a significant component in electricity generation, a fuel for many manufacturing activities, and a key raw material for the basic petrochemical program, the strategy adopted for natural gas use during the first three years of the 1970s aimed at satisfying domestic demand, which, it was calculated, would grow on the average of 7 percent per year.[27] The implementation of such a strategy proved far from easy.

In the early 1970s, apart from the constraints mentioned earlier, the Mexican natural gas industry had to solve a series of problems related to the availability of crude reserves that would assure an increase in the rate of gas extraction. Although some fields producing nonassociated gas were virtually exhausted, the extraction and utilization of associated gas was also dwindling because of the priority given to crude extraction. The country's proven gas reserves declined progressively, and little short of the discovery of new oil fields could be done to replace the volume extracted and mostly flared. All in all, the situation with gas reserves was similar to that of crude reserves.

The Echeverría administration considered the intensification of crude-exploration activities essential. The extraction of gas through the improved regulation of pressures within the mantles from the traditional fields, such as Poza Rica, was not considered of great importance. The exploitation of this district was secondary to the development of new reserves in other areas. Thus, the Poza Rica associated gas, which was the second most important supply in the country at the time, was to be exploited at a later date, when oil production at this traditional oil district had been exhausted.[28]

From 1974 onward the projects for natural gas utilization were closely related to crude oil output at the new fields in Chiapas-Tabasco, where a high ratio of gas to oil (1,000 CF per barrel) was found in the Cretaceous formations. In order to utilize the associated gas from this province, an integrated development strategy was designed, involving collection systems, compressors, desulfurization machines, and cryogenic plants as well as transport facilities. However, the flared gas represented a significant percentage of overall production, averaging 24 percent annually.[29]

From 1974 to 1976, the second half of the Dovall Jaime management of PEMEX, national natural gas production grew at an average of only 4 percent per year, restricting the availability of gas for both domestic consumption and exports, which were suspended in 1975. A large part of the deficit in supplying domestic gas demand, growing at 10 percent annually on the average,[30] was covered with fuel oil.[31] The substitution was feasible in the electricity subsector and in a large number of industries established along the northeastern gas pipeline (Tamaulipas-Nuevo León-Chihuahua) (see Figure 7.2).

Some of the major factors that determined the slow growth in natural gas production over this period follow:

. The exhaustion of some of the nonassociated gas deposits long exploited in the northeast of the country

- The deliberate reduction in associated gas production in Poza Rica with the aim of protecting recoverable oil reserves[32]

- The postponement of production and processing programs in some nonassociated gas deposits in the absence of gas pipelines and compression facilities. (Some already producing wells were closed, and in a number of cases new drilling was not undertaken in expectation of associated gas production in the Tabasco-Chiapas province.)[33]

The priority given to the exploitation of the Tabasco-Chiapas area produced a stagnation in nonassociated gas output, which was compensated by a rapid growth in the contribution of associated gas to total domestic gas supply. This trend was to continue during the later oil boom.

The fact that the emphasis on crude oil production heavily influenced the decision to extract associated gas indicates a serious structural fault in the gas production strategy: the lack of investment coordination in crude exploitation and in gas collection, distribution, and processing. Over several years a large part of the associated gas was flared or released into the atmosphere because of the delay in providing adequate facilities.

POLICIES FOLLOWED FROM 1977 TO 1983

In 1977 with the advent of new management in PEMEX under Diaz Serrano, a basic change occurred in oil industry policy. The belief held during the Dovali Jaime period was that the industry should cover domestic demand primarily if not exclusively. The new policy, however, was that crude exports would no longer be marginal.

The industry's development program for the forthcoming six years sustained that exports should gradually increase to 400 TBD of crude and 610 TBD of refined products by 1982. Thus, the oil production capacity had to be expanded considerably and in 1982 the industry had to be able to produce 2.25 MBD, an increase of 270 percent over 1976.[34] This target was set on the basis of a revision in available resource volumes. In effect, proven hydrocarbon reserves on which the production program for 1977-1982 was based were put at 11,200 MB, of which approximately 63 percent corresponded to crude oil condensates. With reserves of this magnitude, it was deemed feasible to reach the production target set for 1982, except that by then the R/P safety margin would have declined to only 13 years, much below the required minimum of 20 years. In view of this decline it was essential to find additional reserves. Hence, PEMEX had to expand and intensify its exploratory work.

The six-year program estimated that PEMEX's total budget would amount to $45 billion (U.S. $ at 1977 prices), of which 25 percent was to be used for new investment. Most of the investment expenditure (nearly 60 percent) would be spent on primary activity (exploration and exploitation), thus consolidating the industry's role as a producer and exporter of crude oil.[35] A large part of the investment requirement would be covered with revenue coming mainly from PEMEX's exports. Consequently, the volume of oil extracted would no longer be determined by the internal market alone but would increasingly depend on export proceeds.

Exploration

The exploration objective was to locate new areas with the aim of immediately incorporating reserves and evaluating those parts of Mexico's territory where there was the possibility of finding new accumulations. PEMEX hoped that by 1982 exploration would have revealed proven hydrocarbon reserves of 30,000 MB. With a volume of this magnitude, it was hoped to obtain a broader R/P margin, enough to satisfy the country's local and export needs for approximately the next 48 years.[36]

In order to prove reserves in the short term, the evaluation was to be concentrated in Tabasco-Chiapas; the little-explored areas of Campeche Bay, Veracruz (Cotaxtla), and Baja California; and a relatively small section of the Gulf of Mexico (the

Arenque and Barracuda fields) (see Figure 7.2). In the medium and long term, it was hoped that new reserves would be located in previously unevaluated areas such as Coahuila and Chihuahua (in the north), the central plateau, and the Sierra of Chiapas (in the southeast).[37] PEMEX decided to allocate a significant share of financial resources to exploration in the Campeche continental shelf because it was thought to be one of the largest oil provinces in the western hemisphere and that it could provide most of Mexico's fuel exports.[38]

In 1978 when the production mark for the whole six-year term was put forward to 1980, it was decided that exploratory activity should be stepped up to allow a prompt evaluation of hydrocarbon reserves. The aim was to have available by 1982 proven reserves evaluated at 42,000 MB.[39] Exploration was again meant to produce a very large number of locations in the shortest possible time, which would prove that Mexico had vast reserves and sufficient production capacity to become a major crude exporter. At the same time the industry's and the country's access to international credit would become easier because of the backing provided by the hydrocarbon deposits. Nevertheless, PEMEX had to carry out prospecting studies and confirm deposits in promising areas, including those that had been left to one side because of technical and economical difficulties associated with their recognition as deposit sites (for example, Chicontepec). PEMEX also reinforced its policy of concentrating resources in the provinces where the high productivity of wells, such as those in Reforma-Samaria and Campeche Bay, had been verified. In 1980 the exploratory targets had been more than met. Two years ahead of time, proven crude reserves of 47,224 MB had been located. Consequently, the security margin for reserves rose to 59 years, 11 more than had been forecast for 1982.[40]

These results suggested that it was no longer necessary to search for additional reserves. No great increases in crude demand were foreseen for 1980-1982, with a ceiling of 1.5 MB set for exports[41] and no changes expected in expansion trends for domestic demand. However, both SEPAFIN and PEMEX considered it unwise to reduce the intensity of exploratory work. Although at SEPAFIN the quantification of reserves was considered an essential factor for long-term energy sector planning, PEMEX did not wish to limit the prospects for increasing oil production and exports above the determined level.

The oil industry's production capacity is determined by the development of necessary exploitation facilities, transport and distribution networks, and efficient management of oil fields, but reserves nevertheless constitute an essential element in determining production capacity. In 1980 the crude oil reserves, which were estimated at 47,224 MB, provided a potential production capacity of 6.4 MBD of crude over 20 years, or a capacity of 2.7 MBD for 48 years. Thus, with proven reserves of this magnitude, it no longer seemed to be of vital importance to intensify exploration unless the potential hydrocarbon production capacity was to be gradually expanded or crude reserves of a specific density range assured.

In 1981 when the international market for oil showed signs of saturation (there was still a clear preference for light crude) PEMEX found it difficult to increase its output and, consequently, to assure a steady stream of exports. The search for mantles containing light crude was intensified. Available geologic studies seemed to indicate that these mantles could be found near the Tabasco-Chiapas fields and offshore in Campeche Sound. When the offshore Ixtoc exploratory well went out of control because of an oil spill, the existence of very large reserves of semi-light oil in this area was confirmed. Consequently, drilling efforts where concentrated in these areas, and equipment that had been used in the search for new fields in previously unexploited locations was moved to these sites. As a result, new fields in Tabasco -Chiapas were found (for example, Huimanguillo), which proved that the deepest deposits contained superlight oil. Likewise, in Campeche Sound oil was found to be less heavy than that discovered in the earlier wells.

By the end of the López Portillo administration in 1982, exploratory activity had greatly increased proven reserves, thus easily fulfilling the proposed targets. In December 1982 PEMEX estimated hydrocarbon reserves to be as follows:[42]

Reserves	Millions of Barrels
Proven	72,000
Probable	58,650
Potential	250,000

Test-drilling programs were behind schedule for a number of reasons. In the search for new deposits in the Reforma area, wells had to be drilled much deeper than calculated. Offshore drilling platforms required modifications and the setup of communication and backup systems assuring the continuous flow of supporting machinery, equipment, and materials. The complexity of the geologic formations prolonged the wells' completion. Also, adverse climatic conditions forced offshore drilling to be suspended from time to time.[43]

Despite the delay in carrying out the programs, the results of test drilling were the most spectacular in PEMEX's history, with the discovery of 21 areas and 163 fields. Of these fields, 96 were oil, and 67 were gas. Furthermore, the percentage of successful drilling was very high: 40 percent of the wells were found to be productive compared to 26 percent from 1971 to 1976, indicating the qualitative improvement of geologic, geophysical, and interpretative surveys.

The so-called southern zone (Tabasco-Chiapas and the Campeche Bay marine zone) contributed most to the reserves discovered between 1977 and 1982. The additions came fundamentally from Campeche Sound, where 77 percent of the southern zone crude reserves located by 1982 had been found. However, the global magnitude of Mexico's proven reserves continued to be open to discussion mainly because of the controversial incorporation of crude reserves from the Chicontepec zone into the totals.

Information policies about oil reserves

In October 1978 PEMEX's director general announced to the United States that reserves of great magnitude had been proven (24,318 MB of hydrocarbons more than the 1977 figures) and that most of the new reserves (10,960 MB of crude and 5,355 MBCE of gas) were located onshore in the Chicontepec region not far east of the gulf coast.[44]

The hasty process of discovering the new reserves and then announcing them reflected a clear break with the policy concerning information on Mexico's oil wealth that had been enforced by previous administrations. The discretion and caution that had characterized earlier official reserve estimates was substituted by greater "optimism." The new evaluation and information policy reflected a change in the criteria for classifying hydrocarbon resources. Two concepts for reserves appeared that PEMEX previously used only internally (but were not published until Diaz Serrano took over PEMEX)--probable and potential. The new evaluation method followed criteria used by the U.S. consulting firm De Goyler and McNaughton in its certification of the size of Mexico's reserves. The purpose of the external certification was to give PEMEX access to foreign capital markets and, thus, to improve its global financial position.

With the open-door policy concerning reserve information, Mexico gradually became an important participant in the international crude market, acquiring greater bargaining power in many other areas as well. For the United States the announcements regarding Mexico's reserves were of particular interest because they opened up the possibility that Mexico might expand its productive capacity considerably. However, there were doubts both at home and abroad about the alleged Chicontepec reserves because the complex geologic structure of this formation made its crude production both difficult and costly (see Table 7.1).

The profitability and technological feasibility of exploiting the Chicontepec reserves was a necessary condition for them to be classified as proven. Hence, PEMEX outlined a development program for the area, whereby from 800 TBD to 1,600 TBD of oil could be recovered continuously to 1992 when the whole field would go into production. The program assumed continuous drilling for 13 years until 16,000 wells were completed, an extremely ambitious goal if one considers that PEMEX had drilled fewer wells in the 40 years it had existed. Because of the technical difficulties facing the Chicontepec project, PEMEX calculated that development of this area would be more costly than

TABLE 7.1
REGIONAL DISTRIBUTION OF PROVEN CRUDE OIL AND CONDENSATE RESERVES
(in millions of barrels)

Year	Northern zone	Central zone	Chicontepec	Southern zone	Southeastern zone	Offshore
1975	431.2	1,750.0	--	1,772.1	--	--
1976	767.6	1,889.7	--	4,621.3	--	--
1977	820.8	1,886.8	--	7,720.4	--	--
1978	800.8	1,812.7	12,285.0	13,508.4	--	--
1979	689.9	1,757.5	12,260.7	18,852.1	--	--
1980	731.0	1,723.5	12,257.3	32,512.4	--	--
1981	726.9	1,605.9	12,252.1	42,413.5	--	--
1982	726.9	1,605.9	12,252.1	42,413.5	--	--
1983	658.0	1,481.0	12,241.0	963.0	9,734	32,019

Sources: PEMEX, statistics from the Coordinacin de Comercio Exterior, for internal use; PEMEX, Memoria de labores, 1975-1983, Mexico City, PEMEX, 1976-1984.

that of any other potential oil region.[45] However, had the price of crude stayed at 1979 levels ($14/barrel [U.S. $]), the expenditures for the project would not have recuperated for 14 years, but because it was believed that oil prices in the international market would continue to increase, a rapid recovery of investment was expected. The economic feasibility of the exploitation of the Chicontepec proven reserves continued to be a controversial subject in 1983, even though international crude prices were higher than at the time of the calculations and the disclosure of these reserves (1978).

In 1980 the economic viability of utilizing the Chicontepec reserves was refuted by successive reports, first from the interministerial commission composed of experts from SEPAFIN and SPP and later from SPP. Showing a reduction in the reserve figures from 17,595 MB as evaluated by PEMEX to approximately 2,690 MB,[46] both reports stated that total expenditure and investment on the development of Chicontepec would be far greater than originally estimated. Therefore, exploitation was not considered advisable despite increased international crude prices.

The apparent overestimation of oil reserves, which included Chicontepec, their public disclosure, and subsequent doubts expressed by the executive branch of the government coincided with a debate concerning crude-export levels. When compared with the López Portillo administration's economic and social development program, the export levels did not necessarily match with the PEMEX plans.[47] The high-level political critics of the feasibility of the Chicontepec project not only considered PEMEX's expansion plans overambitious and technically unnecessary, they also wanted to restrain the growing political power of the industry's director general who was emerging as the leading candidate for the office of president of the republic. However, even after Díaz Serrano's sudden forced resignation from PEMEX in July 1981, no official revision in the Chicontepec proven reserve figures was announced. Neither PEMEX nor the government felt it advisable to rectify the size of proven oil reserves because the economic and financial crisis prevented the government from endangering its access to international financial sources. The Chicontepec episode confirms that from the early 1960s on official announcements regarding hydrocarbon reserves were highly conditioned by domestic and international political factors. It is no secret that similar conditions exist in many other countries around the world. In some oil-producing and -exporting countries, no information about their oil reserves has ever been made public.

The doubts about the accuracy of PEMEX's estimated proven reserves applied to other areas than Chicontepec as well, such as Campeche Sound and Tabasco-Chiapas. In these cases, however, the doubts were of a different nature. It was calculated that proven offshore reserves could be underestimated by 20 percent. The performance of wells in Campeche Sound had been spectacular, and the percentage of successful exploitation drilling was very high, on the average of 85 percent. Proven reserves in Campeche Sound were underestimated most probably because lower net densities, corresponding to shorter drilling depths, were used for calculation purposes.[48] However, in Tabasco-Chiapas some experts sustained that proven reserves were overestimated and that it was advisable to reevaluate some fields. Here, the errors might have been related to the accelerated rate of extraction, which reduced the amount of recoverable crude. Despite these estimate uncertainties, there does not seem to be any serious doubt about the country's potential as a producer and exporter of crude oil particularly if one considers that the search for hydrocarbons has covered as yet only 15 percent of Mexico's territory.

Oil production

When Díaz Serrano became PEMEX's director general, the prospects for Mexico becoming an important world crude exporter became clear. The production targets were to be reached through an accelerated exploratory drilling program concentrated in Tabasco-Chiapas and Campeche Sound. The number of wells to be exploited was to be adjusted according to the productivity of the deposits discovered, and it was foreseen that nearly half of these deposits would be very deep, between 3,000 and 5,000 meters (the average for 1976 was 2,780 meters).[49,50] The exploitation program stressed the importance of well-managed extraction. Special care was taken in stalling secondary recovery systems because they allowed greater volume to be obtained at a relatively lower cost than drilling additional wells.

It appeared that the prospects of achieving the proposed objectives could not have been better, and just over a year after the new program was started, it was officially announced that the oil output target for 1982 would be reached in 1980. PEMEX's director general also said that because proven hydrocarbon reserves were increasing more rapidly than expected (in 1977 an additional 5,000 MB were discovered), a similar quantity could be added to the reserves each year; consequently, it would be possible to increase the rate of extraction considerably.[51]

International crude-market conditions, the ample availability of reserves, and the country's need for foreign exchange created a favorable framework for reaching the production target ahead of time. The director general assumed that once the desired level was reached, its eventual expansion could be decided easily, with a view not only toward satisfying the domestic market but also toward exporting larger volumes of crude surplus.[52]

PEMEX's management was aware that reaching the production goal would require a very large increase in investment, considerable administrative effort, an accelerated production rate, and a buildup of transport infrastructure. The objective was not only to extract additional crude but also to process greater amounts of the associated natural gas available in the new deposits. If the proper facilities for utilizing gas were not made available, there was the risk of its being wasted through flaring.

The potential production of the Reforma fields was one of the main reasons for believing that the objective could be achieved in such a short time. PEMEX considered that once this area was developed, a crude production level could be maintained around 3.5 MBD. This seemed possible in view of the fact that the industry was technically and financially prepared to manage a daily production to 25 TB in each of the Reforma wells (Bermúdez, Cactus, and Sitio Grande), although their average output at the time was only 5 TBD.[53] Another important reason was the exploitation of Campeche Sound. Because offshore drilling is very costly, it was thought worthwhile to improve operating efficiency by monitoring all drilling parameters by computer.[54] To achieve its production objectives early and in view of the continued discoveries in Campeche Sound, PEMEX augmented the number of its mobile drilling units and modified its initial development plans.[55] Oil from offshore deposits was mainly heavy, but once a light-oil mantle was located, it was expected that the production of this crude type would increase shortly thereafter.

TABLE 7.2
NATIONAL HYDROCARBON PRODUCTION, 1975-1983
(daily average)

Year	Crude Oil (BD)	Annual Increase (%)	Natural Gas (MCFD)	Annual Increase (%)
1975	716,547	--	2,154.7	--
1976	800,770	12.0	2,108.6	-2.0
1977	980,780	22.0	2,046.2	-3.0
1978	1,209,172	23.0	2,561.4	25.0
1979	1,461,176	21.0	2,916.6	14.0
1980	1,935,667	32.0	3,548.0	22.0
1981	2,312,144	19.0	4,060.8	14.0
1982	2,746,383	19.0	4,246.3	4.0
1983	2,665,540	-3.0	4,053.6	-4.0

BD = barrels per day.
MCFD = million cubic feet per day.

Source: PEMEX, Memoria de labores, 1975-1983, Mexico City, PEMEX, 1976-1984.

However, by trying to adjust oil-production targets to the growth needs of the rest of the economy, the rate of extraction would have increased more than was technically advisable, whereby smaller volumes of oil would be recovered. Calling for rational exploitation, SEPAFIN's energy commission made several proposals. These proposals simply stressed the need to keep continuous watch over the rate of crude extraction, giving the deposits periods of quiescence so as to reestablish the balance in pressure and prevent wasting the potential oil wealth.[56]

Despite these recommendations, exploitation was launched without due regard for the indicated technical criteria. In 1978 it was decided to extend the producing sections of some wells in the Reforma field in order to achieve 25 TBD per well. These new drillings were carried out with no consideration for the specific characteristics of the deposit. Furthermore, the rush to extract even further oil led to an indefinite postponement of the periods of necessary quiescence. Consequently, the deposits' response to stimulation from water injection could not be monitored properly. Under such circumstances, 18 TBD of oil were produced at some wells, contributing to a record 32 percent increase in domestic oil production during 1980 (see Table 7.2).[57]

On the basis of the most recent figures for proven reserves (45.8 BB) and particularly on the magnitude and production level of the Campeche Sound offshore deposits, Diaz Serrano informed the federal executive early in 1980 that hydrocarbon production could be increased above the 2.5 MBD forecast for 1982. Diaz Serrano insisted that by December 1980 daily production capacity for oil and liquids could reach 2.8 MBD, with the surplus crude (1.5 MBD) to be exported. By 1982 the production capacity for oil and liquids was to increase to 3.7 MBD, with exports probably reaching 2 MBD.[58]

According to Diaz Serrano, the revised target for production would accelerate the country's development, and the high oil prices prevailing in the international market would permit a considerable increase in foreign-exchange revenue from exports. Several factors seemed to indicate that Mexico could increase its installed production capacity:

- From 1977 to 1979 the exploration policy designed to substantially increase hydrocarbon reserves had produced very good results.

- In Tabasco-Chiapas a daily average of 7 TB per well was produced, at which time the target set for 1982 was brought forward to 1980.

- The production from the Campeche Sound deposits far surpassed initial expectations, and in January 1980 PEMEX extracted 315 TBD from the offshore wells. Campeche Sound thus became the most rapidly developing area in the whole of the industry's history.

- The technical feasibility of increasing production capacity was supported by the hypothesis that the potential of new deposits would be as good as that of earlier recent discoveries.

- A sufficient margin of flexibility existed to produce considerably larger volumes of crude because of the capacity of the drilling and support equipment already used, that under construction, and that still on the drawing board.[59]

- The natural gas sales agreement with the United States, which was signed in 1979, would absorb a large part of the associated gas production.

The most important factors in PEMEX's proposal to increase crude production to 3.7 MBD were as follows:

- The country had several highly interested and insistent clients. Several letters of intent had been signed by different governments for the purchase of the first 200 to 300 TBD available when the Mexican government eventually decided to accelerate production.[60]

- Because of world oil-price trends, revenue from exports would grow substantially.

- PEMEX only had to invest 32 percent more than originally planned to achieve the new targets: Drilling could be reduced because of Campeche Sound's high productivity, and with a project of this kind, Mexico could count on all the credit it needed from the international banking system.[61]

On the basis of these considerations, PEMEX suggested to the executive that more investment be dedicated to exploiting Campeche Sound because it was assumed that this area would supply nearly 90 percent of the additional crude oil production during 1980-1982. The production from Tabasco-Chiapas would only increase from 1.1 MBD to 1.3 MBD during the same period because of the steady decline in the output of some major wells. The Tabasco-Chiapas fields registering contraction in oil production were those that had been operating since 1973, that is, Cactus, Samaria, and Oxiacaque, and had accounted for the highest yields in the whole formation. The drop in production at Cactus was spectacular. In only two years its output was reduced by 39 TBD because of pressure loss in the mantle.[62]

Although PEMEX suggested increasing production and crude-export targets, various groups within the federal government opposed the proposal, supporting the earlier established ceilings placed on exports. Economic advisers to the president and SEPAFIN, among others, undertook a detailed study of the advantages of an increase in oil production and exports. The study concluded that adopting the PEMEX-sponsored program would have no significant effect on the possibilities of real economic growth because of the bottlenecks and constraints within the oil industry and the economy as a whole. Mexico's limited absorption capacity for foreign exchange suggested that additional revenue from oil sales would not be used productively. Consequently, the majority of the government's high-level economic experts thought it advisable to maintain the exports and the investment within the limits originally set for the 1980-1982 period.

The president himself resolved the dispute by deciding to maintain the June 1980 production capacity of 2.5 MBD, with a 10 percent flexibility to guarantee the domestic supply and exports of 1.5 MBD, without surpassing at any time the 2.7 MBD output limit. Therefore, from then on investment and exploitation only had to be maintained at a level that guaranteed production stability and, consequently, the fulfillment of export ceilings.

In 1981 the short-lived second international oil shock, which was related to the outbreak of the Iran-Iraq War, spent its course, and the international oil market changed abruptly. Several countries reduced their demand for Mexican crude and wanted increasing amounts of light crude (Isthmus), showing little interest in the semi-heavy crude (Maya). This change in preference by Mexico's clients affected the country's crude exploitation, and it became necessary to extract larger volumes of light crude in order to maintain Mexico's exports. Although earlier crude -export contracts were based on an equal split of the two types of Mexican crude, it was now necessary to increase the proportion of light crude to 60 percent so as not to lose clients.[63] The task was not at all easy in spite of the unilateral decision of Díaz Serrano to cut crude-export prices considerably, a decision that cost him his post. Under the new management of Rodolfo Moctezuma Cid, who was secretary of the treasury at the beginning of López Portillo's administration, it took PEMEX sometime to recover its export revenues. The difficulties had to do not only with the state of the international crude market but also with declines in domestic production. PEMEX's main problem in supplying exports, even at a 50-50 ratio, arose from the decline in production at the Tabasco-Chiapas fields: Until 1979 this production accounted for 50 percent of the light-crude output; the average decline from 1979 to 1981 was 15 percent. The fall in their output stemmed mainly from pressure loss in the area that could not be rectified by secondary recovery techniques, that is, water injection.[64]

Despite exploration and development efforts undertaken during 1981 and 1982, onshore light-crude production continued to decline, going from 1.3 MBD in May 1981 to 900 TBD in December 1982.[65] In Campeche Sound several wells were partially closed to reduce heavy-crude production because external demand had declined, and domestic processing facilities were not available. From June 1981 to December 1982 200 TBD less of heavy crude were produced on average than in May 1981 alone. Fortunately, this drop was more than compensated for by an increase in light-crude extraction, which rose to 600 TBD late in 1982.[66]

By December 1982 Tabasco-Chiapas was providing 60 percent of the country's light-crude production and the Gulf of Campeche 40 percent. The overall production of light crude rose to 1.5 MBD, its share in domestic oil supply at 55 percent, or slightly less than the target set in 1981 (59 percent). Exports of heavy crude increased because of large world price differentials between the two major crude types produced in Mexico and the subsequent reconditioning of refining facilities in many industrial countries to support the cheaper semiheavy crudes.

In brief, at the end of the 1977-1982 López Portillo term, PEMEX had more than achieved the objectives set for crude production at the beginning of the administration. However, the high priority given to reaching these targets early created serious difficulties in the nationwide coordination of projects; these difficulties, which were accompanied by the emergence of administrative and financial problems, had a serious impact on the crude deposits under exploitation. Although the definition of production levels was subject to some technical considerations, both domestic and external economic and political factors acted as serious constraints upon the oil industry's rational development, particularly in respect to exploration and exploitation activities. The extraction of crude from the subsoil became virtually inevitable because the country needed the foreign-exchange revenue from oil to increase the federal government's income, overcome the economic crisis of the mid-1970s, and set the foundations for Mexico's development. Because the rapid rate of oil production coincided with large new-reserve discoveries, little notice was taken of the need to protect the nonrenewable resources through technically efficient exploitation and the programming of all the oil industry phases so that large-scale waste of both crude and natural gas could be avoided.

Natural gas production

In 1977 a production target of 3,600 MCFD for natural gas was set for 1982, an increase of 70 percent over the output level reached in 1976. This new target was fixed so that this hydrocarbon could be used both as an industrial fuel and as a raw material in the primary petrochemical industry, where the capacity was expected to expand quickly. PEMEX management thought that reaching the new target was feasible in view of the size of the quantified proven gas reserves, which were estimated at 19.4 billion cubic feet (BCF) in December 1976.

As planned at the end of the outgoing administration, projects for natural gas production were closely linked with those for crude. Although gas reserves were located both in the north and the south of the country (41 percent and 50 percent, respectively), it was thought that most of the new gas would come from the south.[67] It was assumed that most of the crude oil production was to come from the same region and that there were easily enough domestic users for the associated gas.

The development of the Tabasco-Chiapas oil fields (Sitio Grande, Cactus, Samaria, Rio Nuevo, Iride, and Cunduacán), where a very high gas-oil ratio had been discovered (in excess of 1 thousand cubic feet [TCF] per barrel), led in 1982 to a gas production in this area of approximately 2,000 MCFD, that is, 55 percent of the total gas output forecast six years earlier.[68]

Although in the initial gas-production plans export targets were not mentioned, six months later in mid-1977 PEMEX's new director general announced the intention to export 2,000 MCFD to the United States, starting in 1979.[69] The plans to sell abroad such a large volume of gas output were based on the expected production of seven new fields in Tabasco-Chiapas, where a gas-oil ratio of 5,000:1 had been confirmed (see Giraldas, Artesa, and Copanó in Figure 7.1).[70] It was argued that because the output of associated gas would exceed domestic demand, it was essential to export the surplus, which otherwise would have to be flared.

Since 1977 various programs for collecting, treating, and transporting associated gas had been aimed at exporting this commodity. These programs included laying out field-gathering systems and expanding the desulfurizing plants (the associated gas was bitter and high in sulfhydric acid) and the cryogenic facilities for extracting liquefiable gases (methane, ethane, and so on). Simultaneously, construction of 48-inch gas pipeline was begun, connecting the fields in the southeast with those in the northeast for transporting gas to the U.S. border.

In 1978 it was decided to push the targets for crude production and gas collection forward. This decision made it important to utilize natural gas locally or export it in growing volumes. By 1980 the target for natural gas production that was forecast originally for 1982 (3,600 MCF) was reached primarily because of the contribution of associated gas from Tabasco-Chiapas, which accounted now for 60 percent of domestic production.[71]

Although gas production rose, exports to the United States were substantially lower than originally planned (294 MCFD instead of 2,000 MCFD).[72] These low exports were the result of a number of factors that related to the gas supply-demand picture on the domestic and U.S. markets and to certain aspects of the U.S.-Mexico bilateral negotiations that transcended the energy issue. Among the factors that helped define the gas-production policy, the following seem to be particularly important:

- Because no agreement was reached with the U.S. government in 1978 on Mexican gas pricing, Mexico decided to switch the gas consumption to the domestic market. It was considered advisable to substitute the fuel oil used in industry, particularly in generating electricity, by natural gas. The construction of the gas pipeline was to be continued because this line carried gas from the southeast to the large domestic gas-consuming centers, such as the Distrito Federal, Salamanca, and Monterrey.

- In 1979 it was finally agreed to sell 300 MCFD to the United States (a fraction of the volume originally forecast). It is probable that this decision was influenced by the possibility that associated gas production in Tabasco-Chiapas was not going to increase at the same rate as in 1977 and 1978 because the biggest gas deposits had already begun to loose pressure, and little could be done to compensate for the loss in the short term. Moreover, the evidence was growing that the gas-oil ratio of the offshore fields was much lower than had been estimated earlier (400 cubic feet [CF] per barrel instead of 1 TCF per barrel from a formation similar in size to that of Tabasco-Chiapas).

From 1978 to 1980 domestic gas sales grew at a much higher rate (15 percent per year) than in the previous years, the industrial and energy sectors contributing the most to the increase in consumption. Late in 1980 the demand of these sectors, to which that of the residential sector must be added, accounted for 69 percent of total gas production and 89 percent of available gas. Consequently, the margin was insufficient to increase gas exports, which in 1980 already accounted for 11 percent of the total gas available.[73]

Had the connections between the collector systems and the processing plants been completed, Mexico would have been in a position to increase its gas sales abroad. The national gas-processing capacity in cryogenic and desulfurization plants (sweeteners)) increased at a slower rate than that needed to use all the gas extracted. Furthermore, not all the pipelines or compression systems required to carry gas inland from the offshore fields were constructed.[74] While these projects were being delayed, increasing amounts of associated gas were flared. In 1980 gas flaring accounted for 22 percent (427 MCFD) of domestic gas production.

Two years later at the end of the López Portillo administration, the situation had not changed much, even though 4,246 MCF had been extracted in 1982.

Exports to the United States continued at the level established in 1979, but the expansion of local sales slowed because of a decline in the Tabasco-Chiapas gas production, the noncompletion of associated gas-recovery systems, and the onset of the economic recession.

In 1982 77 percent of the country's natural gas production was derived from the associated gas extracted from the Tabasco-Chiapas and Campeche Sound deposits.[75] In other words, from 1976 to 1982 the trend to concentrate gas production in crude-producing areas was reinforced.

The case of natural gas is a clear example of planning and coordination problems brought about by the unduly accelerated exploitation of crude deposits with a high percentage of associated gas. The incorrect evaluation of reserves[76] and the waste occasioned by the inadequate infrastructure for the collection of gas from the wells, along with the crude, and its delivery to consumer centers combined to create a situation where investment costs seemed far exceed the benefits accrued by PEMEX. The exploration targets for crude had preference over the integrated utilization of hydrocarbons as a natural resource and an energy source. The errors in quantifying the resources led to haphazard allocation of investment in transport systems, with priority given in the case of gas to exporting quantities that were marginal compared to total domestic gas production and the needs of the domestic market.

EXPLORATION AND EXPLOITATION IN RECENT YEARS

In 1982 at the beginning of the new government term, Mexico faced its most serious economic and financial crisis in many years. Economic policy followed during the oil boom had placed the hydrocarbon industry in a difficult position. On one hand, the industry was considered largely responsible for initiating the crisis, and on the other, its activities were expected to help overcome the most serious economic difficulties. Because the oil industry was the only major source of foreign exchange, the incoming administration was well aware of the importance of crude production and exports.

Hence, primary activities continued to have the highest priority in PEMEX's vertically integrated productive structure. In 1983 exploration policy was modified. The search for new fields through geologic and geophysical test-drilling studies and evaluations was slowed. Keeping in mind the earlier official proven reserve figures (72,000 MB), PEMEX decided to add new reserves only to compensate for actual hydrocarbon extractions and to keep the reserves stable.[77] This decision reflected a high R/P ratio; internal financial constraints that limited investment to top-priority areas; and the fragile equilibrium of the international oil market, where an increase in reserves would have exerted unwarranted pressure on all exporting countries. The policy regarding reserve information was directed toward supporting the equilibrium between world supply and demand in order to prevent a steep drop in crude prices.

As in 1983, exploration revealed new locations in the areas of great productive potential, and reserves increased to 72,500 MB. Furthermore, the existence of other fields offshore not yet in production was confirmed.

The country's economic stagnation and the price increases for domestic oil products jointly helped reduce the local demand for derivatives and contributed to determining the guidelines for a crude-production policy from 1983 onward. It was decided to maintain production at 2.7 MBD, maintain the export ceiling at 1.5 MBD, and concentrate extraction in the country's productive areas.[78] Offshore exploitation in Campeche would continue to compensate for the decline in the Tabasco and Chiapas deposits and to guarantee export coverage.[79]

As the decline in onshore natural gas production continued, offshore production was to be intensified in line with the expansion of the collection and transport systems. Thus, the amount of gas flared would be reduced further. Because it had been publicly acknowledged that the previous estimates of proven gas reserves were incorrect, all the operative measures were to be taken with urgency.[80] It was in natural gas production that the failures of the previous administration's hydrocarbon planning became apparent (see Table 7.3).

CONCLUSIONS AND FUTURE PROSPECTS

During the 1970s both exploration and primary hydrocarbon production went through a number of phases, from a critical shortage in the early years to boom conditions toward the end of the decade.

From 1970 to 1976 exploration and production policies followed resource-conservation criteria and were concerned primarily with providing for the domestic market's needs and assuring regulated exploitation aimed at optimal hydrocarbon recovery from the subsoil. Within these policy considerations, PEMEX was able to accelerate exploration activities, eliminate the crude and natural gas deficit, and recover self-sufficiency. In the early 1970s as a result of exploration, reserves in Tabasco-Chiapas were discovered, and foundations were established for later offshore development in Campeche Sound.

In the face of the international oil situation and the domestic production shortages, the government's decision to provide financial resources through a broad investment and operation program allowed primary production capacity, mainly for crude, to be recovered between 1974 and 1976. Thus, the foundations had been laid that permitted the subsequent administration to rapidly expand crude and gas output.

Under Dovall Jaime's management exploration and development efforts concentrated in the areas that showed the most promise for early exploitation. The results were favorable for both PEMEX and the country despite the subsequent considerable waste of associated gas. Gradually, the possibility of exporting increasing amounts of crude surpluses, which would guarantee increased foreign-exchange revenue for the state, presented itself. Nevertheless, the PEMEX board of directors maintained the cautious conservationist position, restricting the incorporation of new reserves into the category of proven ones and supporting a policy of export-oriented oil production designed only to obtain as much foreign currency as was deemed necessary to support the industry's activities.

TABLE 7.3
GAS-OIL RATIO IN TABASCO-CHIAPAS, 1975-1983

Year	Natural Gas Production in Comalcalco Cretaceous and Mesozoic Formations (MCFD)	Annual Increase (%)	Oil Production in Comalcalco Cretaceous and Mesozoic Formations (TBD)	Annual Increase (%)	Gas-Oil Ratio (CF/barrel)
1975	507.2	–	326.7	–	1,552:1
1976	633.0	25.0	451.3	28.0	1,403:1
1977	820.5	30.0	647.4	43.0	1,267:1
1978	1,205.5	47.0	868.8	34.0	1,387:1
1979	1,747.1	45.0	1,077.2	24.0	1,622:1
1980	1,915.4	10.0	998.5[a]	-7.0	1,917:1
1981	2,132.3	11.0	914.1[a]	-8.0	2,333:1
1982	2,116.6[a]	-0.7	834.3[a]	-9.0	2,537:1
1983	2,014.4[a]	-5.0	734.8[a]	-12.0	2,741:1

CF = cubic feet.
MCFD = millions of cubic feet per day.
TBD = thousands of barrels per day.
[a] These figures are for Mesozoic formations.

Sources: PEMEX, statistics from the Gerencia de Comercio Exterior, for internal use; PEMEX, Memoria de labores, 1975-1983, Mexico City, PEMEX, 1976-1984.

The election of José López Portillo as president of the republic and the nomination of Jorge Díaz Serrano as director general of PEMEX brought about radical changes in the economic and hydrocarbon policies. From this time on economic planning revolved around the oil industry, which was considered the central element for the country's economic expansion. The structure of Mexico's productive system was also to become dependent on foreign-exchange revenue from crude oil and natural gas exports. Until the 1981-1982 crisis the system practiced accelerated exploration, increasing proven reserves and producing crude to satisfy domestic demand and to allow Mexico to enter into export markets in force. Exploration was linked to the speedy quantification of additional reserves in the promising regions, to which large technical and financial resources were channeled. The caution exercised by PEMEX's previous administration in releasing information about reserve magnitude to the public was abandoned. The fear of foreign pressure on the export volumes disappeared as reserve increases assured access to international capital markets and permitted the installation of the production-capacity targets. The desired boom in production and exports led PEMEX to bring its 1982 output target forward 2+ years, and the need for additional increases in capacity was pressed upon the government. Thus, since the late 1970s both production and export volumes have been determined by the outcome of battles between diverging economic and political beliefs rather than by technical factors associated with hydrocarbon exploitation. Long before 1982 PEMEX exceeded the exploration and production targets it had set for itself in 1977. However, grave technical and other problems that accompanied reaching these targets forced the oil industry's performance. The lack of coordination between interlinked activities and closely related goals, the violation of certain basic technical norms, and the neglect of parameters fundamental to the exploitation of oil fields resulted in a policy that ignored the basic principles of nonrenewable resource conservation, all official assurances notwithstanding.

Numerous difficulties arose in exploration activities:

- Incorrect estimates were made of crude oil and gas reserves, as in the case of Chicontepec, Campeche Sound, and the Sabinas Basin.

- As a result of financial resource concentration in regions with greater short-term promise, only 15 percent of the areas with probable hydrocarbon deposits were evaluated; the target had been 65 percent. Geologic studies in sedimentary basins with long-term prospects were neglected.

- Priority was given to geologic surveys on the surface and in the subsoil over seismological studies, and a disequilibrium was created between different prospective activities, making an accurate calculation of proven and potential reserves difficult.

- Drilling was dedicated mostly to certifying oil reserves in only two provinces. As more emphasis was placed on broadening already known fields (mainly Tabasco-Chiapas and Campeche Sound) than on discovering new ones, heavy crude predominated in the proven reserves. Other activities such as refining and petrochemicals fell behind as light-crude production was neglected.

The following occurred as a result of these new priorities:

- The rapid exploitation of deposits led to their premature depletion and reduced hydrocarbon recovery from the subsoil. In the Tabasco-Chiapas fields oil production fell from the 1980 levels (see Table 7.3).

- The lack of coordination in programming and carrying out specific projects caused vast energy losses through the flaring of natural associated gas.

- Urgent expansion needs also implied large increased costs for primary activities contributing to a deterioration of PEMEX's financial situation toward the end of the López Portillo administration.

- The urgency with which the installations were developed prevented adequate coordination between the demand for materials and equipment and their domestic supply, which, in turn, led to a significant part of the earnings from crude exports being spent on equipment imports.

- This same urgency led to the unsatisfactory quality of the projects undertaken, for example, the wells that were not drilled right down to their base, restricting the adequate and timely application of secondary recovery techniques.

With the new PEMEX administration in 1982, the urgency of the problems and constraints arising from the previous oil policy had to be dealt with in the medium term. The PEMEX 1984-1988 investment program offered the framework within which the oil and natural gas industry and, consequently, exploration and primary production were to operate.

PEMEX estimated the decline in the country's future growth rate as a result of the economic crisis and the restrictive financial measures of the new federal administration would be moderate. Although domestic output and external trade were expected to recover, no substantial change in the international hydrocarbon markets was foreseen. Under these assumptions no rapid expansion was expected in domestic and world demand for hydrocarbons, and consequently, domestic hydrocarbon production would not have to expand as rapidly as it had over the previous ten years.

An exploration policy for the remainder of the 1980s was to maintain the level of reserves in the medium and long term. Exploitation's task now was to guarantee domestic supply and exports that contribute to the balance-of-payment equilibrium.

The concrete targets for 1984-1988 were set as follows:[81]

- To extract an average of 2,776 TBD of crude oil and 4,276 MCFD of gas to fulfill export commitments and assure crude supply to refineries and petrochemical complexes

- To add a minimum of 7,000 MB of total liquid hydrocarbons to the proven reserves to compensate for the crude and gas to be produced

- To export 1,560 TBD of crude and 97 MCFD of gas on the average so as to generate $87.5 million a day, assuming continued international price stability

To achieve production and export objectives, PEMEX decided to expand the hydrocarbon-production infrastructure. Most of the increase in productive capacity was to be obtained from the offshore fields. Production, compression, and stabilization platforms would be installed and pipelines laid from the offshore fields to the shore and loading zones. Gas and bitter condensates would be utilized entirely by increasing gas-sweetening capacity to 3,800 MCFD in 1984. A new natural gas-processing complex was to be developed and one of the existing complexes extended.

The guidelines and targets set for exploration and exploitation activities from 1984 to 1988 indicate that no drastic modification to the prevailing situation will take place early in the current administration. The economic, productive, and financial crisis dictated cautions and relatively austere development of the Mexican oil industry this time.

ACKNOWLEDGMENTS

The author thanks Dr. Oscar Guzmán for his assistance in preparing the final draft of this work.

NOTES

1. From 1965 to 1970 hydrocarbon production grew at an average annual rate of 4.5 percent and domestic oil and petrochemical consumption at a rate of 13 percent. See PEMEX, *Informe del director general*

de Petróleos Mexicanos, Mexico City, PEMEX, 18 March 1970, p. 12.

2. In his inauguration speech as PEMEX's new director, Antonio Dovalí Jaime announced the need to revise exploration targets and pointed out that from 1971 to 1976 an additional 976 MB had to be incorporated into the reserves each year to satisfy domestic demand, which was growing a 6.4 percent per year. See PEMEX, Informe del director general, 18 March 1971, p. 5.

3. Idem., p. 3.

4. The head office for exploration requested that technical auditing be done by a specialized firm. See PEMEX, Memoria de labores 1971, Mexico City, PEMEX, 1972, p. 8.

5. In these states hydrocarbon accumulations in Tertiary rock had already been discovered, and it was estimated that at a depth of between 4,000 to 5,000 meters Cretaceous and Jurassic accumulations of the Mesozoic era would be found.

6. The first two wells reached a depth of 3,740 meters and produced 2,500 and 2,800 BD of oil, the national average being 114 BD per well. See Zenteno, Miguel A., "Exploration and Development of the Campeche Sound and Chiapas-Tabasco Areas," paper presented at the XI World Petroleum Congress, London, 1983.

7. During 1973 three test wells were completed in Sitio Grande as well as six in Cactus and five in the north of these fields. Furthermore, the existence of deposits to the east of Samaria, Tabasco, was confirmed. See PEMEX, Informe del director general, Mexico City, PEMEX, 1974, pp. 10 and 11.

8. Late in 1973 14 wells were already producing in Reforma, Chiapas, and Samaria, Tabasco, confirming that the deposits discovered were, in effect, extraordinary, their production amounting to 71,000 BD, or 13 percent of national crude oil production. See PEMEX, Informe del director general, 18 March 1975, p. 10, and PEMEX, Memoria de labores 1973, Mexico City, PEMEX, 1974, p. 12.

9. See "Reunión de la comisión de energéticos", in Carta de México No. 18, Mexico City, Secretaría de la Presidencia, 8 January 1974, p. 4.

10. See PEMEX, Informe del director general, 18 March, 1974, p. 10.

11. See PEMEX, Informe del director general, 18 March 1975, pp. 9, 10, 16.

12. By this time crude production from the Tabasco-Chiapas fields amounted to 41 percent of domestic production. Ibid., pp. 3-6.

13. Zenteno, Miguel A., op. cit.

14. Washington Post, 18 October 1974. This figure was based on a new resource-calculation method not accepted by PEMEX.

15. Moraga, Fernando, "Los yacimientos petroleros del sureste no son de enorme magnitud," in El Universal, Mexico City, 20 October, 1974; El Universal, 3 November 1974.

16. Luis Echeverría, president of Mexico during this period, stated that the Tabasco-Chiapas deposits were extremely large, but they were not "nearly as fantastic as had been announced as part of an international maneuver to weaken oil prices." See "Ford and Mexican leader meet near border today," in The New York Times, 21 October 1974, p. 1.

17. The reserve-quantification method used by PEMEX until December 1976 took into account the existing reserves in the draining area of each of the wells, added together, which meant that estimated volumes increased with the drilling of each new productive well. This method was very safe in that it made it impossible to overestimate reserves, but it was definitely also a conservative measurement.

18. Isguanzo, Francisco, "Recursos energéticos de México y programas de exploración," in IMIQ, Mexico City, IMIQ, January 1976, pp. 4-8.

19. For more details, see Chapter 11, "Foreign Trade."

20. See PEMEX, Informe del director general, 18 March 1971, pp. 1-4.

21. Idem.

22. See "Reunión de la comisión de energéticos," op. cit., pp. 4 and 5.

23. Declarations in the past came from the minister of SEPANAL in Excélsior, 28 July 1973; President Luis Echeverría in Excélsior, 25 January 1974; and PEMEX's director, "900 barriles de petróleo al mes exportará nuestro país a E. U. la semana próxima,", in El Nacional, 17 September 1974.

24. In the Tabasco-Chiapas province there were wells that could have produced an average in excess of 12 TBD. However, PEMEX's adviser, who was also PEMEX's assistant director of primary production, recommended caution and a production of no more than 6 TBD in these wells. Thus, the overall average per well in this area did not exceed 5.5 TBD. The pressure at the sill was constantly under observation so as to avoid overexploitation. Furthermore, production at the main producing field (Sitio Grande) had to be reduced considerably, granting it a period of quiescence before its capacity was measured again. (This information was gathered from interviews with technical personnel working at PEMEX at the time.)

25. The production growth rate in Tabasco-Chiapas was 170.4 percent in 1974, 70.2 percent in 1975, and only 37.0 percent in 1976. See PEMEX, Memoria de labores, 1973-1976, Mexico City, PEMEX, 1974-1977, statistical appendix.

26. This figure was obtained by substracting available volume (in general consumption, domestic sales, and exports) from total production. See PEMEX, Memoria de labores, 1965-1970, Mexico City, PEMEX, 1966-1971, statistical appendix.

27. Ibid., 1969, 1970, and 1971, statistical appendix.

28. PEMEX, Informe del director general, 18 March 1972, pp. 11-13.

29. Based on PEMEX, Memoria de labores, 1974-1976, Mexico City, PEMEX, 1975-1977, statistical appendix.

30. The deficit, or unsatisfied national gas demand, is the amount of gas that theoretically would have been necessary to satisfy the oil industry's internal requirements as well as sales. These calculations were done by the División de Planeación de Petroquímica (Petrochemical Planning Division) of IMP. See IMP, Plan de desarrollo de la industria petrolera y petroquímica básica, Vol. 5, Mexico City, IMP, 1975.

31. This phenomenon was reflected in the fact that fuel oil consumption grew more rapidly than gas consumption. The share of gas in total consumption went from 66 percent in 1971 to 55 percent in 1976, and fuel oil became increasingly important. See PEMEX,

Anuario estadistico, 1982, Mexico City, PEMEX, 1983, pp. 94 and 95.

32. Associated natural gas production in Poza Rica declined at an average rate of 10 percent from 1970 to 1976. See PEMEX, Memoria de labores, 1970-1976, Mexico City, PEMEX, 1971-1977; PEMEX, Anuario estadistico, 1983, Mexico City, PEMEX, 1984, p. 43.

33. During this time approximately 25 percent of the processing capacity for natural gas in cryogenic and absorption plants was idle because not enough collection dumps and compressor and gas-sweetening complexes had been installed. See IMP, op. cit.

34. See PEMEX, "Programa de inversiones, 1977-1982," in El Mercado de Valores, Mexico City, NAFINSA, 17 January 1977, pp. 54 and 55.

35. Ibid., p. 30.

36. Idem.

37. Alvarez Jerzayn, León, "Some aspects of exploration planning for oil and natural gas in Mexico," in PEMEX, Technicians and records of the oil exploration, Mexico City, PEMEX, 9 November 1979, pp. 10-12.

38. PEMEX, Informe del director general, Mexico City, PEMEX, 18 March 1977.

39. Official information in El Economista Mexicano, Vol. XII, 21 April 1978, p. 6.

40. PEMEX, Anuario estadistico, 1983, Mexico City, PEMEX, 1984, p. 29.

41. SEPAFIN and STCE, "Programa de energia: Metas a 1990 y proyecciones al año 2000", in Energéticos: Boletin informativo del sector energético, Year 4, No. 11, Mexico City, SEPAFIN and STCE, November 1980, p. 12.

42. PEMEX, Memoria de labores, 1982, Mexico City, PEMEX, 1983, p. 4.

43. Ibid., 1977 to 1982.

44. The announcement was made at the annual meeting of the American Oil Institute in Chicago.

45. It was estimated that expenditure plus investment would amount to $8.7 million (U.S. $) at 1978 prices. See "Mexico" (supplement), in The Financial Times Survey, 20 June 1979.

46. The interministerial commission study proved that the Chicontepec formation had fewer reserves than originally estimated by PEMEX. The mantle's net den-

sity was found to be less than that described by the company. The original figures for porosity, permeability, and water saturation were neither reliable nor representative. Furthermore, in a fair number of wells it was noted that oil came from contact points between the shale and sandstone, the intercalated shale considerably reducing net density. In light of these factors the Chicontepec proven reserves were estimated at 2,691 MB, with a 5 percent recovery factor without resorting to injection and cracking techniques; 5,382 MB, with a recovery factor of 10 percent; and 8,072.9 MB if recovery reached 15 percent. However, because these figures were not final, detailed studies of recoverable reserves were recommended with the aid of additional test drilling. See Comisión Intersecretarial SEPAFIN-PEMEX-SPP, Las reservas de la formación Chicontepec, Mexico City, SPP, May 1980, pp. 99 and 109.

47. Cp. Part 3, chapters 16 and 17.

48. The technicians assumed that deeper drilling was dangerous because of the highly permeable formation. Additionally, crude was under very high pressure and if not properly controlled could provoke a situation similar to that occurring with the test well Ixtoc I, which spilled the oil. This information was gathered from direct interviews.

49. "México: Plan sexenal de desarrollo petrolero," in Petróleo Internacional, Vol. 35, No. 1, Mexico City, January 1977, pp. 28-34.

50. PEMEX, Anuario estadístico, 1983, Mexico City, PEMEX, 1984, p. 33.

51. Oil Daily, 29 March 1978, p. 25.

52. PEMEX, Informe del director general, 18 March 1978, p. 14.

53. See Díaz Serrano, Jorge, "We are ready to handle 25,000 barrels per day", in Oil & Gas Journal, 5 June 1978, p. 68.

54. See Petróleo Internacional, Mexico City, January 1978, p. 54.

55. See PEMEX, Informe del director general, 18 March 1978, pp. 30 and 31.

56. The most important of the SEPAFIN proposals suggested that before deposit exploitation began, development and drilling maneuvers should continue until the necessary information to undertake optimum ex-

ploitation was made available. SEPAFIN also emphasized the need to modify--and sometimes even suspend--the exploitation of deposits periodically or delay the commencement date in order to allow time for the production-stimulation techniques to be applied.

57. This information was gathered during interviews with oil engineers who collaborated with Díaz Serrano during his management of PEMEX.

58. Oficina de Asesores de la Presidencia, Ultima versión sobre la plataforma de producción y exportación de PEMEX (internal document; mimeograph), Mexico City, 1980, pp. 4 and 5.

59. Ibid., p. 6.

60. Business Week, New York, 11 February 1980, p. 36.

61. Oficina de Asesores de la Presidencia, op. cit., p. 6.

62. This information was gathered from interviews with PEMEX personnel.

63. This information was gathered from direct interviews with PEMEX technical personnel.

64. These statistics were elaborated by the Office of Deputy Director of Primary Production at PEMEX, 1983.

65. Idem.

66. Idem.

67. PEMEX, Memoria de labores, 1977, Mexico City, PEMEX, 1978, p. 77.

68. This information was gathered from direct interviews.

69. See "Nuevas formaciones aumentan el potencial petrolífero del sureste de México," in Energéticos: Boletín informativo del sector energético, Year I, No. 3, Mexico City, SEPAFIN, November 1977, p. 3.

70. PEMEX, Generalidades del proyecto de construcción del gasoducto Cactus-Reynosa (mimeograph), Mexico City, PEMEX, July 1977, pp. 1-3.

71. PEMEX, Anuario estadístico, 1983, Mexico City, PEMEX, 1984, pp. 44 and 45.

72. Ibid., p. 116.

73. PEMEX, Memoria de labores, 1978-1980, Mexico City, PEMEX, 1979-1981.

74. PEMEX, Informe del director general, 18 March, 1983, p. 3.

75. PEMEX, Anuario estadistico, 1983, Mexico City, PEMEX, 1984, pp. 44 and 45.

76. In 1979 it was estimated that 20 percent of the country's proven gas reserves were located in the northern zone. Most of them were in Sabinas Basin, Coahuila, classified as nonassociated gas. However, the formation turned out to be very complex geologically, and the well's productivity was very poor. After three months of operation production began to decline abruptly, making it necessary to reevaluate the area's proven reserves. In 1983 the reserve figure was adjusted sharply downward. See PEMEX, Memoria de labores, 1983, Mexico City, PEMEX, 1984, p. 64; information obtained during interviews with PEMEX technical staff.

77. PEMEX, Memoria de labores 1983, Mexico City, PEMEX, 1984, p. 1.

78. PEMEX, Informe del director general, Mexico City, PEMEX, 18 March 1983, p. 18.

79. PEMEX, Memoria de labores 1983, Mexico City, PEMEX, 1984, p. 5.

80. PEMEX's director general declared late in August 1983 that "currently our endowment of gas is no where near as abundant as we had assumed earlier." See Espinosa, Maria de Jesús, "No contamos con las enormes reservas de gas que se estimaban: Mario Ramón Beteta," in El Dia, 30 August 1983.

81. PEMEX, Aspectos relevantes del plan 1984-1988, Mexico City, PEMEX, 1984, pp. 3 and 4.

8

The Refining Industry

*Oscar M. Guzmán
and Michele Snoeck*

The first refineries were installed in Mexico early in this century when the oil industry was still in the hands of foreign companies.[1] With the oil industry nationalization in 1938, refining activities were affected by the decision to adapt the level of production to domestic demand and to utilize this energy source to support economic development and industrialization efforts.

Planning has been an important factor in the refining industry's development since nationalization. In contrast with other PEMEX's areas the refining programs have usually transcended the six-year government terms, and projects to expand and modify the system have been carried out, although somewhat behind schedule. The global refining policy was aimed at broadening production capacity at a rate dictated by local demand. A low-price policy encouraged petroleum product consumption by diverse consumer sectors. On several occasions this price policy was a hindrance to investment in expanding refining capacity, but it has also stimulated accelerated and sometimes excessive growth in the consumption of derivatives, consequently requiring additional investment to extend installed capacity. It was not until the early 1980s that attempts were made to rationalize demand for oil products through modifications to price policy, eventually allowing a reduction in refining expansion requirements.

Throughout the 1970s an expansion policy for refining facilities was maintained. Although most of the oil-producing countries and enterprises leaned toward a reduction in primary-distillation capacity, particularly after the late 1970s when a worldwide overcapacity appeared, Mexico raised its crude and gas liquid-processing capacity from 996 TBD in 1976 to 1.3 MBD in 1983. It then became the thirteenth most important country in the world regarding refining capacity and the first, together with Brazil, in Latin America.[2]

This chapter provides an analysis of refining policies and their impact on the oil industry's development. The first part presents the most important measures from the time of oil industry nationalization until the mid-1970s. It also covers the problems involved in the steady expansion of the refining system. The second part discusses the policies followed during the oil boom (1976-1980) and the modifications to these policies made as a result of the country's economic and financial crisis in 1981-1982. Other factors influencing the industry's progress and its problems are also briefly analyzed. The final part offers the conclusions derived from the analysis along with the industry's future development prospects.

REFINING POLICY UNTIL THE MID-1970s

Mexico's main objective in nationalizing the oil industry in 1938 was to achieve energy self-sufficiency and to aid industrialization through low energy prices. Because the oil industry's main aim had previously been the extraction of crude for export, the new objective would require a change in the industry's structure, thus allowing it to satisfy the domestic demand for petroleum products. In 1938 the distances separating centers of supply and demand represented a serious problem because 89 percent of the refining capacity was concentrated in the Gulf of Mexico's coastal areas, and 55 percent of the demand came from the country's central and northern zones. The refining system was particularly inefficient, the six refiner-les in operation were old and obsolete, and primary distillation was basically the only process used.[3]

With the aim of adjusting oil production to demand requirements, a series of corrective measures was adopted that later would become part of overall refining policies. These measures, defined during the year immediately following nationalization, included the location of new refineries in such a way as to achieve geographic equilibrium between the production and consumer centers, the expansion of refining capacity, the modification of refinery productivity through the introduction of new processes such as oil-cracking and viscosity-reduction facilities, the construction of pipelines for crude and products, and the development of transport systems.[4] These measures were aimed at improving product quality and increasing the production of light and intermediate products that were increasingly in demand. With the expansion and modification undergone after nationalization, refining capacity evolved rapidly.[5] From 1938 to the mid-1960s PEMEX's primary-distillation capacity for crude and liquids rose from 102 TBD to 439 TBD.[6] Even more significant than the primary refining expansion was the tenfold increase in cracking and viscosity-reduction capacity, giving rise to improvements in yield for distillates as opposed to residual products. Consequently, during this period liquefied gas and light- and middle-distillate production grew rapidly, at 29 percent and 7.5 percent per year, respectively. Heavy-product growth was much lower, registering only a 2.5 percent growth in fuel oil.

From 1938 to 1965 the refining expansion process came up against several problems:

- Consistent with the oil industry's objective to aid the country's economic development, the low-price policy in oil-product sales facilitated the installation of new industries within the framework of an import-substitution strategy and the extension of the transportation system. Consequently, although the foundations were laid for the country's later economic development, a large domestic market demanded a constant increase in oil production. At the same time, the fixed prices maintained over long periods limited PEMEX's own revenue, which made investment financing difficult. During certain periods, particularly from 1954 to 1958, the rate at which the refining industry developed and modernized had to be slowed. The delay in the work program implied that over this period petroleum product imports had to be increased.

- Not only did domestic oil demand grow very quickly, but is also was concentrated in light and middle distillates (gasoline, kerosene, and diesel). Despite the expansion and consequent growth in production, distillate supply was still insufficient to satisfy consumption. The exports of gasoline and diesel surpluses were gradually reduced until they eventually disappeared after the early 1950s. Meanwhile, fuel oil exports grew.

- Despite the improvement in the location of the new installed capacity, it was still a long way from some consumer centers. This location problem, together with a weak transport infrastructure, made it necessary for the western Pacific states and the northern zone to resort to importing petroleum products from the United States.[7]

In the late 1960s a significant change occurred in the oil industry. From 1966 onward crude exports were suspended and petroleum product imports began to increase. By 1970 the imports amounted to more than 10 percent of the apparent domestic consumption of refined products. Concurrently, the nominal refining capacity rose by 150 TBD but was still not sufficient to keep up with the growth in demand. Although the refining project at Mazatlán was canceled, essentially for political reasons, the deterioration in PEMEX's financial situation generally hindered its expansion programs. However, although in 1970 domestic crude production was insufficient to meet refining requirements, the idea of importing crude (particularly light crude, which gives a better yield than other relatively high-consumption products) was rejected by PEMEX's administration.[8]

Although during this period exports of heavy petroleum products still compensated for the oil that had to be imported, it became increasingly difficult for the country to achieve refining self-sufficiency and stay that way when the economy had become heavily dependent on petroleum derivatives.[9] Mexico needed to increase production more than 8 percent per year, with proportionately higher rates for gasoline, jet fuel, and other high-quality products. In 1970 PEMEX announced a development program aimed fundamentally at improving crude utilization in order to make production, both in quantity and in quality, equal to demand.[10] Consequently, particular emphasis was placed on reprocessing residual oil to obtain additional amounts of those products that were in relatively greater demand and whose value in the international market was high. Residual oil would provide the fuel for certain industries mainly to generate electricity.[11]

The program forecast a 175 TBD increase in nominal primary-distillation capacity and proposed three different types of activities: (1) the addition of small-scale equipment to already existing facilities, involving moderate investment, in order to make use of marginal capacity; (2) the construction of new facilities at existing refineries using efficient designs; and (3) the construction of a new refining complex at Tula, Hidalgo.

The Tula refinery was built in response to the central zone's increased demand for petroleum products, which by 1970 represented 30 percent of global domestic demand. Traditionally, this zone received its supply from Azcapotzalco, a refinery located in the outskirts of Mexico City. Moreover, because of the inconvenience of maintaining and expanding a refinery situated in the country's main urban zone, it was decided to convert Azcapotzalco into a product supply center.[12] The decision to locate the refinery at Tula was also motivated by CFE's decision to install a thermoelectric complex there with a fuel oil consumption of 32 TBD.

Tula was to be the first refinery built since the late 1940s. It was composed of a complex of integrated plants so as to take advantage of the economies of scale and to increase conversion capacity of residual oil to light products. Therefore, apart from a combined plant for atmospheric vacuum distillation with a capacity of 150 TBD, the refinery included catalytic-cracking and viscosity-reduction facilities, each with a 40 TBD capacity.

The refining programa presented in late 1970 was reconfirmed two years later with very few modifications.[13] It formed part of a long-term plan that went beyond the six-year government term. It included projects for three refineries to be built during the 1970s.[14]

During the first three years of the 1970-1976 term, the refining activities carried out followed the established program, although efforts were somewhat behind schedule. The Tula refinery, which initially was supposed to start operations in the early 1970s, came on line in 1972. The following year the combined atmospheric and vacuum-distillation plant at Salamanca was completed. It had a capacity of 110 TBD, which meant a 20 percent increase in total primary -distillation capacity. Also, some of the proposed modifications to, and the expansion of, refineries in operation were undertaken at Minatitlán and Ciudad Madero. With only moderate investment processing capacity was increased in the short term to the maximum technical limit. With an awareness of the projects' lead time, it became necessary to go ahead and design the two new refineries at Cadereyta, Nuevo León, in order to cover supply for the industrial complex at Monterrey, and at Salina Cruz, Oaxaca, to provide a solution to the long-standing problem of petroleum product supply to the Pacific coast. The first stage in the construction of these refineries involved only a diluted fuel oil separating facility, with a 100 TBD processing capacity at Cadereyta and 150 TBD at Salina Cruz.

Progress was made under difficult circumstances for the refining industry in particular and the oil industry in general. Late in 1971 when domestic crude supplies became insufficient, the new PEMEX administration decided to import crude oil instead of distillates, hoping to take advantage of the refining plants' marginal capacity. The substitution of distillate imports with crude meant savings in excess of 30 million pesos in 1972.[15] However, the amount of crude that had to be imported to feed the country's refineries gradually increased as national production began to fall behind. Thus, PEMEX's crude and petroleum product imports rose steeply from 9 MB in 1970 to 48 MB in 1973, causing a critical disequilibrium in its trade balance.

The backlog in the oil industry's production over these years, stemming fundamentally from PEMEX's financial constraints, became critical in 1973 when international crude and derivative prices took an upward turn. For PEMEX this turn meant that the value of its imports tripled from 1972 to 1973. These conditions led PEMEX to restructure its domestic sales prices late in 1973. The prospect of additional income, together with the ready availability of crude as a result of the newly discovered fields in the southeast, made it possible for PEMEX to design a new investment program aimed at recuperating domestic self-sufficiency in oil. Therefore, although during the first three years of the government administration, the amount of 1.7 billion pesos was invested in refineries, the new program, which included auxiliary services and pipelines, contemplated an investment of 27 billion pesos for the period from 1974 to 1976, which represented 15.6 percent of PEMEX's overall investment.[16]

In general terms the new refining program followed the same lines of the previous one, but economic resources were much less restricted than before. Once again the need to step up secondary processing capacity was stressed. Production had to be adapted to demand requirements and the quality of products improved to comply with stricter national standards. The program planned to increase capacity, with particular attention to the following processes: hydrodesulfurization and catalytic naphthareforming, middle-distillate hydrodesulfurization, and residual oil processing.[17]

The increased availability of economic resources for investment later in the Dovall Jaime administration made it possible to activate the refining development plan. In 1975 alone the amount of 3 billion pesos was assigned to investment, which is equivalent to the total sum invested from 1970 to 1974.[18] These resources were channeled predominantly into the Tula refinery, with the aim of eventually eliminating gaso-

TABLE 8.1
REFINING PROGRAMS: COMPARISON BETWEEN GOALS AND RESULTS, 1970-1983 (TBD)

Program	1970 actual	1974 actual	1976 target[a]	1976 actual	1977 actual	1982 target[b]	1982 actual	1983 actual
Atmospheric Distillation[c]	533	668	935	865	865	1,670	1,270	1,300
Vacuum Distillation	237	282	382	382	382	794	594	594
Viscosity Reduction	28	28	--	28	69	69	69	69
Catalytic Cracking	122	140	217	180	208	377	328	328
Naphtha and Gasoline Hydrodesulfurization	47	47	142	47	83	266	194	194
Middle Distillate Hydrodesulfurization	73	72	147	72	122	372	272	272
Catalytic Naphtha and Gasoline Reforming	35	35	134	35	65	191	105	105

TBD = thousand barrels per day.
[a]This target was set in 1974 for 1976.
[b]This target was set in 1977 for 1982.
[c]This category does not include fractionation of gas liquids.

Sources: PEMEX, Memoria de labores, 1970, 1983, Mexico City, PEMEX, 1971-1984; President's Office, Carta de Mxico, Mexico City, President's Office, 8 February 1974; "Duplicarn capacidad de refinacin," in Petrleo Internacional, Mexico City, June 1977; and Lara Sosa, Hctor, "Plan sexenal de Petrleos Mexicanos en refinacin," in IMIQ, Mexico City, March-April 1977.

line and diesel imports and starting to export surpluses. Construction of the refinery represented a total investment of around 9 billion pesos. Basic engineering for catalytic-cracking and reforming facilities was contracted abroad. The rest of the basic engineering, and construction and operation technology was undertaken by local contractors.[19]

During the last year of the 1970-1976 government term, primary-distillation capacity for crude increased to 865 TBD, which was over 90 percent of the target established in the 1974 program. The refining system's expansion was accomplished essentially because of the completion of the combined atmospheric and vacuum-distillation complex at Tula. When this plant came on line late in 1976 together with a catalytic-cracking facility, Mexico was able to suspend crude refining abroad, satisfy gasoline and diesel consumption, and substantially reduce fuel oil imports.

However, because of unfinished work at the other facilities at Tula, among other problems, the installation of operating capacity for several secondary processes (particularly product treatment plants) was behind schedule (see Table 8.1). Consequently, product yield underwent no significant change in the 1970-1976 government term, although there was a small increase in some of the light fuels.[20] The increase in light fuels was a result of additional amounts of gas oil and residual oil being converted to lighter products and of lighter crude being processed from the new deposits in the southeast. In addition, larger quantities of gas liquids were obtained from cryogenic and absorption facilities. Progress was also made in improving product quality: The production of special low-sulfur diesel increased, and in 1973 a high-octane, lead-free gasoline known as *Extra* came on the market.

Thus, in spite of the fact that the refining industry went through a difficult period during the 1970-1976 government term, the problems were gradually overcome by channeling considerable amounts of money into investments. Nonetheless, while oil production grew at an annual rate of 7 percent, it was insufficient to cover domestic demand, which increased on the average by more than 10 percent per year. Consequently, the quantities of petroleum products imported by PEMEX and private companies grew to the point where they amounted to more than 10 percent of the country's apparent consumption. Also, exports, which in 1970 were made up exclusively of heavy products, gradually diminished and by 1976 represented less than 1 percent of total production. Still, the refining industry's immediate prospects were favorable because Tula was to start operating at full capacity a year later. Even the long-term outlook was encouraging. Works at the new Salina Cruz and Cadereyta refineries continued and when completed would raise installed crude processing capacity by 400 TBD, thus guaranteeing national distillate self-sufficiency until 1982.[21]

To summarize, from the time of oil nationalization until just before Mexico's oil boom, extensive restructuring and expansion were undertaken in the refining system to accomplish and subsequently maintain national oil self-sufficiency. The growth in demand and PEMEX's financial problems were the main factors that forced the country during certain periods to increasingly rely on the international oil market. The limitations inherent in the oil industry itself had less to do with this situation than did the industrialization strategy based on import substitution, whereby local industry and transport sectors were supplied with low-priced hydrocarbon derivatives.

Over this period refining policy stressed the need to raise the capacity of residual oil that was converted to light products. Although the achievements in this area helped reduce oil imports, they were insufficient to counteract PEMEX's particular production structure, which was characterized by a surplus of heavy products and a deficit in light and middle distillates and liquefied gas. Early in the 1970s domestic production was inadequate for a much wider range of petroleum products because the refining system had become saturated. Even the modernization and expansion of existing refineries was insufficient to cope with the demand. However, the reason for this situation was not a PEMEX's lack of foresight since new refineries were already under development (in various stages). The real problem lay in financial investment constraints.

REFINING POLICIES FROM 1977 TO 1983

With the government changeover in December 1976, crude-production policy was directed toward exports to obtain the foreign exchange needed to finance the country's economic and social expansion. The outlook for future development in the refining industry improved because the foreign exchange earned from international crude sales provided the necessary resources to invest in refining capacity expansion. Since the previous six-year term, PEMEX had established a long-term development plan for this area.[22] However, it was the new 51.4 billion peso investment program for 1977-1982, involving 16 percent of PEMEX's overall investment, that made this plan and such expansion feasible.[23] The target established for 1982 was to double the primary crude distilling capacity installed in 1976 and reach 1.67 MBD. For 1986 the target was 2 MBD.

Complying with PEMEX's policy of integrating large-capacity plants into a small number of refining complexes, PEMEX's six-year program (1977-1982) extended the main projects within three refineries over several stages. Therefore, over the six-year period the first two phases of the Salina Cruz refinery (170 TBD and 200 TBD, respectively), the first stage of the Cadereyta plant (235 TBD), and Tula's second stage (200 TBD) would come on line. Furthermore, the third phase of the Salina Cruz plant and Cadereyta's second phase would also begin operations, each adding 200 TBD of primary crude distilling capacity. An increase in refining capacity was planned, taking into account the decision to make use of large exportable surpluses of products with a high commercial value, such as gasoline and diesel. A target of 212 TBD was established for the last year of the government term, utilizing 13 percent of the available refining capacity for this purpose.

The expansion program forecast that the heavy increase in natural gas production would allow large volumes of fuel oil to be substituted. The yield of fuel oil would have to be reduced in order to raise that of gasolines and middle distillates. Particular emphasis was placed on installing facilities to convert residual oil into distillates. The vacuum-distillation capacity was to be increased 108 percent and catalytic-cracking capacity 153 percent. As in the past, efforts were made to improve product quality, although this time with the idea of competing in the international market. Therefore, it was planned to increase naphtha and middle-distillate desulfurization and gasoline reforming more than 400 percent.

Despite a heavy increase in the demand for petroleum products, in 1977 when the first stage of the Tula project was completed and the remaining facilities began operations, Mexico became practically self-sufficient in light and middle distillates. However, this respite for the refining industry was brief. The reactivation of the economy after the 1976 crisis, together with a drop in real terms in domestic oil prices, encouraged excessive consumption of these products.

The main extension to primary-distillation and secondary processing facilities took place from 1979 to 1981 when the first stages of the Cadereyta and Salina Cruz refineries were completed. These two refineries were planned in the early 1970s and construction began around 1974. However, during the following two years PEMEX gave priority to the completion of the Tula refinery and channeled most of its resources into this effort. When the new government came into office in 1976, Salina Cruz and Cadereyta were again given priority, and the refineries came on line during 1979, allowing the six-year program to be fulfilled almost on schedule. Thus, although certain financial constraints hindered the projects initially, the main cause of delay seems to have been the complexity of the customs formalities involved in requesting and purchasing materials and equipment from abroad, along with certain coordination difficulties between PEMEX, IMP, and domestic manufacturers.[24]

In compliance with PEMEX's policy to situate refineries close to consumer centers to facilitate distribution, the Cadereyta refinery (Nuevo León) was designed to directly supply the north of the country, particularly the Monterrey industrial zone, which is one of Mexico's largest.[25] Cadereyta marked a significant change in the criteria for selecting plant size, its normal primary-distillation capacity (235 TBD) equivalent to 1+ times that of Tula and almost 2+

times that of Azcapotzalco. Bringing the different facilities on line was spread over the three-year period from 1979 to 1981 and represented a total investment of 12 billion pesos. In the first two years the following facilities began operations: primary and secondary distillation (100 TBD and 62 TBD, respectively), combined distillation (135 TBD), and catalytic cracking (40 TBD). In 1981 additional facilities, including a naphtha reformer and a middle-distillate hydrodesulfurization facility, were completed. The refinery supplied crude from Ciudad Madero through pipelines that previously were used to carry diluted fuel oil that had been separated in the old distillation towers at Cadereyta.

In 1979 the refinery was hampered by raw material supply problems and by facilities that were only partially operational. In 1981 its production amounted to 68 MB, representing 16 percent of Mexico's total oil production. 90 percent of total Cadereyta refinery's production was divided equally between gasoline, diesel, and fuel oil.

The Salina Cruz refinery in Oaxaca was the only one to be installed on the Pacific coast. It was built to guarantee energy supply to this heavily developing area.[26] Although Salina Cruz had less primary- and vacuum-distilling capacity than Cadereyta--170 and 75 TBD, respectively--the two refineries included the same type of facilities for catalytic cracking, gasoline and middle-distillate treatment, and power generation, which meant that engineering, lead times, and equipment costs could be economized considerably. Cadereyta and Salina Cruz were not the only cases of refinery construction based on twin plants since such efforts were one of PEMEX's long-term planning goals for refining development. One of PEMEX's intentions has been to distribute the required capacity for each type of process into similar modules, thereby facilitating its installation in the different refining centers.[27]

In 1981 refining production at Salina Cruz was 48 MB, that is, 11 percent of total oil production. With the Salina Cruz plant in operation, pressure was taken off the Minatitlán refinery in Veracruz. Prior to this change the Minatitlán refinery supplied the Pacific coast but had run into distribution problems, particularly in the case of fuel oil, which is difficult to transport.

With operations starting at all the facilities planned for the first stage of the Cadereyta and Salina Cruz refineries, from 1978 to 1981 total oil production grew quickly, at an annual rate of 13 percent, which was higher than apparent consumption (9 percent). Consequently, an important change occurred in foreign oil trade. Although in 1979 PEMEX's import volume was three times that of exports, in 1980 the situation was inverted. However, growth in demand occurred along with a modification in the structure of demand, which did not coincide with the rate at which supplies increased. In effect, from 1978 to 1981 gasoline and liquefied gas consumption rose sharply, whereas fuel oil demand increased at a much slower rate. The participation of these products in overall oil supply remained virtually the same, with the exception of the liquefied gas supply, which increased slightly. Although the disequilibrium between supply and demand was not a serious problem in the short run --witness the favorable results in the commercial balance for these products between 1980 and 1981--the situation would have become critical in the medium term if this trend had continued. Many different factors combined to create this imbalance, and at the same time the policies adopted to counteract them did very little to change the situation.

At the time the Cadereyta and Salina Cruz refineries started up, a change occurred in the composition of crude production, and refining policy was influenced by the consequent modification of expected transformation yields. From 1979 onward the use of heavy Maya crude implied increased density in the processed crude mixture. Product yields were, therefore, modified, and proportionately less light crude was obtained, which did not coincide with the new consumption pattern. Although there was some success in increasing the amount of Maya crude in the mixtures exported by PEMEX, the preference for light crude in the international market made it necessary to increase domestic heavy-crude processing.

PEMEX's short term policy designed to confront the situation, later confirmed in the 1980 PE, consisted of increasing refinery crude load to cover domestic light-crude consumption.[28] Both PEMEX and SEPAFIN felt that the consequent increase in fuel oil production should be used locally. PEMEX management continued to encourage natural gas exports, and domestic consumption of fuel oil surpluses was intended to allow large quantities of natural gas to be freed for sale abroad. SEPAFIN considered the exportation of fuel oil inadvisable because of its high-sulfur content, which meant a lower market value or heavy investment in desulfurization facilities. Therefore, contrary to the measures proposed in the six-year program, natural gas was to be substituted by fuel oil, mainly for electricity generation and for refining.

The initial optimism regarding heavy-crude processing did not last.[29] From 1981 onward the heavier load placed on refineries altered product yields, which meant obtaining a lower proportion of light crude than planned. Attempts were also made to modify production composition by reprocessing high vacuum plant residual oil and reducing fuel oil production. By operating refineries in excess of their optimum capacity, with heavier loads and without residue demetalization, serious damage was caused to several plants because of dirtying and wear; production was eventually suspended while repairs were carried out.[30] Although this situation was the initial response to a change in the processed crude mixture, action was also taken to overcome in the medium term the refining system's new tendency to give a lower yield with light-crude products. PEMEX asked IMP to deign new technology to allow light-product yields to be obtained from Maya crude that were similar to those from less heavy oil. The Demex and Impex processes to eliminate metals and asphaltness from high vacuum-distillation residues were developed as a result, but the new technology was expensive to apply and PEMEX was reluctant to use it. A refining project designed for the Pacific coast (Lázaro Cárdenas, Michoacán) to process only Maya crude through the Demex process had to be suspended in 1982 for budgetary reasons.

The strategy proposed in PE to make the production structure equal to domestic demand implied stepping up the rate of investment in refining. The refineries were to be modified so that from the mid-1980s onward light-product yields would increase despite the different crude mixtures.[31] The program stressed the need to double primary-distillation capacity from 1980 to 1990 to cover domestic demand alone.

Little attention was paid early in the López Portillo administration to the idea of increasing the viscosity-reduction capacity of the refining system so as to obtain greater light-product yields.[32] The six-year program (1977-1982) did not contemplate any kind of expansion in viscosity reduction probably because no increase in heavy-crude production had been forecast when this program was elaborated. Furthermore, it was estimated that the increased capacity foreseen for secondary processors would allow fuel oil production to be reduced to the required minimum. The ambitious natural gas export target established in 1977 made the installation of viscosity reducers even less urgent in view of the possibility of using fuel oil as a natural gas substitute. However, when it was decided to increase viscosity-reduction capacity early in the 1980s, projects were slowed primarily because of budgetary constraints.

Therefore, the change in the outlook for natural gas availability and use was decisive in formulating a hydrocarbon and fuel oil substitution policy. However, the apparent decision to stimulate fuel oil consumption in order to free large volumes of gas for export (considering also the restricted gas supply after 1980) did not progress because effective measures were not introduced to promote this substitution. Until 1980 the lower natural gas price favored its use. Moreover, natural gas offered the added advantage of higher productivity, longer active life and easier maintenance at plants, and lower contamination levels.

The poor progress made in modifying product yield in the 1976-1982 government term cannot be blamed solely on the changes in processing crude mixtures.[33] Despite the guidelines of the 1977-1982 six-year program, the slow progress of several projects also inhibited the system's evolution. Just one year before the end of the López Portillo term, barely half the capacity initially planned for primary and secondary distillation, including naphtha, gasoline, and middle-distillate treatment facilities, had been incorporated (see Table 8.1). Although the extensions made to catalytic-cracking capacity were proportionately greater than the additions to other facilities, it was not sufficient enough to make a significant difference in the refining system's structure. Also, although refining capacity increased, there was no parallel growth in the storage and distribution infrastructure.[34]

Until 1981 the program's slow progress was due to PEMEX's serious financial limitations. The Tula, Cadereyta, and Salina Cruz refineries were completed rapidly because resources were concentrated in these works at the cost of progress in other activities. In general, however, PEMEX's capacity to undertake these projects turned out to be considerably less than foreseen, and the same can be said of many other industries involved in oil development. The financial crisis appearing in PEMEX in mid-1981 brought about a reduction in the resources invested in refining, with a consequent slowing of the program.[35,36]

The heavy pressure exerted by the demand for petroleum products since 1978 and the measures taken to overcome the problems involved in heavy-crude processing meant that the refining plants were worked at their maximum capacity for longer than was technically advisable. Installed capacity could not be utilized at only 85 percent as proposed by the six-year program. The installations were overworked to the point where product quality dropped. In 1982 a generalized plant repair and maintenance program was unavoidable. Operations were detained in several facilities during that year, and the government had to have 100 TBD of crude refined overseas to compensate for the reduction in gasoline and diesel production capacity.[37]

The impact of the fall in oil production in 1982 and the slow progress of the six-year program was mitigated by a change in demand. The annual increase in the volume of domestic sales dropped from more than 8 percent in 1981 to less than 3 percent in 1982. The contraction in the demand reflected the country's economic and financial crisis and was a product of the government's first efforts to rationalize oil use. With PEMEX's financial problems and its inability to satisfy the demand for oil, in late 1981 a readjustment was made to oil prices, which had been so low that they themselves had stimulated excessive oil consumption.[38] Thus, the reduced demand in 1982 gave a respite to the refining industry, and the country's self-sufficiency in oil achieved in 1980 was no longer endangered by growing consumption, as it was in 1977.

After 1980 most oil imports were provoked by seasonal shortfall situations or border imports, which were insignificant compared to the apparent volume of national consumption. However, two products continued to have a production deficit: liquefied gas and lubricants.

Liquefied gas production increased almost threefold from 1976 to 1982 partly because of the refineries' expanded catalytic-cracking capacity but mostly because of the installation of cryogenic plants. In 1982 almost three-fourths of liquefied gas production were obtained from gas treatment facilities, although the possibility of obtaining even greater quantities by this means was restricted by the lack of coordination between programs for natural gas extraction and those involving gathering, distribution, and processing.[39]

Thus, despite an increase from 1977 to 1982 in domestic liquefied gas sales at an average annual rate of 16 percent, imports by PEMEX and private enterprises fell to only one-seventh of the amount required at the end of the previous government term. At the same time, private enterprise import levels fell below those of the mid-1970s because of the advantage in buying from PEMEX at the domestic sale price rather than abroad at an import price. Thus, PEMEX gradually became responsible for all imports. In view of the self-sufficiency achieved in most other petroleum products, from 1980 to 1982 liquefied gas imports represented around 50 percent of PEMEX's total oil imports, even with the heavy reduction in absolute terms.

Although lubricant production was never sufficient to satisfy demand, the situation worsened in 1978 when imports of this product tripled over the previous year. With the high investment needed to build lubricant-processing chains in addition to the very specific quality required for crude, production-capacity expansion during the 1976-1982 government term began to slow and was limited to modifying the main lubricant-producing facilities at the Salamanca refinery. Needless to say, domestic needs could not be covered.

Lubricant imports by private enterprises were stopped after the mid-1970s when PEMEX took over all imports. However, the old policy of letting private enterprises make their own mixtures from basic lubricants and distribute the end product never changed.[40] During the 1976-1982 government term PEMEX manufactured and sold its own finished lubricants and also provided basic lubricants for the other manufacturers, who distributed the final product under their own brand name (these were usually foreign) and at a higher price than PEMEX.[41]

Although the overall volume and number of imported products was reduced during the latter years of the 1976-1982 government term, exports began to increase and diversify. However, with the exception of fuel oil these exports consisted mainly of marginal production surpluses, so that the total exported volume amounted to no more than 30 percent of 1982 production.

A comparison of PEMEX's six-year program objectives with the results shows that the fundamental objective, that is, petroleum self-sufficiency, was more or less achieved, whereas specific goals were not. Crude-processing capacity only reached 1.27 MBD instead of the proposed 1.67 MBD, and the increment in secondary processing capacity aimed at raising light-product yields and improving product quality amounted to barely half the established target. Although imports were reduced to a minimum, they were not totally eliminated, and only 20 percent of the export target set for 1982 was reached.

These results lead one to believe that the six-year program overestimated the oil industry's potential to increase production capacity enough to satisfy demand and avail itself of exportable surpluses. However, for several years plants worked at more than the technically advisable capacity, and to fulfill the export targets and eliminate liquefied gas imports, a far grater production capacity was required. Had the prevailing trend in demand persisted, it is probable that during the late 1970s the refining industry would have found itself in a tight spot when the new government took power in 1982.

In examining the results of the six-year program, one must consider the assumptions on which this planning exercise was based: (1) domestic demand would continue to grow at around 9 percent; and (2) despite the worldwide refining overcapacity, Mexico would be able to place 13 percent of its domestic production in the international market. The first assumption reflects the decision to expand the refining system according to the probable growth rate in the demand for petroleum products, without considering the need to rationalize the use of these products. The forecasts for consumption turned out to be true until 1982 in part because of the oil-price stability from late 1976 to late 1980. Under the prevailing inflationary circumstances, real prices deteriorated, leading to excessive consumption of these products.

The possibility of significantly increasing the participation of Mexico's petroleum products in the international market was not altogether feasible because of the market situation itself. With the continued worldwide refining overcapacity and the oil companies' efforts to retain their sales and their market, the need arose to adjust prices, which had tended to drop in real terms. With the investment and operation costs implied in developing petroleum products and the value given to crude on the international market, the economic viability of exporting derivatives was undermined. The argument that Mexico's oil industry should concentrate on exporting petroleum products of greater aggregate value than crude was no longer valid given international prices, which barely covered real product cost.

In 1983 Mexico's economic and financial crisis strongly affected the refining industry. Domestic oil sales decreased 4 percent that year, with even greater reductions occurring in gasoline and diesel.[42] An overall deceleration in economic activity and intensified measures aimed at rationalizing domestic oil demand through new price increases contributed to the contracted demand. Although consumption of petroleum products was affected in industry, the impact was particularly evident in the transport sector because of the heavy increases in diesel and gasoline prices and the consequent overall reduction in cargo and passenger transport.[43] Consequently, in 1983 large production surpluses, mainly gasoline and diesel, were freed, allowing oil exports to double over those of 1982.

The increase in liquefied gas and lubricant import volumes caused total oil imports to rise by 100 percent. Liquefied gas was one of the few fuels whose demand increased in 1983, its consumption encouraged by the lower increase in price compared to other products.

With the contraction of domestic energy demand and the financial difficulties faced by both PEMEX and the country in general, PEMEX proceeded to revise the refining industry's development programs. Resources were concentrated in the second stages of the Salina Cruz and Tula refineries with the hope that oil self-sufficiency could be maintained during the whole administration term.

CONCLUSIONS AND FUTURE PROSPECTS

Since the oil industry's nationalization in 1938, the refining industry has been the subject of a medium- and even long-term planning exercises, the measures taken in this direction more or less corresponding to established guidelines. Although the programs have had to reflect the particular conditions of the moment, one can observe a continuity in both the objectives and the courses of action taken to achieve them.

The general policy established by PEMEX when it was decided to adjust oil production to domestic demand includes a series of guidelines, the validity of which were to be maintained as time went by. These guidelines included the location of refineries close to consumer centers in order to facilitate distribution to strategic regions; the expansion of production capacity, keeping the number of refining complexes small but with a high degree of large-scale integration to allow maximum advantage of the economies of scale; the concentration of efforts in expanding secondary processing capacity with the aim of increasing light-product yield and improving product quality; and the adaptation of the transport system to the modifications occurring in the refining industry.

In the refining system's expansion plan, activities were programmed systematically at three different levels:

- The construction of new refining complexes, all of which were designed with practically the same production-structure pattern

- The installation of new facilities in existing refineries to broaden the conversion capacity of residual oil to light products and to improve product quality by introducing different secondary processes

- Modifications to operating units requiring limited investment with the aim of improving operational efficiency and utilizing marginal capacity

From 1976 to 1982 the planning efforts primarily initiated in the previous government administration came to fruition. The growing domestic oil demand and the prospect of assured raw material availability led to the expansion of the national refining system. The only three refineries established after the 1950s were designed during the early 1970s. However, because additional economic resources were available for investment from 1977 to 1980, the program could rapidly be carried out.

Although planning had been important for refining, the industry's development was also conditioned by a number of other factors. The changes occurring in primary hydrocarbon production, the subordination of pricing policy to certain macroeconomic objectives, the virtual absence until 1980 of measures aimed at rationalizing demand, a miscalculation of PEMEX's and the country's capacity to carry out given projects, the evolution of the international market, and the change in PEMEX's financial situation since 1981 all helped divert activities from the guidelines established in refining plans and programs. Furthermore, these factors created new problems or brought old ones to light.

The changes occurring in primary production had a heavy impact on refining policy and development. On one hand, the large-scale exploitation of heavy crude since 1980, the difficulties associated with its foreign trade, and the consequent need to utilize it locally caused maladjustments in the refining system, which was designed for light crude processing. In spite of the emphasis placed on secondary processes, the change in conversion capacity from residual oil to light products was insufficient considering the need to process Maya-crude. On the other hand, plans for fuel oil production and consumption were subordinate to the expectations about the availability of natural gas for domestic consumption and the high degree of interfuel substitution. However, the policy containing these changes related to the alternative use of natural gas and fuel oil did not include effective measures to achieve its objectives. Until 1982 relative prices for these two products favored the use of natural gas despite the prevailing policy.

In general, the low-price policy was not always favorable to the refining industry. Although the heavy increase in oil demand was mainly a product of high economic growth rates, the greater importance given to energy-intensive industries and the vast expansion of transport systems and a deterioration in the real price of petroleum products encouraged excessive waste of these products. The refining system was constantly under pressure to broaden its production capacity, but financing for the required investment was hindered by the low income from refining, a direct result of the low-price policy.

The slow progress made in development programs for the refining industry was due in part to financial constraints. However, it also reflects a certain lack of realism on the part of PEMEX about project lead times, particularly when one considers the limited capacity of the other industries involved in the construction and the difficulties inherent in acquiring the material and equipment from abroad. Furthermore, the 1977-1982 six-year plan was elaborated early in the administration when the country's medium-term prospects looked particularly bright.

Early in the 1982-1988 administration, the outlook for the refining industry changed significantly (see Figure 8.1 for a map of the refineries operating in 1983). The country's sharp economic

FIGURE 8.1
PEMEX REFINING CENTERS, 1983

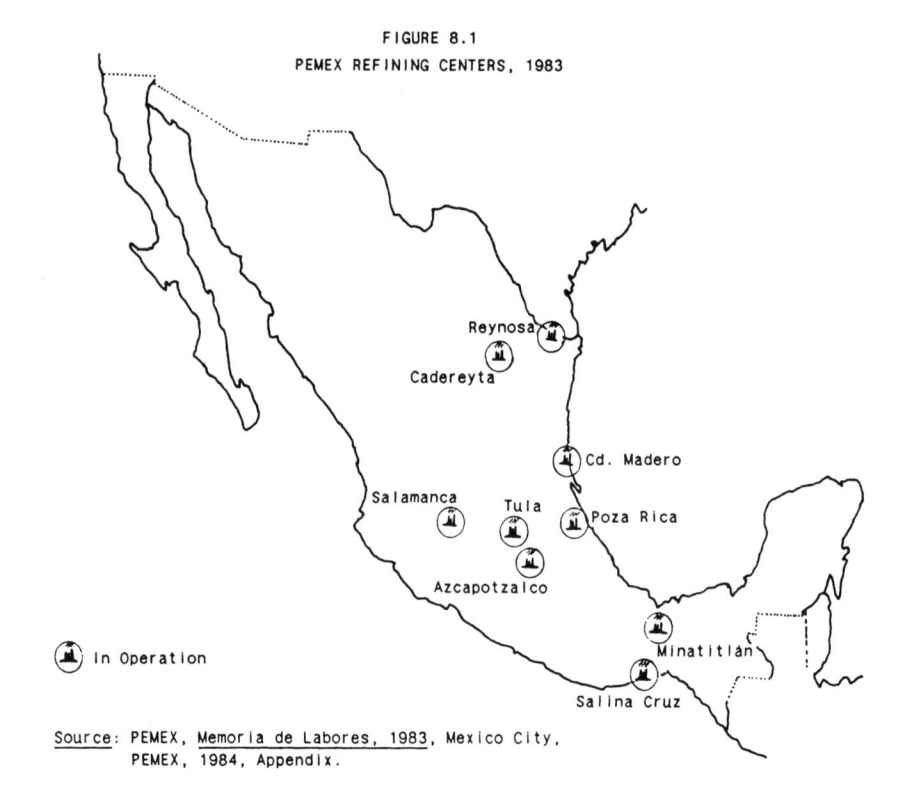

Source: PEMEX, Memoria de Labores, 1983, Mexico City, PEMEX, 1984, Appendix.

crisis, PEMEX's own financial difficulties, and the sudden contraction of oil demand led to readjustments in development plans, and several projects were postponed. Thus, PEMEX's 1984-1988 plan for refining includes a 218 billion peso investment program, which is 8.6 percent of PEMEX's total investment and only two-thirds of the investment planned for basic petrochemicals.[44] With this budget it was originally hoped that the second stage at Tula would be completed in 1987, after which extensions to Salina Cruz would continue and should have been finished in 1989. However, the economic crisis resulted in the postponement of these projects.

The only modifications foreseen for refining complexes in operation consist of installing three 50 TBD viscosity reducers at Minatitlán, Cadereyta, and Salina Cruz, with the aim of increasing light-product yield. PEMEX hopes to adapt the Impex process to the current refining system to get a better yield from Maya crude. With the improved outlook for foreign trade in Maya crude, the plan proposes to keep heavy crude's share in the processed load at the refineries at 20 percent, which is the level that has been maintained in previous years.[45]

Despite the evident reduction in refining development programs, both the PEMEX plan and PNE 1984-1988 estimate that the planned capacity increases will be sufficient to satisfy demand.[46] The growth in demand, estimated at 6 percent per year, will be determined mainly by fuel oil consumption, which will, in turn, depend on the requirements of the thermoelectric plants under construction and the progress made in gas substitution. The export target is considerably more modest than that established in 1977, having been set at 100 TBD. Gasolines and diesels represent more than 80 percent of these exports.

Last, the PEMEX plan for 1984-1988 keeps within the general guidelines of the global energy policy, recognizing the need for rational energy use using a differential price and tariff scale.[47] Under these conditions pressure on the system would be reduced and refining capacity maintained at a sufficiently high level to fulfill the proposed targets. Investment in the area could then be postponed, thus temporarily relieving PEMEX's financial burden.

NOTES

1. The refining industry covers a series of physical and chemical processes, such as distilling, cracking, and purifying oil, whereby hydrocarbons are transformed into a wide range of products, including fuels, special products (lubricants, paraffin, asphalt, grease), and raw products, for the basic petrochemical industry.
2. See PEMEX, Anuario estadístico, 1983, Mexico City, PEMEX, 1984, pp. 17-19.
3. Operating refineries included Madero, with a nominal capacity for primary distillation of 43 TBD; Minatitlán (27 TBD); Arbol Grande (11.5 TBD); Azcapotzalco (11 TBD); Mata Redonda (8 TBD); and Bella Vista (1.5 TBD).
4. See Bermúdez, Antonio, Doce años al servicio de la industria petrolera mexicana, 1947-1958, Mexico City, COMAVAL, 1960, pp. 81-103.
5. The first important modification to the refining system was the updating of, and extension to, Azcapotzalco in 1945 to supply the country's central states. Other refineries were gradually modernized, and in the early 1950s two new refineries were built in Salamanca, Guanajuato, and Reynosa, Tamaulipas. Three of the old refineries were eliminated because of low productivity.
6. The data given in this chapter are taken from Memoria de labores and Anuarios estadísticos de PEMEX, various years, except where otherwise stated in the notes.
7. A typical example was the fuel oil supply to the Pacific coast. Although there were surpluses in the Gulf of Mexico, it was economical and efficient to export them via Tampico in the east and to import fuel oil from the United States for the west.
8. See Bermúdez, Antonio, La política petrolera mexicana, Mexico City, Ortiz, 1979, pp. 63-64.
9. By 1970 oil-product participation in energy and consumption was 99.8 percent for the transport sector, 71.5 percent for the commercial and residential sector, and 31.2 percent for the industrial sector. See SEPAFIN and STCE, Energéticos: Boletín Informativo del Sector Energético, Year 6, No. 11, Mexico City, STCE, November 1982, p. 11.

10. See PEMEX, Memoria de labores, 1970, Mexico City, PEMEX, 1971, pp. 16-17.

11. It was decided simultaneously to increase transport capacity using pipelines leading to the consumer centers because this method was economical and the only option available to convey large quantities.

12. With the growth in the demand for petroleum products, this project did not come to fruition. The possible shift from Azcapotzalco had been continuously postponed primarily because of the magnitude of the investment implied, not to mention the temporary reduction in refining capacity and the trade union problems that such a move would create.

13. See PEMEX, Informe del director general de Petróleos Mexicanos, Mexico City, PEMEX, 18 March 1971, p. 10.

14. In 1972 there were two new refineries at the design stage; locations at Cadereyta and Salina Cruz were to be decided in 1974.

15. See PEMEX, Informe del director general de Petróleos Mexicanos, Mexico City, PEMEX, 18 March 1972, p. 12.

16. See "Reunión de la comisión de energéticos,", in Carta de México (Appendix), No. 18, Mexico City, Secretaría de la Presidencia, 8 January 1974, p. 6.

17. The increased capacity planned for 1973 to 1976 included 23 percent for primary distillation, 35 percent for vacuum distillation, 99 percent for catalytic cracking, 104 percent for middle-distillate hydrodesulfurization, and more than 200 percent for naphtha hydrodesulfurization and reforming and residue processing. See Table 8.1.

18. See PEMEX, Informe del director general de Petróleos Mexicanos, México City, PEMEX, 18 March 1976.

19. See SEPAFIN and STCE, "Refinación en México," in Energéticos: Boletín Informativo del Sector Energético, Mexico City, STCE, December 1981, p. 12.

20. The diesel yield went from 16.6 percent in 1970 to 21.7 percent in 1976; however, gasoline and liquid gas increased their yield only slightly. In the group of heavy products although the asphalt yield

fell from 4.6 percent to 1.6 percent, the yield of fuel oil remained almost the same.

21. See PEMEX, Informe del director general de Petróleos Mexicanos, Mexico City, PEMEX, 18 March 1975, pp. 18-20; PEMEX, Memoria de labores, 1976, Mexico City, PEMEX, 1977, p. 54.

22. See Vázquez Domínguez, Enrique, "Planes de ampliación de capacidad en las refinerías del sistema," in IMIQ, Mexico City, IMIQ, March 1976, pp. 82-89.

23. See Lara Sosa, Héctor, "Plan sexenal de Petróleos Mexicanos en refinación," in IMIQ, Mexico City, IMIQ, March-April 1977, pp. 12-21.

24. Reliable official data are not available on refining equipment and material sources. However, according to a study done in 1979, 70 percent of the refining and petrochemical program's investment in materials and equipment from 1977 to 1986 was to be channeled into purchases abroad. See "Bienes de capital para la industria petrolera," in Comercio Exterior, Vol. 29, No. 8, Mexico City, Banco Nacional de Comercio Exterior, August 1979, pp. 851-856.

25. Prior to this refinery the region was supplied mainly by the Ciudad Madero refinery. Distillates were sent via the Madero-Monterrey-Torreón (Coahuila) polyduct and fuel oil via Madero-Cadereyta fuel oil pipeline.

26. Before the refinery was built, Salina Cruz was an important distribution center, mainly for fuel oil and ammonia.

27. See Vázquez Domínguez, Enrique, op. cit., p. 86.

28. See SEPAFIN, Programa de energía, metas a 1990 y proyecciones al año 2000 (resumen y conclusiones, Mexico City, SEPAFIN, 1980, p. 40.

29. In 1980 Maya crude processing increased, with the refineries programmed to concentrate on converting residues into distillates. Thus, in Cadereyta heavy-crude processing increased from 18 percent to 43 percent with no increase in residual oil production. See PEMEX, Memoria de labores, 1980, Mexico City, PEMEX, 1981, p. 10.

30. See Cardoso, Víctor, "El crudo que se procesa aquí daña las refinerías," in Proceso: Semanario de

Información y análisis, No. 289, Mexico City, CISA, 17 May 1982, p. 27.

31. The program considered the possibility that natural gas production could exceed domestic consumption plus the export volumes recently agreed upon with the United States. In such a case gas consumption could be encouraged instead of fuel oil. "During the mid-1980s, when a relative reduction in fuel oil production has been achieved, it will become necessary to encourage the use of natural gas," SEPAFIN, op. cit., p. 42.

32. The only refineries with viscosity reducers were Azcapotzalco, Madero, and Tula.

33. The yield for gasoline, kerosene, and diesel fell from 1976 to 1982, but the fuel oil yield increased slightly. Liquefied gas yield increased from 7.4 percent to 12 percent.

34. See Chapter 10, "Transport and Distribution."

35. See Chapter 12, "PEMEX's Finances."

36. In 1982 the processing capacity of gas liquids only increased by 242 TBD because of the installation of natural gasoline fractionators at Cactus and La Cangrejera. Thus, primary-distilling capacity as a whole (crude and gas liquids) rose to 1.62 MBD.

37. From 1979 to 1981 refining was limited to an average of 15.5 TBD.

38. During the second half of 1982 industrial fuel was subject to monthly price increases of 5 percent, and on two occasions gasoline, diesel, and liquefied gas prices were increased. See Chapter 12, "PEMEX's Finances."

39. See Chapter 7, "Exploration and Exploitation."

40. Until 1955 when the lubricant facility came on line at the Salamanca refinery, PEMEX did not produce high-quality lubricants. Therefore, the manufacturers imported the basic components and made their mixtures, adapting the end product to the demand.

41. See Chapter 10, "Transport and Distribution."

42. Domestic sales for these products fell by 12 percent and 13.5 percent, respectively, compared to 1982.

43. See PEMEX, Balance de energía, 1983 (synthesis; mimeograph), Mexico City, PEMEX, 1984, p. 10.

44. See PEMEX, Aspectos relevantes del plan 1984-1988, Mexico City, PEMEX, 1984, p. 6.

45. See Chapter 11, "Foreign Trade."

46. Poder Ejecutivo Federal, Programa nacional de energéticos, 1984-1988, Mexico City, SEMIP, 1984, pp. 107-113.

47. See PEMEX, Plan nacional de desarrollo, 1983-1988: Aspectos principales e implicaciones para el sector petrolero, Mexico City, PEMEX, 1983; Poder Ejecutivo Federal, op. cit., pp. 88-89.

9

The Basic Petrochemical Industry

Michele Snoeck

Although petrochemicals cannot be classified as part of national energy supply, the industry is included in this study because of its institutional and operational ties with the energy sector, its development forming part of PEMEX's activity. Furthermore, the basic petrochemical industry is one of Mexico's most energy intensive, using hydrocarbons as a raw material and fuel and electricity for energy purposes.[1]

The decision to nationalize the basic petrochemical industry in the late 1950s reflected an economic policy designed to encourage certain underdeveloped sectors to contribute to import substitution through industrialization. From this point on, the petrochemical industry was considered a strategic area in transforming hydrocarbons into derivatives with a high aggregate value and providing broader possibilities for natural raw material substitution. Thus, by including basic petrochemical development in PEMEX activities, it was hoped that the right conditions for expanding secondary industries could be established and that PEMEX would then have the means of controlling the general course of the industry.

Basic petrochemical policy has always been aimed at achieving national self-sufficiency. Since the mid-1970s the industry has been given considerable thrust, with raw materials and financial resources being made readily available. However, in spite of major expansion in production capacity from 1976 to 1982, self-sufficiency was never achieved primarily because of the dynamics of secondary industries.

This chapter presents an analysis of the policies and programs related to the basic petrochemical industry together with their scope and limitations. The first part of the chapter covers the origin and growth of the industry from its beginnings in the late 1950s until the mid-1970s. The second part is a discussion of the industry's evolution from 1976 to 1983, with particular emphasis on the manner in which policies and programs influenced its development, other factors conditioning its expansion, the results obtained, and the most important problems arising during this period. Last, conclusions drawn from the analysis are discussed and the industry's future development prospects are evaluated.

BEGINNINGS AND GROWTH FROM 1958 TO 1975

The petrochemical industry in Mexico is divided into two branches--basic and secondary--in accordance with legislation passed in 1958 and modified in 1970.[2] Basic petrochemicals are derived from the first transformation of natural hydrocarbon compounds, their development in Mexico being carried out by PEMEX. Secondary petrochemicals include those products resulting from subsequent transformation processes. These processes can be undertaken by private enterprises with 60 percent Mexican capital; state participation is not a requirement.[3]

The law passed in 1970 established that SEPANAL (which became SEPAFIN in 1976 and SEMIP in 1982), with the help of the Comisión Petroquímica Mexicana (Mexican Petrochemical Commission), would decide which products were to be classified as basic petrochemicals and, therefore, developed exclusively by PEMEX. The Comisión Petroquímica is a technical advisory and research agency in which the heads of each of the three public agencies directly related with petrochemicals participate, that is, PEMEX, SEPANAL, and SECOFI.

Once basic petrochemicals were included as part of PEMEX's activities in 1958, the industry's main objective was to attain national self-sufficiency in the majority of the basic products required by the secondary petrochemical and other productive sectors. This target was to counteract the record growth in basic petrochemical demand that had occurred since the 1960s and that had given rise to increasing imports despite PEMEX's efforts to boost the new industry.[4] From 1958 to 1973 the gradual reduction in PEMEX's resources restricted investment programs in its different activities. Although some investment was made in basic petrochemicals over this period, with significant increases in production, this amount was not enough to overcome the country's dependence on the international market.[5] This situation worsened after 1973 because of a sharp rise in international basic petrochemical prices and produced a marked increase in the value of imports.

Early in the 1970-1976 government term, social inequality and the economic imbalance between various regions led the federal government to elaborate an industrial strategy emphasizing the country's organization into regional "poles" of development. The petrochemical industry was important to carry out this policy; production would initially be based on the complex compounds produced at several plants and would contribute to the formation of these regional-development poles. Secondary petrochemicals could be used to strengthen each center because to a certain degree it was possible to control the location of the development poles; thus, location was a factor that the Comisión Petroquímica took into consideration when granting investment permits to private enterprises. However, it was not until several years later, when PEMEX's economic situation had improved considerably, that industrial policy with its double objective —decentralization and the creation of regional-development centers—was to have a major effect on the petrochemical industry's location and development. From 1971 to 1973 PEMEX found itself in a kind of Catch 22 situation. On one hand, PEMEX management thought it would not be long before the petrochemical industry could generate its own resources for investment, that is, as soon as new plants with greater capacity and bigger economies of scale started operating and had personnel experienced in design and operation.[6] On the other hand, PEMEX did not have the initial resources it needed to build these plants.[7]

In 1974 and 1975 different factors combined to make basic petrochemicals of strategic importance, not only for political reasons but also for practical purposes. The discovery of new oil fields, mainly in Chiapas and Tabasco, in 1973 and 1974 and the domestic price increases for PEMEX's products since 1973 made PEMEX decide to step up expansion in petrochemical production capacity. Thus, although self-sufficiency was still the main objective, about half way through the Dovall Jaime administration big changes were introduced into the petrochemical strategy. First, additional funds were to be channeled into expansion. PEMEX budgeted for an investment of 6 billion pesos in basic petrochemicals for 1974 to 1976, a significant amount considering that the branch's total accumulated investment (including integration works) until 1974 barely amounted to 5 billion pesos at current prices.[8] Furthermore, the petrochemical program represented 18 percent of PEMEX's proposed total investment for the same period.[9] In fact, in 1975 PEMEX's investment in this area amounted to double that of the previous year.[10]

Second, the economies of scale that could be derived from large-scale production gained importance as selection criteria for the plant's production capacity. The dimensions planned for certain plants reached levels comparable to other major world petrochemical complexes; capacity would more than cover domestic demand, leaving large exportable surpluses that could hopefully be set at a competitive cost in the international market.

The new strategy introduced late in the 1970-1976 government term involved two project types. The first project chosen was the production of ammonia because of ammonia's importance to the fertilizer industry and, therefore, to agriculture. In 1974 PEMEX contracted with a U.S. company for the engineering of three new ammonia plants. These plants were to start up late in 1976 and would provide 6,300 tons of ammonia per day, as opposed to the 1,700 tons produced in 1974.[11]

However, the project contributing the most to PEMEX's new strategy was a large complex at La

Cangrejera in Veracruz, which would allow PEMEX to take advantage of the vast hydrocarbon resources in the southeast. With a forecasted nominal production capacity of 2.8 million tons per year divided between twenty plants, production capacity would increase by 70 percent. The complex was the biggest of its kind in Latin America and one of the largest in the world. Several of the twenty conditioning and processing plants were to operate at maximum capacity and included the most advanced technology, and together the plants were conceived of as a totally integrated complex in which twenty-odd products and by-products could be developed. It was hoped that the project would allow that ever-present objective, self-sufficiency, to be reached along with large export volumes.

THE POLICIES FOLLOWED FROM 1976 TO 1983

Early in President López Portillo government term (1976-1982) the petrochemical industry was among the nine industrial sectors with the highest priority for investment. This activity amalgamated the essential characteristics of the government's industrial policy. It allowed "better use to be made of hydrocarbons, a more equitable regional distribution of industry, and the intensive use of existing infrastructure and it encouraged the use of local technicians and entrepreneurs' experience and initiative."[12]

PNDI 1979-1982, which was published in 1979, reaffirmed the petrochemical industry's importance and gave it priority because of its high productivity and competitiveness in the international market. It was felt that the petrochemical industry could grow around 18 percent annually, whereas the rate forecast for the whole industrial sector was 12 percent.[13] When PNDI was introduced, major sectors of the Mexican economy were rapidly expanding, and conditions looked good for the economy as a whole. This optimistic situation was reflected in the high target set for petrochemical production from 1979 to 1982.

Because of the close relationship between the two branches of the petrochemical industry in Mexico (basic and secondary) and because various agencies were in charge of developing each of them (state and private enterprise), it was imperative that there be some sort of medium-term plan establishing the overall guidelines for this industry. Certainly, there had been efforts in the past to establish institutional mechanisms to this end. However, after the petrochemical legislation of 1970, the Comisión Petroquímica was made clearly responsible for formulating petrochemical programs that would allow the industry to develop within the guidelines of national policy and with the country's best resources at its disposal. The Asociación Nacional de la Industria Química (National Association of Chemical Industries; ANIQ) periodically published information on both the basic petrochemical branch and the different areas of the secondary petrochemical branch.[14]

However, the mechanisms established previously for maintaining close coordination between those two branches do not seem to have been taken into account in the Programa Sexenal de Petroquímica Básica (Six-Year Basic Petrochemical Program) 1977-1982. Designed exclusively by PEMEX, this very ambitious program was essentially a reflection of PEMEX's intention to establish a major basic petrochemical industry at an international level as quickly as possible, taking advantage of the easy availability of financial resources and raw materials.

The Programa Sexenal de Petroquímica Básica 1977-1982, introduced in 1977 as part of PEMEX's global program, was important in that its outlines were basically followed, although without the success originally hoped for.[15] 53 billion pesos at 1977 prices were to be invested in the petrochemical industry, representing 17 percent of PEMEX's total budget for 1977-1982. It was hoped that with a total production capacity for 1982 of around 20 million tons per year (compared with 5 million tons in 1976), divided between 124 plants, domestic self-sufficiency would be achieved. Furthermore, a capacity of this dimension would facilitate Mexico's participation as an important competitor in the international market for specific products, such as ammonia, paraxylene, aromatics, low-density polyethylene, and some ethylene derivatives.[16] In concrete terms an export target of 26 percent of the basic petrochemical production was set. The availability of large volumes of oil and gas for use as petrochemical inputs was fundamental to the project, as was the construction of integrated complexes involving extremely high level economies of scale and very efficient techniques. La Cangrejera, in particular, whose planned annual production capacity was increased from 2.8 to 3.5 million tons in 1977, was considered a key link in the expansion of the national petrochemical industry. It was the first of a series of petrochemical complexes of this kind to be built by PEMEX.

Although PEMEX's results for 1982 in basic petrochemicals are impressive compared to 1976, none of its targets were met, except perhaps for the total amount invested (see Table 9.1). In 1982 the basic petrochemical industry still had to import over twenty products from abroad, representing 13.5 percent of Mexico's apparent consumption of imports. Exports were restricted to two products only (instead of twenty-one), and PEMEX's petrochemical trade balance showed a deficit of 12 billion pesos. Consequently, self-sufficiency in production and export diversification, PEMEX's two main objectives for the six-year term, were postponed.[17]

Although the petrochemical program for 1977-1982 planned for the production expansion of the four main groups of basic petrochemicals, higher growth was recorded in dry natural gas derivatives (ammonia, and methanol) and ethylene and its derivatives.[18] At the same time, the demand was particularly high for those products with a relatively lower growth rate.[19] The difference between supply and demand was not a result of the incorrect evaluation of future demand but rather of the way in which the production structure took shape and was conditioned by the type and the amount of raw materials made available to Mexico's basic petrochemical industry. During the 1970s this industry increasingly based its development on natural gas derivatives because of the availability of natural gas and the low transformation costs compared to processes utilizing naphthas.[20]

Ethylene production from natural gas derivatives —ethane—has made Mexico one of the world's cheapest ethylene producers. However, a much smaller amount of the by-products (propane-propylene and butane-butylene) is obtained from this process than from the prod-

TABLE 9.1
PEMEX PETROCHEMICAL PROGRAM, 1977-1982: TARGETS AND RESULTS

Economic Indicators	Unit of Measurement	1976 Level	Targets 1977-1982	Targets 1982	Results 1977-1982	Results 1982
Investment	Millions of Pesos		53,000		54,700 (1977-1980)	
Participation in Total Investment	Percentage		15.0		15.6 (1977-1980)	
Nominal Production Capacity	Millions of Tons/year	5.0		19.0 (21.7)[c]		14.9
Operating Plants		54		124 (133)[c]		92
Production	Millions of Tons/year	3.9		17.4		10.6
Utilization of Production Capacity	Percentage	83.5	92.0		82.2	72.8
Number of Products		35		44		40
Integration Coefficient (in terms of volume)[d]	Percentage	86.2		95.0		86.5
Imports (in value)	Millions of Pesos (current prices)	1,659		121.0[a]		18,557

Exports (in value)	Millions of Pesos (current prices)	9	13,689[a]	6,501
Number of Products Exported		2	21	2

[a]This figure represents 1977 prices.
[b]This figure represents current prices.
[c]Target was revised in 1978.
[d]This category represents the share of domestic market production in apparent national consumption.

Sources: De Oteyza, Jos Andrs, "Programa sexenal de petroqumica," in El Mercado de Valores, Year 37, No. 17, Mexico City, NAFINSA, 25 April 1977, pp. 309-311; "Expansin de la petroqumica bsica," in Comercio Exterior, Vol. 28, No. 5, Mexico City, Banco Nacional de Comercio Exterior, May 1978, pp. 544-548; Baptista, Csar, "Industria petroqumica en Mxico," in IMIQ, Mexico City, February 1977, pp. 60-72; Garca Luna, Jos Luis, "Petroqumica," in Ingeniera Petrolera, Mexico City, Asociacin de Ingenieros Petroleros de Mxico, A.C., December 1976-February 1977, pp. 69-74; PEMEX, Memoria de labores, 1976, and Memoria de labores, 1982, Mexico City, PEMEX, 1977 and 1983.

uction of ethylene based on naphthas, which explains the relatively slow progress in producing butadiene and propylene and its derivatives.[21]

PEMEX justified its expansion program for ammonia by alluding to its importance in the development of fertilizers and the growing availability of dry natural gas, which cannot economically be stored or transported any great distance. In fact, production reached such proportions that ammonia became the only product to meet the expectations of the six-year petrochemical program, and from 1978 onward very large quantities were exported.[22] However, the decision to export large volumes was not so much a consequence of the target that had been set but rather of the delay in setting up the Fertilizantes Mexicanos (Mexican Fertilizers; FERTIMEX) urea plants.[23] The consumption of ammonia for use as a fertilizer for direct soil application was much lower than expected because of an inadequate distribution network, insufficient fertilizing equipment, and general ignorance about its use on the part of the peasant farmers. As a result, the market for ammonia as a fertilizer was small even in areas where farming had been encouraged, and there was no problem of supply.[24]

The imbalance between basic petrochemical supply and demand from 1976 to 1982 (see Table 9.1) was also affected by a delay of several years in starting up the La Cangrejera complex. The demand for those products to be developed at La Cangrejera by 1978-1979 grew rapidly, but the complex contributed virtually nothing to the supply of these products until 1982. When the plants finally came on line, the secondary petrochemical branch's demand for some of these products had grown to the point where it overtook the complex's capacity to produce them. Thus, the possibility of achieving self-sufficiency vanished, not to mention the chance of obtaining exportable surpluses.

The delay in the construction of the complex was caused by a combination of factors. PEMEX was faced with numerous internal problems, such as an inadequate internal information system, planning deficiencies, technical and administrative4 irregularities, and inadequate management of materials and equipment storage.[25] The 1976 economic crisis brought the construction to a standstill, and there were other problems specific to establishing a complex of these proportions. The multiple interrelationships between the different units and the services and infrastructure required exponentially increased the logistic, administrative, and coordination problems.[26]

The project's slow progress, the inflationary process, and the peso's consequent loss of value in relation to the U.S. dollar caused a substantial increase in the cost of local and foreign equipment and material, thus augmenting considerably the financial resources absorbed by the complex. In 1982 and 1983 amid an internal financial crisis and consequent economic restrictions, PEMEX had to suspend work at the main complexes under construction---Laguna del Ostión in Veracruz, Dos Bocas in Tabasco, and Altamira in Tamaulipas--in order to complete construction at La Cangrejera.

During this period the first signs of a change in PEMEX's petrochemical strategy appeared. Although officially the medium-term program followed the same expansionist lines introduced early in the López Portillo administration (1976-1972), PEMEX's financial problems restricted petrochemical activities during 1982 and 1983, and resources were concentrated on works with highest priority or where construction was advanced.[27] Late in 1983 it became evident that the complexes under construction would have to be suspended temporarily. Furthermore, studies were undertaken to relocate some of the plants "in order to utilize the already existing infrastructure of other complexes in operation."[28]

Aside from a lack of financial resources during 1976 and from 1982 to 1983, which was caused by the precarious financial situation facing the country and PEMEX in particular, the basic petrochemical industry labored under conditions that prevented it from generating the earnings necessary for reinvesting in its own development. Until mid-1982 no clear criteria or norms for pricing basic petrochemicals had been defined. However, declarations by PEMEX and the state made it clear that a low-price policy was to be adopted.[29] From 1970 to 1982 the basic petrochemical price index evolved at a slower rate than the industrial sector as a whole.[30] Price increases for petrochemicals and, in fact, for almost all PEMEX's products have tended to be sudden, the result of PEMEX's unsustainable financial situation. From late 1976 to 1978 the gap between the domestic and international prices became increasingly wider as a result of both the rise in international prices and the Mexican peso's successive devaluations beginning in 1976.[31] Also during this period the volume of imported basic petrochemicals increased, with PEMEX absorbing the difference between the import cost and the resale price on the domestic market.[32] The importation of basic petrochemicals by PEMEX became a heavy burden for the company. This burden was aggravated by the low domestic price policy and was responsible for the scant profit obtained from basic petrochemicals from 1970 to 1973 turning into a loss, which worsened after 1975.[33]

In 1982 PEMEX for the first time made an announcement regarding petrochemical pricing. Prices were to be revised quarterly so that eventually the difference between international and domestic prices did not exceed 20 percent. The June 1982 price increase was substantial, averaging 60 percent, and was followed by a new increase in September of the same year. However, by the end of 1982 when the current government administration left office, the gap between domestic and international prices was even greater because of the peso's heavy devaluation that year.[34]

Low basic petrochemical prices were maintained until 1982 for two interacting reasons. The first was a certain degree of reluctance by PEMEX to establish clear pricing criteria; this reluctance was aggravated by pressure from the organized secondary petrochemical sector to maintain existing prices (the sector's political strength was derived basically from its economic power and key position in the country's productive apparatus). The second reason for the sustained low-price policy was intervention by the state into PEMEX's affairs. In effect, from the declarations made by PEMEX and other state agencies, it seems that basic petrochemical prices were kept low in order to achieve the following broad economic policy objectives:

. Industrialization: The state considered the petrochemical industry strategic in the country's industrial growth and attempted to stimulate capitalization of the secondary petrochemical branch through low-priced inputs. Thus, with low production costs the branch was able to increase its financial resources for reinvestment and accelerate the industrialization process. In fact, most of the secondary petrochemical industry grew more rapidly than the industrial sector or the economy as a whole.[35]

- Decentralization and the creation of regional-development poles: PNDI 1979-1982 sought to stimulate private investment, particularly in secondary petrochemicals in certain preferential areas, through a system of incentives that included fiscal credit for 25 percent of new investment, a 20 percent credit on additional employment generated, and a 30 percent discount on the price of energy and petrochemical inputs. The priority regions included four industrial ports--Coatzacoalcos, Salina Cruz, Tampico, and Lázaro Cárdenas--three of which involved petrochemical-related activities. This type of subsidy mainly favored large industrial units linked to the international market because subsidies were granted on the understanding that the enterprise had to export 25 percent of its production. Although the policy attracted several industries to some of the poles, the overall benefits for the area were questionable. The absence of adequate urban-industrial planning and infrastructure, particularly at the Coatzacoalcos-Minatitlán industrial chemical complex in Veracruz, provoked a serious socioeconomic imbalance and bottlenecks in production.[36]

- Support for farming development: From the time the basic petrochemical industry began, particular attention was given to the production of ammonia, a major input for nitrogenous fertilizers, because of its possible contribution to farming and to the country's self-sufficiency in food production. This product has had the benefit of an explicit subsidy policy; highly subsidized ammonia is made available to FERTIMEX, but the chemical industry must acquire the product at a much higher price.[37]

On different occasions the secondary petrochemical branch has had difficulties in planning its growth because of insufficient basic petrochemical production and an undefined pricing policy. In addition, the industry's transport system was inadequate, which prevented local and imported basic petrochemicals from being purchased opportunely and the finished products distributed efficiently (see Figure 9.1).[38]

CONCLUSIONS AND FUTURE PROSPECTS

The heavy expansion in basic petrochemicals from the mid-1970s onward reflected PEMEX's efforts to speed up the development of a national petrochemical industry and reduce dependence on foreign imports. From 1977 to 1983 an additional production capacity of 9.7 million tons per year was installed, allowing basic petrochemical production to grow from 3.9 million tons in 1976 to 11.3 million in 1983, or an average annual rate of 16.4 percent.

However, the economy's accelerated growth from 1978 to 1981, the diversification of end and middle markets, and the growing possibility of substituting natural products with petrochemicals resulted in a heavy increase in basic petrochemical demand. Early in the 1980s production still could not keep up with domestic demand; the share of imports in apparent national consumption was practically the same in 1982 as it was in 1976, 13.5 and 13.8 percent, respectively.

Basic petrochemical programming underwent a change during the 1970s. During the 1970-1976 Echeverría government term, expectations for basic petrochemical expansion far exceeded its ability to grow. There were neither financial resources nor raw proucts sufficient to undertake an ambitious program. However, the Programa Petroquímico Sexenal 1977-1982 set production and export targets such that by 1982 the foreseeable increase in domestic demand should have been satisfied and large exportable surpluses made available. The nonfulfillment of the established objectives reflected the program's own limitations as well as the obstacles encountered in its execution.

In spite of the institutional mechanisms aimed at integrating the basic and secondary petrochemical branches, the six-year program was essentially the product of petrochemical advocates within PEMEX who wished to grasp the once-in-a-lifetime opportunity of converting Mexico into a major international producer of basic petrochemicals. With the size of the proposed plants comparable to those in the United States and other industrialized countries, the project was probably motivated by a certain degree of exhibitionism. The targets established were not based on in-depth analyses of the industry and its markets, nor were they the result of collaboration and close coordination with the other agencies involved in the industry's development. For instance, ammonia production represented a major part of the program and in fact grew as planned, but it did not adjust to the expected domestic pattern of consumption. On one hand, expansion in both ammonia and urea production capacity by PEMEX and FERTIMEX, respectively, was not properly coordinated, even though FERTIMEX was a major consumer. On the other hand, no strategy existed to encourage the consumption of ammonia as a fertilizer for direct application, which was what the farmers needed. The economic profitability of exporting ammonia surpluses was questioned in light of its low international price. If the quantity of natural gas utilized as an input for developing ammonia had been exported, it would probably have brought in more foreign exchange earnings than ammonia exports did.[39]

Coordination between the basic and secondary branches was difficult because of project construction delays by PEMEX as well as private companies. Consequently, basic petrochemical production was unable to keep up with consumption. The construction delay is attributable to an unrealistic estimate by PEMEX of its own capacity to carry out the program together with an incorrect evaluation of the economy's capacity to respond to the program requirements. The problems related to the country's industrial and technological underdevelopment were apparently underestimated. Several of the problems PEMEX ran into in executing its program were not new, and they were probably not

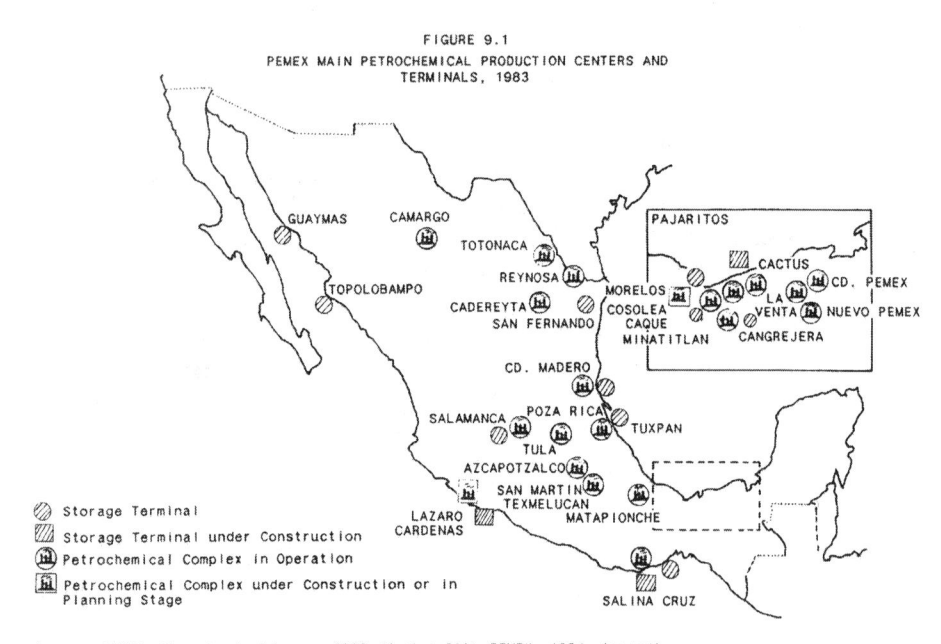

FIGURE 9.1
PEMEX MAIN PETROCHEMICAL PRODUCTION CENTERS AND TERMINALS, 1983

- ◎ Storage Terminal
- ▨ Storage Terminal under Construction
- ⊙ Petrochemical Complex in Operation
- ⊡ Petrochemical Complex under Construction or in Planning Stage

Source: PEMEX, Memoria de labores, 1983, Mexico City, PEMEX, 1984, Appendix.

typical of PEMEX's petrochemical activities. However, there were other problems related specifically to La Cangrejera, a project that had been a real challenge from the start. Undoubtedly, this project's planning and execution were PEMEX's most ambitious integrated effort in this field and a very important industrial and technological experience for the country. With the complexity of La Cangrejera and the lack of financial resources during certain periods, it is not surprising that ten years went by from the time the program was introduced until the plants came on line. Nevertheless, if one considers that the primary objective was to right the domestic basic petrochemical deficit, the question is whether the experience acquired at La Cangrejera compensated for the growing amount of petrochemicals that had to be imported in the interim. In other words, smaller plants established over a relatively shorter time period could have been a better, less costly option in the long run because the economic benefits would have been immediate.[40] Also, La Cangrejera will not even be used as a model as was originally planned because the construction of other similar complexes was suspended due to a lack of resources. Similar difficulties in other new oil-producing countries during their oil industrialization process in the 1970s suggest that strategies such as Mexico's were adopted in other parts of the world.

Last, in Mexico the basic petrochemical industry developed as a function of the characteristics and availability of petrochemical raw materials; preference was given to those processes utilizing natural gas and its derivatives. In time, this preference caused an imbalance between local production and consumption. Although some technicians at PEMEX advocated planning complexes to allow a balance to be restored, it was not until early in the de la Madrid administration that these complexes gained priority in PEMEX's petrochemical program.

In general, the development of the secondary petrochemical industry was highly stimulated by increased diversification and low cost of basic petrochemical production. The secondary petrochemical branch undertook some of the most dynamic industrial activities of the 1970s. However, it was the large firms that intended to export their production that were truly able to take advantage of the subsidies and fiscal advantages. Because of the barriers confronting all new firms entering the petrochemical industry, as opposed to other areas of production, it has been mainly public and direct foreign investment that has penetrated these spheres, despite the fact that legally 60 percent of a company's social capital must be Mexican.[41] Thus, a specific type of investment was promoted, that is, investment of the domestic private sector's dominating group with some participation of multinational companies. This situation has led to a high concentration of production in the firms and plants in the secondary petrochemical branch.[42] With this in mind, were subsidized basic inputs necessary --and how much--to allow the major companies in the secondary petrochemical industry to expand?

As an essential element in fertilizer manufacture, ammonia represents a major part of basic petrochemical production. Undoubtedly, part of agriculture and agro-industry's economic growth in Mexico can be attributed to a policy allowing fertilizers to be produced and distributed at low prices. However, if fertilizers are not used in combination with effective credit and technical and commercialization programs, the benefits never reach the vast majority of small- and medium-scale farmers who live mainly at subsistence level. It seems then that once again the main beneficiaries of subsidized ammonia were multinational companies and agro-exporting concerns.

PEMEX forecasts that the basic petrochemical industry's program for 1984-1988 will satisfy 92 percent of the domestic demand in 1988 with goods produced locally. When construction is completed on the forty new plants, total installed capacity will increase to 18.8 million tons per year, allowing production to rise at an average annual rate of 8.5 percent. It is estimated that the rate of growth in domestic demand will reach 9.2 percent per year. The share of production destined for exports will drop from 9 percent in 1984 to 3 percent in 1988.[43]

The goals for 1988 are considerably less ambitious than those of the six-year program for 1977-1982 and are the product of PEMEX's revision of its petrochemical plans and strategies, with available financial resources taken into account. PEMEX again evaluated the possibility of Mexico becoming a net basic petrochemical exporter, an idea reiterated in political speeches from 1977 to 1980. The government's stance, adopted in 1984, of channeling surpluses alone into the export market rather than building plants expressly to augment export production resulted not only from limited financial resources but also from the low profitability of basic petrochemical exports. A worldwide overcapacity in basic petrochemical production and tough international competition, as well as the fact that the basic petrochemical industry requires large investment and contributes very little to job creation, undermines any advantage this industry could have over alternative gas and oil production. This current situation has led PEMEX to reiterate the petrochemical industry's branch main objective: to promote the secondary petrochemical branch and the industries derived from it.

NOTES

1. In 1982 energy consumption in the basic petrochemical industry represented 14.2 percent of domestic final energy consumption (7.1 percent in raw materials and 7.1 percent in energy). PEMEX, México: Balance de energía, 1982 (summary; mimeograph), Mexico City, PEMEX, 1983, p. 23.

2. "The petrochemical industry involves chemical and physical processes for elaborating compounds either totally or partially from natural hydrocarbons derived from the refining process." SPP, SEPAFIN, PEMEX, and FERTIMEX, Industria petroquímica: Análisis y expectativas, Mexico City, SPP, 1981, p. 21.

3. See "Reglamento de la ley reglamentaria del artículo 27 constitucional en el ramo del petróleo, en materia de petroquímica," in PEMEX, Marco jurídico básico, Mexico City, PEMEX, 1983.

4. The Mexican basic petrochemical industry, which had been practically nonexistent during the 1950s, developed rapidly over the following ten years. From 1960 to 1974 PEMEX's petrochemical production increased from five products with a total volume of 57,000 tons per year to thirty-three products amount-

ing to 2.7 million tons, which meant an average annual growth of 31.7 percent.

5. In 1974 the volume of basic petrochemicals imported by PEMEX and private companies represented 18.6 percent of Mexico's apparent consumption. The value of PEMEX's basic product imports amounted to 880.5 million pesos. PEMEX, Memoria de labores, 1974-1975, Mexico City, PEMEX, 1975, 1976; PEMEX, Anuario estadistico, 1977, Mexico City, PEMEX, 1978, pp. 130-135.

6. See Dovall Jaime, Antonio, "Tendencias de la industria petrolera nacional," in El Mercado de Valores, Year 31, No. 32, Mexico City, NAFINSA, 9 August 1971, p. 506.

7. The investment made in petrochemical works from 1971 to 1973 was 2.028 billion pesos, corresponding to only 32 percent of the investment programmed for this field over the whole six-year government term (6.285 billion pesos). Petrochemical investment represented 12 percent of PEMEX's total investment over this period.

8. See IMP, Plan de desarrollo de la industria petrolera y petroquímica básica, 1976-1985, Vol. 3, Mexico City, IMP, 1975, Part 7, pp. 7-39.

9. See Secretaria de la Presidencia, "Reunión de la comisión de energéticos," in Carta de México (appendix), No. 18, Mexico City, Secretaria de la Presidencia, 8 January 1974, p. 6.

10. Petrochemical investment, including that in the gas-processing area, rose to 2.8 million pesos in 1975 compared with 1.2 million in 1974. See IMP, op. cit., Vol. 1, Table 7.

11. Actually, these plants came on line during 1977 and 1978.

12. De Oteyza, José Andrés, "Programa sexenal de petroquímica," in El Mercado de Valores, Year 37, No. 17, Mexico City, NAFINSA, 25 April 1977, pp. 309-311.

13. SEPAFIN, Plan nacional de desarrollo industrial, 1979-1982, Mexico City, SEPAFIN, 1979, p. 9.

14. ANIQ serves as a kind of collective body for chemical sector problems to negotiate directly with the ministries involved in petrochemical industry development. The ANIQ-PEMEX and ANIQ-SEPAFIN commissions were established for this purpose.

15. The data appearing here are taken from the program as presented in de Oteyza, José Andrés, op. cit., pp. 309-311; "Expansión de la petroquímica básica," in Comercio Exterior, Vol. 28, No. 5, Mexico City, Banco Nacional de Comercio Exterior, May 1978, pp. 544-548; Baptista, César, "Industria petroquímica en México," in IMIQ, Mexico City, IMIQ, February 1977, pp. 60-72; and García Luna, José Luis, "Petroquímica," in Ingenieria Petrolera, Mexico City, Asociacion de Ingenieros Petroleros de México, A.C., December 1976-February 1977, pp. 69-74.

16. For example, an increase in the nominal ammonia production capacity from 910,000 tons per year to almost 3 million tons per year was forecast for the whole government term. The nominal capacity for ethylene was increased from 260,000 tons per year to 2 million tons per year, whereby Mexico would be producing as much or even more ethylene than all of Latin America. Hence, ethylene would not be a starting point for producing large volumes of derivatives. The utilization of naphthas derived from the vast quantity of associated gas extracted during the oil-production development program would allow production of aromatics to increase from 310,000 tons per year to 2.4 million tons per year. Apart from providing sufficient propane for liquefied gas production, the supposed abundance of natural gas would create large surpluses that could be utilized to obtain 300,000 tons of propylene per year.

17. Although in 1982 petrochemical exports surpassed basic petrochemical imports in volume, the situation was not so much a product of the substantial increase in exports as of the reduction in imports resulting from the difficulty in obtaining foreign exchange.

18. There are dry natural gas derivatives, ethylene and derivatives, propylene and derivatives, and aromatics. A fifth group consists of butadiene.

19. A sample of the twenty-six major basic petrochemicals grouped according to origin showed that the AAGR of apparent consumption for aromatics, propylene and its derivatives, and butadiene from 1970 to 1982 was 12.1, 12.8, and 3.2 percent, respectively, although the AAGR of production for these groups only reached 5.9, 9.3, and -3.9 percent, respectively. How-

ever, growth in the demand for dry natural gas derivatives was lower than growth in production, at 11.7 and 15.5 percent, respectively. Despite dynamic growth (AAGR = 17 percent), the production of ethylene and derivatives was insufficient to satisfy consumption because in 1982 29 percent of the demand for petrochemicals considered in this sample was for these products. These data were taken from a broader study of the basic petrochemical industry still being developed.

20. By 1970, of the total volume of basic petrochemicals produced, 76 percent came from natural gas components; in 1982 the figure rose to 89 percent.

21. The consequent deficit in propylene and butadiene production, together with the forecasted easy availability of naphthas, led several PEMEX's petrochemical technicians in the early 1970s to promote a new project for producing propane-propylene and butane-butylene. However, the construction of this complex in Morelos, Veracruz, was continually postponed.

22. The Cosoleacaque petrochemical complex in Veracruz, which includes six ammonia plants, four of which are maximum international capacity (445,000 tons per year), is one of the world's largest ammonia producers. If considered together with the rest of the country's ammonia plants, installed capacity for ammonia production amounted to almost 3 million tons per year in 1982.

23. Mexico's fertilizer industry is in the hands of FERTIMEX, a state-owned monopolistic company.

24. It is calculated that total ammonia supply for 1980 would have covered the fertilizer requirements for the states of Jalisco and Aguascalientes. Ammonia is mainly used for developing nitrogenous fertilizers, which took up 72.8 percent of total domestic consumption in 1980; also in 1980 direct fertilization accounted for 23.1 percent and the secondary petrochemical industry for the remaining 4.1 percent. See SPP, SEPAFIN, PEMEX, and FERTIMEX, Industria Petroquímica: Análisis y expectativas, Mexico City, SPP, 1981, pp. 102, 107; Angeles, Luis, "La industria petroquímica mexicana en la dinámica Internacional," in Unomásuno, Mexico City, 9 February 1984.

25. See SPP, Diagnóstico de Petróleos Mexicanos, Mexico City, SPP, no date, pp. 13-15.

26. Another reason for the project's being behind schedule was red tape; the main bottleneck was import permits for materials and equipment.

27. In 1982 and 1983 PEMEX and certain other public sector agencies insisted that PEMEX's petrochemical expansion projects had not been suspended, although they did admit they had slowed their pace somewhat. See, for example, "La industria petroquímica: Punta de lanza para la recuperación," in Expansión, Vol. 15, No. 366, Mexico City, 25 April 1983, p. 34.

28. See PEMEX, Memoria de labores, 1983, Mexico City PEMEX, 1984, p. 12.

29. The lack of official data on PEMEX's production costs prevents estimates being made of just how much PEMEX was being subsidized by the secondary petrochemical branch.

30. From 1970 to 1979 the price index for basic petrochemical production grew at an average rate of 12.2 percent per year, and the whole industrial sector's index was 16.5 percent. From 1980 to 1982 the rates for the petrochemical subsector and the industrial sector were 21.9 percent and 39.9 percent, respectively.

31. Until the Mexican peso's devaluation in 1976, domestic prices were higher than international prices for most of the basic petrochemicals. The relatively obsolete and small-scale technology used in Mexico compared with the particularly dynamic development of world petrochemical technology probably explains this price difference.

32. The subsidy PEMEX granted to the secondary petrochemical sector with the resale of imported petrochemicals went from 667 million pesos in 1974 to 5.331 billion in 1979. See SPP, et al., Industria petroquímica: Análisis y expectativas, op. cit.

33. These losses, representing 42 percent of the sales in 1978 (4.9 billion pesos), reached 82 percent in 1979 (12 billion pesos). This information is from PEMEX's internal documents.

34. According to PEMEX the subsidy on the resale of imported basic petrochemicals amounted to 12.237 billion pesos in 1982. See "Nuevos precios de

petroquímicos," in Transformación, 9th season, Vol. 1, Nos. 6 and 7, Mexico City, CANACINTRA, June-July 1982. Despite the later adjustments, which jointly represented an average increase of 114 percent from November 1982 to July 1983, in terms of dollars basic petrochemicals were only 2 percent more expensive in July 1983 than they were in 1982 at the end of the previous government term.

35. See SPP, et al., op. cit., p. 16.

36. See Toledo, Alejandro (editor), Petróleo y ecodesarrollo en el sureste de México, Mexico City, Centro de Ecodesarrollo, 1982, pp. 69-70, 221-233; Bosh, Pedro, "Evolución de las inversiones químicas y petroquímicas, 1976-1981," in ANIQ, Memorias: XIV Foro nacional de la industria química, Mexico City, ANIQ, 1981, pp. 15-16.

37. Until 1976 the price was kept below that of 1970.

38. "The highway, railroad, and port transport systems do not have sufficient capacity to unload, store, and transport the basic petrochemical industry's inputs and outputs. This means an additional cost, which is transferred in the end to the local consumer and reduces competitiveness in foreign markets." IEPES, Industria petroquímica nacional, Mexico City, IEPES, p. 87. This same study also mentions that PEMEX's credit policy, whereby clients were given only thirty days credit or were paid after more than ninety days, contributed to the decapitalization of both parties, especially during inflationary periods when an increase in work capital could affect a company's cash flow significantly.

39. When the six-year program was introduced, the Cactus-Reynosa gas pipeline had already been planned, providing the option to export natural gas surpluses once domestic ammonia demand had been satisfied; this option does not appear to have been considered.

40. In 1983 the president of ANIQ stated that the crisis that began to make itself felt in the petrochemical industry in 1982 was beset by liquidity problems as well as technological and organizational difficulties. "In the technological crisis, the introduction of what is known as 'gigantismo' led the chemical industry to become involved in heavy diseconomies

of scale. The fact is that large petrochemical complexes with fifteen or twenty interdependent plants are so difficult to operate they become inefficient; furthermore, it is doubtful whether there are sufficient financial resources available to keep building on the basis of the same technology premises we did in the past." Statement by Lars Cristianson in "Foro nacional de la industria química," in "En industria química, la mayoría del capital debe ser mexicano," in Unomásuno, Mexico City, 15 October 1985.

41. These entry barriers to new petrochemical firms include initial investment, technological complexity, project lead time, the need for highly qualified personnel, plant size in relation to the domestic market, availability of technology on the domestic market, and the vertical integration of existing companies.

42. For example, of the sixteen products developed by the intermediate petrochemical industry, nine are produced by only one company, and another four are produced by only two companies. A single enterprise —Celanese Mexicana, S.A., a branch of Celanese Co. (U.S.A.)—controls 37 percent of the country's intermediate petrochemical production. However, it is estimated that in 1979 four consortiums (Celanese, Cydsa, Desc, and Alfa) controlled at least 22 of the 150 enterprises in the secondary petrochemical branch, accounting for 75 percent of the branch's sales. (OECD, Transfer of technology in the world petrochemical industry, Sectorial Study Number 1, Paris, OECD, 1979, p. 22.) Apart from the major enterprises, many companies' production by 1982 to 1983 was expensive and inefficient and these companies faced the problem of obsolete technology. This situation was in part the result of protectionist measures and the global strategies of the multinational companies involved in the secondary petrochemical branch.

43. Villagómez Arias, Braulio, "Estrategia y desarrollo de la petroquímica básica en PEMEX, 1984-1988," paper presented at the XXIV Convención Nacional del Instituto Mexicano de Ingenieros Químicos, Mexico City, 1984.

10

Transport and Distribution

Sotero Prieto and Miguel Márquez

The expansion of the transport and distribution system after the oil industry was nationalized became of major importance in supplying Mexico's hydrocarbons and derivatives rapidly and efficiently.[1] Although the proposed change in the refineries' geographic situation was aimed at facilitating product distribution, it also meant readapting the crude transport system from the producing fields to the processing units.[2] Furthermore, the growing demand for derivatives in regions both near and far from production centers required continuous expansion of the maritime and overland distribution systems--poliducts, tank trucks, and tank cars--as well as the storage system.

Although PEMEX has always tried to plan according to technical and economic criteria, the development of the physical infrastructure for oil-product transport and commercialization was also conditioned by other factors. Such planning can lead to a certain degree of inefficiency in the system's management, particularly in relation to alternative means of distribution. This chapter presents an analysis of the policies and criteria followed in expanding this system, with special attention to those factors influencing its development. Although PEMEX's strategies have been approached mainly by product type, this chapter is organized according to the different means of transport and distribution. However, comments have been introduced where necessary with specific information on the different products in relation to the way they are transported.

The first part of the chapter covers the period between nationalization and the mid-1970s and deals especially with the criteria, procedures, and external factors that provided a framework for the transport and distribution system's development and functioning. Then the changes occurring during the oil boom are presented together with the transport system's reaction to the expansion of primary production activities and industrial transformation.

TRANSPORT AND DISTRIBUTION UNTIL THE MID-1970s

The expansion and relocation of refineries, the changes in hydrocarbon production and foreign trade, and the sustained growth in the domestic demand for derivative products determined the need to expand PEMEX'S transport and distribution system following nationalization. Although there is no knowledge of global and integrated policies in this field, as time went by PEMEX's guidelines were defined for the use of alternative means of transport. These selection criteria mainly covered initial investment, operation and maintenance costs, travel and type of terrain, volumes transported, and product specifications.

Pipelines

For the sake of this study pipelines include those pipes that are used for transporting crude oil from producing fields to refineries or seaports for export; gas pipelines that constitute the only means by which PEMEX transports and distributes natural gas; and pipelines that are for derivatives, which are sometimes used to convey a variety of products, such as gasoline, kerosene, and liquefied gas.

When dealing with large volumes transported over long distances, the pipeline tends to be the most economic means of transport.[3] However, it does have certain limitations compared to other means. It can only be used to transport products between set points and is not appropriate for carrying those with high viscosity. Although the use of pipelines avoids traffic-congestion problems and environmental contamination, installation costs are particularly prohibitive where the terrain is hilly or where the areas are highly populated, thus requiring detours and greater security measures.

The decision to bring refineries closer to consumer centers also implies expanding the pipeline system and changing worn-out or small-diameter pipes. This alternative is considered less difficult and costly than keeping refineries close to oil fields because of the problems associated with distributing large volumes over long distances, particularly in the case of fuel oil.

Thus, after nationalization the refineries were renovated, and the pipeline network was modified significantly. The larger-diameter pipes were installed and the pipeline itself extended. This construction was complemented by the development of crude oil maritime transport. From 1938 to 1970 around 1,700 kilometers of trunk lines were built, the major lines from Poza Rica to Salamanca, Azcapotzalco, and Ciudad Madero. In 1970 over 400 TBD of crude were conveyed by oil pipelines, and only 66 TBD were transported by sea from the southern zones to the ports of Tuxpan and Ciudad Madero.[4]

Early in the 1970s the discovery of new oil fields in southeast Mexico made it necessary to build new lines for transporting additional crude to the refineries. Furthermore, when Mexico began to export again in 1974, crude also had to be taken to the port of Pajaritos. From 1972 to 1975 oil transport by pipeline doubled.[5] In 1975 construction began on the 30 inch in diameter oil pipeline from Minatitlán to Poza Rica because volumes in excess of 100 TBD had to be transported from the south to the central plateau and the north.[6] It was decided that from now on because of the large volumes of crude required, the refineries should be supplied only by oil pipeline.

By the mid-1970s PEMEX already had an impressive infrastructure for transporting crude, consisting main-ly of the pipeline network. Apart from connecting oil fields with different ports, the pipelines supplied refineries as follows:

- Reynosa in the northeast received oil produced in nearby fields by pipeline.

- Ciudad Madero in the northeast coast was supplied with crude by oil pipeline from neighboring districts and Poza Rica. As production grew in the south, crude was transported by tanker from Minatitlán and later Pajaritos.

- Salamanca and Azcapotzalco in the central plateau received oil by pipeline from Poza Rica and the fixed buoy loaders in Tuxpan, Veracruz, which were fed from the south by undersea pipeline.

- Minatitlán in the southeast was also supplied by oil pipeline except for a small quantity of crude sent by barge.

Very few budgetary restrictions were involved in developing the oil pipeline network because of PEMEX's policy in this respect. However, a few bottlenecks arose in refinery operation because of the somewhat slow progress in pipeline construction. Salamanca, for instance, which had a primary-distillation capacity of 210 TBD in 1974, only received 130 TBD of crude by oil pipeline.[7]

In the late 1940s PEMEX began gas pipeline construction for commercial use. Until then only two private gas pipelines were working, taking gas imported from the United States to Monterrey; meanwhile, Mexican gas could not be utilized because there were no treatment plants, nor was there any way of transporting and distributing the product. Of the pipelines installed during the 1950s, those from Reynosa to Monterrey and Poza Rica to the Distrito Federal were the most important because they allowed a large part of the local gas production capacity to be utilized.

The gas pipeline network continued to expand mainly from the south to the Distrito Federal and Guadalajara and by 1975 had reached a length of 5,400 kilometers.[8] In general, pipeline transport capacity was greater than the availability of natural gas, its utilization extremely limited by the delay in installing collector and processing systems.[9]

The distribution of light refined products (gasoline, kerosene, and diesel) by poliduct was practically nonexistent before 1950, but it became increasingly important over the following twenty years. By 1970 the network had extended approximately 3,500 kilometers, allowing more than 40 percent of the overall light-product volume to be distributed by this means.[10] Although over 1,000 kilometers of poliducts were installed during the following five years, in 1975 IMP studies considered installed capacity insufficient. Because poliducts were more economical than mobile transport for distributing volumes of more than 5 TBD, additional lines would have to be built as a substitute for the overland vehicles carrying products from maritime and poliduct terminals to sales agencies.[11]

However, PEMEX was unable to obtain the budgetary authorizations from the executive to improve the efficiency of the distribution system because it had failed to undertake the studies necessary to determine appropriate selection criteria and because of the pressure exerted by freight companies who wished to continue lending their services to PEMEX. Under these circumstances and because it was easier for the executive to approve a budget for current expenditure than for investment, PEMEX decided to continue leasing oil tank trucks and charging it to current expenses, even though in the long run the alternative would cost more in terms of money, highway deterioration, and environmental contamination than the construction of new pipelines.[12]

PEMEX only established two liquefied gas pipelines from Poza Rica and Minatitlán to the central plateau. In the north of the country distribution was handled by overland vehicles belonging to private companies, a practice begun when PEMEX's production was exceedingly small, and distributing companies were responsible for most of the imports. From the early 1970s onward, PEMEX had pipelines for taking fuel oil to maritime terminals and thermoelectric plants, but because of its high viscosity, this product had to be transported by other means when distances over 50 kilometers were involved.

Last, although the pipelines could be used for transporting petrochemicals, this practice was limited to ammonia, which was conveyed from Cosoleacaque to the Salina Cruz maritime terminal, and to PEMEX's own inputs. All other products were sold at PEMEX plants, which was a headache for clients who had to solve the problem of transport.

Maritime Transport

From the time of the oil industry's nationalization to the mid-1970s it was intended that port infrastructure should evolve according to the needs and characteristics of the ships PEMEX either purchased or rented. Problems such as shallow ports and the risks inherent in leasing tankers forced PEMEX to quickly purchase units and continuously dredge the harbors, with or without the help of the navy.

Until the early 1970s very little crude was transported by sea (no more than 70 TBD). From 1973 onward, however, a substantial increase in oil production in the southeast conferred greater importance on shipping. The increased demand for products in the country's different regions also made maritime transport more important and convenient than overland vehicles, especially to Pacific ports.

Although until 1975 it appears that the program for purchasing and leasing tankers and adapting ports was congruent with the technical and economic selection criteria applied exclusively to maritime transport, the measures adopted did not always agree with the global guidelines established for the hydrocarbon transport and distribution system. Such was the case with the costly maritime maneuvers made when the central plateau's product demands could not be satisfied even with the help of the Minatitlán poliduct. Had a second poliduct been made available, the demand could have been covered.

The fuel capacity of tankers could not be utilized because of the shallowness of some maritime terminals, and their reduced storage capacity forced tankers to carry out maneuvers with less than a full load.[13] Until the early 1970s the oil fleet was used basically for coastal sailing, with crude taken to the refineries and refined products and fuel oil to maritime terminals. Despite these difficulties, very few problems were encountered.[14]

PEMEX's internal reports show that leasing tankers was less costly than purchasing them, even with the risk of being dependent on ship owners. The maximum capacity of PEMEX's tankers did not exceed 21.7 thousand tons of dead weight (TTDW) per unit.[15,16]

Despite the slow increase in crude production, the rise in its demand just prior to 1972 did not warrant additional port capacity and maritime transport installations than what PEMEX's existing fleet and infrastructure could provide. However, because of a significant increase in crude production in the south from this time onward and the sustained increase in demand, PEMEX was forced to lease tankers. In 1975 maneuvers by these tankers were equivalent to 70 percent of those of PEMEX's own fleet.[17] This situation arose despite the fact that PEMEX had increased its capacity and that some of the crude exported was transported by ships hired by the clients themselves.

Overland Vehicles

Derivative transport by railways was of particular importance until the 1950s. Mexico's railroad system became so slow and inefficient that PEMEX began to substitute the method with pipelines, tankers, and tank trucks. By 1975 the relative share of railroad tank cars in global movement for these products had fallen to a bare 3 percent.[18]

The railroads still continued to be used for two reasons. First, railroad tank cars were more economical than tank trucks or pipelines for distributing fuel oil and asphalt over long distances.[19] Second, by using the railways PEMEX was less dependent on private transport companies and could use the railways as a guide for determining the cost of leasing private tank trucks.[20]

Considering the high investment and maintenance costs involved in purchasing railroad tank cars, PEMEX decided it was better to lease; furthermore, the cost of doing so traditionally had been low. However, although no apparent change in policy had occurred from 1973 to 1975, the number of PEMEX's own tank cars involved in total railway movement increased.[21]

While the use of railroad tank cars dropped, the utilization of tank trucks for product distribution underwent a considerable increase and in 1975 represented 7 percent of total movement.[22] The substitution of one form of transport for another took place despite the fact that the volumetric capacity of railroad tank cars was three times that of the tank trucks, which only indicates how slow and inefficient the railroad system was compared to other overland transport.[23]

Undoubtedly, efforts to reduce dependence on railroad transport were a direct response to the need to improve economic profitability. However, PEMEX was forced to disregard established criteria for product distribution and chose tank trucks instead of poliducts because of its financially limited investment program.

Although PEMEX resorted to leased tank trucks for distributing its products, local gasoline, kerosene, and diesel delivery has been carried out mainly by PEMEX's own vehicles. Because this operation involves delivery to gas service stations and wholesalers and is the most visible of PEMEX's services (where the public can judge PEMEX's efficiency), special attention has been given to maintaining an adequate fleet of tank trucks for this purpose. These vehicles have even been used to solve storage problems both at sales agencies and service stations. From 1970 to 1975 the number of tank trucks owned by PEMEX rose from 440 to 743, their capacity standardized to the volume considered appropriate for local delivery, that is, 15 cubic meters.[24] Regulations state that urban delivery must be made solely by PEMEX's unionized personnel, although delivery to nonurban service stations, that is, those outside the town limits where sales agencies are located and that account for 40 percent of total delivery, can be delegated to private companies.

TABLE 10.1
AVERAGE DAILY AVAILABLE STORAGE SPACE CAPACITY IN MEXICO, 1967

Area	(1) Capacity (TB)	(2) Production (TBD)	(1)/(2) Daily Spare Capacity
Poza Rica	1,090	162	7
Northern Zone	2,930	64	46
Southern Zone	1,804	138	13
Total	5,824	364	16
Tuxpan	825	--	--
Catalina	99	--	--
Total	6,748	--	--
Refineries (crude and products)	16,170	--	--

TB = thousands of barrels.
TBD = thousands of barrels per day.

Source: Based upon unpublished information received from PEMEX.

Storage

Because it is impractical to sustain a continuous and uniform flow of crude from the time it is extracted until it is refined or exported, it was obvious that storage deposits would be necessary. Lack of data and analysis on variations in the fuel production cycle prevented PEMEX from determining the appropriate storage capacity for each phase. From the limited information available on installed capacity, it can be deducted that in 1967 the average daily available spare capacity was as shown in Table 10.1.[25]
The situation was quite different in 1975 as a result of increased crude production in the south and diminished production in the north. Because storage capacity did not increase in accordance with the geographic changes observed in relative crude production, spare capacity in the south fell to barely five days. In all the exploitation districts and maritime termi

nals, only twelve-day spare mean production capacity was available (806 TBD).[26]

Variations in derivative flow also occur because of changes in the following phases: (1) crude delivery to refineries; (2) refining production; (3) delivery from refinery to transport vehicles; (4) distribution to the shipment terminal; (5) delivery to next transport vehicle en route to the end plant; and (6) delivery to service stations and retailers. Problems with delivery from refinery to transport vehicles, the temporary suspension of seagoing transport because of adverse weather conditions, and excessive transitory demand at service stations are factors that have made storage capacity necessary.

Although storage plant (sales agencies) location and capacity for delivering light refined products has varied since 1975 and before, the number of plants has remained at around sixty, not including small nonurban plants and private distributors. These plants were situated where development poles or centers arose, which, in turn, stimulated demand for certain products, particularly gasoline and diesel. Their location also depended on the evolution of production centers and refining complexes.

From 1967 to 1975 light-product storage capacity increased from 5.4 MB to 8.1 MB.[27] In order to determine new plant or existing facility extension requirements, PEMEX's assistant trade management took the following parameters into account: average daily demand, maximum demand, means of transport for storage, distance from supplying refinery and reshipment terminal, and medium-term forecast for product demand. These items, however, were applied with a certain degree of flexibility and sometimes inconsistently.

The following days of spare capacity for 1967 and 1975 can be calculated using figures for storage and sales capacity for light refined products and fuel oil:

	1967	1975
Capacity (TB)	5,400	8,100
Sales (BD)	205	383
Days of Spare Capacity	27	22

Although these data show a capacity in excess of that recommended, one must take into account that reshipment terminals dealt with volumes greater than those they sold.[28] Furthermore, the capacity of a number of storage plants was much below the recommended limits.

Service Stations

After nationalization PEMEX continued a policy aimed at avoiding the unnecessary proliferation of facilities, retailers, and service stations.[29] Of the 1,890 service stations that existed in the late 1950s, 90 percent of them were private, and the remaining 10 percent belonged to PEMEX.

In 1975 the number of service stations had increased to 2,694, of which 240 were in the Distrito Federal.[30] 95 percent of the gas stations were in private hands, granted permits after PEMEX's assistant trade management carried out market research studies on safety. Although the property of PEMEX, the remaining 5 percent of the gas stations were administered by different government agencies or public-welfare organizations, PEMEX decided that service stations required at least 20 cubic meters of storage capacity per product, which was sufficient for an average of three days' sales.

Internal Organization

Until 1979 difficulties arose in different phases of transport and distribution activities because of the number of different departments involved:

- Hydrocarbon transport by pipeline was the responsibility of the Subdirección de Producción Primaria (Primary Production Assistant Management), which was also in charge of several other pipelines for transporting products.

- Product distribution by pipeline depended mainly on the Gerencias de Refinación y Petroquímica

. (Refining and Petrochemical Departments) of the Subdirección de Producción Industrial (Industrial Production Assistant Management) as well as the Gerencia de Ventas (Sales Department) of the Subdirección Comercial (Trade Assistant Management) after 1975.

. The same Gerencia de Ventas was in charge of distribution by overland vehicle.

. Maritime transport of crude and derivatives was the responsibility of the Gerencia de Marina (Marine Department) of the Subdirección Comercial.

. Work on pipelines, storage plants, loading wharves, and so on, was handled by the Gerencia de Proyectos y Construcción (Projects and Construction Department).

Responsibilities had been formally assigned; however, the interference of different agencies during operations showed a lack of precision in functions definition. Although a coordinating office was established at management level, it lacked staff and the authority to work effectively.

Mainly because of its multiple functions and the lack of coordination, the Subdirección de Finanzas (Finances Assistant Management) encountered serious problems in controlling expenditure. A detailed record of current investment and expenditure was never kept, a measure that would have allowed the cost of each transport and distribution phase to be determined in relation to the means of transport. Moreover, the absence of an adequate and integrated system for measuring and controlling mobilized volumes from production to sale made it difficult to efficiently program expenditures.

EVOLUTION OF STRATEGIES AND POLICIES FROM 1976 TO 1983

Just before the oil boom the existing transport and distribution infrastructure generally made it possible for PEMEX to deliver its products on schedule.

However, not all operations were carried out efficiently because the technical and economic criteria defined by PEMEX had to be adapted to budgetary constraints. Furthermore, the inherent complexity in the distribution of a large variety of products, complicated by sustained growth in demand, was exacerbated by the lack of coordination between PEMEX's different decision-making departments.

Although the oil industry's large-scale expansion during the 1976-1982 government term placed new and greater quantitative and qualitative demands on the transport and distribution system, the policies followed for this area, most of which were implicit, underwent only slight changes. In other words, PEMEX's technical and economic criteria for determining the alternative uses of the different transport means were also the basis for the strategies proposed by PEMEX technicians. However, in some cases the action taken differed from these criteria because of PEMEX's unusual use of its investment and current expenditure budget, the executive's intervention in certain operations, and private transport company pressure.

The analysis that follows addresses the modifications made to some of the policies in this sector, the causes of theses changes, and their impact on the evolution of PEMEX's physical structure and the degree of efficiency achieved (see Figure 10.1, Figure 10.2, and Figure 10.3).

Oil pipeline construction progressed rapidly between 1976 and 1983 because of higher export targets as well as new refining requirements. Although crude oil exports increased from 94 TBD to 1.5 MBD, primary crude-distillation capacity grew from 693 TBD to 1.3 MBD from 1975 to 1983.[31] With increased crude transport needs, the length of pipelines increased fourfold from 1975 to 1983, and the diameter of the new pipes widened considerably. These changes made it possible to increase crude flow from 12 to 29 billion ton-kilometers over the same period.[32] Thus, even though three more refineries--Tula, Cadereyta, and Salina Cruz--came on line, PEMEX was able to supply the refining complexes mainly through oil pipelines, although some complementary maritime transport had had to be used before 1983 because completion of the pipeline from Poza Rica to Ciudad Madero had been delayed.

FIGURE 10.1

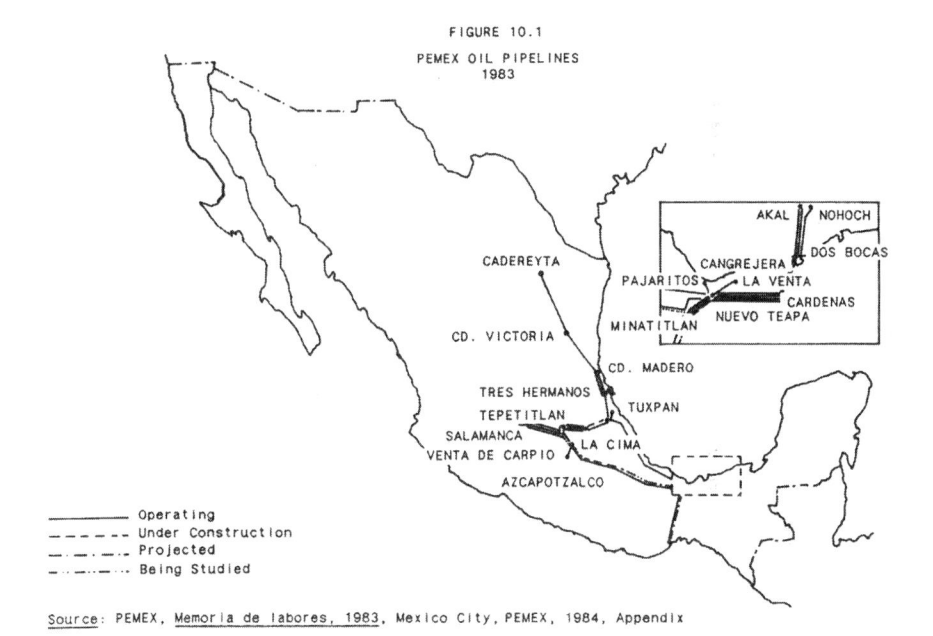

PEMEX OIL PIPELINES
1983

——————— Operating
— — — — Under Construction
—··—··— Projected
—··—··— Being Studied

Source: PEMEX, *Memoria de labores, 1983*, Mexico City, PEMEX, 1984, Appendix

FIGURE 10.2
PEMEX MAJOR GAS PIPELINES IN 1983

Source: PEMEX, Memorias de labores, 1982 y 1983

FIGURE 10.3
PEMEX POLIDUCTS
1983

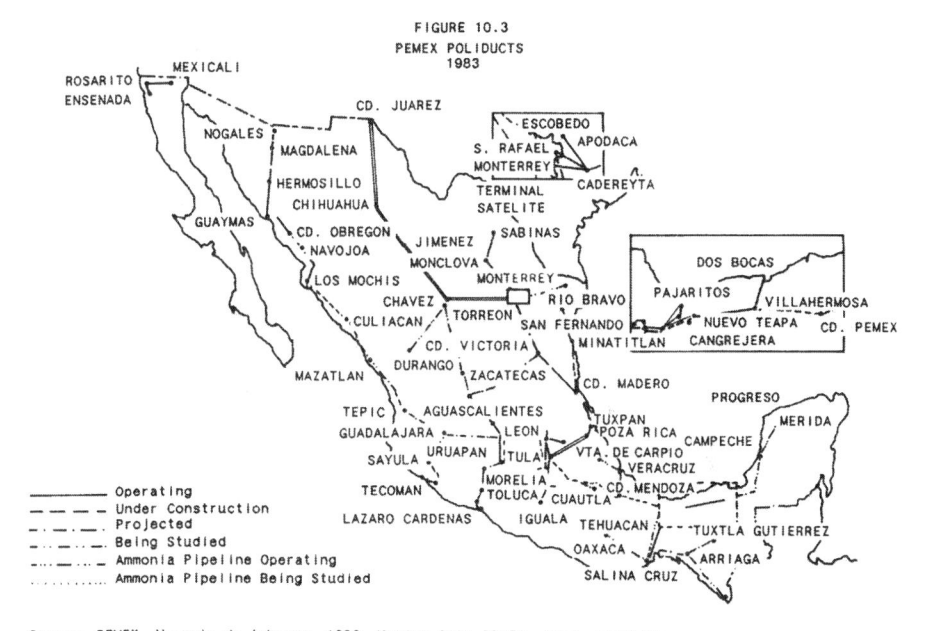

Legend:
— Operating
– – – Under Construction
–··–··– Projected
–···–···– Being Studied
–··–··– Ammonia Pipeline Operating
············ Ammonia Pipeline Being Studied

Source: PEMEX, *Memoria de labores, 1983*, Mexico City, PEMEX, 1984, Appendix.

The heavy increase in crude exports also meant that substantial modifications had to be made to the maritime tankers of over 200 TTDW offshore, such as those at Rabón Grande (near Pajaritos); Dos Bocas; and, recently, Salina Cruz. A reef called Cayo Arcas was also conditioned to load Campeche Gulf crude from a stationary ship. With the improved loading conditions and dredging done at certain ports, tankers with capacity to 55 TTDW were purchased, the number of units increasing from twenty-six with a tonnage of 489 TTDW to thirty-six with a tonnage of 970 TTDW in 1983.

Despite these improvements, information about the movements, although incomplete, indicates that fleet productivity fell considerably in 1983 compared to 1975.[33] With the exception of Pajaritos, Rosarito, Tuxpan, and, to a lesser extent, Ciudad Madero, the improvements and extensions were apparently insufficient to cope with the increased draft and storage capacity required for the tankers that had been purchased. Although the oil fleet increased, so did the number of leased vessels and their contribution to total transported volume, which rose from 43 percent in 1975 to 71 percent in 1983.[34]

Progress in gas pipeline construction between 1975 and 1983 can be divided into two periods: (1) when the prospect of exporting natural gas to the United States was forecast early in 1977 and (2) when the controversy arose as a result of this forecast.[35]

Late in 1976 PEMEX director Jorge Díaz Serrano and some of his closest collaborators decided to begin construction on a 48-inch gas pipeline between Cactus and Reynosa so that large volumes of natural gas could be exported to the United States. This decision was based on the assumptions (1) that such large quantities of exportable natural gas (2 BCFD) actually existed and (2) that the U.S. government would accept the conditions (mainly price) under which the negotiations would take place.[36]

Because of the project's specific characteristics and conditions, not only was the construction of this gas pipeline risky, it was also a mistake.[37] In effect, it was confirmed not only that the assumed volumes of gas were not available but that the volumes and price agreed upon after fifteen months of long and delicate negotiations were very much below Mexico's expectations. It was the assumptions regarding volume and price that were used to justify starting a large part of the construction.[38]

In light of new conditions arising from the negotiation process, a few months before an agreement was reached in September 1979 between PEMEX and Border Gas Inc. PEMEX had to change its strategy radically.[39] Following SEPAFIN's advice it was decided to build a series of gas pipelines. The project turned out to be of very little use and extremely costly because the maximum amount of natural gas available did not even cover the volumes estimated for domestic consumption, let alone for export. In short, extensive gas pipelines were constructed between 1980 and 1983 (an increase from 8,435 kilometers to 14,000 kilometers) and were accompanied by a proportionate increase in transported volumes.[40]

Rapid growth in oil consumption from the mid-1970s onward led to accelerated expansion in the distribution system with almost complete disregard for the criteria established for alternative use of different distribution means.[41] Consequently, the tendency to depend heavily on overland equipment became greater during these years. Tank truck participation in total product movement rose from 22 percent in 1971 to 48 percent in 1980, whereas the amount transported by poliduct fell from 61 percent to 47 percent, even though movement by poliduct was considered to be the most economic means of transporting large volumes over long distances.[42]

Liquefied gas distribution by pipeline was not promoted. Most of the production from Minatitlán was carried to the central plateau by overland vehicles and from Pajaritos in tankers via the Panama Canal, both of which were extremely costly methods.

The ever-increasing inefficiency in dealing with alternative distribution means stemmed mainly from insufficient investment in this field. Both pressure from demand and the new hydrocarbon-export policy led PEMEX to channel investment mainly into primary production and industrial transformation. However, investment in trade activities from 1977 to 1981 represented only 6 percent of total investment, even though PEMEX's petrochemical program for 1977-1982 had budgeted 13 percent for this purpose.[43]

Equally as serious was the deterioration in the efficiency of overland equipment. Products transported by tank trucks fell from 4 million ton-kilometers per unit in 1976 to 1.5 in 1981.[44] Also, movement by railroad tank car decreased nearly 40 percent from 1975 to 1983 despite having the same total volumetric capacity.[45] The inefficient use of overland equipment, together with increased tariffs, implied that PEMEX's payout for transport rose at an average annual rate of 53 percent from 1976 to 1981.[46]

Added to this was a change in the composition of railroad transport capacity, which departed considerably from the economic profitability criteria. PEMEX's own unit share in total capacity increased from 46 percent to 65 percent from 1975 to 1983 despite the lower cost of leasing tank cars.[47]

The slow progress made in extending the poliducts was in part due to the red tape involved in settling the compensation with SEPAFIN for land expropriated for laying the pipeline.[48,49] These conditions did nothing to encourage PEMEX to promote poliduct installation.

Between 1981 and 1983 because storage capacity was insufficient to cope with the frequent changes in crude volume exported and the adverse weather conditions, the company had to resort to leasing tankers in Curaçao. Although foreign demand for crude stabilized after 1982, it was not until late 1983 that leasing, as well as the practice of using oil tankers, was finally suspended. A lack of coordinated technical and economic studies in exploitation, refining, and foreign-trade activities made it impossible to define the appropriate storage capacity for the different crude mobilization phases. Studies undertaken late in 1983, which primary considered probabilistic factors, concluded that the existing 20 MB crude capacity (seven-day production), along with that available at refineries, was more than enough to avoid major risks.[50]

Although oil demand rose at an average annual rate of nearly 10 percent from 1976 to 1982, the number of plants and terminals available for storing products only increased from sixty to sixty-four.

Over the same period total capacity doubled, but by late 1981 it had become insufficient to keep product supply at a reasonable level at all plants.[51] Problems in supply to service stations continued at some plants because of insufficient capacity.[52]

From 1979 onward PEMEX adopted a number of measures aimed at making internal transport and distribution operations efficient. Additional offices were created, such as the Gerencia de Ductos (Pipeline Department) of the Subdirección de Producción Primaria and others related with sales and distribution. Although the specific responsibilities assigned to each office improved the efficiency of certain operations, in general the communication and coordination problems worsened because so many departments were involved. Thus, there was no improvement in activities involving the measurement of product volume and the recording of operation expenditures and investment in new works.

Last, some of the norms followed in transport and distribution operations are derived from agreements established between PEMEX and STPRM. The Contrato Colectivo (Trade Union Contract) specifies that sales agent positions in storage plants have to be occupied by trade union personnel, which means external pressure cannot be exerted to appoint certain candidates for these posts. The same measure is applied to local distributors, who deliver products from storage plants to service stations, and retailers so that the final distribution phase should depend solely on PEMEX personnel (with the exception of nonurban service stations).

However, until 1983 there was an implicit agreement between PEMEX management and STPRM leaders, whereby the union gave contracts to PEMEX, even for activities that according to the Contrato Colectivo (clause I) should have been undertaken directly by PEMEX. The resolutions introduced by the executive in 1983 stipulated that PEMEX had to accept tenders for all contracts; subcontracting was prohibited. (STPRM's contract commission often subcontracted private enterprises.) When confronted with these measures, STPRM began to exert pressure to obtain the contracts. It demanded that clause I of the Contrato Colectivo be applied and maintenance activities be assigned to PEMEX personnel, that is, direct administration. Consequently, most of the maintenance work on transport vehicles was done with insufficient skilled personnel or specialized equipment.

Late in the López Portillo administration (1976-1982), PEMEX publicly recognized he trading system's deficiencies and the need to expand capacity enough to satisfy domestic- and foreign-market requirements. "It must be stressed that we need an infrastructure and commercial organization far superior to that available. We need ports and port services, a modern and efficient fleet, adequate storage facilities, an extended pipeline network, and efficient export operation systems."[53] The PEMEX administration that took office in December 1982 considered the slow trade development, as opposed to production, one of the major problems arising from the changes in the oil industry over the previous years.[54]

The strategy laid down for the new government term consisted of short-term measures to improve the efficiency and flexibility of the major factor involved in distributing derivatives, that is, offshore and onshore terminals and overland and maritime transport:

- Annual growth, operation, and maintenance programs were formulated for the terminals. These programs included the modernization of control and safety instruments and were designed to provide substantially increased storage capacity.

- On the basis of the two existing pipeline networks for oil-product distribution, that is, the northern and south-central, an integrated system was designed, including a double interconnection and access to the Pacific coast. The project made use of those lines that had been intended for conveying quantities of natural gas, which, as it turned out, were superior to those available. Thus, by modifying five gas pipelines and building three additional branches, the national pipeline system would be complete.

- Because of the rise in overland transport tariffs, attempts would be made to improve both transport routes and vehicles, allowing a

- balanced cargo distribution and a reduction in costs. Optimum utilization of pipelines would concurrently be promoted.

- To facilitate maritime transport proper coordination would be established between oil ports; improvements would be made to the infrastructure and dredging and maintenance operations intensified.

- To improve the service's public image the Programa Nacional de Revaloración de Estaciones de Servicio (National Program for Service Station Improvement) was introduced; its aim was to modernize the country's gas station network.[55]

CONCLUSIONS

In general, the physical infrastructure for transporting hydrocarbons and trading derivatives developed quickly enough for it to adapt to the profound changes occurring in the oil industry, on one hand, following nationalization and, on the other, during the oil boom of the 1970s. Save a few exceptions, there have been no bottlenecks in derivative production and delivery that can be attributed to insufficient means of transport and distribution. On certain occasions, though, oil exportation was hindered by the limitations in maritime infrastructure and storage capacity; nevertheless, new measures allowed PEMEX to overcome these obstacles. However, a highly efficient integrated system still has not been developed. In order to deliver its products according to schedule and to fulfill export commitments, PEMEX resorted to measures that were not always congruent with technical and economic criteria and that implied high operational costs.

According to available information, PEMEX's efforts toward integrated planning have been fewer for these activities than for other areas such as refining and petrochemicals. Programming was severely limited from the start because the measurements and control that were needed to track the quantity of hydrocarbons and derivatives transported from production to sale were not carried out with precision and detail. Also, investment and associated operational costs were not itemized for each type and stage of transport. Apart from these deficiencies, studies on criteria for alternative transport use were also lacking. Ignorance of its operating economics is a reflection of PEMEX's inability to overcome the internal complications stemming from the excessive number of departments handling these activities.

In addition to the obstacles inherent in PEMEX's organization, there were external factors that contributed to increased operational costs. Until the early 1980s PEMEX had problems in getting the executive to approve its investment budgets as well as a tendency to concentrate this investment in production; as a result, PEMEX resorted unwisely to its current expenditures to meet the increasing needs of the distribution system. Specifically, restricted investment in trade accompanied by rapid growth in sales soon meant the poliducts could not cope with the demand, and excessive dependence on highway transport became necessary to distribute the product. Not only has this situation led to high operating costs, it has also caused highway congestion and environmental contamination.

Furthermore, the decision to purchase railway tank cars instead of lease them, wasted tanker capacity because of shallow harbors, and insufficient storage capacity at maritime terminals and certain sales agencies only indicate the extent of these deficiencies and the worsening of conditions during the 1976-1982 government term. In addition, gas pipelines were constructed predominantly for political reasons and without solid background information regarding the availability of gas for both export and domestic consumption. Activities such as this, which were devoid of established technical and economic criteria, further restricted the possibility of making the necessary investments in pipelines, storage plants, and so on.

Although PEMEX's program for the late 1980 is still unknown, we can assume the following:

- Crude transport to refineries and wharves will encounter major obstacles, even with the extended processing capacity forecast for Tula and Salina Cruz.[56] Projects for installing pumping stations on the pipeline to Tula and constructing an oil pipeline from Minatitlán to Salina Cruz could experience a certain amount of delay. Although there is still enough time to complete the projects on schedule delays have occurred previously in works of a similar nature.

- Crude storage capacity at oil fields, terminals, and refineries is sufficient to cope with unforeseen changes that might occur over the next few years. There is also a project to drill saline domes near the port of Pajaritos and the Rabón Grande buoys in the south, although detailed studies have not been undertaken to determine the feasibility of using caves (as opposed to other options) for storing crude.

- Although the capacity of the 48-inch gas pipeline being constructed between Veracruz and the central plateau would be excessive, two 24-inch lines will be freed and could convey crude to the Tula refinery and liquefied gas to the Distrito Federal from Minatitlán.

- The prospects for improving light-distillate distribution are not encouraging because dispersed responsibilities and a lack of coordination within PEMEX make evaluation activities and modifications based on rational criteria difficult. As recent as 1984 the purchase of one thousand railroad tank cars was approved, with a cost equivalent to the construction of over 1,000 kilometers of poliducts.

- Plans made years ago to reduce costs and solve liquefied gas distribution problems are still being modified; as yet not one has been put into practice. The projects include readapting little-used gas pipelines, although these works will probably not be finished before 1988. Until then high distribution costs are still expected with the continued use of overland vehicles to convey products to the central plateau and of tankers to carry the products to the Pacific ports via the Panama Canal. Another unsolved problem is insufficient liquefied gas storage capacity.

In short, it appears that no significant changes in the distribution system are programmed that might improve its efficiency. However, in view of the heavy reduction in the growth rate of oil product demand since 1982, no bottlenecks are expected for product delivery, even with the existing system (see Tables 10.2, 10.3, and 10.4).

TABLE 10.2
COMPARATIVE COSTS OF TRANSPORT AND DISTRIBUTION*

Transport Means	Costs (%) Minimum	Maximum
Tank Truck[a]	100	100
Railroad Tank Car (excluding rental)	80	105
Tanker		
Less than 500 km	30	70
Less than 2,500 km	10	25
Pipelines[b]		
Crude Greater than 100 TBD	10	25
Products Greater than 5 TBD	15	30
Fuel Oil (hot)	30	70

TBD = thousand barrels per day.
*This figures are an estimate average cost per ton-kilometer compared with a tank truck.
[a]An average of 4.5 pesos per ton-kilometer for a mean distance of 300 kilometers is estimated for the tank truck, considering an average exchange rate of 150 pesos per dollar (1983).
[b]The flow of other products is lower in barrels per day than crude; therefore, its conveyance is more costly. Fuel oil cannot be carried over distances exceeding 60 kilometers because cooling occurs, increasing viscosity and impeding its transport by pipeline.
Source: These estimates are based upon information received from PEMEX and IMP, internal documents.

TABLE 10.3
INSTALLED AND UTILIZED CAPACITY FOR TRANSPORT AND
DISTRIBUTION, 1971-1983

Capacity	1971[a]	1975	1980	1983
Transport (Tm^3)				
Own Tank Trucks[b]	430	578	1,082	1,162
Own Tank Trucks (for delivery)	10	11	16	19
Rented Tank Trucks (for distribution)	30	44	144	182
Own Railroad Tank Cars	43	69	87	98
Rented Railroad Tank Cars	90	82	99	52
Pipeline Length (km)				
Oil Pipelines	1,795	2,770	9,134	11,000
Gas Pipelines	4,544	5,418	8,435	14,000
Petroleum Product Pipelines	3,423	5,418	5,199	5,777
Petrochemical Pipelines	473	529	1,676	2,521
Capacity Utilized (Movements in millions of ton/kilometers/year)				
Rented Tank Trucks[c]	1,800	3,425	--	4,795
Railroad Tank Cars Used by PEMEX	1,405	1,170	--	742[d]
Own Tank Trucks	10,000	12,092	17,031	15,070[d]
Rented Tank Trucks	4,435	8,288	28,115	10,380[d]
Oil Pipelines	5,420	11,722	--	29,000[d]
Gas Pipelines	5,090	5,896	--	13,000[d]
Petroleum Product Pipelines	4,015	74	--	--
Petrochemical Pipelines[e]	--	--	--	--

[a]Full information for previous years is not available.
[b]A weighted record of rented units is not available.
[c]Records of PEMEX-owned truck tank movement for delivery are not available.
[d]Data corresponding to 1982.
[e]Data are not available.

Sources: PEMEX, *Memoria de labores*, Mexico City, PEMEX, various years; PEMEX, *Anuario estadistico, 1983*, Mexico City, PEMEX, 1984, pp. 73-79.

TABLE 10.4
STORAGE CAPACITY (MB)

Crude at Fields and Terminals	1967[a]	1983
Poza Rica and Tuxpan	2.0	2.0
Northern Zone	2.8	3.0
Southern Zone (Includes Barcos and Salina Cruz)	1.9	15.0
Total	6.7	20.0
Products in Sales Agencies and Terminals		
Oil Products	5.4	16.0[b]
Liquefied Gas at Terminals	--	1.0
Petrochemicals (thousands of tons)	--	318.0
Crude and Products at Refineries		
Crude	--	9.1
Liquefied Gas	--	1.2
Gasoline	--	10.2
Fuel Oil	--	6.5
Other	--	12.0
Petrochemicals	--	1.5
Total	16.0[c]	40.5

MB = Millions of barrels.
[a] The only year for which information is partially available is 1967.
[b] 2.2 MB correspond to fuel oil.
[c] Partial data are not available.

Sources: IMP, *Plan de desarrollo de la industria petrolera y petroquímica básica, 1976, 1985*, Mexico City, IMP, 1975; PEMEX, internal documents.

NOTES

1. The term "transport" refers to moving crude oil from storage and dehydration centers to refineries or seaports for export. It also applies to conveying natural gas from collecting centers and treatment plants to distribution networks. "Distribution" involves carrying by-products from processing plants, maritime or pipeline terminals, and importation depots to storage plants (sales agencies) and wholesalers.

Local delivery or distribution is made from storage plants to service stations and retailers.

2. See Chapter 8, "The Refining Industry."
3. See Table 10.1.
4. See PEMEX, Memoria de labores, 1971, Mexico City, PEMEX, 1972.
5. See Table 10.2.
6. See Figure 10.1. From Poza Rica, crude oil was to be pumped to the refineries in the central plateau and Ciudad Madero. This line would then be connected to another oil pipeline to be pumped to the refinery under construction at Cadereyta, Nuevo León.
7. See PEMEX, Memoria de labores, 1974, Mexico City, PEMEX, 1975, p. 17.
8. See Table 10.2. In some cases pressure from certain consumer groups led to branch construction being given priority over the main trunk line.
9. See Chapter 7, "Exploration and Exploitation."
10. See Table 10.2 and IMP, Plan de desarrollo de la industria petrolera y petroquímica básica, 1976-1985, Mexico City, IMP, 1975, Chapter 8.
11. Idem. It is estimated that the investment needed to install a pipeline is equivalent to less than four times the annual cost of moving products by oil tank trucks over the same distance.
12. An example of this situation was a project to amplify the capacity of liquefied gas being transported from the Minatitlán refinery to San Juan Ixhuatepec (Valle de México) via an additional poliduct that could also be utilized for distributing other products. Despite the savings involved in eliminating the use of tank trucks, the project was abandoned for these reasons. See IMP, Plan de desarrollo de la industria petrolera y petroquímica básica, 1970-1980, Mexico City, IMP, 1970.
13. The exception was port of Pajaritos, Veracruz, which was conditioned to load tankers of 50 TTDW that were carrying cargo for export or crude refining.
14. Between 1938 and 1975 the PEMEX fleet included the following units:

Units	1938	1958	1970	1975
Tankers	1	18	22	26
Tugboats	5	23	27	30
Barges	82	110	117	113
Other	49	45	45	39
Total	137	196	211	208
Gross Tonnage (Tton)	35	157	264	342

Source: PEMEX, Anuario estadístico, 1983, Mexico City, PEMEX, 1984, pp. 83-84.

15. PEMEX tanker capacity rose from 1.3 to 3.7 MB over this period.

16. This figure is equivalent to 157 TB of capacity.

17. See Table 10.2.

18. Authors' calculation is based on PEMEX, Memoria de labores, Mexico City, PEMEX, various years, and interviews with SCT personnel.

19. See Table 10.1.

20. In general, it was intended that tariffs should be not more than 15 percent over those of the railways.

21. Over this period the use of PEMEX's own units in the total volume conveyed by railway rose from 30 percent to 45 percent. PEMEX, Memoria de labores, 1974-1976, Mexico City, PEMEX, 1975-1977; PEMEX, internal documents.

22. See Table 10.2.

23. Idem. However, in some cases tank cars could also be utilized for storing products.

24. See PEMEX, Memoria de labores, Mexico City, PEMEX, various years.

25. Until 1980 PEMEX did not publish data on storage capacity at exploitation districts and refineries.

26. Authors' estimates are based on data from interviews with PEMEX technicians, specialists, and officials.

27. These figures do not include refinery storage plants, although they appear as product distributors. See IMP, Plan de desarrollo de la industria petrolera y petroquímica básica, 1976-1985, Mexico City, IMP, 1975, Chapter 8.

28. In general terms the following ranges for days of spare capacity for mean daily demand are recommended in order to determine maritime, poliduct, and onshore plant storage:

Plants	Light-Product Days	Fuel Oil Days
Maritime	20-30	25-35
Poliduct	15-25	- -
Onshore	5-10	- -

29. See Bermúdez, Antonio, Doce años al servicio de la industria petrolera mexicana, 1947-1958, Mexico City, COMAVAL, 1980, pp. 129-138.
30. Between 1970 and 1975 the number of service stations went from 2,560 to 2,694. Total Nova and Extra gasoline sales in 1975 were 187 TBD, which meant an average station had around 69 BD.
31. See PEMEX, Anuario estadístico, 1983, Mexico City PEMEX, 1984, pp. 49, 115.
32. See Table 10.2.
33. PEMEX's Memoria de labores for both years show that transported volumes fell from 99 MB to 65 MB, although the distances covered were greater.
34. In 1982 the leased fleet contributed even more than in 1983, transporting 333 MB in 1982 and 155 MB the following year. The situation in 1982 was a result of the deliveries made to storage terminals at Curaçao.
35. See Chapter 11, "Foreign Trade."
36. See Chapter 7, "Exploration and Exploitation."
37. Adequate and reasonable proposals suggested by some PEMEX technicians and SPP officials to construct a smaller 46 inch in diameter line to Monterrey, Nuevo León, via the central plateau (Distrito Federal) were disregarded. This alternative responded to the need to supply parts of the country whose demand for natural gas was greater and also to the somewhat remote possibility of being able to produce the exportable surpluses offered to the United States.
38. See Chapter 11, "Foreign Trade."
39. Border Gas Inc. was a consortium representing six North American gas companies and created for

the sole purpose of negotiating purchase conditions for Mexican natural gas.

40. See Table 10.2.

41. From the mid-1970s until the early 1980s petroleum product sales grew at an average annual rate of nearly 10 percent, rising to 14 percent in the case of gasoline. See Chapter 8, "The Refining Industry."

42. See Escobedo Villalón, Gilberto, "Distribución de productos petrolíferos para consumo interno," in IEPES, <u>Reunión popular para la planeación sobre energéticos y desarrollo nacional: Estrategias de expansión y diversificación del sector energético; Estrategia de expansión de la industria petrolera</u>, Mexico City, IEPES, 1982.

43. See Chapter 12, "PEMEX's Finances."

44. Escobedo Villalón, Gilberto, op. cit.

45. See Table 10.2.

46. Through the intervention of SCT transport companies managed to get approval to increase their tariffs considerably. The increase applied late in 1983 to tank truck tariffs was 30 percent higher than that granted to the railways. This information is based on a personal interview with PEMEX officials in the Gerencia de Ventas.

47. The annual charge for purchase and maintenance is several times greater than yearly rental. This information is based on PEMEX internal documents.

48. During this period less than 900 kilometers of pipeline were constructed for petroleum products, implying an increase of only 17 percent. However, 2,000 kilometers of pipeline for petrochemicals were installed, thus extending the network fivefold. These figures appear to reflect a greater effort on the part of the Gerencia de Petroquímica in promoting pipeline construction for conveying petrochemical imports between PEMEX's different plants and for distributing products. See Figure 10.2.

49. The delay in these payments caused a holdup of several years in completing the Distrito Federal-Toluca-Cuernavaca and Rosarito-Mexicali poliducts. This information is based on interviews with PEMEX personnel. For an in-depth study of the problem, see Chapter 15, "The Impact of Oil Exploitation on the Environment."

50. This information is based on PEMEX internal documents.

51. In October 1977 available local distilled products covered twenty-five days and in December 1981 only eleven days. Information based on PEMEX internal documents.

52. Escobedo Villalón, Gilberto, op. cit.

53. PEMEX, Informe del director general de Petróleos Mexicanos, Mexico City, PEMEX, 18 March 1982, p. 6. Also, at the meeting on planning organized by IEPES during the electoral campaign, PEMEX's assistant trade director declared, "We can say without exaggerating that the nation's product distribution system is in a critical situation." Escobedo Villalón, Gilberto, op. cit.

54. "A reduced storage and distribution capacity and the country's inadequate pipeline network have made it excessively costly to try and satisfy local demand. Petróleos Mexicanos has only recently begun to participate in world markets and more ideal infrastructure still has to be developed." PEMEX, Informe del director general de Petróleos Mexicanos, Mexico City, 18 March 1983, pp. 12-13.

55. PEMEX, Presentación al C. Presidente de la República, Lic. Miguel de la Madrid, de los avances y perspectivas de Petróleos Mexicanos, en los primeros dos años de su administración, Mexico City, PEMEX, 1985, pp. 68-72.

56. See Chapter 8, "The Refining Industry."

11

Foreign Trade

Michele Snoeck

Oil exports have been of major economic importance for Mexico from the moment the oil industry was established early in this century. Until the oil industry was nationalized these activities were in the hand of multinational companies whose prime objective was to extract crude for sale on the international market. Growing crude oil exports by these companies made Mexico one of the major actors in the international oil scene around 1920. The situation changed radically from 1938 onward, though, when the new national industry decided to dedicate most of its production to supplying and developing the domestic market. As a result of nationalization, the changes it brought, and the reaction of the countries whose companies were affected by it, exports fell rapidly. From then on the dynamics of foreign trade began to change; it was based essentially on the exchange of those derivatives that Mexico had in surplus for those that were in deficit. This process was conditioned by the way the refining structure evolved (see Chapter 8, "The Refining Industry"); the consequent imbalance between domestic production and demand; and the development of primary hydrocarbon production, especially crude.

During the 1970's PEMEX managed to correct Mexico's domestic crude-supply deficit, which had forced it to import until 1974, thus gradually restoring the country's importance in the international market. At the same time the natural gas trade with the United States ran into difficulties because of the negotiations and the internal controversy that arose as a result. Apart from primary hydrocarbons petroleum products and petrochemicals were also exported. This subsector had undergone considerable change as a result of PEMEX's efforts to expand its basic petrochemical industry.

This chapter examines PEMEX's foreign-trade dealings during the oil industry's boom, with reference to certain events considered relevant to understanding the magnitude of what took place. Crude oil, natural gas, derivatives, and petrochemicals are all dealt with separately in order to give a clearer picture, although evidently it is the interaction of these products that defines the evolution of PEMEX's trade balance.

BASIC CHARACTERISTICS OF FOREIGN TRADE IN THE OIL INDUSTRY FROM 1966 TO 1977

The Mexican oil industry's involvement in foreign trade underwent a major change in 1966 when oil exports were suspended. Although Mexico's trade balance for crude and petroleum products was positive until 1970, during the mid-1970s PEMEX found it increasingly difficult to satisfy its domestic market. In 1971 crude and petroleum product imports exceeded petroleum product exports by 0.5 MB, the deficit increasing to 39.1 MB in 1973.[1] PEMEX's total trade-balance deficit grew from 49.1 million (U.S. $) in 1971 to 252.7 million in 1973.[2]

The domestic supply crisis reflected in these data stemmed essentially from PEMEX's limited financial resources, which prevented the investment necessary to increase its production capacity and keep up with demand. From the time the oil industry was nationalized until 1970, exploration expenditures were given a back seat to the numerous problems in the different industrial areas that the government had to attend to on its reduced budget.[3]

The situation worsened in 1973 when PEMEX was forced to increase oil imports at a time when international crude prices had quadrupled. The discovery of oil deposits in the southeast helped overcome this situation, and crude imports were suspended in 1974. During the same year Mexico began to export, reaching a total of 5.8 MB.

The discovery of major reserves in Tabasco and Chiapas and the forecast growth in oil production gave rise for the first time since nationalization to two apparently opposing strategies existing side by side. One strategy advocated production for the domestic market according to the guidelines established in 1938, and the other aimed to generate foreign exchange by exporting large surpluses. Although certain internal discrepancies prevailed about the role oil exports should play in the future, pressure from the United States, motivated by its interests in obtaining access to Mexican crude exports for strategic reasons, obliged the Mexican government to publicly define a conservative production and export policy.[4,5] The government dealt with the country's new wealth with a profound sense of nationalism, restraining production at the new deposits with supply for future generations in mind.

Late in 1974 a 39 TBD ceiling was set for crude exports, that is, 15 percent of the crude production planned for that year. The purpose of this target was to establish an equilibrium in PEMEX's trade balance and to allow the financing of the technology and capital goods imports required to expand the oil industry.[6] When the three new refineries under construction and the planned petrochemical complexes eventually came on line, derivatives could then be exported instead of crude.

Notwithstanding previously established targets, oil exports increased on the average from 55 TBD in the second half of 1974 to slightly more than 94 TBD in 1975 and 1976. A number of factors appear to have created a certain degree of flexibility in the way the conservative policy for crude oil exports was managed:

. Mexico's lack of the refining capacity needed to fully utilize the crude oil produced

- The oil industry's increasing need for foreign exchange (PEMEX's expansion, which included everything from exploration to basic petrochemical production, would require very large amounts of material, equipment, and technology imports)

- The possibility of compensating for reduced growth in manufactured exports with oil exports, thus improving the country's balance of payments, particularly in view of a threatened economic recession

- The favorable international oil scene brought about by increases in crude oil prices since 1973[7]

Although crude exports were taken up again in 1974, natural gas exports were suspended in 1975 following a fall in production and a relative increase in national consumption. Because Mexico's border industries required natural gas, small volumes were still imported from the United States.

In view of the characteristics of the newly discovered oil deposits, associated gas production targets were set according to crude oil production. Unfortunately, however, crude exploitation and the infrastructure for natural gas recovery, processing, and distribution did not develop at the same rate. Hence, by 1976 only 10 percent of domestic natural gas demand could be covered, and exports were obviously nil.[8]

Growing domestic demand, a reduced availability of crude oil until 1971, and insufficient refining capacity forced the government to import petroleum products continuously from 1970 to 1976. Goods imported by both PEMEX and private enterprises represented 11 and 10 percent of domestic consumption in 1970 and 1975, respectively, and consisted mainly of gasoline, diesel, and liquefied gas. When the Tula refinery came on line late in 1976, it was possible to cut PEMEX's imported volumes from 18.2 MB in 1975 to 9.3 MB in 1976. Because domestic demand had grown steadily from 1971, traditionally exportable heavy-oil surpluses (fuel oil and asphalt) fell progressively, reaching only 0.5 percent of production in 1976. From 1970 to 1976 imports were the dominant factor in PEMEX's foreign trade in basic petrochemicals because domestic demand had grown heavily as a result of the recent accelerated growth in production capacity. The petrochemical trade balance rose from 25,000 tons in 1970 to 35,000 tons in 1976.

By the end of the Dovall Jaime administration in 1976, PEMEX's foreign-trade balance in hydrocarbons and derivatives was positive, at 206 million (U.S. $), because of crude exports, which represented 96 percent of total exports, that is, 436 million. Imports amounted to 230 million and were made up more or less of equal amounts of petroleum products and petrochemicals.

FOREIGN-TRADE POLICIES FROM 1977 TO 1983

In this section various aspects of Mexico's foreign-trade policies from 1977 to 1983 are presented. Topics include oil program policies, the hydrocarbon and derivative trade balance, oil exports, natural gas exports, and the petroleum product and basic petrochemical imports and exports.

Policies governing oil programs

The Mexican government changeover late in 1976 occurred in the midst of a profound economic crisis. The possibility of increasing oil exports, generating foreign exchange, and establishing a new source of financing that would aid the country's economic recovery brought about a change in foreign-trade policy, whereby oil exportation became one of its major objectives.

In 1977 the new PEMEX administration announced the Programa Sexenal 1977-1982, which should have made it possible to produce large exportable surpluses (mainly oil) as well as oil derivatives and petrochemicals.[9] The 1982 export target for crude and refined product was 1.1 MBD, 82 percent of this corresponding to oil. This target was based on a crude-production ceiling that jumped from 0.9 MBD in 1976 to 2.25 MBD in 1982, a doubling of refinery production over the same period, and a 7 to 8 percent AAGR in domestic hydrocarbon consumption.[10] The program aimed at exporting 26 percent of the basic petrochemical production for 1982 by increasing production from 4 to 17 million tons per year.

Although it involved one-third of all public investment and was designed to increment foreign-exchange earnings, PEMEX's six-year program was not derived directly from Mexico's broad industrialization and socioeconomic development objectives. PEMEX's new director general, Jorge Díaz Serrano, saw the possibility of exporting oil under such favorable international market conditions as the solution to the country's economic crisis and its limited financial resources.[11] Although by 1977 the López Portillo government had already stressed that oil was becoming the cornerstone of its economic grow strategy, the role hydrocarbons were to play in achieving the established economic and social objectives was still far from clear.[12] It was felt that the resources from oil exports should be used as a lever for development and that the export target should be defined in terms of the economy's capacity to absorb foreign exchange. However, no definite alternative was elaborated for utilizing resources.

PNDI, PGD 1980-1982, and PE 1980-1982 reflected attempts to coordinate the oil industry's activities with the country's productive sector amid intense political and economic debate about the role oil surpluses should play in the country's development and the costs and benefits associated with the oil boom.[13] The debates became heated when PEMEX subsequently presented new proposals for expanding production and export targets. In 1978 PEMEX management announced that by 1980 the production and export targets set for 1982 would already have been reached. In view of its success PEMEX proposed in 1979 and again in 1980 that its programs be revised, setting the 1982 crude oil export target in 1979 at 1.4 MBD and in 1980 at 2.0 MBD.[14]

In March 1980 López Portillo put an end to the internal debate by establishing the crude oil production and export targets at 2.5 and 1.5 MBD, respectively, with a 10 percent degree of flexibility.[15] Although PEMEX's original program had not specified a target for natural gas exports, it was set at 300 MCFD.

PE, which was publicly announced in late 1980, established for the first time certain guidelines for foreign trade in hydrocarbons, particularly in regard to the conditions under which oil was to be exported:

- The hydrocarbon -export market had to be diversified in order to avoid concentrating any more than 50 percent of Mexico's oil exports in any one country or supplying any more than 20 percent of a given country's foreign-crude requirements.

- Cooperation between Mexico and other developing countries on oil exploitation and supply issues would be intensified; as a result, Mexico's share in crude oil supply to Central American and Caribbean countries rose from 20 to 50 percent.

- Efforts were to be made to achieve higher aggregate value for hydrocarbon exports by increasing derivative exports.

- Income from oil exports was not to be allowed to exceed 50 percent of the country's total foreign earnings in order to avoid the economy's undue dependence on any one product.

- Foreign oil and gas sales would be used to acquire modern technology, develop national capital goods manufacturing, obtain access to new manufactured goods export markets, and improve financing conditions.

An overview of the hydrocarbon and derivative trade balance

For a clear picture of PEMEX's foreign-trade situation (see Table 11.1), an analysis of its trade balance should show the following: (1) hydrocarbon and derivative exports along with other items such as services lent by PEMEX abroad; (2) PEMEX's hydrocarbon and by-product imports, with separate classifications for those inputs used directly by PEMEX and those received by it only as an intermediary; (3) materials, equipment, and machinery imports along with payments made for technical aid, licensing and technology contracts, royalties, and so on; and (4) service payments on foreign debt contracted directly for financing operations, thus enabling foreign-exchange flows to be clarified. The limited amount of available information, however, only allows a sound analysis of a few areas, such as foreign trade in hydrocarbons and derivatives, with data on imports including products not utilized directly by PEMEX.

PEMEX's favorable hydrocarbon and derivative trade balance resulted in an accelerated growth of the Mexican oil industry's foreign earnings from 1977 to 1983.[16] The trade balance showed a positive remnant of $1.5 billion (U.S. $) in 1977, which increased to $9.7 billion in 1980 and $15.6 billion in 1983 at current prices. This progress in attributable not only to an increase in crude export volume, which went from 73.7 MB in 1977 to 561.0 MB in 1983, but also to the sharp rise in international crude oil prices.[17] The average annual price of exported Mexican crude increased from $13.4 per barrel (U.S. $) in 1977 to $33.2 per barrel in 1981 and then took a downward turn to $26.4 per barrel in 1983. Consequently, although the volume of crude exports increased by 40 percent annually from 1977 to 1983, the corresponding increase in earnings averaged 57 percent per year.

Over the same six-year period petroleum product, basic petrochemical, and natural gas exports were somewhat less spectacular than crude exports. Although petroleum product exports were not of major importance to start with, they increased from 3.7 MB in 1979 to 17.5 MB in 1980 and then to 30.8 MB in 1983 because fuel oil surpluses and increased exportable petroleum product surpluses—that is, fuel oil, diesel, gasolines, liquefied gas, and jet fuel—became available in 1983. The income from these exports, which in 1983 amounted to $865.8 million (U.S. $), boosted their relative share in PEMEX's overall exports from 1.7 percent to 5.4 percent from 1977 to 1983.

In 1978 Mexico began to export large ammonia surpluses, thus providing a basis for broadening

TABLE 11.1*
HYDROCARBON AND DERIVATIVE FOREIGN-TRADE BALANCE
1976-1983 (in millions of dollars)

Year	Crude	Natural Gas	Petroleum Products	Petro-chemicals	Total
1976	420.0	- -	15.7	0.3	436.0
1977	987.3	5.4	22.8	3.3	1,018.8
1978	1,760.3	- -	9.3	67.6	1,837.2
1979	3,811.3	- -	67.6	107.7	3,986.6
1980	9,449.4	447.8	390.7	125.3	10,413.2
1981	13,305.2	526.2	589.0	153.6	14,574.0
1982	15,622.7	475.5	355.9	140.4	16,594.5
1983	14,821.3	353.9	865.7	123.9	16,164.8

IMPORTS[a]

Year	Crude	Natural Gas	Petroleum Products	Petro-chemicals	Total
1976	- -	- -	126.3	103.8	230.1
1977	- -	- -	51.7	156.5	208.2
1978	- -	- -	144.0	163.6	307.6
1979	- -	- -	208.6	331.6	540.2
1980	- -	- -	243.1	522.9	765.9
1981	- -	- -	159.2	523.4	682.6
1982	- -	8.7	140.5	400.8	550.0
1983	- -	- -	263.3	336.5	599.8

aFigures do not include imports by private firms.

Source: PEMEX, Memoria de labores, 1977-1983, Mexico City, PEMEX, 1978-1984.

foreign basic petrochemical sales. However, because ammonia international market price was very low, the income from these exports, which in 1983 amounted to $124 million (U.S. $), constituted less than 1 percent of PEMEX's total export earnings.

Last, Mexico began exporting natural gas in 1980 but until 1983 exports were well below the 300 MCFD agreed upon with the United States after the protracted negotiations (see Table 11.2). The contribution of natural gas exports to PEMEX's earnings dropped from 4.3 percent in 1980 to 2.2 percent in 1983.

TABLE 11.2
NATURAL GAS PRODUCTION, TRADE, AND APPARENT CONSUMPTION (MCFD)

Year	Production	Imports	Exports	Apparent Consumption
1970	1,822.5	48.8	106.3	1,764.9
1971	1,762.7	53.2	55.9	1,760.0
1972	1,803.8	43.2	27.0	1,820.0
1973	1,854.0	42.4	5.5	1,890.7
1974	2,040.3	34.2	1.1	2,073.4
1975	2,154.5	15.9	--	2,170.4
1976	2,108.7	17.2	--	2,125.9
1977	2,046.0	9.6	6.6	2,049.0
1978	2,561.4	8.5	--	2,569.0
1979	2,916.7	11.0	--	2,927.7
1980	3,548.1	--	280.9	3,267.2
1981	4,060.8	--	288.2	3,772.1
1982	4,246.3	5.3[a]	273.1	3,978.5
1983	4,053.6	4.7[a]	217.1	3,841.2

MCFD = millions of cubic feet per day.
[a] Figure does not include imports by private firms.

Sources: SPP, La industria petrolera en México, Mexico City, SPP, 1980, p. 329; PEMEX, Memoria de labores, 1970-1983, Mexico City, PEMEX, 1971-1984.

In order to complement national petroleum product and basic petrochemical production, in 1983 PEMEX imported very large quantities of these products. Their value increased from $208 million (U.S. $) in 1977 to $600 million in 1983, with slight fluctuations over the years. In spite of a marked variation in the value of petroleum product imports over this period, the value of petrochemicals increased steadily from 1977 to 1982 when it reached $401 million (U.S. $), that is, 75 percent of total imports. The figure later dropped as a result of a sharp increase in petroleum product imports and a decrease in imported petrochemicals.

Petroleum product imports consisted primarily of lubricants and liquefied gas because of the traditionally deficient local production. Light products, particularly diesel and gasoline, were imported primarily to border regions or in temporary shortfall situations. Marked variations in imported volumes were due to fluctuations in domestic demand combined with the effect of new refineries coming on line. In 1977 and 1983 light products amounting to 3.5 MB and 6.3 MB, respectively, were imported; an import maximum of 10.6 MB was recorded in 1978 and a minimum of 3.0 MB in 1982.

A heavy increase in basic petrochemical demand was responsible for increased imports of the same, which jumped from 460,000 tons in 1977 to 702,000 tons in 1982. However, the following year the volume imported dropped to 582,000 tons in response to a contraction in domestic demand. Even so, during 1983 additional quantities of twenty-one of the forty-four petroleum products developed by PEMEX had to be imported in order to satisfy local needs.

Oil exports from 1977 to 1980, the years of prosperity

From 1977 to 1980 Mexican oil exports grew sharply. In 1977 the daily average reached 202 TBD, whereas in 1980 828 TB were exported daily, a figure similar to the amount forecast for 1982 in PEMEX's Programa Sexenal 1977-1982. Because of their rapid growth, oil exports represented 42.8 percent of the country's total crude production compared with 20.6 percent in 1977. The increase in the export volume, together with a tripling of international crude oil prices, caused crude-export earnings to jump from $987 million (U.S. $) in 1977 to $9.449 billion in 1980. The more than satisfactory results of exploration and exploitation, along with the international oil market situation, encouraged the accelerated expansion that Mexico's oil exports underwent during this period.

At home, the higher productivity of fields in the southeast made it possible to increase production even more than had been planned initially, but internationally the oil scene's relative stability was abruptly upset late in 1979. Iran reduced its oil exports in 1979, the exporting countries' stocks increased, and war broke out between Iran and Iraq in 1980. Between 1979 and early 1981 there was a 4 MBD drop in world oil supply, followed by a steady increase in oil prices.[18] The international oil shortage provided the opportunity for Mexico to define its international oil policy essentially on the basis of domestic factors. Although not a member country, it was able to take advantage of the high prices set by OPEC. The gradual increase in Mexico's negotiating power in the world oil market was reflected in its pricing policy. This negotiating power was also directly responsible for the share of heavy crude in exported mixtures; a diversification in PEMEX's clientele; a reduction in the time given to clients to settle export contract payments; and the insistence that oil would be exported on the condition that Mexico in return be given favorable technological contracts, joint investments, and financing facilities.

Until mid-1979 Mexico adjusted its pricing policy for light crude (Isthmus) in accordance with the OPEC crude marker (Light Arab). The Isthmus price was quoted slightly higher than the OPEC crude marker, but this increase was basically to compensate for the lower costs of transport to the United States, Mexico's main client.[19] The OPEC crude-marker price served as a guide for Mexico to determine its own prices and maintain its solidarity with OPEC However, the Mexican government affirmed its decision to abstain from joining OPEC on the grounds that such a move would be inadvisable because of the economic and political pressures the United States would exert on Mexico and would contradict Mexico's established principle of self-determination. The government felt that it would not be able to act freely on issues regarding price and export markets and that its trade flexibility and negotiating capacity would be undermined. In fact, on different occasions after July 1979, Mexico increased the Isthmus crude price to well above that of the OPEC crude marker, taking advantage of its position as a sure supplier and a nonmember of OPEC.[20]

In 1979 Mexico began producing a heavy crude called *Maya*, and by 1980 production had increased considerably. Because of the increased complexity of heavy-crude processing compared with light crude and a general shortage of processing facilities in importing countries, Mexico found it difficult to sell its Maya crude abroad. However, Mexico's strong position in the international oil market and the fact that the

Maya crude fluctuated between $3 and $5 per barrel less than Isthmus crude made it easier to increase the amount of Maya exported in relation to the other types of crude.[21] From a 20 percent share of exports in late 1979, Maya crude jumped to an average of 44.6 percent in 1980, with the prospect of it increasing to 60 percent.

From 1977 to 1980 as oil exports grew, foreign markets gradually diversified. At the beginning of the 1976-1982 government administration, President López Portillo adopted a favorable attitude toward the United States, which was reflected, among other things, in talks with North American gas companies about natural gas exports and with the U.S. government about the sale of crude for its strategic reserves.[22] Furthermore, major North American companies were invited to participate with PEMEX in its expansion plans, and in winter 1976-1977 Mexico was able to supply its northern neighbor with emergency oil and gas. In general, subsequent political and economic relations between both countries were friendly. Although heavily dependent on the United States, Mexico hoped that its hydrocarbon exports would be a key to negotiating a solution to certain delicate aspects of its bilateral relations, which mainly concerned undocumented workers' immigration to the United States and the U.S. tariff policy.[23]

The United States looked with interest on the growing prospects for Mexico's oil production because it represented a potential source of large-scale imports. Mexico's political situation was relatively stable, it shared the same border with the United States, and it was a long way from the disturbances in the Middle East, which made it a sure source of supply and also presented transport advantages. This situation was reinforced by the fact that one of the U.S. energy policy's main objectives at this time was to reduce its dependence on crude imports from OPEC countries.[24] Needless to say, the United States looked kindly on the fact that Mexico had refrained from joining the organization.

However, with almost 90 percent of Mexican oil exports in 1977 and 1978 concentrated in the United States, the government began negotiations with different countries in an attempt to diversify its clientele.[25] The international scene looked kindly on Mexico's search for new markets. With the 1973 oil crisis and the new role taken by OPEC, several industrialized countries were on the lookout for alternative markets in order to reduce oil imports from the OPEC-member countries.

The Mexican government's efforts to reduce its dependence on the North American market were based on the following:

- Increasing export volumes to traditional clients with the exception of the United States

- Exporting to new clients, giving priority to those willing to contribute to developing strategic sectors of the Mexican economy and to open their economic doors to Mexican manufactures.

- Exporting oil to Central America and the Caribbean nations with the aim of fulfilling part of Mexico's commitment to economic cooperation with this region.

Mexico managed to increase its crude oil exports to Spain from 14.3 TBD in 1978 to 92.5 TBD in 1980, which amounted to 11 percent of PEMEX's total oil exports for that year.[26] In 1977 Israel's imports of Mexican crude made Israel PEMEX's second most important client, a situation with very definite political connotations. By 1980 these imports had gradually increased to 56.6 TBD.

In 1977 the Mexican government started the difficult process of negotiating with Japan. An agreement was reached in mid-1979, whereby Mexico promised to sell 100 TBD of crude through the 1980s. Japan offered economic and technical cooperation in developing ports, electricity facilities, and railway systems, among others, and agreed to encourage tourist exchange. These promises were fulfilled in some cases, but problems arose in the negotiations that caused the remainder to be postponed. Japan's needs for crude became acute late in 1980 with the conflict between Iran and Iraq, two of its major suppliers. When Japan requested a 200 TBD increase in oil imports for 1982, the Mexican government stated that it was not in a position to satisfy this demand unless Japan was willing to offer additional cooperation and a comprehensive economic, technical, and cultural exchange.[27]

France's Compagnie Française du Pétrole started importing 42.5 TBD of oil in 1980, which was considerably less than the 100 TBD agreed upon in 1978. However, oil negotiations formed part of the broader framework of economic relations between France and Mexico that primary involved the steel, automobile, urban transport equipment, and nuclear industries. In 1980 both countries signed a contract, whereby Mexico, in exchange for a 100 percent increase in crude exports and an extensive supply of raw materials, would benefit from additional French investment in its economy, increased joint investment, additional technology transference, a progressive opening of the French market to nonpetroleum products, and ample collaboration in training personnel for those sectors considered most important to Mexico's development.[28]

In August 1980 Mexico's economic cooperation with Central America and the Caribbean began to materialize with the Programa de Cooperación Energética para Países de Centroamérica y el Caribe (Program for Energy Cooperation for Central America and the Caribbean), better known as the Acuerdo Petrolero de San José. The purpose of this program was to "take care of the area's net internal oil imports and aid official financing of the same."[29] To this end, Mexico and Venezuela promised to equitably provide these countries with crude oil to a maximum of 160 TBD, agreeing to grant credit to beneficiary countries for 30 percent of their respective oil invoices for a period of five years at a 4 percent annual interest rate. The program also contemplated prolonging these credits twenty years at a 2 percent annual interest rate under the condition that the money be channeled into priority economic development projects, particularly those related to the energy sector. Numerous difficulties were encountered in setting up the program, such that in 1980 the agreed volume could not be covered.[30] From August to December of that year Mexico only delivered 10.7 TBD to the region, which included Costa Rica, Nicaragua, and El Salvador, and granted credit for nearly 19 million (U.S. $), which was equivalent to 30 percent of the value of the sales.

From 1978 to 1980 efforts to diversify foreign markets brought the relative share of the United States in Mexican crude oil exports from 89 percent to 69 percent.[31] The number of buyer countries went from seven to twelve.[32] Despite this trend, exports to the United States in absolute terms rose from 324 TBD in 1978 to 571 TBD in 1980, the greatest increase received by any country.

Oil-export growth meant that major investments had to be made in the industry's infrastructure because of the inadequate port facilities, deficient transport system, and insufficient storage capacity. In spite of the efforts to improve the infrastructure, on various occasions in 1979 and 1980 PEMEX was unable to satisfactorily fulfill its crude-export contracts (as was the case with France) because of adverse weather conditions in the Gulf of Mexico, inadequate wharf loading facilities, and insufficient storage capacity. To help solve storage problems a space at the Curaçao terminal was rented at a very high cost. Bottlenecks usually had to be solved through emergency programs involving expenditures well above those planned for investment programs.

Late in 1980 PEMEX's clients began to express their doubts about Mexico's trade strategy, especially its high crude prices and heavy crude's growing share in exported mixtures. By this time a major change was expected in the international oil market as a result of an excess of available crude; this excess was to alter Mexico's negotiating power drastically.

The worldwide oil market glut: Economic crisis and the new government policy

The years 1981 and 1982 saw a series of adjustments to Mexico's crude-export policy in relation to prices and clients. These adjustments occurred in response to new international oil market conditions and the resulting confusion and internal controversy. The second quarter of 1981 was marked by a glut on the international crude oil market and the consequent price drop.[33] This glut, coupled with several clients' threats to reduce their purchases from Mexico, prompted PEMEX's Director General Diaz Serrano to adjust Mexican crude oil prices to prevailing market conditions, reducing them substantially in April and again in May 1981.[34] The decision was severely frowned upon both in Mexico and in other oil-exporting countries that felt that by jumping the gun and cutting prices (instead of adjusting prices according to OPEC policy) Mexico had confirmed expectations of a fall in oil prices and contributed to a disequilibrium in the international oil market.

At home Diaz Serrano's decision was disliked for several reasons: it lacked careful analysis of the international oil market situation (which some classified as transitory), the advice of other internal institutions was not sought, and the possible deterioration in relations with OPEC and the substantial reduction in foreign earnings that would result from a fall in export prices were not taken into account.

The political and institutional conflict that arose between SEPAFIN and PEMEX led to Diaz Serrano's forced resignation in June 1981. PEMEX's new director general, Julio Rodolfo Moctezuma Cid, decided to increase Mexican crude oil prices by $2.00 (U.S. $) per barrel, and measures such as augmenting the proportion of light crude in exported mixtures were taken to restore Mexico's competitiveness. The new price increase was part of what was considered an aggressive role by Mexico in the international oil market. The list of clients was selectively reduced, and contracts were negotiated directly between governments.

Because its pricing policy had created a certain degree of confusion in the world market, PEMEX's began to face serious problems in its foreign-trade relations. Several clients, such as the United States, France, Sweden, India, and the Philippines, suspended or reduced their purchases, adhering strictly to the contractual clauses, and Mexico's search for new buyers was not as successful as had been hoped.[35] Thus, by July 1981 Mexican crude oil exports had fallen 50 percent, with a consequent loss of around $1 billion (U.S.. $) in foreign earnings.

In order to reestablish its initially planned export volume, in August 1981 PEMEX had to reduce its crude oil prices once again, increase the proportion of light crude in the exported mixture, and abandon its selective client policy. In the third quarter of 1981 Mexico managed to recover its planned export volume with essentially the same clients as before. However, successive price reductions meant that the expected income for 1981 had shrunk by nearly 30 percent.

By early 1982 the gradual slide in international oil prices had become an avalanche.[36] OPEC-member countries agreed to reduce production levels in an attempt to arrest the fall in prices, but Mexico continued to maintain its expanded development policy by increasing its production and export volume. From 1980 to 1982 Mexico's crude production increased from 1.9 MBD to 2.75 MBD, making the country the fourth largest crude oil producer in the world.[37] Crude exports increased from 0.8 MBD to 1.6 MBD over the same two-year period and surpassed the export level of most of the OPEC-member countries. Despite the weak market conditions for exporters, Mexico's strategy was to reduce its export prices below those of the OPEC crude marker and to channel exploration and hydrocarbon production efforts into light-crude products, with the aim of improving its own foreign-trade situation.[38]

Although the relative participation of the United States in Mexican crude exports dropped to 49 percent in 1982, which, strictly speaking, conformed with the clientele diversification principle established in the 1980-1984 energy program, Mexico's relative participation in U.S. oil imports increased.[39] By late 1981 Mexico had supplied 50 percent of U.S. strategic reserve and, consequently, enhanced its geopolitical importance for the United States.[40] By agreeing to supply this reserve, Mexico was granting a series of major concessions to the United States. The price established for this purpose was lower than the OPEC crude-marker price and caused friction between Mexico and OPEC, which had always considered the U.S. strategic reserve contrary to its interests. Furthermore, this preferential price was even lower than that established for the rest of Mexico's crude exports. Also agreed upon was a maximum price for mexican oil; this factor, intended as a medium-term protection measure, could easily have placed Mexico at a disadvantage in future negotiations between the two countries. Last, although it was Mexico's policy to deal directly with buyer-country governments because government contracts also usually included broader economic agreements, the contract drawn up for supplying the U.S. strategic reserve had no such accompanying agreement. For the first time Mexico had granted preferential treatment to one of its foreign hydrocarbon clients, apart from those included in the Acuerdo Petrolero de San José. The incipient economic and financial crisis was definitely making mexico dependent on the sale of a product that was of strategic importance to the United States. This commercial fact of life seriously restricted the progressive activities of mexican foreign policy.

Thus, the worldwide oil glut had major repercussions for mexico in 1981-1982:

- The impact caused by the fall in oil prices seriously undermined Mexico's economic expansion programs, which were elaborated under the assumption that the country would continue to benefit from increases in international oil prices. Furthermore, the international oil crisis occurred at a time when Mexico's domestic economic and financial situation was less than stable, and crude oil exports were a key factor in economic development. The country was now confronted with a question vital to its foreign oil trade strategy: In view of the growing needs for foreign exchange, could the crude-export level be maintained in a saturated market without provoking an even greater deterioration in international oil prices and in relations with OPEC?[41]

- Mexico's negotiating power in the international oil market was substantially reduced and was reflected in the fall of crude-export prices, an increase in the share of light crude in the exported crude mixture, and the adaptation of Mexico's crude trade policy to changing international market conditions. The need to improve foreign-trade conditions meant that Mexico had to abandon some of its international oil policy principles, such as its solidarity with OPEC and the reduction of its dependence on the United States for the sale of its oil exports.

With the change in government in 1982, Mexico began to redefine its foreign oil policy in accordance with world oil conditions.[42] With the world oil market's particularly difficult situation early in 1983, which was brought about by contracted demand and continuing oil glut, Mexico was not going to be able to play the starring role in reducing oil prices as it had in 1981. Its crude-export prices were modified in response to changes registered in the international market, and the government attempted a reconciliation with OPEC and other oil-producing countries.[43] After the emergency OPEC meeting in March 1983, Mexico agreed to establish a closer working relationship with other oil-producing countries, help elaborate and apply a long-term strategy for establishing the market, respect OPEC prices, and maintain production and export ceilings.[44] For the first time the Mexican government had coordinated its policies with those of OPEC and adopted a position different from that of other oil producers not affiliated with this organization.[45]

Mexico's decision to refrain from raising production and export ceilings was particularly significant, considering how critical the country's economic and financial situation was. Its foreign debt was being renegotiated, and new loans were needed to render the economic recovery strategy viable; such a situation made the possibility of increasing its foreign earnings from oil export extremely tempting. Moreover, it would have been technically feasible to increase crude exports because Mexico's crude production capacity at both onshore and offshore deposits at the time was 3.1 MBD. However, this time Mexico chose to try and maintain the international market's fragile stability for exporters.

Natural gas exports

PEMEX's Programa Sexenal 1977-1982 did not include plans or export targets for natural gas, but the possibility of exporting arose late in 1976 because of the following (see Table 11.2):

- The amount of associated natural gas already obtained, along with the expected future production, made it seem almost certain that there would be an exportable surplus even after domestic demand had been covered.[46]

- Natural gas exports represented a potential source of financing for oil sub-sector expansion and for the reestablishment of Mexico's international credit. This source would help alleviate the balance-of-payment deficit and reactivate the economy as a whole.

- Associated natural gas utilization implied major investment in a whole series of related systems, such as collectors, compressors, absorption and cryogenic plants, and so on, that could never be covered with domestic natural gas prices because they were so low. Therefore, by exporting gas surpluses at a price much higher than domestic prices the necessary investment could be amortized in the short term and considerable benefits obtained.

- Of all the natural gas export alternatives the most feasible and economically viable was to sell it to the United States.

These considerations prompted PEMEX to begin pertinent negotiations with the United States. In May 1977 PEMEX made it clear that it wished to export natural gas through a letter of intent to Border Gas Inc., a consortium that represented the interests of six North American gas companies and was created for the sole purpose of facilitating negotiations. The letter essentially contemplated the sale of 2,000 MCFD of natural gas from 1979 onward at $2.60 (U.S. $) per thousand cubic feet or its equivalent in BTUs, wherein the vendor agreed to build adequate facilities for transporting the gas. The agreement was to be submitted to the respective governments late in the same year for their approval.

Although Border Gas Inc. had agreed to the price proposed by mexico, the U.S. government refused to accept the terms of the letter, dispatched it without signing the contract, and suspended the negotiations. The U.S. government and a number of congressmen argued that the price Mexico asked for the gas was too high and that if it were accepted, it would cause serious problems with the North American producers that had been offered $1.75 per thousand cubic feet. Furthermore, if the proposed price were accepted, Canada would be prompted to insist on parity; the current price for Canadian gas was $2.16 per thousand cubic feet.

The United States also objected to PEMEX's periodic revision, whereby the mexican gas price was linked to the behavior of certain international hydrocarbon prices. This proposal was unacceptable to Washington because it linked the price of gas to international crude oil prices, which were highly influenced by OPEC.

By the time negotiations were suspended, work had already been started on a gas pipeline, 49 inches in diameter, designed for exporting the large quantities of gas offered in the 1977 letter of intent. This project gave rise to great controversy: Not only was a vast sum invested in its construction, which amounted to around $1 billion (U.S. $) at 1977 prices, and Mexico given unfavorable credit conditions to finance the work, but the gas pipeline's course was a long way from domestic consumer centers, and no alternative uses had been considered in case negotiations broke down.

Early in 1979, fifteen months after the first negotiations, the talks were taken up again, but the conditions under which the letter of intent had initially been discussed had changed radically:

- The increases in natural gas production were insufficient to provide the planned 2,000 MCFD surplus that was to be used for exports. Consequently, the quantities offered by PEMEX fell during the course of the negotiations from 1,200 MCFD to 800 MCFD, eventually reaching 300 MCFD.

TABLE 11.3
PETROLEUM PRODUCT IMPORTS AND EXPORTS, 1977-1983 (TB)

Imports

Product	1977	1978	1979	1980	1981	1982	1983
Gasolines	50	44	47	46	462	45	46
Kerosenes	200	193	228	225	221	439	385
Diesel	525	934	--	333	105	--	--
Fuel Oil	1,403	6,498	5,593	--	--	--	--
Lubricants	238	712	2,035	1,732	948	1,147	2,059
Grease	2	21	14	19	34	42	--
Paraffins	3	9	7	17	17	19	58
Liquefied Gas	1,022	2,155	2,944	3,054	1,911	1,315	3,793
Other	23	50	9	3	7	10	6
Total	3,466	10,616	9,877	5,429	3,705	3,017	6,347

Exports

Product	1977	1978	1979	1980	1981	1982	1983
Gasolines	1,183	613	--	482	355	57	7,030
Kerosenes a	39	20	--	138	146	173	1,151
Diesel	238	40	98	447	3,124	947	8,928
Fuel Oil and Residues	192	--	1,442	10,559	19,073	12,981	9,462
Lubricants	--	--	--	108	14	--	75
Liquefied Gas	--	--	2,161	5,328	931	431	1,598

Naphthas				481	563	768	875
Virgin							
Stock	—	—	—	—	—	—	1,633[b]
Total	1,652	673	3,701	17,543	24,206	15,357	30,752

TB = thousands of barrels.
[a]This figure includes mainly jet fuels.
[b]This figure includes 1,633 TB of virgin load.

Sources: PEMEX, Memoria de labores, 1978–1983, Mexico City, PEMEX, 1979– 1984; PEMEX, Anuario estadístico, 1983, Mexico City, PEMEX, 1984, pp. 115–116, 121–122.

- The reduced supply of exportable gas was also a product of local industry's growing demand, which had gradually reduced the exportable margin.

- The prices that had served as a reference for determining the original price of $2.60 per thousand cubic feet had changed.

After prolonged negotiations an agreement was signed in October 1979. It was agreed that (1) PEMEX would sell the United States 300 MCFD of natural gas, this figure subject to increases by mutual accord; (2) there would be a minimum consumption of 180 MCFD; and (3) a formula would be elaborated allowing Mexico to obtain the highest price of a group of five different crudes--Mexican Isthmus, Saudi Arabian Light Arab, Algiers' Sahara Blend, North Sea Forties, and Venezuela's Tia Juana Medium 26x--and of the price the United States paid for Canadian natural gas.

The initial delivery price was fixed at $3.625 (U.S. $) per thousand cubic feet, and two important clauses were included in the contract. The first covered the possibility of canceling the contract, with 180 days notice stipulated for both parties; the second clause covered available gas volume. It was explicitly stated that Mexican domestic demand would have first priority; the exportable volumes were determined by this factor alone.

The importance of the negotiations and the final agreement reached between PEMEX and Border Gas Inc. was evidenced by the fact that the contracted sale volume, with its possible fluctuations, remained stable until late 1984. The subsequent evolution of Mexican natural gas exports brought to light some of the factors that were to affect not only policy but also the desire to continue exporting under the contract's terms. The most important of these factors was competition from Canadian gas, and the second, which was derived in part from the first, was that Mexican natural gas exports had lost ground in terms of overall U.S. imports.

According to the agreement, which took effect in January 1980, natural gas exports, which did not exceed 300 MCFD, were begun in February of that year.[47]

By 1983 exports had reached 217 MCFD. With the strict application of the original pricing formula, the $3.625 (U.S. $) per thousand cubic feet agreed upon initially was constantly modified until it reached a maximum of $4.94 in the second quarter of 1981, falling to $4.40 per thousand cubic feet and remaining there until late 1983.

The natural gas trade balance favored PEMEX because during this period imports were virtually marginal, at 17.2 MCFD in 1976, none in 1980 and 1981, and 4.7 MCFD in 1983. These imports were indispensable, covering the needs of Mexico's border industries.

Petroleum product trade balance

PEMEX's commercial balance for petroleum products showed a deficit from 1977 to 1979 and a surplus from 1980 to 1983.[48] This change was brought about by a heavy increase in the production of refined products because of the growing installed refining capacity at Salamanca, Tula (1976), Cactus (1979), Salina Cruz (1979-1980), and Cadereyta (1979-1980).[49] However, the trade surplus from 1980 onward is attributable more to an increase in exports than to the steady fall in imports (see Table 11.3).

Despite increased foreign sales, the 42 TBD exported in 1982 amounted to only 20 percent of the target established in PEMEX's Programa Sexenal 1977-1982. If one looks beyond the official emphasis given to the need to sell products on the international market that have a higher aggregate value than crude, it becomes clear that the expansion of refining capacity was aimed more at satisfying domestic consumption than at creating exportable surpluses. With the world excess in refining capacity at this time, the high investment costs in constructing new refineries, and the sudden increase in international crude prices, it simply was not economical to construct refineries for export purposes.

An in-depth analysis of the petroleum product trade balance shows that the evolution of foreign trade in refined products differs according to the type of product (see Table 11.3). After 1976 light

—product imports, mainly gasoline and diesel, tended to fall and were gradually replaced by exports. This situation was particularly evident in 1983 because domestic demand for these products had dropped.

Although domestic demand for gasoline grew steadily until 1982, gasoline exports gradually exceeded imports from 1977 to 1983 because of the expanded refining capacity and the utilization of natural gas in Cactus for obtaining liquefied gas and gasoline. Imports fell from 2.4 MB in 1976 to 50 TB in 1977 and stayed at this level during most of the following years.[50] In other words, after the new PEMEX administration took office in 1977, these imports were relatively insignificant, amounting to less than 1.5 percent of annual domestic consumption. Gasoline had to be imported not because production capacity was insufficient but because the demand in the country's northeastern region, which is a long way from the refining complexes, rose temporarily.

Like gasoline, some diesel imports were necessary because of the problem in transporting diesel to border regions as well as the seasonal fluctuations in the demand (which occurred only during certain years from 1977 to 1983), which represented an average of less than 1 percent of apparent domestic consumption. Diesel's unimpressive export figures grew steadily from 1980 until they reached 11 percent of production in 1983. In general, the value per unit of the light refined products, such as gasoline and diesel, that Mexico had to import was higher than the same type of product Mexico exported because Mexican fuel was of a lower quality and because the imports were urgent and transitory. Foreign trade in kerosene was different from other light refined products in that imports exceeded exports from 1977 to 1982 because of the priority given to gasoline production.

A heavy increase in the demand for industrial fuels in 1978 made it necessary to cover the domestic demand for fuel oil with purchases from abroad, which totaled 1.4 MB in 1977 and 6.5 MB in 1978.[51] The 1978 amount represented 57 percent of total petroleum product imports for that year. However, after 1980 production at the new Cadereyta and Salina Cruz refineries brought about a reversal in the country's production deficit, and large surpluses were made available for export. Also influencing this situation was the higher density of the Mexican crude extracted after 1980 and the consequent improvement in fuel oil yield in relation to the total volume of crude oil processed. Fuel oil exports reached a maximum in 1981 at 19.1 MB, which was equivalent to 15 percent of production, only to fall again in 1983 to 9.5 MB, that is, 7.5 percent of production, in response to increased domestic demand.[52] Fuel oil made up a major part of Mexican petroleum product exports from 1980 to 1983, reaching a maximum of 85 percent in 1982.

Although PEMEX's lubricant production had been insufficient to yield exportable surpluses, the problem became serious after 1978 when the input requirements for the oil industry, among others, rose sharply. Imported lubricants covered 29 percent of apparent domestic consumption in 1982, increasing to 46 percent in 1983. Except for new purchases made for the northeast of the country, lubricants were imported almost exclusively by PEMEX, which distributed them at prices lower than international market prices.

Finally, liquefied gas constituted one of Mexico's major petroleum product imports, but because most of the gas trade was in private hands until the late 1970s, these figures do not appear in PEMEX's trade balance. Although liquefied gas production tripled between 1976 and 1983, the amount was insufficient to satisfy both PEMEX's internal demand and national sales, which had been encouraged by sustained low prices. From 1979 to 1982 PEMEX organized a commercial exchange arrangement abroad under the assumption that there would be fewer losses than with importing alone. However, the operation was suspended in 1983 to give Mexico greater trade flexibility; also, the terms of the transaction would have been unfavorable to PEMEX.

In brief, until 1980 the petroleum product trade balance was adversely affected by fluctuations in the domestic demand for each individual product and the heavy load put on the refineries, even though refining capacity had been expanded. After 1980, however, Mexico's trade balance for these products had a surplus, with fuel oil providing a major share of the exports. The liquefied gas and lubricant deficits were a reflection of the unsolved structural problems in developing a refining infrastructure that forced these industries to continue with their respective imports.

Foreign trade in basic petrochemical products

PEMEX's foreign trade in petrochemicals had persistently showed a negative balance until 1978 when a heavy increase in dry natural gas derivative production made it possible to introduce large surpluses of ammonia and methanol to the international market. The petrochemical trade balance then began to show a 224,000 ton surplus, which it maintained until 1982 except for a slight deficit in 1980.

However, the overall domestic picture was somewhat different because PEMEX was responsible only for part of the basic petrochemical imports, its share amounting to 35 percent in 1982. If the import volumes of private firms had been included in the basic petrochemical industry's foreign-trade balance, it would have showed a deficit from 1970 to 1983. The foreign basic petrochemical trade was almost limited to the United States, which in 1979 provided more than 80 percent of Mexico's imports and absorbed nearly one-third of its sales.[53]

Despite the major contribution of foreign ammonia and methanol sales after 1978, the foreign-trade deficit had grown steadily; international commercial value of these products was low in comparison to the value of the products PEMEX had to import. At current prices the deficit went from $153.2 million (U.S. $) in 1977 to $212.6 million in 1983. Thus, although basic petrochemical production has grown steadily since 1977, this industry has not yet managed to achieve self-sufficiency; so, in 1983 PEMEX paid out $336.6 million for petrochemical purchases abroad.[54]

In general, basic petrochemicals were imported because of a sustained growth in demand encouraged by the government's low-price policy and the increasing possibilities of natural product substitution offered by the petrochemical industry. However, certain aspects of petrochemical industry development in Mexico did have an effect on imports. During the 1970s the Mexican petrochemical industry based its development on natural gas derivatives, mainly methane and ethane, because of the easy accessibility and lower transformation costs of natural gas compared to other processes using naphthas as a raw material. By broadening its productive base in this way, the petrochemical industry was able to produce exportable surpluses of ammonia and methanol and, after 1983, ethylene. However, this situation also meant that the production of certain by-products from naphtha-based transformation processes would be limited. These limits were seen in propylene and butane-butylene derivative production, which over the years became a structural void in basic petrochemical production. Certain products, particularly aromatics, had to be imported for longer than planned because some of PEMEX's petrochemical projects were not completed on schedule, as was the case with the La Cangrejera complex.[55]

From the mid-1970s onward, PEMEX publicly stressed the need for the active participation of the Mexican basic petrochemical industry in the world market. For this purpose sufficient large-scale production capacity was to be installed for several different products to provide large exportable surpluses. However, the results appear to indicate that the target was set more on the basis of wishful thinking than on fact. In 1982 the 873,000 tons exported represented only 8.2 percent of total basic petrochemical production as opposed to the 26 percent proposed in PEMEX's Programa Sexenal de Petroquímica Básica 1977-1982. Moreover, efforts concentrated on two products, ammonia and methanol, instead of the twenty-one initially planned. To make things worse the very large volumes of ammonia that were exported could not be used locally as planned because Mexico's main ammonia consumer, the FERTIMEX urea plants, had still not come on line.

Although Mexico's basic petrochemical exports have not been substantial, since the early 1980s the country has felt the impact of the industrialized countries' general policy of reinforcing protectionist measures against petrochemical-exporting countries.[56] Thus, in 1982 U.S. ammonia producers asked the trade department to apply compensatory tariffs on Mexican ammonia imports because they felt that the ammonia production was subsidized by the government. In 1983 after a thorough investigation, the U.S. government rejected the petition.

In 1981-1982 because of its financial difficulties, PEMEX looked again at the possibility of becoming a net basic petrochemical exporter. However, it was decided that it would be not economically worthwhile to construct facilities for the sole purpose of exporting. Consequently, the 1984-1988 petrochemical program was designed to include new plants that would first cover domestic demand and, having done so, reserve any surplus for exporting. The policy change was obviously a reflection of the current domestic economic crisis and the difficult international petrochemical market conditions.

CONCLUSIONS AND FUTURE PROSPECTS

Late in the Luis Echeverria administration (1970-1976), the possibility arose of Mexico becoming a major oil producer and exporter. During the next government term this possibility became a reality. Providing a marginal contribution to world oil supply in 1976, Mexico by 1982 had become the world's fourth largest oil producer. Because of the Mexican government's decision early in the 1976-1982 administration to transform oil exports into a new source of financing for the country's economic and social development, oil contributed enormously to the public income and the country's foreign-exchange earnings. However, determining how these economic resources should be used to benefit the economy as a whole was a particularly speculative and difficult task, so much so that the influx of oil earnings gradually made the country's economy subordinate to oil industry activity and triggered a series of problems that eventually led to the economic and financial crisis in mid-1981.

The high priority given to the oil industry by the López Portillo government led to unprecedented expansion. The crude production and export targets established in 1977 for 1982 were reached 2+ years ahead of schedule. Technically, it would have been possible to double the original export target of 0.9 MBD after 1982, but the proposal was rejected by the executive, who felt that the earnings coming in from exports of

2 MBD would far exceed the economy's capacity to absorb foreign exchange. Although by 1982 PEMEX had reached the new 1.5 MBD export level set in 1980, on several occasions it ran into serious problems with its export commitments because of the limitations of the existing infrastructure and trade organization. The ports and port services, the marine fleet, storage facilities, pipeline networks, and operative export systems could not be developed at the rate required to keep up with the country's growing exports.

When PEMEX began to produce heavy Maya crude, it came up against serious entry barriers to the international market. Although its lower price was an advantage over light crude, its high-sulphur and -vanadium content corroded and contaminated the refining systems. These drawbacks were gradually overcome by the technological progress made in refining processes. In fact, Mexico currently finds it easier to sell its heavy crude on the world market than its light crude, a favorable situation for the country because the price difference between the two types of crude compensates for the degree of complexity involved in processing heavy crude. Furthermore, the current prices for Mexican crudes make Maya very competitive on the international market, more so than Isthmus crude, which is lower in quality than the other light crudes with which it must compete.

The López Portillo government's oil policy was basically elaborated according to the short-term world oil market scenario. Statements made by Mexican oil industry personnel show that it was the government's intention to keep the international market value of hydrocarbons high to benefit the producer countries as well as keep the market stable. Despite this intention, the strategies and courses of action taken were not altogether consistent with the public statements.

The Mexican international oil policy during the 1976-1982 government term was subject to changes in local conditions during the first three year and later to changes in the international market. However, the de la Madrid government has adopted an active role in the international oil market, assuming a position that is in accord with its principles and that promotes Mexico's importance in this market.

After 1983 it became obvious to the current administration that Mexico could no longer sustain its main oil policy objective, that is, to obtain as much foreign exchange as possible regardless of the interests of the other producer and exporter countries. Hydrocarbon foreign policy has since aimed at maintaining market stability through orderly readjustments to prices and production that have been agreed upon by all the producer countries.

World oil market prospects do not indicate a large enough increase in oil demand to curb the current tendency for prices to drop. Furthermore, the international crude market still leans toward oversupply and will probably continue to do so for some time in view of the fact that (1) there are no clear signs of sustained world economic recovery, (2) the industrialized countries continue promoting their energy-saving policies, (3) no one knows just how long the OPEC-member countries can continue oil production at levels far below their full capacity, and (4) new oil producers are entering the international market. Under these conditions it is unlikely that Mexico will be able to increase its oil-export earnings in real terms. Also, since 1983 there has been a tendency toward a reduction in foreign-exchange earnings. Future decisions in this respect depend on Mexico's position in relation to the other oil producers. In 1984 the government confirmed its decision to maintain oil exports around 1.5 MBD, and it agreed not to adopt commercial practices that might endanger international oil market stability.[57,58] It also appears that Mexico endorses its policy of cooperation with OPEC. However, the country's experience in the world oil market and in international oil policy making is relatively limited, and a series of economic and political and national and international issues that could potentially have an effect on Mexico's relations with its clients and other oil-producing countries still remain unsolved.

The obstacles to a major expansion of natural gas exports during the 1976-1982 administration were not related to transport infrastructure problems as they had been with crude oil because a large-scale gas pipeline for exporting gas to the United States was already under construction, even though an agreement still had not been reached. However, political and commercial problems arose in the course of the Mexico-U.S. negotiations, and a lesser than expected quantity of exportable natural gas was available for export because of insufficient processing and production capacity and a lack of facilities for salvaging the gas otherwise flared in the Gulf of Campeche. This reduced quantity meant that the contracted volume was established at 300 MCFD for 1979 instead of the original 2 BCFD proposed earlier.

Although natural gas featured prominently in the plans proposed for 1984-1988 in regard to foreign-exchange earnings, Mexico was forced to suspend its natural gas exports temporarily in November 1984.[59] This decision was made after the North American gas companies declared they would be willing to import Mexican natural gas only if the price was considerably lower than that quoted, with which PEMEX decided to use the gas locally.[60] Economically, this alternative was considered attractive given the increased domestic demand and the restricted availability of natural gas reserves.

Even with the possibility of increased domestic natural gas supply due to the canceled exports, efficient harnessing of associated gas, and the potential for large volumes from the Huimanguillo area, it is quite probable that production will still not be sufficient enough to satisfy the industrial sector's and the electricity subsector's demands. Thus, fuel oil will continue to be used, even though it means a reduction in exports.

The goals for PEMEX's Programa Sexenal 1977-1982 included a heavy increase in refining capacity, with which exports were supposed to reach 13 percent of total refinery production by 1982. In spite of these intentions and repeated government statements that Mexico should export products adding value to crude, the increases in refining capacity have been absorbed by domestic consumption, with only occasional surpluses made available for export because (1) domestic demand for refined products expanded at a particularly high rate from 1976 to 1982, (2) there was a worldwide excess of refining capacity, and (3) work on Mexico's expanded production has been suspended since 1981.

NOTES

1. Crude imports started in 1971 in part because of policy changes. Considering the low price of rude in comparison to refined products, PEMEX new director general, Antonio Dovall Jaime, decided to import crude and process it in Mexican refineries. However, the director general during the 1964-1970 administration, Jesús Reyes Heroles, preferred to import refined products because he felt that Mexico's image both at home and abroad might suffer if it were to become a net oil-importing country.

2. Foreign trade in petrochemicals and natural gas includes products not easily integrated into PEMEX foreign-trade volumes. The data quoted in this chapter, unless otherwise indicated in the notes, are taken from PEMEX, Memoria de labores, 1970-1984, Mexico City, PEMEX, 1971-1985; PEMEX, Anuario estadistico, 1983, Mexico City, PEMEX, 1984, pp. 115-126.

3. See Chapter 7, "Exploration and Exploitation."

4. PEMEX's director general, Antonio Dovall Jaime, would not commit himself to exporting large quantities of crude, but President Luis Echeverría and the SEPANAL minister, Horacio Flores de la Peña, seemed open to this possibility initially.

5. See Chapter 7, "Exploration and Exploitation."

6. The government announced its intention to base its pricing policy on international oil market trends.

7. During the last quarter of 1973 OPEC announced two increases in its crude oil prices; thus, the international price went from $2.40 (U.S. $) per barrel to $10.50 per barrel. In october 1975 the price was set at $11.51 per barrel and stayed there until late 1976.

8. See Chapter 7, "Exploration and Exploitation."

9. "México: Plan Sexenal de desarrollo petrolero," in Petróleo Internacional, Vol. 35, No. 1, Mexico City, January 1977.

10. Expanded production was based on a renewed assessment of proven reserves (11 BBCE), which represented an increase of 76 percent compared with the

official figure published during the previous administration.

11. PEMEX, Informe del director general de Petróleos Mexicanos, Mexico City, PEMEX, 18 March 1977, p. 19.

12. "Aspectos económicos del discurso de toma de posesión del Presidente de México," in Comercio Exterior, Vol. 26, No. 12, Mexico City, Banco Nacional de Comercio Exterior, 1976, pp. 1459-1466.

13. See SEPAFIN, Plan nacional de desarrollo industrial, 1979-1982, Mexico City, SEPAFIN, 1979; SPP, Plan global de desarrollo, Mexico City, SPP, 1980; SEPAFIN, Programa de energía, metas a 1990 y proyecciones al año 2000 (resumen y conclusiones), Mexico City, SEPAFIN, 1980.

14. Oficina de Asesores de la Presidencia, Ultima versión sobre la plataforma de producción y exportación (internal document; mimeograph), Mexico City, 1980, pp. 1-8.

15. See Chapter 7, "Exploration and Exploitation."

16. This analysis only takes into account PEMEX's own imports and excludes those of private concerns.

17. PEMEX, Memoria de labores, 1977-1983, Mexico City, PEMEX, 1978-1984.

18. Iran's decision to reduce its oil exports after its revolution, which began in 1979, meant a 4 percent reduction in world crude supply (excluding socialist countries). The ensuing rush by most of the oil-importing countries to increase their stocks pushed crude prices even higher, which was reflected in a doubling of spot-market prices early in 1979. The outbreak of war between Iraq and Iran in September 1980 caused an additional 6 percent reduction in world crude oil supply despite efforts by Saudi Arabia and other exporting countries to increase production. The price of the Light Arab crude marker went from $12.70 (U.S. $) per barrel in December 1978 to $32.00 per barrel in December 1980. See Weyant, John, and David Kline, "Crisis energética y sobreoferta de crudo," in Wionczek, Miguel S. (editor), Mercados mundiales de hidrocarburos, Mexico City, El Colegio de México, 1983, pp. 81-82.

19. If one takes into account the difference in transport expenditure, for the United States Mexican oil was substantially lower in price than Light Arab. This situation appears to indicate that Mexico did not capitalize sufficiently on the comparative advantages it had with transport. See <u>Petroleum Intelligence Weekly</u>, New York, 17 July 1978.

20. Following the prices trend established by the radical OPEC countries, or <u>hawks</u>, in July 1979 Mexico increased the price of Isthmus crude to $4.60 per barrel more than the crude-marker price of $18.00 per barrel. Prior to this, the gap between these two crude prices was less than $1.00 per barrel. The price gap was reduced even further late in 1979, but in January 1980 it widened again, reaching $6.50 per barrel by the end of the year. For details regarding Mexico-OPEC relations, see García Silva, Marcelo, "Las relaciones entre México y la Organización de Países Exportadores de Petróleo (OPEP): De la ambigüedad a la cooperación," in <u>Cuadernos sobre Prospectiva Energética</u>, No. 62, Mexico City, El Colegio de México, Programa de Energéticos, March 1985.

21. In 1979 and 1980 OPEC elaborated a policy, whereby the difference in prices between light and heavy crudes was increased with the aim of stimulating the demand for heavy crude. Most of the OPEC countries' oil reserves consisted of heavy crude.

22. In 1975 the U.S. Congress approved the implementation of a strategic oil reserve, the aim being to allow the country to cover all of its crude oil imports for a period of ninety days in case of an emergency. Setting up the strategic reserve program was a difficult task because of a number of internal and external factors. The government began to build up the reserve in mid-1977, but late in 1978 these efforts were suspended for two years in part because of Saudi Arabia's refusal to provide oil for this purpose. Until 1979 the only foreign country to continue supplying oil for the reserve was Mexico, which had agreed to do so in 1978. For an analysis of this subject, see Wionczek, Miguel S., <u>Strategic Oil Reserves and Stocks in Industrial Countries</u> (mimeograph), Mexico City, El Colegio de México, September 1984.

23. Both then and now Mexico's economic dependence on the United States has stemmed from the

following: (1) the United States was Mexico's main client, but commercial transactions between them invariably resulted in a deficit for the mexican economy and its consequent vulnerability to U.S. tariff policy; (2) Mexico's foreign debt was primarily held by private American institutions or international agencies controlled by the Unites States; (3) the North American multinational companies operating in Mexico had considerable influence over the Mexican economy; and (4) Mexico depended heavily on the United States for technology and capital goods.

24. In 1977 the United States faced a critical situation because of its growing trade deficit, which basically was attributable to oil imports amounting to approximately 45 percent of its total crude oil consumption. Most of these imports came from OPEC-member countries.

25. The data appearing on buyer countries' relative participation in Mexican oil exports were taken from SPP and PEMEX, La industria petrolera en México, Mexico City, SPP, 1983, pp. 96-97; PEMEX, Memoria de labores, Mexico City, PEMEX, various years.

26. In addition to this Mexico signed a contract with another Spanish company in 1980 for exporting 60 TBD of crude as of 1981. This agreement was complemented by another, whereby Spain would convert crude oil into light lubricants destined for the Mexican and European markets. Moreover, in 1980 PEMEX entered into a joint investment in a Spanish refinery that was to import Mexican crude and export refined products to Europe.

27. See Wionczek, Miguel S., and Miyokei Shinohara (editors), Las relaciones económicas entre México y Japón, Mexico City, El Colegio de México, 1982, pp. 106-111.

28. Idem.

29. "Declaración conjunta de los presidentes de Venezuela y México," in Energéticos: Boletín Informativo del Sector Energético, Year 4, No. 10, Mexico City STCE, October 1980, pp. 27-28.

30. This instance was the first time the governments of beneficiary countries had intervened directly in crude oil purchases; therefore, they lacked experience. However, the facilities at the beneficiary countries' refineries were designed for processing

oil, a mixture of crude and derivatives exported by Venezuela, whereas the oil that Mexico was exporting to them was heavy crude. Modifications to the refineries were, therefore, necessary, but the major transnational oil companies who owned most of them were reluctant to make these changes. Last, storage capacity in these countries was limited, and distribution networks were inadequate. See Rosenzweig, Gabriel, "La cooperación económica de México con Centroamérica a partir de 1979," in Pellicer, Olga (editor), La política exterior de México: Desafíos en los ochenta, Mexico City, CIDE, 1983, pp. 235-272.

31. Although Mexico's diversification policy implied a lower relative share for the United States in Mexican oil exports, it did not affect U.S. interests to any real extent. "Even if most of Mexico's petroleum exports are not shipped to the United States, as long as a significant proportion goes to major U.S. Allies, the market power of OPEC would still be reduced and U.S.-Allied energy security enhanced." Ronfeldt, David, Richard Nehring, and Arturo Gándara, Mexico's Petroleum and U.S. policy: Implications for the 1980s (executive summary prepared for the U.S. Department of Energy), Santa Monica, California, The Rand Corporation, 1980, p. 2.

32. Apart from the countries already mentioned, in 1980 the buyer countries included Canada, Brazil, Yugoslavia, and Bermuda, which together accounted for less than 5 percent of Mexico's total crude oil exports. In 1981 crude was exported to twenty-five countries, but if oil and petrochemical products are taken into account, the total number of buyer countries is thirty-two.

33. The conditions that contributed the most to an excess of world crude supply were a worldwide reduction in hydrocarbon consumption because of the economic recession and the industrialized countries' energy-saving policies; the oil companies' policy of reducing existing stocks, which was provoked by high interest rates and storage costs; and the participation of an even greater number of oil producers in the international oil market.

34. In April 1981 the price of Maya crude fell by $2.50 (U.S. $) per barrel; in May of the same year the price of both Isthmus and Maya crudes fell by

$4.00 per barrel. The new prices were then set at $34.50 per barrel and $28.00 per barrel, respectively.

35. The North American companies, Mexico's major buyers, cut back their purchases from 750 TBD to 105 TBD. The French oil company canceled the purchase of 100 TBD, prompting Mexico to cancel industrial contracts for a total of almost $1 billion. However, Mexico tried to negotiate the increase that Japan had originally requested in crude oil sales, from 100 TBD to 300 TBD, but Japan refused on the grounds that it lacked sufficient storage capacity. Salas, Federico, "La crisis petrolera internacional y la renegociación de la venta de crudo mexicano," in Cuadernos de Política Exterior Mexicana, Year 1, No. 2, Mexico City, CIDE, May 1984, pp. 17-20.

36. Spot-market prices for Light Arab crude fell between $6.00 and $7.00 below the official price of $34.00 (U.S. $). In the official market the non-OPEC -member producers, along with other economically weaker oil-producing countries, began to cut their prices and give discounts, thus creating even greater confusion and competition in the international oil market. Although OPEC managed to stabilize crude oil prices during the second quarter of 1982, it still faced serious problems that threatened its internal cohesion and its ability to control prices in the future.

37. From 1980 to 1982 Saudi Arabia's crude production went from 9.6 to 6.5 MBD, Nigeria's went from 2.1 to 1.3 MBD, Libya's from 1.8 to 1.1 MBD, Indonesia's from 1.6 to 1.3 MBD, Kuwait's from 1.4 to 0.7 MBD, and so on.

38. Early in 1982 the price of Isthmus crude went from $35.00 per barrel to $32.50, and for Maya crude the price went from $28.50 per barrel to $25.00. These prices remained stable for the rest of the year.

39. Crude-export distribution for 1982 was as follows: United States, 48.9 percent; Central America and the Caribbean, 3.8 percent; Brazil and Uruguay, 4.0 percent; Canada, 3.2 percent; Europe, 26.1 percent; Israel, 4.3 percent; and the Far East, 9.7 percent.

40. Mexico's agreement with the United States to supply crude for the strategic reserve set the sale of 200 TBD of crude during 1981 and 50 TBD from 1982 to

1986. By 1983 the strategic reserve was to consist of 132.3 MBD of Mexican crude, making Mexico's participation in the reserve, 36 percent, the most important.

41. See González, Guadalupe, "Los cambios recientes en el mercado petrolero internacional y sus repercusiones en las relaciones de México con la OPEP," in *Cuadernos de Política Exterior Mexicana*, Year 1, No. 1, Mexico City, CIDE, May 1984, pp. 21-28.

42. "The aim is to establish fairer and more stable conditions and, at the same time, adapt our prices according to market fluctuations. We do not wish to compete disloyally with other producers, but neither do we wish to lose competitiveness by charging prices above the general consensus." PEMEX, *Informe del director general de Petróleos Mexicanos*, Mexico City, PEMEX, 18 March 1983, p. 16.

43. By February 1983 the price of a barrel of Isthmus crude was set at $10.00, that is, $3.50 lower than the price maintained since March 1982. The price of Maya crude registered a $2.00 per barrel drop to $23.00 per barrel. However, because heavy-crude demand increased that year, the price of Maya crude recovered, rising to $25.00 per barrel in October.

44. Because of world-market movements, OPEC was forced to reduce its crude-marker price by $5.00 per barrel and redistribute the member countries' production quotas.

45. See García Silva, Marcelo, *op. cit.*, pp. 12-17.

46. See chapter 7, "Exploration and Exploitation."

47. Natural gas exports were suspended in 1975, the exception being 6.6 MCFD exported to the United States in winter 1976-1977.

48. In 1979 the deficit was 6.2 MB, equivalent to 3.2 billion pesos. In 1980 there was a surplus of 12 MB (3.4 billion pesos), which increased to 24.4 MB in 1983 (12.4 billion pesos).

49. See Chapter 8, "The Refining Industry."

50. In addition to this, because on occasions maintenance was carried out at the refineries, there was a temporary suspension of supplies to those regions farthest away from other supply centers.

51. Domestic sales increased 16.9 percent from 1977 to 1978, but production only increased 4.5 percent.

52. This situation was the result of increased thermoelectric plant requirements and an unsatisfied natural gas demand.

53. In 1979 there were eleven basic petrochemical buyer countries, the most important being the United States with 36.4 percent of total volume; Brazil followed with 17.0 percent, Spain with 14.2 percent, and Sweden with 9.1 percent. SPP, La industria petrolera en México, Mexico City SPP, 1980, pp. 288-289.

54. The total volume of basic petrochemical imports by both PEMEX and private companies represented 13.5 percent of apparent domestic consumption in 1982 and 13.8 percent in 1976.

55. In 1982 of the forty basic petrochemicals developed by PEMEX twenty of them had to be complemented with imports to satisfy domestic demand. These imports, expressed as a percentage of total petroleum imports, were the following: ethylene and derivatives, 27.4 percent; butadiene, 5.9 percent; and aromatics, 30.4 percent.

56. The industrialized countries' protectionist measures were reinforced after the oil-exporting countries decided to invest vast sums in expanding their industrial capacity in order to give a higher aggregate value to extracted crude. Consequently, world-level petrochemical supply sources multiplied very quickly. With the increased number of petroleum product suppliers and a world recession, the industry suffered from excess capacity, which meant that most plants had to work at less than full capacity and that inefficient facilities were forced to close down.

57. See Poder Ejecutivo Federal, Programa nacional de energéticos, 1984-1988, Mexico City, Subsecretaria de Energia, 1984, p. 111.

58. See PEMEX, Las nuevas politicas comerciales de Petróleos Mexicanos, Mexico City, PEMEX, 1984, pp. 2-4.

59. PEMEX had hoped to export 180 MCFD in 1984 and 1985. See Poder Ejecutivo Federal, Programa Nacional de Energéticos, 1984-1988, op. cit., p. 111;

PEMEX, Aspectos relevantes del plan 1984-1988, Mexico City, PEMEX, pp. 3-4.

60. The conditions that made it possible for the United States to pressure Mexico to lower its gas price were (1) the North American gas market in late 1984 in which there was a surplus of around 2.6 BCFD; (2) the surplus of available Canadian natural gas for export, which was estimated at 17 BCFD; (3) the North American gas market deregulation in January 1985, which lifted controls on the domestic price of more than half the gas produced in the country; and (4) Canada's acceptance of a downward price revision for exported natural gas sent to the United States.

12

PEMEX's Finances

Oscar M. Guzmán

After the mexican oil industry was nationalized in 1938, the federal government's prime objective became the maintenance of national self-sufficiency in hydrocarbons. By providing industry with the energy it needed for expansion, the oil industry was laying the foundation for the country's economic and social development. Mexico's economic and energy low-price policy has followed this basic principle to the present day, and PEMEX has had to supply the energy needs of the domestic market and ensure that the expansion of the various consumer sector activities was not inhibited by a lack of energy resources. In other words, this low-price policy followed by the oil industry was intended to activate the rest of the economy.

However, these basic tasks assigned to PEMEX became incompatible over time. In the mid-1970s PEMEX began to run into serious problems in satisfying domestic demand and, consequently, in guaranteeing the country's oil self-sufficiency. It began to lag behind in production because the economic resources it generated were not its own. This highly restricted financial situation prevented the timely and well-planned expansion of productive facilities that would have enabled PEMEX to keep up with the consumer sector's requirements. The price freeze imposed on PEMEX's products in 1958 eroded its financial resources at a time when it faced constant increases in operating costs and the unavoidable need to invest in broadening its production capacity. This financial deficit forced PEMEX to make only those investments that were absolutely necessary to support the demands of the different operational phases.

The crux of PEMEX's expansion problem was in its commitment to satisfying the increasing demand when its own financial resources were severely restricted. State policy provided a petroleum product subsidy for the local consumer and restricted PEMEX from expanding into areas that obviously needed investment and where operating costs were growing constantly.

By the mid-1970s credit obtained from financial institutions and its own suppliers was PEMEX's major economic resource. This practice was an accepted part of general public finance policy and was encouraged by the government itself. Foreign indebtedness progressively became an essential mechanism, for the country's overall economic growth and for that of the energy sector in particular.

PEMEX's FINANCIAL SITUATION FROM 1970 TO 1976

In 1970 PEMEX's finances began to show the effects of the progressive deterioration that had been occurring for more than a decade. Although its financial structure was relatively well balanced, PEMEX had insufficient working capital at its disposal, its short-term debt was larger than its long-term debt, and it had a serious liquidity problem.[1]

When Antonio Dovall Jaime became PEMEX director general in December 1970, priority was given to restoring and maintaining PEMEX's economic and financial stability. It was the management's intention to revise and modify trade policy and introduce price increases for its products. By doing so, PEMEX would provide itself with enough income and respect as a worthy credit risk to be able to finance, in one way or another, the well-balanced expansion of its production facilities. PEMEX management was fully aware of the problem and of the course it must take in order for it to develop without damaging its production or finances.[2] However, despite an awareness of the current situation, until late 1973 financial policy was centered on aspects that although important did not attack PEMEX's basic financial problem. This situation was a clear indication of the constraints placed on PEMEX by the treasury and the executive, in whose hands rested the power to dictate how the oil industry had to operate. Moreover, these guidelines were subject to the economic and social policies elaborated by the federal government. Thus, the same basic economic policy guidelines used to achieve stable development during the previous decade were followed until 1974. Private investment, rather than public, was necessary to reactivate and stimulate production, which faced a severe recession. Investment and expenditure in PEMEX and other state-owned enterprises was very restricted. Although "redistributed growth" was maintained within these enterprises, PEMEX was obliged to somehow guarantee hydrocarbon supply and subsidize domestic consumption.

With the federal government's refusal to authorize a price increase, which meant that there was no real change in the level or structure of the company's financial resources, PEMEX elaborated and implemented a financial policy aimed at assuring the oil industry's continued operation and expansion even with the imposed restrictions. The intention was to resort to measures that would complement the revenue obtained from domestic and foreign sales. Two important factors were stressed in this policy:

- Internal saving, which was to be achieved through cutbacks and an efficient use of financial, productive, and human resources

- Control over the level and structure of PEMEX's borrowing and debt-servicing conditions

The PEMEX administration proposed a policy of cutbacks in current expenditure, which meant reducing its rate of growth in relation to its income in order to avail itself of a proportionately greater amount of economic resources and reduce the amount of credit required. A series of administrative and productive measures was implemented to increase labor productivity. Work loads and methods and the efficiency level of the different complexes were revised, and a substantial reduction was made in the number of workers taken on. Strict control over new purchases, mechanized storage administration, the limiting of investment to priority projects, construction supervision, and project budgetary control were among the other measures taken to promote savings within the oil industry.

To avoid the danger of a financial crisis, PEMEX's debt commitments had to be controlled by a series of policy-related measures in order to achieve the following:

- To regulate PEMEX's indebtedness according to its capacity to pay without having a negative effect on the public sector's financial structure as a whole

- To suspend, where possible, financing by contract and from national suppliers because of the high financing costs for PEMEX (This measure, together with a reduction in the terms of undocumented liability payments, were aimed at allowing PEMEX to get better purchase and construction prices.)

- To contract financing with major credit institutions; improve and diversify internal and external financial sources; and standardize the criteria governing credit conditions, taking into account the creditor's origin

- To reduce the short-term debt where possible and substitute it with new long-term international credit in order to improve the structure of the debt (In other words, amortization periods should be delayed as long as possible and advantageous periods of grace obtained.)

- To improve credit conditions by negotiating the lowest possible interest rates and attempting to eliminate almost all legal expenditure

International market conditions, the problems involved in supplying Mexico's domestic market, and PEMEX's financial strangulation put the United States in a position where it could influence development in exploring and exploitation Mexico's new oil deposits and fields with a view toward placing the extracted crude on the American market. In late 1972 the United States offered Mexican oil industry technological advice in exploration and exploitation as well as credit to back up these activities. Both the services and the credit would be given on the condition that the payments be made with part of the hydrocarbon production, the volume and price of which were subject to negotiation.

Despite pressure from abroad, PEMEX, with the approval of the executive, reaffirmed its decision to utilize the hydrocarbons it produced to satisfy the country's domestic needs, thus consolidating a prudent nationalistic oil policy. PEMEX's attitude implied a refusal to resort to accelerated foreign indebtedness as a means of financing development and obtaining fast earnings from crude-surplus exports. Therefore, it was decided to continue with the finance policy defined early in the administration, wherein PEMEX was provided with a larger share of its own profits, which, in turn, would became greater if the oil industry improved efficiency.

Although some improvements were made from 1970 to 1973, the finance policy based on internal savings was not effective in providing PEMEX with the economic stability it needed to expand. Low energy prices had reduced profits, thus postponing investment and causing fiscal-debt payments to fall behind. After a few years reduced profits became losses and, in fact, constituted a transference of income to other sectors of the economy.

Late in 1973 the government introduced substantial modifications to its economic policy, whereby investment and public expenditure were to become the economy's driving force. The state-owned enterprises then took up the role private companies had been unwilling to assume. The stable development model that had been in force for over a decade had definitely been abandoned.

In the face of PEMEX's serious financial situation, its inability to satisfy domestic market requirements, and the growing need to import goods as well as credit, the state intervened directly to alleviate PEMEX's tight financial situation with the introduction of two measures.[3] In accordance with the economic policy turnaround, it was announced late in 1973 that the government had released PEMEX from its 3 billion peso fiscal debt and had authorized an increase in energy prices.

The price increase that PEMEX had wanted for so long finally came into effect in December 1973 after the different production sectors recognized the need for it. The increase, however, was not indiscriminate; it followed the government's economic policy guidelines and tried to reduce the impact on low-income consumers. Hyaline, tractor gas, and *tractomex* prices were left unchanged, and although the price of diesel rose slightly, its cost to the consumer was still only 20 percent of what PEMEX paid to import it. Gasoline prices received the most marked increase because the consumers of this fuel belonged mainly to the upper- and middle-income brackets. However, the gasoline price increase also affected freight transport and was consequently reflected in end prices with a general inflationary effect.

The state capitalization of PEMEX's fiscal debt was a mechanism that had been used before in the 1960s and early 1970s. This contribution complement that established in 1970, whereby the federal government channeled PEMEX's explicit subsidies into some of the country's regions and specific organizations. The higher income derived from the price increases, Mexico's proven hydrocarbon potential from new-found oil deposits in the southeast, and the need to regain oil self-sufficiency prompted PEMEX to elaborate a 36.6 billion peso investment plan for the last three years of the 1970-1976 government term, which meant that 12.2 billion pesos would be invested every year.

By raising oil prices, capitalizing PEMEX's debt, and authorizing its investment budget, the government had taken definite steps toward changing the direction of its hydrocarbon and derivative policy. The main priorities of the investment plan were to intensify the search for hydrocarbon deposits, increase both onshore and offshore test and exploitation drilling, and increase refining and reprocessing capacity. Furthermore, accelerated development was proposed for PEMEX's other areas, from transport to petrochemicals, constituting the most ambitious expansion program proposed for many years. It was hoped that a program of this nature would avoid the recurring deficits in the oil industry's different productive areas and pave the way for a healthy financial situation within PEMEX.

In 1974 the increase in income from sales was the combined result of two factors: price increases and, to a lesser extent, an increase in volumes traded. PEMEX's financial situation improved, and the amount of credit contracted from abroad fell. During 1974 financing amounted to only 60 percent of that for the previous year, that is, 4.179 billion pesos, or 11.4 percent of PEMEX's total income.

The financial respite brought about by the 1973 measures appeared to indicate the possibility of PEMEX operating with enough economic solvency to fulfill its objectives. However, early in 1974 the federal government changed its stance. In January a new price structure was imposed on the oil industry: The tax on oil-product sales rose from 12 to 16 percent, and for petrochemicals it rose from 7.8 to 12 percent. In addition to the tax increase, a 50 percent tax was placed on crude-export sales. Consequently, the recent price increases were undermined by a greater tax burden, the government presumably compensating costs of servicing the foreign debt.

The conditions under which PEMEX was to operate during the second half of the Echeverria Alvarez administration were established in 1974, the foundation thus being laid for the events of the next government term. PEMEX's expansion was no longer held back, and the investment program for the years to come was broadened considerably on the basis of resources provided by the new price structure, which was reinforced by sustained growth in domestic sales.

Although in 1974, the first year of the investment plan, PEMEX was in a better position to operate effectively, the financial requirements to cover operating expenditures and investment in its different areas were so great that they could not be covered by the income from domestic oil sales alone, not even when combined with the small revenue from international crude oil sales. According to PEMEX management, the revenue obtained from oil sales would be concentrated first and foremost on efforts to help the country become self-sufficient again in hydrocarbons, derivatives, and petrochemicals and to guarantee a reasonable security margin so as to avoid any possibility of a shortage in the domestic market supply.[4]

With comparatively high international prices, revenue from PEMEX's growing exports, although relatively small compared to the major oil-exporting countries, became increasingly important to PEMEX's total income from sales. However, the amount still was not enough to cover all of PEMEX's commitments. This situation, together with the ineffectiveness of the internal saving policy, left PEMEX with no other alternative than to resort to credit in order to carry on with its expansion plans. The favorable outlook for oil production in the southeast, the rapid progress made in exploration, the addition of vast new reserves, and the prevailing international market conditions for both hydrocarbons and capital prompted PEMEX to seek foreign credit to finance investment and operating expenditure. With the element of foreign credit, the financial policy elaborated in 1970 took on a new shape.

From 1973 to 1976 PEMEX's total liabilities grew faster than its equity, causing an imbalance in its financial structure. In 1976 liabilities were equivalent to 64.7 percent of total assets and only 35.3 percent of total equity. Two factors helped produce this situation: PEMEX's rapidly increasing foreign debt and the Mexican peso's devaluation this same year. PEMEX's situation was not unusual. It reflected a general policy for financing expenditure and public investment that was followed from the middle of the government term onward. Recourse to foreign credit was one of the main aspects of the policy and was encouraged by a growing liquidity in the international capital market.

From 1970 to 1976 Mexican credit institutions provided very little in the way of funds for the oil industry; of the 4.770 billions (U.S. $) borrowed during this period, only 11.9 percent was in local currency.[5] Consequently, the annual balance for PEMEX's total debt grew 3.5 times between 1970 and 1976, and the foreign debt's annual balance increased 5.6 times, reaching a total of 2.799 billions (U.S. $)

by 1976. Although PEMEX settled part of its commitments, the amount borrowed increased again after the mid-1970s; most of the credit came from foreign banks, as opposed to suppliers, with the short-term payments representing 45 percent of the total debt in 1976.

Although the 1973 price increases meant higher income from domestic sales, with foreign sales providing almost 15 percent of total sales for 1976, borrowed funds once again became an important part of the oil industry's total income, covering 33 percent in 1973, 15.4 percent in 1974, and 31 percent in 1976. It was necessary not only to borrow for investment, but also to cover increased operating costs, which grew 24 percent per year between 1974 and 1976, that is, 5 percent faster than the income from sales over the same period.

By late 1976 PEMEX's financial situation had deteriorated even further, and short-term liquidity problems partially solved a few years before had arisen once again. A reduction in working capital had become evident by 1976 and indicated the trend the oil industry was to follow in the years to come.

The Dovali Jaime administration completed its term of office in 1976, leaving PEMEX in a relatively precarious financial situation even after avoiding a serious mid-term crisis. Meanwhile, Mexico's growing hydrocarbon reserves pointed to the possibility of increasing earnings through international crude oil sales, and conditions seemed to indicate that PEMEX's financial problems were only transitory. Undoubtedly, exports were seen as the solution to the oil industry's dwindling finances and the foundation of the country's future development.

PEMEX's FINANCIAL POLICY BETWEEN 1977 AND 1982

The government changeover and the consequent changes in the PEMEX administration in the midst of the economic crisis sped up the transformation process that had begun to occur in the oil industry during the second half of the previous administration. The conviction that oil-export earnings would be the answer to the crisis and essential to PEMEX's economic recovery was a decisive factor in determining the development policy for both PEMEX and the country as a whole.

Primary production and industrial transformation were given priority in order to satisfy domestic demand and, above all, to provide enough crude oil and derivatives for export. These objectives were accompanied by a policy designed to administer the economic resources for this purposes without further compromising the oil industry's financial stability. The production targets for the next six years were laid down early in the administration and involved increasing refining capacity, and tripling basic petrochemical production capacity.[6] A crude oil and gas liquid production of 2.25 MBD was planned for 1982, along with 3.63 MCFD of natural gas and an exportable surplus of 1.1 MBDCE in crude and refined products. A processing capacity for petrochemicals was set at 18.6 million tons per year and refining capacity at 1.67 MBD.

To reach these targets PEMEX had to invest more money than ever before. Its total budget for 1977-1982 was calculated at 960 billion pesos, 310 billion assigned to investment.[7] The funds were distributed between exploration, which was assigned 8 percent; exploitation, 46 percent; refining, 15 percent; petrochemicals, 17 percent; distribution and transport, 13 percent; and others, 1 percent. Most of the resources would be used in primary production and a lesser proportion in industrial transformation. With resources distributed in this way, it was obvious that hydrocarbon extraction, particularly petroleum, for domestic consumption and international trade was PEMEX's main concern.

The financial program designed to complement that for production was based on the assumption that operating costs plus 50 percent of the investment made would be covered by earnings from sales. The program also took into account that given PEMEX's situation in 1977, it would not be possible to achieve these objectives for an additional few years. It was estimated that 78 percent of the investment would have to be financed in 1977, that is, 43 billion pesos, but that the amount needed would be much smaller by 1980, around 15.5 billion pesos. By 1982 a surplus of 9.772 billion pesos was expected.[8]

These forecasts were based on the assumption that the earnings from sales would cover nearly 40 percent of the accumulated income for 1977-1982. Operating expenditures were calculated at 33 percent of total expenditure; federal taxes at nearly 20 percent; and debt servicing, including the interest on loans, at 16 percent. The prospects for a steady improvement in the financial situation, particularly after 1979, were good, and there was no sign of PEMEX exceeding its debt-servicing capacity. More than a year after Jorge Diaz Serrano took control of PEMEX, the situation remained basically unchanged, and it was announced that by 1982 PEMEX's total debt would be 40 percent lower than in 1976, or 34 billion pesos.[9]

The situation could not have looked brighter. PEMEX not only was going to be able to finance oil industry development but also would be able to generate a surplus of 24.9 billion pesos during the six-year government term, which was equivalent to nearly 30 percent of PEMEX's income over this same period. In short, PEMEX's analysis of its future financial situation supported and fully justified the oil industry program and the state's global economic project. The new administration's concept of the oil industry's future development contrasted with that of members of the previous administration, who warned of the risk of decapitalizing PEMEX if the financial situation deteriorated or if the rate of borrowing and the credit conditions were not adequately controlled.

PEMEX's finances during the 1977-1979 oil boom

The guidelines for administering PEMEX's finances were defined early in the Diaz Serrano administration in PEMEX's Programa Sexenal. Those heading the oil industry were convinced that the income from exports would guarantee PEMEX's unrestricted development. It was hoped, therefore, that operating expenditures would gradually fall in line with sales and that the working force's global productivity would increase as hydrocarbon production grew. Proper rotation of stock in storage would postpone the need to purchase new materials and equipment and with careful selection of suppliers and purchase conditions would contribute to internal savings. The policy would be further complemented by a strict selection of investment projects, favoring those with a higher return on investment in the short term. Furthermore, priority would be given to works not requiring external financing.

In light of these measures to consolidate the oil industry's general economic situation, PEMEX was only to use external financing that could be balanced by income from foreign oil sales. All financing from abroad had to be free from conditioning factors that might influence the decisions concerning industrial development and, especially, hydrocarbon production and export policy. There were assurances on the part of PEMEX management that future borrowing had been calculated not to exceed the institution's debt-servicing capacity, particularly where foreign debt was concerned. Borrowing averages would be controlled so as not to endanger PEMEX's financial equilibrium.[10]

The basic financial policy for the first half of the Díaz Serrano administration followed the same general principles that had been formulated and applied during the early stages of the previous administration. However, the oil industry's situation and future prospects had changed, and its financing priorities were also headed in a different direction. From the start the Díaz Serrano administration insisted on the careful selection of investment projects and control over the rate of borrowing and credit conditions. These conditions constituted the major considerations of PEMEX's policy and were stressed on several occasions between 1977 and 1979. The measures designed to increase internal savings during the previous administration no longer carried the same weight. The prospect of high earnings from oil exports relaxed the control over internal resources.

The consequences of this course of action were felt a few years later. By 1979 (halfway through the López Portillo term) with the influx of financial resources, it became evident that although the oil industry's global development policy offered certain benefits, there were also restrictions, disadvantages, and risks. Between 1977 and 1979 sustained growth in the domestic demand for derivatives caused a progressive increase in income from local sales. However, this tendency was the result of an increase in the traded volume because sales prices were not modified over this period. The low energy price policy took hold during this stage; the last time prices had been increased was late in 1976 to compensate for the Mexican peso's devaluation. With the prevailing inflationary situation, price stability in fact meant a reduction in real terms. Consequently, by December 1979 PEMEX's income from domestic sales had fallen 9 percent compared to 1977.

The composition of PEMEX's income changed considerably over this period. In 1976 exports had accounted for nearly 15 percent of PEMEX's income from sales, and in 1979 they had jumped to 56 percent, that is, a total of 166.153 billion pesos in one year, which is equivalent to around $7.22 billion (U.S. $).[11] Therefore, with its growing international sales, PEMEX's total real income increased 19.5 percent per year between 1977 and 1979. PEMEX also benefited from the price increase for Isthmus crude, which went from $14.1 (U.S. $) per barrel in January to $24.6 per barrel in December. The income policy had produced its first results: PEMEX had increased economic resources of its own and still maintained the subsidy on petroleum products for local consumption.

The expansion in PEMEX's productive activities meant greater operating expenditures both at the wellhead and at the oil refining and petrochemical plants. Between 1977 and 1979 expenditure in these areas, which does not include federal taxes and liability settlements, increased 30 percent more than inflation, that is, 13.7 percent in real terms. Although the increased expenditure can be attributed to greater activity within the oil industry, the rate at which this activity occurred began to have a negative effect on the financial balance. Early in 1978 PEMEX announced that the production target set for 1978 would be reached in 1980. However, to reach this target production capacity had to be expanded, which implied the need for additional material and equipment. Mexico's industrial capacity was insufficient to supply PEMEX with the quantity and quality of merchandise needed for the expansion program. PEMEX increasingly had to resort to purchasing abroad, which inevitably pushed up costs in the different areas of production. At the same time, increased borrowing meant that financing had become a major part of total expenditure.

PEMEX had achieved some of its goals because expenditure fell in relation to sales from 66.5 percent in 1977 to 60.4 percent in 1979. However, this apparent improvement was mainly the result of increased income from exports rather than control over operating expenditure. PEMEX's profits--that is, its total income from sales less total operating expenditures, including other net expenditures and income from sales--before taxes and worker profit sharing increased 33.3 percent in real terms from 1977 to 1979.

PEMEX's higher profit margin could have provided it with the means to cope financially with its investment programs and debt-servicing commitments. However, the federal government and PEMEX management had clearly stated that the profits from hydrocarbon exports would go to financing the country's development. Accordingly, the government subjected the oil industry to additional fiscal pressure. Federal tax on income grew and profit margins fell. In 1977 federal taxes took away 59.4 percent of PEMEX's profits, and by 1979 the figure had reached 92.6 percent, an amount equivalent to $2.953 billion (U.S. $). In 1978 the rate at which the different items were taxed increased: The tax on the sale of refined products went to 17 percent in 1978 and to 18 percent in 1979; the tax on petrochemical sales set at 12 percent in 1976 rose to 13 percent in 1979, and late in 1979 the 50 percent tax plus 2 percent ad valorem on exports set in 1975 was modified.

The federal government intended to overcome the crisis of the mid-1970s under the conditions laid down in the agreement signed with the IMF in 1976, which was to conclude in 1979. Production was stimulated in order to obtain foreign exchange as quickly as possible and give impetus to the development plans. The government had the oil industry following an exceptionally harsh regime compared to other industries so that it could collect part of the oil revenue from PEMEX's international sales. With growing expenditures and fiscal taxes, PEMEX decided to go ahead with its investment program in order to reach the production targets it had set for itself.

From 1977 to 1979 more than 146 billion pesos (1977 rates) had been invested in the oil industry, or nearly $8.3 billion (U.S. $). There are no definite figures for the amount invested annually or for the proportions assigned to each of PEMEX's productive sectors. The figures given indicate that by 1979 only 47 percent of the investment budget programmed early in 1977 had been utilized.. If one considers the oil industry's later evolution and its financial situation it seems that the amount quoted did not take all expenditures into account.[12]

From 1977 to 1979 income in the form of credit went from approximately $1.228 billion (U.S. $) to $3.280 billion, representing 26.2 percent and 32.3 percent of PEMEX's total income, respectively. More than 80 percent of this financing was obtained from the international capital market. Unlike circumstances during the previous government term, the national banking system had greater resources at its disposal, some of which were channeled into the oil industry. A greater portion of the financing was done with local currency, but increased borrowing from abroad added to the already existing debt. Although in 1977 and 1978 net borrowing was slightly lower than in 1976, around $645 million (U.S. $), in 1979 it rose to nearly $1.474 billion, indicating a need for resources to finance projects. The total debt rose sharply during the first three years of the Díaz Serrano administration; by midterm the total debt had almost tripled. Late in 1979 PEMEX owed nearly $9.9 billion (U.S. $). Moreover, after 1978 a slight tendency toward short-term borrowing existed, which became particularly marked later on.

Both PEMEX and Mexico in general had good credit ratings in the various world capital markets and enjoyed plenty of support from the international bankers. The prevailing international financial situation and hydrocarbon market conditions made it very easy for them to borrow money. However, the cost of financing began to weigh heavily upon the oil industry, and the need to amortize the debt started to restrict the availability of economic resources. The shortage of working capital became acute, and liquidity problems worsened as a result. The first signs of financial problems associated with accelerated industrial expansion began to appear. However, PEMEX thought these difficulties would disappear just as soon as additional oil was placed on the international market, where prices continued to rise.

Consolidation and crisis in the oil industry, 1980 to 1982

The basic criteria for managing financial resources established during the Diaz Serrano administration and, to a certain extent, even earlier changed very little from 1980 to 1982. On numerous occasions PEMEX management explicitly stated the measures that had to be taken as part of its financial policy were based on efficient resource administration and geared toward counteracting possible financial imbalance. PEMEX's achievements were pointed out, and any mention of possible problems was avoided. Then, the crisis broke.

From 1980 to 1982 PEMEX's income followed essentially the same lines as before, with exports accounting for an increasingly greater share of total sales, reaching 85 percent in 1982. In other words, in six years the relative importance of earnings from internal and external sales was inverted. PEMEX's income increased 2.3 times in real terms from 1980 to 1982 and by 1982 totaled $18.9 billion (U.S. $).[13]

The decisions about the amount of surplus oil to be placed on the international market and to whom it should be assigned were a major cause of disagreement between different interest groups in the country.[14] The dispute arising between those who proposed differing developmental strategies gave way to mutual agreement on two points: the production ceiling and export levels. The energy program introduced in 1980 reflected the position of those who advocated moderation in exports, whereby exports would be a direct function of the economy's ability to absorb foreign exchange. The crude-export target was raised to 1.5 MBD and that for natural gas to 300 MCFD. Experts insisted that the income from these exports could be absorbed by the growing economy and would not cause any economic imbalance. The level of export earnings, therefore, would be subject to changes in international oil prices.

In 1980 international market conditions were an advantage for PEMEX; its export volume increased, as did both Isthmus and Maya crude prices.[15] However, the world oil glut gradually forced the oil-exporting countries to consider reducing their prices. In May 1981 Diaz Serrano ordered a reduction in Mexican oil prices of $4 and $2 (U.S. $) per barrel for the two types of crude exported, respectively, Isthmus and Maya. This decision was considered rash and Diaz Serrano was forced to resign, relinquishing his hopes for presidential candidacy. PEMEX's new director general, Julio Moctezuma Cid, announced a $2 increase in crude-export prices in July 1981. This measure was unacceptable to many clients who either canceled their account with PEMEX or reduced their purchases. This last price increase was intimately related to Mexico's political situation and its international policy, but it clashed with the prevailing international market trends and had to be modified later. These price fluctuations cost PEMEX $1 billion in lost income as a result of their clients' reaction. Mexico had expected to receive $20 billion (U.S. $) for its exports in 1981, but its earnings only amounted to $14.3 billion.

In 1982 Mexico's oil-export prices, along with world-market prices, continued their downward trend and by December had reached $32.5 (U.S. $) and $25 per barrel, respectively, for Isthmus and Maya crude. In spite of this decrease, the income from exports rose by $2 billion. The international market conditions now tended to favor the buyer-consumer and began to restrict to an even great extent both PEMEX's income policy and the country's economic policy.

For more than four years the oil industry's development had been planned under the assumption that real export prices would at least remain constant. The events that occurred indicate that due notice was not taken of the warning signals present in the steady decline in the major consumer countries' demand for crude.

For almost three decades the domestic natural gas and derivative prices had been subject to the government's general economic policy, with no concern for the oil industry's financial needs. Late in 1980 after four years of nominal price stability, attempts were made to modify the traditional low energy price policy. Several consecutive increases in domestic gasoline, diesel, natural gas, and other derivative prices were aimed at reducing the gap between Mexico's domestic prices and the prevailing international prices, but the increases only had an indirect effect on PEMEX's finances. The increases were sufficient only to reestablish real 1976 prices. Also designed to regulate demand, the price rises, in fact, caused a reduction in consumption; as a result the investment that would have been required for extraction and industrial transformation had this measure not been effective was postponed. This instance is probably the only time the pricing policy had a favorable effect on PEMEX's finances because the price increases had been introduced with the state's well-being in mind and not the oil industry's. During this period of deteriorating public finances, the sale of fuel was indeed the government's mainstay.

From late 1979 to late 1982 production in all PEMEX areas grew rapidly: crude and condensate production rose 23.1 percent per year; natural gas, 13.3 percent; derivatives, 7.8 percent; and petrochemicals, 18 percent. The aim of this development was to cover the rapidly expanding domestic demand and fulfill export commitments to the 1.5 MBD ceiling established for crude and the 300 MCFD for natural gas. The very high rate of crude oil extraction and industrial transformation brought an increase in total operating expenditures. However, although the oil industry's increased activity obviously required greater expenditures, the available economic resources were not administered as efficiently as they could have been. From 1977 to 1979 operating expenditures increased 8.9 percent per year in real terms, but from then until late 1982 expenditures grew at a rate of 20.4 percent per year. Over this last three-year period PEMEX's operating expenditures grew at a 13.2 percent lower rate than that at which crude oil and condensate extraction grew, but in the case of natural gas extraction and industrial production, growth in expenditure was higher. Thus, the degree of efficiency in expenditure became less and less despite increased production in the different areas.[16]

The real rise in operating costs that undermined PEMEX's efficiency in resource management was brought about by a combination of factors: (1) PEMEX's expansion and an increase in the price of its inputs, (2) the added cost implied in purchasing these goods because of the oil industry's urgent requirements, (3) inadequate rotation of goods in warehouses because of the magnitude of PEMEX's operations, (4) excessive borrowing, (5) lack of coordination in programming and carrying out works, (6) administrative red tape, and (7) corruption. However, compared with the income from sales, operating expenditures fell from 60.4 percent in 1979 to 31.8 percent in 1982. The revenue from oil sales camouflaged operational inefficiency and minimized the effect the sales' evolution had on PEMEX's development.

The relative variation in PEMEX's own income and expenditures gave way to a large increase in before-tax profits. The federal government's policy was to appropriate most of PEMEX's international earnings and redistribute them according to the priorities established in government programs; thus, the oil industry's remaining profit, which was to be used for investment, was severely reduce. In 1982 the government again increased its tax on the sale of refined products to 27 percent; for petrochemicals it was set at 15 percent and exported crude at 58 percent plus 3 percent ad valorem. Consequently, the federal tax PEMEX had to pay in 1982 amounted to 91 percent of its before-tax profits, that is, around $11.724 billion (U.S. $), which was 5.4 times more than it had paid in 1979 in constant 1977 currency.

In 1980 PEMEX stepped up its investment program, and the amount of borrowed currency invested was double that of 1979. From 1980 to 1982 facility expansion in all the different areas of the oil industry absorbed a minimum total of about $21.154 billion (U.S. $), that is, nearly $7 billion each year. This figure is 2.6 times higher than the total investment for the three previous years. No precise information is available on the way in which funds were assigned to the oil industry's different areas, and the total amount invested during this period is still open to conjecture. According to available figures, accumulated investment for the 1986-1982 government term was nearly 36.5 percent higher than that programmed in PEMEX's 1977 Programa Sexenal. Despite all this investment and the fact that targets for crude oil production and export had been reached, PEMEX failed to fulfill the goals established for both petrochemical and refining capacity and production.

Although in 1981 PEMEX received less revenue from exports than expected, the rate at which facilities were built or expanded continued to be high, so much so that more money was invested at this time than in the whole government term or, in fact, ever in the history of the Mexican oil industry, that is, about $9.5 billion (U.S. $).

Although PEMEX's before-tax profits grew substantially, the fiscal cuts left very little margin for financing the oil industry's development and operations; so, the financial policy that had been elaborated in 1973 lingered on. However, by the end of the 1970s the oil industry's growth and the amount of revenue in circulation reached such unprecedented dimensions that the whole country's economy was brought into play. PEMEX's borrowing for financing purposes represented 28.3 percent of its total income in 1980, that is, 5.4 times more than during the first half of the 1976-1982 administration.

PEMEX sought out virtually every possible credit method, from direct and revolving credit to credit from independent institutions and banking syndicates. Funds were gathered from the different international capital markets with the aim of diversifying the source of borrowed currency; however, it was the U.S. banks that provided most of the credit. Although heavy liability payments were being made, PEMEX's debt balance continued to grow steadily, reaching $25.2 billion (U.S. $) by 31 December 1982. By this time the international banking system had financed 80 percent of the debt, the remaining 20 percent made available by Mexican financiers. Short-term borrowing was on the increase, induced by the oil industry's growing commitments, the heavy increase in interest rates on capital, and PEMEX's decision to finance some of its investment with short-term loans. Late in 1980 the international banking system began to show concern over Mexico's excessive borrowing and consequent indebtedness; nevertheless, credit continued to flow freely until mid-1982 when the crisis finally broke.

The oil industry's debt increasingly became a burden, and financing costs grew because of the high interest rates on short-term loans; so, in order to service its debt PEMEX was forced to borrow even further. Between 1980 and 1982 financing expenditures recorded in operating expenditures almost doubled in current dollars, as did expenditures capitalized in investment; the total sum for both was estimated at $2.7 billion (U.S. $) for 1982.

Early in the second half of Díaz Serrano's administration period, PEMEX figures clearly indicated a growing deterioration in its finances; however, instead of making moves to right the imbalance, Díaz Serrano allowed it to get worse. Not only was the future market interpreted incorrectly, but the decision to try and reverse the decline was never made. By 1982 the rapid deterioration in PEMEX's financial situation had reduced its equity to a mere 25 percent of its total assets. In 1977 PEMEX had had a liquidity problem, and during the following years it worsened. Current cash assets fell drastically in relation to current liabilities, and if current assets and receivables are taken into account, the coverage for every peso of current liability in 1982 was 0.26. PEMEX's working capital, insufficient in 1979, reached an all-time low in 1982 (-47 billion and -739 billion current pesos in 1979 and 1982, respectively).[17]

Early in the López Portillo administration the government decided that the country's social and economic development should be financed with the revenue from hydrocarbon exports. By the end of the administration PEMEX was providing nearly 40 percent of all public income and 75 percent of Mexico's foreign-exchange earnings, but it was also responsible for one-third of the country's overall debt.

There is no doubt that between 1977 and 1982 the Mexican oil industry's productive capacity underwent a kind of development that had never before been seen in its history; Mexico was one of the fastest-growing producer-exporter countries to emerge during the 1970s. However, PEMEX's financial situation deteriorated because of the relative shortage of the resources it needed to carry out its investment and operation program. Its dual commitment to satisfy the domestic market and keep the price of its products low was complicated even further when the oil industry became the "lever for the country's development." Just as had happened on several other occasions after the oil industry's nationalization, the contradictions inherent in the government's mandates led to a major crisis, but this crisis was the most serious in many a decade.

CHANGES IN PEMEX's FINANCIAL SITUATION IN 1983

When the new government took office in December 1982, Mexico was in the throes of the most serious economic crisis of the last few decades; seemingly brought about by the aftermath of the oil boom, this crisis was, in fact, the result of the economic policy followed after the 1940s. Now, as in the past, the government observed the economic measures recommended by IMF to aid its financial recovery. With Mexico's high foreign debt it was absolutely necessary to improve the oil industry's financial situation because it was here that there was the most hope for generating economic resources and the greatest chance for aiding the country's economic recovery. As a result, the new PEMEX management implemented a series of measures aimed at improving its financial situation.

The level of crude oil exports was maintained at 1.5 MBD, and an international sales policy was designed to maintain market stability. Crude oil export prices were to be adjusted according to international market prices, taking OPEC decisions into consideration. Although this practice had essentially been followed by the previous administration, the Miguel de la Madrid government tended toward greater and more obvious cooperation with OPEC, even though Mexico only participated as an observer. The revenue from crude exports became indispensable for combating the country's critical economic and financial situation and prompted the government to assume an active position in the efforts to stabilize the international crude oil market.

A pricing policy was applied to domestic oil sales in order to prevent real price deterioration and maintain the subsidies to certain consumer sectors. These measures were partly responsible for the proportionate increase in income from domestic sales in 1983, which represented 23 percent of PEMEX's total income from sales compared to the 15 percent recorded for 1982. Fuel sales still constitute one of the state's most important sources of income and it is for this reason that price increases have very little effect on PEMEX's own income.

The new PEMEX management acknowledged the lack of coordination between its technical and administrative departments, the excessive red tape within the institution, the inadequate management of stocks and supplies, and the widespread corruption and overpricing by PEMEX officials. Consequently, an administrative policy was designed to correct these irregularities and achieve efficient administration of operating and investment expenditures. PEMEX's debt servicing was restructured and essentially became part of Mexico's public debt. As a result, the short-term debt was rescheduled, and medium-term settlements were extended from 2.2 years in 1982 to 3.7 years in 1983. Payments on capital were rescheduled so that 65 percent of the foreign debt would be paid between 1984 and 1987 and 35 percent in 1987. The reduction in short-term liabilities through debt renegotiation, the settling of the previous years' fiscal debits, and the increase in current assets made it possible for PEMEX to operate with a positive working capital and noticeably improve its liquidity indexes.

The federal government thus abandoned the tax regime in force until December 1982 and substituted one with an emphasis on income from crude oil exports rather than on crude production through the application of the derecho de explotación de hidrocarburos (tariff on hydrocarbon exploitation).[18] After a year there was a real reduction in the taxes paid on income from sales, which fell from 63 percent in 1982 to 35 percent in 1983. Under these circumstances PEMEX's future financial situation had to improve, and it did in 1983.

CONCLUSIONS AND FUTURE PROSPECTS

The true nature of the financial and productive evolution of the Mexican oil industry is best understood in its role as a state-owned company operating in an area of utmost strategic importance to the country's economy. The close relationship between PEMEX and the state has always been a determining factor in the course followed by both. Therefore, no evaluation of the oil industry's finances should be reduced to the criteria commonly used for private firms. This close relationship has been maintained from the time the government's general economic policy was implemented until the government intervened in the regulation of the conditions of PEMEX's foreign debt.

After the oil industry's nationalization, successive governments maintained within their respective development policies the double commitment assigned to PEMEX of satisfying the domestic oil market and contributing to the development of the different productive sectors through a low hydrocarbon and derivative price policy. Late in the 1950s considerable growth in domestic demand was foreseen. PEMEX continued to operate under these conditions and soon its financial resources became insufficient to sustain a balanced expansion of its facilities and assure domestic market supply. PEMEX's financial situation became progressively worse. Late in 1973 the state modified its economic policy guidelines, abandoned its stable development principles, and based the country's growth on public expenditure channeled into productive areas and institutions for social well-being.

The upward movement of international crude oil prices and problems of supply made the oil industry's rehabilitation essential. In 1970 PEMEX's financial deficit was lessened when the state began transferring resources to the institution in different ways. It was not until 1974, however, when there was a turnaround in economic policy, that attempts were made to revert PEMEX's tight financial situation by increasing domestic fuel prices as well as borrowing from foreign institutions; the latter measure was to become the major source of financing for public expenditure until 1982. During the second half of the Echeverria Alvarez administration, the foundations were laid for PEMEX's future financial policy. Furthermore, economic resources now began to flow in the opposite direction, that is, from the government to PEMEX.

The oil industry was further subjected to state development policy during the mid-1970s when oil became a major source of financing. It was then that the highest investment budget in PEMEX's history was authorized and an exploration infrastructure established. Financing for this expansion program was subject to the needs of both PEMEX and the state within the framework of the international economic and energy situation. PEMEX collected considerable revenue from the international oil market that for the most part was passed to the state through steadily increasing taxation. The credit used to finance the oil industry also came from the international capital market, which at that time had large amounts of capital at its disposal for this purpose. Thus, the Mexican state was financed with foreign credit through PEMEX, which, together with the latter's growing inefficiency as a result of its precipitated expansion, gave way to the oil industry's critical financial situation in late 1982.

Once again, in accordance with state priorities, PEMEX defined its domestic policy for resource administration but this time on the basis of increased internal saving, improved productivity in all areas, and the regulation of borrowing conditions according to the institution's capacity to pay. The extent to which these guidelines were actually put into practice and the efficiency achieved varied according to the prevailing conditions in the oil industry. It was during the period of austerity between 1970 and 1973 that greater attention was paid to these guidelines. Later, as economic resources became readily available and a race against time took place to reach production targets, the basic principles of PEMEX's economic policy were virtually forgotten. After the mid-1970s the situation became serious, with unprecedented increases in operating expenditures, wasted resources, excessive borrowing from abroad, and a lack of liquidity because of the transference of resources to the state (see Table 12.1).

In 1984, a year after the new administration took office, measures were introduced that helped

TABLE 12.1
PEMEX INCOME AND OPERATING AND INVESTMENT EXPENDITURES, 1977-1982
(in millions of current pesos and in percentages)

Income and Expenditures	1977	1978	1979	1980	1981	1982
Income						
Own Income						
Earnings from Net Sales	76,729	100,595	166,053	335,461	460,924	1,078,982
Other	936	1,235	2,199	4,767	4,757	6,174
Total Own Income	77,665	101,830	168,252	340,228	465,681	1,085,156
Income from Financing[a]	27,635	51,306	74,654	134,000	397,963	603,300
Total Income	105,300	153,136	242,906	474,228	863,644	1,688,456
Expenses						
Operating Expenditures	44,265	62,427	99,970	131,087	205,273	341,660
Other Operating Expenditures	6,802	3,926	372	4,523	5,988	3,974
Total Operating Expenditures	51,067	66,353	100,342	135,610	211,261	345,634
(Percentage of Sales)	(66.6)	(65.9)	(60.4)	(40.4)	(45.8)	(31.8)
Liability Payments[a]	13,821	18,380	40,805	70,500	165,657	564,716
Investment						
Auditor's Reports	39,429	72,038	77,614	152,292	234,106	— —
Annual Reports[a]	33,888	61,358	83,472	121,800	227,502	284,700

Total (operating expenditures,
liability payments,b and investment
--auditor's reports) 104,317   156,771   218,761   358,402   611,024   1,195,050

Percentages

	1977	1978	1979	1980	1981	1982
Income and Expenditures	73.8	66.5	69.3	71.7	53.9	64.3
Own Income	26.2	33.5	30.7	28.3	46.1	35.7
Income from Financing	100.0	100.0	100.0	100.0	100.0	100.0
Total						

aPEMEX, Memoria de labores, 1977-1982, Mexico City, PEMEX, 1978-1983.
bTotal for 1982 includes annual report investment figure because Auditor's report data for 1982 are not available.

Source, Based on data from Estados financieros de PEMEX, 1977-1982.

avoid a serious financial situation within the institution. PEMEX's future financial equilibrium and the fulfillment of its production targets will still be conditioned by the state taxes placed on oil earnings, the evolution of the international hydrocarbon market, and the as yet uncertain recovery of both the Mexican and world economies.

NOTES

1. By financial structure is meant the way in which a company's capital assets and total liabilities are distributed among its total assets. In 1970 PEMEX's total assets amounted to 47.9 percent, and its total liabilities ran to 50.3 percent. The information presented in this chapter was taken from data gathered for an in-depth study of PEMEX's finances. The main source was PEMEX's financial reports for 1970 to 1982 and was complemented with data from the Memoria de labores. Some of the basic information for 1977-1982 is found in Table 12. 1.

2. In March 1972 after slightly more than a year in office, the new management announced that the economic resources PEMEX generated should provide the financial support for the oil industry's expansion and that for the sake of national economic development, local prices that were so much lower than international prices were no longer justified. The low-price policy had seriously endangered PEMEX's growth, forcing it to depend heavily on both internal and external loans.

3. The need to import crude oil coincided with a heavy international price increase, which only worsened PEMEX's and Mexico's financial problems.

4. See Chapter 8, "Exploration and Exploitation"; Chapter 9, "The Refining Industry"; and Chapter 10, "Petrochemical Industry."

5. These figures are for 1971 to 1976, inclusively.

6. PEMEX, Informe del director general de Petróleos Mexicanos, Mexico City, PEMEX, 18 March 1977, pp. 12-13.

7. See PEMEX, Programa sexenal de Petróleos

Mexicanos, Mexico City, PEMEX, 1977. These sums are equivalent to $43.636 and $14.090 billion (U.S. $), respectively. See Banco de México, S.A., Información Económica: Monedas y Banca, Mexico City, Banco de México, S.A., July 1980, p. 96.

8. Idem.

9. PEMEX, op. cit., 18 March 1978. This sum is equivalent to $1.495 billion (U.S. $). See Banco de México, S.A., op. cit.

10. PEMEX, op. cit., 18 March 1977, 1978, and 1979.

11. The average exchange rate for 1979 was 23 Mexican pesos per dollar.

12. According to financial reports, the 146 billion pesos correspond to "additions to net permanent investment from write-offs and postings." If the "gross" additions to permanent investment are considered, the sum for the three years would amount to $255 billion (U.S. $) and would be 43 percent higher than in the case of "net" additions. If this were in fact nearer the true figure, in 1979 PEMEX invested 73.6 percent of the amount programmed for the whole six-year term.

13. An exchange rate of 57.4 pesos per U.S. dollar is used here, which was the average for 1982.

14. See Chapter 8, "Exploration and Exploitation," and Chapter 9, "The Refining Industry."

15. In January 1980 oil prices for Isthmus and Maya crude went from $32 (U.S. $) and $28 per barrel to $34 and $29 per barrel, respectively. In January 1981 PEMEX set its prices at $38.5 and $34.5 per barrel.

16. Here, the degree of efficiency in expenditure is evaluated on the basis of the relationship between operating expenditures and production.

17. In 1982 PEMEX's working capital was equivalent to $12.875 billion (U.S. $) at the average exchange rate for that year, 57.4 pesos per dollar.

18. From 1983 onward PEMEX acted as a tax collector in the case of the impuesto sobre el valor agregado (value-added tax) and the impuesto especial sobre producción y servicios (special tax on production and services). In 1983 these taxes amounted to 3.7 and 7.1 percent of PEMEX's total income, including financing, respectively.

13

Domestic Pricing Policy

Oscar M. Guzmán

REFLECTIONS ON THE YEARS FROM 1938 TO 1976

One of the determining factors in the rapid growth rate in the domestic demand for derivatives after oil was nationalized in 1938 was PEMEX's low-price policy. This policy contrasted with the domestic trade strategy of the foreign companies working under concession in Mexico and was aimed at reducing the impact of energy costs in production while stimulating trade through a low-cost transport system.[1] It was hoped that expanding the domestic oil market would also promote the development of the oil industry itself. Among other things, the low-price policy promoted the use of hydrocarbons, as opposed to other energy forms, to the extent that from the 1950s onward they represented more than 90 percent of end energy consumption.[2]

As time went by a serious financial problem began to build within PEMEX as a result of this practice. The prices that had initially been established at a level that covered production costs began to lose ground in real terms. Readjustments to oil prices implemented from 1938 to 1954 were much lower than the country's general price increases, particularly those corresponding to the goods and services used by the oil industry; this situation progressively restricted PEMEX's real income.[3] Its own economic resources were further eroded as a result of the state's explicit subsidies policy, whereby PEMEX had to grant differential prices to certain consumer groups, such as public transport services, users in regions with low economic activity, and users supplied with imported products.

Both these policies forced the national oil industry to hold back its development programs on more than one occasion. Such was the case from 1954 to 1958 when PEMEX management insisted on a price and subsidy revision, which would allow the oil industry to expand and to satisfy the growing demand.[4] However, pressure on the government from the industrial and transport sectors forced it to postpone any talks on this subject.[5] Then, in November 1958, only a few days before the Adolfo Ruiz Cortines government term was to end, a price raise was authorized for the major petroleum products.[6] A period of nominal price stability followed that lasted fifteen years, until 1973.

During these fifteen years a low inflationary index made it easier for PEMEX to adhere to the federal government's economic and social policy and continue providing low-priced energy for promoting other industrial activities.[7] Upon taking office as PEMEX's director general, Antonio Dovalí Jaime began pressing the government to relax price restrictions and allow prices to finance development in the oil industry's different areas. However, it was not until 1973, when PEMEX's financial condition was critical, that a price increase was authorized; its production had fallen behind, making imports increasingly necessary, and the conditions on world crude oil market had deteriorated because of sharp price increases. By this time the proposed price increase, which was also advocated by the Comisión Nacional Tripartita (National Tripartite Commission), was essential in order to keep PEMEX afloat financially.[8]

The price increase did not apply to all petroleum products because it was elaborated with continued protection for low-income groups. The price of some products consumed by the farming sector, such as hyaline and tractor fuel, remained unchanged, whereas products consumed mainly by high- or medium-income groups, such as gasoline and lubricants, were subjected to considerable increases.[9] With the introduction of these measures, both PEMEX and the state were able to prepare the oil industry's new productive expansion program on which its subsequent boom would be based.

During the latter half of the Dovali Jaime PEMEX term prices were modified twice. The first increase was late in 1974 when the tax on gasoline consumption was raised, a fiscal measure aimed solely at augmenting the federal government's income. The second, introduced in 1976, was an attempt to compensate for the Mexican peso's devaluation and the consequent price increase in goods imported by PEMEX.

In brief, from the time of the oil industry's expropriation until the eve of the oil boom, PEMEX was continually confronted with financial problems caused basically by the low-price levels maintained over long periods; only on rare occasions were these problems overcome through price increases. Far from constituting an adequate means of financing investment, the pricing policy was subordinated to the overall economic and social objectives of successive governments. The two last increases, of 1974 and 1976, were an indication of the course pricing policy was to take in the following six-year government term: The prime objective of any subsequent increase was aimed at augmenting federal government income rather than benefiting PEMEX.

CONTINUITY AND CHANGE IN THE PRICING POLICY FROM 1976 TO 1983

The first few years of the López Portillo government saw no real change in the traditional low-price policy for PEMEX's domestic products. With an ease in the availability of economic resources earned from oil exports, the smaller income from local sales did not necessarily mean an immediate bottleneck in the oil industry's investment programs as it had earlier. PEMEX was able to avail itself of foreign exchange and had access to international credit, and no substantial modifications to domestic hydrocarbon derivative and natural gas prices were necessary. However, the federal tax applied to oil exports allowed the government to receive additional income without having to introduce a price-increase policy, which undoubtedly would have been very unpopular.

From late 1976 to late 1980 the economy's inflationary process and the oil-price freeze resulted in a deterioration of oil prices in real terms. This situation encouraged petroleum product consumption at an even greater rate than during the early 1970s, it gave rise to wasteful and inefficient use of fuel, and energy-intensive technologies were adopted, all of which forced PEMEX to assign additional resources to the expansion of refining capacity.[10] Furthermore, maintaining much lower gasoline and diesel prices than those in the United States encouraged the consumption of both these fuels in Mexico by U.S. residents living on the border, thus reinforcing the upward trend of demand.[11]

Concern about the impact of the low-price policy was not limited to the oil subsector. PGD 1980-1982, which was introduced in mid-1980, clearly stated that Mexico's dependence on hydrocarbons had been exacerbated by the price and tariff structure prevailing in the energy sector.[12] An irrational consumption pattern had arisen, and there was no longer any incentive to exploit or use energy sources other than hydrocarbons.

PGD deemed it necessary to modify energy-pricing policy, assigning it three functions: (1) to finance the energy sector's development, (2) to fortify public finances, and (3) to rationalize consumption. PGD proposed establishing a pricing structure, whereby energy-saving measures would be adopted by all the consumer sectors, and consumer patterns for electricity consumption would be corrected. Also, the gap between domestic and international prices would gradually be reduced, maintaining a small margin in favor of local industry, although this margin would be a bit wider in those regions the global economic policy considered a priority.[13] Thus, continuity would be given to utilizing the country's endowment of natural resources in order to improve industrial productivity.

The first attempt to define a pricing policy aimed at rationalizing energy consumption and, in particular, hydrocarbons was reinforced late in 1980 when PE was introduced.[14] Although the program's prime objective was still to satisfactorily meet domestic energy demand, its second aim was to rationalize energy use and diversify primary energy sources by implementing a series of direct measures and modifying the existing price structure.

Among the policies defined in the program, that related to pricing was of particular importance. It was seen as a means of achieving established goals; it constituted a mechanism for regulating growth in demand as well as helping to achieve the broader objectives of the country's economic and social policy.[15] An indiscriminate low-price policy maintained over prolonged periods as a means of promoting industrialization was at last questioned. Selective mechanisms were introduced to encourage development in priority areas of production. Domestic hydrocarbon prices were to be raised in the medium term by 70 percent of the value of international reference prices for industrial fuels and diesel and to 100 percent for other petroleum products.

It was felt that the increase in gasoline prices would be reflected in reduced consumption, which, in turn, would have a favorable effect on the global economic structure. By raising the public tax on oil, revenue would be absorbed from the middle and upper social strata and then distributed by the state. In December 1980 the new policy for rationalizing hydrocarbon consumption through regular price adjustments put an end to stagnant domestic oil prices. The first increase agreed upon, which gave rise to diverse reactions from the public, was selective so that it didn't counteract the anti-inflationary measures already implemented and lessened the impact on the lower-income consumer.[16,17] Price increases were only introduced on high-octane gasoline (Extra), jet fuel, liquefied gas, and natural gas for industrial use.[18] This price raise was, in fact, a tax increase and did not affect derivative consumption, which in 1981 continued to grow at rates similar to previous years.[19]

During the last two years of the López Portillo government, prices were modified twice, which barely helped most of the petroleum derivatives to recuperate their real 1973 value. These increases came at a very difficult moment for both PEMEX and the economy as a whole. In 1981 the federal government's revenue shrank because of a fall in export volume and in international crude prices. The following year, as the country's economic and financial crisis worsened, the government gave first priority to reducing the budgetary deficit. With this new state of events the price increases were aimed more at augmenting federal revenue than improving PEMEX's financial situation. With the 1981 price increases the proportion of federal tax in the end price of gasolines went from 33 percent to 69 percent for Nova and from 62 percent to 73 percent for Extra.[20] This measure meant that PEMEX's share in these prices was reduced from 1.66 and 2.42 pesos per liter for Nova and Extra, respectively, to 1.54 and 2.31 pesos. Probably the only price increases to benefit PEMEX were those applied to diesel.[21]

The first sign that thE price increases had had an effect on fuel consumption was in 1982 when domestic sales fell considerably; however, the country's economic crisis also had much to do with this situation.[22] Thus, the successive price increases over the last few years of the 1976-1982 government term were introduced mainly in response to the objectives proposed in PGD 1980-1982: to fortify public finances and regulate hydrocarbon demand.

Sustained low prices for petroleum derivatives sold within the country were not an isolated phenomenon; they were part of an overall government policy to restrict (or prevent) price and tariff increases on products and services supplied by public enterprises. Between 1976 and 1982 the prices charged by the state for goods and services remained practically the same, even though products and services supplied by the other sectors of the economy underwent generalized price increases.[23]

Upon taking office in December 1982, President Miguel de la Madrid announced a restructuring of the public tariff and pricing system within the framework of the Programa Inmediato de Reordenación Económica (Immediate Program for Economic Reorganization; PIRE).[24] The government felt that the system tended to create a deficit for the state-owned companies and that it concealed inefficiencies and subsidized the high-income groups, thus worsening the public sector's budgetary deficit and nurturing the country's economic crises. One of the measures introduced with PIRE was "to increase price and tariffs on the goods and services produced by the public sector, greater increases being placed on those consumed by the higher-income social groups.[25]

PND 1983-1988 simply reinforced the course of action defined in 1980 as part of the energy-pricing policy.[26] The policy was designed essentially to promote rational energy use and allow the state-owned enterprises in the energy sector to generate sufficient income to finance their own expansion. A realistic outline of differential prices and tariffs was elaborated to help regulate the demand, and the price scale was adapted to the productivity level of the corresponding entities.

Although the course of action proposed both by PIRE and PND did not involve major changes in the pricing policy defined early in the 1980s, the specific measures adopted were quite drastic. A quarterly price revision was introduced and the Extra gasoline price adjusted according to international oil market conditions; the price adjustments for liquefied gas, fuel oil, and natural gas for industrial use were carried out on a monthly basis. By 1983 the price increases had helped PEMEX make a profit on its domestic sales for the first time. PEMEX's income tripled from 1982 to 1983, even though the actual sales volume had fallen 4.5 percent.[27]

After the long period of gradual deterioration in real hydrocarbon prices, accentuated from 1976 to 1980 by static domestic prices, the 1980 price policy had to avail itself of several successive and somewhat drastic price adjustments to achieve its objectives. From 1980 to 1983 Nova and Extra gasoline price went from 2.80 and 7.00 pesos per liter to 30.00 and 41.00 pesos, respectively; diesel went from 1.00 to 19.00 pesos per liter; liquefied gas from 2.50 to 10.60 pesos per kilogram; and natural gas for industrial use from 0.42 to 6.19 pesos per cubic meter.

Although hydrocarbon-pricing policy was used to achieve certain economic and social objectives, clear criteria for defining a relative-price policy, particularly for complementary or substitute products, have not been established. This situation apparently stems in part from problems within PEMEX itself because the pertinent production cost studies have not been done, making it impossible to establish prices in accordance with costs and on the basis of selectivity criteria. However, modifications made to relative prices from 1980 onward were not aimed at promoting product substitution but rather at obtaining an overall reduction in petroleum product consumption and fortifying public finances. The low-price precedent and pressures from industrialists and transport authorities made it difficult to raise the federal tax on certain products, such as natural gas, diesel, and fuel oil, which is one of the reasons why the price increases were particularly steep for the gasoline types consumed mainly by the high- and medium-income groups.

Because relative pricing did not always correspond to clearly defined criteria, some of the prices were even incongruent with each other. In the relationship between relative prices and fuel consumption, several points are worthy of note. First, the considerable difference in the price of gasoline and diesel in calorific terms encouraged diesel consumption. However, this situation tended to change after 1980 when price increases for diesel were proportionately higher than for other fuels.[28] Preferential use of diesel was more apparent in public transport vehicles than in private automobiles.

Second, until the early 1970s liquefied gas was used increasingly in internal combustion engines because it was much lower in price than gasoline. Insufficient liquefied gas production capacity made it impossible to satisfy demand; so, after 1975 special taxes were added to its sale price in order to reduce consumption. Nevertheless, after 1980 the price increases for liquefied gas were proportionately lower than those for gasoline, and its use in automobiles began again, accounting for 20 percent of total gas consumption in 1986.[29] With this renewed use the demand for one of the few derivatives still imported in fairly large amounts increased considerably.

Third, certain amount of kerosene mixtures was substituted for diesel in freight-transport vehicles, even though it meant less efficient fuel consumption.[30] Fourth, the real price of natural gas fell continuously compared to fuel oil, leading to a certain degree of substitution.[31] This process is congruent with the natural gas and fuel oil substitution policy elaborated in the early 1980s, particularly if one considers that there are a number of disadvantages in using fuel oil as opposed to natural gas. The 1983 price increases were aimed at reversing this situation; natural gas rose 55 percent in price and fuel oil only a mere 5 percent.

Last, the price of certain products was established according to the type of consumer. For example, until 1981 the price of natural gas for industrial use was three or four times higher than gas for domestic use. At the same time, the use of hyaline for domestic consumption was encouraged by a lower price than that for industrial use. This situation gave rise to a resale business, whereby hyaline was bought at the domestic rate and sold to industry at a profit. However, this practice was curtailed in 1977.[32]

The differences between domestic and international prices were such that the resale of products imported by PEMEX was clearly subsidized: PEMEX absorbed the price difference. A subsidy was not given for all products, however; the price of many of them, such as jet fuel and lubricants, was the same at home as it was abroad. There was a transference of resources to the consumer through the sale of goods imported by PEMEX, but the consumer did not benefit in the same way from the price structure elaborated for other goods.

The persistent deterioration in real petroleum product prices, which brought the oil industry to the verge of financial crisis on numerous occasions, leads one to suspect that income was being transferred to the consumer through the pricing system despite the increases introduced over the years. PEMEX's cyclic productive and financial strangulation reinforces the notion of the oil industry's consumer subsidy. To analyze this concept, one must compare sales price and the costs associated with the production chain for the different forms of energy. However, there is no record of oil industry production costs for a period of more than four decades. Only recently has PEMEX attempted to set up a system for gathering and processing the information necessary to evaluate the costs incurred in the different industrial phases and for each product. This task is not easy because many areas must be covered, from exploration and primary production to industrial transformation, for a whole range of products, which, in most cases, are related, that is, derived from a single transformation process (for example, refining), and whose costs must be distributed accordingly. Such an analysis also requires a detailed revision of indirect costs, such as operational, financial, and administrative costs, depreciation of assets, and so on, where financing and fiscal contributions are key factors. Only careful analysis of this information can shed light on the true extent of the subsidy and establish clear reference points for analyzing the oil industry's economic productivity and comparing it with its sister organizations, whether state or private, in other parts of the world. The evaluation of this subsidy is vitally important to precisely formulating a pricing policy as a basis for elaborating and implementing any state economic policy.

The basic guidelines for the present and future hydrocarbon- and derivative-pricing policy are laid down in PNE 1984-1988.[33] The program basically synthesizes those principles designed and reiterated in previous planning exercises, such as PGD, PE, PIRE, and PND, and makes certain aspects of its content explicit.

First, domestic prices will be kept lower than prevailing international prices except where the product is imported or contains a high percentage of imported inputs. The country's economy should be allowed to benefit from Mexico's comparative advantage as a hydrocarbon producer.

Second, the price of each product will be adjusted, taking into account its availability, the consumer pattern to be encouraged, and the reduction to be given to the consumer sector in question, be it rural, domestic, industrial, or transport. The lowest price level will be set for derivatives of most importance to the rural sector, such as hyaline and tractor fuel.

Third, the price structure for products used in transport will be established according to social priorities. Preference will be given to diesel because it is used mainly in public transport and freight. However, internal gasoline prices will be similar to prevailing international levels to promote less wasteful consumption and discourage the use of private transport.

The program establishes general criteria as a reasonable basis for determining pertinent aspects of pricing policy in regard to internal price levels versus international prices as well as specific criteria, such as fuel substitution and complementarity. Pricing is dealt with in such a way as to leave open the possibility of implementing seemingly opposite measures, but they must not contradict the course of action established in the program. For example, gradual price adjustments will be made utilizing the end-user sector and the desired consumer patterns as the basic pricing criteria. Thus, prices are ultimately determined by the general aspects of state economic policy. With the country's generalized economic and financial crisis, economic policy is clearly oriented toward restrictive measures, such as cutbacks in public expenditure, which unavoidably affect the viability of certain social objectives favoring the lower-income bracket.

In view of Mexico's prolonged crisis, keeping domestic prices low seems to counteract the aim of achieving PEMEX's financial well-being. It is true that the oil industry obtains considerable revenue from exports, but this income is not used solely by PEMEX; it is committed to servicing the country's heavy foreign debt, and any surplus is channeled into other sectors of the economy.

Now, as before, PEMEX is under pressure from other economic areas to provide them with resources. This situation will be decisive in determining the direction that the general pricing guidelines will take and, more specifically, the rate at which price increases will occur both in absolute and in relative terms. Last, any attempt to establish the different price levels and their interrelationships is still subject to the conflicting interests of the country's social and economic sectors; it is these interests that first must be worked out.

NOTES

1. Before oil nationalization domestic market prices were set by the foreign oil companies at levels higher than export prices. For example, between 1934 and 1936 a company called El Aguila established domestic prices for its products that exceeded its external sale prices by 35 to 250 percent. See Navarrete, J. Eduardo, "Nacionalización de la industria petrolera: La experiencia de México," in Comercio Exterior, Vol. 24, No. 4, Mexico City, Banco Nacional de Comercio Exterior, April 1974, pp. 390-392.

2. See Bermúdez, Antonio J., Doce años al servicio de la industria petrolera mexicana, 1947-1958, Mexico City, COMAVAL, 1960, p. 12.

3. Over this period the average price increase for oil derivatives was 66 percent, whereas the general wholesale price index rose by 330 percent. See Bermúdez, Antonio J., op. cit., p. 239.

4. "(...) the main factor holding back Petróleos Mexicanos's development(...) is its diminished resources brought about by an uneconomic pricing system governing the domestic market, as well as subsidies granted to the whole nation in the form of further discounts on already underpriced goods(...) This, however, does not mean a change from low-price policy, one of the most important justifications for oil nationalization(...) what we are dealing with is an attempt to reduce the vast gap existing between certain costs and prices, without losing sight of the country's interests. Nevertheless, we should(...) consider this readjustment an essential condition for oil industry growth at the rate required by Mexico's own development." See "Informe anual, 18 de marzo de 1956," in Bermúdez, antonio J., op. cit., pp. 304-306.

5. By mid-1958 the prices of the major oil derivatives had fallen on average and in real terms to one-third their 1939 level. See Bermúdez, Antonio J., op. cit., p. 240.

6. Gasoline prices increased around 10 percent; dry cleaning gasoline, 29 percent; naphtha gas, 33 percent; diesel, 100 percent; jet fuel, around 10 percent; and kerosene, around 10 percent. See PEMEX, Anuario estadístico, 1983, Mexico City, PEMEX, 1984.

7. See Chapter 12, "PEMEX's Finances."

8. The Comisión Nacional Tripartita, created early in President Luis Echeverría Alvarez's regime, was formed by the representatives of the worker, business, and state sectors.

9. The gasolines available at the time were substituted by two new types--PEMEX Nova and PEMEX Extra--that cost 0.80 to 1.40 pesos per liter and 1.20 to 2.00 pesos per liter, respectively.

10. From 1975 to 1980 hydrocarbon end consumption grew at an annual average rate of 10 percent, that is, 40 percent higher than the GNP; the rate for the previous five-year period was 20 percent. See Gastelum, Raúl, "La política de precios internos de productos petroleros en México, 1976-1982," in Wionczek, Miguel S. (editor), Problemas del sector energético en México, Mexico City, El Colegio de México, 1983, p. 97.

11. See Lajous Vargas, Adrián, "La política a largo plazo de los precios de la energía," in IEPES, Reunión popular para la planeación: Energía y desarrollo nacional, Mexico City, IEPES, 1982.

12. Poder Ejecutivo Federal, Plan global de desarrollo, 1980-1982, Mexico City, 1980, p. 144.

13. Differential prices were set for electric power, fuels, and petrochemical inputs used at new plants to be established in geographically important industrial-development regions.

14. SEPAFIN, Programa de energía: Metas a 1990 y proyecciones al año 2000, Mexico City, SEPAFIN, 1980.

15. See Part 3 of this book.

16. "The Confederación de Trabajadores de México was in favor of the increase; there was disagreement between businessmen, some of whom felt that the economic situation would improve, and other who though the measure would have a serious effect on costs; the representatives of the Partido de Acción Nacional (PAN) and the leftist coalition disagreed with the increase, whereas PEMEX's Director General pointed out that the oil company's stability would allow prices to be kept constant." Gastelum, Raúl, op. cit., p. 98.

17. See SPP, Primer Informe de avance del Plan Global de Desarrollo, 1980-1982, Mexico City, SPP, 1980, p. 42; Juárez, Víctor Manuel, "Siete pesos, nuevo precio de la gasolina tipo extra," in Unomásuno, Mexico City, 22 November 1980.

18. The increase in the price of Extra gasoline was almost 100 percent, bringing it nearer the price of the same type of product in the United States. It was hoped that the increase would bring consumption down on Mexico's northern border.

19. PEMEX's director general announced that the price increase was a fiscal measure designed to benefit SHCP alone. See Ferreyra, Carlos, "PEMEX no tiene ningún programa inmediato de aumento de precios, afirmó Díaz Serrano," in Unomásuno, Mexico City, 25 November 1980.

20. See "México: (Punta de lanza en el ajuste de precios?" in Energy Detente, Vol. 3, No. 2, North Hollywood, California, 2 February 1982, p. 6.

21. In this case the tax on consumption only increased from 18 to 26 percent over the 1975-1982 period, although it was diesel that showed the highest real increase. PEMEX's revenue per unit of product sold was twice as high for diesel as it was for gasoline, even though the price of gasoline was double that of diesel.

22. Although the volume of domestic oil sales had increased to 8.5 percent in 1982, the following year their growth had fallen to 2.6 percent. See PEMEX, Anuario estadístico, 1983, Mexico City, PEMEX, 1984, pp. 94-95.

23. The general price index grew 579 percent during this period.

24. See de la Madrid Hurtado, Miguel, "Criterios generales de política económica para 1983," in Comercio Exterior, Vol. 32, No. 12, Mexico City, Banco Nacional de Comercio Exterior, December 1982, pp. 1287-1296.

25. Ibid., p. 598.

26. Poder Ejecutivo Federal, Plan nacional de desarrollo, 1983-1988, Mexico City, PEMEX, 1983, pp. 337-345.

27. See PEMEX, Memoria de labores, 1983, Mexico City, PEMEX, 1984, pp. 132-133.

28. From 1973 to 1983 the gasoline-diesel price ratio fell from 4.9 to 1.8. See Guzmán, Oscar M., Antonio Yúnez-Naude, and Miguel S. Wionczek, Uso eficiente y conservación de la energía en México: Diagnóstico y perspectivas, Mexico City, El Colegio de México, 1985, pp. 179-181.

29. The price ratio of liquefied gas to Nova gasoline was 0.24 in 1983 compared with 0.41 in 1973. Ibid.
30. Ibid.
31. In terms of calories and with the 1973 fuel oil price (100) as a basis, the price of natural gas went from 100.5 in 1973 to 75.2 early in 1977. See Willars Andrade, Jaime Mario, op. cit., p. 5.
32. In 1977 SECOFI decided to standardize hyaline prices in order to eliminate the transference that benefited the resellers and not the users.
33. Poder Ejecutivo Federal, Programa nacional de energéticos, 1984-1988, Mexico City, SEMIP, 1984, pp. 88-89.

14

The Role of Strategies and Policies in Fortifying Domestic Technological Capacity

Rogelio Ruíz

After oil nationalization in 1938 PEMEX emerged upon the national scene particularly vulnerable to variations in material and equipment supply. When the necessary capital goods and other inputs were not available, the oil industry's productive capacity fell considerably. It then became obvious to those heading the new entity that the introduction of modern technology was essential to improving production.

Forty years later PEMEX was producing 2.7 MBD of crude and condensates and 4.426 BCFD of natural gas it had quantified oil reserves to a total of 72 BB and had nine refineries and ninety-two petrochemical plants at its disposal.[1] This capacity could not have been achieved without the experience of PEMEX and IMP technicians; the advanced material, equipment, and systems; and the technical assistance acquired either locally or abroad.

This chapter addresses (1) the frame of reference for the policies and activities designed to encourage local job training in petroleum technology, (2) the nature of these policies and activities, (3) their evolution, and (4) their results. Generally speaking, this chapter deals with those policies promoting basic research and technological development, the local capital goods sector, and engineering firms.

EFFORTS TO STIMULATE THE OIL SUBSECTOR'S TECHNOLOGICAL CAPACITY

One of the major drawbacks of Mexican development policy has been the lack of a global science and technology policy capable of bringing about a progressive improvement in the different sectors of the country's economy. A policy of this kind would imply sustained financial, material, and institutional aid from one six-year term to the next. The energy sector has been one of the few to attempt any sort of coordination efforts in technological R&D primarily because of the state's considerable participation in this area.

Of particular importance to the stimulation of the oil subsector's technological capacity was the creation of IMP by presidential decree in 1965. The Gustavo Díaz Ordaz administration thought that the newly formed institution would have a very positive impact on the country's industrial transformation. As a state-owned company responsible for Mexico's oil and petrochemical development, PEMEX was urgently in need of technical know-how and adequate worker ability. It was for this reason that IMP was created. It was clearly defined from the start as a center for technological innovation for the national oil and petrochemical industry.[2]

In 1970 another organization was created that would eventually give further support to the development of the oil industry's technology.[3] The Consejo Nacional de Ciencia y Tecnología (National Council for Science and Technology; CONACYT) was given the task of elaborating a national scientific and technological development policy that would provide a frame of reference for the otherwise independent activities of the different sectors of the Mexican economy. This government mandate implied considerable efforts in carrying out this task because the newly formed institution would have to start from scratch. Very few economic resources were available at the time, and furthermore, a comprehensive system of cooperation had to be established between the various parties responsible for the implementation of finance, education, and industrial policy, among others.

During the first six years after its formation, CONACYT's activities included the following steps:

(1) between June and December 1973 the "bases para la formulación de una política científica y tecnológica en México" (basis for formulating scientific and technological policy in Mexico) were elaborated; (2) from July 1974 to September 1975 the "lineamientos de política científica y tecnológica para México" (guidelines for scientific and technological policy in Mexico) were formulated; (3) the "política nacional de ciencia y tecnología: estrategia, lineamientos y metas" (national science and technology policy: strategy, guidelines, and goals) was determined between October 1975 and June 1976; and (4) between July and October 1976 the final document titled "Plan Nacional Indicativo de Ciencia y Tecnología" ("Guidelines for the National Plan for Science and Technology") was published. The first positive results were a diagnosis of the Mexican scientific and technological system and a definition of the foundations on which the future R&D activities would be based. Upon establishing the basis for implementing a general science and technology policy, CONACYT was contributing to the eventual advancement of the country's technological capacity and particularly that of the oil industry. The national guidelines defined the country's scientific and technological shortcomings and set forth the goals, priorities, and policies for achieving scientific development and technological self-sufficiency.[4] Between 1971 and 1976 CONACYT was also responsible for a large number of measures designed to build up technological and scientific infrastructure, particularly in regard to statistics, computing, equipment imports, the dissemination of information, and the setting of technical standards. These measures were also aimed at establishing permanent scientific and technological planning mechanisms duly linked to the country's educational and productive systems.

From 1977 to 1982 CONACYT's very limited participation in promoting the development of national capacity in oil technology was centered mainly in (1) providing support for scientific exchange between IMP and different universities and research institutions both at home and abroad, (2) coordinating with IMP the visits of foreign scientists and the elaboration of the national census on scientific activities,

(3) granting scholarships to IMP professionals, and (4) organizing the exchange of scientific documents.[5]

Although it had been intended that CONACYT coordinate its activities with institutions such as IMP, this coordination did not occur. Instead of combining the different activities to have a broader view of the whole problem, each institution scrutinized the wisdom, points of view, and activities of the other from their own perspective, thus making it very difficult to achieve any sort of institutional coordination in support of the oil subsector's technological development.

The establishment late in 1972 of another agency, the Registro Nacional de Transferencia de Tecnologia (National Register for Technology transfer; RNTT), could have had an indirect effect on the development of the technological capacity for oil.[6] The new organization's main objective was to control the internal and external flow of technology in order to attenuate the growing disequilibrium in the balance of payments, which had been aggravated by the increase in royalties and charges for technical assistance, and to regulate the remittances abroad corresponding to foreign investment.

These measures attempted to stimulate interest in areas traditionally abandoned by postrevolutionary regimes. Of all the scientific, technological, and industrial policy measures designed, perhaps the most important was the creation of these institutions and the action taken to stimulate the country's industrial capacity. Concentrated efforts were made during this period to promote local capital goods industry development, and the government acknowledged the need for an appraisal of the general engineering and consulting services available in Mexico.

The Instituto Mexicano del Petróleo

In 1975 most of the activity and resources for promoting the oil industry's technological capacity were concentrated in IMP, PEMEX's exploration department, and INEN. Each of these had more resources at their disposal than any other national research institution. Around 90 percent of national expenditure in R&D activities was channeled into these three institutions.[7]

Previous policies endowed the energy sector with a large share of both financial and human resources and allowed the national oil industry to achieve a high degree of expertise in exploration and exploitation technology. Even so, Mexico still had to import a lot of technology for industrial plant design and then the corresponding materials and equipment. From the moment it was founded, IMP has participated in the gradual development and adaptation of oil-exploration technology and has been involved in studying and perfecting geologic and geophysical science and techniques. IMP has, therefore, been able to offer its services in these areas to PEMEX and other clients both at home and abroad.[8]

From 1973 to 1982 an average of five seismological processing studies were undertaken each year, and in twelve years seven gravimetric and six magnetometric studies were done for PEMEX. These studies, in particular, were those most utilized, even though there were others that were faster and more efficient, such as those involving the measurement of phenomena occurring at great depths. Neither electric methods nor optic processes were available (see Table 14.1).

Most of the IMP services lent to PEMEX involved using shot-point processing, bringing gravimetric and magnetic interpretation programs up to date, and developing geologic-magnetic models. Seismological processing is still being done for countries such as Jamaica, Costa Rica, Cuba, Nicaragua, China, and India. Quality control has been kept locally and data collected and parameters identified for the seismic areas in five zones: northern, Poza Rica, northeastern, southern, and the Gulf of Mexico. From 1973 to 1982 PEMEX's exploration activities were concentrated in offshore areas. During the first year 258,283 shot points were processed, and for the entire ten-year period the figure was 2,024,843.[9]

Oil was first discovered in the Campeche Basin in the Gulf of Mexico when seismologic, gravimetric, and magnetometric studies were undertaken simultaneously in 1972. In 1974 these same studies led to the discovery of one of Mexico's most important deposits, know as Chac I, after drilling had reached a depth of

TABLE 14.1
IMP SUBDIRECCION DE TECNOLOGIA DE EXPLORACION*:
SERVICES LENT TO PEMEX EXPLORATION DEPARTMENT, 1973-1982

Services	1973	1974	1975	1976	1977	1978	1979	1980	1981	1982	Total
Seismological Processing											
Onshore	4	4	4	4	4	4	4	4	4	4	40
Offshore	1	1	1	1	1	1	1	1	1	1	10
Gravimetry	1	0	0	1	1	1	1	1	0	1	7
Magnetometry	1	0	0	1	1	1	1	1	0	1	7
Electric Methods	0	0	0	0	0	0	0	0	0	0	0
Optic Processes	0	0	0	0	0	0	0	0	0	0	0

*Assistant management for exploration technology.

Source: IMP, Informes de actividades, 1973-1982.

5,000 meters. This achievement and the development of all the exploratory activity and information analysis behind it was carried out by Mexican technicians.

The hiring and instruction of personnel for oil exploration was undertaken mainly by IMP and local as well as foreign engineering firms and consultants. The foreign firms were obliged to train Mexican personnel and use them for their exploration activities as much and as soon as possible. Although PEMEX demonstrated its ability to organize the different exploration activities assigned to the foreign contractors, the contractual clauses referring to training and hiring local personnel were still insufficient to really introduce Mexican technicians to modern exploration technology. However, by 1982 practically all the personnel of the different foreign geophysical companies working in Mexico were Mexican. A number of local engineers who had previously worked in foreign companies providing technical exploration services established their own companies locally and became contractors for PEMEX. In general, despite the far from adequate educational level of personnel in scientific and technical areas, PEMEX, IMP, and local private companies all employ professional technical personnel with sufficient training to allow them to participate in most oil exploration activities.

IMP's technological participation in the exploration activities leading to the new discoveries in the Gulf of Mexico was conditioned, among many other things, by PEMEX's policy for contracting local and foreign technology, the unbalanced relationship between the user company (PEMEX) and the producer of services (IMP), the participation of foreign capital and technology, and Mexico's incipient scientific-technological system. Nevertheless, there was also an interesting correlation between those areas of intense exploration and the higher concentration of technical and human resources in the seismological processing development undertaken by the Subdirección de Tecnología de Exploración (Management Office for Exploration Technology). The assistance IMP provided in this area, as well as the technical services offered PEMEX by private local and foreign companies, were of major importance in the discovery of the new oil deposits in southeast Mexico.

Mexico's technical personnel have developed the ability to process and interpret exploratory data, but the technology incorporated into the analytic systems still was coming from abroad. Existing local ability had been inadequate for developing software because the technology was still very avant-garde and not commercially accessible to local industry, even assuming that it could be integrated properly. The integration and interpretation of geological and geophysical information was of the utmost importance in exploration. Bruno Mascanzoni, IMP's first director general is quoted as stating that

> Everywhere, the success of oil exploration has been based up until now, not on the knowledge of a given technique—advanced as it may be—but on the adequate integration and interpretation of all data, be it geological or geophysical.[10]

This observation implicitly acknowledged that in order to progress in this field it is essential to master mathematical techniques, such as communications theory, numeric analysis, analog and digital computation, and so on. Analog data processing began in Mexico about two years after IMP was founded, and digital processing began in 1970. According to Mascanzoni, "we can confidently state that data interpretation has been done almost totally by Mexican geologists and geophysicists." Such an interpretative activity was developed by the Subdirección de Tecnología de Exploración and was complemented by knowledge adapted from organic geochemistry, diagenesis, gravimetry, magnetometry, seismology, and biostratigraphy, all of which relevant to oil exploration activities.

In 1970 IMP established the first digital processing center for geophysical data with the technical assistance of the Western Geophysical Company in the United States. By 1978 the center had processed mote than 800,000 shot points, which is equivalent to 80,000 kilometers of seismological lines. In 1982 after ten years of operations, the center with its modern equipment was able to cover most of PEMEX's seismic data processing requirements, allowing better control and integration of subsoil information, not to mention a savings in time and money.

Before the processing center was installed, all the geophysical information PEMEX obtained from both its onshore and offshore exploration teams was processed in the United States. Without a doubt being able to locally process the strategic information needed for planning hydrocarbon exploration activities has been a major achievement; however, until 1982 PEMEX still depended on foreign firms for the software needed to process and analyze all the data on the Mexican subsoil. The software packages were imported from the United States, and the potential users were ignorant about how these systems worked; they were used mechanically and were thought of as a kind of "little black box." Mexican technicians had learned to utilize costly and sophisticated equipment and processes, but the country was still dependent upon foreign technological innovation and paying a very high price for it.[11]

In 1979 when Mexico increased its hydrocarbon production, PEMEX requested the assistance of the United States in processing the data on its financial situation and well exploitation; the reason was that

> the data processing needed as a result of PEMEX's increased production should not become a bottleneck, therefore in view of PEMEX insufficient resources information on the well system was processed in INFOTEC's international network; furthermore, the company began to use shared computer time to process the company's financial information.[12]

The satellite ERTS-a has been utilized to elaborate tectonic plans for the north of the country since 1973. These activities gave rise to the first tectonic study of the northern part of Coahuila and the Sierra Madre Oriental. The study was followed by others of Baja California and Sonora, and studies were started also on Mexico's central region and the areas of Oaxaca and Chiapas. Two years later the Comisión Nacional de Energéticos requested that IMP, in collaboration with the Western Geophysical Company, begin a study to determine the extent of Mexico's hydrocarbon reserves.[13] Consequently, with the help of radiometric and geochronometric information, all the areas explored by PEMEX were subjected to stratigraphic, diagenetic, paleontological, palynological, geochemical, and tectonic-petrographic studies. From 1977 to 1982 IMP tried to provide viable solutions to the oil industry's technological requirements, but it lacked the guidelines of an intersectorial policy for scientific and technological development that would coordinate the different activities developed at random and precipitately in Mexico's oil industry.

During these five years much of IMP's longer-term technological R&D was almost totally abandoned in an attempt to cover some of PEMEX's most urgent needs. PEMEX gave very little specific support to these activities, with the argument that most of the modern technology it needed could be acquired immediately from abroad, already tried and tested. Nevertheless, IMP has contributed considerably to Mexico's technological progress, particularly in developing new processes, equipment, and techniques for exploration, exploitation, refining, and petrochemicals. Some of these achievements have meant a major breakthrough, such as the PEMEX process for demetalizing crude oil, now in use in different plants, even in the United States.[14] In this case commercialization of the patented know-how was successful, but it is generally acknowledged that IMP has encountered particular difficulty in commercializing its newly developed processes.

Exploratory activity carried out by contractors

An indication of the amount of exploratory activity carried out from 1970 to 1982 is shown in the fieldwork done by PEMEX and local and foreign contractors. During this period the number of teams working in the field increased, as did field activities. After 1978 efforts were intensified to such an extent that in five years the number of work teams more than doubled. This unprecedented activity was a reflection of the government's interest in discovering new hydrocarbon reserves. The exploration teams concentrated their efforts in surface, subsoil, and seismological geology. However, progress in the activities involving gravimetric, ground gravimetric, and gravimetric-magnetometric techniques was much slower.[15]

Offshore exploration was particularly successful with the use of marine seismological, gravimetric-seismological, and ground-magnetometric techniques. Aerial magnetometry was seldom used in exploration except on three occasions, as shown in Table 14.2.

The teams involved in these exploratory activities were supervised by PEMEX as well as by both local and foreign contractors (see Table 14.3). The preference for local contractors is clear. In 1972 Mexican companies were responsible for twelve exploration teams, and by 1981 the figure had risen to ninety-one. The participation of foreign contractors was considerably less, with an average of ten teams per year; this average decreased gradually, reaching seven in 1981. These data appear to indicate certain trends but should not be interpreted too hastily. Although foreign intervention seems low in terms of the number of teams provided by foreign contractors (see Table 14.3), a common practice was a joint venture with both national and foreign capital. Legally, nothing can stop the use of foreign technology and capital in establishing local companies that could later be contracted by PEMEX to undertake hydrocarbon-exploration activities. Therefore, one can assume that foreign firms probably decided to enter into joint-investment schemes with local companies, whereby their participation in exploration activities would have been much higher and their technology more advanced than that available in Mexico.

Hydrocarbon-exploitation technology

In 1973 IMP Subdirección de Tecnología de Explotación concentrated its activities in four specific areas: oil pools, drilling, evaluation of formations, and corrosion. Its general activities included establishing standards and quality control for drilling fluids. Experimental work was concentrated on developing equipment for studying the liberation phases in hydrocarbon mixtures, carrying out steady-state displacement laboratory tests, recovering oil by steam

TABLE 14.2
NUMBER OF EXPLORATION TEAMS EMPLOYED BY PEMEX, 1970-1982

Exploration Type	1970	1971	1972	1973	1974	1975	1976	1977	1978	1979	1980	1981	1982
Onshore Exploration													
Surface													
Geology	27	27	26	26	29	30	32	30	46	56	60	66	60
Subsoil													
Geology	15	16	17	23	23	23	23	20	20	19	20	20	20
Seismology	24	23	23	22	23	21	19	23	25	25	28	28	24
Gravimetry	3	5	7	5	10	11	9	12	14	18	22	23	--
Ground Magnetometry	1	1	1	1	1	--	--	--	--	--	--	--	2
Mixed Gravimetry and Magnetometry	1	1	--	2	6	4	3	1	3	7	25	32	22
Total (onshore teams)	71	73	74	79	92	89	86	86	108	125	155	169	128
Offshore Exploration													
Marine													
Seismology	--	--	1	1	1	5	2	2	4	8	4	6	10
Gravimetric and Magnetometric Seismology	--	--	--	2	--	--	--	--	--	--	--	--	--

Total (offshore teams)	--	--	1	3	1	5	2	2	4	8	4	6	10
Aerial Exploration											
Aerial Magnetometry	--	--	--	--	1	2	--	--	--	--	--	--
Total (onshore, offshore, and aerial)	71	73	75	82	94	96	88	88	112	133	159	175	138

Sources: PEMEX, Comentarios sobre la situación financiera, 1982, Mexico City, PEMEX, 1982; for 1970, 1971, and 1982, PEMEX, Anuario estadístico, 1982, Mexico City, PEMEX, 1983.

TABLE 14.3
PEMEX EXPLORATION TEAM MANAGEMENT, 1972-1981
(in numbers and percentages)

Work Teams	1972 (No.)	1973 (No.)	1974 (No.)	1975 (No.)	1976 (No.)	1977 (No.)	1978 (No.)	1979 (No.)	1980 (No.)	1981 (No.)	Total (No.)
Managed by PEMEX	53	56	58	56	58	52	59	69	74	77	612
Managed by Local Contractors	12	15	22	26	22	25	39	56	79	91	387
Managed by Foreign Contractors	10	11	14	14	8	11	14	8	6	7	103
Total	75	82	94	96	88	88	112	133	159	175	1,102

Work Teams	1972 (%)	1973 (%)	1974 (%)	1975 (%)	1976 (%)	1977 (%)	1978 (%)	1979 (%)	1980 (%)	1981 (%)	Total (%)
Managed by PEMEX	71	68	62	58	66	59	53	52	46	44	55.53
Managed by Local Contractors	16	18	23	27	25	28	35	42	50	52	35.12
Managed by Foreign Contractors	13	14	15	15	9	13	12	6	4	4	9.35
Total	100	100	100	100	100	100	100	100	100	100	100.00

Source: PEMEX, Comentarios sobre la situacin financiera, 1982, Mexico City, PEMEX, 1983.

injection, and designing thermal stimulators for oil and gas wells.

Work reports for 1973-1980 show that the Subdirección de Tecnología de Explotación developed a large number of projects for designing and building equipment for several IMP divisions and PEMEX departments. For the first time IMP was successful in designing constant-pressure test porosity meters, gas permeability meters, mercury distillers, flash separators, and other similar technological instruments. In IMP's facilities a pulse digitalizer and register was manufactured for PEMEX and equipment repair and servicing facilities provided for both the state-owned company and the private firms. Other products, such as plugging and foaming agents, wax and scale inhibitors, new and basic emulsion breakers, mud surfactants, and lubricants, were also developed. One of the most intense activities was the development of mathematical models for the study of oil pools. Work was mainly concentrated on simulating the behavior of volumetric reservoirs (crude and dissolved gas) and both saturated and undersaturated reservoirs that have undergone water injection.

After 1973 the same subdirección concentrated on evaluating the behavior of fields such as Sitio Grande in Chiapas-Tabasco and Cinco Presidentes, San Ramón, and Ogarrio in Tabasco. Consequently, the number of projects under way at this technical subdirección began to increase rapidly. (Reports on IMP exploitation-technology activities appear to indicate that projects were considered synonymous with problems.) From 35 projects in 1973 the figure jumped to 106 in 1976, at which time PEMEX began to insist that IMP find solutions to new problems related to the exploitation of crude-condensate deposits in the Chiapas and Tabasco Cretaceous region. In response to this a mathematical model for simulating behavior of these deposits was elaborated. This work used up a large portion of the resources assigned to R&D and adversely affected the progress of other projects for equipment manufacture.[16]

The Subdirección de Tecnología de Explotación used computer programs for designing primary foundations and analyzing rod-pump dynamometer graphs. By 1975 this project had let to self-sufficiency in the traditional secondary recovery processes, although high-yield recovery was still not possible. Theoretical and experimental research continued, however, in the search for improved methods for crude displacement. In 1975 work began on a simulation model for studying the effect of waves on marine platforms in order to find information useful to platform design. Products of this work were alternating current potentiometers, highly sensitive digital and inductive wave sensors, temperature-control devices, and a phototype for a dual-channel laboratory tape recorder. Work continued on oceanographic studies in areas of interest to PEMEX; the information obtained from these studies contributed to a well-boring platform design. After two years these efforts resulted in the design of a marine exploration platform.

In view of the importance for PEMEX of the Campeche hydrocarbon production in 1979, IMP and PEMEX jointly worked on a priority project called the Desarrollo Integral de la Sonda de Campeche (Integrated Development for the Campeche Basin). With the oil boom in the Campeche Basin, the Subdirección de Tecnología de Explotación became responsible for monitoring and supervising well drilling by computer.

When it was realized that most of Mexico's crude was located in naturally fractured reservoirs and that there was no completely satisfactory model for analyzing exploitation under these conditions, the Subdirección de Tecnología de Explotación invested considerable time and effort in studying fluid flows in porous and permeable media and in developing the first stage of a mathematical simulation of the same. As a result, a good number of mathematical models were developed, which, when applied to information on some of the wells in different exploitation zones, provided PEMEX with some very useful results.

By 1982 the heavy demand for services by PEMEX meant that the subdirección was making intensive use of computer models and programs developed by IMP. Increasing use was made of coding, digitalizing, transcribing, and processing services for the data rcorded in the geophysical well logs, which included well-bottom pressure. Work was also done to improve existing automatic well-drilling systems. The results obtained are a gauge of the experience obtained in calculating drilling variables and in installing and calibrating electric registers and automatic drills. Despite this experience, IMP's capacity in design and construction is still very limited; the only equipment developed is for fluid analysis, heaters, and special-range voltage sources (sensors and equipment for measuring electric current).[17] Much time was spent evaluating automatic drilling equipment purchased abroad.

The Subdirección de Tecnología de Explotación also contributed to PEMEX's exploitation capacity by developing general hydrocarbon-exploitation plans, feasibility studies, and basic and detailed engineering as well as organizing the purchase of equipment and materials and supervising project construction and control. Other projects also received considerable attention, such as those dealing with onshore and offshore crude oil and gas handling and transport and distribution facilities.[18]

The technical services lent by this subdirección to private industry involved chemical analyses; tests; repairs to viscosímeters; and the sale of certain products, such as barium oxide and clay. Until 1982 IMP's income from services rendered to private enterprises amounted to 80,000 pesos, the number of jobs per year averaging barely seven.

In brief, IMP managed to achieve considerable proficiency in the technology associated with hydrocarbon exploitation, but it was still limited in its capacity for research and design and equipment construction as well as in advisory services to the oil industry's local goods and service producers. However, there has been a considerable increase in the institute's personnel. In 1972 it had 1,750 people in its employ, but by 1982 the figure had risen to 4,250.

The Programa de Energía of 1980 acknowledged that energy self-sufficiency could be maintained only if Mexico participated actively in technological development. However, no policy of any kind was incorporated into this plan to promote such a development within the energy sector, let alone in the oil subsector. It was taken for granted that the state had several organizations at its disposal that were dedicated specifically to scientific and technological research; that is, IMP, IIE, ININ and CONACYT would support the universities and research institutes so that energy-related areas would receive the most attention.[19]

From 1977 to 1980, the time of the oil industry's accelerated expansion, IMP's role in general policy, although important, was in fact secondary and had no real normative effect on technological decisions. Had this not been so, it might have been possible to gradually substitute domestic participation for foreign in certain areas of the oil industry's development. The reason for IMP's secondary role was PEMEX's tendency to look abroad for its technological needs, arguing that oil had to become the Mexican economy's lever for development as soon as possible.

According to IMP data on the oil and basic petrochemical industries' technological capacity for 1981, approximately 82 percent of the demand for technology was satisfied locally, with 18 percent coming from abroad. Ninety-one percent of the engineering requirements were covered by Mexican sources. Technological capacity in capital-goods design still lagged behind, evidenced by the fact that only 45 percent of the country's requirements were covered locally. However, recent emphasis placed on import substitution will probably bring about a substantial increase in the utilization of local capacity.[20] Hence, the basic problem still to be solved is how to avoid excessive dependence on foreign inputs. From 1979 to 1983 PEMEX's total imports amounted to $4.2 billion (U.S. $), 42 percent of which was equipment and 58 percent materials.[21] The least contribution to local technology has been made in petrochemical plants, where licensing only amounts to 27 percent. Engineering's contribution, however, was greater, at 62 percent.[22]

Most of the IMP technological research efforts have been directed toward the search for efficient methods of determining oil potential, recovering oil from the subsoil, and designing computer simulations of hydrocarbon deposit behavior. Considerable efforts have also been made in improving materials and equipment. The basic engineering in refining and petrochemicals undertaken in Mexico has made it possible to develop process simulators for efficiently calculating material and energy balances for the operations involved in separation, distillation, absorption, flash calculations, energy- and heat-exchange optimization, and calculation of thermophysical properties of the most common compounds used in the oil industry.[23]

IMP continues to work on finding efficient means of utilizing energy in chemical and physical processes and improving existing knowledge of molecular processes and catalysis. Efforts are also being made in material research and atmospheric contamination in order to reduce the adverse side effects of heavy crude on the environment. The Institute is aware of the need to dedicate additional time to those refining processes capable of converting a higher percentage of the heavy-crude fractions into valuable fuels:

> The search for better yields is not only a result of greater availability of the heavier crudes but also because of the demand for lighter products, which will hopefully continue. Apart from the hydrotreatment needed to enrich heavy fractions with hydrogen, there are two major obstacles to obtaining greater yield, for instance, the presence of sulphur and a high metal content, mainly nickel and vanadium. At present the most viable means of hydroprocessing residua appears to be with new catalyzers, protector guards (traps) and beds for use in reactors. Current plans involve a combination of desulphurization or vacuum flashing, slow coking, hydrodisintegration, and catalytic disintegration in fluidized beds.[24]

Research work is carried out mainly in the Subdirección de Investigación Básica de Procesos (Department for Basic Process Research):

> Here research involves basic studies in different areas on specific subjects, some of which lead to definite projects. First, basic research is done in the same way it would be done in any academic institution. The activities related to specific projects, on the other hand, are similar to those carried out in companies dealing with technological development. There has been a considerable degree of success in this type of

research, even though the number of people working in this field is small.[25]

TECHNOLOGY TRANSFER TO THE OIL AND BASIC PETROCHEMICAL INDUSTRIES

Two years after it was founded in 1973, RNTT was only just realizing the magnitude of the tasks assigned to it in bringing into check the abuses accompanying the buying and selling of technology. The scant evidence available about the register's operations seem to indicate its ineffectiveness in regulating oil technology contracts. Apparently, private engineering and consulting companies took the need to keep a register of these transactions very lightly. This reaction was the result of a deep-rooted misunderstanding and bias in the private industrial sector. High officials and technicians in this sector thought RNTT was just another bit of red tape obstructing trade in technology.

The attitude of the public industrial sector was not much different. PEMEX registered its local and international technical-assistance agreements more to give the impression of a disciplined institution than to contribute to the organization or optimization of the oil industry's technological input. The contracts registered by PEMEX over these first few years were imprecise and invalidated any efforts to bring order to technology transfer. RNTT not only lacked the experience, professional staff, and financing, it also lacked the authority to demand PEMEX's cooperation in directing the inflow and outflow of technology through official channels.

RNTT's political impotence with the oil industry was obvious. IMP's reaction was similar. The first agreement registered in 1973, wherein IMP loaned its services to PEMEX, refers vaguely to

> the transfer of technical know-how in applied scientific research and studies of problems specific to the field of oil-exploration and -exploitation technology, refining and petrochemicals, project engineering, economic and

industrial studies, personnel training, and any other services (sic).[26]

With this sort of information it would be virtually impossible to keep specific track of the technology IMP produced for the oil industry. Contracts of this kind, together with RNTT's own internal problems, did not help RNTT to gain adequate regulatory power over the technical and financial viability of IMP's technological contributions to the national oil industry.

Any impact RNTT might have had on the oil industry's technological capacity was limited by the lack of facilities and technical personnel needed to evaluate the viability of the technology contracted by PEMEX. The enormous de facto autonomy adopted by the enterprise in its pursuit of the developmental objectives for oil was the main cause of RNTT's inability to keep an adequate record of technology transfer within the oil industry. The most plausible explanation for RNTT's limitations was the insufficient financial, technical, and administrative resources necessary to allow it to coordinate with PEMEX from an appropriate political position.

Most agree that from the time it was founded until 1982, RNTT acted as an agency whose sole purpose was to formally process technology transfers for the oil and basic petrochemical industries, the fundamental technological decisions having already been handled by PEMEX high-level personnel.[27]

Although RNTT's limitations were undeniable, certain anomalies and abuses were detected in a sample of basic-petrochemical contracts between PEMEX and local and foreign contractors. Examples include (1) handing improvements free of charge to the entity selling the technology, (2) exporting, also freely, patented manufactured products or processes to other countries, (3) accepting limitations on R&D by the purchaser, and (4) allowing contract expiration dates in excess of ten years. All clauses of this type were to be eliminated before the contracts could be recorded in the technology transfer register.

The technical-assistance agreements for exploration between PEMEX and local and foreign companies lacked the detailed technical information needed to determine their real effect on the development of local technological capacity in the corresponding field. No data are available on the exact nature and cost of the technology purchases abroad made for other branches of the oil industry. However, the data that are available indicate that between 1973 and 1982 PEMEX entered into nearly 149 agreements for technical assistance in exploration, 2 in exploitation, 55 in refining, and 87 in basic petrochemicals. The official inflow of technology to PEMEX is shown in Table 14.4.

Mexican and U.S. companies covered more than 95 percent of PEMEX's demand for technical assistance in exploration. It was found that 125 agreements involved local participation, and 24 agreements belonged to foreign companies. Most of the services were related to seismological geophysics, gravimetry, magnetometry, and field and laboratory electric means as well as processing and analyzing of geophysical and geologic information and studies on surface and subsoil geology. Assistance agreements were also made in computer software--five with U.S. companies, one with a French company, two with local companies, and one with a company from Panama. There was local participation in practically every facet of exploration but particularly in geophysical and geologic information processing and surface and subsoil geologic study. Mexican, U.S., and English companies all participated in studies on marine seismological geophysics, and according to RNTT data virtually no technology transfer was related to exploitation. In 1982 only two agreements of this kind were registered.

The refining industry received the most assistance from local technology. Initially, IMP entered into joint ventures with The Fluor Corporation, a U.S. company, to carry out the project engineering for cryogenic ethane recovery as well as natural gas liquid recovery. After 1974 Bufete Industrial became the private Mexican engineering firm that participated the most in refining and basic petrochemical projects. The field of basic petrochemicals probably has the highest demand for modern technology, either incorporated, as with automatic process-control equipment, or nonincorporated, as with know-how transfer for manufacturing industrial products.

TABLE 14.4
PEMEX TECHNOLOGY INFLOW ACCORDING TO ORIGIN

Country	Number of Agreements
United States	70
Germany	6
Japan	10
England	6
France	4
Mexico	192
Panama	2
Canada	3
Total	293

Source: RNTT, Convenios de transferencia de tecnología nacional y extranjera para PEMEX, 1973-1982.

Mexican petrochemicals could be promising if the international markets were propitious and if the industry were given sufficient technological and scientific resources to compete internationally. In 1976 development in basic petrochemicals was achieved with the help of licensing and foreign-engineering transfer. The exceptions were those projects designed to expand ethylene production capacity, which were undertaken jointly by PEMEX, IMP, and the Lummus Company.

Until 1982 foreign companies participated in a variety of basic petrochemical projects. British Petroleum, Houndry/Shell, The Kellogg Company, and B. F. Goodrich Co. were involved in acrylonitrile, butadiene, and ammonia projects; S. D. Plants, Ltd., participated mainly in ethylene projects; Lummus, Monsanto Corp., and Imperial Chemical Industries worked on vinyl chloride, ethylene, and polyethylene projects; and the French worked on process licensing for obtaining ethylbenzene and xylene.

After 1977 under foreign license, PEMEX and IMP began to develop project engineering for iso-propanol, toluene, xylene, ethylene, and ethylene oxide. In 1979 Bufete Industrial and the S. D. Plants, under license from Halcon International, collaborated on the engineering design for an ethylene-oxide production project. In 1980 Bufete Industrial was totally responsible for the engineering in a similar project under license from S. D. Plants. A year later IMP began participating as licensee in charge of project engineering for alkyl-benzene acrylonitrile and acetonitrile production.

Currently, sufficient local capacity in basic petrochemicals is available to design and construct industrial complexes. However, some assistance with the high technology is still required because of the imbalance between the insufficient know-how in Mexico's different scientific and technological fields and the rapid rate of innovation in the basic petrochemical industry.

Calculations have also been made by other researchers of the origin of the technology used in oil and petrochemical facilities and the expenditure involved. The percentages presented in Table 14.5 are only a guide and are not intended as a reflection of any facility in particular. Furthermore, these percentages vary considerably according to the type of plant.[28] A brief look at these figures is enough to tell that Mexico will have to pay special attention to R&D in materials and equipment for the oil industry.

The capital goods sector

In 1975 the presence of foreign capital was particularly noticeable in the capital goods industry, with foreign firms holding 47.3 percent of all shares. Furthermore, branches of the multinational corporations were mainly located in the dynamic sectors; the branches development was based on labor-saving technology. The intensive use of capital was encouraged by the existing fiscal structure and protectionist tariffs that favored investment and machinery and equipment imports. Labor policy in general promoted the use of labor-saving technology.[29] This type of technological development occurred essentially because there was no coordinated policy to promote the development of local technology tailored to existing production factors and the size of the market. The development was further reinforced by Mexican entrepreneurs who were reluctant to take technological risks.

TABLE 14.5
TECHNOLOGY DISTRIBUTION (in percentages)

Item	Expenditure per Item	Expenditure in Technology Item	Expenditure in Technology Total	Origin of Technology Local Item	Origin of Technology Local Total	Origin of Technology Foreign Item	Origin of Technology Foreign Total
Know-How License	2	100	2.0	75	1.50	25	0.50
Basic and Detailed Engineering	8	100	8.0	90	7.20	10	0.80
Material and Equipment							
Imported	25	10	2.5	– –	– –	100	2.50
National	25	10	2.5	70	1.75	30	0.75
Construction	35	15	5.0	100	5.00	– –	– –
Administration	5	– –	– –	– –	– –	– –	– –
Total	100		20.0		15.45		4.55

Source: Malo, Salvador, "Políticas y programas de investigación en petróleo," en Ángeles, Luis (compiler), El petróleo y sus perspectivas en México, Mexico City, UNAM, Programa Universitario Justo Sierra, 1983, pp. 85-100.

Local capital goods production was undertaken in production units of varying proportions, but it was limited by low-technology machinery that in most cases was made up mainly of imported parts. In 1971 the royalties and technical-assistance payments by the capital goods sector represented 31.2 percent of all payments of this kind in the manufacturing industry. Of all the manufacturing sector's products, 1.9 percent of the payments corresponded to metallic products, 3.7 percent to nonelectric machinery, 4.7 percent to electric machinery, and 2.5 percent to transport equipment.[30]

To date, virtually no basic research or technological development has been achieved in the local capital goods industry. In 1976 this industry had technological problems, particularly in smelting, manufacturing, and production engineering. After three years the situation still remained the same.[31] The major obstacles to development in the capital goods industry were the lack of an effective policy with an emphasis on international markets, inadequate development in local engineering firms, and a shortage of large smelting and heavy-machinery works and skilled personnel.[32] Early in the 1970s the Comisión Coordinadora para el Desarrollo de la Industria de Maquinaria y Equipo (Commission for Coordinating Machinery and Equipment Industry Development) was created with the aim of coordinating the different departments of the executive working in the capital goods industry.

General statements were made in PE 1980 about support for the energy sector's technological development, but PNDI 1979-1982 gave maximum priority to capital goods manufacture because it was considered the basis for technological self-determination. With this in mind, PNDI was to be implemented by means of a combination of fiscal stimuli, low energy prices and tariffs, preferential credit rates, new sources of capital, and a reorganized buying program on the part of the public sector.[33]

There were several attempts to supply PEMEX locally with capital goods, equipment, and spare parts in order to protect both the industrialists and the workers. However, these efforts were abandoned after a very short time because of the opposing interests associated with this type of activity. A further hindrance to sustained domestic supply was PEMEX's somewhat disorderly search abroad for the goods needed to reach the crude-production targets that had been set.

Accelerated oil expansion and the coordination problems associated with investment programming contributed little to the success of the import-substitution policy. The share of national capital goods in PEMEX's purchases increased but so did the volume of imported goods, leading to even greater indebtedness for PEMEX and the country in general. Import substitution was not as successful as expected mainly because the companies involved in covering PEMEX's demand could not fulfill efficiency requisites and because the government failed to use PEMEX's buying power to make the rest of the economy dynamic. Consequently, PEMEX looked to satisfy its demand abroad to the detriment of local industry.

In the late 1970s the big local capital goods manufacturers were the major suppliers for oil industry projects, to the virtual exclusion of small- and medium-sized industries. The demand was so disorderly and inconsistent that suppliers were reluctant to become specialized and invest in projects whose long-term profitability was uncertain. The use of intermediaries, both unnecessary and uncalled for, was marked and had obvious repercussions on costs. All these factors combined had a negative effect on the develop-ment of a local technological capacity that could help to keep PEMEX finances independent and promote competitive development in strategic sectors of local industry.

Reliable data on the production and finances of the local machinery manufacturers for the oil industry are limited. In 1980 very few companies were still producing machinery for the oil industry alone. Because these manufacturers also produce tools for use with their own machinery, some of the data lump machinery and tool manufacture together, which tends to complicate the situation.[34] Installed capacity is especially difficult to calculate because the local machinery suppliers generally just assemble parts and components, 70 percent of which are imported; thus, the local contribution to the finished product is relatively small. Also, the market is apparently monopolized by one or two suppliers for each type of equipment.

Selective protectionism appears to explain the capacity achieved in building relatively simple machinery. However, this situation does not exist with the complex technology utilized by national firms, which most often is imported from abroad. The simple machinery produced by local industry is utilized more in exploitation and refining than in exploration and petrochemicals where automatic processes tend to raise productivity levels.

The local producers of oil-field machinery still do not have the capacity to compete with foreign manufacturers even in the local market. According to a U.S. source, the sustained growth in Mexican material and equipment imports for the oil industry began after 1971 when these imports cost the country $8.6 million (current U.S. $); this trend continued until 1981 (see Figure 14.1) Reliable local data are not available for materials and machinery purchased by PEMEX and the companies contracted to carry out hydrocarbon-exploitation activities from 1970 to 1982; however, U.S. Department of Commerce figures show that oil-field machinery exported from 1970 to 1983 had an accumulated value of $1.4965 billion (see Figure 14.1). A drop in this value was registered in 1982 and further increased in 1983. The value of U.S. machinery exports to Mexico in 1981 was $260 million (current (U.S. $); it was 180 million in 1982, and $55 million in 1983.[35] This reduction in PEMEX's machinery and equipment imports occurred as a result of the following:

. The present administration's policy of rationalizing imports and promoting foreign capital goods substitution with locally produced goods

. An oversupply of hydrocarbons that gradually made its appearance felt in the international market

. The extent of the energy sector's foreign debt and that of the country in general

FIGURE 14.1

U.S. OIL-FIELD MACHINERY EXPORTS TO MEXICO
1970-1982

(In millions of current dollars)

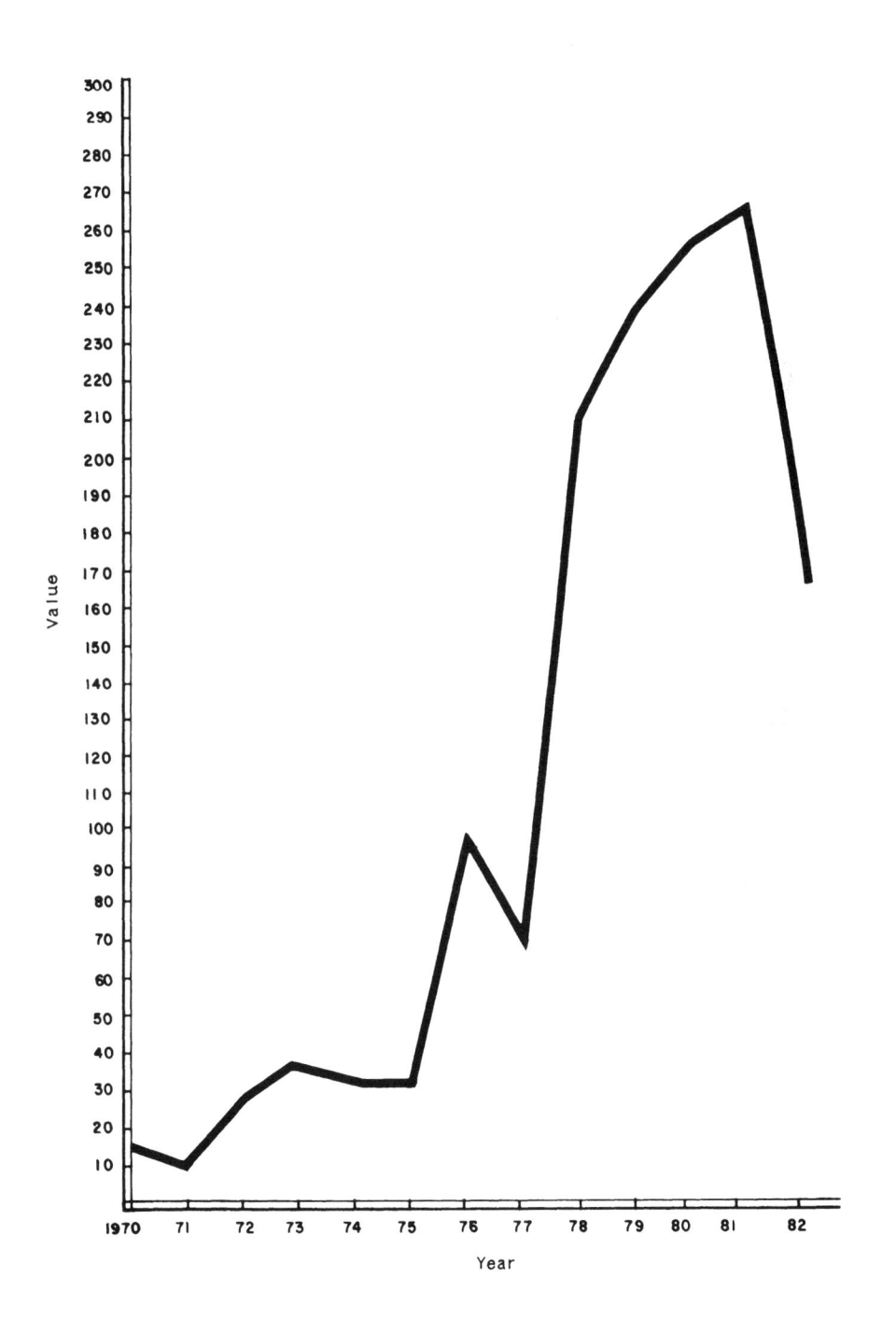

- The attempts made to reorganize the Mexican economy and reduce its dependence on hydrocarbons

- The international money market's closed doors to Mexico's requests for credit

In 1982 Mexico's oil-field machinery imports came from the following countries:[36]

Country	%
United States	70
Switzerland	18
Italy	4
Japan	3

The market for automatic industrial process-control equipment in Mexico basically consists of the major energy sector organizations, that is, PEMEX and CFE.[37] More than one-half of this equipment sold in Mexico is acquired by these two institutions. In 1978 there was a $83.4 million (U.S. $) market (see Table 5.1), and one assumes that until 1981 this market increased considerably. It is thought that by 1983 the market had reached $182 million.

Imports were particularly important in satisfying the oil industry's needs for capital goods and technology. In 1980 external sources provided 93 percent of the oil industry's electric and electronic instruments, 40 percent of its nonelectric and nonelectronic control equipment, 60 percent of its control valves, and 100 percent of its process-control computers.[38] Mexican manufacturers are essentially subsidiaries of U.S. corporations. They assemble simple equipment but lack the capacity to provide the oil and petrochemical industries with sufficient high-quality automatic process-control equipment.

In 1978 of the twelve manufacturers established in Mexico, only one, Termo Industries, was Mexican, although 49 percent of it was owned by American-based Masoneilan (see Table 5.2). The rest of the local automatic process-control equipment manufacturers were subsidiaries or branches of U.S. companies, such as Bayley, Foxboro, and Leeds & Northrup, which assemble thermocouples; Bristol, Fisher & Porter, and General

Electric, which produce manometers; Honeywell and Taylor, which produce control valves; and Fisher Govemor, which is dedicated to gate and butterfly valves. At this time Siemens was the only German subsidiary producing analog panels. Approximately 1,000 people were employed in these industries.[39] Although their components comply with the users' strict specifications, Mexican manufacturers produce very simple pneumatic or mechanical instruments and control valves. The limited size of the domestic market and the high cost of technology makes it unlikely that Mexico could ever produce technologically sophisticated equipment at prices low enough to compete on the international market.[40]

In 1978 oil and gas extraction absorbed 14 percent of the automatic process-control equipment sold to the oil industry that year. Refining operations undoubtedly boosted the purchase of these goods considerably. PEMEX is one of the largest enterprises in the world involved in well drilling. More than one-half of its equipment purchases are imports, almost three-fourths of them from the United States (see Table 5.3).

When pressure was placed on the oil industry to produce additional hydrocarbons, many PEMEX technicians and high officials felt that process-control instruments should be improved because petrochemical and other facilities required sophisticated equipment. From 1978 onward there was a gradual conversion within PEMEX to electric and electronic equipment. Before 1980 Foxboro installed a computerized system in Tula refinery in Hidalgo. It was thought that this pilot program would encourage the computerization of all modern refining operations.

Local engineering and consulting services

In 1976 the development of private engineering services was conditioned by a series of adverse factors: (1) demand was highly irregular because of periodic fluctuations in investment; (2) the domestic market was so small that engineering services tended to become diversified, which, in turn, made it difficult to master high technology; (3) there were no norms, standards, or technical or administrative procedures for designing and undertaking complex projects; (4) the lack of qualified personnel persisted because of the limitations of the educational system and the little importance given to training by companies; (5) with few exceptions engineers maintained little contact with national research institutions; and (6) a limited capacity for technological development in basic engineering led to a heavy dependence on foreign sources of technology, thus generating a vicious circle that inhibited the development of technology.[41,42,43]

The lack of communication between engineering firms and national experimental R&D institutions was due in part to the fact that private firms in Mexico usually took care of their own detailed engineering, which required very little research. Engineering and consulting firms operating in 1976 and, in fact, most of those existing today were not specialized companies. Each company was involved in a wide range of fields, which implied that personnel had to be very diversified, thus raising operating costs considerably and reducing capacity. Such a situation put Mexican firms at a disadvantage compared to foreign engineering firms, which tended to be highly specialized in specific industries.

By 1976 the number of private local engineering firms had risen to forty-three; these firms were employing nearly 5,000 people. The size of the companies in terms of working personnel varied considerably. Work was concentrated in only a few companies, with two of them absorbing 35.2 percent of all personnel.[44] In IMP the situation was somewhat different. Ten years after it was founded in 1966, it had participated in fifty-five refining and petrochemical projects, and basic engineering was imported for only sixteen of the projects. The remaining thirty-nine used technology developed by the Departamento de Ingeniería de Proyectos (Department of Project Engineering) and other IMP departments.[45]

By 1985 local basic and detailed engineering services had developed sufficiently to cover 90 percent of the country's demand, with the rest brought in from abroad. However, in those plants with complex processes and projects financed with package loans, the work was done in collaboration with foreign engineering firms, mainly North American. With the origin of project engineering determining the source of the equipment and materials, the importance of promoting local engineering becomes obvious.

Market instability is bad for any company, but for those dedicated to engineering it is particularly damaging. The company cannot maintain production when demand is low and store the goods in anticipation of increased demand. Furthermore, because these services are highly specialized, the volume of work cannot be increased suddenly during peak periods without having an adverse effect on quality, reliability, and project lead times.

One specialist, having studied the activities of twenty private detailed engineering firms from 1977 to 1982, drew two conclusions. First, when the demand for engineering services is at its height, private companies tend to grow at an uncontrolled rate. New, poorly structured companies are created; there is a rapid changeover in qualified personnel; and improvised methods with unskilled technical personnel become the order of the day. The resulting incompetence and slow progress in undertaking projects consequently leads to low quality, delays, increased costs, and unsatisfactory results. Second, when the demand for engineering services is low, there is unemployment and wasted skilled or semiskilled worker capacity. The company either goes bankrupt, or its situation becomes critical. The personnel, trying to retain their jobs, are uncertain and discontent.[46] The circumstances cause slow growth and instability in the company and lead to unreliability and a consequent drop in competitiveness in the local market. The situation becomes particularly serious when local companies cannot compete with specialized foreign companies.

CONACYT's Plan Nacional Indicativo de Ciencia y Tecnología (National Guideline Plan for Science and Technology) estimated that in 1975 there were around 35 major consulting firms, although for this same year the archives of the Fondo Nacional de Estudios de Preinversión (National Fund for Preliminary Investment Studies) registered 200 such local companies and 226 international firms 89 of which were Canadian, 78 North American, and 59 European. No one really knows what percentage of the domestic market was actually covered by local firms, although it is thought that the participation of foreign companies was considerable, particularly in the larger industrial projects. The 35 major consulting companies had staffs totaling 1,810, and as in the engineering firms, employees were concentrated in only a few of these companies, with fours firms absorbing more than 50 percent.[47]

At this time the growing consulting services were coming up against problems similar to those faced by the engineering firms. The industrialists, particularly those in small- and medium-scale industry, saw no need to hire consultants to solve their technical problems in part because of the expense but also because they were unaware of their importance. The lack of skilled human resources and access to institutional financing limited the expansion possibilities of the consulting companies. The Instituto Mexicano de Investigaciones Tecnológicas (Mexican Technological Research Institute; IMIT) was established to provide support for local industry with preliminary engineering studies designed to improve projects and make good use of existing engineering services.[48]

As a consulting agency, IMP in 1975 had already developed or improved some of the technology and was in a position to export its technical consulting services. These achievements were only possible because of IMP's relationship with PEMEX. For the first time in Mexico the integration of a consulting, engineering, research, and development agency with a production company had produced results and raised the technological capacity of one of the economy's most strategic subsectors.

During the López Portillo administration (1977-1982) PNDI's final measure designed to achieve technological self-sufficiency was to give support to engineering and consulting firms. Nevertheless, the plan only pointed out the importance of these companies in the transfer, adaptation, and diffusion of technology: "These services are situated in a strategic position because they are the link between financial resources and their transformation into investment, between research institutes and the productive sector, and between the capital goods industry and the machinery and equipment consumers."[49] PNDI considered that the number of engineering and consulting firms could be increased and directed into priority industrial sectors through sustained and orderly demand.[50] All these measures would be facilitated by the public revenue from oil surpluses.

The implementation of policies promoting the development of national engineering and consulting services for the oil industry was hindered when (1) neither engineering nor construction could be completed according to PEMEX's schedule; (2) the projects involved facilities in which PEMEX lacked experience, that is, efforts for new products; (3) only one or two companies in the world had sufficient experience and technology to produce a particular product, as was the case with ammonia; and (4) the machinery and equipment needed at the facilities was highly specialized.[51] Until 1978 the fourth problem was particularly common, especially in basic petrochemicals.

No official policy has ever been defined explicitly for consolidating local engineering and consulting services. However, there has been a series of incentives and government regulations, such as the Ley de Propiedad Industrial (Industrial Property Law); RNTT; the Fideicomiso de Información Técnica a la Industria (Technical Information Trusteeship for Industry; INFOTEC); and, in general, the fiscal incentives applicable to technological expenditures, which until 1982 were not particularly effective.

The fact remains, however, that the growth in local engineering capacity has occurred in large industrial firms and particularly in stage agencies, such as PEMEX, that are backed up by IMP engineers, who, in turn, are assisted by high-level engineering services from abroad. The services given to PEMEX by IMP in this field have been many and varied, but efforts in developing basic and detailed engineering for different branches of the industry and in designing heat transference equipment have been outstanding.

Despite the progress made in local engineering and consulting services, the fact that a good part of the high-level basic engineering is still brought from abroad is a sure indication of the oil industry's limitations. The company providing the basic engineering might guarantee its project on the condition that it choose the machinery and equipment that is going to be used, and more often than not foreign companies require that these goods be purchased abroad. Also, when preliminary investment studies are requested of foreign companies, decisions about the type of process, machinery, and equipment to be used can be made without even considering local production.

CONCLUSIONS AND FUTURE PROSPECTS

The financial and human resources granted to the energy sector for developing its energy technology have been the largest given to any government sector. The national oil industry's efforts in developing energy technology are reflected in the mastery of the operational aspect of exploration, exploitation, and process technology. However, a lot of high-technology materials and equipment still have to be imported, for example, automatic industrial process-control equipment.

One of the major problems affecting IMP's ability to effectively transfer and apply its technology to PEMEX has been communication between the two institutions. As the official institution in charge of the oil industry's technological development, IMP is a direct link between government policy and the activities that result. It must act within its own technological field and maintain the continuity of the decision-making process. IMP is in a position to orient groups, such as engineering firms and manufacturers, so that their coordinated efforts can have a positive effect on national oil industry development. Unfortunately, such coordination has not been possible. Although IMP has become a recognized center for engineering, it still has not been able to fully proceed with its work in basic research and technological development and its promotion of technological innovations because of inadequate financing and insufficient qualified personnel.

The most obvious problem between IMP and PEMEX was PEMEX's inability to effectively define for IMP its problems and medium- and long-term technological needs. If PEMEX had been precise, IMP could have used its full capacity and resources to help solve some of PEMEX's problems. As a result of this poor communication, IMP, CONACYT, and RNTT tended to disassociate themselves from PEMEX, offering little advice on PEMEX's technological operations. Only in a few occasions have IMP's consulting services been of particular consequence in orienting PEMEX's technological activities. PEMEX's argument for this lack of communication was that it had to give priority to oil industry expansion. Furthermore, CONACYT and RNTT were limited by the amount of technical and administrative resources at their disposal as well as by their own internal regulations.

To overcome obstacles such as these, new policies need to be implemented. This procedure implies undertaking a serious evaluation of the technological capacity of the oil industry and the private industrial sector that supplies it. This evaluation would allow the government to do the following:

- To determine which technological needs were covered by local industry and which had to be covered by imports, thus allowing the areas in which competent organizations would have to join forces to reduce dependence on foreign technology to be determined as well

- To specify all PEMEX's requirements in both capital goods and technology in order to compare these data with available local productive ability

- To promote those activities related with national technological development and coordinate the effective involvement of pertinent organizations, especially PEMEX and IMP (not only would this effort aid basic engineering development in priority areas, but it would also be an added stimulus for the local development of previously imported technology)

Engineering and consulting services have a very large potential market in both the public and private sectors. Although the development plans for both these sectors are ambitious, they lack continuity; they are constantly being modified, postponed, or even canceled. This situation is true in private and public engineering firms alike, and the causes are many and varied. It seems that inadequate planning and a lack of continuity during the changes in the Mexican political cycle are mainly responsible for the underdevelopment of local engineering capability. If capacity could be increased, the quality and price of capital goods and technology could be improved, which would lead to successful import substitution. Aside from inadequate planning and development, the situation is also aggravated by the absence of highly specialized engineering. The structural renovation of the oil industry to obtain greater added value, higher productivity, additional jobs, and higher income has also been restricted by a predominantly unskilled work force, which has made it difficult to supply those sectors with a higher degree of aggregate value with the trained workers they need.

The most important factors influencing the Mexican oil industry's technological development are (1) the technological underdevelopment of local companies because of a lack of R&D, (2) PEMEX's irregular demand for technology, (3) the bottlenecks arising in the metallurgic and metal-mechanic industry, (4) PEMEX's financial requirements, and (5) the lack of coordination between PEMEX and other technological agencies.

Innovative policies are also needed to overcome those problems in which the intimate relationship between technology and foreign capital must be defined and the role of each in national development clearly determined. The elaboration and implementation of these policies necessarily implies a complete awareness of the extent of their political effects.

Despite the real or assumed limitations associated with both energy and scientific and technological planning in Mexico, since 1970 the Mexican state has made considerable efforts to organize these areas, with varying degrees of success because the state is fully aware of their strategic value in the country's socioeconomic development. President de la Madrid's administration has tried to coordinate a series of activities and policies aimed at boosting the capacity of Mexico's capital goods and science and technology sectors.

PNE 1984-1988 states that the energy sector will give support to industries contributing to technological development and in coordination with its state-financed technological R&D organizations will encourage the development of local technology or the adaptation of technology from abroad. Efforts to standardize raw materials, parts, components, substances, and equipment will be made, and basic and detailed technology transfer will be negotiated.

The course of action laid down by PNE for IMP is as follows:

. Continue developing technology for processing heavy crude and its by-products and assimilate and innovate hydrocarbon-exploration and -exploitation technology.

. Continue providing the oil, petrochemical, and related industries with engineering services and technical aid, thus broadening their scope, improving their efficiency, and promoting the elaboration of technology in line with the country's needs.

. Support the manufacture of local inputs and capital goods for the oil and petrochemical industries, making use of technology already developed by the institute.

. Intensify training schemes for workers in the oil, petrochemical, and related industries, thus contributing to efficient use of available human resources.[52]

In regard to the strategy for effectively coordinating the energy sector with the rest of the economy, it has been stated that

the energy sector is Mexico's main user of capital goods and other products of major importance to industry and is therefore one of the key actors in the country's industrial development. The strengthening of the bonds between the energy sector and the rest of the economy is one of the energy policy's highest priorities.(. . .) This will be stimulated through directing demand toward local industry, technological development, and support to those activities using inputs produced by the energy sector. In the short term continued support will be given to the Programa de Defensa de la Planta Productiva y el Empleo and as the sector gradually becomes modernized, to productive activities in accordance with the policy for industrial promotion.[53]

PNE 1984-1988 specifically states the importance of the country's scientific and technological potential. It is estimated that the most important scientific and technological activities in the oil industry are concentrated in IMP, where "basic and applied research and development programs are undertaken by highly qualified personnel."[54]

PNE works under the assumption that the energy sector has at its disposal adequate qualified human resources, productive and technological capacity, legal assistance, and a solid organic and operational structure.[55] With the current problems facing the technological R&D centers, the local capital goods sector, local engineering firms, and institutions assigned to train highly qualified personnel, these assumptions appear too optimistic.

Nevertheless, some specific action has already been taken toward achieving PNE's objectives. In December 1984 the Mexican Congress approved the Ley para Coordinar y Promover el Desarrollo Científico y Tecnológico de México (Law for Coordinating and Promoting Mexico's Scientific and Technological Development). Under this law CONACYT was given the power to coordinate the Programa Nacional de Desarrollo Tecnológico y Científico (National Program for Technological and Scientific Development; PRONDETYC).

PEMEX has introduced an import-substitution program aimed at reinforcing the capital goods firms supplying the Mexican oil industry. By July 1984 PEMEX had spent almost half of its annual budget of 430 billion pesos on purchasing capital goods by tender. Almost 80 percent of these purchases were made in the domestic market:

During the first four months of 1984 the institution acquired capital goods, material, and other inputs with a value of 73 billion pesos, apart from the accumulation of stock from previous years, and for May-June tenders were accepted for a sum of around 130 billion pesos. Thus, during the first six months of the year the total amount invested in this area amounted to nearly 200 billion pesos, that is, practically half PEMEX's budget for the year.[56,57]

In conjunction with attempts to direct local demand toward the local market, efforts have also been made to promote the exchange of capital goods within Latin America.[58] At the fifteenth Ministers' meeting of LAEO, the assistant minister for SEMIP, representing Mexico, proposed the creation of a capital goods technology bank for the energy sector so that the LAEO-member countries could have priority access to the sector's capital goods technology.[59]

With similar objectives in mind, a company called Latinequip was created in Mexico on 20 November 1984. It is a joint venture formed by the Banco de la Provincia de Buenos Aires, the Banco del Estado do Sao Paulo, and Mexico's NAFINSA. Latinequip's main aim is to promote the exchange of high-technology capital goods and services in Latin America and assure optimum export conditions for other regions.[60] Latinequip was organized "in response to the irreversible transnationalization of the world economy(. . .) and was aimed at promoting local business particularly in the local market."[61]

Although measures such as these have been taken to promote high-technology and capital goods development in Mexico, serious impediments still exist. The current director general of CONACYT has stated that

In Mexico, a complete lack of realistic policies and appropriate programs, a private sector with very little interest in national scientific and technological development, and the absence of administrative links between research and production had created a system that is 90 percent dependent on foreign expertise in these fields.(. . .) The science and technology sys-

> tem is still very inadequate—it is small, incomplete, and disorganized. All its subsystems are insufficient for the size of the Mexican market and even though there are many active elements, others are very weak and lack key components. The system's greatest defect is perhaps poor coordination between subsystems and their different parts.(. . .) There are no established norms or general practices for evaluating researchers and research groups.[62]

There are enormous bottlenecks in the capital goods sector. Local specialized equipment manufacturers are given very little financial support. No definite measures exist for providing technical assistance to local suppliers. There is no quality control. The sector lacks a realistic pricing system where prices are structured to assure its producers a certain degree of security in their operations. Two major firms in the sector habitually delay payments to the suppliers and are sometimes the cause of bankruptcy and unemployment. Also to blame are the ignorance, the erroneously interpreted instructions, and the administrative mistakes occurring in most of the public sector companies.

For the Cámara Nacional de la Industria de la Transformación (National Chamber of the Transformation Industry; CANACINTRA), prospects are not very gratifying:

> Mexico does not have the capacity to produce high-technology capital goods due both to structural inadequacies and lack of information.(. . .) The weakness in this area, according to the President of the CANACINTRA's Capital Goods Industry Coordinating Council, are caused by inadequate assimilation and development of technology, insufficient qualified working technicians, a lack of standardization, a tendency toward excessive integration or insufficient horizontal integration, and major deficiencies in technology use.(. . .) All this makes for inadequate project preparation, a reduction in efficiency and productivity, and higher risks in

programming capital goods-manufacturing projects in both private and public sectors.[63]

The problems dealt with in this chapter are still present even under the prevailing adverse economic and financial conditions. It is imperative that this situation be reversed through policies and measures sustained from one government term to the next. The general guidelines have been established, but precision is still needed in determining objectives and concrete measures. The infrastructure for Mexico's scientific, technological, and industrial capacity is still weak, but the state is aware of how important infrastructure is for national economic development. The viability of any policy for achieving technological self-sufficiency in energy depends necessarily on the use of the national and regional markets as frames of reference.

NOTES

1. PEMEX, Anuario estadistico, 1982, Mexico City, PEMEX, 1983.
2. "Decreto que crea el Instituto Mexicano del Petróleo como organismo descentralizado," in Diario Oficial, Mexico City, 26 August 1965, p. 2.
3. "Ley que crea el Consejo Nacional de Ciencia y Tecnologia," in Diario Oficial, No. 27, Mexico City, 29 December 1970.
4. CONACYT, Plan nacional indicativo de ciencia y tecnologia, Mexico City, CONACYT, 1979.
5. IMP, Informe de actividades, Mexico City, IMP, 1973-1982.
6. "Ley sobre el registro de transferencia de tecnologia y el uso de explotación de patentes y marcas," in Diario Oficial, Mexico City, 30 December 1972.
7. CONACYT, op. cit., 1976, p. 193.
8. IMP, Informe de actividades, Mexico City, IMP, 1970-1982.
9. Idem.
10. Mascanzoni, Bruno, "Comentario a la ciencia y la tecnologia del petróleo: Situación actual y perspectivas futuras en México," in Las perspectivas del

petróleo mexicano, Mexico City, El Colegio de México, 1979, p. 88.

11. García Colín Scherer, Leopoldo, "La ciencia y tecnología del petróleo: Situación actual y perspectivas futuras en México," in Las perspectivas del petróleo mexicano, Mexico City, El Colegio de México, 1979, pp. 65-82.

12. Statements by the Gerencia de Informática de PEMEX in Weisser, Teresa, "Los datos sobre la producción petrolera en México del año 1900 a la fecha se envían a procesar a los Estados Unidos," Unomásuno, Mexico City, 24 September 1979.

13. PEMEX, Memoria de labores, 1976, Mexico City, PEMEX, 1977.

14. Malo, Salvador, "Políticas y programas de investigación en petróleo," in Angeles, Luis (editor), El petróleo y sus perspectivas en México, Mexico City, UNAM, 1983, pp. 85-100.

15. IMP, Informe de actividades, op. cit.

16. Idem.

17. IMP, Instituto Mexicano del Petróleo, Mexico City, IMP, Department of Industrial Promotion and Technical Assistance, 1980.

18. Ibid., p. 27.

19. SEPAFIN, Programa de energía, metas a 1990 y proyecciones al año 2000 (resumen y conclusiones), Mexico City, SEPAFIN, 1980.

20. Bazán, Gerardo, "Petróleo y tecnología" (mimeograph), paper presented at the roundtable discussions on Petróleo: El mercado y sus opciones, UNAM, Programa Universitario Justo Sierra-Programa Universitario de Energía, Mexico City, 25-26 March 1985.

21. Ibid., p. 3.

22. Idem.

23. ONUDI-IMP, Efectos del origen de la ingeniería en el desarrollo de la industria de bienes de capital, Mexico City, ONUDI-IMP, c. 1978.

24. Malo, Salvador, and Manuel Guerrero, "Tecnologías futuras para combustibles fósiles," in Programa Universitario de Energía, Tecnologías energéticas del futuro, Mexico City, UNAM, 1983, pp. 181-202.

25. Malo, Salvador, op. cit.

26. This information was obtained from RNTT internal records, 1973-1982.

27. Apparently neither IMP nor foreign suppliers shared this point of view because they felt that "Mexico's technology transference law was recognized by major supplier-countries of technology and capital goods as being consistent with and adequate for the purpose of protecting Mexico's capital goods and technology development." See ONUDI-IMP, op. cit.
28. Maio, Salvador, op. cit., p. 99.
29. CONACYT, op. cit., 1976, p. 61.
30. Ibid., p. 178.
31. NAFINSA-ONUDI, La oferta nacional de bienes de capital, in Monografías sectoriales sobre bienes de capital, No. 1, Mexico City, NAFINSA, 1978, p. 3.
32. Ibid., p. 4.
33. SEPAFIN, Plan nacional de desarrollo industrial, 1979-1982, Mexico City, SEPAFIN, 1979.
34. SPP, Escenarios económicos de México: Perspectivas de desarrollo para ramas seleccionadas, 1981-1985, Mexico City, SPP, 1981.
35. U.S. Department of Commerce, Statistics, 1970-1983, Washington, D.C., 1984.
36. Idem.
37. This equipment consists of computers and process-control accessories, control valves, nonelectronic and nonelectric instruments, and electric and electronic instruments.
38. U.S. Department of Commerce, Office of Export Planning and Evaluation, country market survey 80-210, Mexico: Industrial Process Controls, Washington, D.C., September 1980, p. 3.
39. Ibid., p. 3.
40. Ibid., p. 4.
41. Engineering services deal with engineering development in industrial projects, and consulting services refer to advice given in evaluating industrial projects for purchasing equipment and materials.
42. One or two firms have actually given training courses to their personnel, but only a few institutions for higher education, such as the chemistry faculty at UNAM, have made any effort to provide specialized training in project engineering.
43. CONACYT, op. cit., 1976, p. 98.
44. Ibid., p. 100.

45. De la Fuente, José Luis, "La ingeniería de proyectos de plantas industriales," in IMIQ, Mexico City, IMIQ, November 1976.

46. Berjón Rodríguez, J. Luis, "La ingeniería de detalle en México," paper presented at the VII Congreso Nacional de la Sociedad Mexicana de Ingeniería Económica y de Costos: La estructura nacional de los costos, realidad y perspectiva, Mexico City, 1983, pp. 3-17.

47. CONACYT, op. cit., 1976, p. 100.

48. Idem.

49. SEPAFIN, Plan nacional de desarrollo.

50. Ibid., pp. 178-186.

51. CONACYT, op. cit., 1976. p. 99.

52. Poder Ejecutivo Federal, Programa nacional de energéticos, 1984-1988, Mexico City, SEMIP, 1984, pp. 66, 86.

53. Ibid., p. 65.

54. Idem.

55. Poder Ejecutivo Federal, op. cit., p. 43.

56. "Por lo menos 10 mil millones de pesos en bienes de capital puede producir el país," in El Día, 2 July 1984.

57. Idem.

58. "Ahorro y divisas por compras mutuas (México-Venezuela)," in Excélsior, Mexico City, 7 April 1984.

59. "Creará la OLADE un banco tecnológico y de bienes de capital energéticos," in El Día, Mexico City, 6 October 1984.

60. "Creará Latinequip tecnología para América Latina," in Excélsior, 25 February 1985.

61. "Se fortalecerá la industria de bienes de capital en América Latina," in Excélsior, Mexico City 22 December 1984.

62. Mayagoitia D., Héctor, "De 93% es nuestra dependencia tecnológica," in Excélsior, Mexico City, 1 September 1984.

63. "Incapacidad para producir bienes de capital, por desinformación," in Excélsior, Mexico City, 10 June 1984.

15

The Impact of Oil Exploitation on the Environment

*Miguel Márquez
and Roberto López*

In response to widespread international concern over the impact of industrialization on the environment, the Mexican state adopted legal and institutional measures early in the 1970s that were designed to protect the environment. At this time PEMEX was one of the only industries to have organizations at its disposal that were specifically dedicated to this type of work and to have taken a number of preventive measures, although they were only partially effective.

Since the mid-1970s the development and expansion of oil-related activities has brought about a series of major transformations, which affected not only the quality of the environment but also the social and productive structure of several different regions, particularly the southeast. Although measures have been adopted since this time, they have not been able to cope with the extent of the territory and the intensive exploitation of new energy resources without the support of a global ecological policy with effective measures and sufficient legal power to deal with the rapid pace of some of the oil industry's activities.

The major role of hydrocarbons in the Mexican economy since the mid-1970s has tended to reinforce the general opinion that the oil industry is one of the country's main contaminating agents and the cause of major transformations in the social-productive structure of the oil-producing regions. Although only a small section of the general public was aware of the serious impact of oil exploitation on the environment and on certain regions, the administration was well aware of the problem and firmly intended to systematically attend to the problems because they related to the development of the society as a whole. In 1983 the Secretaria de Desarrollo Urbano y Ecologia (Ministry of Urban Development and Ecology; SEDUE) was created, making these problems the concern of state policy and indicating a definite change in official policy.

This chapter deals with the oil industry's impact of the ecology and the regions involved and the measures implemented by PEMEX and the state to counteract the problems. By bringing to light these aspects of the problem, one might also determine to what extent environmental issues represent a hindrance to the oil industry's recent development and how much attention should be given to environmental conservation in future industrial development.

THE OIL INDUSTRY AND ITS IMPACT ON THE ENVIRONMENT UNTIL THE MID-1970s

From the period immediately following expropriation until the early 1970s, the oil industry was limited to certain regions, and its rate of expansion was very slow compared to later years. Consequently, the ecological impact of its activities was insignificant. Because the oil region's growth was so reduced, it did not represent any kind of threat to either social organization or the environment: The activities of the oil industry had very little attraction for the migrant work force, the city lifestyle had been based for many decades on an already consolidated social-productive structure, and PEMEX's presence was accepted tacitly by the respective townships as a source of jobs and a means of progress.

As far as environmental conservation was concerned, PEMEX's contribution was somewhat halfhearted and limited by the instruments and technological procedures available at the time. In a few facilities there was equipment for reducing the amount of contamination emitted, such as storage tanks for drilling wastes, oil separators, field burners, and a preventive system developed by IMP technicians to treat waste water from refining and oil facilities before releasing it into the rivers.

With the introduction of new federal environmental legislation in 1971, PEMEX took formal steps to counteract the harmful effects of oil in Mexico's ecosystems by creating the Comisión de Protección Ambiental (Environmental Protection Commission), which was designed to elaborate policies and general guidelines and determine priority activities.[1] This commission was headed by PEMEX's subdirectors and managers, with the director general as president. The first steps included training the personnel at the main refineries and petrochemical facilities in environmental protection, making an inventory of contamination sources and contaminating agents, and organizing agreements and activities in conjunction with decentralized public organizations and state ministries.[2] In January 1972 when the Department of the Environment, a branch of the Secretaria de Salubridad y Asistencia (Health Ministry), was created, the commission was renamed the Oficina de Protección Ambiental (Environmental Protection Office) and made responsible for coordinating and supervising the subcommittees established in PEMEX's three administrative zones.

Despite these apparent changes, PEMEX's anticontamination efforts during the early 1970s continued at more or less the same rate and used the same technology and procedures as before. Little attention was paid to such problems as a given plant's closeness to urban centers or the effects of contamination on large areas of land. The head of the environmental protection department later acknowledged that despite their complexity and high operating costs, the procedures followed were still not sufficient to do much good.[3]

Early in the 1970s problems began to arise with certain social sectors that interfered with some of PEMEX's projects and its work at the plants.[4] Generally, these conflicts involved powerful economic concerns, the invasion of land in the process of exploitation activities, and the effect of transformation on the zones with little or no previous contact with the oil industry. There were also fears concerning possible harmful effects on the environment and the acquisition of lands by PEMEX. Although private landowners were in a position to negotiate the price of their land, the peasant farmers were ousted in exchange for an indemnity that was usually well below the amount requested. This situation led the peasant farmers to form a protest organization in 1976. However, some social and political sectors were in favor of the oil industry's expansion because it meant new jobs and community modernization.

The ecological issue was a cause for concern among some state agencies, including IMP and CFE, as well as some private organizations. Aside from the partially effective efforts of these institutions to reduce contamination, the issue received no response from any other industry or company. The measures implemented by the federal government did not have the whole-hearted cooperation of state and municipal authorities. Therefore, until the early 1970s the measures adopted by PEMEX for preserving and protecting the environment, which were in accord with the oil industry's own ecological policy and federal government legislation, were of little consequence because of (1) PEMEX's restricted technology, (2) its limited jurisdiction in certain geographical areas and industrial processes, (3) the uncertain nature of the measures implemented, and (4) the absence of an overall view of the environmental contamination problem.

OIL EXPANSION AND THE EVOLUTION OF THE ENVIRONMENTAL CONTAMINATION PROBLEM FROM 1976 TO 1983

The negative impact of Mexico's industrialization on the environment was accentuated by accelerated oil exploitation during the López Portillo administration and brought a major change in Mexico's oil regions. During the 1950s and 1960s over three-fourths of Mexico's crude and gas production came from the Huasteca in the northeast, with the southern zone supplying one-tenth of the same.[5] However, from the early 1970s onward the discovery of rich resources in the south brought about a redistribution of production; after 1977 the southern zone was producing approximately 80 percent of Mexico's crude and liquids.[6] In less than a decade the socioeconomic profile of Mexico's oil regions was to change dramatically.

PEMEX's oil policy followed the guidelines of the state industrial policy designed during the Luis Echeverria government (1970-1976), which was aimed at redistributing economic activity by creating growth poles. Among other things, the purpose of these poles was to create job opportunities away from the main urban centers. This development model was given even greater thrust during the following government term when hydrocarbons became a major factor in Mexico's economy.

The state economic and political stance during this period gave priority to those industries geared toward export and decentralized industry, for example, relocating a plant on the coast away from a major city. The government dealt first and foremost with oil industry activities and to a lesser extent with those of the iron and steel industry.[7] The development of the basic petrochemical industry typifies the model used. In addition to the fifty-nine existing processing facilities for basic petrochemicals, thirty other complexes were built between 1976 and 1982. Most of these new facilities were built to the south of Veracruz, the largest of them the La Cangrejera petrochemical complex with twenty plants and the Cosoleacaque complex with seven plants.[8]

Because of high world-market prices for hydrocarbons, decisions about the location of industrial facilities and the territory to be occupied met with very few administrative problems and did not have to consider measures for preventing environmental deterioration. From this point on the rapid dissemination of oil centers into different parts of Mexican territory had an important effect on regional development.

The impact of the oil industry on the environment became intense and extensive; the number of accidents occurring at oil installations increased, resulting in human, material, and ecological losses; and there was a considerable increase in oil exploitation. These circumstances meant additional friction between PEMEX and the various social sectors.

A brief description of the effects the oil industry has had on the environment in the various regions brings to light the real impact the oil industry had on the Mexican ecosystems. This impact was such that the way of life was affected everywhere the oil industry was established.

Economic and social repercussion at a regional level

The changes in the socioeconomic profile of Mexico's oil regions, mainly in the southeast, during the last ten years show how the introduction of a high-cost, high-technology industrial process into a traditionally agricultural system with no infrastructure can produce dynamic development with alarming results. The impact of oil-related activities on the southeastern region's social-productive structure can be seen in the soil use, unemployment rates, migration, urbanization, and inflation. The number of farmers who abandoned their land or reduced their traditional farming activities is considerable. In many regions land was only partly farmed. Farming activities in general appeared to have been particularly affected by the dramatic transformations brought about by oil-related activity. Expropriation by the state-owned enterprise reduced the amount of available farmland and created urban and industrial zones, bringing about changes in the pattern of land tenure and use. There was a growing tendency by the peasant farmer to abandon the land, but an increasing amount of land was used for cattle farming.[9]

In regard to unemployment, oil industry expansion gave rise to the emigration of the farming work force toward the oil-rich zones where farming services were not always assured. Work was usually temporary, and when oil production fell or natural sources were exhausted, serious unemployment problems arose, as they did during the Tabasco crisis in 1982.[10]

Two kinds of migration occurred with oil industry expansion. The first involved PEMEX and its technical and professional personnel as well as nonqualified workers who hoped to find work within the industry, and the other involved the rural areas. The first type was characterized by a working population that moved according to the industry's needs and was encouraged by the prospect of higher wages, fringe benefits, and an improved social status. The rural migration was a response to the high wages offered by the oil industry and the excellent job opportunities for nonskilled workers that were available during the construction phase. The accelerated urbanization process in these zones is probably attributable more to migration than to normal population growth.

Between 1970 and 1980 the southeastern oil states rapidly became urbanized. In 1970 the national urban-population average was 40.4 percent; the rate for Chiapas being 8.1 percent, for Tabasco 10.2 percent, and for Campeche 27.6 percent. (No data are available for Veracruz.) However, in 1980 the panorama had changed drastically, with Chiapas at 12.5 percent, Tabasco at 22.5 percent, and Campeche at 43.5 percent.[11] These figures clearly show the rapid population growth of Mexico's oil cities.

Another factor affecting life in these regions was inflation. Because of the lifestyle in the oil cities, PEMEX workers, whose wages and fringe benefits were better than those of the average local worker, created a permanent inflationary process involving all the basic goods and services in these cities.

Land expropriation policy

During the years of high hydrocarbon prices, it seemed the policy was to take maximum advantage of the benefits of these prices, at the expense of certain ecological and social considerations. The oil industry's accelerated development and the lack of a formal land-expropriation policy created discontent among the peasant farmers. They demanded either that the state legalize their proprietary deeds or that if their land was expropriated by PEMEX, they be fairly compensated or given an equivalent plot of farmland.

The manner in which PEMEX expropriated properties and compensated farmers depended on whether the transaction involved big landowners with coercive power, who were more likely to receive the compensation they demanded, or peasant farmers and small landowners, who had insufficient power or influence to negotiate a fair price for their land. Where the oil industry's expanded activities affected fishing areas they were particularly damaging to the local fishermen because they did not own a property that could be used to fix or negotiate some sort of compensation for the lost of their source of income. The organization and mobilization of farm workers and other people affected in protest against PEMEX's activities was a direct result of this situation. In August 1976 the Ribereño Pact was formed, with a membership of approximately seven thousand peasant farmers and small property owners. Their first protest was to picket at the La Venta oil fields on November 20 that same year and demand compensation and fulfillment of the promises made by PEMEX authorities. PEMEX appears to have taken no notice of the farmer's protests, directing its oil policy in such a way as to overcome the constitutional obstacles placed in its path by the Ley de Reforma Agraria (Agrarian Reform Law).

PEMEX urgently needed to incorporate land, be it federal or communal, in order to develop new oil fields and build processing plants, gas pipelines, oil pipelines, and poliducts. Because it was unable to move on to this land before first fulfilling the necessary expropriation formalities, it managed to have existing law reformed.[12] Previously, any agreement to expropriate land had to be approved by the SEPAFIN (now SEMIP) Comisión Nacional de Avalúos (National Evaluation Commission; COMAVAL) or a local commission made up of representatives from SARH and the Secretaría de la Reforma Agraria (Agrarian Reform Ministry; SRA), PEMEX and the peasant farmers. With the new law PEMEX only had to obtain authorization from SEPAFIN for expropriation; the corresponding formalities and demands for compensation were taken care of by peasant-farmer organizations.[13]

As a result of these new expropriation procedures, the peasant farmers became even further united and increased their activity. Their boycotting efforts were so extensive that in 1978 PEMEX announced losses of 1.5 billion pesos.[14] Despite the protesters' removal by the military and attempts by various political groups to divide the farmers and elect their own candidates to strategic posts, the farmers' demands and boycotting activities persisted and, in fact, increased.

In 1981 an attempt was made to treat this explosive situation. The Comité de Participación Múltiple (Multiple Participation Committee) decided to join the warring sectors, providing solutions to the problems caused by oil activity, especially expropriation and pollution.[15] These measures were meant to demonstrate PEMEX's willingness to come to terms with these external organizations, but the underlying aim was to reduce or even completely eliminate the power of the farm-worker trade unions.

A PEMEX work report announced that between 1977 and 1982 there had been over 6,000 requests for compensation from those affected by expropriation. By late 1983 this figure had increased sixfold, to 36,000.[16] PEMEX's policy for dealing with the complaints of the affected social sectors was superficial and unsystematic. Because no adequate expropriation policy existed that duly considered the peasant farmers' interests and rights, conflicts frequently arose.

Oil's effects on the environment and the measures taken to counteract them

The oil policies adopted with the accelerated expansion of the oil industry took little note of environmental considerations despite the fact that both urban and rural contamination was a growing concern in certain sectors of the general public. Warnings about the irreversible damage to Mexico's ecosystems as a result of oil expansion came from a number of specialized circles, all of which unanimously agreed on the urgent need for effective plans and programs to protect the environment. Studies and research conducted in various cities and regions of the country openly corroborated these observations and proposals. According to the Centro de Investigaciones Ecológicas del Sureste (Southeastern Ecological Research Center; CIES), 40 percent of the land used by PEMEX for oil-related activities was farmland, which points to the destruction of some of the country's agricultural wealth.[17, 18]

In 1982 the Ecology Department of the Secretaría de Asentamientos Humanos y Obras Públicas (Ministry for Human Settlements and Public Works) published an evaluation of the ecological changes occurring in Tabasco. It revealed that the land had become highly contaminated with the salts used in drilling oil wells; the salts had filtered into the subsoil and reached the roots of trees. The state SPP representative in Tabasco stated that approximately 60,000 hectares of lagoons, rivers, and farmland belonging to the state had been contaminated with PEMEX's waste, directly affecting more than 740,000 peasant farmers, a figure representing 60 percent of the region's population.[19]

At a seminar on ecology organized by IPN in 1979, it was announced that with crude extraction taking place in a vast area of the Campeche Basin, the fishing industry would lose tons of its yearly prawn catch. In 1981 the Veracruz state Subsecretaría del Medio Ambiente (Underministry for the Environment) called attention to the critical level of pollution in oil cities such as Minatitlán, Coatzacoalcos, Poza Rica, and Veracruz. He stated that the high level of contamination was one of the main causes of respiratory ailments, skin disorders, cardiovascular disease, and imbalances in red blood cell counts among the local inhabitants. The Veracruz state government reported that the Coatzacoalcos River had been polluted by substances tipped into it, such as ammonia, lead, cyanide, phenols, detergents, phosphates, sulfites, and mercury.

In addition to the economic impact of the oil industry's productive activities, there has been ecological damage and water pollution. For example, the pipeline from Salina Cruz, Oaxaca, to Coatzacoalcos, Veracruz, burst, spilling oil into the lagoons. There have been oil-well leaks, as in the case of Soledad Doblado, Veracruz, which polluted the San Antonio River, and there have been numerous explosions in various parts of the country where oil activity has been responsible at least in part.[20]

Overwhelming evidence indicates that air pollution caused either directly or indirectly by the oil industry has far surpassed acceptable levels in some human settlements and in the ecosystem as a whole.

Although other productive units have also done much damage to the environment, PEMEX has been labeled the main contaminator by some sectors.[21] A major cause of air pollution has been plant location. For years the public has insisted to no avail that the government move the Azcapotzalco refinery away from Mexico's capital because the presence of a refinery of this size in one of the largest industrial zones in the Valley of Mexico has made the valley one of the most contaminated areas--if not the most--in the whole country.[22] Mexico City's immense industrial activity and its overpopulation have created conditions that exacerbate the pollution affecting the city. The oil industry's contribution to this situation is by no means insignificant. Among the main causes of pollution are solid, gas, and volatile wastes; insecticides; and radioactive contaminants.[23]

Atmospheric pollution is directly related to engine combustion, and until now the fuel used in Mexico has not been purified to reduce its contaminants, such as lead. It is most certain that if this purification process were carried out, contamination would be reduced, albeit at a high cost. Although the environment department announced that PEMEX would withdraw its Nova gasoline from the market and introduce lead-free Gasol in order to reduce fumes and noise pollution, this effort has only partially been carried out.

There is no doubt that the oil industry's greatest damage to the environment resulted from the accident at the Ixtoc I well in the Campeche Basin on 3 June 1979. The well was out of control and spilling crude into the ocean for almost ten months. According to articles in both local and foreign newspapers and other publications, as well as research on the subject, this oil spill was the most disastrous in the history of hydrocarbon exploitation: Between 3.5 and 4.0 MB of crude were lost, of which 4.5 percent was recovered, 28.5 percent was left floating on the ocean's surface, 17 percent evaporated, and 50 percent was burned. The incident at Ixtoc I was also the oil industry's most expensive accident. With the value of the crude spilled, the compensation demands by the United States, and the amount PEMEX spent to control the leak and reduce pollution, the catastrophe cost slightly more than $620 million (U.S. $).[24]

However, the Ixtoc I accident did provide the opportunity to scrutinize the political, economic, and diplomatic interests involved in developing the oil industry and paved the way for open discussion by the public of the ecological issue.[25] The crisis and its resulting public awareness led PEMEX to raise the Oficina de Protección Ambiental to the level of assistant management under the jurisdiction of the Gerencia de Desarrollo Petroquímico (Department of Petrochemical Development), which was subordinated to the Subdirección de Refinación y Petroquímica (Assistant Administration for Refining and Petrochemicals). At the same time PEMEX introduced other measures designed to give the oil industry a positive image as Mexico's passport to social progress and modernization.[26]

The upheaval created in political circles led the government to institute the House of Representatives' Comisión de Ecología y Medio Ambiente (Ecology and Environmental Commission), whereby PEMEX Director General Jorge Díaz Serrano was called to report on the industry's efforts to control pollution.[27] The time was ripe for the House of Representatives to make environmental conservation a constitutional matter. The government and PEMEX came to an agreement on several measures for preventing pollution and protecting the environment.[28] PEMEX also established different agreements with state ministries, federal entities, universities, and other organizations working on the environmental issue.

With the second half of 1981 the environmental problem took on quite a different character with events such as the forced resignation of Díaz Serrano, the naming of the presidential candidate whose election was assured for late 1982, and the ratification of the new federal law for environmental Protection, which came into force in January 1982. Many new ideas concerning the ecological problem were being translated into institutional changes.

The Gerencia de Protección Ambiental (Environmental Protection Department) became part of the Subdirección Técnica Administrativa (Technical Assistant Administration), and the Subdirección the Protección Ecológica y Social (Ecological and Social Protección Assistant Administration) was substituted for the Comité de Participación Múltiple under the control of the Subdirección Técnica Administrativa.[29] Thus, it was intended that all activities related to the ecological and socioeconomic impact of oil industry development would be managed under one roof, so to speak, and not dealt with separately.

PEMEX official documents and reports show that the Gerencia de Protección Ambiental formulated a vast plan of activities consisting mainly of preventive measures to be introduced into different facilities and productive processes.[30] However, the effectiveness of these measures in counteracting ecological deterioration was questioned because the magnitude of PEMEX's activities made it virtually impossible for the institution to abide by the new regulations.[31]

CONCLUSIONS AND FUTURE PROSPECTS

The growth pattern followed during the 1970s and PEMEX's tendency to overlook environmental considerations in its planning activities were responsible for the progressive deterioration of the environment and the relationship between society and the oil industry in some parts of Mexico. In addition, the ongoing migration into urban centers and the accelerated expansion of industrial activity and the oil industry in particular only made matters worse.

By the 1970s signs of environmental deterioration were unmistakable, but the measures taken by PEMEX and other state organizations were insufficient to satisfy the vastness of the problem and the oil industry's intense activity. The oil industry's central and dynamic role in the Mexican economy caused the government to overlook the need for programs that at least could have provided norms and effective measures to protect the environment while productive activities continued.

Quite rightly, PEMEX has been and still continues to be the target for criticism for its participation in Mexico's serious ecological problem. However, the oil industry is only one of several agents responsible. The liability rests not only with PEMEX but also with the state and oil end users. PEMEX's environmental conservation measures were halfhearted and took a back seat to the institution's main objective of producing as much oil as possible in as short a time as possible. The state's global development policies formulated during the mid-1970s failed to take the ecological problem sufficiently into account, and the government failed to see the problems the policies would create between society and the industry. Also, because these problems were not foreseen, the subsequent social conflicts were well out of hand before solutions were considered, causing even further deterioration of the environment.

Even when legal standards and measures were implemented, it was only done halfheartedly and sometimes not at all because of the lack of any real institutional support. These same measures were sometimes badly formulated and gave rise to serious problems in the expropriation and compensation process that still have not been solved.

Because of Mexico's existing transport structure, low fuel prices, and an inadequate public transport system, air pollution in Mexico City has reached alarming proportions. These factors have encouraged the excessive use of private cars, and 95 percent of the gasoline stations carry Nova gasoline, which is 83 percent octane and contains tetraethyl lead; the inefficient combustion of this fuel results in the release of residual gases that pollute the atmosphere.[32] It is clear that PEMEX, the state, and oil end users are all responsible for this situation.

Peasant farmer protests and the Ixtoc I accident brought the oil industry's social, economic, and ecological problems to the public's attention. The government reacted by elaborating the Programa Nacional de Ecología (National Ecology Program) 1984-1988, which was published during the current administration.[33] This program is aimed at eliminating the fragmentary way in which the ecological issue has been managed and introduces policy measures for effectively conserving the environment and attenuating the impact of industry in general and the oil industry in particular.

The oil industry's attempts to implement an effective environmental conservation policy have raised serious doubts about several policy-related matters. Although the national ecology program confronts the environmental problem, using the past experience as a basis and defining clear, precise objectives for prevention and correction, there are still concerns about whether these measures will be applied effectively and other important institutional changes made. Evidence suggests that the measures are not legally binding and that the institutions and organizations created to enforce them have the power to do so only in theory. Consequently, the state will possibly be forced to take another look at the power these organizations have been granted.

The program has raised hopes, but these could easily be dashed because the plans have not been taken seriously enough by either the industrial sector or society. Although the government took note of public opinion during several ecology meetings, as well as the first national ecology symposium, neither of the sectors directly involved, that is, the contaminators and those affected by them, were consulted. Had their opinions been taken into account, they would probably have contributed to a realistic and feasible series of measures.

With the drastic disequilibrium in Mexico's oil regions, substantial human and economic resources are required to successfully coordinate the harmonious development of oil and farming activities and to implement the legal norms to assure environmental conservation. Mexico's economic and financial situation makes it very difficult for these resources to be channeled appropriately to satisfy the present and future needs of this field; pressing issues in other sectors of the country's economy make such use a rather remote possibility.

The fair distribution of the country's relatively scarce resources requires a clear and precise definition of the society Mexico intends to build to support and develop worthwhile and effective policies. Although industrial activity and oil in particular can be blamed for most of Mexico's pollution problems, a radical change in attitude by institutions, industry, and the individuals in Mexican society is the only way the program's objectives can truly be successful.

NOTES

1. On 23 March 1971 the "Ley Federal para Prevenir y Controlar la Contaminación Ambiental" (federal law for preventing and controlling environmental contamination) was published in the Diario Oficial, wherein the measures introduced to avoid contamination of air, water, and soil were laid down along with the corresponding fines. On September 17 of the same year the "Reglamento para la prevención y control de la contaminación atmosférica originada por la emisión de humos y polvos" (regulations for preventing and controlling atmospheric contamination from smog and dust) was published as part of the aforementioned law. The Secretaría de Salubridad y Asistencia (Ministry of Health) was responsible for the implementation of these regulations in coordination with SECOFI. The measures were aimed at combating the following sources of contamination: burning rubbish, refineries, thermoelectric plants, railroads, motor vehicles, industrial manure plants, fertilizer producers, and concrete plants. All new industries creating smog and dust had to apply for a license from the Ministry of Health. See Secretaría de la Presidencia, Medio ambiente humano, Cuadernos de Documentación, serie Estudios No. 1, 2d. ed., Mexico City, Litoral, 1974, 185 pp.

2. PEMEX, Memoria de labores, 1975, Mexico City, PEMEX, 1976.

3. García Lara, Miguel Angel (head of PEMEX Oficina de Protección Ambiental), "Petróleos Mexicanos pone en práctica las medidas necesarias contra la contaminación," in El Nacional, Mexico City, 27 May 1974, p. 6.

4. One month after President Echeverría came into office, construction work on a refinery in Mazatlán was canceled; the explanation given by PEMEX high officials was that the project "was impractical and unprofitable." However, the real reason was that the major hotel owners and others involved in tourist services had protested, finally managing to get the refinery site moved to Salina Cruz, Oaxaca. PEMEX's losses were estimated at more than 200 million pesos for the investment made in preliminary works and equipment at these sites. See "Doscientos millones

perdidos entre maleza y huizachales," in Excélsior, Mexico City, 22 July 1972; "No habrá refinería en Sinaloa, confirma PEMEX," in El Sol de México, Mexico City March 1973, p. 4. In 1973 representatives of the Chamber of Tourism and the Mexican Hotels and Motels Association also objected to PEMEX's plans to install a petrochemical plant in Mazatlán, arguing that the plant's location would seriously affect tourism at the port, which brings in 20 percent of the state of Sinaloa's tourism income. See "PEMEX pretende instalar una planta despuntadora en Mazatlán," in Excélsior, Mexico City, 1 September 1973, p. 4.

5. Bassols Batalla, Angel, "Impacto regional del petróleo en México," in Problemas del desarrollo, Vol. 10, No. 37, Mexico City, UNAM, Instituto de Investigaciones Económicas, 1979.

6. SPP and PEMEX, La industria petrolera en México, 1979, Mexico City, SPP, 1980.

7. López, Roberto, and Angelina Alonso, "Petróleo, desarrollo regional y cambio social en las zonas petroleras de México a partir de 1970" (mimeograph), paper presented at the Seminar on Energy and Society, Mexico City, IPN, 1984.

8. PEMEX, Memoria de labores, 1982, Mexico City, PEMEX, 1983.

9. Several authors sustained this thesis, among them are Baños Ramírez, Othón, "Campesinos y petróleo en Tabasco," in Cuadernos del CES, No. 31, Mexico City, El Colegio de México, Centro de Estudios Sociológicos, 1984; Thompson, Roberto, Estado y explotación petrolera en Chiapas. Marco jurídico y conflictos sociales: 1970-1980, Tuxtla Gutiérrez, Centro de Investigaciones Ecológicas del Sureste and Congreso del Estado de Chiapas, 1984.

10. See Frias Cerino, José, "Tabasco, víctima de su propia riqueza," in Revista de Revistas, No. 3815, Mexico City, Excélsior, 9 March 1983.

11. See García, Brígida, "Dinámica del empleo rural y urbano en el sureste de México: 1970 y 1980" (mimeograph), Mexico City, El Colegio de México, Centro de Estudios Demográficos y de Desarrollo Urbano, 1984, 40 pp.

12. This law was the Ley Reglamentaria del Artículo 27 Constitutional in which modifications to Article 10 established the oil industry's priority

"over any other use given to land or its subsoil, including its socialized use by peasant farmers or the community. The said land will be occupied either temporarily or permanently or expropriated with due legal compensation wherever the needs of the country or the industry require it." Quoted in Proceso, Semanario de Información y Análisis, No. 56, Mexico City, 28 November 1977, p. 17.

13. The most important-peasant farmer organization is CNC, which is affiliated with PRI. There was also very active participation on the part of the Liga de Comunidades Agrarias (The Agrarian Communities League) and the Central Campesina Independiente (Independent Peasant-Farmers Organization).

14. Maza, Enrique, "Todo el apoyo para la acción devastadora de Pemex," in Proceso, Semanario de Información y Análisis, No. 140, Mexico City, 9 July 1979, p. 13. In 1979 presidential expropriation decrees numbering 2,428 and with a value of 3 billion pesos were published. More than 3,000 applications were still waiting to be processed, their value calculated to be over 3.5 billion pesos. See document published by CNC, in Unomásuno, Mexico City, 28 September 1979; El Día, Mexico City, 11 March 1982.

15. Read further for the circumstances behind the creation of this committee as well as its objectives.

16. PEMEX, Informe del director general de Petróleos Mexicanos, Mexico City, PEMEX, 18 March 1984, p. 6.

17. "PEMEX quiere mayor producción sin importar el costo social; CIES," in Excélsior, Mexico City, 19 March 1978.

18. Excélsior, Mexico City, 10 April 1980. Statements were made to the press by the director of the Instituto Nacional de Investigaciones sobre Recursos Bióticos (National Institute for Biotic Resources Research).

19. "Arrasa la inflción petrolera a Tabasco," in Excélsior, Mexico City, 20 March 1983, p. 4.

20. Excélsior, Mexico City, 24 August 1981.

21. UNAM's Instituto de Investigaciones Económicas (Economic Research Institute) studied the impact of the petrochemical industry on the environment and discovered that of the whole hydrocarbon subsector it

was this area that contributed the most to pollution.

22. PEMEX, "Alto al deterioro ambiental," in Nosotros los Petroleros, No. 38, Mexico City, PEMEX, Subdirección Técnica Administrativa, 1983.

23. Visibility in the Valley of Mexico went from 12 kilometers in 1940 to less than 2 kilometers in 1970. Secretaría de la Presidencia, op. cit., p. 46.

24. Márquez, Miguel, "Las lecciones del accidente del pozo Ixtoc I," in Cuadernos sobre Prospectiva Energética, No. 48, Mexico City, El Colegio de México, Programa de Energéticos, 1984, p. 7.

25. The impact on the marine ecosystem was undoubtedly serious, but according to the experts, even now the real damage to the ecosystem and the flora and fauna of the coasts is impossible to determine because of the slow rate at which biodegradation occurs.

26. Different official spokesmen for PEMEX insisted that oil's negative effects "were of lesser importance than the benefits it would bring, that is, an industrial infrastructure, job creation, the opportunity for community economic growth, and, more importantly, its positive effect on society." PEMEX, Nosotros los Petroleros, No. 32, Mexico City, PEMEX, Subdirección Técnica Administrativa, p. ii. The same points of view were expressed by different high officials in PEMEX as well as the governors of the southeastern states.

27. A detailed account of this interview appeared in Impacto, No. 24-25, Mexico City, 10 April 1981, p. 28.

28. By presidential accord the Comisión Intersecretarial de Saneamiento Ambiental (Interministerial Commission for Environment Sanitation), consisting of seven state ministries and PEMEX, was formed. The commission in turn drew up the Plan Nacional de Contingencias (National Hazard Plan) designed to control spills of hydrocarbons and other harmful substances into the sea. The plan was published in Diario Oficial on 15 April 1981, and PEMEX, Nosotros los Petroleros, No. 32, p. 22. In April 1981 PEMEX introduced the Subdirección de Protección Ecológica y Social (Ecological and Social Protection Assistant Administration), with the Environmental Protection Office under its jurisdiction. Its main objectives were to use anticontamination facilities to a maximum, encourage agreements

with other states involved in similar activities, and tighten up industrial security and pertinent social services. The Environmental Protection Office became a head office in September of this same year. PEMEX, Nosotros los Petroleros, No. 25, p. 19.

29. This committee consists of federal, state, and municipal agencies; private organizations of fishermen, farmers, cattle farmers, and peasant farmers; members of STPRM; and PEMEX's assistant managers and heads of the various departments of the technical assistant administration, that is, medical services, industrial security, complementary technical services, legal services, and personnel. The representatives of the department of personnel involved mixed commissions for security and hygiene representing STPRM. PEMEX, Nosotros los Petroleros, No. 22, Mexico City, PEMEX, January 1982. The Comité Participativo de Protección Ecológica de Tabasco (Participative Committee for Tabasco's Ecological Protection) was formed soon afterwards in February that same year. The idea was to establish committees in PEMEX's other four regional administrative centers, all of which would be coordinated by the Comité de Participación Múltiple. See El Día, 10 February 1982.

30. In April 1981 PEMEX Director General Jorge Díaz Serrano gave a detailed account of the oil industry's expenditures for environmental conservation: 6 million pesos for sulphur elimination facilities, 2.128 billion pesos for waste-water treatment plants, 913 million for smokeless burners, and 112 million for equipment to confine and recover accidental hydrocarbon spillage. The expenditures came to almost 10 billion pesos per year. Not included here was the total amount paid as compensation for expropriated lands. Unomásuno, Mexico City, 5 July 1980.

31. This opinion was held by the Ministry of the Environment and SARH. Unomásuno, Mexico City, 5 July 1980.

32. For more information on the transport sector, see Guzmán, Oscar, Antonio Yúnez-Naude, and Miguel S. Wionczek, Uso eficiente y conservación de la energía en México: Diagnóstico y perspectivas, Mexico City, El Colegio de México, 1985, pp. 165-194.

33. Poder Ejecutivo Federal, Programa nacional de ecología, 1984-1988, Mexico City, SEDUE, 1984.

PART THREE

Energy Planning Between 1970 and 1988

16

Energy Planning for 1970-1976

Manuel Boltvinik

The development model Mexico adopted after the late 1940s made it possible for the country to sustain high economic growth rates between 1950 and 1970, notwithstanding the rising consumption of oil derivatives and electric power. In the 1950s once the main organizational, technical, and labor problems had been overcome, the oil industry took its first steps forward in planning. Its aim was to define the main expansion guidelines, with the trend toward vertical integration in refining in order to cover the growing domestic demand for petroleum products. This approach, however, was subject to the budgetary and credit restrictions imposed by the state and restricted by the sustained low-price policy for hydrocarbon derivatives. As a result, during this period PEMEX was forced to postpone or even cancel many of its projects for expanding refining capacity.

PEMEX's internal planning and budgetary problems were further aggravated by the state's decision in 1958 to make the oil industry responsible for developing the basic petrochemical industry. The vast amount of capital required to promote this field placed added pressure on PEMEX's overall investment budget. These restrictions, the uncertain availability of financial resources, and the intense competition for these resources within PEMEX itself meant that oil industry planning was limited to projects with lead times of less than two or three years. PEMEX made the first attempt to overcome these limitations in 1958 when it ordered the exploration and primary production departments to elaborate a ten-year investment program.[1]

When the formerly independent power companies had been incorporated into CLFC, CFE began a program of studies to be able to forecast the probable overall electricity demand and its sectorial and regional distribution for the following ten-year period. Toward the end of the 1960s these planning activities came to fruition with the formulation of the ten-year program for works and investment in the electricity subsector (POISE), which would be adjusted annually. In the early 1960s CFE began broadening and improving its data banks and developed the technical capacity to forecast aggregate electricity demand through econometric models. These models were complemented with regional polls designed to obtain information on new industrial projects and their developmental guidelines. With this information the country's future electricity requirements, including the installation of new power lines, could be forecast precisely.

Also during the 1960s period, having exhausted Mexico's major hydraulic potential with the construction of dams such as those at Malpaso and Infiernillo in the southeast, which started producing electricity during the 1960s, CFE began to study the diversification of primary energy sources for generating electric power. These efforts produced Cerro Prieto I for tapping geothermal power close to Mexicali in Baja California Norte, the Laguna Verde nucleoelectricity facility in Veracruz (still not in operation; see Chapter 5, "Nuclear Electricity Planning and Development), and the Rio Escondido coal-burning electricity facility in Coahuila. The Rio Escondido project was undertaken after a pilot project in Nava, Coahuila, had shown the technical and economic viability of a coal-burning electric plant in Mexico. In order to supply the Rio Escondido plant with coal and under the assumption that development would continue at other similar plants, MICARE was created to search for and mine the noncoke coal needed by CFE for its coal-burning electricity projects.

Although coal tends to be considered as a single resource, development planning has revolved around its two different applications. While the demand for coke stems from the need for steel, mainly in the capital goods and construction industries, the demand for noncoke coal depends on the government's plans to diversify primary energy sources for generating electricity.

A POLITICAL AND ECONOMIC FRAME OF REFERENCE

The political stance assumed by the Echeverria Alvarez administration was at least initially an attempt to revindicate the state's image before the Mexican people. Two phenomena had had a profound effect on Mexican society: (1) the forceful repression of the student movement in 1968 and (2) the generalized opinion within the government that the development model in force from 1940 to 1970, commonly referred to as "stabilizing development," had run its course.

The new politico-economic model, designated "shared development" and "democratic aperture," aimed at a just distribution of income with immediate attention to the social demands that had been relegated to second place under the previous development model. In order to reduce Mexico's dependence on foreign powers, particularly the United States, the new administration established two priorities: (1) creating institutional infrastructure and (2) providing the financial resources needed to build up local scientific and technological capacity and develop the country's exporting potential based on the principle of market diversification and exportable products with a higher added value. Apart from its intention to strengthen and rationalize the activities of state-owned enterprises, the executive also established a legal and administrative framework for monitoring and controlling the public sector.[2]

Early in 1971 the federal executive passed a new Ley Orgánica de Petróleos Mexicanos (the PEMEX law) and announced a series of norms the enterprise had to follow in order to modify the oil industry's tendency to reduce oil reserves and import increasingly greater amounts of crude.[3,4] In 1972 the executive announced that PEMEX's growth was to be based on the following points: (1) scrupulous conservation of Mexico's oil wealth because squandering or waste due to technical or administrative ineptitude would be like plundering the heritage of future generations, (2) the distribution of the wealth and benefits reaped from hydrocarbon exploitation among the whole population and not just between a few privileged sectors of the community, and (3) maximum yield from the country's raw materials by using the most modern industrial processes possible. These intentions materialized in 1974 when investment amounting to 36.6 billion pesos was programmed to cover the rest of the government term.

In 1972 SEPANAL was put in charge of all energy-related activities. As a result, in January 1973 the Comisión Nacional de Energéticos, a group of professionals responsible for formulating pertinent national policy, was created by presidential accord.[5] Its most important functions involved coordinating policies within the sector and encouraging efficient energy use in view of existing reserves and the country's requirements. Although led by the minister for SEPANAL, the commission had representatives from the president's office and the ministers for SECOFI, SHCP, and SRH, as well as from PEMEX, CFE, and INEN.

By the end of 1973 the increased importance given to the energy sector, the subsequent legal and administrative adjustments, the decisions to raise domestic oil prices and to substantially increase investment expenditure had allowed the energy sector and the oil industry in particular to overcome its chronic stagnation problem. They were able to reduce the imbalance between exploration and exploitation activities and oil refining and distribution and the petrochemical industry.

The new investment programs made it possible for PEMEX to develop the newly discovered oil fields in the southeast, with the aim of eliminating all crude imports. At the same time it was able to finish building refineries still under construction and speed up the installation of several petrochemical plants. With the discovery of Mexico's new oil potential and the increase in international hydrocarbon prices, two options arose. The first was to continue producing oil exclusively for the domestic market, which had been the oil industry's sole objective since its nationalization. The second was for Mexico to become a major oil-exporting country. Although this dilemma arose between 1974 and 1975, late in the Echeverría Alvarez administration, it was the cause of considerable controversy for many years afterwards, during the oil boom and until the crisis of 1982.

The oil industry's option to expand was subject to the limits of economic policy, which, in view of the private sector's feeble response to the government's repeated pleas for investment, continued to sustain economic growth with state intervention in production and in development of the infrastructure to cover the production sector's needs. However, domestic inflationary pressure after 1973, the United States's economic recession that began in 1974, and the overvalued Mexican peso caused an imbalance in foreign trade in 1975 that resulted in a drop in manufactured goods and raw material exports.[6,7]

To restore a healthy trade balance and a current-payment account, the Echeverría Alvarez administration resorted to foreign financing and increased oil exports. With an excess of available credit in the international money markets, on one hand, and the keen interest of the international oil companies and the U.S. government to reduce their dependence on crude oil supplies from the Middle East, on the other, neither policy met with any resistance. Unfortunately, the global economic policy that had been adopted by the Echeverría Alvarez regime about midterm was unable to solve the economy's structural problems, such as disorganization within the industrial sector, lack of coordination between the industrial and the primary sectors, the rural population's low productivity and stagnant income, regional disequilibrium, technological backwardness, and noncompetitiveness of exportable products. The slow return on public investment, whether productive or part of the social infrastructure, persistent inflation, heavy foreign indebtedness, and the magnitude of the public sector's deficit gave rise to considerable discontent among business groups, who considered these factors to be the result of growing state intervention in the country's economy. Serious clashes between certain business groups and the executive resulted in a big reduction in private investment and capital flight to foreign banks.[8] The combined effect of these economic and political factors brought about the August 1976 crisis and the devaluation of the peso, which had been stable, although increasingly overvalued, for twenty-three years.

With the severe crisis and the Echeverria Alvarez administration coming to a close, it became obvious during the presidential campaign that Mexico's oil resources would increasingly be relied upon to overcome the country's problems. The future president entrusted the task of analyzing industrial problems and, in particular, those of the energy sector to one of his most important advisers, Jorge Diaz Serrano, who immediately proceeded to quantify crude resources, using new criteria and obtaining much higher figures than those published by the outgoing PEMEX administration. These optimistic estimates contrasted strongly with the position of certain nationalistic groups within the oil industry that had traditionally advocated hydrocarbon conservation. The "old oilmen's" position was shared by CFE, which also advocated an energy-diversification policy but for different reasons. Although the position of these two groups was eventually taken into account in the energy commission's plans in 1976, the victory was shortlived considering the course taken by energy policy after the new six-year term began late that year.

ENERGY POLICY GUIDELINES, 1976

At the end of the Echeverria Alvarez administration, SEPANAL entrusted the elaboration of energy policy guidelines to the energy commission.[9] This effort was undoubtedly a first attempt at integrated planning for the energy sector, which previously was characterized by independent activities by participating state-owned enterprises whose only coordination consisted of budgetary constraints and some control mechanisms. For the first time the production and use of energy resources in Mexico was openly discussed. In view of the fact that energy policy has to be designed for the long term, it is clear that the document produced was a reflection of the commission's concern for far-reaching planning in the sector. Efficient energy use was advocated and so was primary energy-source diversification away from hydrocarbons, which would involve developing coal resources and establishing the basis for the use of nuclear energy as well as other energy forms.[10] Because the proposals for accelerated oil development presented by the incoming Díaz Serrano group clashed with the position of PEMEX high officials and technicians led by outgoing Dovalí Jaime, the energy commission guidelines gave particular attention to the criteria it considered fundamental to long-term hydrocarbon exploitation.[11] These criteria can be summarized as follows:

- Mexico's proven hydrocarbon reserves will not be sufficient to cover the country's future energy needs, not even the first couple of decades of the next century.

- By this time new energy sources will have displaced hydrocarbons as fuel, and both crude and natural gas will be used as raw materials for other purposes.

- Future electricity generation will mainly use alternative sources, and if estimated hydrocarbon reserves are, in fact, greater than expected, this fuel substitution will create a hydrocarbon surplus than can be exported.

- Planning in energy sector administration and control, as well as in organization and labor issues, are considered even more important than planning energy supply. Also of particular importance is the energy sector's financial and pricing policy.

- To rationalize energy consumption and its structure requires realistic prices that take shortfall costs into account.

- In order to reduce Mexico's disadvantage in relation to industrialized countries, energy research should be promoted and plans elaborated for a smooth transition from hydrocarbons to other energy sources.

- To minimize the risks of shortfall situations, strategic hydrocarbon reserves should be established to maintain supply at reasonably safe levels.

- In order to define the normative concepts for immediate application, it is essential to adopt a long-term approach to planning for the energy sector.

Despite its undeniable merits, the energy commission's energy policy failed to leave an impression on the president-elect's work team, and although the proposals put forward brought the need for long-term energy sector planning to the forefront, the planning did not progress. Faced with a severe crisis at the end of the 1970-1976 administration, the incoming economic policy makers decided on a development strategy designed to promote hydrocarbon exports.

NOTES

1. A major concern of Jesús Reyes Heroles, one of PEMEX's director generals, was a balanced distribution of resources between PEMEX's industrial and primary activities and the reactivation of exploration and development programs designed to maintain reliable reserve levels and counterbalance the trend to import crude and refined products. These issues were, however, given little attention because of the heavy pressures on the state from private concerns in secondary petrochemicals and the technocrats engaged in expanding basic petrochemicals. Philip, George, Oil and politics in Latin America, Cambridge, Massachusetts, Harvard University Press, 1982, pp. 341-352.

2. Late in December 1970 a law was passed giving the executive the power to control state companies and decentralized organizations. See "Ley para el control por parte del Gobierno Federal de los organismos descentralizados y empresas de participación estatal," in Diario Oficial, Vol. 303, No. 49, Mexico City, 31 December 1970.

3. On 6 February 1971 the Ley Orgánica de Petróleos Mexicanos was published, repealing the 7 June 1938 decree. According to the new law PEMEX was to be governed by an administrative council composed of eleven members, six of whom were to be elected by the federal executive and the other five by STPRM; a director general was to be nominated by the federal executive. "Ley Orgánica de Petróleos Mexicanos," in Diario Oficial, Vol. 304, No. 30, Mexico City, 6 February 1971.
4. PEMEX, Informe del director general de Petróleos Mexicanos, Mexico City, PEMEX, 18 March 1972, pp. 5-6.
5. "Comisión de Energéticos," in Carta de México, No. 26, Mexico City, Oficina de la Presidencia, 30 April 1973, pp. 18-19.
6. The most important state projects are the Lázaro Cárdenas-Las Truchas iron and steel complex, the first stage of which cost $500 million (U.S. $) plus another $300 million to double its capacity in 1980, and the Chicoasén hydroelectric project with an investment calculated at $300 million. Tello, Carlos, La política económica de México, 1970-1976, Mexico City, Siglo XXI, 1978, pp. 194-199.
7. The Echeverría Alvarez regime also attempted to overcome some of the obstacles seriously inhibiting the country's economic and social development, such as the low income in rural areas and insufficient skilled labor, by financing agro-industries and rural enterprises and by creating technical and farming colleges and regional technological institutes.
8. The conflicts arising from this situation led the entrepreneurs to unite in organizations such as the Consejo Coordinador Empresarial (Entrepreneur Coordinating Council), which allowed them to effectively defend their interests from the threat of state intervention. In fact, this sector's response was far more drastic than expected--private investment decreased and capital flight increased. The consensus that existed between entrepreneurs and the government in previous decades had come to an end--at least temporarily. Luna, Matilde, "Los empresarios y el régimen político mexicano: Las estrategias tripartitas de los años setenta," in Estudios Políticos, Vol. 3,

No. 1, Nueva Epoca, Mexico City, January-March 1984, pp. 28-34.

9. SEPANAL, Propuesta de lineamientos de política energética, Mexico City, SEPANAL, Comisión de Energéticos, 1976, 91 pp.

10. The electricity industry's expansion program included the installation of 9,000 MW of capacity in coal-burning electricity facilities by the year 2000. It is estimated that coal consumption could reach 27 million tons by the same year. A tentative figure of 40,000 nuclear MW was also established for the year 2000, which would require approximately 220,000 tons of U_3O_8 to operate the plants for thirty years without plutonium recycling or 200,000 tons with plutonium and uranium recycling. Ibid., pp. 39, 72.

11. SEPANAL, op. cit., pp. 84-90.

17

Energy Planning for 1977-1982

Cecilia Escalante

From 1977 on the economic crisis gave rise to numerous shifts in power and new political alliances both within the government and without. This crisis was the impetus for a search for new ways to encourage Mexico's future development. The serious deterioration in the Mexican economy not only affected the country's economic structure but also had grave repercussions on the traditional relationship of the state with the different sectors of society. A particularly low level of political activism and the government's loss of credibility undermined the very legitimacy of the state itself. It was considered advisable to formulate a global politico-economic project that would voice the demands of the different social sectors and satisfy the country's need for internal saving to finance investment. This proposal gave rise to the Alianza Nacional Popular para la Producción (Popular National Alliance for Production) with leanings toward social reform as a means of confronting the crisis.[1] The government attempted to gain the cooperation of Mexico's different productive sectors by stimulating private investment through incentives and industrial promotion, which would pave the way for a reactivated and restructured productive sector and restore the confidence of business groups in the state's ability to successfully conduct the country's development. For the recovery program to work a wage-restraint policy acceptable to the major workers' organizations affiliated with the Congreso del Trabajo (Work Congress) was necessary. The successful implementation of this project for economic and social reform, which was designed to cope with the country's immediate problems, was seriously jeopardized by IMF's short-term stabilizing policies, which called for a reduction in public expenditure, severe wage restraint, and limits on foreign borrowing.

In light of this situation oil industry development was to constitute the cornerstone on which the hopes of Mexico's economic recovery were to rest. Favorable international market conditions for hydrocarbons and capital, together with the promising prospects for the country's oil reserves, prompted the federal government to draw up an economic- and social-development project on the basis of its oil-export earnings.

Although the López Portillo cabinet was considered to be "an excellent example of equilibrium based on heterogeneity(. . .) and indicated an attempt to reconcile the nation's many interests,"[2] it was initially agreed that the old conservationist notions should be discarded and oil industry development given top priority.[3] Oil was essentially the focal point of the whole state project, and because of the politi-cal and bureaucratic tug-of-war between the various groups interested in promoting their particular view of economic policy, policy formulation and implementation and energy planning took on a character all of its own.

PROGRAMA DE ENERGIA 1980-1982

As part of the new government's administrative reform, the functions of some ministries were restructured and other new ones formed. SPP, the new ministry for programming and budget, was responsible for global, sectorial, and regional programming as well as for budgeting and assigning resources for the whole public sector. The reformed SEPAFIN was given the responsibility of state-owned industry programming and control and support for private industry.[4] The different plans introduced by the state to make the decision-making process rational and congruent brought to light a whole range of divergent political and economic projects and points of view associated with the different roles assumed by public institutions and the political interests of those concerned.

The 1980 energy program was the first of its kind in the country and was largely a product of the confrontation between two opposing views of development.[5] One view proposed that economic development should be based on the oil industry's expansion and growing crude exports, at the expense of manufactured exports. The other proposed a much slower growth in hydrocarbons while Mexico's industry built up with a view toward participating in the international market later under favorable conditions. With the first view most of the foreign earnings would be reinvested in the oil subsector, and in the second they would be channeled mainly into programming industry as a whole.[6]

Diverse proposals were made prior to the final draft: SPP's first attempt at programming, the industrial-development alternative laid down in PNDI, the discussion to broaden Mexico's oil production, and the energy proposal contained in PGD.[7]

The SPP proposal, 1977

In 1977 the first differences of opinion about the nature of Mexico's economic policy made themselves felt. SPP was of the opinion that state activities should be funded through increases in public expenditure, which would help the country overcome its serious economic problems as well as bridge the vast differences between social classes. It was suggested that oil earnings be used to cover the public deficit arising from increased public spending and foreign-debt servicing.

The proposal was strongly objected to by the representatives of private banks and the landed authorities acting as spokesmen for the Mexican government in negotiations with IMF. The income-redistribution strategy underlying the increased spending policy was no longer viable because of IMF restraints that established clear limits to foreign indebtedness and increases in public expenditure. Thus, the possibility of introducing an economic policy based on greater public expenditure was thwarted. Consequently, a contradiction arose in the López Portillo economic cabinet ending in the resignation of the SPP and SHCP ministers, and the project for economic growth that had been designed to solve priority social problems was postponed.[8,9] Despite the sudden withdrawal of the SPP minister, a number of aspects in his economic policy concerning the redistribution of income were sustained by other cabinet members and later appeared as part of PNDI.

SEPAFIN's energy proposals for the Plan Nacional de Desarrollo Industrial, 1979

March 1979 saw the introduction of PNDI, the national industrial development plan, which pointed to two basic socioeconomic problems in Mexico: (1) unemployment, a major cause of social unrest and the weakening of political institutions, and (2) the oligopoly existing within the production sector, with the resulting exclusion of small- and medium-sized business.[10] This type of production structure was characterized by the absence of a strong capital goods industry and of companies capable of competing efficiently in the international market; manufacturing activities were concentrated mainly in the capital city and surrounding areas. The plan's general objectives were to create employment, thus helping redistribute income and attain a balanced productive structure.

The idea of an economic policy capable of promoting productive investment, lessening the industrial sector's structural problems, and contributing to social equality led PNDI's creators to propose an industrial-expansion strategy.[11] This strategy would promote labor-intensive activities, such as basic consumer goods manufacture mainly carried out by small- and medium-sized industries, as well as capital-intensive enterprises linked basically to the energy sector, such as refining and petrochemicals, and the capital goods sector.[12] This approach clashed with others advocating a reduction in public spending and monetary credit restraints in order to pull the country out of the crisis. Those endorsing this second approach felt that PNDI's expansion strategy would cause an "overheating" of the economy and accentuate the inflationary spiral.

Because the financing for the industrial strategy came from hydrocarbon-export earnings, PNDI intended to establish a frame of reference for growth in this subsector. Development here should not become an end in itself but rather be a function of the industrial strategy, which implied determining a ceiling for oil production and exports. The resources generated here would be used to achieve a balanced industrial growth and an adequate distribution of income rather than to expand the oil industry itself. The plan's financial proposal included three stages. During the first stage, from 1977 to 1978, the earnings from oil exploitation would be used to overcome traditional financial limitations. During the second, planned for 1979, the foundations for the country's sustained development would be established, achieving gradual independence from hydrocarbons. During the third stage, from 1980 to 1982, it was intended that Mexico begin a phase of rapid development lasting well into the 1990s.

PNDI acknowledged the inadequacies of Mexico's productive sector, its inefficiency and international noncompetitiveness. One of its objectives was, therefore, to develop highly productive areas capable of exporting goods and efficiently substituting imports.[13] A major share of oil-export earnings were used to import everything necessary to establish a capital goods industry. In the meantime a protectionist policy was introduced, which was designed to promote and protect industry, particularly those areas producing basic consumer goods. These areas covered more than 50 percent of the industry's manufacturing production.

PNDI's success was conditioned by certain external economic and political factors, which showed little sign of change. By the late 1960s the value of industrial production was double that of primary production, and by the early 1970s heavy industry, such as the iron and steel, oil, petrochemical, and automotive industries, had overtaken light industry, becoming the economy's driving force. Although these development trends indicated a growing integration into the world market, they also showed a fall in the competitiveness of medium-sized industries.[14] PNDI's basic weakness was in trying to change these trends that in fact did not depend on local conditions but were a consequence of a severe decline in the growth rate of the international economy. Apart from the fact that PNDI gave very little consideration to the prevailing international economic conditions, it assumed that heavy state investment, financed with oil-export earnings, would restore the export sector's growth rate to the level it had enjoyed years before.

In 1979 after certain declarations by the president that seemed to indicate his undecidedness about the approach to take, those responsible for elaborating PNDI set out to look for other political alternatives, establishing alliances with certain energy sector groups in order to strengthen their expansionist strategy and define the guidelines for the oil industry's development.[15]

However, PNDI was outdated all too soon by events both at home and abroad that brought about marked changes in the circumstances and assumptions on which the plan was based. The boom in Mexico's economy in 1980 brought to light its structural weaknesses, which were made manifest in serious bottlenecks in the transport sector and at port terminals; the inability of local industry to respond quickly to the increased domestic demand for goods and services; the investors' feeble reaction to the incentives designed to promote a capital goods industry to serve the energy sector; and the delays in the big state iron and steel, petrochemical, and fertilizer projects.

Proposals for accelerated expansion by PEMEX and the redefinition of oil policy

In 1977 congruent with the long-standing view that oil was the solution to the crisis and the key to Mexico's economic recovery, the new administration elaborated PEMEX's six-year program.[16] This program meant increasing crude production 2+ times, doubling refining capacity, and tripling basic petrochemical industrial production capacity. Targets for 1982 included the production of 3.6 BCFD of natural gas and 2.25 MBD of crude; 1.1 MBD of this crude production would be exported. However, the oil industry developed at such a rate during the first three years of the government administration that the production targets set for 1982 had already been reached by the first quarter of 1980.

These achievements prompted PEMEX's director general to suggest increasing hydrocarbon production and broadening the export program originally set for 1982.[17] Access to the international capital market, the significant increase in Mexico's crude reserves, and the unconditional support given by the president to PEMEX policies also played an important part in the oil industry's rapid expansion.[18]

With PEMEX's proposal the economic cabinet's debate on the role oil should play in Mexico's development strategy further intensified. The main worry in the debate between those who endorsed industrialization strategy proposed by PNDI and those in PEMEX and certain other sectors who urged speeding oil industry development even further was whether the disequilibrium and inequality in the economy's nonoil sector would get worse.[19] If PEMEX were assigned more public resources, the development of other industrial activities would have to be postponed.

Those in favor of PNDI's proposals tried to gain the political favor of other groups whose economic and political interests would benefit if Mexico were to become closely involved in international economic scene by exporting its oil and joining the General Agreement of Tariffs and Trade (GATT). When PEMEX presented its proposal to increase oil production early in 1980, there were differences of opinion between the different schools of thought that considered oil to be the basis of Mexico's economic and social development. The first signs of the economic boom brought about by the high income from oil exports only served to make the differences greater and the confrontation worse.[20] To those against accelerated economic devel-opment, the particular characteristics of the boom were, in fact, manifestations of artificial growth. Also, with the high concentration of foreign earnings from oil exports now in the hands of the state, the struggle for a bigger share of the budget intensified both within the government and without.

By 1979 oil earnings had given the state a broader margin for action, and certain business groups, such as the Confederación Patronal de la República Mexicana (Employers' Confederation of the Mexican Republic; COPARMEX), tried to convince the government to limit its activities in the public sector and concentrate more on catering to the short- and long-term interests of the private sector. However, some fractions of the workers' movement called for an alliance between the workers and the state in order to strengthen the state's role in administering the economy, with the condition that priority be given to overcoming local problems and creating an equitable distribution of wealth.

With the broad difference of opinion in the government's economic cabinet and the heightened controversy within Mexican society, the president ordered the presidential advisory office to carry out an evaluation of the opinions of all the government offices involved in defining economic policy and the oil subsector's development.[21] The advisory office report concluded that both investment and oil exports should be kept within the limits set in the original program for the 1980-1982 period. Thus, average daily crude exports should not exceed 1.1 MB of crude, with the rest of the production assigned exclusively to the growing domestic demand.

The main arguments upon which the advisory office based its conclusion were the following:

. The original oil-production program was designed to allow a high and sustained growth of GDP along with a high employment rate.

. The additional earnings from oil exports could not be absorbed productively because of the bottlenecks and constraints inherent in Mexico's existing production capacity, a situation that would cause serious inflationary problems and make it further difficult to adequately implement economic policy.

- If additional resources were concentrated in the oil subsector, those activities not related to oil would tend to stagnate; the country's economy would evolve in a disorderly fashion, thus affecting the prospects for industrial expansion; the farming sector's participation would fall significantly; and the contribution of the oil subsector and the services sector to GDP would increase disproportionately.

- The employment growth rate would fall noticeably because the oil industry is capital intensive.

- The country's inflation rate would tend to rise above 30 percent per year, causing a considerable reduction in real wages.

- Because of the low real cost of foreign credit and the expected increase in international oil prices, it was not considered advisable to increase exports to accumulate international reserves, pay debts before time, or not make use of the country's credit worthiness.

- The decision to increase oil exports would probably have been irreversible considering the prevailing worldwide hydrocarbon shortage. Under these circumstances it would be difficult to reduce export volumes later because the major crude buyers would probably see the act as unfriendly and press Mexico into continuing to produce at full capacity.

Informed sources suggested that apart from providing a technico-economic evaluation of the risks of increasing oil production, the study also helped limit the excessive power enjoyed by PEMEX's director general within the López Portillo cabinet. Díaz Serrano's power gave him considerable advantage in the race for presidential succession and consequently undermined the chances for other candidates.

The opinion of the advisory office was that to accept PEMEX's proposal meant substantially lower growth for the rest of the economy, distorting the country's productive structure even further. The office felt that if Mexico were to take an active role in the world economy, it would have to drastically relax its protectionist foreign-trade policies, perhaps by joining GATT. Mexico would have no way of knowing whether other oil-exporting countries would limit production in order to protect the real crude price in the face of a fall in hydrocarbon demand brought about by the economic recession in the major industrialized countries. Internal social contradictions reflected in unemployment would be even further marked, and there would be a fall in real wages, a regional lack of compensation caused by the sudden changes in areas where oil activity was concentrated, and much greater autonomy for PEMEX management. Politically, these arguments pointed to the fact that by increasing the rate of oil industry activity, Diaz Serrano would be given much more power than the rest of the state ministers involved in the decision-making process.

In reply to the economic cabinet's conclusions based on the advisory office's arguments, Diaz Serrano stated that it might be worthwhile to consider "a gradual increase, not exactly in production" (for the study had made the inadvisability of this step quite clear) "but in production capacity," thus giving the oil industry a margin of "flexibility."[22]

On 18 March 1980 after reviewing Diaz Serrano's annual report, the president of the republic defined the oil-production target between 2.5 and 2.7 MBD, that is, 10 percent higher than before, which meant there would be enough foreign exchange to attain other priority goals. The executive also announced the Sistema Alimentario Mexicano (Mexican Alimentary System; SAM) and the decision to reject the proposal to join GATT. These announcements ended the controversy about expanding Mexico's economic role in international trade, an approach strongly opposed by the PNDI planners, the Work Congress, and the groups of small- and medium-scale businessmen who would have been particularly affected by such a policy. Strangely enough, many of the multinational companies established in Mexico would also have been affected adversely.[23]

The Plan Global de Desarrollo, 1980

The idea behind a national planning system was to elaborate a master plan containing the criteria and foundations for sectorial planning. This task was entrusted to SPP. However, a change of leadership was made within SPP because of the differences of opinion within the economic cabinet during 1977-1978 about the state's future economic policy;[24] as a result, the appearance of PGD in 1980 was simply an extemporaneous attempt to coordinate the different sectorial plans already introduced.[25]

The new plan was an attempt to restructure the country's development process using the earnings from foreign oil sales to finance economic growth and public works.[26] Thus, in accordance with PGD's general objectives, the surplus from oil-exploitation earnings, with its redefined target, was to be channeled into the priority sectors established in the plan. Of the total profit to be used for financing investment and the country's development, around 32 percent was to be reinvested in PEMEX. The remaining 68 percent was to be distributed as follows: farming and rural development, 25 percent; industrial sector (except PEMEX), 16 percent; social works, 24 percent; and the states and municipalities, 15 percent.

The plan's broad coverage, together with the excessive optimism associated with the oil boom, was reflected in the proposal to give particular impetus to the farming and social-work sectors. Incorporated within PGD 1980 was the plan to support SAM as well as measures designed to create employment, redistribute income, and provide the essentials for the population's social well-being. By including these social goals in its policy, the state was able to justify the economic policy followed until then. For three years the government's activities were conditioned partly by IMF's economic restrictions, such as wage restraints, but according to PGD 1980, by the end of this same year the growth strategy based on oil expansion should have begun to bear fruits in terms of economic, social, and political well-being.

Even with the prevailing oil boom PGD 1980 was based on a lower rate of economic growth than that proposed in PNDI perhaps because of a less optimistic view by the planners about the future of international hydrocarbon prices and the Mexican economy's real possibilities. This lower rate constituted one of the major differences between the two plans. PGD 1980 set the annual GDP growth rate at 8 percent and at 10.8 percent for the industrial sector, which included energy, manufactures, mining, and construction. In 1979 PNDI had forecast a 10 percent annual growth rate for GDP and 12 percent for the industrial sector. For certain areas such as the capital goods sector and the petrochemical subsector, PNDI proposed an annual expansion rate between 18 and 20 percent. Although both documents agreed on the idea of promoting the nonoil sectors' development by placing a ceiling on oil production and, thus, diversifying exports, the measures each included were quite different. While PNDI's export-promotion strategy involved granting local industry energy discounts to 30 percent, depending on their location, and maintaining the price of energy for industrial use at lower than international prices, PGD, however, stated that energy prices should be adjusted to cover production and distribution costs and generate the savings needed to finance, to a large extent, the energy enterprises' productive capacity. Furthermore, PGD pointed out that reduced internal saving, a result of the pricing and tariff policy, and long investment-maturation periods in the energy sector had forced these enterprises to increasingly resort to foreign borrowing or fiscal resource transference by the federal government. If this trend continued, it was feared that oil earnings would increasingly be used to subsidize the rest of the economy. To reduce this risk PGD insisted that the productivity of public enterprises had to be increased and their physical and financial resources efficiently administered.[27] However, the adjustments to energy-pricing policy proposed by PGD were postponed until late 1981 for oil and its derivatives and until mid-1982 for electricity tariffs. Another difference between PGD and PNDI involved foreign-trade policy. For example, PGD recommended maintaining the current account deficit within reasonable limits, diversifying exports to reduce the tendency to depend completely on oil, and rationalizing industrial protectionism.[28]

Mexico's planning process as expressed in its various plans and programs was again cause for political debate between those who argued in favor of an economic development model based on growth from within and those who advocated growth based on income from exports. This situation, together with the executive's apparent vacillation, gave rise to pendular movement: The economic policy program of one party was given preference only to be substituted later by another and so on and so forth.

The all-encompassing nature of PGD, whose scope was designed to reach all the main areas of economic activity, also took into account a series of basic guidelines related to different aspects of the energy sector. These guidelines were, in fact, a forerunner of the energy program introduced in November 1980. The intention of the energy sector's general guidelines was to relieve the pressure of energy generation that had been placed on hydrocarbons. PGD strongly advocated diversifying energy sources and adopting measures to counteract the excessive energy waste prevailing at the time by establishing a pricing and subsidy policy that would reflect the real cost of producing energy.

It was felt that exploration efforts should continue to be channeled into locating primary energy reserves, with particular attention to nonhydrocarbon resources. Concurrently, continued efforts would be made to encourage industry to convert to natural gas; the measures necessary to make better use of hydraulic, nuclear, coal, and geothermal resources would be introduced; and rational and efficient energy use would be encouraged. Energy-pricing policy was designed to fortify public finances and provide the energy sector with financing for development, which, in turn, would allow the cost of diversifying primary energy sources to be absorbed as well as provide an incentive to export manufactured goods. In the field of hydrocarbon industrialization it was intended that refining capacity should increase 25 percent; this measure, together with energy-diversification efforts, would help create a major demand for capital goods, thus encouraging local production of the same.

The activities proposed by PGD for the energy sector were so general that they could not have positive effect on the prevailing situation. Apart from repeated statements to the effect that oil should be used as a "lever for development," the proposed measures were no more than good intentions, lacking specific indications about the way in which the objectives should be achieved. Thus, what was still needed was a specific program containing an in-depth diagnosis and the definition of a workable energy policy based on precise proposals.

THE 1980 PROGRAMA DE ENERGIA

Although the energy program published in November 1980 by SEPAFIN was the first attempt at any detailed planning in the sector and was designed to cover PGD inadequacies, it made its appearance in the middle of a political vacuum. The controversy within the state organization continued about the type of economic and social project that with the oil industry as a starting point would reconcile all the different interests and restore the balance between the different social forces. These political circumstances made coordinated action between the different government entities difficult and converted energy sector planning in 1980 into a battleground for continued political and institutional strife; thus, the technical and economic viability of the energy program was limited considerably and its introduction postponed.
If the energy program is considered not only a technical document but also a political one, it is evident PE 1980 managed to retrieve the basic principles of PNDI that had fallen by the wayside with the introduction of PGD. It also attenuated the power of PEMEX's director general by formalizing the executive's decisions regarding oil-export targets. It did not go unnoticed that Diaz Serrano did not comment on the program's content, which had been elaborated mainly at SEPAFIN.
Technically, PE 1980 took up some of PGD's original guidelines, such as reducing Mexico's hydrocarbon dependence, diversifying energy sources, promoting efficient energy use, and so on. However, these objectives were integrated into the program and redefined in accordance with the development concept defined in

PNDI. In addition, CFE's proposals were also incorporated into PE 1980, giving it a broader dimension than PGD.

Having decided to consider growth in energy demand as a function of economic expansion, the designers of PE 1980 put forward the need to expand hydrocarbon reserves and establish a production structure and energy-consumption pattern that would bring about a gradual and orderly change in Mexico's energy as well as economic situation; thus, by the beginning of the twenty-first century, Mexico would be able to take full advantage of the world hydrocarbon shortage expected by PE's designers. These general objectives could be attained by expanding energy production only as much as necessary to sustain balanced economic growth. The financial resources from oil exploitation were to be used to promote priority activities such as industrialization, regional development, and foreign trade, as indicated earlier in PNDI. Thus, oil production would be regulated according to domestic needs and not as a function of the reserve volume (Díaz Serrano's basic argument in favor of a sustained increase in production) or of the crude oil requirements of other countries.

PE's specific objectives were the following: (1) to satisfy local primary energy requirements; (2) to rationalize energy production and use; (3) to diversify primary energy sources, with particular attention to renewable resources; (4) to incorporate the energy sector into the rest of the economy; and (5) to fortify Mexico's scientific and technical infrastructure for utilizing new energy technology.

In regard to the relationship between energy and industrialization, the document proposed broadening refining capacity, promoting balanced growth in the petrochemical industry, controlling the introduction of energy-intensive activities, and giving priority to local manufacturers producing capital goods for energy companies. It was argued that although rapid expansion of the energy sector's enterprises would be assured if capital goods were imported, the local manufacturing industries' development would be inhibited.

As far as energy production and foreign trade were concerned, hydrocarbon exports would be regulated according to the economy's capacity to absorb foreign exchange productively and to export those petroleum products with the highest added value. Oil exports were seen as an aid to foreign policy and foreign-trade negotiations with importing countries, in turn reinforcing Mexico's policy of cooperation with other regions, which eventually would include other developing countries. Mexico's negotiating position would be enhanced by the consequent increase in manufactured exports and the improvement in foreign financing conditions.

The export target, considered to be the backbone of development, was as follows:

- The ceiling for oil and gas production could not exceed at any given period between 8 and 10 MBDCE.

- Exports would be limited to 1.5 MBD of crude and 300 MCFD of natural gas.

- In view of the possible variation in international hydrocarbon prices, oil-export earnings should not exceed 50 percent of current foreign income.

- No more than 50 percent of all Mexican hydrocarbon exports should be concentrated in a single importing country. Mexican crude's share in a given country's imports should not exceed 20 percent of its total foreign-crude purchases. Only in Central America could Mexico's share in global oil demand reach as much as 50 percent.

Macroeconomic framework of the Programa de Energía

The energy program's goals were defined within the general macroeconomic framework of PNDI and adjusted according to the changes occurring in the international scene, that is, the rise in crude oil prices and their impact on the country's economic development. According to PE 1980 oil was no longer to be the fund raiser whose prime objective was to cover the balance-of-payments deficit and the public sector's bills. Oil was to become a vehicle for the economy's structural transformation, whereby Mexico would sustain its own growth.

To justify its basic proposals for the national hydrocarbon supply growth rate and export ceilings, PE 1980 elaborated two alternative economic policy scenarios for Mexico (see Figure 17.1). The political objective of this exercise was to justify a constant crude-export level such that the economy would not have to depend much longer on oil exports alone and would be less vulnerable to pressure from abroad. The rest of the economy would have to adjust to the oil-export level established by the government while it promoted other types of exports. In both of the program's scenarios hydrocarbon export levels represent the variable with the most weight in the long-term global economic policy.

One of the energy program's major assumptions was that until 1982 the export volumes established by the government (1.5 MBD of crude and 300 MCFD of natural gas) would be sufficient to cover Mexico's balance of payments, taking the GNP growth rate as 8 percent per year regardless of the economic policy followed. However, the level of oil exports for 1990 would depend on the balance-of-payment situation and, therefore, on the course of economic policy. According to the first scenario the need for foreign exchange would be so great that technical constraints would affect crude extraction even before the late 1980's. With the second scenario by maintaining exports at predetermined levels, sufficient foreign exchange would be earned to sustain a growth in the GNP of 8 percent per year until 1995. In this case the problems related to reserve exhaustion or technical constraints would appear much later in the century. However, by this time the transition toward a self-sustained industrial economy and a diversified energy structure would be complete.

In retrospect, it is obvious that some of the basic assumptions of the second economic policy scenario were not given enough thought, particularly those related to the annual growth rate of international crude prices, which was calculated at 5 to 7 percent until the year 2000, and the GNP growth rate, which was taken as 8 percent per year. The second sce-

FIGURE TABLE 17.1
ECONOMIC GROWTH AND HYDROCARBON PRODUCTION
FORECAST based on total reserves of 60 MMB

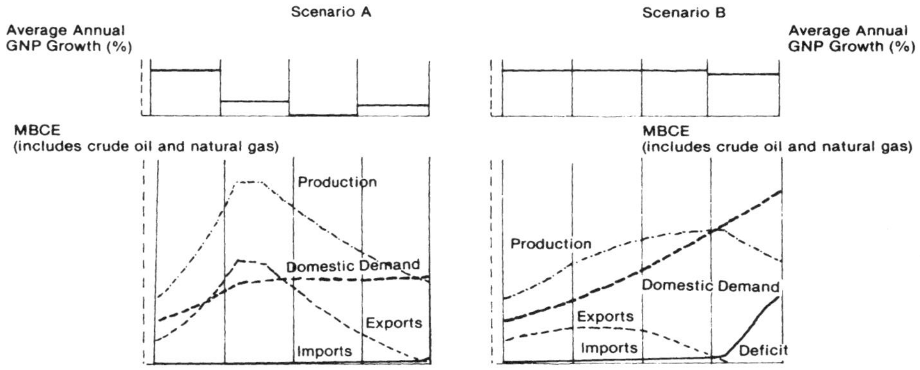

Scenario A

Average Annual GNP Growth (%)

MBCE (includes crude oil and natural gas)

Production
Domestic Demand
Exports
Imports

Scenario B

Average Annual GNP Growth (%)

MBCE (includes crude oil and natural gas)

Production
Domestic Demand
Exports
Imports
Deficit

The graph shows the long-term implications of two alternative scenarios for economic policy. Both consider current proven hydrocarbon reserves included although the results are essentially the same if probable reserves are also included. Scenario A assumes a deterioration in foreign trade for non oil areas and requiring an increase in hydrocarbon exports to cover the balance of payment deficit and assure sustained economic growth. However, after the mid 1980s oil and gas production was to face certain restrictions that prevented exports from being increased. To give the reserves longer life, production would in fact have to be reduced. In order to maintain the foreign deficit within financil limits, economic growth would have to be curbed in order to cut goods and service imports. Scenario B proposes an economic policy similar to the one adopted by the current government which is designed to strengthen industry and stimulate agriculture. In this case with the need to satisfy foreign exchange requirements considering and a growth rate of 8 percent in the long term, it would be sufficient to export 1.5 MBD of oil sectors along with 300 MCFD of natural gas because cause the productive sectors would produce the rest. Although hydrocarbon production would continue to increase, it would tend to provoke increased domestic demand. However, if by the end of the century there were an energy deficit that had to be covered with imports or other sources, the transition toward a self-sustained industrial economy would already have been completed and a diversified energy structure attained.

GNP = gross national product.
MBCE = millions of barrels of crude oil equivalents.
MCED = millions of cubic feet per day.
MBD = millions of barrels per day.
MMB = billions of barrels.

SOURCE: SEPAFIN *Programa de energía, metas y proyecciones al año 2000 (resumen y conclusiones), Mexico City, SEPAFIN November 1980, p. 27.*

nario's hypothesis underestimated the duration of the economic recession in the major industrialized countries and the consequent effects on crude prices; the success of widespread energy-saving and energy-conservation programs; the high cost of international credit; the protectionist measures adopted in all the industrialized world; and the basic trends in Mexico's own development, particularly in regard to major world credit institutions.

Once they had established the hydrocarbon export volume the economy required to grow, PE's creators proposed a series of goals for restraining local energy demand until 1990 and made forecasts regarding the same to the year 2000. The first set of targets covered rational energy use and energy-resource conservation. These measures were, in fact, thought of as an additional energy source that would help reduce hydrocarbon dependence considerably. It was estimated that by 1990 energy saving could result in a reduction of energy consumption per unit of GNP amounting to 1 million barrels per day of crude oil equivalent (MBDCE). Specific measures for promoting energy saving were defined, such as careful use of energy, efficient new technology, and technology for recovering residual industrial heat.

The important indirect measures involved pricing policy. Appropriate adjustment to energy prices to the consumer, whether middle or end, would moderate the growth in domestic demand and help achieve economic policy objectives. Although still helping promote industrial development through cheap energy, PE 1980 proposed that local oil prices should increase gradually until they caught up with international ones.[29] Although PE 1980 established definite targets for the amount of energy saved, it failed to introduce concrete measures for modifying prevailing consumer patterns. Measures such as careful energy use, the introduction of modern conservation technology, and control over waste were not explained in detail. PE's designers expected rather naively that these measures would be adopted almost spontaneously by the consumers despite the fact that previous experience by other countries in adopting such measures showed very poor results except when the measures were accompanied by drastic changes in oil-pricing policy.

Although pricing and subsidy policies were less effective than other measures in energy saving, it was believed that government subsidies and low energy prices would continue to be of major importance in the country's industrialization (only 34 percent of energy saving could be contributed to pricing and subsidies, whereas other measures contributed 66 percent). Nevertheless, it had long been shown by past experience that policies such as these applied indiscriminately more often than not tend to promote inefficient industrial growth, with consequently little hope of competing in world markets.

     Apart from these measures, PE 1980 elaborated in detail a series of specific targets and proposals for developing oil and natural gas, coal and electric power as well as other energy sources that would contribute to the energy-diversification process. The targets and policies were based on forecasts for growth in domestic hydrocarbon and electricity demand that form part of Mexico's industrial model incorporated in PNDI.[30]

     Oil and natural gas. The hydrocarbon subsector's development targets were established on the basis of the projected growth contained in the program's macroeconomic framework. Production had to cover domestic demand, whatever that might be, and generate a constant exportable surplus of 1.5 MBDCE plus 300 MCFD of natural gas. According to the program's forecasts, crude oil and gas liquids would be extracted at a rate of 3.5 MBDCE in 1985 and 4.1 MBDCE in 1990. The figure for natural gas would reach 4.3 BCFD by 1985 and 6.99 BCFD by 1990.

     PE 1980 advocated satisfying domestic demand for light products, particularly gasoline and kerosene, in view of their high commercial value on the international market. With Mexico's increased heavy crude oil production and the need to process more of it locally in a short amount of time, the refining load would have to be increased and major technical modifications undertaken. In the medium term domestic demand could be covered if refining capacity were doubled by 1990.

     PE 1980 was opposed to flaring natural gas and proposed reducing the amount burned from 12 to 3 percent of gross production. The use of natural gas instead of fuel oil was to be encouraged, especially

In the energy sector itself, implying a reduction in exports. Should there be any surplus that could not be absorbed by either local or foreign markets, it would be channeled into the manufacturing and residential sectors. Like PGD, PE 1980 overestimated the amount of associated gas extracted from the southeastern fields and the Campeche marine zone. Although a surplus of fuel oil and a probable shortage of gasoline was foreseen for the next three years, natural gas shortage forced CFE to continue using fuel oil for electricity generation.

Coal. According to PE 1980 the main reason for not promoting the exploitation of coal further was the small potential market. Although the iron and steel industry's expansion demanded increasing amounts of coke, which was not easy to find, the electricity subsector needed only small amounts of noncoke coal to implement its new coal-burning electricity program.

PE 1980 also attempted to evaluate the comparative advantages of the two iron and steel processes available, one using blast furnaces and an oxygen converter with coke as a reducing agent and the other involving direct reduction with electric ovens and using natural gas. With these two processes coke would be used in the major plants and natural gas in projects of lesser importance.

Coal's contribution to energy diversification was to be even greater with the program's proposed Rio Escondido coal-based electric plant with 1,200 MW capacity and the construction of two other plants during the 1980s each with a capacity of 1,400 MW. It was estimated that 120 TBD of fuel oil could, therefore, be substituted with coal in 1990 and almost 11 percent of the country's electric power generated by this means.[31]

Electric energy. The growth targets for this subsector were based on forecasts for an expanded electricity demand similar to that recorded over the las few decades. The electricity subsector's expansion plan was based on figures for the estimated growth in demand in the long term, that is, 20 to 30 years.[32] With the influence of the prevailing economic situation on electricity subsector development, future demand was forecast on the basis of the direct relationship between per capita energy consumption and the

GNP. CFE forecasted that demand would be such that the electricity subsector's generating capacity would have to triple between 1980 and 1990. However, the calculations on which these forecasts were based lacked foundation because they failed to consider that energy-saving measures could be introduced and that probable variations would occur in economic parameters, such as a growth in GNP.

Other energy sources. Apart from providing sure energy supply the program's aim was to diversify primary energy sources for generating electricity. Therefore, work had to start on coal-based power generation; two nuclear electric plants were planned to come on line by 1990; and special attention was given to further developing hydroelectricity, geothermal power, and solar energy. Although the major sources of hydroelectric power had already been exploited, some medium- and small-size sources could still be tapped, a possibility that would provide local industry with the opportunity to produce the equipment needed for these projects.

With the drilling and operating problems at geothermal fields and the lack of experience even at a world level, it would have been unrealistic to consider geothermal power as a viable energy source before the 1990s. A minimum target of 620 MW was set for the end of the century, but the program's designers recommended that the energy commission organize a research group to analyze the country's geothermal potential. With this information criteria could be established for determining how this potential should be exploited.

PE 1980 estimated that by 1990 Mexico would have an installed nuclear electricity capacity of 2,500 MW and that by the year 2000 the capacity would reach 20,000 MW. Given the long lead times for this type of project, work would have to begin immediately. The intention was to begin in 1981 by selecting the sites and the technology to be used in the nuclear industry and giving a boost to uranium-exploration programs. Solar energy was expected to contribute only marginally to the energy balance because the technology needed for operating on a large scale was not available commercially.

The specific development goals established for the various energy sources and the importance given to each in the energy diversification process were strongly biased. Despite recommendations to carefully ponder the advantages and practical aspects (such as financing, technological development, and human resources) of the different options available and SEPAFIN's stress on the advantages of developing geothermal power in Mexico, extremely ambitious goals were established for developing nuclear power. The motivation behind these goals was purely political, but technical and economic arguments were used to justify them. In order to strengthen the politicoeconomic option offered in PNDI and counterbalance PEMEX's politicoeconomic project and PGD's subsequent development strategy, certain tactical alliances were formed by those involved in defining Mexico's energy policy.[33]

Including these goals in PNN brought about a major controversy.[34] ' CFE's proposals were based on two alternative forecasts for electricity demand to the year 2000. The first option was known as basic and included PNDI's assumptions that electricity consumption would grow yearly at a rate around 11 percent, reaching 550 TWh by the year 2000. The second forecast was based on an extrapolation of historical trends and an estimated consumption for the year 2000 of 374 TWH, considering an annual growth rate in electricity consumption around 8 percent. CFE felt that electricity consumption for the year 2000 would more than likely be somewhere between these two figures.

In order to justify the magnitude of the nuclear project, maximum limits were placed on the contribution of hydroelectricity, geothermal power, and coal-based electricity to global electricity supply (a ceiling of 140 TWh from a total between 374 and 550 TWh). The rest was to come from nuclear electricity and the hydrocarbon-fed thermoelectric systems. Therefore, it was concluded that to prevent even greater dependence on hydrocarbons and at the same time assure electricity self-sufficiency, the only viable option was nuclear power.

The nuclear industry's proposed 20,000 MW capacity encountered open resistance from another important group involved in energy sector decision making.[35] The advocates of greater caution in nuclear electricity development urged that a nuclear program be formulated to include a detailed study of available technology in order to make an optimum selection; propitiate better conditions under which technology transfer could occur; and contribute to the creation of a nuclear capacity that would lead to greater scientific, technological, and financial self-sufficiency. Such an effort would mean limiting considerably the proposed activity in both PE 1980 and PNN.

Despite the group's insistence on a cautious approach to nuclear development, early in 1981 the government invited companies internationally to offer proposals to select the appropriate reactor and technology for Mexico's second nuclear plant, which was scheduled to come on line in 1990. However, with the financial restrictions that arose after 1981 because of the fall in international crude oil prices, the project had to be abandoned.

The severe crisis of 1981-1982 also invalidated the economic models that advocated rapidly establishing Mexico's nuclear electricity industry. Apart from its lack of financial liquidity, the country did not have sufficient human resources, the scientific, technological, and industrial infrastructure, or uranium reserves large enough to embark on a program of this magnitude.

SCOPE AND LIMITATIONS OF THE PROGRAMA DE ENERGIA

The efforts of SEPAFIN's industrial sector planners and the Comisión Nacional de Energéticos' specialists materialized in Mexico's first formal energy program, which was designed to attack all aspects of the energy problem in an integrated way. The project was not fully endorsed by the various political groups tacitly in favor of delaying oil industry expansion. However, the program became an additional argument in support of presidential decisions regarding hydrocarbon export ceilings and the foreign-trade model to be adopted, and it represented an alternative economic policy that could have had considerable influence over the whole process of presidential succession.

The energy program's most important contribution was its proposal to coordinate energy policy with the rest of the economy, particularly with the industrial and foreign sectors, in order to promote the saving and rational use of energy as well as energy diversification. The program also defined the incentives for developing the local capital goods industries that were related to the energy sector (proposed earlier in PNDI). One of the program's more important political proposals concerned the criteria to be adopted in exporting hydrocarbons in order to avoid excessive dependence on certain importing countries. This particular policy was taken up again by PNE 1984, which was introduced by the Miguel de la Madrid administration and is still in force today.

The 1980 program took steps to determine ways to achieve rational energy use and even set definite primary energy-saving goals. The pricing policy, designed to encourage rational use of energy, also proposed gradually closing the gap between domestic and international prices while offering protection to industrialists and low income consumers through low energy prices. The program also took definite steps toward solving the problem of energy diversification. Progress was made in evaluating the potential of the different sources of electric energy, and for the first time in the country's energy-planning history, a comparative cost analysis per unit of electricity generated was introduced together with an itemization of required investment, operation costs, and fuel consumption for each case. The program stated production and electric installed capacity targets by source for 1990 except for hydroelectricity, where potential was evaluated in qualitative terms only.

The program clearly pinpointed the oil and electricity industries' main problems, bottlenecks, and feasible options. Of particular importance were its proposals for making use of natural gas, recommendations concerning the potential primary energy reserves the electricity industry would need to provide reliable service, and a listing of the energy-related implications of the iron and steel industry's technological options.

Despite the program's valuable contributions to integrated energy sector planning, its undeniable merits in pinpointing the major obstacles facing energy planning in Mexico, and its concrete proposals for action, the implementation of definite solutions was constrained by a series of external factors, such as the prevailing international situation, Mexico's financial circumstances, and political and institutional friction.

The program was formulated on the basis of SEPAFIN's political project, expressed earlier in PNDI, rather than as an attempt to find an effective way to deal with the energy sector's complicated problems. The program was used as a political instrument to contain the oil industry's growth--PEMEX's exceedingly rapid growth had placed its director general in a very advantageous position in the 1981-1982 race for the presidency. However, because the document was associated with PNDI and put forward as a sectorial program by SEPAFIN without presidential endorsement, its political strength was automatically undermined.

The energy program was incomplete, and its presentation by the minister for SEPAFIN, the macroeconomic framework on which it was based, and the sectoral proposals and targets were inconsistent with each other. For example, the presentation stressed the advantages of Mexico's geothermal resources and their major contribution to the country's energy development, but the program's targets for the year 2000 showed a marked preference for nuclear energy as opposed to other sources. With sustained annual growth rates for the electricity industry between 11 and 12 percent and with the uncertain availability of energy from other sources, such as hydroelectricity and geothermal and coal-based power, the program concluded that to cover the 3 MBDCE energy deficit foreseen for the year 2000, the only solution possible was to build a nuclear electric capacity of 20,000 MW, which was clearly impossible for both technological and financial reasons.

This contradiction can be explained by the assumptions on which the SEPAFIN macroeconomic framework was based and by the ministry's political alliances and commitments with the group promoting nuclear energy within CFE, whose influence on the 1980 energy policy was particularly strong. CFE group offered its experience and planning know-how and supported the energy program's political stance, and the high officials in SEPAFIN agreed to support the proposal for an ambitious nuclear program despite their leanings toward energy diversification using local renewable resources. Perhaps this latter view of Mexico's energy future was influenced by the prospect of a diversified and high-technology local manufacturing sector that promised to provide most of the equipment and components demanded by the nuclear industry by the late 1980s. Other observers suggest Mexico was influenced by the major foreign suppliers whose sales had been affected by the reduced demand for nuclear facilities in their own countries.

The energy program assumed a 5 to 7 percent annual increase in real hydrocarbon prices on the international market working in conjunction with the domestic energy-saving proposals and energy-source diversification. This meant a contradiction since Mexico would be the exception, reducing hydrocarbon dependence while the rest of the world continued to intensively use hydrocarbons. It was evident after the first oil shock of 1973-1974 that the trend was beginning to change.

The maintenance of an export ceiling and the industrial-development strategy associated with the energy program were based on the assumption that international hydrocarbon prices would continue to increase until the year 2000. However, this assumption could only hold under certain conditions, which were not valid after the early 1970s. These conditions were as follows:

- World hydrocarbon consumption would continue to grow indefinitely at the same rate as in the past.

- World hydrocarbon supply would not be affected by price rises.

- The supply of alternative energy sources would remain the same because of the energy consumers' unconditional preference for hydrocarbons, even though the higher price of hydrocarbons would make alternative sources economically worthwhile.

- World energy-consumption patterns would be relatively unaffected by the price increases.

- The political instability in the Middle East would continue to seriously affect hydrocarbon supply to the rest of the world.

It would only be fair to those who elaborated the energy program to admit that similar conditions held weight in many OPEC countries and for most of the major international oil companies.

Even when the SEPAFIN planners realized that international oil transactions and the world energy system in general were not behaving according to their original thesis, they still continued to assume a hydrocarbon shortage for the medium term brought about by the major oil-producing countries and hydrocarbon importers. This assumption can first be explained by the government's distorted view of the world energy situation (despite the second oil shock in 1979-1980), an idea that was sustained and reinforced by the oil syndrome affecting the country's leaders.[36] Second, it might be that the SEPAFIN planners and decision makers were unaware of the structural changes occurring in the world's energy systems, such as the appearance of new oil-producing regions, policies related to energy saving, fuel substitution, and strategic reserve formation in the industrialized countries. Because these facts were not completely unfamiliar to the experts and analysts within the energy commission, one is forced to ask the following questions: Were these people unable to express their doubts about the validity of the assumptions concerning the future behavior of hydrocarbon prices? If their doubts were raised, why was there no response from the SEPAFIN planners?

A possible explanation is that although those responsible for designing the energy plan were more or less aware that the domestic's basic assumptions were probably not valid, by outwardly supporting them they were likely to achieve their short-term political objectives. For the authors of the energy plan who had also been involved in elaborating PNDI, it was worth supporting the proposal to place a ceiling on crude exports, under the pretext that the foreign exchange earned was sufficient for the country's growth requirements, in order to curb the oil industry's expansion toward foreign markets that threatened to tip the scales in favor of Jorge Díaz Serrano in the presidential race.

According to CFE, particularly those involved in promoting electricity industry expansion, the expected inflow of abundant financial resources and the high rate of growth in electricity demand justified the subsector's rapid expansion, which was even more rapid than that forecast in CFE's ten-year program.[37] Under the auspices of the energy program and with the support of the ministry responsible for energy sector development, CFE representatives were able to justify a large budget; thus, the electricity industry was able to overcome its chronic shortage of economic resources, a situation that had severely inhibited its development and was responsible for the blackouts in 1980 that consequently damaged its public image as a reliable power supplier.

To be able to interpret some of the key decisions contained in PE 1980, one would have to carry out careful and detailed reconstruction of the facts and know far more about the real motivations of the various actors. The events occurring after 1981, which brought about the country's worst political and financial crisis since World War II, seriously affected the chances for putting the program into practice. However, several of the program's basic principles and guidelines were taken up again in PNE 1984-1988.

To summarize, the implementation of the energy program was seriously affected by the fact that the economic policy expressed therein was supported neither by the executive, who advocated PGD's approach, nor by PEMEX. Furthermore, because the program appeared late in the government term, it was not supported by those political groups that were preparing for the government changeover and that had economic and political projects that were different from those presented in PE 1980. Once again it became clear that with the characteristics of the Mexican political system, any economic planning, whether global or sectoral, extending beyond the traditional six-year term has little chances for success.

ENERGY PLANNING AND THE ECONOMIC AND FINANCIAL CRISIS OF 1981-1982

During mid-1981 a number of national and international events that ended in crisis brought to light the growing structural weaknesses of the country's economy. Despite the vast income from oil exports and international borrowing, the inadequacy of Mexico's productive system was obvious.[38] The economy's dependence on oil, the imbalance between the industrial and farming sectors, the existence of a growing work force with no job possibilities, a high rate of inflation, and overvalued currency all indicated the ineffectiveness of the development model followed during the postwar period. Domestic problems became noticeably worse because of the prolonged world economic crisis, growing interest rates in the capital market with their consequent effect on foreign-debt servicing, and the fall in international crude oil prices precipitated by the oil market glut.[39] With the sudden reduction in the state's foreign earnings and the growing fiscal deficit, the development plans financed by oil earnings were no longer viable. The state thus resorted to short-term borrowing in the international capital market in order to compensate for the income lost with the drop in oil prices and the temporary suspension of some of its sales.[40]

In addition to foreign borrowing the state adopted a series of local measures designed to cope with the initial manifestations of the crisis. In mid-February 1982 the Banco de México withdrew from the international exchange market and devalued its peso. Uncoordinated attempts were also made to set up an economic adjustment program in August that same year.[41] These measures were insufficient to even cope with the immediate problems. During the rest of 1982 and in 1983 the country suffered an economic and financial crisis that was unparalleled in its recent history. Although a slight fall in total commodity production was registered in Mexico during the 1930s crisis, the GNP growth had been sustained without interruption from 1940 to 1981.[42] The negative economic growth rate recorded in 1982 and 1983 shows a qualitative difference with the rates of the 1930s. Furthermore, most of Mexico's work force lives off its wages, and the severe contraction in production brought about a major deterioration in living standards for most of the population, particularly with the closing of job sources and severe cuts in real wages.

The economic crisis that began in Mexico in the early 1980s coincided with a rather erratic fall in international growth rates, which was characterized by the inflationary tendencies and unemployment in technological fields. Compared with the first twenty years after World War II when the world economy underwent sustained growth and financial resources were easy to acquire, today, in addition to the international recession, international credit conditions have become very tight, the international oil boom has come to an end, and everyone has resorted to protectionism. These factors have had serious consequences for Mexico because its economy is heavily dependent on the international market for the sale of crude oil, certain raw materials, and nondurable consumer manufactured exports. Furthermore, it has major import requirements, the result of inadequate vertical integration in the industrial sector and technological backwardness.

In light of these internal and external circumstances, the present crisis is clearly neither cyclical nor circumstantial—it is, in essence, structural, which is evident in the constant deterioration of the economy. The state has been forced to attempt both political and economic reorganization in order to modernize its political institutions and increase its economic efficiency. It is still too soon to tell the outcome of these attempts.

NOTES

1. José López Portillo stated, "Let us pause for a moment in order to get back on to our feet and not stray from our course(...) to establish new foundations and recover lost confidence." "El gabinete: Arcón navideño," in Expansión, Vol. 3, No. 206, Mexico City, 22 December 1976.

2. "El gabinete," 22 December 1976.

3. Jorge Díaz Serrano was appointed director general of PEMEX, and other high officials were given

key posts in the PEMEX administration in fields such as exploration, primary and industrial production, trade, and financing, replacing some of the most respected technicians of the 1938 generation who were asked either to retire or to resign. No doubt these outgoing officials would have actively supported the conservationist stance. Grayson, George, <u>The Politics of Mexican Oil</u>, Pittsburgh, University of Pittsburgh Press, 1980, pp. 59-60.

4. SPP took over the planning and programming activities related to public investment that previously were the responsibility of the president's office. It also dealt with current expenditure budgeting that had been undertaken by the treasury ministry's expense department and other regulatory functions associated with the public sector that earlier were the responsibility of SEPAFIN. SEMIP would see to the programing and control of energy enterprises, such as PEMEX and CFE, as well as energy research institutes and organizations, such as IMP, ININ, and IIE.

5. SEPAFIN, <u>Programa de energía, metas y proyecciones al año 2000 (resumen y conclusiones)</u>, Mexico City, SEPAFIN, November 1980, 60 pp. The complete text has never been published.

6. The first view was clearly represented by PEMEX Director General Jorge Díaz Serrano and the second by SEPAFIN Minister José Andrés de Oteyza. The difference of opinion on energy development between the two, with the support given by the president to the development concept sustained by PEMEX's director general, made it difficult for SEPAFIN to control PEMEX the way it was supposed to. Continual confrontations arose and were reflected in PEMEX's proposals to increase oil production and exports, on one hand, and, on the other, in the elaboration by SEPAFIN of PNDI in 1979 and the energy program proposals one year later, which were designed to attenuate the power of Díaz Serrano.

7. SEPAFIN, <u>Plan nacional de desarrollo industrial, 1979-1982</u>, Mexico City, SEPAFIN, 1979; SPP, <u>Plan global de desarrollo, 1980-1982</u>, Mexico City, SPP, 1980; Bueno, Gerardo, "Petróleo y planes de desarrollo en México," in Wionczek, M. S. (editor), <u>Energía en México: Ensayos sobre el pasado y el presente</u>, Mexico City, El Colegio de México, 1982, pp. 209-228.

8. On 6 November 1976 Carlos Tello Macias and Julio Rodolfo Moctezuma Cid, ministers of SPP and of SHCP, respectively, resigned office.

9. For the deposed minister of SPP the question still remained open: Should oil resources be used as an instrument for economic policy or as a way to solve the serious problems of social inequality? Declarations by Carlos Tello Macias in Kraft, Joseph, "A Reporter at Large: The Mexican Oil Puzzle," New York, The New Yorker, 15 October 1979.

10. PNDI was published in Diario Oficial, Vol 311, Mexico City, 17 May 1979.

11. Productive investment was promoted with the help of two kinds of measures. The direct measures involved public investment in economic and social infrastructure by state-owned companies. The indirect measures comprised tax incentives, financial backing, an industrial protectionist mechanism, the regulation and development of technology, and the promotion of investment projects. For details see SEPAFIN, PNDI, 1979, pp. 28-32.

12. The implementation of the expansionist project would mean that industry would have to grow at a rate of 12 percent per year and some areas, such as the capital goods sector and the petrochemical subsector, between 18 and 20 percent per year. Thus, growth in the GNP and employment would reach 10 and 5 percent per year, respectively, in the medium and long term. SEPAFIN, PNDI, 1979, pp. 9, 23.

13. The policy for protecting and promoting exports established by PNDI included the substitution of previously granted import permits for tariffs plus discounts on energy and other raw materials. Discounts on fuel oil, natural gas, and basic petrochemicals for those industries established in industrial complexes was 30 percent on current local reference prices and 10 percent in the regions distributed along the national gas grid. In addition, the price of energy for industrial use was kept below the international price. SEPAFIN, PNDI, 1979, pp. 30-32.

14. Jacobs, Eduardo, et al., "Competencia y concentración: El caso del sector manufacturero," in Economia Mexicana, No. 3, Mexico City, CIDE, 1980.

15. Story, Dale, "Development strategies in an oil exporting advanced developing nation: The case of

Mexico" (mimeograph), paper presented at the International Studies Association annual reunion, Cincinnati, Ohio, March 1982, p. 7.

16. "México: Plan sexenal de desarrollo petrolero," in Petróleo Internacional, Vol. 35, No. 1, Mexico City, January 1977.

17. PEMEX's new proposal estimated that by December 1980 crude and liquid production capacity could reach 2.8 MBD, and 1.5 MBD could be made available for export. By 1982 capacity could increase to 3.7 MBD; it was calculated that Mexico could produce 4.7 BCFD of gas by late 1980 and 6 BCFD in 1982. It was added that the increase in investment would not be directly proportional to the increase in production capacity because of the high productivity of recently discovered oil fields. According to verbal and written declarations by PEMEX representatives, the new production target was introduced to accelerate national development by taking advantage of favorable international hydrocarbon market conditions. Oficina de Asesores de la Presidencia, Ultima versión sobre la plataforma de producción y exportación, internal document (mimeograph), Mexico City, 1980, pp. 1-8.

18. The centralized power within the executive and the close relationship between the president and PEMEX's director general made the latter's position of prime importance in energy sector decision making until 1981. Despite the fact that PEMEX was officially controlled by SEPAFIN and that the president of the PEMEX administrative council was also the minister for SEPAFIN, a decision-making process was established at an unofficial level, and on various occasions the legal authorities of other sectors were overridden by PEMEX's autonomous decisions.

19. There was a forerunner to this proposal to speed up expansion. In 1979 a revised six-year program was submitted to the governmental authorities. It proposed increasing oil production for 1982 to 2.5 MBD for crude and liquids, with an increase in exports to 1.4 MBD. However, this program was not approved. Oficina de Asesores de la Presidencia, op. cit.

20. Income also increased because of the sudden jump in international crude oil prices after the revolution in Iran and late with the war between Iran and Iraq.

21. The study made a careful analysis of PEMEX's proposal and the points of view of SEPAFIN, SPP, and SHCP. Oficina de Asesores de la Presidencia, op. cit.

22. "Oil under the ground is a valuable asset and the irrefutable patrimony of the Nation. But once the oil is located, work can go on for years to exploit it. In order for Mexico to have a greater maneuverability during its development in the international oil scene, we should perhaps consider a gradual increase, not precisely in production but in production capacity. In this way we would enjoy flexibility in a much more rigid and convulsed world where development possibilities are nil for many countries." Díaz Serrano, Jorge, Informe del director general de Petróleos Mexicanos, 18 March 1980, p. 39.

23. This transaction occurred between PEMEX's 1979 proposal in the revised six-year program and its 1980 proposal, which stated that "with the hydrocarbon consumption forecast for 1982(...) a relatively set figure, the fact is that this apparently unimportant change is really quite substantial. On one hand, it means a 48 percent increase in the export target in terms of volume before 1982 and, on the other, this increase occurs at the same time that a 100 percent increase in the international price of oil. In other words, we are talking of practically tripling expected income from foreign oil sales between 1980 and 1982. Therefore, it is not surprising that as was quietly pointed out in the Global Development Plan, this will give the country sufficient bargaining power to solve any problem that may arise." Bueno, Gerardo, "Petróleo y planes de desarrollo en México," op. cit., p. 8.

Aurelio Tames, vice-president of CANACINTRA, announced at the close of the ceremony on 18 March 1980, that "the organization I represent approves of the president's decision to postpone Mexico's entry into GATT." Ramiro Ruiz Madero, coordinator of the Work Congress, pointed out that "the country still does not possess an adequate productive apparatus to be able to compete with GATT-member nations." Excélsior, Mexico City, 19 March 1980.

24. SPP's planning attempts gave rise to the first version of the Programa de Acción del Sector Público (Action Program for the Public Sector) 1978-1982, which was elaborated by SPP Minister Carlos

Tello Macías. His successor, Ricardo García Sáinz, decided to include the private sector in the program, but his version of the document, presented to the president in March 1979, did not prosper. In May that year García Sáinz left the ministry; his place was taken by Miguel de la Madrid, who in April 1980 publicly announced PGD 1980-1982.

25. Among these were PNDI, the Plan Nacional de Desarrollo Pesquero (National Fishing Development Plan), the Plan Nacional de Turismo (National Tourism Plan), and the Programa Nacional de Empleo (National Employment Plan).

26. The plan's general objectives were (1) to reaffirm Mexico's independence; (2) to provide the population with jobs and a minimum social well-being, that is, food, education, and housing; (3) to promote rapid, sustained, and efficient growth; and (4) to improve the distribution of income between people, production areas, and geographical regions. Cf. SPP, Plan global de desarrollo, p. 15.

27. SPP, Plan global de desarrollo, pp. 104-106.

28. Ibid., pp. 122-124.

29. The aim was to increase local hydrocarbon prices until they were equivalent to 70 percent of external reference prices for industrial fuels and diesel and to practically eliminate the gap between local and international prices in all other petroleum products over a period of ten years. An electricity tariff policy was proposed with the aim of maintaining the low consumers' buying power and the offer of a certain degree of protection to industry through prices lower than international ones. Furthermore, the program proposed a formula to prevent the average price for electricity from deteriorating in real terms. SEPAFIN, Programa de energía, p. 17.

30. The basic forecast was made on the assumption that past trends in local energy demand would continue, modified by technological changes. It also assumed an energy-pricing policy that would prevent energy prices from deteriorating in real terms with respect to domestic inflation. The energy program forecast incorporated specific goals for energy rationalization and conservation and included a direct pricing policy. SEPAFIN, Programa de energía, pp. 19-20.

31. The Carbón I and Carbón II projects were planned on the basis of expected economic growth during the oil boom. With the economic recession that followed, the coal-burning electricity project had to be slowed, and to date only three of the four Carbón I units and none of the Carbón II units are operating. As a result, MICARE has had to close some of its open-cut mines and operate underground mines at a very inefficient rate.

32. CFE, "El programa de desarrollo del sector eléctrico," in Energéticos, Year 2, No. 3, Mexico City, CFE, March 1978.

33. The most important alliance was between those who formulated the frame of reference for PE 1980 and the CFE group interested in promoting nuclear development in Mexico, represented by the Subsecretario de Energía y Minas (Undersecretary for Energy and Mines), Fernando Hiriart; CFE's director, Alberto Escoffet; and the CFE planning coordinator, Juan Eibenshutz.

34. CFE, Programa nucleoeléctrico nacional, Mexico City, CFE, 1981, pp. 4-7.

35. Those who strongly opposed these targets were ININ director, Dalmau Costa; SEPAFIN's energy director, Adrián Lajous; and one of the president's economic advisers, Jaime Corredor E.

36. For the purpose of this book the term oil syndrome is defined as a series of concepts and expectations generated among decision makers about the benefits of hydrocarbon exports. The expectations are reinforced with the favorable results obtained in the short term, which, in turn, provides feedback in the form of associated benefits; eventually, the country's development rests on this resource alone. Under these circumstances any analysis of reality tends to be subjective and shallow, and any questioning of the established premises is rejected as pessimistic and unrepresentative of assumed future prosperity.

37. For the period 1977-1986 CFE calculated an annual growth of 9.75 percent in electricity consumption as opposed to the 11-12 percent forecast by PE. CFE, Programa nucleoeléctrico nacional, 1981, p. 3.

38. An example of the inadequacy of Mexico's productive system was the fall in the share of manufactured exports in overall exports. It went from

47 percent in 1976 to 15 percent in 1982. Meanwhile, the oil industry's share in exports increased from 21 percent to 79 percent over the same period. Banco de México, Producto interno bruto y gasto, 1970-1979, Mexico City, Banco de México, 1980; information was also obtained from the bank's annual reports.

39. In August 1982 the rise in U.S. interest rates forced the state to declare itself incapable of servicing its foreign debt and to insist on the need for renegotiation.

40. The state's foreign-borrowing policy adopted in the mid-1970s largely substituted for tax reforms. During most of the postwar period taxes in Mexico were among the lowest in the world because the government feared that any major modification in the tax structure would frighten the private sector and induce capital flight. However, in 1964 and 1972 attempts were made to promote tax reform. Both efforts were unsuccessful because of the opposition of entrepreneurial groups and their allies in the government. When the private sector refused to accept higher taxes, the Echeverría Alvarez government opted for large-scale deficit expenditures and a major increase in money supply. During the first two years of his administration, José López Portillo tried to reverse the tendency to increase the government deficit, but his efforts were abandoned when the public treasury began to fill with the revenue from oil exports.

41. This program included the following points: a 3 percent reduction in public expenditures, support for the Programa de Productos Básicos (Basic Products Program), a reduction in public sector imports, assimilation of the losses of companies whose liabilities were in dollars (to 42 percent), and a flexible interest rate policy. On 5 August 1982 a double parity was established temporarily. On August 12 all bank transferences abroad in dollars were canceled, and the mexdollar was established at 69.50 pesos. On August 17 an increase was announced in the oil supply to the U.S. strategic reserve. BANAMEX, Examen de la situación económica de México, Mexico City, BANAMEX, February-September 1982.

42. With the fall in production in 1971 and 1976 the GNP growth rate did not fall any lower than 2 percent per year.

18

Energy Planning for 1982–1988

Manuel Boltvinik

POLITICAL AND ECONOMIC CIRCUMSTANCES SURROUNDING THE PROGRAMA NACIONAL DE ENERGETICOS, 1984-1988

The unsuccessful growth strategy built around the transient oil boom, the private sector's insistence that the crisis was caused by mismanagement of state funds and excessive foreign borrowing, growing discontent in the working sector, and the demands of farm-worker groups affected by the oil industry's accelerated development led the new presidential candidate to incorporate in his campaign a call to the various social sectors to participate in formulating the new development strategy. In many ways the political challenges facing the system were as dangerous as its economic and financial problems.

Miguel de la Madrid's political strategy concentrated on two main issues: democratic planning and moral renovation.[1] The concept of democratic planning answered the need to rationalize economic policy and at the same time provide the opportunity for those social sectors whose opinion had been traditionally ignored to participate in policy making and the definition of development models. Public opinion forums were held at regional and state levels to allow these sectors to state their demands and express their inconformity with proposed policy, or so it was said. These forums were, in fact, the state's way of justifying the economic and social measures it intended to introduce, which incorporated some of PNDI's proposals. The other important aspect of the new administration--moral renovation--was designed to fulfill a double objective: to revindicate the state, which had lost prestige as a result of a campaign launched by the business sector and the conservative and socialist opposition, and to reconcile the conflicting interests of the different groups and strengthen the state's role as leader in the country's economy.[2]

The government's economic strategy took into account the urgent need to reorganize the economy and establish the right conditions to overcome the crisis and to make the qualitative changes needed to tackle the underlying structural problems. This strategy appeared in the form of PIRE, which was announced in December 1982, and PND, which was introduced in May 1983.[3,4] Because of oil's strategic importance to the López Portillo economic policy and the subsequent frustration of the government's plan to use oil as the lever of development, the new energy strategy became one of the most important subjects of Miguel de la Madrid's campaign; it was also given preferential treatment in the national development plan.

ENERGY'S ROLE IN THE PLAN NACIONAL DE DESARROLLO

PND's analysis of Mexico's industrial development appeared to back up previous criticism; particular reference was made to the energy sector's inability to sustain Mexico's national development single-handedly. The plan also referred to the anomalies occurring within the energy sector in general and the oil subsector in particular. According to the plan the excessive importance given to achieving the oil subsector's quantitative targets had repercussions in the development of the national capital goods industry and was responsible for the growing amount of imports demanded by the oil industry itself. The anomalies created by the low energy price policy not only gave rise to generalized waste and excessive overconsumption in the industrial and transport sectors, they also postponed the adjustment necessary to make exportable manufactured goods competitive internationally. Thus, oil subsector expansion was not, as it had been hoped, the means of achieving Mexico's industrialization and modernization, nor was it capable of transforming its productive structure.

Mexico's dependence on hydrocarbons to cover primary energy supply resulted in serious problems. Hydroelectricity became of secondary importance, and fuel oil was used extensively in thermoelectric plants. Apart from causing contamination, fuel oil's high-sulphur content had a negative effect on productivity, the active life of the facilities, and the maintenance cost of electricity generating plants.

In view of the energy sector's importance in national development, PND planners insisted that the main objectives of the national energy plan should be to guarantee the country's energy self-sufficiency, gradually incorporating both rural and urban communities still without electricity into the national grid; to increase the energy sector's contribution to economic development by using local capital goods and other imports and by providing foreign revenue and taxes for the national treasury; to improve productivity and efficiency in energy sector companies through budgetary discipline; and to achieve a rational and coherent energy balance with the gradual and orderly diversification of energy sources, nonrenewable resource conservation, and energy saving.

The general action guidelines for the energy sector stressed the need for the following:

- Increased control over energy companies to assure cooperation with the national development strategy

- Differential price and tariff system, including price scales that would encourage rational use of energy

- Greater efficiency in hydrocarbon production and distribution to be achieved by adapting and expanding refining capacity, completing petrochemical projects, and giving priority to construction of those facilities contributing to the use of refined-product storage capacity and marketing and projects for creating port infrastructure and facilities designed to optimize oil reservoir exploitation

. Greater efficiency in the electricity subsector through strict control over plant maintenance, optimization of operating margins with the aim of satisfying peak-hour demand, and the promotion of joint generation

. The energy sector's efficient integration into the whole productive system by using technological processes and purchasing equipment and materials, preferably locally, that would rationalize energy requirements, including those of the energy sector

. Efficient participation in foreign trade by maintaining hydrocarbon exploitation at a level conducive to the country's orderly development (Export policy should assure domestic energy supply and take into account agreements reached with OPEC and other exporters, thus contributing to international crude-market stability.)

. Energy-source diversification, implying an economic and social evaluation of the various options; their raw material input; capital intensity; technological complexity; and sources of strategic input, components, and spare parts

. The increased productivity, efficiency, and self-financing capacity of the energy companies through a disciplined budget, the elimination of nonproductive expenditures, and the creation of only those jobs strictly necessary to operate the new plants (The energy companies' financial recovery should be based on a combination of the newly established prices and productivity so that the sector can gradually generate sufficient resources to finance its own expansion.)

- The promotion of technological development and the training of personnel with pure and applied research in priority fields and through collaboration agreements between the energy sector companies, energy consumer industries, and equipment suppliers in order to reduce the technological gap between Mexico and the industrialized nations

GUIDELINES FOR THE PROGRAMA NACIONAL DE ENERGETICOS, 1984-1988

SEMIP, in coordination with the representatives of the energy companies and the ministries of state dealing with energy problems, undertook the elaboration of the national energy program, PNE 1984-1988, according to the economic and social policy contained in the national development plan, PND.[5] The program was formally approved by the president and published in mid-August 1984. It placed special emphasis on the three fundamental points of energy strategy stressed by the current administration: productivity, energy saving, and diversification.

The productive strategy was designed to eliminate the lack of coordination and the bottlenecks in the energy sector that had worsened considerably from 1978 to 1981 when the oil industry--and Mexico's economy as a whole--expanded so rapidly. The strategy was aimed at taking maximum advantage of existing production capacity and the energy sector's backup infrastructure. It also looked to solve specific problems related to flared associated gas, the recovery of gas liquids, the low quality of some petroleum products, inadequate facility maintenance, and operational problems caused indirectly by the delay in adjusting end-consumer energy tariffs and the intervention of the trade unions in energy company management.

These measures are clearly related to general economic reorganization criteria, such as restrained expenditure and budgetary restraints together with a smaller investment than previously required (although large enough to still allow an increase in the energy sector's productivity). The political measures taken in this area were based on the assumption that in the short term it is possible to save from 7 to 9 percent on the energy-consumption forecast for 1988 with an effective pricing policy for transferring energy within the energy sector itself and to the external users through a series of technical, financial, and publicity measures. It was also assumed that with the imposition of norms in the energy sector and in the state-owned industry, it will be possible to achieve these results and at the same time help stimulate the rest of the economy.

The energy-diversification strategy directed mainly at the electricity subsector proposes gradually substituting thermoelectric plants for those using uranium, coal, and hydraulic and geothermal energy and establishing criteria for selecting energy sources other than oil. The purpose of diversification is essentially to eliminate the pressure on nonrenewable resources; to begin an orderly transition to alternative sources; and to achieve a balanced use of energy forms, taking all available sources into consideration.

THE ENERGY SECTOR'S EVOLUTION AND CURRENT SITUATION

The 1984-1988 program was the first in Mexico to provide a panorama of the world's energy development. It gave special attention to the behavior of the international hydrocarbon market and the tendency by industrialized countries to reduce their dependence on hydrocarbons through energy saving, diversification of energy sources, and fuel substitution. The prospects and trends for world energy for the year 2000, including the risks and uncertainties that will probably affect the national energy sector in its international relations, were also listed in the program.

Also contained in this section of the program was a description of the energy sector's progress since 1970. The view of the industry's technological and administrative capacity, its physical infrastructure, and potential energy resources known to date is somewhat idealistic. Brief mention is made of the most outstanding anomalies related to high energy consumption, Mexico's heavy hydrocarbon dependence, the disorganization and bottlenecks in the electricity subsector, and the unsatisfactory coordination with the capital goods industry and other suppliers. The program also acknowledges the harmful effects the oil industry has had on the environment and on regional social organization.

The analysis maintains that should the behavior observed during the past years continue, domestic energy consumption for the year 2000 would be 3.3 times higher than in 1983, resulting from an annual average growth in energy demand between 6 and 7 percent and an income elasticity of consumption between 1.3 and 1.5. Under these circumstances hydrocarbon dependence would remain the same as it is currently, that is, 93 percent because an additional 0.5 MBD of fuel oil would be required just to feed the conventional thermoelectric plants.

Because the analysis was kept at a general qualitative level, it did not go into sufficient depth about the structural and circumstantial factors affecting the levels of consumption recorded during 1978-1982. Also, assumptions regarding consumption structure and the opportunities and potential for energy saving, which were used as the basis for both strategies and action guidelines, were inadequately formulated. The program gave very little attention to the economic, technical, administrative, and institutional factors influencing the level of consumption, which only recently have aroused the interest of academic circles and those responsible for energy-policy design and implementation. The analysis does not give sufficient details on the financial and budgetary constraints imposed on the electricity industry, which were a determining factor in the limited availability of generating plants, nor does it explain the reasons why the energy-source diversification strategy introduced early in the 1970s was abandoned. One reason why little detail on these subjects is given is that the political problems and interests within the energy sector, which are beyond the program's scope, would have to be dealt with.

PNE considers that with its energy-saving strategy Mexico could save energy at a rate of 18-22 percent by the year 2000 based on a growth pattern using traditional figures. This saving would be equivalent

In absolute terms to the calorific power of the oil produced for domestic consumption in 1983, that is, 1.3 MBD. PNE maintains that with the proposed strategy Mexico's current hydrocarbon dependence could be reduced from 93 percent of domestic primary energy consumption to 68-73 percent by the year 2000. By this time conventional thermoelectric plants would also have reduced their contribution to power generation from 65 percent to 42-47 percent. The expected contribution of nonconventional alternative energy sources to total energy supply by the end of the century is around 5 percent. PNE's target for energy saving is 7-9 percent of total consumption, an estimate based on historical trends.

The diversification strategy in the electricity subsector would reduce the participation of hydrocarbon-based plants from 61.4 percent in 1983 to 59 percent in 1988. The expected growth in production for the electricity subsector ranges from 28 to 32 percent, measured in GWh sold per employee in this subsector. Overall thermal efficiency is expected to increase from 30.5 percent to over 31 percent. No increases are planned for oil production. The ceiling for hydrocarbon exports was confirmed at 1.5 MBD for crude, and there were indications that after 1985 large volumes of gasoline and diesel would be available for export, which was indeed the case in 1986 (100 TBD).

The targets set in the 1984-1988 program include neither those for energy production for the year 2000 nor those for hydrocarbon production for 1988. Also, the document admits that no reliable indicators exist at present on which to base calculations for the electricity subsector. No productivity criteria are given on which to base qualitative and structural changes required by the energy sector to cope effectively with future challenges, particularly those associated with designing and building electricity facilities not dependent on hydrocarbons.

The 7-9 percent energy-saving goal for 1988 is not based on specific estimates of savings for each of the different consumer sectors, nor is it known to what extent specific political measures would contribute to this target. In other words, the individual contribution to energy saving of each of the various measures--financial austerity and rationalized expenditure, lower economic growth, pricing policy, obligatory policies for energy companies, and programs introduced in the private and social sectors--is unknown.

The proposed strategy and the action guidelines for promoting energy diversification are congruent and contain a view of long-term possibilities. However, the diversification strategy still lacks sufficient information on the probable evolution of the consumer sectors and the patterns of energy demand, and it appears that very little is known about alternative energy resources or the costs involved with each. With the scant amount of detailed information on energy supply and demand, it is not surprising that the PNE diversification strategy for 1984-1988 only refers to the convenience of energy diversification, some of its limiting factors, and the range of possibilities available to the country in the long term. The program does not venture to point out the contribution of each source to global primary energy supply.

Forecasts state that for the year 2000 Mexico's hydrocarbon dependence will decrease from 93 percent of total primary energy to 68-73 percent, implying a reduction in petroleum product consumption of 50-57 percent based on historical trends extrapolated to the year 2000. However, the program proposes only a 1-2 percent reduction in hydrocarbon dependence for 1988; the colossal technological and industrial challenge of establishing the many nonconventional electric plants needed will be undertaken during the remaining twelve years of the century.

Additionally, with the contribution of alternative nonconventional energy sources to global primary energy supply estimated at 5 percent for the year 2000, the lack of coordination between short-term and long-term efforts is evident. For example, for 1988 no production targets for nonconventional energy have been set, but by the year 2000 these sources are supposed to be able to generate between 450 and 500 TBDCE. This goal implies that the energy supply from these sources has to grow 13.2 percent annually from 1984 onward.[6]

The diversification strategy's first stage involves only limited effort in diversifying primary energy sources for generating electricity. Therefore, in 1988 thermoelectric facilities fed with fuel oil will still provide 54 percent of the capacity of the country's electricity plants. These calculations do not take into account possible delays in planned coal-burning, geothermal, and nuclear project schedules, even though in the past there has always been a high incidence of unforeseen technical and operational problems involved in setting up this type of project.

REFLECTIONS ON MEXICO'S ENERGY STRATEGY FOR 1985-2000

A review of the strategic aspects of PNE brings to light two major contradictions; one concerns the strategy's time schedule and the other the almost unavoidable clash between its different objectives. During the first stage, from 1984 to 1988, efforts will be directed toward eliminating the major bottlenecks that adversely affect operational efficiency in the sector and establishing appropriate prices and tariffs. Among other things it is hoped that the level of idle or wasted resources can be reduced and that better use can be made of investment in order to free financial resources for the state's other productive and social priorities.

In the second stage, from 1989 to 2000, it is assumed that the technical and financial adjustments made during the current administration in the sector's operations and in the different consumer groups will have laid the foundation for the application of intensified adjustment measures and the undertaking of the investment needed to achieve energy-saving and -diversification objectives and contribute to the country's economic and social development. The measures taken during this stage will probably encounter fewer financial restrictions, and international market conditions will probably be favorable for Mexican hydrocarbon exports during the 1990s.

Although PNE insists on the need to carry out long-term energy planning, that is, to the year 2000, current targets and courses of action are based on the country's immediate need to consolidate and rationalize operations in the energy sector and not on the intermediate targets that would still have to be fulfilled before long-term objectives could ever be contemplated. This statement is supported by the following:

- Energy-diversification strategy will not be implemented until after PNE 1984-1988 term has been completed.

- Despite the fact that by the year 2000 nonconventional alternative energy sources, such as biomass, solar energy, and mycrohydroelectricity, will supposedly be providing 5 percent of the primary energy needed for domestic consumption, PNE does not specify any targets in this respect for 1988, nor does it mention any concrete action to be taken from 1984 to 1988.

As the PNE strategic approach stands, it seems that the aims to increase productivity, rationalize expenditure, and promote energy saving do, in fact, converge and complement each other to a certain extent. This fact is evident in the pricing and tariff guidelines, which were designed to improve the financial situation of the sector's companies and stimulate rational use of energy. The program also intends to elicit specific productivity commitments from the energy companies so that operating inefficiency will not be passed on to consumers through price increases.

The diversification strategy clashes with the state's earlier economic reorganization program in that the technical and economic stance of PNE, its short-term approach, and the priority given to profitability, budgetary restraint, and the limited use of foreign exchange tend to support the program for conventional thermoelectric plants. Furthermore, a relative abundance of hydrocarbons, lower investment costs, and fewer restrictions on plant location are added incentives to build this type of facility. However, the implementation of a diversification strategy implies higher costs in technical infrastructure and manpower, higher initial investment, and longer lead times.

In the case of coal-burning electricity plants short-term prospecting and exploration programs would have to be stepped up, or the country would have to resort to imports and, consequently, use up its foreign exchange. The short-term nuclear alternative still implies considerable imports of costly capital goods, large sums would have to be spent on uranium prospecting, and the nuclear industry's as-yet weak scientific and technological infrastructure would have to be reinforced.

Rational use of finances, cutbacks in expenditure, and increased technical and economic productivity appear to contradict the energy sector's social objectives. One objective is to extend the electricity grid to rural areas and install between 12,000 and 13,000 kilometers of new power lines between 1985 and 1988, thus extending the service to 10 million additional inhabitants. The enormous initial investment and the low return on investment this service would generate would seriously affect the electricity industry's finances. Moreover, the rural electricity program is congruent with efforts to promote the development of technology designed to satisfy the energy needs of rural communities with local resources and with a much lower investment than that needed to put up electric power lines.

The national energy program does not mention specific programs and, therefore, does not state the financial requirements involved in each. In other words, as with many other planning exercises in Mexico, past and present, rather than a plan of action PNE is a large catalog of problems, good intentions, and possible solutions. However, it is not the author's intention to detract from an exercise that takes the whole energy sector into consideration and that acknowledges that any attempt at planning for just one six-year term makes little sense.

INTERNAL AND EXTERNAL FACTORS RESTRICTING THE IMPLEMENTATION OF THE PROGRAMA NACIONAL DE ENERGETICOS

Although PNE was elaborated with the aid of suggestions, proposals, and points of view of different interest groups, certain doubts still exist about the practical viability of the program. Those implementing the program have had to deal with complacency, vested interests, and bureaucratic criteria that tend to give individual interpretations to new policies and can even result in the refusal to apply these policies.

Some of the structural changes currently needed by the energy sector and included in PNE were actually part of a previous planning experience but were left to one side when the politics and the policies changed hands. Even now there is still the risk that even the best intentions might be waylaid or simply ignored in the event of new political and economic circumstances. The section on PNE's implementation is very general, and although it specifies a series of administrative and institutional measures for carrying the program out and evaluating its results, it does not provide the criteria for making the necessary adjustment should unforeseen circumstances arise.

Like other government programs (or perhaps even more so), PNE faces a series of constraints and uncertainties, some general and some specific to the energy sector. International hydrocarbon market instability, changes in international interest rates, the protectionist tendencies of industrialized economies, and the serious doubts about Mexico's ability to diversify its exports are variables that could seriously affect PNE's success. Should there be a further drop in international crude prices, the continuity of investment projects could be affected, as could the income PEMEX needs to finance its own expansion. Mexico's economic policy has suffered many modifications since 1970 for many reasons. Therefore, if the economy were to remain stagnant for too long, it would not be surprising if the State, under both social and political pressure, be forced again to adopt an expansionist policy, which would bring about changes in the distribution of financial resources and energy-price freezes.

The energy sector's bureaucratic and institutional barriers, their causes, and possible solution have received very little attention and, therefore, are not properly understood. Of particular importance are those problems stemming from inadequate information and communication, unreliable indicators about the efficiency and productivity of public companies in the energy sector, the imbalance of power between SEMIP and the two major energy enterprises, the coordination of institutional efforts, and the operational restraints arising from worker contracts and certain trade union practices.

Serious problems still persist when applying policy, particularly when the points of view and the interests of planners do not coincide with those of the individuals carrying out the policy. This situation is complicated even further by the presence of certain power groups determined to hinder or even sabotage those measures that threaten to undermine their power or interfere with their interests. Very few incentives exist for motivating self-improvement in unionized technical personnel because their promotion depends on years of service in the company or union militancy. Additional problems arise when organizing complex projects requiring coordination between specialized teams and greater interinstitutional collaboration.

The six-year government cycles with their consequent administrative changes create serious limitations for all three phases of the energy-planning process, that is, formulation, implementation, and control. Although energy policy is reformulated at least every six years, its basic principles have not changed significantly for some time. This situation exists in part because at the beginning of every government term the high posts are assumed by people with limited experience in the field they come to be responsible of. Moreover existing basic studies or research are seldom examined by the incoming administration, although they could provide ample key information on energy sector conditions during the previous term.

The recent history of the Mexican economy and public administration shows continual six-year economic cycles. The last year of the outgoing administration and the first year of the new one are characterized by a period of economic recession; this situation is mainly the result of three factors: First, public investment tends to fall toward the last year of the administration: No new projects are authorized, and resources are assigned only to works and projects that can be completed and inaugurated that same year. Other ongoing projects are postponed or continued at a very slow rate.

Second, private contractors and industries supplying the energy sector have reacted similarly because of (1) administrative disorganization during the last few months of the concluding term and the first year or two of the next, causing indefinite delays in payments to suppliers and considerable worry, and (2) the waiting period used by industrialists and investors during the government changeover to make sure the rules of the game in this mixed economy are not going to change with the new administration.

Third, the last three six-year cycles have ended in crisis, the first with the 1968-1970 political crisis, the second with a serious economic crisis and a confrontation between the federal executive and the major business groups in 1975-1976, and the last in 1981-1982 with the worst economic crisis in the country's postwar history and a generalized loss of confidence in government institutions and the existing political system. Although these crises were influenced partially by the prevailing international situation, they were made worse by persistently inadequate economic policy.

The process of presidential succession, which begins during the fifth year of each six-year term, causes previously formed alliances between different groups to break off as each vies for power. Public officials in high posts dedicate their time to maintaining a political image that coincides with that of the president still in power while forming new political and economic alliances that will allow them to participate one way or another in the incoming administration.

In such a political climate the implementation and continuity of existing programs has very little importance. While presidential succession is still undecided, adjustments to government policy that might appear to question the rate and style of the current executive are avoided. All projects extending beyond the six-year cycle are postponed, and everyone assumes a cautious noninnovative approach. With the administrative changeover a kind of musical chairs occurs between the high officials, who seldom take up policies where their predecessors left off. The real results of the previous administration have little to do with the granting of important posts in the new government, dealing rather with political affiliations and work related to the efforts of the president-elect. Clearly, these political practices make the economic and social planning process in Mexico very cumbersome.

NOTES

1. On 11 October 1981 PRI announced Miguel de la Madrid's presidential candidacy. The new government's basic principles would be the following: (1) revolutionary nationalism; (2) integrated democracy; (3) an equal society; (4) moral renovation; (5) decentralization; (6) development, employment, and reduced inflation; and (7) democratic planning.
2. De la Madrid Hurtado, Miguel, Nacionalismo revolucionario: Siete tesis fundamentales de campaña, Mexico City, PRI, 1982, pp. 48-58.
3. PIRE established the following ten points: (1) reduced growth in public expenditure; (2) job conservation; (3) investment only in priority areas; (4) reinforced standards of discipline, adequate programming, efficiency, and scrupulous honesty in administering authorized public expenditure; (5) protection and encouragement for production, importing, and distribution programs for basic foodstuffs for human consumption; (6) increased public income to slow excessive growth in the deficit and the consequent disproportionate increase in the public debt (this would mean tax reform and an increase in the price of goods and services produced by the public sector); (7) the channeling of credit into national development priorities; (8) restored government control over the exchange market; (9) the restructuring of public administration to make it efficient and effective; and (10) action according to the principle of state guidance and under the mixed economic regime defined in the general constitution speech. BANAMEX, Examen de la situación económica de México, Vol. 63, No. 685, Mexico City, BANAMEX, December 1982, pp. 597-600.
4. Poder Ejecutivo Federal, Plan nacional de desarrollo, 1983-1988, Mexico City, SPP, May 1983.

5. Poder Ejecutivo Federal, <u>Programa nacional de energéticos, 1984-1988</u>, Mexico City, SEMIP, August 1984.

6. Calculations were made by Dr. Manuel Martinez of the UNAM Material Testing Institute and presented at the meeting organized by the Centro Tepoztlán, A.C., in "Perspectivas del Programa Nacional de Energéticos 1984-1988" (mimeograph), Tepoztlán, Morelos, Mexico, August 1984.

Abbreviations and Units of Measurement

Acronyms and abbreviations

AAGR	average annual growth rate
AHMSA	Altos Hornos de México, S.A. (Blast Furnaces of Mexico)
ANIQ	Asociación Nacional de la Industria Química, A.C. (National Association of Chemical Industry)
BANAMEX	Banco Nacional de Mexico, S.A. (National Bank of Mexico)
BWR	boiling-water reactor
CANACINTRA	Cámara Nacional de la Industria de la Transformación (National Chamber for the Transformation Industry)
CARBOMEX	Carbón de México, S.A. (Mexican Coal Company)
CEC	Centro de Estudios Carboníferos (Center for Coal Studies)
CEMEX	Cenizas de México, S.A. de C.V. (Mexican Ash Company)
CFE	Comisión Federal de Electricidad (Federal Electricity Commission)
CFM	Comisión de Fomento Minero (Commission for the Promotion of Mining)
CIDE	Centro de Investigación y Docencia Económica (Center for Economic Research and Teaching)
CLFC	Compañía de Luz y Fuerza del Centro Central Light and Power Company)
CNC	Confederación Nacional Campesina (National Paysan-Farmers Confederation)
CNE	Comisión Nacional de Energéticos (National Energy Commission)
CNEA	Comisión Nacional de Energía Atómica (National Atomic Energy Commisslon

CNEN	Comisión Nacional de Energía Nuclear (National Nuclear Energy Commission)
CNSNS	Comisión Nacional de Seguridad Nuclear y Salvaguardas (Nation Commission for Nuclear Safety and
COMAVAL	Comisión de Avalúos de Bienes Nacionales (Commissión for the Appraisal of National Property)
CONACYT	Consejo Nacional de Ciencia y Tecnología (National Council for Science and Technology)
COPARMEX	Confederación Patronal de la República Mexicana (Employers' Confederation of the Mexican Republic)
CRM	Consejo de Recursos Minerales (Council for Mineral Resources)
CTM	Confederación de Trabajadores de México (Mexican Workers' Confederation)
CUF	Comité de Unificación de Frecuencias (Committee for the Unification of Frequencies)
DEH	derecho de explotación de hidrocarburos (tariff on hydrocarbon exploitation)
DGDE	Dirección General de Documentación y Evaluación (General Department of Documentation and Evaluation)
FERTIMEX	Fertilizantes Mexicanos, S.A. (Mexican Fertilizers)
FMMNM	Fondo Mexicano de Minerales no Metálicos (Mexican Trusteeship for Nonmetalic Minerals)
GATT	Acuerdo General sobre Aranceles Aduaneros y Comercio (General Agreement on Tariffs and Trade)
GDP	gross domestic product (producto interno bruto)

GNP	gross national product (producto nacional bruto)
IDB	Banco Interamericano de Desarrollo (Inter-American Development Bank)
IEPES	Instituto de Estudios Políticos, Económicos y Sociales (Institute for Political, Economic, and Social Studies)
IEPS	Impuesto especial sobre producción y servicios (special tax on production and services)
IIE	Instituto de Investigaciones Eléctricas (Institute for Electric Research)
IMF	Fondo Monetario Internacional (International Monetary Fund)
IMIQ	Instituto Mexicano de Ingenieros Químicos (Mexican Institute of Chemical Engineers)
IMIT	Instituto Mexicano de Investigaciones Tecnológicas (Mexican Technological Research Institute)
IMP	Instituto Mexicano del Petróleo (Mexican Petroleum Institute)
INEN	Instituto Nacional de Energía Nuclear) (National Nuclear Energy Institute)
INFONAVIT	Instituto del Fondo Nacional de la Vivienda para los Trabajadores (Institute of the National Fund for Workers' Housing)
INFOTEC	Fideicomiso de Información Técnica a la Industria (Technical Information Trusteeship for Industry)
ININ	Instituto Nacional de Investigaciones Nucleares (National Nuclear Research Institute)
IPN-ESIA	Instituto Politécnico Nacional-Escuela Superior de Investigaciones Avanzadas (National Politechnical Institute-School for Advanced Research)

IVA	impuesto al valor agregado (value-added tax)
LAEO	Organización Latinoamericana de Energía (Latin American Energy Organization)
LWR	light-water reactor
MICARE	Minera Carbonífera de Río Escondido (Río Escondido Mineral Coal)
NAFINSA	Nacional Financiera, S.A. (National Finance Bank)
NRC	U.S. Nuclear Regulatory Commission
OECD	Organización para la Cooperación y el Desarrollo Económicos (Organization for Economic Cooperation and Development)
ONUDI	Organización de las Naciones Unidas para el Desarrollo Industrial (United Nations Industrial Development Organization; UNIDO)
OPEC	Organización de Países Exportadores de Petróleo (Organization of Petroleum-Exporting Countries)
PDSE 1977-1986	Programa de Desarrollo del Sector Eléctrico 1977-1986 (Electricity Sector Development Program 1977-1986)
PE 1980-1982	Programa de Energía 1980-1982 (Energy Program 1980-1982)
PEMEX	Petróleos Mexicanos (Mexican Petroleum Company)
PESE 2000	Plan de Expansión del Sector Eléctrico al año 2000 (Expansion Plan for the Electricity Sector to the Year 2000)
PGD 1980-1982	Plan Global de Desarrollo 1980-1982 (Global Development Plan 1980-1982)
PIRE	Programa Inmediato de Reordenación Económica (Immediate Program for Economic Reorganization)
PND 1983-1988	Plan Nacional de Desarrollo 1983-1988 (National Development Plan 1983-1988)

PNDC	Plan Nacional de Desarrollo Carbonífero (National Plan for Coal Development)
PNDI 1979-1982	Plan Nacional de Desarrollo Industrial 1979-1982 (National Plan for Industrial Development 1979-1982)
PNDU	Plan Nacional de Desarrollo Urbano (National Plan for Urban Development)
PNE	Programa Nacional de Energéticos 1984-1988 (National Energy Program 1984-1988)
PNEC	Programa Nacional de Exploración de Carbón (National Program for Coal Exploration
PNN	Programa Nucleoeléctrico Nacional (National Nuclear Electricity Program)
POISE	Programa de Obras e Inversión del Sector Eléctrico (Program of Works and Investment for the Electricity Sector)
PRI	Partido Revolucionario Institucional (Institutional Revolutionary Party)
PROFIEX	Programa de Fomento Integral a las Exportaciones (Program for the Integrated Promotion of Exports)
PRONDETYC	Programa Nacional de Desarrollo Tecnológico y Científico (National Program for Technological and Scientific Development)
R&D	research and development
R/P	reserve-production
RNTT	Registro Nacional de Transferencia de Tecnología (National Register for Technology Transfer)
SAM	Sistema Alimentario Mexicano (Mexican Alimentary System)
SARH	Secretaría de Agricultura y Recursos Hidráulicos (Ministry of Agriculture and Hydraulic Resources)

SCT	Secretaría de Comunicaciones y Transportes (Ministry of Communications and Transport)
SECOFI	Secretaría de Comercio y Fomento Industrial (Ministry of Commerce and Industrial Promotion)
SEDUE	Secretaría de Desarrollo Urbano y Ecología (Ministry of Urban Development and Ecology)
SEMIP	Secretaría de Energía, Minas e Industria Paraestatal (Ministry of Energy, Mines, and State-Owned Industry)
SEN	Sistema Eléctrico Nacional (National Electricity System)
SEPAFIN	Secretaría de Patrimonio y Fomento Industrial (Ministry for National Patrimony and Industrial Promotion)
SEPANAL	Secretaría del Patrimonio Nacional (Ministry for National Patrimony)
SHCP	Secretaría de Hacienda y Crédito Público (Ministry of Finance)
SIC	Secretaría de Industria y Comercio (Ministry for Industry and Commerce)
SICARTSA	Siderúrgica Lázaro Cárdenas-Las Truchas (Lazaro Cardenas-Las Truchas Iron and Steel Company)
SIDERMEX	Siderúrgica Mexicana (Mexican Iron and Steel Company)
SIN	Sistema Interconectado del Norte (Northern Interconnected System)
SIRDO	Sistema Integral de Reciclaje de Desechos Sólidos (Integrated System for Recycling Solid Wastes)
SIS	Sistema Interconectado del Sur (Southern Interconnected System)

SPP	Secretaría de Programación y Presupuesto (Ministry for Programming and Budget)
SRA	Secretaría de la Reforma Agraria (Ministry for the Agrarian Reform)
STCE	Secretariado Técnico de la Comisión de Energéticos (Technical Secretariat for the Energy Commission)
STPRM	Sindicato de Trabajadores Petroleros de la República Mexicana (Mexican Oil Workers' Trade Union)
SUTERM	Sindicato Unico de Trabajadores Electricistas de la República Mexicana (Mexican Electricity Workers' Trade Union)
SUTIN	Sindicato Unico de Trabajadores de la Industria Nuclear (Nuclear Industry Workers' Trade Union)
UNAM	Universidad Nacional Autónoma de México (Autonomous National University of Mexico)
UNO	Organización de las Naciones Unidas (United Nations Organization)
URAMEX	Uranios Mexicanos (Mexican Uranium Company)

Units of Measurement

BB	billions of barrels
BBCE	billions of barrels of crude oil equivalent
BBD	billions of barrels per day
BBDCE	billions of barrels per day of crude oil equivalent
BCF	billions of cubic feet
BCFD	billions of cubic feet per day
BD	barrels per day
BTU	British thermal unit
Cal	calories
CF	cubic feet
cm^2	centimeter squared
GWh	gigawatt-hours

HP	horsepower
Kcal	kilocalories
Kg	kilograms
Km	kilometers
Km/l	kilometers per liter
KW	kilowatts
KWh	kilowatt-hours
l	liters
m	meters
m^3	cubic meters
MB	millions of barrels
MBCE	millions of barrels of crude oil equivalent
MBD	millions of barrels per day
MBDCE	millions of barrels per day of crude oil equivalent
MCF	millions of cubic feet
MCFD	millions of cubic feet per day
m/s	meters per second
MW	megawatts
TB	thousands of barrels
TBD	thousands of barrels per day
TBDCE	thousands of barrels per day of crude oil equivalent
TCF	thousands of cubic feet
TCFD	thousands of cubic feet per day
TJ	terajoules
Tm^3	thousands of cubic meters
TTDW	thousands of tons of dead weight
TW	terawatts
TWh	terawatt-hours
U.S. $	U.S. dollars

Bibliography

Official documents

Banco de México, S.A.,
- 1977   *Estadísticas de cuentas de producción*, Mexico City, 1977.
- 1980   *Producto interno bruto y gasto, 1970-1979*, Mexico City, 1980.
- *Indicadores Económicos*, Mexico City, various years.

Banco Nacional de México, S.A.
- 1982   *Examen de la situación económica de México*, Mexico City, February-September and December 1982.

Comisión Federal de Electricidad
- 1977   *La evolución del sector eléctrico de México*, Mexico City, 1977.
- 1979   *Plan nacional de electrificación rural*, Mexico City, 1979.
- 1981   *Programa nucleoeléctrico nacional*, Mexico City, 1981.
- *Instalación del programa nucleoeléctrico*, Mexico City, June 1981.
- *Programa de obras e inversión del sector eléctrico*, Mexico City, July 1981.

Consejo Nacional de Ciencia y Tecnología
- 1976   *Plan nacional indicativo de ciencia y tecnología*, Mexico City, 1976.

Instituto de Investigaciones Eléctricas
- 1982   *Diagnóstico y pronóstico sobre fuentes de energía en México*, Vol. 1, Mexico City, October 1982.

Instituto Mexicano del Petróleo
- 1976   *Plan de desarrollo de la industria petrolera y petroquímica básica, 1975-1986*, Mexico City, 1976.
- 1977-1982   *Informe de actividades*, Mexico City, data obtained for the years 1977 to 1982.

Latin American Energy Organization
- 1981   *Balances energéticos de América Latina*, Quito, Ecuador, 1981.

Nacional Financiera, S.A.
- 1980-   *La economía mexicana en cifras*, Mexico

1984 City, data obtained for the years 1980 to 1984.

Nacional Financiera, S.A., and United Nations Organization for Industrial Development

1978 "La oferta nacional de bienes de capital," in <u>Monografías sectoriales de bienes de capital</u>, No. 1, Mexico City, 1978.

1979 "La demanda de bienes de capital para las industrias petroleras y petroquímicas básicas de México," in <u>Monografías sectoriales de bienes de capital</u>, No. 5, Mexico City, 1979.

Oficina de Asesores de la Presidencia

1980 <u>Ultima versión sobre la plataforma de producción y exportación</u>, internal document (mimeograph), Mexico City, 1980.

Organization for Economic Cooperation and Development

1979 <u>Transfer of Technology in the World Petrochemical Industry</u>, Sectorial Study No. 1, Paris, 1979.

1984 <u>Energy Policies and Programmes of IEA Countries</u>, Paris, 1984.

Partido Revolucionario Institucional, Instituto de Estudios Políticos, Económicos y Sociales

1981 <u>Plan básico, 1982-1988, y plataforma electoral</u>, Mexico City, October 1981.

1981 <u>Memoria: Gira de prioridades nacionales. Desarrollo regional en zonas petroleras</u>, Ciudad Madero, Tamaulipas, Mexico, December 1981.

1982 <u>Reunión popular para la planeación. Tema: "Energéticos y desarrollo nacional,"</u> 10 months work, Mexico City, Subdirección de Coordinación Regional, May 1982.

Petróleos Mexicanos

1965-1984 <u>Memoria de labores</u>, Mexico City, data obtained for the years 1965 to 1984.

1971-1984 <u>Informe del director general de Petróleos Mexicanos</u>, Mexico City, data obtained for the years 1971 to 1984.

1977 <u>Programa sexenal de Petróleos Mexicanos</u>, Mexico City, 1977.

1977-1983 <u>Anuario estadístico</u>, Mexico City, data obtained for the years 1977-1983.

1983   Plan nacional de desarrollo, 1983-1988: Aspectos principales e implicaciones para el sector petrolero, Mexico City, 1983.
1984   Aspectos relevantes del "Plan 1984-1988," Mexico City, 1984.
1984   Balance de energía de 1982 a 1983, (summary; mimeograph), Mexico City, 1984.
1985   Presentación al C. Presidente de la República, Lic. Miguel de la Madrid, de los avances y perspectivas de Petróleos Mexicanos en los primeros dos años de su administración, Mexico City, 1985.

Poder Ejecutivo Federal
1983   Plan global de desarrollo, 1983-1988, Mexico City, Secretaría de Programación y Presupuesto, May 1983.
1984   Iniciativa de ley reglamentaria del artículo 27 constitucional en materia nuclear, Mexico City, November 1984.
Programa nacional de ecología, 1984-1988, Mexico City, Secretaría de Desarrollo Urbano y Ecología, 1984.
Programa nacional de energéticos, 1984-1988, Mexico City, Subsecretaría de Energía, 1984.

Ronfeldt, David, et al.
1980   Mexico's Petroleum and U.S. Policy: Implications for the 1980s, document prepared for the U.S. Energy Department, R-2510-DOE, Santa Monica, Calif., The Rand Corporation, 1980.

Secretaría de Agricultura y Recursos Hidráulicos
1981   Plan nacional hidráulico, Mexico City, March 1981.

Secretaría de Energía, Minas e Industria Paraestatal
1983   Foro de consulta popular sobre energéticos y minería, Síntesis (conclusions and recommendations), Mexico City, February 1983.
Diagnóstico sobre fuentes alternas de energía (mimeograph), Mexico City, Dirección General de Investigación y Desarrollo, June 1983.
La energía en México y en el mundo, Cuernavaca, Morelos, Mexico, November 11, 1983.

Secretaría de la Economía Nacional
    1939   Boletín de petróleo y minas, Mexico City, January 1939.

Secretaría de la Presidencia
    1972   Medio ambiente humano, col. Cuadernos de Documentación, series Estudios, No. 1, 2d. ed., Mexico City, 1972.
    1973   "Comisión de energéticos," in Carta de México, No. 26, Mexico City, April 30, 1973.
    1974   "Reunión de la comisión de energéticos," in Carta de México (offprint), No. 18, Mexico City, January 8, 1974.

Secretaría de la Presidencia,
Secretaría de Hacienda y Crédito Público,
Petróleos Mexicanos, and
Comisión Federal de Electricidad
    1971   Dictamen sobre el proyecto nucleoeléctrico de la Comisión Federal de Electricidad, Mexico City, February 11, 1971.

Secretaría de Patrimonio y Fomento Industrial
    1978   Propuesta de lineamientos de política energética, Mexico City, August 1978.
    1979   Plan nacional de desarrollo industrial, 1979-1982, Mexico City, 1979.
    1980   Programa de energía, metas a 1990 y proyecciones al año 2000 (resumen y conclusiones), Mexico City, 1980.

Secretaría de Patrimonio y Fomento Industrial,
Instituto Nacional de Investigaciones Nucleares, and
Comisión Federal de Electricidad
    1980   Informe sobre los estudios de factibilidad del programa nucleoeléctrico nacional, Mexico City, September-October, 1980.

Secretaría de Patrimonio y Fomento Industrial and
Secretaría de Programación y Presupuesto
    1981   Escenarios económicos de México: Perspectivas de desarrollo para ramas seleccionadas, 1981-1985, Mexico City, Secretaría de Programación y Presupuesto, 1981.

Secretaría de Programación y Presupuesto
    1980   Plan global de desarrollo, 1980-1982, Mexico City, 1980.
    1981   Escenarios económicos, Mexico City, 1981.

Informe de avance del plan global de desarrollo, 1980-1982, Mexico City, 1981.
n.d. Diagnóstico de Petróleos Mexicanos, Mexico City, no date.
Secretaría de Programación y Presupuesto and Petróleos Mexicanos
1980- La industria petrolera en México, Mexico
1983 City, SPP, Dirección General de Integración y Análisis de la Información, data obtained for the years 1980 to 1983.
Secretaría de Programación y Presupuesto, Secretaría de Patrimonio y Fomento Industrial, Petróleos Mexicanos, and Fertilizantes Mexicanos
1981 Industria petroquímica: Análisis y expectativas, Mexico City, 1981.
United Nations Organization. Preparatory Comittee for
1981 the United Nations Conference on New and Renewable Energy Sources, third period of sessions from March 20 to April 17, 1981 (Summary of Technical Group Reports), New Delhi, 1981.
United Nations Organization for Industrial Development and Instituto Mexicano del Petróleo
n.d. Efectos del origen de la ingeniería en el desarrollo de la industria de bienes de capital, Mexico City, no date.
U.S. Congress, Office of Technology Assessment
1984 Nuclear Power in an Age of Uncertainty, OTA-E-216, Washington, D.C., 1984.
U.S. Department of Commerce
1980 Industrial Process Controls: Mexico, CMS-80-120, Washington, D.C., September 1980.

Books

Atlantic Council's Nuclear Fuels Policy Working Group
1976 Nuclear Fuels Policy, Lexington, Mass., Lexington Books, 1976.
Bermúdez, Antonio
1960 Doce años al servicio de la industria petrolera mexicana, 1947-1958, Mexico City, COMAVAL, 1960.

1979 La política petrolera mexicana, Mexico City, Ortiz, 1979.

Bullard, J. Freda
1968 Mexico's Natural Gas, The Beginning of a New Industry, Austin, Tex., The University of Texas, 1968.

Echaniz, Jorge
1958 Petróleo y cuestiones nacionales, Mexico City, Fondo de Cultura Económica, 1958.

Grayson, George
1980 The Politics of Mexican Oil, Pittsburgh, Penn., University of Pittsburgh Press, 1980.

Guzmán, Oscar, and Hugo Altomonte
1982 Perspectivas energéticas y crecimiento económico en Argentina, Mexico City, El Colegio de México, 1982.

Guzmán, Oscar, Antonio Yúnez-Naude, and Miguel S. Wionczek
1985 Uso eficiente y conservación de la energía en México: Diagnóstico y perspectiva, Mexico City, El Colegio de México, Programa de Energéticos, 1985.

Hernández, E.
1979 La distribución de la radiación global en México evaluada mediante la fotointerpretación de la nubosidad observada por satélites meteorológicos, master degree thesis, Mexico City, Universidad Nacional Autónoma de México, Facultad de Ciencias, 1979.

Pellicer, Olga (editor)
1983 La política exterior de México: Desafíos en los ochenta, Mexico City, Centro de Investigación y Docencia Económica, 1983.

Philip, George
1982 Oil and Politics in Latin America, Cambridge, Mass., Harvard, University Press, 1982.

Reynolds, Clark W.
1972 La economía mexicana, su estructura y crecimiento en el siglo XX, Mexico City, Fondo de Cultura Económica, 1972.

Shulgovskii, Anatoli
1977 México en la encrucijada de su historia, Mexico City, Ediciones de Cultura Popular, 1978.

Tello, Carlos
1978 La política económica de México, 1970-1976, Mexico City, Siglo XXI Editores, 1978.

Thompson, Roberto
1984 Estado y explotación petrolera en Chiapas: Marco jurídico y conflictos sociales, 1970-1980, Tuxtla Gutiérrez, Chiapas, Mexico, Centro de Investigaciones Ecológicas del Sureste and Congreso del Estado de Chiapas, 1984.

Willars, Jaime Mario
1984 El petróleo en México: Efectos macroeconómicos, elementos de política y perspectivas, Mexico City, El Colegio de México, 1984.

Wionczek, Miguel S. (editor)
1982 Capacidad tecnológica interna y sector energético en los países en desarrollo, Mexico City, El Colegio de México, 1982.
Energía en México: Ensayos sobre el pasado y el presente, Mexico City, El Colegio de México, 1982.
Mercados mundiales de hidrocarburos: Situación presente, perspectivas y tendencias futuras, Mexico City, El Colegio de México, 1983.
Problemas del sector energético en México, Mexico City, El Colegio de México, 1983.

Wionczek, Miguel S., Gerald Foley, and
Ariane van Buren (editors)
1983 La energía en la transición del sector agrícola de subsistencia, Mexico City, El Colegio de México, 1983.

Wionczek, Miguel S., and Miyokei Shinohara (editors)
1982 Las relaciones económicas entre México y Japón, Mexico City, El Colegio de México, 1982.

Articles

Aburto Avila, José Luis
1982 "Costos y beneficios de la fabricación nacional de mauinaria y equipos para el sector eléctrico," in Instituto de Estudios Políticos, Económicos y Sociales del PRI, Consulta popular para la planeación. Tema: Energéticos y desarrollo nacional, ninth week session, Subdirección de Coordinación Regional, May 25, 1982.

Almanza, Rafael, and Gerardo Hiriart
1978 "Conversión fototérmica de la energía solar a electricidad y a energía mecánica," in Boletín IIE, Vol. 2, No. 6, Mexico City, Instituto de Investigaciones Eléctricas, 1978.

Alonso, Angelina, and Roberto López
1984 "Petróleo, desarrollo regional y cambio social en las zonas petroleras de México a partir de 1970" (mimeograph), paper presented at the Seminar on Energy and Society, Mexico City, Instituto Politécnico Nacional, 1984.

Baños Ramírez, Othón
1984 "Campesinos y petróleo en Tabasco," in Cuadernos del CES, No. 31, Mexico City, El Colegio de México, Centro de Estudios Sociológicos, 1984.

Baptista, César
1977 "Industria petroquímica en México," in IMIQ, Mexico City, Instituto Mexicano de la Industria Química, February 1977.

Bassols Batalla, Angel
1979 "Impacto regional del petróleo en México," in Problemas del Desarrollo, Vol. 10, No. 37, Mexico City, Universidad Nacional Autónoma de México, Instituto de Investigaciones Económicas, 1979.

Berjón Rodríguez, José Luis
1983 "La ingeniería de detalle en México," paper presented at the VII National Congress of the Mexican Society for Economic Engineering and Costs, in La estructura nacional de los costos: Realidad y pers-

pectiva, Mexico City, Sociedad Mexicana de Ingeniería Económica y de Costos, 1983.

Bosch, Pedro
1981 "Evolución de las inversiones químicas y petroquímicas, 1976-1981," in ANIQ, Memorias, XIV Foro Nacional de la Industria Química, Mexico City, Asociación Nacional de la Industria Química, 1981.

Bueno, Gerardo
1981 "Petróleo y planes de desarrollo en México," in Cuadernos sobre Prospectiva Energética, No. 19, Mexico City, El Colegio de México, Programa de Energéticos, 1981.

Castañeda, Miguel, and Roberto Iza
1982 "Plan carboeléctrico nacional" (mimeograph), Mexico City, September 1982.

Castellanos, Alfonso, and Margarita Escobedo
1980 "La energía solar en México: Situación actual y perspectivas" (mimeograph), Mexico City, Centro de Ecodesarrollo, 1980.

Colegio Nacional, El, and
Universidad Nacional Autónoma de México, Programa Universitario de Energía
1982 Planeación energética en México, (mito o realidad? Mexico City, October 1982.

Comisión Federal de Electricidad, Gerencia General de Estudios e Ingeniería Preliminar
1978 "El Programa de Desarrollo del Sector Eléctrico," in Energéticos: Boletín Informativo del Sector Energético, Year 2, No. 3, Mexico City, Comisión de Energéticos, Secretariado Técnico, March 1978.

Consejo Nacional de Ciencia y Tecnología
1980 "Diez años del CONACYT", in Comunidad CONACYT, Year 6, Mexico City, November-December 1980.

Corredor, Jaime
1981 "El significado económico del petróleo en México," in Comercio Exterior, Vol. 31, No. 11, Mexico City, November 1981.

de la Fuente, José Luis
1976 "La ingeniería de proyectos de plantas industriales," in IMIQ, Mexico City, Instituto Mexicano de la Industria Química, November 1976.

de Oteyza, José Andrés
1977 "Programa sexenal de petroquímica," in El Mercado de Valores, Year 37, No. 17, Mexico City, Nacional Financiera, April 25, 1977.

Dovall Jaime, Antonio
1971 "Tendencias de la industria petrolera nacional," in El Mercado de Valores, Year 31, No. 32, Mexico City, Nacional Financiera, August 9, 1971.

Eibenschutz, Juan
1982 "Mexico," in Katz, Everett J., U. Marwah, and A. Onkar, Nuclear Power in Developing Countries, Lexington, Mass., Lexington Books, 1982.

Escobedo Villalón, Gilberto
1982 "Disminución de productos petrolíferos para consumo interno," in IEPES, Reunión popular para la planeación. Tema: Energéticos y desarrollo nacional. Estrategia de expansión de la industria petrolera, Mexico City, PRI, Instituto de Estudios Políticos, Económicos y Sociales, Subdirección de Coordinación Regional, May 1982.

Escofet, Alberto
1981 "El programa nucleoeléctrico mexicano," in Energéticos: Boletín Informativo del Sector Energético, Year 5, No. 12, Mexico City, Comisión de Energéticos, Secretariado Técnico, December 1981.

Farrán Riquelme, Flavio
1980 "Formulación de un programa de investigación sobre pequeñas centrales hidroeléctricas" (mimegraph) Mexico City, Instituto de Investigaciones Eléctricas, November 1980.

1984 "Energía hidráulica para generaciones de electricidad a pequeña escala," paper presented at the Interdisciplinary Forum on Alternative Energy Sources, Mexico City, Instituto Politécnico Nacional and Instituto de Investigaciones Eléctricas, April 2, 1984.

Frias Cerino, José
   1983   "Tabasco, víctima de su propia riqueza," in Revista de Revistas, No. 3815, Mexico City, Excélsior, March 9, 1983.

Galindo, Ignacio
   1979   "Situación actual y perspectivas de la energía solar en México," in Problemas del Desarrollo, Mexico City, Universidad Nacional Autónoma de México, February-April 1979.

García, Brígida
   1984   "Dinámica del empleo rural y urbano en el sureste de México: 1979-1980" (mimeograph), Mexico City, El Colegio de México, Centro de Estudios Demográficos y de Desarrollo Urbano, 1984.

García Luna, José Luis
   1978   "Petroquímica básica," in IMIQ, Mexico City, Instituto Mexicano de la Industria Química, March-April 1978.

Gastelum, Raúl
   1983   "La política de precios internos de productos petroleros en México, 1976-1982," in Wionczek, Miguel S. (editor), Problemas del sector energético en México, Mexico City, El Colegio de México, 1983.

González, Guadalupe
   1982   "Los cambios recientes en el mercado petrolero internacional y sus repercusiones en las relaciones de México con la OPEP," in Carta de Política Exterior Mexicana, Year 2, No. 4, Mexico City, Centro de Investigación y Docencia Económica, July-August 1982.

Gutiérrez, Roberto
   1979   "La balanza petrolera de México, 1970-1982," in Comercio Exterior, Vol. 29, No. 8, Mexico City, Banco Nacional de Comercio Exterior, 1979.
   1981   "Cambios de matiz en la estrategia económica de México: Los años sesenta y ochenta," in Comercio Exterior, Vol. 31, No. 8, Mexico City, Banco Nacional de Comercio Exterior, August 1981.

Guzmán, Oscar
    1982   "Las nuevas fuentes de energía en México. Situación actual y perspectivas," in Cuadernos sobre Prospectiva Energética, No. 30, Mexico City, El Colegio de México, Programa de Energéticos, 1982.
    1983   "Nuevas fuentes energéticas," in Wionczek, Miguel S. (editor), Problemas del sector energético en México, Mexico City, El Colegio de México, 1983.

Inguanzo, Francisco
    1976   "Recursos energéticos de México y programas de exploración," in IMIQ, Mexico City, Instituto Mexicano de la Industria Química, January 1976.

Jacobs, Eduardo, et al.
    1980   "Competencia y concentración: El caso del sector manufacturero," in Economía Mexicana, Mexico City, Centro de Investigación y Docencia Económica, 1980.

Lajous Vargas, Adrián
    1982   "La política a largo plazo de los precios de la energía," in IEPES, Reunión popular para la planeación. Tema: Energía y desarrollo nacional, Mexico City, PRI, Instituto de Estudios Políticos, Económicos y Sociales, 1982.

Lara Sosa, Héctor
    1977   "Plan sexenal de Petróleos Mexicanos en refinación," in IMIQ, Mexico City, Instituto Mexicano de la Industria Química, March-April 1977.

Malo, Salvador
    1983   "Políticas y programs de investigación en petróleo," in Angeles, Luis (editor), El petróleo y sus perspectivas en México, Mexico City, Universidad Nacional Autónoma de México, Programa Universitario Justo Sierra, 1983.

Márquez, Miguel
    1984   "Las lecciones del accidente del pozo Ixtoc I," in Cuadernos sobre Prospectiva Energética, No. 48, Mexico City, El Colegio de México, Programa de Energéticos, 1984.

Martínez, Ana María
   1983   "Biomasa," in UNAM, Programa Universitario de Energía, Tecnologías energéticas del futuro, Mexico City, Universidad Nacional Autónoma de México, March 2, 1983.

Mercado, Sergio
   1983   "Posibilidades de participación de la UNAM en el desarrollo de la energía geotérmica," in UNAM, Programa Universitario de Energía, Tecnologías energéticas del futuro, Mexico City, Universidad Nacional Autónoma de México, March 1983.

Mulás, Pablo, and Sergio Mercado
   1983   "Investigación y desarrollo en apoyo de la geotermia," in Wionczek, Miguel S. (editor), Problemas del sector energético de México, Mexico City, El Colegio de México, 1983.

Navarrete, Jorge E.
   1974   "Nacionalización de la industria petrolera: La experiencia de México," in Comercio Exterior, Vol. 24, No. 4, Mexico City, Banco Nacional de Comercio Exterior, April 1974.

Navarro, Jaime
   1984   "Economía de carbón en el sector eléctrico," paper presented at the Forum on Coal and Uranium: Energy Sources in Mexico, Mexico City, Universidad Nacional Autónoma de México, Programa Universitario de Energía, August 1984.

Organización Latinoamericana de Energía
   1980   "El desarrollo de pequeñas centrales hidroeléctricas en Latinoamérica y el Caribe," in Boletín Energético, No. 16, Organización Latinoamericana de Energía, October-December 1980.

Ortiz Mena, Antonio
   1969   "Desarrollo estabilizador: Una década de estrategia económica en México," speech before the International Monetary Fund and the World Bank, Washington, D.C., September 1969.

Petróleos Mexicanos
- 1977 "Programa de inversiones, 1977-1982," in El Mercado de Valores, Mexico City, Nacional Financiera, January 17, 1977.
- 1982-1983 Nosotros los petroleros, Nos. 22, 32, and 38, Mexico City, Petróleos Mexicanos, Subdirección Técnica Administrativa, 1982 and 1983.

Programa de Energéticos
- 1985 "Energía eólica" (mimeograph), Mexico City, El Colegio de México, March 1985.

Ruiz, Rogelio
- 1983 "La problemática de la planta nuclear de Laguna Verde," in Wionczek, Miguel S. (editor), Problemas del sector energético de México, Mexico City, El Colegio de México, 1983.

Salas, Federico
- 1981 "La crisis petrolera internacional y la renegociación de la venta de crudo," in Carta de Política Exterior Mexicana, Year 0, No. 1, Mexico City, Centro de Investigación y Docencia Económica, July-August 1981.

Secretaría de Energía, Minas e Industria Paraestatal
- 1983 "Demanda de energéticos alternos: Diagnóstico preliminar de fuentes alternas de energía," in Energéticos, Year 2, No. 1, Mexico City, Secretaría de Energía Minas e Industria Paraestatal, Dirección General de Investigación y Desarrollo, 1983.

Secretaría de Patrimonio y Fomento Industrial, Comisión de Energéticos, Secretariado Técnico
- 1977 "Plan carboeléctrico nacional," in Energéticos: Boletín Informativo del Sector Energético, Year 1, No. 1, Mexico City, August 1977.
- 1978 "Programa de desarrollo del sector eléctrico," in Energéticos: Boletín Informativo del Sector Energético, Mexico City, March 1978.
- 1980 "Programa de energía, metas a 1990 y proyecciones al año 2000" (summary), in Energéticos: Boletín Informativo del Sec-

tor Energético, Year 4, No. 11, Mexico City, November 1980.

Silva García, Marcelo
1985 "Las relaciones entre México y la Organización de Países Exportadores de Petróleo (OPEP): De la ambigüedad a la cooperación," in Cuadernos sobre Prospectiva Energética, No. 62, Mexico City, El Colegio de México, Programa de Energéticos, March 1985.

Story, Dale
1982 "Development Strategies in an Oil Exporting Advanced Developed Nation: The Case of Mexico," paper presented at the annual meeting of the International Studies Association, Cincinnati, Ohio, March 1982.

Strikovich, M.A., and Ju Sinyak
1983 "Posibilidades y limitaciones de la utilización de las fuentes de energía renovables," in Cuadernos sobre Prospectiva Energética, No. 42, Mexico City, El Colegio de México, Programa de Energéticos, July 1983.

Troeller, Ruth
1984 "El futuro de la obtención de la energía, con especial referencia a las áreas rurales de los países del Tercer Mundo," in El Día, supplement, March 16, 1984.

Vázquez Domínguez, Enrique
1976 "Planes de ampliación de capacidad en las refinerías del sistema," in IMIQ, Mexico City, Instituto Mexicano de la Industria Química, March 1976.

Villagómez Arias, Braulio
1984 "Estrategia y desarrollo de la petroquímica básica en PEMEX, 1982-1984," paper presented at the Instituto Mexicano de Ingenieros Químicos 24th National Convention, Mexico City, 1984.

Villarreal, René
1980 "El petróleo como instrumento de negociación en los 80's," in Cuadernos sobre Prospectiva Energética, México City, El Colegio de México, Programa de Energéticos, 1980.

Weyant, John, and David Kline
    1983   "Crisis energética y sobreoferta de crudo," in Wionczek,Miguel S. (editor) Mercados mundiales de hidrocarburos, Mexico City, El Colegio de México, Programa de Energéticos, 1983.

White, Margaret Evans
    1984   "Aspectos socioeconómicos de la carencia de combustibles domésticos: Un estudio empírico del México rural," in Cuadernos sobre Prospectiva Energética, No. 55, Mexico City, El Colegio de México, Programa de Energéticos, 1984.

Willars Andrade, Jaime Mario
    1983   "Perspectivas de la demanda interna y posibilidades de ahorro y sustitución de los energéticos en México," in Wionczek, Miguel S. (editor), Problemas del sector energético de México, Mexico City, El Colegio de México, Programa de Energéticos, 1983.

Wionczek, Miguel S.
    1964   "Electric Power, The Uneasy Partnership," in Vernon Raymond (editor), Public Policy and Private Enterprise in Mexico, Cambridge, Harvard University Press, 1964.
    1980   "¿Es viable una política de ciencia y tecnología en México?" in Foro Internacional, No. 81, Mexico City, El Colegio de México, July-September 1980.
              "Fuentes alternativas de energía," paper presented at the Forum on Energy Alternatives, Jalapa, Veracruz,Mexico, August 20, 1980.
    1984   Strategic Oil Reserves and Stocks in Industrial Countries (mimeograph), Mexico City, El Colegio de México, September 1984.

Zenteno,Miguel A.
    1983   "Exploration and Development of the Campeche Sound and Chiapas-Tabasco Areas," paper presented at the 11th World Oil Congress, United Kingdom, 1983.

Newspapers and magazines

<u>Business Week</u>, New York
<u>Comercio Exterior</u>, Mexico City
<u>El Día</u>, Mexico City
<u>El Nacional</u>, Mexico City
<u>El Sol de México</u>, Mexico City
<u>El Universal</u>, Mexico City
<u>Diario Oficial</u>, Mexico City
<u>Energy Détente</u>, North Hollywood, California
<u>Excélsior</u>, Mexico City
<u>Expansión</u>, Mexico City
<u>Financial Times</u>, London
<u>Fortune</u>, New York
<u>Oil & Gas Journal</u>, Tulsa, Oklahoma
<u>Petróleo Internacional</u>, Mexico City
<u>Petroleum Economist</u>, London
<u>Petroleum Intelligence Weekly</u>, New York
<u>Platts Oilgram News</u>
<u>Proceso</u>, Mexico City
<u>Razones</u>, Mexico City
<u>Siempre</u>, Mexico City
<u>Tiempo</u>, Mexico City
<u>Unomásuno</u>, Mexico City
<u>The Wall Street Journal</u>, New York